Readings in Greco-Roman Culture and Civilization

First Edition

Edited by John Bauschatz
University of Arizona

University Readers
Custom Publishing Evolved.
An Imprint of Cognella, Inc.

www.universityreaders.com   800-200-3908

Bassim Hamadeh, CEO and Publisher
Michael Simpson, Vice President of Acquisitions
Jamie Giganti, Senior Managing Editor
Miguel Macias, Graphic Designer
Marissa Applegate, Senior Field Acquisitions Editor
Gem Rabanera, Project Editor
Michael Skinner, Licensing Specialist
Claire Yee, Interior Designer

First published in the United States of America in 2016 by Cognella, Inc.

Trademark Notice: Product or corporate names may be trademarks or registered trademarks, and are used only for identification and explanation without intent to infringe.

Cover image copyright © 2012 Depositphotos/EpicStockMedia.

Printed in the United States of America

ISBN: 978-1-63487-348-2 (pbk) / 978-1-63487-349-9 (br)

University Readers
Custom Publishing Evolved.
An imprint of Cognella, Inc.

Contents

Book 1 of The Iliad

By Homer, translated by Richmond Lattimore

Sing, goddess, the anger of Peleus' son Achilleus
and its devastation, which put pains thousandfold upon the Achaians,
hurled in their multitudes to the house of Hades strong souls
of heroes, but gave their bodies to be the delicate feasting
of dogs, of all birds, and the will of Zeus was accomplished   5
since that time when first there stood in division of conflict
Atreus' son the lord of men and brilliant Achilleus.

What god was it then set them together in bitter collision?
Zeus' son and Leto's, Apollo, who in anger at the king drove
the foul pestilence along the host, and the people perished,   10
since Atreus' son had dishonored Chryses, priest of Apollo,
when he came beside the fast ships of the Achaians to ransom
back his daughter, carrying gifts beyond count and holding
in his hands wound on a staff of gold the ribbons of Apollo
who strikes from afar, and supplicated all the Achaians,   15

but above all Atreus' two sons, the marshals of the people:
"Sons of Atreus and you other strong-greaved Achaians,
to you may the gods grant who have their homes on Olympos Priam's
city to be plundered and a fair homecoming thereafter,
but may you give me back my own daughter and take the ransom,   20
giving honor to Zeus' son who strikes from afar, Apollo."

Then all the rest of the Achaians cried out in favor
that the priest be respected and the shining ransom be taken;
yet this pleased not the heart of Atreus' son Agamemnon,
but harshly he drove him away with a strong order upon him: 25
"Never let me find you again, old sir, near our hollow
ships, neither lingering now nor coming again hereafter,
for fear your staff and the god's ribbons help you no longer.
The girl I will not give back; sooner will old age come upon her
in my own house, in Argos, far from her own land, going   30
up and down by the loom and being in my bed as my companion.
So go now, do not make me angry; so you will be safer."

So he spoke, and the old man in terror obeyed him
and went silently away beside the murmuring sea beach.
Over and over the old man prayed as he walked in solitude   35
to King Apollo, whom Leto of the lovely hair bore: "Hear me,
lord of the silver bow who set your power about Chryse
and Killa the sacrosanct, who are lord in strength over Tenedos,
Smintheus, if ever it pleased your heart that I built your temple,
if ever it pleased you that I burned all the rich thigh pieces
of bulls, of goats, then bring to pass this wish I pray for: 40
let your arrows make the Danaäns pay for my tears shed."

So he spoke in prayer, and Phoibos Apollo heard him,
and strode down along the pinnacles of Olympos, angered
in his heart, carrying across his shoulders the bow and the hooded   45
quiver; and the shafts clashed on the shoulders of the god walking
angrily. He came as night comes down and knelt then
apart and opposite the ships and let go an arrow.
Terrible was the clash that rose from the bow of silver.

First he went after the mules and the circling hounds, then let go   50
a tearing arrow against the men themselves and struck them.
The corpse fires burned everywhere and did not stop burning.

Nine days up and down the host ranged the god's arrows,
but on the tenth Achilleus called the people to assembly;
a thing put into his mind by the goddess of the white arms, Hera,   55
who had pity upon the Danaäns when she saw them dying.
Now when they were all assembled in one place together,
Achilleus of the swift feet stood up among them and spoke forth:
"Son of Atreus, I believe now that straggling backward
we must make our way home if we can even escape death,   60
if fighting now must crush the Achaians and the plague likewise.
No, come, let us ask some holy man, some prophet,
even an interpreter of dreams, since a dream also
comes from Zeus, who can tell why Phoibos Apollo is so angry,
if for the sake of some vow, some hecatomb he blames us,   65
if given the fragrant smoke of lambs, of he goats, somehow
he can be made willing to beat the bane aside from us."

He spoke thus and sat down again, and among them stood up
Kalchas, Thestor's son, far the best of the bird interpreters,
who knew all things that were, the things to come and the things past,   70
who guided into the land of Ilion the ships of the Achaians
through that seercraft of his own that Phoibos Apollo gave him.
He in kind intention toward all stood forth and addressed them:
"You have bidden me, Achilleus beloved of Zeus, to explain to
you this anger of Apollo the lord who strikes from afar. Then   75
I will speak; yet make me a promise and swear before me
readily by word and work of your hands to defend me,
since I believe I shall make a man angry who holds great kingship
over the men of Argos, and all the Achaians obey him.
For a king when he is angry with a man beneath him is too strong,   80
and suppose even for the day itself he swallow down his anger,
he still keeps bitterness that remains until its fulfillment
deep in his chest. Speak forth then, tell me if you will protect me."

Then in answer again spoke Achilleus of the swift feet:
"Speak, interpreting whatever you know, and fear nothing. 85
In the name of Apollo beloved of Zeus to whom you, Kalchas,
make your prayers when you interpret the gods' will to the Danaäns,
no man so long as I am alive above earth and see daylight
shall lay the weight of his hands on you beside the hollow ships,
not one of all the Danaäns, even if you mean Agamemnon, 90
who now claims to be far the greatest of all the Achaians."

At this the blameless seer took courage again and spoke forth:
"No, it is not for the sake of some vow or hecatomb he blames us,
but for the sake of his priest whom Agamemnon dishonored
and would not give him back his daughter nor accept the ransom. 95
Therefore the archer sent griefs against us and will send them
still, nor sooner thrust back the shameful plague from the Danaäns
until we give the glancing-eyed girl back to her father
without price, without ransom, and lead also a blessed hecatomb
to Chryse; thus we might propitiate and persuade him." 100

He spoke thus and sat down again, and among them stood up
Atreus' son the hero wide-ruling Agamemnon
raging, the heart within filled black to the brim with anger
from beneath, but his two eyes showed like fire in their blazing.
First of all he eyed Kalchas bitterly and spoke to him: 105
"Seer of evil: never yet have you told me a good thing.
Always the evil things are dear to your heart to prophesy,
but nothing excellent have you said nor ever accomplished.
Now once more you make divination to the Danaäns, argue
forth your reason why he who strikes from afar afflicts them, 110
because I for the sake of the girl Chryseis would not take
the shining ransom; and indeed I wish greatly to have her
in my own house; since I like her better than Klytaimestra
my own wife, for in truth she is no way inferior,
neither in build nor stature nor wit, not in accomplishment. 115
Still I am willing to give her back, if such is the best way.
myself desire that my people be safe, not perish.
Find me then some prize that shall be my own, lest I only

among the Argives go without, since that were unfitting;
you are all witnesses to this thing, that my prize goes elsewhere."   120

Then in answer again spoke brilliant swift-footed Achilleus:
"Son of Atreus, most lordly, greediest for gain of all men,
how shall the great-hearted Achaians give you a prize now?
There is no great store of things lying about I know of.
But what we took from the cities by storm has been distributed;   125
it is unbecoming for the people to call back things once given.
No, for the present give the girl back to the god; we Achaians
thrice and four times over will repay you, if ever Zeus gives
into our hands the strong-walled citadel of Troy to be plundered."

Then in answer again spoke powerful Agamemnon: 130
"Not that way, good fighter though you be, godlike Achilleus,
strive to cheat, for you will not deceive, you will not persuade me.
What do you want? To keep your own prize and have me sit here
lacking one? Are you ordering me to give this girl back?
Either the great-hearted Achaians shall give me a new prize   135
chosen according to my desire to atone for the girl lost,
or else if they will not give me one I myself shall take her,
your own prize, or that of Aias, or that of Odysseus,
going myself in person; and he whom I visit will be bitter.
Still, these are things we shall deliberate again hereafter.   140
Come, now, we must haul a black ship down to the bright sea,
and assemble rowers enough for it, and put on board it
the hecatomb, and the girl herself, Chryseis of the fair cheeks,
and let there be one responsible man in charge of her,
either Aias or Idomeneus or brilliant Odysseus,   145
or you yourself, son of Peleus, most terrifying of all men,
to reconcile by accomplishing sacrifice the archer."

Then looking darkly at him Achilleus of the swift feet spoke:
"O wrapped in shamelessness, with your mind forever on profit,
how shall any one of the Achaians readily obey you   150
either to go on a journey or to fight men strongly in battle?
for my part did not come here for the sake of the Trojan

spearmen to fight against them, since to me they have done nothing.
Never yet have they driven away my cattle or my horses,
never in Phthia where the soil is rich and men grow great did they   155
spoil my harvest, since indeed there is much that lies between us,
the shadowy mountains and the echoing sea; but for your sake,
O great shamelessness, we followed, to do you favor,
you with the dog's eyes, to win your honor and Menelaos'
from the Trojans. You forget all this or else you care nothing.   160
And now my prize you threaten in person to strip from me,
for whom I labored much, the gift of the sons of the Achaians.
Never, when the Achaians sack some well-founded citadel
of the Trojans, do I have a prize that is equal to your prize.
Always the greater part of the painful fighting is the work of   165
my hands; but when the time comes to distribute the booty
yours is far the greater reward, and I with some small thing
yet dear to me go back to my ships when I am weary with fighting.
Now I am returning to Phthia, since it is much better
to go home again with my curved ships, and I am minded no longer   170
to stay here dishonored and pile up your wealth and your luxury."

Then answered him in turn the lord of men Agamemnon:
"Run away by all means if your heart drives you. I will not
entreat you to stay here for my sake. There are others with me
who will do me honor, and above all Zeus of the counsels.   175
To me you are the most hateful of all the kings whom the gods love.
Forever quarreling is dear to your heart, and wars and battles;
and if you are very strong indeed, that is a god's gift.
Go home then with your own ships and your own companions,
be king over the Myrmidons. I care nothing about you.   180
I take no account of your anger. But here is my threat to you.
Even as Phoibos Apollo is taking away my Chryseis.
I shall convey her back in my own ship, with my own
followers; but I shall take the fair-cheeked Briseis,
your prize, I myself going to your shelter, that you may learn well   185
how much greater I am than you, and another man may shrink back
from likening himself to me and contending against me."

So he spoke. And the anger came on Peleus' son, and within
his shaggy breast the heart was divided two ways, pondering
whether to draw from beside his thigh the sharp sword, driving   190
away all those who stood between and kill the son of Atreus,
or else to check the spleen within and keep down his anger.
Now as he weighed in mind and spirit these two courses
and was drawing from its scabbard the great sword, Athene descended
from the sky. For Hera the goddess of the white arms sent her,   195
who loved both men equally in her heart and cared for them.
The goddess standing behind Peleus' son caught him by the fair hair,
appearing to him only, for no man of the others saw her.
Achilleus in amazement turned about, and straightway
knew Pallas Athene and the terrible eyes shining.   200
He uttered winged words and addressed her: "Why have you come now,
O child of Zeus of the aegis, once more? Is it that you may see
the outrageousness of the son of Atreus Agamemnon?
Yet will I tell you this thing, and I think it shall be accomplished.
By such acts of arrogance he may even lose his own life."   205

Then in answer the goddess gray-eyed Athene spoke to him:
"I have come down to stay your anger—but will you obey me ?—from the sky;
and the goddess of the white arms Hera sent me,
who loves both of you equally in her heart and cares for you.
Come then, do not take your sword in your hand, keep clear of fighting, 210
though indeed with words you may abuse him, and it will be that way.
And this also will I tell you and it will be a thing accomplished.
Some day three times over such shining gifts shall be given you
by reason of this outrage. Hold your hand then, and obey us."

Then in answer again spoke Achilleus of the swift feet: 215
"Goddess, it is necessary that I obey the word of you two,
angry though I am in my heart. So it will be better.
If any man obeys the gods, they listen to him also."

He spoke, and laid his heavy hand on the silver sword hilt
and thrust the great blade back into the scabbard nor disobeyed   220
the word of Athene. And she went back again to Olympos
to the house of Zeus of the aegis with the other divinities.

But Peleus' son once again in words of derision
spoke to Atreides, and did not yet let go of his anger:
"You wine sack, with a dog's eyes, with a deer's heart. Never   225
once have you taken courage in your heart to arm with your people
for battle, or go into ambuscade with the best of the Achaians.
No, for in such things you see death. Far better to your mind
is it, all along the widespread host of the Achaians
to take away the gifts of any man who speaks up against you.   230
King who feed on your people, since you rule nonentities;
otherwise, son of Atreus, this were your last outrage.
But I will tell you this and swear a great oath upon it:
in the name of this scepter, which never again will bear leaf nor
branch, now that it has left behind the cut stump in the mountains,   235
nor shall it ever blossom again, since the bronze blade stripped
bark and leafage, and now at last the sons of the Achaians
carry it in their hands in state when they administer
the justice of Zeus. And this shall be a great oath before you:
some day longing for Achilleus will come to the sons of the Achaians,   240
all of them. Then stricken at heart though you be, you will be able
to do nothing, when in their numbers before man-slaughtering Hektor
they drop and die. And then you will eat out the heart within you
in sorrow, that you did no honor to the best of the Achaians."

Thus spoke Peleus' son and dashed to the ground the scepter   245
studded with golden nails, and sat down again. But Atreides
raged still on the other side, and between them Nestor
the fair-spoken rose up, the lucid speaker of Pylos,
from whose lips the streams of words ran sweeter than honey.
In his time two generations of mortal men had perished,   250
those who had grown up with him and they who had been born to
these in sacred Pylos, and he was king in the third age.
He in kind intention toward both stood forth and addressed them:
"Oh, for shame. Great sorrow comes on the land of Achaia.
Now might Priam and the sons of Priam in truth be happy,   255
and all the rest of the Trojans be visited in their hearts with gladness,
were they to hear all this wherein you two are quarreling,
you, who surpass all Danaäns in council, in fighting.

Yet be persuaded. Both of you are younger than I am.
Yes, and in my time I have dealt with better men than   260
you are, and never once did they disregard me. Never
yet have I seen nor shall see again such men as these were,
men like Peirithoös, and Dryas, shepherd of the people,
Kaineus and Exadios, godlike Polyphemos,
or Theseus, Aigeus' son, in the likeness of the immortals.   265
These were the strongest generation of earth-born mortals,
the strongest, and they fought against the strongest, the beast men
living within the mountains, and terribly they destroyed them.
I was of the company of these men, coming from Pylos,
a long way from a distant land, since they had summoned me.   270
And I fought single-handed, yet against such men no one
of the mortals now alive upon earth could do battle. And also
these listened to the counsels I gave and heeded my bidding.
Do you also obey, since to be persuaded is better.
You, great man that you are, yet do not take the girl away   275
but let her be, a prize as the sons of the Achaians gave her
first. Nor, son of Peleus, think to match your strength with
the king, since never equal with the rest is the portion of honor
of the scattered king to whom Zeus gives magnificence. Even
though you are the stronger man, and the mother who bore you was immortal,   280
yet is this man greater who is lord over more than you rule.
Son of Atreus, give up your anger; even I entreat you
to give over your bitterness against Achilleus, he who
stands as a great bulwark of battle over all the Achaians."

Then in answer again spoke powerful Agamemnon: 285
"Yes, old sir, all this you have said is fair and orderly.
Yet here is a man who wishes to be above all others,
who wishes to hold power over all, and to be lord of
all, and give them their orders, yet I think one will not obey him.
And if the everlasting gods have made him a spearman,   290
yet they have not given him the right to speak abusively."

Then looking at him darkly brilliant Achilleus answered him:
"So must I be called of no account and a coward

9

if I must carry out every order you may happen to give me.
Tell other men to do these things, but give me no more   295
commands, since I for my part have no intention to obey you.
And put away in your thoughts this other thing I tell you.
With my hands I will not fight for the girl's sake, neither
with you nor any other man, since you take her away who gave her.
But of all the other things that are mine beside my fast black   300
ship, you shall take nothing away against my pleasure.
Come, then, only try it, that these others may see also;
instantly your own black blood will stain my spearpoint."

So these two after battling in words of contention
stood up, and broke the assembly beside the ships of the Achaians.   305
Peleus' son went back to his balanced ships and his shelter
with Patroklos, Menoitios' son, and his own companions.
But the son of Atreus drew a fast ship down to the water
and allotted into it twenty rowers and put on board it
the hecatomb for the god and Chryseis of the fair cheeks
leading her by the hand. And in charge went crafty Odysseus.

These then putting out went over the ways of the water
while Atreus' son told his people to wash off their defilement.
And they washed it away and threw the washings into the salt sea.
Then they accomplished perfect hecatombs to Apollo,   315
of bulls and goats along the beach of the barren salt sea.
The savor of the burning swept in circles up to the bright sky.

Thus these were busy about the army. But Agamemnon
did not give up his anger and the first threat he made to Achilleus,
but to Talthybios he gave his orders and Eurybates   320
who were heralds and hard-working henchmen to him: "Go now
to the shelter of Peleus' son Achilleus, to bring back
Briseis of the fair cheeks leading her by the hand. And if he
will not give her, I must come in person to take her
with many men behind me, and it will be the worse for him."   325

He spoke and sent them forth with this strong order upon them.
They went against their will beside the beach of the barren

salt sea, and came to the shelters and the ships of the Myrmidons.
The man himself they found beside his shelter and his black ship
sitting. And Achilleus took no joy at all when he saw them. 330
These two terrified and in awe of the king stood waiting
quietly, and did not speak a word at all nor question him.
But he knew the whole matter in his own heart, and spoke first:
"Welcome, heralds, messengers of Zeus and of mortals.
Draw near. You are not to blame in my sight, but Agamemnon 335
who sent the two of you here for the sake of the girl Briseis.
Go then, illustrious Patroklos, and bring the girl forth
and give her to these to be taken away. Yet let them be witnesses
in the sight of the blessed gods, in the sight of mortal
men, and of this cruel king, if ever hereafter 340
there shall be need of me to beat back the shameful destruction
from the rest. For surely in ruinous heart he makes sacrifice
and has not wit enough to look behind and before him
that the Achaians fighting beside their ships shall not perish."

So he spoke, and Patroklos obeyed his beloved companion. 345
He led forth from the hut Briseis of the fair cheeks and gave her
to be taken away; and they walked back beside the ships of the Achaians,
and the woman all unwilling went with them still. But Achilleus
weeping went and sat in sorrow apart from his companions
beside the beach of the gray sea looking out on the infinite water. 350
Many times stretching forth his hands he called on his mother:
"Since, my mother, you bore me to be a man with a short life,
therefore Zeus of the loud thunder on Olympos should grant me
honor at least. But now he has given me not even a little.
Now the son of Atreus, powerful Agamemnon, 355
has dishonored me, since he has taken away my prize and keeps it."

So he spoke in tears and the lady his mother heard him
as she sat in the depths of the sea at the side of her aged father,
and lightly she emerged like a mist from the gray water.
She came and sat beside him as he wept, and stroked him 360
with her hand and called him by name and spoke to him: "Why then,
child, do you lament? What sorrow has come to your heart now?
Tell me, do not hide it in your mind, and thus we shall both know."

Sighing heavily Achilleus of the swift feet answered her: 365
"You know; since you know why must I tell you all this?
We went against Thebe, the sacred city of Eëtion,
and the city we sacked, and carried everything back to this place,
and the sons of the Achaians made a fair distribution
and for Atreus' son they chose out Chryseis of the fair cheeks. 370
Then Chryses, priest of him who strikes from afar, Apollo,
came beside the fast ships of the bronze-armored Achaians to ransom
back his daughter, carrying gifts beyond count and holding
in his hands wound on a staff of gold the ribbons of Apollo
who strikes from afar, and supplicated all the Achaians,
but above all Atreus' two sons, the marshals of the people. 375
Then all the rest of the Achaians cried out in favor
that the priest be respected and the shining ransom be taken;
yet this pleased not the heart of Atreus' son Agamemnon,
but harshly he sent him away with a strong order upon him.
The old man went back again in anger, but Apollo 380
listened to his prayer, since he was very dear to him, and let go
the wicked arrow against the Argives. And now the people
were dying one after another while the god's shafts ranged
everywhere along the wide host of the Achaians, till the seer
knowing well the truth interpreted the designs of the archer. 385
It was I first of all urged then the god's appeasement;
and the anger took hold of Atreus' son, and in speed standing
he uttered his threat against me, and now it is a thing accomplished.
For the girl the glancing-eyed Achaians are taking to Chryse
in a fast ship, also carrying to the king presents. But even 390
now the heralds went away from my shelter leading
Briseus' daughter, whom the sons of the Achaians gave me.
You then, if you have power to, protect your own son, going
to Olympos and supplicating Zeus, if ever before now
either by word you comforted Zeus' heart or by action. 395
Since it is many times in my father's halls I have heard you
making claims, when you said you only among the immortals
beat aside shameful destruction from Kronos' son the dark-misted,
that time when all the other Olympians sought to bind him,
Hera and Poseidon and Pallas Athene. Then you, 400

goddess, went and set him free from his shackles, summoning
in speed the creature of the hundred hands to tall Olympos,
that creature the gods name Briareus, but all men
Aigaios' son, but he is far greater in strength than his father.
He rejoicing in the glory of it sat down by Kronion,   405
and the rest of the blessed gods were frightened and gave up binding him.
Sit beside him and take his knees and remind him of these things
now, if perhaps he might be willing to help the Trojans,
and pin the Achaians back against the ships and the water,
dying, so that thus they may all have profit of their own king,   410
that Atreus' son wide-ruling Agamemnon may recognize
his madness, that he did no honor to the best of the Achaians."

Thetis answered him then letting the tears fall: "Ah me,
my child. Your birth was bitterness. Why did I raise you?
If only you could sit by your ships untroubled, not weeping,   415
since indeed your lifetime is to be short, of no length.
Now it has befallen that your life must be brief and bitter
beyond all men's. To a bad destiny I bore you in my chambers.
But I will go to cloud-dark Olympos and ask this
thing of Zeus who delights in the thunder. Perhaps he will do it.   420
Do you therefore continuing to sit by your swift ships
be angry at the Achaians and stay away from all fighting.
For Zeus went to the blameless Aithiopians at the Ocean
yesterday to feast, and the rest of the gods went with him.
On the twelfth day he will be coming back to Olympos,   425
and then I will go for your sake to the house of Zeus, bronze-founded,
and take him by the knees and I think I can persuade him."

So speaking she went away from that place and left him
sorrowing in his heart for the sake of the fair-girdled woman
whom they were taking by force against his will. But Odysseus   430
meanwhile drew near to Chryse conveying the sacred hecatomb.
These when they were inside the many-hollowed harbor
took down and gathered together the sails and stowed them in the black ship,
let down mast by the forestays, and settled it into the mast crutch
easily, and rowed her in with oars to the mooring.   435

They threw over the anchor stones and made fast the stern cables
and themselves stepped out onto the break of the sea beach,
and led forth the hecatomb to the archer Apollo,
and Chryseis herself stepped forth from the sea-going vessel.
Odysseus of the many designs guided her to the altar   440
and left her in her father's arms and spoke a word to him:
"Chryses, I was sent here by the lord of men Agamemnon
to lead back your daughter and accomplish a sacred hecatomb
to Apollo on behalf of the Danaäns, that we may propitiate
the lord who has heaped unhappiness and tears on the Argives."   445

He spoke, and left her in his arms. And he received gladly
his beloved child. And the men arranged the sacred hecatomb
for the god in orderly fashion around the strong-founded altar.
Next they washed their hands and took up the scattering barley.
Standing among them with lifted arms Chryses prayed in a great voice: 450
"Hear me, lord of the silver bow, who set your power about
Chryse and Killa the sacrosanct, who are lord in strength over
Tenedos; if once before you listened to my prayers
and did me honor and smote strongly the host of the Achaians,
so one more time bring to pass the wish that I pray for.   455
Beat aside at last the shameful plague from the Danaäns."

So he spoke in prayer, and Phoibos Apollo heard him.
And when all had made prayer and flung down the scattering barley
first they drew back the victims' heads and slaughtered them and skinned them,
and cut away the meat from the thighs and wrapped them in fat,   460
making a double fold, and laid shreds of flesh upon them.
The old man burned these on a cleft stick and poured the gleaming
wine over, while the young men with forks in their hands stood about him.
But when they had burned the thigh pieces and tasted the vitals,
they cut all the remainder into pieces and spitted them   465
and roasted all carefully and took off the pieces.
Then after they had finished the work and got the feast ready
they feasted, nor was any man's hunger denied a fair portion.
But when they had put away their desire for eating and drinking,
the young men filled the mixing bowls with pure wine, passing   470

a portion to all, when they had offered drink in the goblets.
All day long they propitiated the god with singing,
chanting a splendid hymn to Apollo, these young Achaians,
singing to the one who works from afar, who listened in gladness.

Afterward when the sun went down and darkness came onward   475
they lay down and slept beside the ship's stern cables.
But when the young Dawn showed again with her rosy fingers,
they put forth to sea toward the wide camp of the Achaians.
And Apollo who works from afar sent them a favoring stern wind.
They set up the mast again and spread on it the white sails,   480
and the wind blew into the middle of the sail, and at the cutwater
a blue wave rose and sang strongly as the ship went onward.
She ran swiftly cutting across the swell her pathway.
But when they had come back to the wide camp of the Achaians
they hauled the black ship up on the mainland, high up   485
on the sand, and underneath her they fixed the long props.
Afterward they scattered to their own ships and their shelters.

But that other still sat in anger beside his swift ships,
Peleus' son divinely born, Achilleus of the swift feet.
Never now would he go to assemblies where men win glory,   490
never more into battle, but continued to waste his heart out
sitting there, though he longed always for the clamor and fighting.

But when the twelfth dawn after this day appeared, the gods who
live forever came back to Olympos all in a body
and Zeus led them; nor did Thetis forget the entreaties   495
of her son, but she emerged from the sea's waves early
in the morning and went up to the tall sky and Olympos.
She found Kronos' broad-browed son apart from the others
sitting upon the highest peak of rugged Olympos.
She came and sat beside him with her left hand embracing   500
his knees, but took him underneath the chin with her right hand
and spoke in supplication to lord Zeus son of Kronos:
"Father Zeus, if ever before in word or action
I did you favor among the immortals, now grant what I ask for.

Now give honor to my son short-lived beyond all other   505
mortals. Since even now the lord of men Agamemnon
dishonors him, who has taken away his prize and keeps it.
Zeus of the counsels, lord of Olympos, now do him honor.
So long put strength into the Trojans, until the Achaians
give my son his rights, and his honor is increased among them."

She spoke thus. But Zeus who gathers the clouds made no answer
but sat in silence a long time. And Thetis, as she had taken
his knees, clung fast to them and urged once more her question:
"Bend your head and promise me to accomplish this thing,
or else refuse it; you have nothing to fear, that I may know   515
by how much I am the most dishonored of all gods."

Deeply disturbed Zeus who gathers the clouds answered her:
"This is a disastrous matter when you set me in conflict
with Hera, and she troubles me with recriminations.
Since even as things are, forever among the immortals   520
she is at me and speaks of how I help the Trojans in battle.
Even so, go back again now, go away, for fear she
see us. I will look to these things that they be accomplished.
See then, I will bend my head that you may believe me.
For this among the immortal gods is the mightiest witness   525
I can give, and nothing I do shall be vain nor revocable
nor a thing unfulfilled when I bend my head in assent to it."

He spoke, the son of Kronos, and nodded his head with the dark brows,
and the immortally anointed hair of the great god
swept from his divine head, and all Olympos was shaken.   530

So these two who had made their plans separated, and Thetis
leapt down again from shining Olympos into the sea's depth,
but Zeus went back to his own house, and all the gods rose up
from their chairs to greet the coming of their father; not one had courage
to keep his place as the father advanced, but stood up to greet him.   535
Thus he took his place on the throne; yet Hera was not
ignorant, having seen how he had been plotting counsels

with Thetis the silver-footed, the daughter of the sea's ancient,
and at once she spoke revilingly to Zeus son of Kronos:
"Treacherous one, what god has been plotting counsels with you ?   540
Always it is dear to your heart in my absence to think of
secret things and decide upon them. Never have you patience
frankly to speak forth to me the thing that you purpose."

Then to her the father of gods and men made answer:
"Hera, do not go on hoping that you will hear all my   545
thoughts, since these will be too hard for you, though you are my wife.
Any thought that it is right for you to listen to, no one
neither man nor any immortal shall hear it before you.
But anything that apart from the rest of the gods I wish to
plan, do not always question each detail nor probe me."   550

Then the goddess the ox-eyed lady Hera answered:
"Majesty, son of Kronos, what sort of thing have you spoken?
Truly too much in time past I have not questioned nor probed you,
but you are entirely free to think out whatever pleases you.
Now, though, I am terribly afraid you were won over   555
by Thetis the silver-footed, the daughter of the sea's ancient.
For early in the morning she sat beside you and took your
knees, and I think you bowed your head in assent to do honor
to Achilleus, and to destroy many beside the ships of the Achaians."

Then in return Zeus who gathers the clouds made answer: 560
"Dear lady, I never escape you; you are always full of suspicion.
Yet thus you can accomplish nothing surely, but be more
distant from my heart than ever, and it will be the worse for you.
If what you say is true, then that is the way I wish it.
But go then, sit down in silence, and do as I tell you,   565
for fear all the gods, as many as are on Olympos, can do nothing
if I come close and lay my unconquerable hands upon you."

He spoke, and the goddess the ox-eyed lady Hera was frightened
and went and sat down in silence wrenching her heart to obedience,
and all the Uranian gods in the house of Zeus were troubled.   570

Hephaistos the renowned smith rose up to speak among them,
to bring comfort to his beloved mother, Hera of the white arms:
"This will be a disastrous matter and not endurable
if you two are to quarrel thus for the sake of mortals.
and bring brawling among the gods. There will be no pleasure   575
in the stately feast at all, since vile things will be uppermost.
And I entreat my mother, though she herself understands it,
to be ingratiating toward our father Zeus, that no longer
our father may scold her and break up the quiet of our feasting.
For if the Olympian who handles the lightning should be minded   580
to hurl us out of our places, he is far too strong for any.
Do you therefore approach him again with words made gentle,
and at once the Olympian will be gracious again to us."

He spoke, and springing to his feet put a two-handled goblet
into his mother's hands and spoke again to her once more: 585
"Have patience, my mother, and endure it, though you be saddened,
for fear that, dear as you are, I see you before my own eyes
struck down, and then sorry though I be I shall not be able
to do anything. It is too hard to fight against the Olympian.
There was a time once before now I was minded to help you,   590
and he caught me by the foot and threw me from the magic threshold,
and all day long I dropped helpless, and about sunset
I landed in Lemnos, and there was not much life left in me.
After that fall it was the Sintian men who took care of me."

He spoke, and the goddess of the white arms Hera smiled at him,   595
and smiling she accepted the goblet out of her son's hand.
Thereafter beginning from the left he poured drinks for the other
gods, dipping up from the mixing bowl the sweet nectar.
But among the blessed immortals uncontrollable laughter
went up as they saw Hephaistos bustling about the palace.   600

Thus thereafter the whole day long until the sun went under
they feasted, nor was anyone's hunger denied a fair portion,
nor denied the beautifully wrought lyre in the hands of Apollo
nor the antiphonal sweet sound of the Muses singing.

Afterward when the light of the flaming sun went under   605
they went away each one to sleep in his home where
for each one the far-renowned strong-handed Hephaistos
had built a house by means of his craftsmanship and cunning.
Zeus the Olympian and lord of the lightning went to
his own bed, where always he lay when sweet sleep came on him.   610
Going up to the bed he slept and Hera of the gold throne beside him.

Book 9 of The Odyssey

By Homer, translated by Ian Johnston

Note that in the following translation the line numbers without brackets refer to the English text and those without brackets refer to the Greek text. In the former, short indented lines have normally been counted with the shorter line immediately preceding them.

Resourceful Odysseus then replied to Alcinous:

"Lord Alcinous, most renowned of men,
it is indeed a truly splendid thing
to listen to a singer such as this,
whose voice is like a god's. For I say
there's nothing gives one more delight
than when joy grips entire groups of men
who sit in proper order in a hall
feasting and listening to a singer,

with tables standing there beside them   10
laden with bread and meat, as the steward
  draws wine out of the mixing bowl, moves round,   [10]
and fills the cups. To my mind this seems
the finest thing there is. But your heart
wants to ask about my grievous sorrows,
so I can weep and groan more than before.
What shall I tell you first? Where do I stop?
For the heavenly gods have given me
so much distress. Well, I will make a start
  by telling you my name. Once you know that,   20
if I escape the painful day of death,
then later I can welcome you as guests,
though I live in a palace far away.
I am Odysseus, son of Laertes,
well known to all for my deceptive skills—
    my fame extends all the way to heaven.   [20]
I live in Ithaca, a land of sunshine.
From far away one sees a mountain there,
thick with whispering trees, Mount Neriton,
and many islands lying around it   30
close together—Dulichium, Same,
forested Zacynthus. Ithaca itself,
low in the sea, furthest from the mainland,
lies to the west—while those other islands
are a separate group, closer to the Dawn
and rising Sun. It's a rugged island,
but nurtures fine young men. And in my view,
nothing one can see is ever sweeter
than a glimpse of one's own native land.
When Calypso, that lovely goddess, tried   40
to keep me with her in her hollow caves,
    longing for me to be her husband,   [30]
or when, in the same way, the cunning witch
Aeaean Circe held me in her home
filled with keen desire I'd marry her,
they never won the heart here in my chest.

That's how true it is there's nothing sweeter
than a man's own country and his parents,
even if he's living in a wealthy home,
but in a foreign land away from those   50
who gave him life. But come, I'll tell you
of the miserable journey back which Zeus
arranged for me when I returned from Troy.[1]

"I was carried by the wind from Troy
    to Ismarus, land of the Cicones.
I destroyed the city there, killed the men,   [40]
seized their wives, and captured lots of treasure
which we divided up. I took great pains
to see that all men got an equal share.
Then I gave orders we should leave on foot—   60
and with all speed. But the men were fools.
They didn't listen. They drank too much wine
and on the shoreline slaughtered many sheep,
as well as shambling cows with twisted horns.
Meanwhile the Cicones set off and gathered up
their neighbours, tribesmen living further inland.
There are more of them, and they are braver men,
skilled at fighting enemies from chariots
and also, should the need arise, on foot.   [50]
They reached us in the morning, thick as leaves   70
or flowers growing in season. Then Zeus
brought us disaster—he made that our fate,
so we would suffer many casualties.
They set their ranks and fought by our swift ships.
We threw our bronze-tipped spears at one another.
While morning lasted and that sacred day
gained strength, we held our ground and beat them back,
for all their greater numbers. But as the sun
moved to the hour when oxen are unyoked,
the Cicones broke through, overpowering   80
Achaeans. Of my well-armed companions,   [60]

---

1   Odysseus' first adventure, at Ismarus with the Cicones, seems to have been on the mainland north of Troy.

six from every ship were killed. The rest of us
made our escape, avoiding Death and Fate.

"We sailed away from there, hearts full of grief
at losing loyal companions, though happy
we had eluded death ourselves. But still,
I would not let our curved ships leave the place
until we'd made the ritual call three times
for our poor comrades slaughtered on that plain,
killed by the Cicones. Cloud-gatherer Zeus   90
then stirred North Wind to rage against our ships—
a violent storm concealing land and sea,
as darkness swept from heaven down on us.
The ships were driven off course, our sails   [70]
ripped to shreds by the power of that wind.
We lowered the masts into the holds and then,
fearing for our lives, quickly rowed the ships
toward the land. For two whole days and nights
we lay there, hearts consumed with sorrow
and exhaustion. But when fair-haired Dawn   100
gave birth to the third day, we raised the masts,
hoisted white sails, and took our place on board.
Wind and helmsman held us on our course,
and I'd have reached my native land unharmed,
but North Wind, sea currents, and the waves
pushed me off course, as I was doubling back   [80]
around Malea, driving me past Cythera.[2]

"Nine days fierce winds drove me away from there,
across the fish-filled seas, and on the tenth
we landed where the Lotus-eaters live,   110
people who feed upon its flowering fruit.[3]
We went ashore and carried water back.
Then my companions quickly had a meal

---

2 Malea is a cape on the coast of the Peloponnese, one of the most southerly points in main-land Greece. Cythera is an island off the south coast of the Peloponnese.
3 The land of the Lotus Eaters is commonly placed in North Africa.

by our swift ships. We had our food and drink,
and then I sent some of my comrades out
to learn about the men who ate the food
the land grew there. I chose two of my men   [90]
and with them sent a third as messenger.
They left at once and met the Lotus-eaters,
who had no thought of killing my companions,   120
but gave them lotus plants to eat, whose fruit,
sweet as honey, made any man who tried it
lose his desire ever to journey home
or bring back word to us—they wished to stay,
to remain among the Lotus-eaters,
feeding on the plant, eager to forget
about their homeward voyage. I forced them,
eyes full of tears, into our hollow ships,
dragged them underneath the rowing benches,
and tied them up. Then I issued orders   130   [100]
for my other trusty comrades to embark
and sail away with speed in our fast ships,
in case another man might eat a lotus
and lose all thoughts about his journey back.
They raced on board, went to their places,
and, sitting in good order in their rows,
struck the grey sea with their oar blades.

"We sailed away from there with heavy hearts
and reached the country of the Cyclopes,
a crude and lawless people.[4] They don't grow   140
any plants by hand or plough the earth,
but put their trust in the immortal gods,
and though they never sow or work the land,
every kind of crop springs up for them—

---

4   The Cyclopes (singular Cyclops) are hairy monsters, rather than people, with only one eye in the middle of their foreheads. They originated from the primal gods, Ouranus and Gaia, and had been imprisoned in Tartarus. But they helped Zeus in his fight against his father, Cronos, and Zeus freed them. Odysseus, one assumes, either doesn't know about the Cyclopes before this adventure or is not aware he is about to meet one, since he assumes he is moving into a place where the laws of hospitality apply. We learn later that the Cyclops Odysseus meets has a name (Polyphemus) and is a son of Poseidon. Most geographical interpretations place the incident with the Cyclops in Sicily.

wheat and barley and rich grape-bearing vines, [110]
and Zeus provides the rain to make them grow.
They live without a council or assembly
or any rule of law, in hollow caves
among the mountain tops. Each one of them
makes laws for his own wives and children, 150
and they shun all dealings with each other.

"Now, near the country of the Cyclopes,
outside the harbour, there's a fertile island,
covered in trees, some distance from the shore,
but not too far away. Wild goats live there
in countless numbers. They have no need
to stay away from any human trails.
Hunters never venture there, not even those [120]
who endure great hardships in the forest,
as they roam across the mountain peaks. 160
That island has no flocks or ploughed-up land—
through all its days it's never once been sown
or tilled or known the work of human beings.
The only life it feeds is bleating goats.
The Cyclopes don't have boats with scarlet prows
or men with skills to build them well-decked ships,
which would enable them to carry out
all sorts of things—like travelling to towns
of other people, the way men cross the sea
to visit one another in their ships— 170
or men who might have turned their island
into a well-constructed settlement. [130]
The island is not poor. All things grow there
in season. It has soft, well-watered meadows
by the shore of the grey sea, where grape vines
could flourish all the time, and level farm land,
where they could always reap fine harvests,
year after year—the sub-soil is so rich.
It has a harbour, too, with good anchorage,
no need for any mooring cable there, 180

or setting anchor stones, or tying up
with cables on the stern. One can beach a ship
and wait until a fair wind starts to blow
and sailors' hearts tell them to go on board.
At the harbour head there is a water spring—   [140]
a bright stream flows out underneath a cave.
Around it poplars grow. We sailed in there.
Some god led us in through the murky night—
we couldn't see a thing, and all our ships
were swallowed up in fog. Clouds hid the moon,   190
so there was no light coming from the sky.
Our eyes could not catch any glimpse of land
or of the long waves rolling in onshore,
until our well-decked ships had reached the beach.
We hauled up our ships, took down all the sails,
went up along the shore, and fell asleep,   [150]
remaining there until the light of Dawn.

"When rose-fingered early Dawn appeared,
we moved across the island quite amazed.
Some nymphs, daughters of aegis-bearing Zeus,   200
flushed out mountain goats, food for us to eat.
We quickly brought our curved bows from the ships
and our long spears, as well. Then, splitting up,
we fanned out in three different groups to hunt.
The god soon gave us our heart's fill of game—
I had twelve ships with me, and each of them
received nine goats by lot. I was the only one   [160]
to be allotted ten. So all day long
until the sunset, we sat there and ate,
feasting on that rich supply of meat,   210
with sweet wine, too—we'd not yet used up
the red wine in our ships and had some left.
We'd taken many jars for everyone
the day we'd seized the sacred citadel
of the Cicones. Then we looked across
toward the country of the Cyclopes,

which was nearby. We observed their smoke,
heard their talk and sounds of sheep and goats.
Then the sun went down, and darkness fell.
So on the seashore we lay down to sleep.   220

"As soon as rose-fingered early Dawn appeared,   [170]
I called a meeting and spoke to all the men:

'My loyal comrades, stay here where you are.
I'll take my ship and my own company
and try to find out who those people are,
whether they are rough and violent,
with no sense of law, or kind to strangers,
with hearts that fear the gods.'

"I said these words,
then went down to my ship and told my crew
to loose the cables lashed onto the stern   230
and come onboard. They embarked with speed,
and, seated at the oarlocks in their rows,
struck the grey sea with their oars. And then,   [180]
when we'd made the short trip round the island,
on the coast there, right beside the sea,
we saw a high cave, overhung with laurel.
There were many flocks, sheep as well as goats,
penned in there at night. All around the cave
there was a high front courtyard made of stones
set deep into the ground, with tall pine trees   240
and towering oaks. At night a giant slept there,
one that grazed his flocks all by himself,
somewhere far off. He avoided others
and lived alone, away from all the rest,
a law unto himself, a monster, made   [190]
to be a thing of wonder, not like man
who lives by eating bread, no, more like
a lofty wooded mountain crag, standing there
to view in isolation from the rest.

"I told the rest of my trustworthy crew   250
to stay there by the ship and guard it,
while I selected twelve of my best men
and went off to explore. I took with me
a goatskin full of dark sweet wine. Maron,
Euanthes' son, one of Apollo's priests,
the god who kept guard over Ismarus,
gave it to me because, to show respect,
we had protected him, his wife, and child.
He lived in a grove of trees, a piece of ground   [200]
sacred to Apollo. He'd offered me fine gifts—   270
seven finely crafted golden talents,
a pure silver mixing bowl, and wine as well,
a total of twelve jars poured out unmixed,
drink fit for gods. None of his servants,
men or women in his household, knew
about this wine. He was the only one,
other than his wife and one house steward.
Each time they drank that honey-sweet red wine,
he'd fill one cup with it and pour that out
in twenty cups of water, and the smell   280
arising from the mixing bowl was sweet,   [210]
astonishingly so—to tell the truth,
no one's heart could then refuse to drink it.
I took some of this wine in a large goatskin,
a pouch of food, as well. My soldier's heart
was warning me a man might soon attack,
someone invested with enormous power,
a savage with no sense of law and justice.

"We soon reached his cave but didn't find him.
He was pasturing his rich flocks in the fields.   290
We went inside the cave and looked around.
It was astonishing—crates full of cheese,
pens crammed with livestock—lambs and kids
sorted into separate groups, with yearlings,   [220]
older lambs, and newborns, each in different pens.
All the sturdy buckets, pails, and milking bowls

were awash with whey. At first, my comrades
urged me to grab some cheeses and return,
then drive the lambs and kids out of their pens
back to our swift ship and cross the water.   300
But I did not agree, though if I had,
things would have been much better. I was keen
to see the man in person and find out
if he would show me hospitality.
When he did show up, as it turned out,
he proved no joy to my companions.   [230]

"We lit a fire and offered sacrifice.
Then we helped ourselves to cheese and ate it.
We stayed inside the cave and waited there,
until he led his flocks back home. He came,   310
bearing an enormous pile of dried-out wood
to cook his dinner. He hurled his load
inside the cave with a huge crash. In our fear,
we moved back to the far end of the cave,
into the deepest corner. He then drove
his fat flock right inside the spacious cavern,
just the ones he milked. Rams and billy goats
he left outside, in the open courtyard.
Then he raised up high a massive boulder   [240]
and fixed it in position as a door.   320
It was huge—twenty-two four-wheeled wagons,
good ones, too, could not have shifted it
along the ground—that's how immense it was,
the rock he planted right in his doorway.
He sat down with his bleating goats and ewes
and milked them all, each in turn, setting
beside each one its young. Next, he curdled
half the white milk and set aside the whey
in wicker baskets, then put the other half
in bowls for him to drink up with his dinner.   330
Once he'd finished working at these tasks,   [250]
he lit a fire. Then he spied us and said:

30

'Strangers, who are you? What sea route brought you here?
Are you trading men, or wandering the sea
at random, like pirates sailing anywhere,
risking their lives to injure other men.'

"As he spoke, our hearts collapsed, terrified
by his deep voice and monstrous size. But still,
I answered him by saying:

'We are Achaeans
coming back from Troy and blown off course   340
by various winds across vast tracts of sea.   [260]
Attempting to get home, we had to take
a different route and chart another course,
a scheme, I think, which gave Zeus pleasure.
We boast that we are Agamemnon's men,
son of Atreus, now the best-known man
beneath wide heaven—the city he wiped out
was such a great one, and he killed so many.
As for us, we're visitors here and come
as suppliants to your knee, in hope that you   350
will make us welcome or provide some gift,
the proper thing one does for strangers.
So, good sir, respect the gods. We're here
as suppliants to you, and Zeus protects   [270]
all suppliants and strangers—as god of guests,
he cares for all respected visitors.'

"I finished speaking. He answered me at once—
his heart was pitiless:

'What fools you are,
you strangers, or else you come from far away—
telling me to fear the gods and shun their rage.   360
The Cyclopes care nothing about Zeus,
who bears the aegis, or the blessed gods.
We are much more powerful than them.
I wouldn't spare you or your comrades

to escape the wrath of Zeus, not unless
my own heart prompted me to do it.
But now, tell me this—when you landed here,
where did you moor your ship, a spot close by
or further off? I'd like to know that.'   [280]

"He said this to throw me off, but his deceit   370
could never fool me. I was too clever.
And so I gave him a cunning answer:

'Earthshaker Poseidon broke my ship apart—
driving it against the border of your island,
on the rocks there. He brought us close to land,
hard by the headland, then winds pushed us
inshore from the sea. But we escaped—
me and these men here. We weren't destroyed.'

"That's what I said. But his ruthless heart
gave me no reply. Instead, he jumped up,   380
seized two of my companions in his fist,
and smashed them on the ground like puppy dogs.
Their brains oozed out and soaked the ground below.   [290]
He tore their limbs apart to make a meal,
and chewed them up just like a mountain lion—
innards, flesh, and marrow—leaving nothing.
We raised our hands to Zeus and cried aloud,
to witness the horrific things he did,
our hearts unable to do anything.
Once Cyclops had stuffed his massive stomach   390
with human flesh and washed it down with milk,
he lay down in the cave, stretched out there
among his flocks. Then, in my courageous heart
I formed a plan to move up close beside him,
draw the sharp sword I carried on my thigh,   [300]
and run my hand along his chest, to find
exactly where his midriff held his liver,
then stick him there. But I had second thoughts.
We, too, would have been utterly destroyed,

there in the cave—we didn't have the strength   400
with our own hands to roll from the high door
the massive rock he'd set there. So we groaned,
and stayed there waiting for bright Dawn.

"As soon as rose-fingered early Dawn appeared,
he lit a fire and milked his flock, one by one,
with a new-born placed beside each mother.
When this work was over, he once again   [310]
snatched two of my men and gorged himself.
After his meal, he easily rolled back
the huge rock door, drove his rich flock outside,   410
and set the stone in place, as one might put
a cap back on a quiver. Then Cyclops,
whistling loudly, drove his fat flocks away
towards the mountain. He left me there,
plotting a nasty scheme deep in my heart,
some way of gaining my revenge against him,
if Athena would grant me that glory.
My heart came up with what appeared to me
the best thing I could do. An enormous club
belonging to Cyclops was lying there   420
beside a stall, a section of green olive wood   [320]
he'd cut to carry with him once it dried.
To human eyes it seemed just like the mast
on a black merchant ship with twenty oars,
a broad-beamed vessel which can move across
the mighty ocean—that's how long and wide
that huge club looked. Moving over to it,
I chopped off a piece, six feet in length,
gave it to my companions, telling them
to smooth the wood. They straightened it, while I,   430
standing at one end, chipped and tapered it
to a sharp point. Then I picked up the stake
and set it in the blazing fire to harden.
That done, I placed it carefully to one side,
concealing it beneath some of the dung

33

which lay throughout the cave in massive piles.   [330]
Then I told my comrades to draw lots
to see which men would risk their lives with me—
when sweet sleep came upon the Cyclops,   440
we'd lift that stake and twist it in his eye.
The crew drew lots and picked the very men
I would have chosen for myself, four of them,
with me included as fifth man in the group.
In the evening he came back, leading on
his fine-skinned animals and bringing them
inside the spacious cave, every sheep and goat
in his rich flock—not leaving even one
out in the open courtyard. Perhaps he had
a sense of something wrong, or else a god
had given him an order. He picked up   450   [340]
and put his huge rock door in place, then sat
to milk each ewe and bleating goat,
one by one, setting beside each mother
one of her young. When this task was over,
he quickly seized two men and wolfed them down.
Then I moved up and stood at Cyclops' side,
holding in my hands a bowl of ivy wood
full of my dark wine. I said:

'Cyclops,
take this wine and drink it, now you've had
your meal of human flesh, so you may know   460
the kind of wine we had on board our ship,
a gift of drink I was carrying for you,
in hope you'd pity me and send me off
on my journey home. But your savagery   [350]
is something I can't bear. You cruel man,
how will any of the countless other men
ever visit you in future? How you act
is so against all human law.'

"I spoke.
He grabbed the cup and gulped down the sweet wine.

Once he'd swallowed, he felt such great delight,   470
he asked me for some more, a second taste.

'Be kind and give me some of that again.
And now, without delay tell me your name,
so, as my guest, I can offer you a gift,
something you'll like. Among the Cyclopes,
grain-bearing earth grows clusters of rich grapes,
which Zeus' rain increases, but this drink—
it's a stream of nectar and ambrosia.'

"He spoke. So I handed him more fiery wine.   [360]
Three times I poured some out and gave it to him,   480
and, like a fool, he swilled it down. So then,
once the wine had addled Cyclops' wits,
I spoke these reassuring words to him:

'Cyclops, you asked about my famous name.
I'll tell you. Then you can offer me a gift,
as your guest. My name is Nobody.
My father and mother, all my other friends—
they call me Nobody.'

"That's what I said.
His pitiless heart replied:

'Well, Nobody,
I'll eat all your companions before you   490
and have you at the end—my gift to you,   [370]
since you're my guest.'

"As he said this,
he collapsed and toppled over on his back,
lying with his thick neck twisted to one side.
All-conquering sleep then overpowered him.
In his drunken state he kept on vomiting,
his gullet drooling wine and human flesh.
So then I pushed the stake deep in the ashes,

to make it hot, and spoke to all my men,
urging them on, so no one, in his fear,   500
would hesitate. When that stake of olive wood,
though green, was glowing hot, its sharp point
ready to catch fire, I walked across to it   [380]
and with my companions standing round me
pulled it from the fire. And then some god
breathed powerful courage into all of us.
They lifted up that stake of olive wood
and jammed its sharpened end down in his eye,
while I, placing my weight at the upper end,
twisted it around—just as a shipwright   510
bores a timber with a drill, while those below
make it rotate by pulling on a strap
at either end, so the drill keeps moving—
that's how we held the red-hot pointed stake
and twisted it inside the socket of his eye.
Blood poured out through the heat—around his eye,
lids and brows were singed, as his eyeball burned—   [390]
its roots were crackling in fire. When a blacksmith
plunges a great axe or adze in frigid water
with a loud hissing sound, to temper it   520
and make the iron strong—that's how his eye
sizzled around the stake of olive wood.
His horrific screams echoed through the rock.
We drew back, terrified. He yanked the stake
out of his eye—it was all smeared with blood—
hurled it away from him, and waved his arms.
He started yelling out to near-by Cyclopes,
who lived in caves up on the windy heights,   [400]
his neighbours. They heard him shouting out
and came crowding round from all directions.   530
Standing at the cave mouth, they questioned him,
asking what was wrong:

'Polyphemus,
what's so bad with you that you keep shouting
through the immortal night and wake us up?

36

Is some mortal human driving off your flocks
or killing you by treachery or force?'

"From the cave mighty Polyphemus roared:

'Nobody is killing me, my friends,
by treachery, not using any force.'

"They answered him—their words had wings:

'Well, then,   540
if nobody is hurting you and you're alone,   [410]
it must be sickness given by great Zeus,
one you can't escape. So say your prayers
to our father, lord Poseidon.'

"With these words,
they went away, and my heart was laughing—
my cunning name had pulled off such a trick.
But Cyclops groaned, writhing in agony.
Groping with his hands he picked up the stone,
removed it from the door, and sat down there,
in the opening. He stretched out his arms,   550
attempting to catch anyone who tried
to get out with the sheep. In his heart,
he took me for a fool. But I was thinking
the best thing I could do would be to find
if somehow my crewmen and myself   [420]
could escape being killed. I wove many schemes,
all sorts of tricks, the way a man will do
when his own life's at stake—and we were faced
with a murderous peril right beside us.
To my heart the best plan was as follows: 560
in Cyclops' flocks the rams were really fat—
fine, large creatures, with thick fleecy coats
of deep black wool. I picked three at a time
and, keeping quiet, tied them up together,
with twisted willow shoots, part of the mat

on which the lawless monster Polyphemus
used to sleep. The middle ram carried a man.
The two on either side were for protection.   [430]
So for every man there were three sheep.
I, too, had my own ram, the finest one   570
in the whole flock by far. I grabbed its back
then swung myself under its fleecy gut,
and lay there, face upwards, with my fingers
clutching its amazing fleece. My heart was firm.
We waited there like that until bright Dawn.

"As soon as rose-fingered early Dawn appeared,
males in the flock trotted off to pasture,
while the females, who had not yet been milked
and thus whose udders were about to burst,
bleated in their pens. Their master, in great pain,   580   [440]
ran his hands across the backs of all his sheep
as they moved past him, but was such a fool,
he didn't notice how my men were tied
to their bellies underneath. Of that flock
my ram was the last to move out through the door,
weighed down by its thick fleece and my sly thoughts.
Mighty Polyphemus, as he stroked its back,
spoke to the animal:

'My lovely ram,
why are you the last one in the flock
to come out of the cave? Not once before   590
have you ever lagged behind the sheep.
No. You've always been well out in front,
striding off to graze on tender shoots of grass
and be the first to reach the river's stream.   [450]
You're the one who longs to get back home,
once evening comes, before the others.
But now you're last of all. You must be sad,
grieving for your master's eye, now blinded
by that evil fellow with his hateful crew.
That Nobody destroyed my wits with wine.   600

But, I tell you, he's not escaped being killed.
If only you could feel and speak like me—
you'd tell me where he's hiding from my rage.
I'd smash his brains out on the ground in here,
sprinkle them in every corner of this cave,
and then my heart would ease the agonies
this worthless Nobody has brought on me.'   [460]

"With these words, he pushed the ram away from him,
out through the door. After the ram had moved
a short distance from the cave and courtyard,   610
first I got out from underneath its gut
and then untied by comrades. We rushed away,
driving off those rich, fat, long-legged sheep,
often turning round to look behind us,
until we reached our ship—a welcome sight
to fellow crewmen—we'd escaped being killed,
although they groaned and wept for those who'd died.
But I would not allow them to lament—
with a scowl I told everyone to stop.
I ordered them quickly to fling on board   620
the many fine-fleeced sheep and then set sail   [470]
across the salty sea. They climbed aboard
at once, took their places on the rowing bench,
and, sitting in good order in their rows,
struck the grey sea with their oars. But then,
when I was as far from land as a man's voice
can carry when he yells, I shouted out
and mocked the Cyclops:

'Cyclops,
it seems he was no weakling, after all,
the man whose comrades you so wished to eat,   630
using brute force in that hollow cave of yours.
Your evil acts were bound to catch you out,
you wretch—you didn't even hesitate
to gorge yourself on guests in your own home.
Now Zeus and other gods have paid you back.'

"That's what I said. It made his heart more angry.   [480]
He snapped off a huge chunk of mountain rock
and hurled it. The stone landed up ahead of us,
just by our ship's dark prow. As the stone sank,
the sea surged under it, waves pushed us back   640
towards the land, and, like a tidal flood,
drove us on shore.[5] I grabbed a long boat hook
and pushed us off, encouraging the crew,
and, with a nod of my head, ordering them
to ply their oars and save us from disaster.
They put their backs into it then and rowed.   [490]
But when we'd got some distance out to sea,
about twice as far, I started shouting,
calling the Cyclops, although around me
my comrades cautioned me from every side,   650
trying to calm me down:

'That's reckless.
Why are you trying to irritate that savage?
Just now he threw a boulder in the sea
and pushed us back on shore. We really thought
he'd destroyed us there. If he'd heard us speak
or uttering a sound, he'd have hurled down
another jagged rock and crushed our skulls,
the timbers on this ship, as well. He's strong,
powerful enough to throw this far.'

"That's what they said.   [500]
But my warrior spirit did not listen.   660
So, anger in my heart, I yelled again:

'Cyclops, if any mortal human being
asks about the injury that blinded you,
tell them Odysseus destroyed your eye,

---

5   As in many other translations, line 483 in the Greek (which mentions how the rock just missed the steering oar) has been omitted, on the ground that if the projectile falls in front of the ship, it is nowhere close to the steering oar in the stern. The omitted line occurs a few lines later with the description of the second rock thrown.

a sacker of cities, Laertes' son,
a man from Ithaca.'

"When I said this,
he groaned and spoke out in reply:

'Alas!
Now an ancient prophecy about me
has truly been fulfilled! Telemus,
fine, tall son of Eurymus, a seer   670
who surpassed all men in prophecy,
reached old age among the Cyclopes   [510]
as a soothsayer. He said all these things
would come to pass someday—I'd lose my sight
at the hand of someone called Odysseus.
But I always expected he'd be large,
a noble man, with enormous power.
But now a puny, good-for-nothing weakling,
after overpowering me with wine,
has destroyed my eye. Come here, Odysseus,   680
so I can give you your gift as my guest,
and urge the famous Shaker of the Earth
to escort you home—I am his son,
and he boasts he's my father. If he wishes,   [520]
he himself will cure me. No other blessed god,
nor any mortal man, can do that.'

"He finished speaking. I answered him and said:

'I wish I were as certain I could end your life,
rob you of your living spirit, and send you
off to Hades' home, as I am confident   690
not even the great Shaker of the Earth
will fix your eye.'

"After I'd said this,
he stretched out his hands to starry heaven
and offered this prayer to lord Poseidon:

'Hear me, Poseidon, Enfolder of the Earth,
dark-haired god, if I truly am your son
and if you claim to be my father,
grant that Odysseus, sacker of cities,   [530]
a man from Ithaca, Laertes' son,
never gets back home. If it's his destiny   700
to see his friends and reach his native land
and well-built house, may he get back late
and in distress, after all his comrades
have been killed, and in someone else's ship.
May he find troubles in his house, as well.'

"That's what he prayed. The dark-haired god heard him.
Then Cyclops once again picked up a rock,
a much larger stone, swung it round, and threw it,
using all his unimaginable force.
It landed right behind the dark-prowed ship   710
and almost hit the steering oar. Its fall   [540]
convulsed the sea, and waves then pushed us on,
carrying our ship up to the further shore.

"We reached the island where our well-decked ships
were grouped together. Our comrades sat around them,
in great sorrow, always watching for us.
We rowed in, drove our ship up on the sand,
then climbed out through the surf. From the ship's hold
we unloaded Cyclops' flock and shared it out.
I took great care to see that all men there   720
received an equal part. But when the flock
was being divided up, my well-armed comrades   [550]
awarded me the ram, my special gift,
one just for me. I sacrificed that ram,
there on the shore, to Zeus, Cronos' son,
lord of the dark cloud, ruler of all,
offering him burnt pieces of the thigh.
But he did not care for my sacrifice.
Instead he started planning to destroy

all my well-decked ships and loyal comrades.   730

"So then, all day long until the sunset,
we sat feasting on the huge supply of meat
and sweet wine, too. When the sun went down
and darkness came, we lay down to rest
and slept there on the shore beside the sea.

"As soon as rose-fingered early Dawn appeared,   [560]
I roused my shipmates and ordered them aboard.
They untied cables fastened to the sterns
and got in at once, moved to the rowing bench,
and sitting in good order in their rows,   740
they struck the grey sea with their oar blades.
So we sailed away from there, sad at heart,
happy to have avoided being destroyed,
although some dear companions had been killed."

NOTES

Odysseus' first adventure, at Ismarus with the Cicones, seems to have been on the mainland north of Troy.

Malea is a cape on the coast of the Peloponnese, one of the most southerly points in main-land Greece. Cythera is an island off the south coast of the Peloponnese.

The land of the Lotus Eaters is commonly placed in North Africa.

The Cyclopes (singular Cyclops) are hairy monsters, rather than people, with only one eye in the middle of their foreheads. They originated from the primal gods, Ouranus and Gaia, and had been imprisoned in Tartarus. But they helped Zeus in his fight against his father, Cronos, and Zeus freed them. Odysseus, one assumes, either doesn't know about the Cyclopes before this adventure or is not aware he is about to meet one, since he assumes he is moving into a place where the laws of hospitality apply. We learn later that the Cyclops Odysseus meets has a name (Polyphemus) and is a son of Poseidon. Most geographical interpretations place the incident with the Cyclops in Sicily.

As in many other translations, line 483 in the Greek (which mentions how the rock just missed the steering oar) has been omitted, on the ground that if the projectile falls in front of the ship, it is nowhere close to the steering oar in the stern. The omitted line occurs a few lines later with the description of the second rock thrown.

Works and Days

FROM *Theogony & Works and Days*

By Hesiod, translated by Stephanie Nelson

[Prologue]¹

Muses who dwell on Pieria², you who, through song, give glory,
come, speak of Zeus, hymn your father, through whom mortal men
are known and unknown, famous, forgotten, at the will of great Zeus.   5
For with ease he makes a man strong and gives a strong man over to hardship,
and with ease he dims the great and makes the obscure bright,
and with ease he straightens the crooked and withers the mighty,
Zeus who thunders on high, who dwells at home in the highest.
Hear, see, and attend, and through justice keep our law righteous—
for your part. For mine, I would speak truth to Perses.   10

---

1   Headings are placed in brackets because they have been added by the translator. Lines bracketed in the text have been thought by some editors to be later additions to the poem. For ease of cross-reference, the line numbers follow those of the Greek text rather than of the translation.
2   Pieria, north of Mount Olympus in Thessaly, had a well-known cult of the Muses. *Theogony* 53 identifies Pieria as the Muses' birthplace

There is not, it turns out,
only one kind of Strife; rather, over the earth, there are two.[3]
The first someone would praise when he knew her, the second's
worth blame; their natures are different, completely. The one
fosters war, that evil, and quarrels and contests, the hard-hearted one.
Her no man would be close to; it is by necessity,   15
through the design of the gods, men honor this strife, this burden.
But the other, the first born, the child of dark Night,
Zeus, son of Cronus, high-throned, who dwells in brightness,
set in the roots of the earth, and for men she is better.
It is she who stirs an unhandy man, even him, to start working,   20
for one man watches another and feels then a longing for work,
when he looks at a rich man, who hastens to plow and sow
and set his household in order; so neighbor
envies his neighbor as he hastens towards wealth—for this strife is a good one for mortals—
and potter is rival to potter and craftsman to craftsman   25
and beggar is jealous of beggar, and poet of poet.

[Perses and the Kings]

Perses, set these things in store in your heart; don't let the Strife
who relishes evil keep your heart back from work, with you looking
after quarrels in the marketplace, a listener-in and a cheat.
The season for quarrels is short, and care for the marketplace,   30
when the year's living is yet to be stored, inside in the barn
in its season—the living the earth bears, the grain of Demeter.
When you have plenty of that, go on with your quarrels, disputing
after other men's goods. But you'll get no second chance
for that work. So come, let us settle our quarrel instead, right now   35
with straight judgments; straight judgments are from Zeus and the best.
For already we had divided the farm, but you kept on grabbing,
carrying off the most of it, feeding the kings with great glory,

---

3   In the *Theogony* Night gives birth to a single Strife (Eris) (*Th.* 225) who goes on to bear a long list of evil abstractions. Hesiod's "so it turns out" (*ara*) seems to be a deliberate reference to this passage.

gift-gobblers, who like judging this kind of justice.
Idiots. They don't know that the half is more than the whole   40
nor what is good about mallow and asphodel.[4]

[Prometheus and Pandora][5]

For the gods have hidden
our livelihood and hold it from us. Otherwise, easily, you could work
for a day and have enough for a year and do no more work.
You could put the boat's rudder up over the fireplace in the smoke   45
and let the works of the oxen go hang, and of the long-laboring mules.[6]
But Zeus hid it, enraged in his heart because crooked-minded Prometheus
tricked him. And so for men Zeus plotted grief and trouble.
He hid fire. And Prometheus, bold son of Iapetus, stole it back   50
from the side of wise Zeus, in a fennel stalk, and gave it to men
and Zeus who delights in the thunder did not notice.
So in anger Zeus spoke to him, Zeus, who gathers the clouds:

"Son of Iapetus, all-cunning, wily in plots,
you delight in your stealing of fire and in outwitting me—   55
it will be a plague, a great one, to you, and to men to come.
I too will give them a gift, an evil one, answering fire,
in which all will delight in their hearts, as they embrace their own evil."

So he spoke, and laughed, the father of gods and men.
And he ordered famous Hephaestus, as quick as he could,   60
to mix earth with water, and to put in a human voice

---

4   The advantage of mallow and asphodel appears to be that it is poor fare (asphodel grows freely in the underworld, as *Odyssey* 11.523) and so is not grudged by the gods, much like the "half" which is therefore better than the whole. See the Introduction, pp. 63-64, for this theme and for Hesiod's quarrel with his brother Perses. The word "idiot" here (*nepios*) is elsewhere translated "fool." See n. 13.

5   In the *Theogony* version of this myth Hesiod presents the theft of fire as the second stage in Prometheus' challenge of Zeus, which begins with the division of the sacrifice. Prometheus' name means "Fore-thought" as contrasted, in this version, to his brother Epimetheus, or "After-thought." See the *Theogony* 521–616 for parallels to this story, as well as the Introduction, pp. 65–66. *Bios*, translated as "livelihood" below, can also mean simply "life."

6   As below (l. 629) the rudder is hung up over the fireplace so that the smoke will preserve it.

and human strength and make the face like a goddess immortal
and shape a maiden's most beautiful form. And Zeus bid Athena
to teach her her works—how to weave the varied, intricate web—
and he told Aphrodite, the golden, to pour grace around her   65
and hard longing and knee-weakening care; and he told Hermes
to put in the mind of a bitch and the heart of a thief,
Hermes the guide, the messenger, and the slayer of Argus.[7]

So he spoke; and they obeyed him, lord Zeus, Cronus' son.
Right away Hephaestus, the famous lame god, formed from earth   70
one like a revered, modest maiden, as was Cronus' son great counsel.
And bright-eyed Athena, goddess, clothed and adorned her
and the Graces, bright goddesses, and the lady Persuasion
put gold adornments on her, and the Horae, the lovely-haired
Seasons, crowned her with flowers of springtime,   75
[and all her ornaments Pallas Athena shaped to her body.]
And then Hermes, the slayer of Argus, the guide, put into her breast
lies and wheedling words and the heart of a thief,
[fashioned at the plan of loud-thundering Zeus, and speech]
the gods' herald placed in her too, and he gave this one, the woman,   80
a name—Pandora, "All-gift," since the gods on Olympus
gave her all as a gift, a bane to men who eat bread.[8]

But when the deceit, sheer and without cure, was finished,
Zeus the father sent Hermes, Argus' slayer, the gods' famed messenger
to Epimetheus, Afterthought, bearing the gift.   85
And Epimetheus never thought of what his brother, Prometheus, had told him:
to take no gift from Olympian Zeus, but send it right back
lest it turn out some kind of evil for men. So Epimetheus took it,
and then, when the evil was his, knew what it was.

---

7   Hephaestus, the blacksmith and god of fire, is also the god of crafts and so of anything "man-made." Athena is a goddess
not only of war and intelligence (as *Theogony* 924–6) but also of weaving, the essential work of a woman. Hermes is a god of
boundaries and also of violating boundaries, hence his role as a messenger and his association with theft. In the *Homeric Hymn
to Hermes* for example, while still a baby, Hermes steals Apollo's cattle. See also the note on *Theogony* 938–9.
8   The line could mean either that all the gods gave a gift to Pandora, or that they all gave her as a gift to men. I have tried
to keep my translation ambiguous. In this version Pandora brings with her a jar of evils (which could themselves be the gods'
gifts) while in the *Theogony* version Pandora herself is the evil that Zeus send to men. See the Introduction, p. 65.

For before this human tribes
had lived on the land clear of evils, distant from harsh toil   90
and pain and diseases, the givers of doom to men
[since mortal men grow old quickly in evil and hardship.]
But the woman took the great lid of the jar in her hands
and scattered them, and contrived grief and trouble for humans.   95
Only Hope stayed inside there, in its unbreakable home,
under the lip of the jar—for she threw back the lid
before Hope flew out the door; so willed great cloud-gathering Zeus.

But ten thousand other afflictions wander among us;   100
the earth has its fill of evils, and the sea is full, and sicknesses
come by day to men and by night, roaming at will,
bringing their evils in silence—for Zeus, the wise-minded,
took out their voices.[9] So there is no way at all to avoid Zeus' mind.   105

[The Five Ages]

And, if you like, there is another account; I can sum it up
well and with knowledge, and you store it deep in your heart—
how mortal men and the gods came to be from one source.
Golden were the first kind of men who could speak,
made by the undying gods who live on Olympus;   110
they lived in Cronus' time, while he was king of high heaven.[10]
These men lived like the gods; their hearts had no trouble;
toil and sorrow were far from them. Old age and its wretchedness
did not come upon them; they rejoiced in abundance

---

9   Since Zeus removed the voices from the diseases, human beings cannot hear them coming and so cannot protect themselves.
10   The time of Cronus, Zeus' father, is traditionally associated with a Golden Age, as here, just as in Italy Saturn was associated with a time before violence and injustice and before human beings were forced to work. Zeus enters into Hesiod's scheme when he, as opposed to "the gods," is said to destroy the second, Silver, age and create the third, the Bronze (138, 143). Hesiod calls each stage a *genos*, "kind" or "race" or "age," but does not see one as descended from another. Since the gods are said to "make" the men of each age, Hesiod's statement that "mortal men and the gods came to be from one source" (108) must mean that men and gods at first lived similarly, before hardship came into human life. Plato will adapt this myth in the *Republic* (415 a–b, and 547a) to portray the different kinds of citizens in his city. See also the Introduction, page 66.

with arms and legs never weakened, out of the reach of all evil.[11]   115
They died as if conquered by sleep, and all that is good
was theirs. The fertile plowland brought them crops without stinting
—in plenty all on its own. They tended their fields as they pleased,
at ease and at peace in abundance; their blessings were many.
They were rich in flocks and close to the gods who are happy.   120

But when earth covered over this kind—
who are spirits over the land, through great Zeus' designs,[12]
kindly, warding off evil, guardians for mortal men, keeping close watch
over judgments and pitiless deeds, clothed in mist, everywhere roaming   125
over the land, and givers of wealth, for this kingly prize was theirs too—
then the gods on Olympus made another, a second kind,
one made of silver and worse, not like the gold in body or mind.
A hundred years a child stayed by the side of his lady mother,
a great infant,[13] being raised and skipping about in the house.   130
Then, when they were grown and had come to the measure of youth,
through their folly they lived short lives full of pain.
For they could not hold back from wrong; they outraged one another;
they would not serve the immortals nor sacrifice on their altars,   135
which for humans, by custom, is right.[14] So Zeus, son of Cronus,
hid them in his anger, since they would not give honor to the gods
who, blessed, hold Mt. Olympus.

But when earth had covered these too—   140
who are called the mortal and blessed ones under the earth,
a second kind of protector, but they have their honor as well[15]—
then Zeus the father created another, a third kind of men of clear speech,
a bronze race, not like the silver, of ash trees,[16]

---

11   Literally, "with hands and feet always the same."
12   This is the manuscript reading. In the *Cratylus* Plato quotes the line rather differently: "who are called blessed spirits upon the land." "Spirits" here is *daimones*, often seen as a kind of intermediary between the human and the divine.
13   "Infant" (etymologically, "not-speaking") is a literal gloss of Hesiod's word *nepios*, which elsewhere in the poem is translated as "fool" or "idiot."
14   *Kata ethea*, "according to custom," could also mean "according to their location / usual place."
15   These spirits may be identified with the cults of heroes who, like Oedipus at the end of Sophocles' *Oedipus at Colonus*, were worshipped as powers guarding the area around their burial place.
16   Hesiod may mean that the race was born from the ash-tree nymphs (the Meliae, *Theogony* 187), or the reference may be, as often, to ash-tree spears.

mighty and terrible. Their only care was the works of the war god,   145
groans, outrage, and insolence; they did not eat bread
and the strong hearts in their breasts were of adamant. Their huge force
was unapproachable. Ungraspable hands
reached from the strong arms of their shoulders.
Their weapons, their houses, were bronze; their work was with bronze—   150
they had no black iron.[17] And they, mastered by their own hands,
went down to cold Hades' home in the shadows,
nameless, taken, for all of their terrible power,   155
by dark death, and they left the bright light of the sun.

But when the land had covered this kind too, Zeus, Cronus' son,
made another on the nourishing land, a fourth kind, more just and better,
of heroes like gods, men called half-gods—the race before ours   160
over the unmeasured earth.[18] And of these, cruel war and the battle cry
destroyed some, some under Thebes' seven gates in Cadmus' land,
fighting for Oedipus' flocks, and some went in ships
and crossed the great gulf of the sea to Troy to fight for fair Helen.   165
There, for some, the end that is death enfolded them,
while for others Zeus, Cronus' son, gave custom and livelihood far from mankind,
a living at the edge of the earth, and the father settled them there.
And there they live, by deep-flowing Ocean on isles of the blessed—   170
heroes, and happy, with hearts free from care, for whom the grain-giving plowland
bears crops thrice yearly, abundant and honey-rich[19]

But for the fifth—
I wish I had never been born in this age, but either died first   175
or been born after. For the age now is iron, and neither by day

---

17 Hesiod here links his overall scheme of degenerating metals to what is still known as the "Bronze Age," the period before
the discovery of iron. The heroes celebrated by Homer, whom Hesiod places in the next generation, traditionally used bronze,
but also possessed iron, as *Iliad* 23.826–9, and *Odyssey* 1.184.
18 Literally, "the earlier race." Here, as in his abrupt introduction of his own age, the iron age, Hesiod blurs over the fact
that the aristocracy of his own time traced their descent back to the heroes. He seems to want each "kind" to be considered
separately. Oedipus, along with heroes such as Heracles or Jason, was traditionally of the older generation of heroes while the
heroes of Troy, Achilles, Agamemnon, Odysseus, etc. were of the younger generation.
19 Two papyri preserve some fragmentary lines, 173a-d, which may have been added to parallel the earlier generations: "far
from the immortals. And for them Cronus is king / whom the father of men and of gods released from his chains / and now,
among these, he has always his honor, as is right. / Then Zeus made yet another kind of men with clear speech / of those who
live now upon the earth that feeds many."

can men rest from labor and sorrow, nor by night, as they perish away,
and the gods will give more harsh trouble.

Yet, all the same, for these
some good will be mixed with the evil. But Zeus will destroy them, this race 180
of men with clear speech, when the children are born with grey heads.
Then a father will fight with his children, children with their fathers,
a guest will fight with his host, and comrade with comrade,
and brothers will no longer be close, as once they were.
Parents, unhonored, blamed and reproached, will quickly grow old; 185
hard children will give them hard words, knowing no fear of the gods,
and when they grow old will grudge to give back their rearing,
manhandling justice.[20] One man will ravage another man's city;
no thanks and no grace for keeping of oaths, 190
none for a just man or a good one; they honor a man who does evil
and praise outrage. Their justice lies in their hands; shame and respect
will be gone. A bad man will harm his better with false speeches
and swear an oath to affirm them. Envy will be men's companion, 195
harsh-worded, delighting in evil and hateful, and men will have misery.
And then, their forms covered in white, forsaking mankind
for Olympus to be with the gods, away from the wide paths of the land,
will go Retribution and Shame[21]—and what will be left for men 200
is bitter pain, and no help against evil.

[The Hawk and the Nightingale][22]

And now I will tell a tale for the kings, who know it themselves,
how a hawk, high in the clouds, spoke to a nightingale

---

20 Literally: "hand-justicers" a condensed version of "justice (lies) in their hands", l. 192 below.

21 *Aidos* (Shame, and above, at line 192, translated as "shame and respect") is the force that keeps men from doing wrong out of respect for the opinions of others. Nemesis (Retribution or Righteous Indignation) is the anger men feel at injustice whether or not they themselves are the victims. See also the note on *Theogony* 223.

22 The usual interpretation of this fable is that the nightingale, a singer, represents Hesiod and the hawk represents the kings. It is also possible, however, that the nightingale represents the kings who are themselves in the grip of a higher power, that of Zeus. See the Introduction, p. 67. "Strange one" below translates *daimonie*, otherwise "divine one."

clutching the speckle-necked bird, as he carried her off in his claws;
she wailed, pierced by the hooks of his nails,   205
but he gave speech in his strength: "Strange one, why do you cry?
One greater than you now has you. You will go where I take you,
singer though you are—a dinner for me, if I wish, or I may let you go.
Only a fool stands up to oppose the stronger;   210
he loses his victory, has that disgrace, and more—he has pain as well."
So he spoke, the hawk of swift flight, the long-winged bird.

[Justice and the Kings]

So Perses, you listen to justice; don't breed outrage and insult.[23]
Outrage is an evil for a poor man; not even a great one can carry it lightly
when he meets with ruin—then he bows down under its weight.[24]   215
The road to travel lies on the other side—the better road, the one to justice.
At the end justice is strong over outrage, the lesson a fool learns
by suffering. For Oath runs alongside crooked judgments,
and when men haul Justice about, forcing her to go where she's dragged,
there's a commotion—gift-gobblers, men who judge right with bent justice.   220
Then Justice follows mourning the city and customs of the people
clothed in mist, bringing evil where men drove her out and dealt her not straightly.[25]

But where men give straight judgments   225
to strangers and citizens, where they do not step outside justice,
they prosper; their city prospers; and the people blossom within it.
Peace is a nurse to their children. There far-seeing Zeus never
marks out war's pain. Famine is no companion to them, nor ruin,[26]   230

---

23   "Outrage and insult" here, as "outrage" in the next line translates the Greek word *hubris* which, between human beings,
implies a failure to respect the integrity, or in the modern concept, "rights," of another.

24   "Ruin" (Greek *atê*) here as at line 231 also has connotations of the destruction or blind infatuation that results from
overweening pride, as *Iliad* 9.504.

25   Throughout this passage, and Hesiodic poetry overall, there is no strict division between personifications, such as Oath
and Justice, and the entities they represent. The capital letters introduced here to distinguish personifications were not used in
ancient Greek texts. See the Introduction, pp. 67–68.

26   "Ruin" translates *atê*, as in note 24 above. The tradition of the earth flourishing under a just king appears as well in
Odyssey 19.109-14, while the plague and infertility which strike as a result of unpunished murder features prominently in the

but straight in their justice, in abundance, they care for well-tended
fields. The earth gives them livelihood. The mountain oaks,
high in the branches, bear acorns; in the trunks the bees have their hives;
their sheep are heavy with fleeces; their children look like their fathers.   235
They flourish with good things throughout and do not sail on ships,
and the grain-giving plowland bears them crops.

But for those given to
outrage, evil, and hard-hearted deeds, for them far-seeing Zeus marks a
judgment. And often a whole city suffers for one evil man,   240
presumptuous, who contrives evil. On them, from the sky, Zeus brings calamity,
famine together with plague; the people die off; no children
are born to the women; the households diminish—all through
the contriving of Olympian Zeus. And then, at another time,   245
he destroys their wide army or their walls, or else Cronus' son
plucks off their ships on the sea.

You kings, take heed; mark for yourselves
this judgment. For immortals, close-by, note your crooked judgments   250
where men wear down one another, blind to the wrath of the gods.
Thrice ten thousand immortals guard mortal men, watchers
for Zeus over the flourishing land; they are guardians of judgments
and hard-hearted deeds, clothed in mist, roaming the land.   255
And there is Justice, a maiden, the child of great Zeus. She has renown
and reverance from the gods. When a man's crooked scorn
does her harm, she sits down by Zeus, her father, Cronus' son,
and speaks about men's unjust minds. Then a people pay back   260
the kings' insolence, kings who, thinking ruin, turned their judgments aside
and spoke crookedly. Keep watch over this; keep your words straight, you kings,[27]
you gift-gobblers—and forget everything about crooked judgments.

A man sets up evil for himself when he sets up evil for others;   265
the evil design is worst for the one who designed it.[28]

Oedipus Tyrannus. There is also, of course, a pragmatic relation between a sound political condition and the flourishing of
agriculture, as implied at *Theogony* 901-3, for which see the Introduction, p. 68.

27   Other manuscripts read "keep straight your judgments".

28   Here, as often, Hesiod rounds off specific advice by citing what appear to be proverbs that demonstrate his point.

The eye of Zeus, that sees all, knows all, surveying all things,
sees this too if he wishes; it does not escape him
what kind of justice this is in the city.

Nor would I myself   270
now be just among men, nor want my son to be just,
since justice is an evil where good things go for injustice[29]—
but I don't expect, yet, that wise Zeus will bring that to pass.

And you Perses, you store these things up in your mind,
you listen to justice—and forget about force altogether.
For this is the way men are to live;[30] this is what Zeus has ordained,   275
that for fish and for beasts and for swift-flighted birds,[31]
they eat one another, since they have no justice among them.
But to men he gave justice, and that, in the end, is the best.
For if someone knows what he says and willingly speaks what is right,   280
to him Zeus, the far-seeing, gives wealth. But if someone bears witness,
swears an oath, and deliberately lies, he harms justice,
a wrong without cure—and feeble and dim generations are left to his house.
But for the man who swears truth, the generations after are better.   285

[Reciprocity and Hard Work]

To you then, Perses, fool though you are, I will speak with fair thought.
Evil is easy to take; crowds come upon her; the road is smooth
and she lives close by. But excellence, the gods put sweat before that;   290
the path that leads there is long; that road is steep
and at first rough. When you come to the top, then it starts
to come easier, but it's hard all the same.

---

29 Hesiod puns here on *dikê*, which can mean "justice," "judgment" or even (as line 239) "punishment." Literally the line
reads: "if the more unjust man will have the greater justice / judgment (*dikê*)".
30 "Way" here translates *nomos*, which also means "custom," and later "law," as well as the characteristic "way" of a group.
At *Theogony* 74, Zeus is said to give to the immortals their "ways" (*nomos*) and honors (*timê*).
31 The reference to birds here has been taken as a comment on the fable of 202-12. If the fable there identifies the kings with
the hawks this line would then point out that human beings should not behave similarly.

That man is best,
altogether, who thinks things through for himself—who figures
what will be best later on and finally.
Someone who can listen is good too; he hears when someone speaks well.   295
But a man who won't listen and knows nothing himself,
who takes nothing to heart, he is useless.

But for you,
keep what I tell you in mind: work, Perses, work,
you offspring of Zeus; make famine hate you; make   300
Demeter your friend. Then she, revered with rich crowns,
will stuff full your barn with livelihood, for famine
is the constant companion of one who won't work. Nemesis
follows such men, men the gods hate and men hate, a man who won't work,
like the drone, with no sting, wasting the hive's labor, idle, and eating.   305

But you rather, prize the work; arrange it in measure;
make your barns, in their season, full of livelihood.
Men's flocks prosper from work; work makes men rich;
and you will be close to the undying gods, much more
if you work, [and to men, for they hate the unworking].   310
Work is no shame; not working is the disgrace.
Work, and envy will come soon enough from the idle,
and admiration, as you grow rich; fame and excellence attend on wealth.[32]
Whatever your lot, work is best, if you can manage
to turn your witless mind from other men's goods   315
back to your work, and, as I tell you, care for your living.

Shame is no good at looking after a man who is needy,[33]
shame is a great harm to men, and a great benefit too—
shame leads to no great prosperity; boldness goes with wealth.

Property is not there to be grabbed; what is better is god-given.   320
A man can take wealth by force, with a strong hand,

---

32 "Excellence" (*aretê*) also "status" or "virtue," is the primary goal of the Homeric hero, whose heroic values Hesiod seems here to be undermining by associating them primarily with wealth. "Admire and envy" translates *zelos*, the complex of feelings that comes from looking at someone above oneself. "Lot," below, translates *daimon*, otherwise "spirit" or "fortune."
33 An alternative reading would give "A not good shame looks after a needy man."

or steal with his tongue, as often, when gain
tricks a man's mind and shamelessness tramples his shame,
but then easily the gods blot him out, bring down his household,   325
and wealth, his valet, soon leaves his service.
It is the same to injure a guest-friend, or to do evil
to a man at your mercy,[34] or climb up into your brother's bed
and lie with his wife, doing in secret an act out of season,
or if some fool offends against fatherless children,   330
or when his father is old, on that evil threshold,
gives him abuse, quarreling with harsh words—with him
Zeus is angry; and Zeus himself in the end
imposes a rough exchange as the price of those unjust deeds.

But you, hold off your witless heart from these things   335
and, where you can, sacrifice as is due to the deathless gods
pure and clear, and kindle the gleaming thigh-bones. Other times
have libations and incense appease them, when you lie down to sleep
and when the holy light comes, so they may see you with kindness
and have a heart that is gracious, and you buy the farm of another   340
and not have another buy yours.[35]

Call your friend to a feast; leave an enemy be.[36]
Most of all invite the man who lives nearest; since if something is wrong
on the place, neighbors come as they are—in-laws take time to dress.   345
A bad neighbor is a plague, just as much as a good one is a gain.
To have a good one to your share is to have a share in distinction
already.[37] If you had no bad neighbors your cattle would never be lost.[38]
From your neighbor, then, take fair measure and pay back

---

34 These are the classic offenses punished by Zeus himself, in particular injuring a suppliant (here "a man at your mercy") or a guest-friend. Hesiod's point is that stealing money is an offense just as bad as these.

35 As money was not yet used in Hesiod's Ascra one would acquire the allotment of another by exchange of goods, probably by having someone gradually borrow so much that the only way to settle was to give over his land. The translation gives a modern equivalent.

36 To regard others as either "friends" (*philoi*) or "enemies" (*echthroi*), that is, as either one's own people or not one's own people, is common in the Greek tradition. Elsewhere, as lines 15, 184 etc. I translate "be friendly" as "be close to."

37 "Distinction" here translates the Greek word *timê*, "honor" or "prerogative," as in note 30 above. Here, however, it may simply mean "good value."

38 Although this line has been interpreted as referring to the need to defend oneself against a cattle raid, given Hesiod's generally unwarlike tendencies it is more likely that he has in mind the ubiquitous tendency of cattle to break out and wander off. The battle over the flocks of Oedipus (WD 163) belonged to an earlier time.

in the same measure, what is fair; pay him back with more if you can;   350
then later, when you are in need, he will be there.

Make no evil profits;
evil profits are doom.[39] Be friendly with people friendly to you; visit
those who come visiting; give to those who give too, not to those who do not.
Anyone gives to a giver; a man who won't give won't get either.   355
For Give is a good thing, but Grab is an evil—she gives death.
When you give a gift willingly, even a large gift,
you will be glad in it; it will rejoice your heart as well,
but when a man grabs for himself, persuaded by shamelessness,
even only a small thing freezes his heart. For even a small thing,   360
when piled on a small thing, done often, grows large. Add to what you have
and keep off hunger.

Anything stored in the house
gives no grief. Things are better at home; something gone from the house   365
has harm standing by it. It is good to have things at hand
and a plague to want something gone missing—keep all that in mind.

When you open a jar use it freely and don't spare at the end—
skimp in the middle; to spare at the dregs is just wretched.

When you hire a friend agree on the wage; let it be sure.   370
If you hire your brother, smile; be pleasant—and see there's a witness;
trusting and mistrusting have both been known to destroy men.

For women, don't let a tricked-out rear end fluster your mind.
Women wheedle and coax; all the time what they want is your barn.
Trust a woman—you might as well trust a thief.   375

One son is best for the house;
he will nourish it and wealth will increase in the halls. If another is left,

---

39   "Doom" here translates *atê*, as in note 24 above. I follow David Grene's translation in Nelson, 1998: "Make no ill profits; ill profits are just so much loss."

dividing the property, plan to die an old man.[40] But still, Zeus
can provide riches even to more—more help is more care, and more increase.   380
So for you, if your heart hopes for wealth, do this, and work and work and work more.

[The Farmer's Year]

When Atlas' children, the Pleiades, rise, start your harvest;
plow when they set.[41] Forty nights and days they lie hid,   385
and then, as the year comes round, when the iron for mowing
is first sharpened, they appear.

This is the way of the plains,[42]
of those who live near the sea, and of those in the clefts
of the mountains, in rich land, away from the tossing sea: 390
strip to sow; strip to plow; strip to harvest,[43] if each in its season
you would care for the works of Demeter. So each in its season
will flourish—or else, afterwards, lacking, you may beg   395
at other men's households and gain nothing—as you have come now to me.
But I will give you no further measure. Work, Perses you fool,
work the works that the gods marked for men—lest someday you, children,
wife, and an ache in your soul, look for a living from neighbors
who don't care. Twice maybe, or three times, you may gain   400
your end; trouble them further and you will get nothing—
your fine speeches in vain, your words ranging useless. Instead, as I bid you,
think about undoing your debts and a way to shun hunger.

---

40   Literally "may you die old leaving behind another child". An alternate reading would give "may he [i.e. your child] die old leaving behind another child".
41   The Pleiades, identified mythologically as the seven daughters of Atlas, rise (that is, are visible just before sunrise) in the first half of May and set (no longer visible at sunrise) in late October or early November. From the end of March to May they are not visible at all, that is, they are "hidden." In a Mediterranean climate, in which the winter is a season of rain and the summer of heat and drought, the land is plowed and the crop sown in late fall to be harvested the following spring, after the rains.
42   "Way" here translates *nomos*, as above, note 30.
43   The precept combines "works" and "days": one strips because effort is required and because one should plow and sow early, while it is still warm.

A house is the first thing, and a woman, and an ox for the plowing   405
—a woman you buy in, not one you marry, who can follow the oxen—[44]
and implements in the house, prepared and ready. Otherwise you may
ask another and he turn you down, and then you go lacking,
and the time in season pass by and the work is diminished. Don't put things off   410
to tomorrow and then to the next day; no sluggish worker
fills up his barn, and neither does a man who delays.
It is care that prospers the work; Do-it-tomorrow wrestles with ruin.

[Autumn]

When the sun's strength leaves off its sweat and sharpness, in mid-autumn,   415
and strong Zeus sends rain and mortal complexions are eased
—for then the star Sirius travels little by day, over the heads of men
raised to destruction, and takes a greater share of the night,[45]
then the wood split with your iron ax is least worm-eaten, as the tree   420
pours its leaves to the ground and leaves off its sprouting.
Then be mindful of wood-cutting—for that is this season's work.

A mortar takes three foot of wood, a pestle about four and a half;
for an axle you need seven foot—that is best suited—[46]
but if you cut eight, use what is left for a mallet. Cut a length   425
just over two feet for the wheel of a cart three feet long.
It is good to have many curved timbers: wood for a plow-tree,
whenever you find it, bring back to the house—look in the fields
for a holm-oak or else in the mountains; holm-oak is strongest
for plowing, when a wood-worker, Athena's servant, has fastened   430

---

44 Hesiod seems to have slyly amended a proverbial saying: "A house first, and a wife, and an ox for the plow" by adding the next line. This is possible because the Greek *gunê* means both "wife" and "woman." The Greeks used oxen for farm-work; horses being considered a luxury of the rich (as *Prometheus Bound* 466).
45 Late September and early October.
46 Hesiod opens the farming section, which will, overall, be more descriptive than informative, with detailed instruction designed to give it a businesslike air. Some of the details may have become distorted in transmission as in the wheel for the (literally two and a half foot) cart below. Here, for example, a seven-foot long axle seems excessive, although West *WD* 264 reports wheel-ruts in Classical times from wagons six feet wide.

the blade of the plow in with pegs and fitted it tight to the pole.[47]
Keep two plows—toil on them at home—one naturally bent
and one joined together; it is best to have two. Then, if one breaks
throw the other on the backs of the oxen.

Laurel and elm   435
are least eaten by worms—they are best for the plow-pole;
use oak for the stock, holm-oak for the plow-tree, and get nine-year-old oxen,
two bulls, since their strength is unspent and their measure of youth
at its prime. These two are best at the work; they will not contend
in the furrow, breaking the plow, and leave the work there undone.   440
To follow them, a man in his forties is best, but a strong one.
Give him a decent sized loaf for his dinner, cut into eight slices.[48]
He will take care for the work and drive a straight furrow. Being past
looking around all the time for his friends, he will keep his mind
on the work. Another, no younger than him, is best to scatter the seed   445
and avoid over-sowing. A man more of a boy has his mind wandering
after his friends.

When you hear overhead the voice of the crane, mark well
her clamor, high up out of the clouds; she brings the year's sign
for plowing and points out the season of winter and rain,[49]   450
and she gnaws at the heart of a man with no oxen. That is the time
to fodder your crooked-horned oxen inside in the barn.
For it is easy to say to a neighbor: "Give me your oxen and wagon,"
but the answer is easy too: "I have work for the oxen."
A man rich in daydreams sees a wagon already completed;   455
the fool forgets—a hundred planks are needed as well.
Take care for that first, and have them laid up in the house.

47

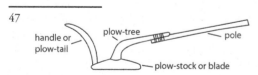

The pole connects the plow to the oxen for pulling; the plow-tree connects this to the plowstock or, (here) "blade" which cuts the soil and which would probably be fitted with an iron blade or "plowshare". The farmer holds the handle or "plow-tail". As the plow-tree takes most of the strain Hesiod advises that it be made of holm-oak, scarce in Boeotia, but very tough. Illustration taken from West *WD* p. 266.

48   Literally "a four-part, eight-piece loaf". Although the meaning is unclear the detail seems designed to produce a vivid image, hence my translation.

49   Late October and early November. See note 41 above for growing crops in a Mediterranean climate.

But then when the plowing shows itself first to men who are mortal,
make haste, both you and your slaves, in both wet and dry, plowing   460
in the season of plowing, at the first light in the morning, hurrying
so that later your fields might be full. Plow land plowed first in springtime[50]—
though fallow land broken in summer will not deceive you. Sow fallow
while the plowland is still light; fallow land defends against ruin; it quiets the children.

Pray to Zeus, god under the land, and to holy Demeter, that the grain   465
might be heavy, the grain of Demeter, and come to completeness.
Pray as you first start to plow, when the plow-handle is firm in your hand
and your stick comes down on the oxen, and they, with straps straining,
struggle to drag on the plow.[51] Let a small boy follow behind, a slave boy,   470
with a mattock, to cover the seed and make work for the birds.[52]
Have things arranged well; this for men is the best, as disorder is worst.
And so your grain-stalks will nod to the earth with their ripeness
if afterward the lord of Olympus himself gives good completion.
Then you may sweep the cobwebs from the grain bins, and, I think, then   475
you will be glad as you take from the livelihood stored up inside,
and in plenty you will come to grey spring, and not be looking to others
—but have another in need of you.

But, if you wait to plow
the good land until the sun turns at the solstice, you may sit down
to harvest, grasping thin handfuls of undergrown sheaves and,   480
dusty, bind them awry. So, not very pleased, you will bring home
a harvest that fits in a basket, and not many will be impressed.
But one way at one time, at another another is the mind of Zeus,

---

50   Literally "plow in spring; in summer plowing fallow [or, land lying fallow] will not deceive you". The elliptical expressions, like the jump below to prospects of the harvest, seem to follow the farmer's thoughts as he begins to plow, wonders if the land has been prepared well enough, and looks forward with pleasure or dread to the results of his labor. A field would normally be sown every other year and lie fallow in between, being broken with the plow as often as possible.

51   Literally "dragging the peg [that fastens the yoke on the oxen to the plow-pole] by the strap". As above, Hesiod uses technical detail to render the picture vivid: the peg would be the first thing the farmer would see taking up the strain as the plow begins to move.

52   This line has been emended to read "let a slave follow a little behind", on the grounds that the work is too hard for a child. Hesiod, however, does not tend to be easy on his servants, and the image of a boy covering the seeds increases the vividness. "Work" here translates *ponos*, otherwise translated as "toil."

who bears the aegis;[53] it is hard for mortals to know. For if you
plow late, there could be this cure: when the cuckoo first cuckoos   485
from the oak trees, and men on the unbounded earth are made glad[54]
if Zeus should then rain on the third day and leave off
just when the tracks of the ox-hooves are filled but not overflowing—
then the late-plowing man may match one who plowed early.   490
Keep these things well in mind, all of them; don't let them escape you,
neither the time of grey spring nor the season of rain when it comes.

[Winter]

Pass right by the blacksmith's; keep away from its warmth and its chatter
in winter season, when the cold keeps a man from his fields; then a man   495
with no fear of work can do much to prosper his household.
Be careful of winter; it is a hard thing to deal with. It can catch you up
helpless and poor, using a thin hand to rub a foot that is swollen.
A man who won't work, with no livelihood, waits on a hope that is empty,
laying evils to heart. For no good hope keeps a poor man company   500
as he sits in the chatter-house[55] without any sure living.

Tell your servants while it is mid-summer still:
"Summer won't last forever: now is the time to build sheds."

But for the month of Lenaion[56]—avoid it; those days are evil;
they would take the skin off an ox, and the frosts that Boreas blows,   505
the North Wind, avoid them—they are cruel. He bellows
through horse-breeding Thrace and through the wide-ranging sea,
stirring it up with his blasts. The earth moans; the forest moans; in the valleys

---

53   The *aegis*, also commonly associated with Athena, is a goat-skin emblem made by Hephaestus that terrifies enemies and can create thunderstorms. See *Theogony* note 3.
54   The farmer who put off his plowing did not get to it until the winter solstice, December 21st. The cuckoo arrives the following March, heralding spring. In England, where the cuckoo arrives later, Shakespeare described King Richard as like the cuckoo in June—heard but not regarded (*Henry IV.1* 3.2.75).
55   The Greek word Hesiod uses, *leschê*, could mean either lounge/hall or talk/chatter.
56   The second half of January and the beginning of February.

the lofty-leaved oaks and thick pines, brought down, as he falls on them,
crash to the nourishing earth. Then the whole forest,   510
uncountable, roars. The beasts shudder, tucking their tails over their
privates, even those covered with fur. But for them too the cold
blowing goes through them, shaggy as they are. And it goes through
the hide of the ox—that cannot hold it back—and through the long hair   515
of the goat, but not the sheeps' fleeces; their wool is enough; the North Wind
does not blow through them, though it curves an old man like a wheel.
And through the soft skin of a girl the wind does not blow,
one who keeps in the house by her fond mother, not knowing yet   520
golden Aphrodite and her works; well bathed, her delicate skin
rich with rich oil, on a winter day she naps in a nook of the house,
while the squid, boneless one, gnaws his foot, deep in his fireless home   525
and pitiful haunts. The sun shows him no pasture to head for,
but goes instead to and fro over the cities and people
of men who are dark—and it sluggishly shines on all Greece.

Then the beasts whose home is the woods, with horns and without,
take flight, wretched, their teeth chattering, through the thickets,   530
each with one care only at heart: it searches for shelter,
a thick-wooded corner, a rocky hollow to hide in.
Then, like an old man with bent back who sees only the ground,
his three legs barely enough—like him, wandering, they flee the white snow.[57]   535

Then wrap yourself up, and watch out for yourself as I bid you—
put on a soft cloak and clothes going down to your feet; make them
of thick cloth, with more warp than woof; wrap them around you
to keep your skin calm, lest the cold raise the hair on your body.   540
Wear thick boots, close-fitting ones; make them from the hide of an ox
you have slaughtered. Line the insides with felt.
The skins of young goats, stitched together with ox-gut, thrown over your back,
keeps off the rain when the chill season comes. On your head wear a cap   545
of worked felt, to keep the wet from your ears—for dawn, in a north wind, is cold.
And at dawn, all over the earth, down from the sky of stars,

---

57 As in the Sphinx's riddle (what goes on four legs in the morning, two in the afternoon and three at night?) the "three-footed mortal" is an old man with his stick.

a wheat-growing mist spreads over the fields of the blessed,[58]
drawn from the ever-flowing rivers, raised by the gusts of the winds   550
high over the earth; at one time it rains down near evening,
at another blows on, when a Thracian north wind clusters the clouds.
Before it comes finish your work and go home. Don't let the dark cloud down from the sky   555
wrapping round you, wet your skin, soaking your clothes. Avoid it,
for this month is the hardest, hard for flocks, with its winter and storms,
hard for men. Give the oxen just half their rations. For your man, though,
give him more—for the glad nights are long and can be great helpers.[59]   560
Keep this in mind until the year finds its end; balance the nights and days,
until earth once again, the mother of all, bears her commingled fruits.

[Spring]

When sixty wintry days from the solstice, sun's turning, are done
and accomplished by Zeus, then Arcturus leaves Ocean' stream   565
to rise, shining out in the twilight.[60] After him comes the swallow,
Pandion's shrill-calling child, who appears when spring is beginning.
Before she comes, prune the vines; that is the best way to do it.   570

But when the house-bearing snail climbs up the plants from the land
fleeing the Pleiades, then the time for digging the vineyard is over.[61]
Rather sharpen your sickle and stir up your slaves—
no sitting around in the shade and sleeping to dawn, when the time
for the harvest has come, the season the sun withers your skin.   575
Then be busy and gather your crops back to the house, rising early,
so your livelihood may be ensured. For dawn takes off a third
of man's work and dawn sends a man on his way,
and dawn sends on the work; dawn, who, in her shining   580
sets many a man on the road and puts many a yoke on the oxen.

---

58   "Fields" here is *erga*, also "works", as Introduction, p. 68.
59   The servant gets more than half-rations, but not full rations, since with the long nights (great helpers) and little work to
do one can sleep rather than eat. Since the word "night" can be ill-omened Hesiod uses *euphronae*, "the glad ones" instead.
60   The second half of February.
61   Mid-May. The Pleiades have returned, as predicted in lines 383-4, to signal the harvest-time.

[Summer]

But when the thistle flowers, when the cicadas sit in the trees,
shrill-chirping, and pour down in crowds their whistling whirring song
from under their wings, in the season of wearying heat,
then goats are the fattest, and wine the sweetest, and women   585
most randy—and men then are most feeble, when the star,
Sirius, parches their heads and their knees and skin dries up
in the heat.[62] Then is the time for cool shade by a rock,
for Biblos' wine, cakes made of milk, the milk of a goat drying-off,
and the meat of a heifer with no calf, grazed in the woods, and   591
of first-born kids. Then drink the bright wine, and sit in the shade,
with a heart glad of its dinner, a face turned to fresh-blowing Zephyrus.
Then you may pour from the springs always flowing   595
three measures of untroubled water, and the fourth a measure of wine.

But for the slaves—hasten them on to Demeter's pure grain;
they need to get to the winnowing. Put them at it as soon as Orion
appears.[63] Let the floor be well-rolled; make the place for the threshing
an airy one; then measure the grain and store it in jars—do it well.   600
And then, when the livelihood is put away in well-locked containers,
put your man out of doors.[64] A girl for a servant is best then—
one with no child; a worker with a calf under her is a trouble.
And attend to the watchdog; let him keep his teeth sharp
and don't spare his food, lest the man that does his sleeping in daytime
use some night to make off with your goods. Bring in fodder   605
and bedding for the oxen and mules, enough for the season—but then
let the men have a rest. There is time to relax; you can unyoke the oxen.

---

62   Mid-July.

63   Orion first rose, for Hesiod, around June 20. He has switched the order of the summer picnic and the threshing, which would naturally follow the harvest, in order to create and then interrupt a sense of relaxation—there is always work to be done on the farm.

64   This line has also been taken as meaning "get a servant without a household" but after the harvest, when help is least needed, is a time for firing not hiring. The *thes*, or hired servant, is in some regards lower even than a slave, who at least has a household he belongs to. In the *Odyssey* (11.589-91) to be a *thes* to a poor farmer is the worst existence Achilles can imagine.

But when Orion and Sirius move south, into mid-sky[65]

and rose-fingered Dawn sights Arcturus, then you, Perses,   610

cut off all the grape-clusters and carry them home. Show them the sun

for ten days and nights, then for five more shadow them over. The wine

will be ready to draw on the sixth. Put it in the jars; it is the gift

of glad Dionysus. And then when the strength of Orion, the Hyades,   615

and the Pleiades go below the horizon, remember—it is time for the plowing;

the season is here; may the full year lodge in fitness under the land.[66]

[Sailing]

But if longing for sailing takes you, with its rough storms, then when the Pleiades

run from Orion's rude strength and plunge into the cloudy sea,   620

then all the winds rage; keep your ship well away from the wine-colored sea;

remember the land; as I tell you, work the earth.[67] For your ship,

haul it up onto shore and pack it round, on all sides, with stones

to hold off the winds' wet strength, and draw out the plug   625

to let out the bilge-water, so when Zeus rains the boat doesn't rot.

Get the rigging and the tackle all ready; store it away in the house.

Take down the sails, the boat's wings on the sea, and pack them up neatly,

and take off the rudder; hang it up over the fire to dry in the smoke.

And you, wait for the season for sailing; it will come soon enough—   630

then drag your ship to the sea; fill its swiftness with cargo,

and have the cargo well readied and fitted to win back gain for the house.

That was what your father and mine did, Perses, you fool—he used

to sail ships, stuck in the need for a livelihood. And then he came here,   635

crossing great stretches of sea in his black ship, leaving Aeolian Cyme behind,

not fleeing wealth or from an excess of riches or substance

but to escape need, evil poverty, that Zeus gives to men—

---

65   Mid-September. As above, note 41, Hesiod means when the stars are in mid-sky at dawn, that is, when the farmer emerges from his house and takes a first survey of the farm and the jobs for the day.

66   With the Pleiades' setting in October the year, and the description of the year, has come back to its starting point.

67   November. This is also the time that Perses should be using for plowing, as in lines 383-4. Despite his father's experience as a sailor (or, perhaps, because of it, 633-40), sailing for Hesiod seems to be purely an adjunct to farming, a way to gain a greater market for surplus goods, most likely olive oil and wine.

and he settled here, in a miserable village near Helicon,
Ascra, evil in winter, unpleasant in summer, never much good.   640

But you, Perses, remember your work, all of your work,
in due season, but most of all about sailing.
A small boat is fine to praise, but your cargo should go in a big one,
for the greater the cargo, the greater the profit, and more upon that
in the future—if the winds hold back blasts of evil.   645
And if ever you turn to trade in your misguided heart, designing
escape from unlovely hunger and debt, I will point out
the measures of the much-sounding sea—not that I am much skilled
in sailing, since I never yet crossed the broad sea on a ship,   650
except once, when I went to Euboea from Aulis, where the Achaeans
lingered a long winter through[68] with a great host of the men
of holy Greece, gathered for Troy, land of fair women.[69]
From there I crossed over too, for the games of war-minded[70]
Amphidamas, over to Chalcis. Many prizes were promised beforehand   655
by the sons of the great-hearted hero—and one, I may boast,
was mine, for my victory in song, a tripod with elegant handles.
That prize went to the Muses of Helicon. It was my offering,
where the goddesses set me first on the way to clear song.[71]
That is all my experience of many pegged-ships, but even so   660
I can speak Zeus' mind, for the Muses taught me unutterable hymn.[72]

For fifty days after the solstice when the sun is done turning,
and the season's wearying heat has come to an end, then sailing
comes seasonable for mortals.[73] Then you are less likely to shatter   665
the ship and the sea drown the sailors—except when Poseidon,

---

68   The distance from Euboea to Aulis, according to West, is about 65 meters of water—hardly an epic voyage. The Greek for "a long winter" could also mean "a long storm". Like Homer, who has no general word for "Greek," Hesiod uses "Achaean" to denote the Greek forces under Agamemnon.

69   Hesiod's epithets reverse the usual Homeric descriptions: "holy Troy" and "Hellas, land of fair women" (for Homer a region of Greece). In general Hesiod uses the regular epic descriptions ("formula"), as the "wine-dark" sea or "many-pegged" ships (660), but with a distinct lack of enthusiasm for sailing.

70   Plutarch says that Amphidamas was killed during the Lelantine War between Chalcis and Eretria, which would date the contest to 730-700 B.C.

71   As described at *Theogony* 22–34.

72   "Unutterable," *athesphatos*, means, literally, beyond a god's uttering, hence both portentous and immense or immeasurable. Homer uses the word of vast entities, such as a storm, night, or the sea.

73   From the end of June through to August.

land-shaker, or Zeus, king of immortals, is set on destruction—
for in them is the end of all, good and evil alike.

At that time
the winds are set in good order; the sea is without harm.   670
Be of good cheer then; trust the winds; drag your ship to the sea
and load in the cargo; but hurry, and come home again quick as you can.
Don't wait for the new vintage of wine—and the strong rain in autumn
and the storms that come with it and fierce blasts of Notus, the south wind,   675
who stirs up the sea, keeping company with Zeus' strong storms,
the great rains of autumn, and makes the sea a harsh place for a sailor.

There is another time for men to go sailing—in spring,
just at first, when a man sees the leaves on the fig tree, on the
very top branches, about the size of the track a crow makes   680
when she lights in her passing.[74] Then you can embark on the sea.
This spring sailing time—I don't like it; I wouldn't praise it;
it brings no joy to my heart. It is something men grab[75]—you
will hardly escape from disaster. And yet humankind, in its folly,   685
will do even this, since possessions, for wretched mortals, are life.

It is a terror to die in the waves; think about this, I bid you;
as I speak it out. Don't load all your livelihood into the hollow ships;
leave most behind; the smaller part take as your cargo.   690
For it is a terror to find misfortune at sea, in the waves,
and terrible if, when loading your wagon, the load overstrains it
and smashes the axle and the goods are all ruined.
Take care; keep watch on right measure; in all things fitness is best.[76]

---

74 At the end of April. Just as the summer sailing fit in between the threshing and the vintage (producing the new wine one might bring back in trade, but that it is dangerous to wait for, 674) the spring sailing fits, just, between the time for pruning the vines and the harvest (564–73), a sign for Hesiod that Zeus (not necessarily out of the goodness of his heart) has set this as a time to sail.

75 As with ill-gotten wealth (lines 320, 356) the need to "grab" is a bad sign for Hesiod. "Disaster" in the next line is literally "evil."

76 "Fitness" here is *kairos*, which came to mean primarily the right moment or the critical time for something.

[Marriage, Friendship, Society]

Bring a wife to your house in good season—when your age   695
is not much short of thirty, nor much over—marriage is seasonable then.
Your wife should be four years past girlhood; marry her in her fifth year
as a woman. She should be young so you can teach her customs and care.[77]
Most of all, marry someone who lives near. Look well about you   700
in this, for fear your marriage become a treat for the neighbors.
The best thing a man can seize is a wife—if she's a good one;
a bad one will freeze you. A wife who wants only dinners
burns a man up, even a strong man, without fire, and gives him
to an unripe old age.   705

Watch well for the wrath of the gods,
the blessed immortals. Do not make your comrade the same
as a brother. If you do, don't wrong him; don't be first doing evil.
Don't tell lies just to talk. But if he wrongs you first, with a word
that vexes, or a deed, remember, and pay him back double.   710
Then, if he is brought back into friendship, and will make amends,[78]
take it. A man who makes now this one his friend and now that one,
is worthless; looks and thoughts should keep company—see that yours do.[79]

Don't be called every man's friend; don't be called no one's.   715
Don't get a name for having bad friends or for picking quarrels
with good people. And never taunt a poor man—don't dare;
poverty eats up the heart; it destroys a man, and it is given
by those blessed forever.

A sparing tongue is a treasure
among men; to speak in measure the greatest grace. Those who speak evil   720
very quickly hear evil, and more evil, of themselves. Do it
and you will find out.

---

77 A *parthenikê* or *parthenos* is an unmarried woman, and at four or five years past puberty (her "girlhood") she would be 18
or 19. As she is unmarried she is assumed to be a virgin, as Athena Parthenos is "Athena the Maiden" or "Athena the Virgin".
78 Literally: "he is willing to provide *dikê* ('justice')". Hesiod's relation to Perses seems to be hinted at here as also above:
"With a brother smile, and get a witness" (371).
79 Literally: "Do not let your mind (*noos*) convict your appearance of falsehood (*katelenchô*)".

And do not be rude at a pot-luck—
it's held for many; the pleasure and grace are the greatest,
and the cost least.

[Observances and Prohibitions]

When at dawn you pour the flashing-eyed wine to Zeus,
don't do it with unwashed hands—or for the other immortals;   725
they will not hear you; they will spit back your prayers.

Do not stand turned to the sun to make water. When he has set
and up to the time when he rises—remember—do not piss in the road,
nor just off the road as you walk. And do not uncover yourself;
the blessed gods are the keepers of night. A man who is godly,   730
who understands what is prudent, crouches or stands by the wall
of the well-fenced courtyard.

After sex, when your privates are wet,
don't stand exposed by the hearth—avoid this. And don't beget generations
when home from a burial—that is ill-omened—but after a feast of the gods.   735

Never, in the mouths of the rivers that flow out to the sea,
nor in the springs, make your water—and never relieve yourself.   758
Take care to avoid this, for it is far better so.[80]   759

Don't cross a river's fair-flowing, ever-running water on foot
without prayer; look at the river's fair stream, and first wash your hands
in the water, well-loved and clear.[81] The gods' nemesis follows
a man unwashed in hands and in evil, later they give him sorrow.   740
Do not, at the gods' abundant feast, trimming the dry from the green,

---

80 These lines, 757–9, have seemed to a number of editors better suited here than closing the section, after the warning against mocking a sacrifice.
81 In Greece, as elsewhere, many people now cross themselves before traveling across water. The word translated "sorrow" below, *algea*, is elsewhere "pain."

pare the nails of your five-branching fingers with bright iron.
Do not set the wine-ladle on the bowl when people are drinking
—a ruinous fate is set there.[82] When building a house don't leave it unfinished   745
or rough—lest a crow make his seat there and screech.

Take nothing from unblessed cauldrons, either to eat
or to wash with; there is requital set also on that.
Do not put a twelve-day old boy on anything fixed, like altars and tombs;   750
it is bad and could unman him—the same for a boy of twelve months.
Don't brighten your body with water used by a woman
—a man should not—for the requital is dire there, at least for a time.
And, if you happen upon sacred rites, do not cast blame   755
as the sacrifice burns—the gods' indignation lies also on this.   756

Do these things, and avoid mortal talk, for talk can be fearful.   760
It is an evil, a light thing to lift up—very easy—but painful to carry,
and hard to be rid of. No talk dies when many people have voiced her;
she too is a kind of a god.[83]

[The Days]

Watch for the days that are Zeus';   765
keep their right portions; point them out to your household. The thirtieth
is best to look over the work and allot the provisions—
where a people who distinguish the truth conduct their affairs.
For these are the days of the wise-minded Zeus:

To begin, the first, fourth,   770
and seventh are all holy days, the seventh most, since then
Leto bore gold-bladed Apollo—also the eighth and ninth. Two days

---

82 The bowl (*krater*) is used for mixing the wine with water, as was usual among the Greeks, the ladle for pouring it into cups.
83 Literally "avoid the fearful (*deinê* as also *WD* 687, 690, 691, where I translate as "terror" and "terrible") talk of mortals." Other manuscripts read "avoid the wretched (*deilê*) talk of mortals." Any entity that has a power beyond human control has, for Hesiod some element of the divine in it.

when the month is increasing are best for the toil of men's work—
the eleventh and twelfth.[84] Both are good, either to shear or to reap   775
the glad crops—but the twelfth is better, since then, in the full of the day,
the air-swinging spider weaves and the ant, the wise one, reaps his store.
On that day a woman should set up her loom; it will forward the work.

The thirteenth, in the first of the month, is a bad day   780
for starting to sow, but best for bedding in plants. The sixth
of the mid-month suits plants least, but for boys is a good day
to be born. For girls it is bad, a bad day to be born, a bad day to marry.
The first sixth is bad too for a girl's birth. On that day geld goats or sheep   785
or fence in a place for your flocks—the day smiles kindly on that.
And it is good for a boy's birth, a boy with a fondness for lies,
guileful words, taunts, and hidden whispers.

On the eighth geld a boar   790
or a strong-bellowing ox; mules, hard-workers, geld on the twelfth.

The twentieth, a mighty day, at high afternoon, gives birth
to a wise man, one whose thoughts will be strong and close-packed.
The tenth is good for a boy to be born, the fourth for a girl
–in-mid month. On that day too gentle to the touch of the hand the sheep   795
and the shambling, crooked-horned cattle and a sharp-toothed dog
and hard-laboring mules. But take care on the fourth, at the month's waning
and its waxing—avoid the pain that eats out a man's spirit;
the fourth is a fateful day.

Bring a wife home on the fourth,   800
when you have looked at the omens, the ones that are best for the job.

All fifth days are bad; avoid them; they are hard days and dire.
They say on the fifth Oath was born, with the Furies attending,
and Strife was the mother, and she bore him, the perjurer's plague.

---

84   Hesiod calculates days from the first to the thirtieth, as we do, but also in three groups of ten, the waxing or increasing,
the middle, and the waning or decreasing (originally following the waxing and waning moon), so that the third day of the
middle month, for example, would be the 13th and the third of the waning month the 23rd.

In mid-month, on the seventh, throw Demeter's pure grain   805
onto the threshing floor, but have a good look at it first,
and have the wood-smith cut wood for a bedroom, and for a ship,
plenty of it—the sort of thing suited to ships—but wait to the fourth
to put together the ship's narrow hull.

The ninth of the mid-month   810
is better towards evening; the first ninth has no harm at all;
it is an excellent day, good to plant, good to be born in—
both for a man and a woman; it is never just bad.
The twenty-seventh—few know this—is the best day
to open a storage-jar. Yoke the necks of the oxen or mules then,   815
or the swift-footed horses. And on the thrice-nine haul a swift ship,
many-benched, down to the wine-colored sea. Few name this day truly.[85]

Open a jar on the fourth. Above all, the fourth of the mid-month
is holy. Also, the day after the twentieth not many know—   820
it is best just as dawn breaks; towards evening the day is less good.

These days bring succor to earth-dwelling men. The others
fall here and there, unfraught; they bring nothing. One man praises one,
another another—few know for sure. Sometimes those days are
a stepmother, sometimes a mother. A man flourishes in them and prospers   825
when, with these things in mind, he works, blameless to the immortals,
judging the birds' omens, and keeping away from transgression.

---

85   West takes the true name to be the one Hesiod uses, the "thrice-nine" day, presumable as opposed to the "twenty-seventh" or the "seventh of the waning month."

Politeia of the Spartans

FROM *Aristotle and Xenophon on Democracy and Oligarchy*

By Xenophon, translated by J.M. Moore

1   I was reflecting one day on the fact that, although Sparta has one of the smallest populations, it has become the most powerful and famous of all Greek states, and I wondered how
this could have come about. However, when I examined the way of life of the Spartiates, I

2   ceased to be surprised. None the less I do admire Lycurgus, the man who established the laws under
which they flourished; I consider him a remarkably wise man. Not merely did he not imitate other
states, but he adopted opposite institutions to the majority with outstandingly successful results.

3   Let us begin our survey at the very beginning, with the begetting of children. In other
cities, the girls who are to become mothers, and are brought up in the approved fashion, arc
reared on the simplest possible diet, and with a minimum of luxury foods; they either drink
no wine at all, or only drink it diluted. Girls are expected to imitate the usually sedentary life
of craftsmen, and to work their wool sitting quietly. How could one expect girls brought up

4   in such a way to produce outstanding offspring? Lycurgus felt that slave girls were perfectly
capable of producing garments, and that the most important job of free women was to bear
children; he therefore decreed that women should take as much trouble over physical fitness
as men. Moreover, he instituted contests of speed and strength for women parallel to those
for men, on the grounds that if both parents were strong the offspring would be more sturdy.

5   He saw that, generally, husbands spent a disproportionate amount of time with their wives when
they were first married, and decreed the opposite here too, for he made it disgraceful for a man to

be seen entering or leaving his wife's apartment. Thus their desire would inevitably be heightened when they did meet, and any offspring which might result would therefore be stronger than if the

6 parents were surfeited with each other. Furthermore, he did not allow men to take wives as and when they wished, but decreed that marriage should take place at the period of physical prime,

7 thinking that this also was likely to produce fine children. He realised that old men with young wives tend to be particularly jealous, and again made the opposite customary, for he made it possible for an old man to introduce to his wife a man whose appearance and character he approved

8 and so have children. Further, if a man did not wish to live with a wife, but wanted children worthy of note, Lycurgus made it legal for him to select a woman who was noble and the mother

9 of fine children, and, if he obtained the husband's consent, to have children by her. He approved many such arrangements, for the women wish to run two households, and the men to get more brothers for their children—brothers who will share in the honour and position of the family, but

10 will make no financial claims. Lycurgus thus took the opposite position to the rest of the Greeks on the begetting of children; it is up to the observer to decide whether he managed to make the Spartans outstanding in stature and strength.

II Having discussed the subject of birth, I wish to turn to the educational systems of Sparta and the rest of Greece. Outside Sparta, those who claim to educate their children best put servants in charge of them as *paidagogoi* as soon as the children can understand what is said to them, and immediately send them to teachers to learn to read and write, to study the arts, and to practise gymnastics. Moreover, they soften their children's feet by giving them shoes, and weaken their

2 bodies by changes of clothes; their diet is limited only by their capacity. Instead of leaving each man to appoint a slave *paidagogos* privately for his children, Lycurgus put in charge of all of them a man who was drawn from the same class as those who hold the major offices of state; he is called the *Paidonomos*, and Lycurgus gave him authority to assemble the children, inspect them and punish any faults severely. This official was also given a group of young men provided with whips for floggings where necessary; the result is considerable respect and obedience there.

3 Instead of softening their feet with shoes, Lycurgus decreed that they should harden them by going barefoot; he believed that if this were their practice, they would climb more easily, go downhill more sure-footedly, and that a man would leap, jump up and run more swiftly barefoot

4 than wearing shoes, as long as his feet were accustomed to it. Instead of pampering them in matters of dress, he decreed that they should habitually wear one garment all the year round to

5 make them more tolerant of heat and cold. He laid down each Eiren's contribution at such a level that nobody should be burdened by overeating or be without experience of going short. He thought that those brought up under such a regime would be better able to labour on without food if the situation demanded it, and to hold out longer on the same rations if ordered to do so; they would miss delicacies less, be less interested in food altogether, and live a healthier life. He

thought that food which tended to produce slimmer figures would make them grow taller, rather

6 than that which produces fat. To prevent their being too distressed by hunger, while he did not make it possible for them to take whatever they wanted without trouble, he did permit them to

7 steal something to alleviate their hunger. As I am sure everyone realises, he did not allow them to feed themselves through their own resourcefulness because he lacked the means of providing for them. Obviously, a man who intends to steal must stay awake at night, and deceive and lie in ambush during the day, and if he is to succeed he must also have spies out. It is clear then that he included this element in their education to make the boys more resourceful in obtaining the

8 necessities of life, and more suited for war. Someone may ask why, if he thought theft a good thing, he decreed a severe flogging for anyone who was caught. My answer is that this is parallel to the way in which punishment is always handed out for not carrying out well what one is

9 taught—those who are caught they punish for stealing badly. Lycurgus made it honourable to steal as many cheeses as possible from the altar of Artemis Orthia, and detailed others to whip the thieves in the process, wishing to demonstrate in this way that a brief moment's pain can bring the joy of enduring fame. This shows that where speed is needed the idler gains nothing

10 except a mass of trouble. To prevent the children being without control even if the supervisor left them, Lycurgus laid it down that any citizen who was present could give the boys whatever instructions seemed necessary, and punish any misconduct. By this means he produced more respect in the boys; in fact, adults and boys alike respect nothing more than the men who are in

11 charge of them. In order that they might not be without someone in charge even when there was no adult present, he put the keenest of the Eirens in charge of each company; therefore boys at Sparta are never without someone to control them.

12 It seems that I must say something also about affection for boys since this too is relevant to education. Elsewhere there are varying practices: in Boeotia, men and boys live together as if they were married; in Elis, they attract a young man by favours;* again, there are states where men

13 are absolutely forbidden even to speak to boys in these circumstances. Lycurgus yet again took a totally different course; if an honourable man admired a boy's character, and wished to become his friend in all innocence, and spend time with him, he approved, and thought this a very fine form of education. If, however, a man was clearly physically attracted to a boy, he classed this as a heinous disgrace, and so ensured that in Sparta there is no more physical love between men and boys than

14 there is between parents and children or brother and brother. I am not surprised that some find this difficult to believe, for many cities tolerate love between men and boys.

Such, then, are the educational systems of Sparta and of the other Greek States; which of them produces men who are more obedient, respectful and self-controlled is again for the reader to decide.

---

* Or possibly: 'in Elis they win short periods with young men by favours.'

III When a boy begins to grow up, the other Greeks release him from his *paidogogos* and no longer
2 send him to school; no one controls him, and he is totally his own master. Lycurgus again chose the
opposite. Realising that at this age pride is greatest, insolence at its height and temptations towards
pleasures most insistent, he selected this period in which to subject them to the most demanding
3 regime, and arranged for them to have as little free time as possible. By adding the provision that
if anyone should avoid this stage of the training he should be deprived of all future privileges, he
ensured that not merely those appointed by the state but also those who cared for each individual
would take care that the boys did not, by shrinking from these duties, utterly destroy their standing
4 in the city. Apart from this, because he wanted modesty to be firmly implanted in them, he decreed
that they should keep their hands inside their cloaks in public, walk in silence, and not look about
them, but keep their eyes fixed on the ground in front of their feet. Here it has become clear that
5 in self-control as well as other fields men are stronger than women—you would be more likely to
hear a stone statue speak than them, more likely to catch a wandering glance from a bronze figure,
and would think them even more modest than the pupil of the eye.* At the common meals you
have to be content if you can even get an answer to a question.

Such, then, was his care for those who were growing up.

IV He took by far the greatest care about those who had just reached manhood, thinking that if they
became the sort of people they ought to be, they would have a very great influence for good in the
2 city. He realised that the greater the rivalry involved, the better choruses are to listen to and athletic
contests to watch; therefore, he thought that if he could induce a spirit of competition among the
young in the field of virtue, this would bring them to the highest levels of manliness. I will explain
3 how he brought it about. The Ephors pick three men in their prime who are called *Hippagretai*; each
4 of these chooses a hundred men, giving his reasons for choosing some and rejecting others. Those
who do not achieve this honour are at odds with those who rejected them and with those selected
instead of them, and keep a close watch on each other for any lapse from the accepted standards
5 of honour. This is the strife most favoured by the gods and most beneficial to the city, since it
demonstrates what a good man ought to do; each group individually aims at being outstanding,
6 and collectively they protect the city with all their might if the need arises. They are compelled to
take care of their physical fitness, for this strife leads to scuffles wherever they meet; however, any
passer-by has the right to separate the combatants. If such an order is disobeyed, the *Paidonomos*
takes the offender to the Ephors, who punish him severely, wishing to ensure that passion never
becomes stronger than obedience to the laws.

---

* Accepting a reading found only in ancient quotations, this sentence contains an untranslatable (and very frigid) play on words; the Greek word translated 'pupil' normally means 'maiden'—hence Xenophon plays on the modesty of a 'maiden' who has no chance of being anything but modest, and also gives a strict parallel to the other two illustrations.

7   The men who have reached maturity, who also fill the highest offices in the state, are relieved by the other Greeks of the duty of preserving their fitness, although they are still required to undertake military service. Lycurgus, on the other hand, established the principle that hunting was the noblest occupation for them, unless prevented by public duties, so that they, no less than the young men, should be able to stand the strain of campaigning.

V   After this description of the occupations laid down by Lycurgus for each stage of a Spartan's
2   development, I will now try to describe the type of life which he arranged for everyone. The Spartiates were in the habit of living at home like the other Greeks, and he realised that this led to considerable neglect of duty; he therefore instituted public messes, believing that this would be
3   the most effective check on disobedience. He specified a quantity of food which would not be too much nor leave them short; however, many unexpected additions come from hunting, and rich men sometimes contribute wheat cakes instead. The result is that as long as they are together their
4   table is never without food, and yet is not extravagant. He stopped anything involving compulsory drinking, which harms the body and fuddles the wits, but permitted each to drink when he was thirsty, believing this to be the least harmful and most pleasant form of drinking. When men live together like this, how could anyone ruin himself or his family through gluttony or drunkenness?
5   In other cities it is usually contemporaries who meet, and in their company there is the minimum of restraint; Lycurgus mingled the age groups in Sparta so that the younger learn from their more
6   experienced elders.*   It is customary for noble deeds in the city to be recounted in the messes, with the result that there is the minimum of insolence, drunkenness, wickedness or foul talk there.
7   The custom of eating in public has a further beneficial consequence, in that men are compelled to walk home; they know that they will not spend the night where they eat, and must be careful not to stumble through drink; they must walk during the night as they do by day, and men of military age may not even use a torch.
8   Lycurgus realised that the same food gives someone who is working a good colour, health and strength, but makes an idle man fat, flabby and feeble. He did not neglect this either, but, noticing that even when someone works hard of his own free will in doing his duty, he clearly stays satisfactorily fit, he required the senior members of each gymnasium to ensure that the rations were
9   not out of proportion to the exercise undertaken,†   In my judgement he was again right; it would be difficult to find a healthier or physically more well- developed people than the Spartans, for they exercise their legs, arms and necks equally.

VI   Another field in which Lycurgus' institutions differed from the normal was that of authority; in other cities each man controls his own children, servants and property, but Lycurgus, because he

---

*   There appears to be an omission in this sentence; a suggested restoration has been incorporated in the translation.

†   The text of this sentence is uncertain; the translation contains a possible free interpretation.

wished the citizens to benefit from each other without doing any harm, gave fathers equal authority

2 over all children, whether their own or those of others. When a man realises that such men have the authority of fathers, he will inevitably control those he has authority over as he would wish his own sons to be controlled.* If a boy tells his father that he has been beaten by another man, it is a disgrace for his own father not to beat him too—to such an extent do they trust each other not

3 to give improper commands to the children. Lycurgus made it possible for someone to use another man's servants in case of need, and established a similar system of sharing hunting dogs; those who need dogs invite the owner to join them, and if he has not time himself, he lends his pack with pleasure. Similarly with horses, when someone is ill, needs a carriage, or has to get somewhere

4 quickly, if he sees a horse, he takes it, uses it carefully and returns it. Another unique custom concerns hunting parties which are caught out late and need food but, have none prepared; they open sealed caches of food which others, according to Lycurgus' rule, have left ready after eating,

5 take what they need, and reseal them.† Because they share in this way, even those who are not well off have some part in all the resources of the country when they need something.

VII There is yet another respect in which Lycurgus' institutions are unique in Greece. In other states, every-one, I suppose, makes as much money as he can; one farms, another is a ship-owner, another

2 is a merchant, and others follow trades for their living. In Sparta Lycurgus forbad the free citizens to have anything to do with making money, and ordered them to devote themselves solely to

3 activities which ensure liberty for cities. Anyway, what need was there to worry about wealth in a society where the establishment of equal contributions to the messes and a uniform standard of living excluded the search for wealth in order to obtain luxury? They do not even need wealth for

4 clothes, since, for them, adornment is not rich fabrics but bodily health. Money is not even to be acquired to spend on the other members of one's mess; he made working physically to help one's companions more honourable than spending money to this end, showing that the former involves

5 the use of character, the latter of wealth. He prevented the acquiring of money by dishonesty. First, he established a currency such that even ten minas could not be brought into the house without the knowledge of the master and servants—it would take up a lot of space, and need a wagon to

6 move it. There are also searches for gold and silver, and if any is found, the possessor is punished. Why, then, should anyone devote himself to making money when the pains of possessing it must outweigh the pleasure to be had from spending it?

VIII Everyone knows the outstanding obedience of the Spartans to their rulers and laws; in my view, however, Lycurgus did not even try to instil this discipline until he had secured agreement among

2 the leading men of the state. I deduce this from the fact that in other cities the most powerful citizens

---

* The text of this sentence is uncertain; the translation contains a possible free interpretation.
† Freely translated to make the sense clear.

do not even wish to give the impression that they are afraid of the magistrates, thinking that this is illiberal, while in Sparta the leading citizens show the greatest respect for the magistrates, and pride themselves on being humble, and running rather than walking in answer to a summons. They think that if they set an example of exaggerated obedience the rest will follow; this has proved to be the

3　case. It is likely that these same people helped to establish the power of the Ephorate. They realised that obedience was of vital importance in the city, in the army and in the home, and they thought

4　that the greater the power of the office, the more likely it was to over-awe the people. Ephors have the right to inflict punishments at will, to require immediate payment of fines, to depose magistrates during their term of office, to imprison them, and even to put them on trial for their lives. Since they have so much power, they do not always allow office-holders to complete their year of office as they see fit, as is done in other cities, but, like tyrants or presidents of the games, they punish an offender

5　as soon as the offence is detected. Among many other excellent ways in which Lycurgus encouraged the citizens to obey the laws willingly, one of the finest seems to me the fact that he did not deliver his laws to the people before going to Delphi with the leading citizens, and asking the oracle whether it would be more desirable and better for Sparta to be governed under his proposed laws. Only when the reply was that it would be better in every way did he deliver his laws; thus he made it not merely illegal but sacrilegious to disobey laws sanctioned by Delphi.

IX　Another aspect of Lycurgus' institutions which may properly be a source of wonder is his establishment of the principle that a noble death is preferable to living in dishonour. Investigation shows that fewer of those who believe this are killed than of those who choose to retreat from danger.

2　In fact, one is more likely to avoid an early death through courage than cowardice, for courage is easier, more pleasant, more resourceful and stronger. Manifestly glory goes particularly with valour,

3　for all wish somehow to be the allies of the brave. It is proper not to omit the means by which Lycurgus achieved this; he made it clear that the reward for the brave would be happiness, for the

4　cowardly misery. In other cities the coward suffers nothing more than tlie stigma of cowardice—he goes to the same market-place as the brave man, sits with him, and attends the same gymnasium if he wishes. In Sparta anyone would think it a disgrace to take a coward into his mess or be matched

5　against him in a wrestling bout. When teams are being selected for the *sphairai* contests, such a man is often not picked, and in the chorus he is relegated to the most ignominious position; he must give way to others in the street, and rise even for younger men when seated. He must keep the unmarried women of his family at home, and answer to them for the disadvantages his cowardice inflicts on them;*　he must endure a house without a wife, and yet pay the penalty for being a bachelor. He must not go about the city looking cheerful, nor must he imitate those who are

6　without reproach; if he does, he must submit to a beating from his betters. When such disabilities are attendant on cowardice, I am not surprised that Spartans prefer death to such a deprived and disgraceful existence.

---

*　Or: 'answer to them for the fact that they are unmarried'.

X   The provision by which Lycurgus required men to practise virtue even into old age seems to me good. By placing selection for the *Gerousia* toward the very end of life he ensured that they would

2   not neglect the virtues of an upright life even in old age. The protection he offered to good men past their prime is also worthy of admiration; by putting the members of the *Gerousia* in charge

3   of capital trials he made old age more honourable than the strength of youth. The contest for the *Gerousia* is correctly regarded as the most important that a man can enter. Gymnastic contests are noble, but they depend on the body; selection for the *Gerousia* depends on nobility of character. Just as the character is more important than the body, so rivalries hinging on it are worth more effort than physical contests.

4   Another admirable feature of Lycurgus' institutions was based on his realisation that where the encouragement of virtue is left to individual initiative the result is not sufficient to promote the good of the state; he therefore decreed that all citizens must practise all the virtues in public life. Just as individually those who practise virtue surpass those who disregard it, so it is reasonable that Sparta is outstanding above all cities in virtue because she is the only one where nobility is

5   consciously practised in public life. For is it not also noble that, where other cities punish a man for wronging someone, Lycurgus decreed no less severe penalties for a man who openly did not live

6   as nobly as possible? His principle, it seems, was that if someone enslaves people, deprives them of something or steals, then only those who are directly harmed are wronged, but that wickedness and cowardice are a betrayal of the whole city. It therefore seems to me right that they should receive the severest punishment. He laid down an inflexible requirement to practise all political virtue. Those

7   who carried out their legal duties were given an equal share in the life of the states. He did not take into account physical infirmity or poverty; if anyone shrank from fulfilling what was required of

8   him, Lycurgus decreed that he should no longer even be considered one of the *Homoioi*. It is obvious that these laws are very old, for Lycurgus is said to have lived at the time of the sons of Heracles. Old as they are, they arc very strange to the other Greeks; it is a most extraordinary phenomenon that they all praise such practices, but no city is willing to imitate them.

XI   The aspects I have discussed up to now are blessings common to times of peace and war; I will now demonstrate how Lycurgus' arrangements are superior to those of other states for military purposes.

2   First, the Ephors proclaim the age-groups to be called up, listing cavalry and infantry, and then also craftsmen, with the result that the Spartans have a sound supply of everything which is available in the city while on campaign as well. All equipment that the army needs centrally is specified, to be produced on wagons or baggage animals; in this way omissions are least likely to be overlooked.

3   He devised the following costume for battle: red cloaks, thinking that this was least effeminate and most warlike, and bronze shields since they are quickest to polish and slow to tarnish. He also allowed those who were grown up to wear their hair long, on the basis that they would thus appear taller, more noble, and more terrifying.

4   Having equipped them in this way, he divided infantry and cavalry into six regiments. Each infantry regiment has one commanding officer, four company commanders, eight section officers and sixteen junior officers. At the word of command, each regiment forms up in platoons two,*

5   three or six abreast. The prevalent impression that Spartan formation under arms is extremely complicated is the opposite of the truth; the front rank man in the Spartan formation is in com-

6   mand, and each file is self-sufficient.† The formation is so easy to understand that anyone who can recognise another man cannot go wrong, for some are designated to lead, others to follow. Deployments are ordered by the junior officers orally, acting as heralds, and the depth of the line

7   of battle is established as they deploy. There is nothing remotely difficult to learn in this. However, to fight on with whoever is at hand after the line has been disrupted is a secret not easily mastered

8   except by those trained under the system of Lycurgus. The Spartans also carry out with considerable ease manoeuvres which instructors in tactics think very difficult. When they are marching in column, obviously with every platoon following the one in front, if an enemy force appears in front of them, the word is passed to the junior officers to deploy to the left, and so down the column until the line is drawn up facing the enemy. If the enemy appears from the rear when the Spartans are in this formation, each file takes up reverse order so that the best men always face the enemy.

9   The fact that the leader thus finds himself on the left is not regarded as a disadvantage, but on occasions as a positive gain; should the enemy attempt an encircling movement, they would do so not on the unprotected side but on the shield side. If it seems right at any time or for any reason for the commander to have the right wing, they reverse the stations of the army by countermarching

10   until the commander is on the right wing and the rearguard on the left. If the enemy appear on the right flank while the Spartans are in column, they just swing each company to face them head on, like a trireme; thus the rear ranks occupy the right wing. They are no more disturbed by an enemy appearing on the left, but run forward,*   or swing the companies to face them; this time the rear company will be on the left.

XII   A word about the type of camp approved by Lycurgus. Because he realised that the corners of a square were useless, he used a circular camp except where a hill provided security, or there was a

2   wall or river in the rear. By day sentries were stationed by the arms dumps looking inwards, for they watch out for friends, not enemies. Cavalry keep watch for the enemy from points where they

3   have as wide a view as possible to detect an enemy approach. By night the Skiritai were assigned to the outposts around the main force, though now this duty may also be undertaken by mercenaries

4   if there happen to be any present. One must be quite clear that the rule that spears should always be carried has the same purpose as the banning of slaves from the arms dumps, and the fact that

---

*   This number is missing from the text; two is the most likely restoration, though single file is possible.
†   There is some doubt about the exact text here which renders the sense doubtful.
*   There is some doubt about the exact text here which renders the sense doubtful.

5   those who leave their posts for necessary purposes go only so far from their companions and their weapons as they must to avoid giving offence; the common basis is safety. They change the sites of their camps frequently to harm the enemy and help their friends. It is laid down that all Spartans must take exercise all the while they are on campaign, with the result that they improve their own splendid physique and appear more dignified than other men. The exercise area and running track must not exceed in size the area covered by the camp so that no one may get far from his arms.

6   After exercise the senior officer present has the order given to sit down; this is a form of inspection; after this comes the order to break their fast, and to relieve the outposts quickly. There follow

7   amusements and a period of relaxation before the evening exercise. The order is then given for the evening meal, and, after singing a hymn to the gods to whom they have sacrificed with good omens, to rest by their arms.

There is no cause for surprise in the length of my account; it would be very difficult to find anything meriting attention in military matters which the Spartans have overlooked.

XIII   I will now describe the power and the honour which Lycurgus decreed for the king on campaign. First, the king and his entourage are maintained at public expense when in the field. The regimental commanders eat with the king, so that, since they are always present, they may take a larger part in any necessary deliberations. Three others of the *Homoioi* also eat with them and see to their every need, so that nothing may distract them from concentrating on matters connected with the war.

2   But I will go back to the beginning, to the moment when the king leaves the city with the army. First, he sacrifices in Sparta to Zeus the Leader and to the gods associated with him. If the omens here are good, the fire-bearer takes fire from the altar and leads the way to the frontiers of the state.

3   There the king sacrifices again to Zeus and Athena; when the omens from both are good, then he crosses the frontier. The fire from these sacrifices is carried in front, and never put out, and sacrificial victims of all sorts follow. Whenever the king sacrifices, he starts the rites before dawn, wishing to

4   obtain the favour of the gods before the enemy. There are present at the sacrifice the regimental and the company commanders and the section officers, the commanders of foreign detachments and of the baggage train, and any of the commanders of the detachments from individual cities who wish

5   to be present. Two of the Ephors are also present, but take no part unless the king invites them to do so; needless to say, by watching each man's conduct they exercise a restraining hand on all. When the sacrifice is over, the king summons everyone and issues the orders for the day. Watching this, one might think that the other Greeks were amateurs in military matters, and the Spartans the

6   only true professionals. When the king is leading the army, if no enemy appear, nobody marches in front of him except the Skiritai and cavalry outriders. If they expect a battle, the king takes the first company of the first regiment and wheels to the right until he takes up his position between

7   two regiments and two regimental commanders. The senior member of the king's council arranges the necessary supporting troops. The council consists of the *Homoioi* who share the king's mess,

prophets, doctors, *aulos*-players, the commanders of the army and any volunteers present. There is
8 therefore no problem about making the necessary arrangements, for nothing is unforeseen. Other
Lycurgan provisions affecting battles seem to me useful: when a goat is sacrificed with the enemy
already in sight, it is the custom that all the *aulos*-players present should play and all the Spartans
9 wear garlands; all armour must be polished. Young men are also permitted to go into battle with
their hair oiled, looking cheerful and impressive. Words of encouragement are spoken by the junior
officers, for not even a whole platodn can hear the words of the junior officer of the next platoon.
10 The regimental commander is responsible for seeing that the process is effectively carried out.
When they decide that it is time to camp, the king is in charge, and indicates the site; however,
he has no authority to despatch embassies, whether to friends or enemies. All are subject to the
11 king's authority when they have any business to transact. Lawsuits are referred by the king to the
Hellanodikai, applications for money to the treasurers, and any booty which is brought in is handed
over to the auctioneers. With this system, the king is left with no duties on campaign except those
of a priest in the religious field and a general in human affairs.

XV*   I would also like to describe the agreement which Lycurgus made between king and state. The royal
authority at Sparta is the only one which remains to-day unchanged in its original form; investigation would show that all other constitutions have undergone modifications and are even now in
2 the process of change. He laid it down that the king should make all public sacrificcs for the state
3 because of his divine descent, and should lead the army on any foreign campaign. He granted the
king the choice parts of the sacrificial victims, and set aside enough land in many of the surrounding
4 cities to ensure that he was not without adequate means, and yet was not too rich. So that the kings
should eat in public, he established a state *sussition* for them; he also honoured them with a double
portion at meals, not so that they should eat twice as much but so that they should have the means
5 of honouring anyone they wished. He also gave them the right of choosing two companions each
for their *sussition*, who are called *Puthioi*. They also received the right to take one pig from each
6 litter, so that a king would never be without victims should he need to consult the gods. A spring
near their houses provides a plentiful supply of water; those without such an amenity will realise its
manifold uses. Everyone stands when the king enters except Ephors seated on their official thrones.
7 Oaths are exchanged every month, the Ephors swearing on behalf of the city, the king for himself.
The king swears to rule according to the established laws of the city, the city to maintain the royal
8 authority unimpaired as long as the king keeps his oath. Such are the honours the king receives in
Sparta during his lifetime; they do not greatly exceed the position of a private citizen. Lycurgus did
not wish to encourage a tyrannical attitude in the kings, nor to make the people envy their power.

---

*   Chapter XIV appears to be an intrusion in its present position, and may well be a later addition to the main treatise; it is
therefore printed at the end. For discussion, see the Introduction, and the Commentary on XIV.

9 The honours given to a king after death by Lycurgus' legislation are intended to demonstrate that kings of Sparta are honoured not as men but as heroes.

*   *   *

XIV If someone were to ask me whether I felt that the laws of Lycurgus still remained unchanged,
2 I could not confidently say yes. I know that in the past the Spartans preferred to stay in Sparta in moderate prosperity rather than expose themselves to the flattery and corruption involved in
3 governing other cities. In the past they were afraid of being proved to have gold, but there are those
4 now who even pride themselves on possessing some. In the past the purpose of the expulsion of foreigners and the ban on foreign travel was to prevent citizens from being infected with idleness by foreigners; now I understand that the apparent leaders of the state are eager to govern foreign
5 cities for the rest of their lives. There was a time when they worked to be worthy to lead, but now
6 they are far more interested in ruling than in being worthy of their position. This is the reason why, whereas formerly the Greeks used to come to the Spartans and ask them for leadership against
7 reputed wrongdoers, now many are encouraging each other to prevent a revival of Spartan power. There is, however, no cause for surprise that such reproaches are being cast at them; they obviously do not obey either the gods or the laws of Lycurgus.

Commentary

I, 1–2 Sparta was certainly one of the most famous and powerful states of Greece at the time of writing, but one might well question the assertion that she had one of the smallest populations of all, though the exact size is a vexed question. Xenophon is clearly confining himself to the Spartiates; Herodotus gives a figure of 8000 adult males for the year 480 (vii, 234), and this corresponds well with a field force of 5000 at Plataea; by the time of Mantinea (418), the figure has dropped to 3,072 on a slightly reduced call-up (Thucydides v,68,3); by 371, the field force of Sparta is said to have fallen to 700 (Xenophon, History vi, iv, i5), implying a total of men of military age of about 1,200. These numbers may be compared with the effective fighting forces of Athens in 432-1; Thucydides (11,13,6) lists 13,000 hoplites, and a further force of 16,000 reserves to man the walls and forts of Attica; the latter would have included those under training and some metics. On the other hand, there were many Greek cities notably smaller than Sparta; for example, Plataea's garrison during the siege at the beginning of the Peloponnesian War included 400 Plataeans (Thucydides 11,78,3); one can hardly believe that the Athenians had tolerated the evacuation of any able-bodied defenders before the siege started. Further, just as the Athenian figures are in a sense misleading in that they take no account of the large number of Athenians occupied in naval affairs, so the figures for Sparta do not include the forces of the *Perioikoi* nor the armed Helots who often formed a part of her army. The commonplace that Sparta was a small state may well have arisen from a combination of the fact that she was *relatively* small for a state with such an important position in the affairs of Greece, and the way in which the Spartiates were obviously and heavily outnumbered by the Helots and others who lived under their domination.

The steady decline in the size of the Spartan population can be ascribed to a large number of factors, but not least will have been economic pressure arising from the land tenure system (see below), and the fact that Sparta was a rigid and exclusive oligarchy—there was virtually no question of recruitment to their number from outside the charmed circle. Loss of life in the earthquake normally dated to about 465 was considerable, and had long-term effects. It is also likely that Xenophon thinks in terms of Spartiate numbers in the fourth century rather than the fifth.

On the other hand, in ascribing the success of Sparta to her system of training, Xenophon must be right; the whole of this work shows the way in which the young Spartans were brought up to be efficient members of what was undoubtedly the finest military machine the Greeks had yet produced.

On the position of Lycurgus, and the claim of 'originality', see the Introduction.

I, 3–4 In beginning his discussion of the Spartan system with women in what he conceived as their only important role, as mothers of future Spartiates, Xenophon appears to have followed the lead of the Athenian oligarchic leader Gritias, who wrote on the constitution of Sparta in verse and prose towards the end of the fifth century. In one of the surviving fragments of his works Gritias says: 'I will begin with the birth of a man; how would one produce the best and strongest physique? If the father exercises energetically, eats well and tests his endurance to the limit, and the mother of the potential child is strong and takes exercise herself' (Dicls-Kranz, 11,88,32). Plutarch gives greater detail in his description of the exercise which the Spartan girls took: 'Lycurgus made the girls take exercise by running, wrestling and throwing the discus and javelin' (*Lycurgus* 14), and other sources add that Spartan girls learned to manage horses and drive carts. Again, the motive given is physical fitness for the bearing of children.

The contrast drawn in the text with 'other cities' no doubt applied to many other Greek states (though not to all*), but is aimed mainly at the upbringing of Athenian girls. The question of the position of women in Athens is much debated, and the present commentary is no placc for a full analysis. The extreme on the one side alleged that they virtually never went out of doors unattended, and generally led a dull and extremely cloistcred existence. This was questioned very strongly by Gomme,† who amassed much evidence which showed that there must at least have been considerably greater freedom for some women at certain times. It seems that Cimon's sitcr Elpinike (to take an upper class example)

* See for example Chios (Athenacus XIII, 586c) and Elis (Pausanias v, 16,2–6).
† 'The position of women in Athens in the fifth and fourth centuries', *C.Ph.*xx (1925) 1–25 = *Essays in Greek History and Literature* 89–115.

led a very free life, and common sense suggests that in the poorest families the women must frequently have left home on their own unaccompanied. There were many families without slaves, and while the women probably did not usually do the day-to-day buying of household necessities in the market-place, many did have market stalls at which they *sold* produce; it is difficult to believe that they were chaperoned. On the other hand, it seems that many Athenian girls led their lives in seclusion for much of the time before marriage, and were not much freer afterwards. The reason for the former is probably the high value put on virginity at marriage—hence the tight control and presence of chaperones; for the latter, we have the evidence of two court speeches where an advocate takes considerable pains to prove that a man's wife existed, which suggests strongly that she had been so little seen in public that the other side had been able to suggest that she did not exist.*   In sum, it appears that Xenophon represents 'accepted' ideas and standards, as one might expect; he disapproved of (and disregarded) the greater freedom arrogated to themselves by the wealthy and aristocratic, and also the greater freedom forced on the lowest classes by economic pressures.

Granted that many women led a cloistered existence, it is not really surprising that many of their occupations were sedentary—there was hardly space for anything else, and not even the wealthiest houses had anything like the long galleries of stately homes in England, designed to make exercise practical within the house. Economic necessity reinforced the other pressures; a house had to be as nearly self-supporting as possible, and obvious tasks for the women were the spinning and weaving of cloth, and the making of clothes; these were in fact the normal occupations of most women in Greece for much of their time. For the poorest, the household routine would also have taken up a good deal of time, though in better-off families slaves undertook the heavier jobs. Xenophon himself elsewhere recommended that a wife should take some part in the general running of the household, and should mix flour and knead dough to get some exercise (*Oeconomicus*, x, 11). Such occupations were a meagre substitute for the Spartan training, or for that matter, for the life of the peasant women, who, then as now, worked in the fields.

Whatever the modern reaction to the average life of Greek women or the Spartan deviation from the norm, Xenophon makes it clear that the reasons behind the Spartan system (and his approval of it) were not humanitarian; the motivation was purely eugenic, and the approach here, as in the section dealing with the begetting of children where the husband was incapable or unfit, was as totalitarian as any that has ever been proposed. Just as for military reasons Spartiates were relieved of the day-to-day problem of obtaining a living by the grant of a plot of land, so the women were relieved of menial work which could be done by slaves so that they could concentrate solely on their most important function—to produce healthy and acceptable children to serve the state.

The difference of diet stressed by Xenophon is given the same nominal motive, but is in all probability also connected with the amount of exercise the girls took. In the classical period the diet of most Greeks was poor by modern standards and relatively deficient in proteins; they ate meat only a

---

* See W. K. Lacey, *Family*, 168.

few times a year after a major state sacrifice, though fish was more readily available. It is not likely that the Spartan girls' diet was noticeably superior in this respect, but at least they appear to have had a reasonable quantity of food. It is quite possible that Xenophon has exaggerated the contrast.

The freedom of life enjoyed by the Spartan girls and women was no doubt of benefit to them, and certainly of practical value in a society where the men were away from home on service to the state even more than was the general rule elsewhere; at such times the women had to manage all the affairs of the household. However, they came in for some stinging criticism from other Greeks: Ibycus (sixth century BC) called Spartan girls 'thigh-showers', and Peleus in Euripides, *Andromache* 595–601 elaborates: 'No Spartan girl could lead a respectable life even if she wanted to; they leave their houses in loose dresses showing naked thighs, and race and wrestle with boys; intolerable behaviour. It is hardly surprising if Spartan women are not respectable.' Although Peleus goes on to discuss Helen as the classic case, the reference of the earlier diatribe is surely contemporary. Aristotle says that Spartan women 'live without restraint in respect of every sort of dissoluteness' (*Politics* 1269, b, 22); Plutarch refers to 'the laxity of morals which *later* affected them' (*Moralia* 228 B; my italics), and elsewhere is clearly at pains to deny what he takes to be a common charge: 'Marriage was so regulated for physical and political reasons, and was so far removed from the immorality which was later attributed to Spartan women …' (*Lycurgus* 15), and '(Lycurgus) freed (the girls) from all weakness and effeminacy of all sorts by making them, like boys, only wear one garment in processions. … There was nothing disgraceful in the light clothing of the girls, for they were modest, and there was no outrageous behaviour; in fact, it produced simple ways, and a desire for health and beauty' (*Lycurgus* 14).

Spartan marriage customs were in some measure bound to produce such charges (see below) and prejudice was inevitable where behaviour differed so radically from that in the rest of Greece; one may compare the accusations levelled at the first women to take advantage of Ata- turk's reforms in Turkey after the First World War, and the similar attitude of the older generations in many Moslem countries today to girls who, with government encouragement, áre taking to Western styles of dress, even when these are, to European eyes, very conservative.

I, 5–6 These sections continue the general theme of the paragraph, that Lycurgus' motive was eugenic. The provision that men and women should marry in their prime is in distinct contrast to the rest of Greece, where it was normal for men to be above thirty when they married, while their brides were often only about fourteen. Xenophon, speaking probably of Athens, comments on the fact that it is very unlikely that a man and wife will have anything in common as a basis for conversation (*Oeconomicus* 111,12), and a factor in this must have been the wide disparity in their ages, as well as the girl's relative lack of education. There is some evidence to suggest that the normal age of marriage for a Spartiate was in his twenty-fifth year; for girls it is more difficult to be definite, but Xenophon and Plutarch suggest that they were fully mature. The eugenic reasoning advanced appears to be biologically sound only in that mothers who are too young tend to have smaller children and greater problems in childbirth. On the other hand, while infrequency of meeting may make conception marginally more likely, there is no evidence that it has any effect on the physique of the child. Similarly, the better diet and superior physical fitness of Spartan mothers would be likely to make childbirth easier and less dangerous, but will hardly have affected the children except during pregnancy.

The attribution of these marriage customs to Lycurgus is one of the more blatantly obvious anachronisms in the traditional account of Sparta. The common life of the men in the *sussitia* looks like a survival of an extremely primitive tribal arrangement, and the existence of similar institutions in Crete makes it likely that these customs antedate the arrival of the Dorians in Southern Greece. Again, Plutarch has a fuller description (*Lycurgus* 15): 'Women were carried off by force at their marriage, not when they were small and not ready for marriage, but when they were in their prime and fully grown. The woman who was called the bridesmaid received the bride, cut her hair short, and dressed her in a man's cloak and sandals, and laid her on a mattress alone in the dark. The bridegroom came, not drunk or feeble through excesses, but sober as always, after dining with his companions. He entered, untied her ceremonial belt and carried her to the bed. Then, after spending a short time with her, he left for his usual accommodation soberly, to sleep with the other young men. Such also was his way of life thereafter, spending the day and sleeping with his comrades, and only visiting his bride secretly and with circumspection, afraid of the shame if anyone in the household should hear him. His bride also joined in the planning to facilitate their clandestine meetings as opportunity offered. This was not just a brief period, but sometimes long enough for children to have been born before the father had seen his wife by the light of day. These meetings not only instilled self-restraint and control, but meant that children were likely to be begotten whenever they met, and there was always something new and fresh in their love; they were not sated or exhausted by unlimited association.' Here are relics of a society where marriage by capture was the rule, though it is only symbolic in Plutarch's account. Many of the rules governing early married life originate in a situation where a man's military commitments had to outweigh all else; it is not without significance that the Spartiates were allowed to set up house with their wives at the age of thirty, that is after ten years of fully effective military life. Similarly, the way in which husband and wife met suggests some sort of trial marriage which did not become fully valid until a child was born.*   The dressing of the bride as a man is paralleled from Argos (another Dorian state), where the bride wore a false beard on her marriage night; there is probably some trace of primitive *riltes de passage* here.

I, 7–10 The provisions outlined in these sections are most unattractive to the modern reader, and Plutarch's similar description is an attempt to defend them without much confidence that he will succeed (*Lycurgus* 15). The arguments advanced are eugenic, and, above all, based on the interest of the state; it is vital that there should be children, and that these children should be born of healthy stock. An idea traceable in some primitive societies is that the 'noble seed' of the great warrior must be utilised as widely as possible for the future benefit of the tribe, and some remains of this feeling may lie

---

*   On Spartan marriage, see Lacey, *Family*, 196ff, to which the above discussion is much indebted.

behind the controlled permissiveness at Sparta. The personal feelings of the individual must be totally subordinate to the needs of the community. Such arguments are at least comprehensible, if distasteful, in the context of historical Sparta's perilous man-power position. In contrast, the justification offered by Xenophon is very naïve; if the Spartans really felt as he suggests they did, this must surely have been the result of long habituation to the practices described, and a rationalisation of the strains involved, rather than the reason for introducing them. One feels that he is being as naïve as Plutarch is when he says that these measures 'freed marriage of the hollow and effeminate vice of jealousy, and kept it free of all irregularities' (*ib.*). It is notable, and typical of the attitude of most ancient Greek writers, that the feelings of the women involved are barely considered.

On points of detail: clearly some Spartans did not marry at the usual age, despite the penalties which this involved (see below), and others will have remarried; from these will come the older husbands with young wives. It is to be presumed that those who 'did not wish to live with a wife' must have been either widowers, since the disgrace of the unmarried was such that they can hardly have been acceptable partners for someone else's wife within the terms laid down in this passage, or those whose wives had behaved in some way disgracefully so as to disqualify them in their husband's eyes, although he did not wish to divorce them and remarry. In either case, it is likely that these extreme steps were usually only taken when the man did not have male offspring already.

As to the concluding sentence, it is open to doubt whether Xenophon has made his point, for the answer to the question is clearly meant to be that Spartans *were* outstanding. Their excellence could as well be attributed to the rejection of weakling children at birth and the rigorous efficiency and single-mindedness of their upbringing as to the stress on eugenics.

II, 1 In switching to a discussion of education, Xenophon opens, as is his normal practice, with a contrast with non-Spartan practice, and here again it appears that he is considering Athens. He picks out the two features which offend him most : the entrusting of children to slaves at an impressionable age, and the physical pampering implicit in their clothes and diet. The *paidagogos* was a slave whose duty it was to supervise his charges' discipline, though inevitably he also had considerable general influence over them; however, there is no evidence of widespread harm resulting from this, and one must assume that parents took some care in selecting a *paidagogos*. Pericles answers the criticism which was widely levelled at Athens even in his day in philo-Laconian circles, that her education was 'soft' in the funeral speech put into his mouth by Thucydides (11,39,1): 'Their educational system imposes laborious discipline from early years in their search for manly courage, while we live in a more relaxed fashion; none the less, we meet equal dangers no less effectively than they.' For a full description of the Athenian educational system, see F. A. G. Beck, *Greek Education* 450-350 BC, 72–146.

II, 2–4 Xenophon omits one feature which might well be most offensive to other Greeks, the inspection of children at birth and their exposure if there was any suspicion of weakness. Exposure of infants was accepted in Greece, but the motive is presumed to have been economic, and it is more than likely that the average Greek would have looked askance at the eugenic reasoning behind the Spartan system; for details, see Plutarch, *Lycurgus* 16.

The Lycurgan *Paidonomos* was a senior citizen—in Xenophon's eyes the exact opposite of the Athenian *paidagogos*, since he was a man of proved excellence. Plutarch says: 'one of the respected leading men was appointed *Paidonomos*, and the boys were organised in companies under his direction, each under the most prudent and warlike of the Eirens' (*Lycurgus* 17). One must assume that he took only a general supervisory role in the organisation of the children, not a detailed part in their education, because of the numbers involved. One imagines that his job was not so dissimilar from that of the Headmaster of a Comprehensive School, who, because of its very nature, cannot know his pupils well, but is responsible for the general outline of their courses, and also for the administration of the most serious punishments— though, fortunately, we do not nowadays tolerate the floggings which are implicit in the description here, and were more severe in Sparta than was normal in the rest of Classical Greece; W. G. Forrest described the Spartan system as 'increasingly brutal and brutalising training schedules which passed for education'.*   One is not totally surprised that the result of the system 'is considerable obedience'—'respect' is slightly more surprising, and is perhaps a tribute to the efficiency of the 'brain-washing' element in Spartan education.

Plutarch says more than Xenophon about clothing: it was not until the twelfth year that the young Spartans had only one garment each, and it is quite possible that the regulation about going barefoot was not applied in winter until they were adult members of the *Krupteia*. The arguments from agility, hardiness and sure-footedness advanced in support of this practice might be reinforced by pointing out that the *Krupteia* had to operate night and day with great stealth, and if the members were used to going barefoot and not bothering about changes of clothing this might increase their silence and efficiency. However, going barefoot was not confined to Spartans—vases show that it was normal for Greeks to exercise barefoot; it could be a positive disadvantage in battle for obvious reasons.

II, 5–8 Xenophon now switches to a discussion of the life of the Spartan man, looking first at the age group referred to as 'Eirens'; Plutarch describes them as follows (*Lycurgus* 17): 'they call those who are already in their second year beyond the class of boys Eirens, and the oldest boys Melleirens. This Eiren, then, who is twenty, controls those under him in the practice battles, and has them as servants at table indoors; he orders the older ones to carry wood, the younger vegetables. They steal what they bring, some going to gardens, others slipping very subtly and cautiously into the men's *sussitia*. Anyone who is caught receives a severe beating for stealing carelessly and unskilfully.' Thus the Eirens were young men in their twentieth year and upwards, though it is not clear whether they remained in this 'class' for the whole of their twenties or only a part. Their main duties were military service of all kinds, supervising the younger members in the educational system, and controlling the Helots.

---

* *A History of Sparta* 950–192, 52.

The whole section smacks of rationalisation; Xenophon (presumably drawing on commonly held views about Sparta which were more than likely believed by the Spartans themselves) produces fairly plausible arguments to justify the sparse fare at the common tables where the Spartans ate, but the reasons are much more likely to have been produced to explain an existing situation than to be causes for establishing such a system from the beginning. Sparta did not import on a large scale, and her food supply was probably adequate for subsistence and no more. Theft to alleviate the pangs of hunger was a standard part of the ancient traditions of Spartan education—Plutarch (*Lycurgus* 18), amongst others, preserves the story of the young Spartan who had stolen a fox-cub and concealed it under his garment, and, rather than reveal what he had done, allowed it to tear his guts out; obviously an improving tale about Spartan courage, but it is surely in order to ask why he should *steal* a fox—and who from!

II, 9 The text of this section is obscure. Later there was a ceremony at Sparta which is first mentioned by Cicero (*Tusculans* 11,34), whereby the young men (authorities differ about their exact age) were whipped in front of the altar, and those who endured for the longest time received great honours. Oilier (and others) rightly question the detailed authenticity of such a ceremony for classical Sparta when the first mention of it is found so late; Sparta used her 'quaint old customs' very much as 'tourist bait' in the Roman period, and it is more than likely that there were some half-understood revivals which were all the more savage because brutality was expected. If the ceremony were merely a test of endurance, why the cheeses? On the other hand, the theft of cheeses from the altar could have formed some part of a ceremony connected with Artemis as presiding over agriculture; if the stealing were central, the aim would presumably be agility, swiftness and coolness, and the object to receive as *few* blows as possible.*   It looks as if Xenophon may hint at a partial survival of a primitive ceremony, which was later modified into the one described by Cicero, and combined it with some other ceremony involving agility; it is impossible to be sure. He may have been led to include the garbled version here by the combination of the references to stealing in the previous sections, and the general theme of toughness and endurance which runs through his whole description of Spartan education.

II, 10–11 Finally Xenophon reverts at considerable length to the question of authority, and stresses the importance attached to arrangements which ensured that the boys throughout their whole training were never not under authority of some sort. This obsession with control, which Xenophon stresses to the exclusion of much interesting detail which he might have included about what Spartan children were taught, may reflect Xenophon's own interest in discipline, but it is also a comment on the whole Spartan system, which assumed that children were basically wild animals that needed training and controlling with great care in order to preserve useful wild instincts, while adapting them to the state's purposes.

---

*   The whipping may have some parallel in the rites of the Lupercalia at Rome, and den Boer sees the theft of the cheeses as a survival of a puberty rite in the course of which the young men attained full manhood by seizing the cheeses, and acceptance as warriors by demonstrating their hardihood.

II, 12–14 The whole discussion of pederasty is clearly defensive, and very naïve. Such practices were widely accepted, though controlled, in Classical Greece, and may have formed an even more important part of life in a primitive tribal structure, where military needs dominating everyday life dictated that young men should grow up in an all-male society. Further, such bonds were useful in warfare, encouraging loyalty and comradeship. Xenophon's distinction between the spiritual and physical aspects of such attachments is interesting as an example of ingenious and ingenuous special pleading, but it is tempting to wonder how much even he expected to be believed.

To call chapter II a description of the 'educations of Sparta and of the other Greek states' is a travesty; Xenophon has given us an outline of what he regarded as the most important of those features of Spartan education which were geared to produce the qualities in which he claims, overtly or by implication, that Sparta excelled: obedience, respect and self-control. Simonides said 'They say that Sparta was called the man-tamer because its citizens were subservient to the laws … as horses are broken right from the outset' (Plutarch, *Agesilaus*, 1, frag. 218 Bergk). While den Boer is broadly right in saying that 'children of genuine Spartans are regarded as the property of the state', one must beware of the tendency to regard this as unusual or to read back modern prejudices; the whole tenor of Pericles' funeral speech in Thucydides is similar—the individual is subservient to the needs of the city. The difference in Sparta is one of degree, not of basic outlook.

Some of the omissions in Xenophon's account emerge later; for example, they had some musical training because it had practical application in war time (see below on xiii, 6–11). On literacy, Plutarch said 'their letters they learnt only for practical purposes' (*Lycurgus* 16), and the traditional Greek belief about Spartan anti-literacy is summed up, probably about 400 BC, in a curious philosophical rag-bag called the *Dissoi Logoi* (11,10; Diels-Kranz 11,90,2,10). 'The Spartans think it is a good thing for children not to pursue musical and literary studies, the Ionians that it is disgraceful for them not to have a good knowledge of the whole field.' Sparta was not quite the cultural desert which this implies. Ceremonies connected with the worship of Artemis Orthia imply at least some form of literary competition, though not necessarily any form of originality in the entrants; perhaps Homer and the Spartan poets were known at least. Further, there was singing and dancing; see (e.g.) Aristophanes, *Lysistrata* 1296ff.

Xenophon, then, has concentrated exclusively on the aspect of Spartan education which was summarised by Plutarch immediately after the passage quoted above: 'The whole of the rest of their training is designed to produce obedience, fortitude in distress and victory in battle.'

III Xenophon approves of the Spartan approach of keeping 'teenagers' as busy as possible to exclude time for other, less desirable occupations. In this he claims that Sparta is again the opposite of the rest of Greece, and seems to be describing a much exaggerated parody of the extremely 'hearty' Public School of the 1920s. Such a full-time educational system was only practical, of course, in a society where the state took financial responsibility for maintaining the children, for in the rest of Greece most children of this age were contributing to the family income. In Athens, for example, only those boys wealthy enough not to have to work seem to have spent their 'teens' in further education like the Spartans, though it was not state-controlled or organised, and the objectives were totally different. Secondly, the Spartan system could only work in a rigidly authoritarian society; in any other, the boys would revolt against an arrangement designed 'for them to have as little free time as possible' (§2). A small point worthy of note à propos of 111,3 is that the heirs-apparent of the kings were exempt from the *Agoge*; Plutarch points out that Agesilaus was unusual in that he had been through the full training since he was not heir-apparent in his youth. The simplest explanation of this is that the Spartans did not wish to risk the possibility of their future kings performing poorly. Alternatively, the Spartans perhaps regarded qualities other than those instilled by the *Agoge* as more important for their rulers; they may have realised that the stress on obedience was not an ideal training for a future king.

The modesty of the Spartans was proverbial (§4–5), but the logic of the comparison between men and women which Xenophon makes does not bear a moment's scrutiny. One suspects that he was led to draw this conclusion because, while the Spartan men were notably more modest than the average Greek, the women *appeared* to be much less so because of the greater freedom of their lives. The whole passage is a rhetorical exaggeration.

The last sentence is a passing hint at the fact that the adolescents were from time to time admitted to the adult *sussitia* for the main meal, a process which was regarded as part of their education: 'Boys also used to attend the *sussitia* regularly, as if they were going to schools of self-control. They used to listen to the political discussions, and watch the examples of gentlemanly behaviour ; they got used to humour and jesting without ribaldry, and learnt to take a joke without being offended' (Plutarch, *Lycurgus* 12).

IV, 1–6 It was natural and essential that Lycurgus should take particular care of those who had just reached manhood, not merely for the obvious reason given, true as this was, but also because it was from this group that the Eirens were drawn who controlled in detail the education of the next generation of Spartiates. Thus it would matter not merely that the individual Eirens chosen for this job should be outstanding, but also that the whole group should be seen to stand for the virtues which the Spartan state held to be most important; this necessity sprang from the right and duty of all Spartiates to take a hand in the upbringing of the children (vi, i). Naturally also, in such a male- orientated and authoritarian society, the 'teenagers' would admire and imitate those who were a little older than themselves. There is a further element involved in this spirit of competition which Xenophon saw as central at this stage: the Spartan education as outlined up to now must have killed initiative and personal ambition—its main aim appears to have been to produce a uniform body of highly disciplined robots. Again, Plutarch: 'overall, Lycurgus trained the citizens neither to wish nor to be able to live as individuals. Like bees, they were always to be integrated with the state, swarming round their leader, almost beside themselves in their eagerness and rivalry to belong wholly to the state.' (*Lycurgus* 25) By providing a motive for individual self-improvement at a late stage in the educational process, Lycurgus encouraged them to develop beyond the universal minimum which had been achieved by their earlier training.

The group of 300 picked by the *Hippagretai* (apparently officials whose sole job was to select and manage these three groups of 100 men) were the élite of the young Spartan army, and formed the bodyguard of the king on campaign (cf. Thucydides v, 72, 4), and were sometimes mounted, hence their title of 'knights'. The picture of rival groups fighting whenever they met is hardly attractive, but perhaps comprehensible if the primary objective was to prove one's physical strength; despite the right of any passer-by to separate the contestants, ill-feeling must have been generated, and this cannot have helped the unity which Xenophon claims was generated by the system in national crises. Élite units within modern armies are sometimes similarly unpopular. Some have connected this passage with the *sphairomachia* of ix,5, which is probably to be interpreted as some form of boxing rather than a ball game, the name deriving from boxing gloves shaped like modern ones, as opposed to the thongs with which Greek boxers normally bound their hands ; however, such an assumption would lead to the deduction that the whole of the 20–30 age group wore, or at least carried their gloves whenever they were out, which is surely too ludicrous to be conceivable. It is implicit in this passage that the membership of the group of 300 could change in the course of the ten years, and one is at liberty to doubt whether the rivalry was as pure and admirable as Xenophon implies. It is also likely that it led to a good deal of suspicion, hypocrisy and jealousy; the opposite is stressed in Pericles' funeral speech, and may be a conscious contrast: 'We not only have freedom in public life, but we do not indulge in anger and suspicion towards our neighbours in private if he does as he likes; we do not even put on disapproving looks, which, although harmless, are hurtful' (Thucydides II, 37, 2).

IV, 7 That the 'other Greeks' did not require their senior citizens to keep fit in centrally organised programs is merely an extension of the normal freedom of approach to adult life which they adopted. A reasonable sense of self-preservation must have made them keep moderately fit : they knew they would in all likelihood have to take part in hoplite battles involving considerable exertion, and that their survival depended on their ability to 'last the course'. In point of fact, many Athenians did go to the gymnasia every day before dinner (Xenophon, *Symposium* 1, 7). That hunting was a major part of an adult Spartan's way of life not only arose from the terrain which surrounded Sparta, where they had within their own territory extensive and good hunting areas, but is also another example of the survival of the values of a fairly primitive community. Xenophon, himself a 'country gentleman', was interested in hunting, and a treatise on the subject survives which may at least be based on his own ideas; it is interesting that in it the author defends hunting against those who attack it as a waste of time (*on Hunting* xii, 1 of).

V, 1–6 Xenophon has now described some aspects of the Spartan educational system up to the age of thirty, at which point the Spartiate was entitled to some relaxation of rigid discipline; he could, for example, set up house with his wife. It is important to be clear that Xenophon's account is selective, confined to the aspects which the author wishes to emphasise in contrast to the systems of other Greek states, those which he believes contribute most to the outstanding position of Sparta; witness the rhetorical questions with which he concludes each section.

In turning to a general discussion of Spartan life, Xenophon starts, not unnaturally, with the feature which was most noticeably different from the Greek norm, the communal life in *sussitia*. The nearest equivalent is a modern army mess, but the parallel is not close. All Spartiates had to eat the main meal of the day in their *sussition* until they were sixty, and between the ages of twenty and thirty had to spend the night with their companions also. Membership of a *sussition* was an essential prerequisite of full citizenship, and election at the age of twenty was dependent on satisfactory completion of the *Agoge*, physical fitness and acceptance by the members; one negative vote barred election. How membership was decided is uncertain; it may either have been a matter of being invited to join a certain group (or putting oneself up for it), or the *sussitia* may have had some territorial basis linked to land tenure. Whichever is correct, one cannot imagine that there was any significant wastage due to 'black-balling' because of the chronic shortage of manpower. It is perhaps marginally more likely that membership was not tied to land tenure because it appears from Plutarch (*Lycurgus* 12) that each *sussition* usually had about fifteen members; any territorial basis would be likely to lead in time to numerical disparity.

Xenophon again suggests that the institutions described were established with social motives, whereas they must surely have been survivals of a traditional way of life, which were probably later tightened up and systematised. From them may well have sprung *as results* the aspects of life which are here claimed as *motives* for the institution of the system. The military value of *sussitia* was universally recognised, and commented on as early as Herodotus (1, 65); the mixing of age groups was a reflection of the army organisation (see below), and is paralleled in the modern army mess. Now, as then, the mixing of age groups may bring shared experience and some degree of restraint as well. The recounting of noble deeds (§ 6) is reminiscent of Achilles signing of the 'famous deeds of heroes' (Homer *Iliad* ix, 189), and in a wider field is typical of any similar gathering of military men off duty.

The *sussitia* drew monthly contributions from each member. Plutarch gives the following figures: a bushel of barley, eight *choes* (about three and a half imperial gallons) of wine, five minas of cheese (either five or seven lb. approximately, depending on the standard used by Xenophon), two and a half minas of figs, and a small sum of money for meat and delicacies (*Lycurgus* 12). Dicaearchus, a historian of the fourth century quoted by Athenaeus (rv, 141c), gives figures which are a half as much again for barley and wine, indefinite for cheese and figs, and 'around some ten Aeginetan obols' for meat. Assuming the figures to be somewhere in the right region, they do not represent a princely diet, and it is not surprising that Spartan food had a poor reputation in Greece, nor that they found it necessary to supplement their basic provisions by hunting. Plutarch tells how a king of Pontus bought a Spartan cook in order to have some of their famous *zomos*; when he tasted it, he was disgusted, and the cook's answer implied that it could only be appreciated after the rigours of a Spartan day (Lycurgus 12).*

---

*   A slightly different version of the story is given elsewhere by Plutarch (*Moralia* 236 F). It is not clear exactly what *zomos* was; A. H. M. Jones describes it as 'a peculiarly nauseous haggis', and Plutarch implies that it was made of blood, salt and vinegar, possibly with meat added. (*Moralia* 128 C).

The restrictions on drink refer to drinking parties, which normally followed dinner; in the rest of Greece, the toasts were announced and the wine passed round so that each should drain his cup to it in turn. It is this practice which Lycurgus is said to have banned, since it meant that individuals did not have control over the strength of what they drank (Greeks normally drank their wine diluted with water), nor over how much they drank, since they were expected to respond to the general toasts. Lycurgus' provisions are here clearly good, and were widely noticed in the ancient world.

A verse fragment of Critias preserves a contrast between Spartan drinking parties 'and others (Diels, 11,88,6,9ff): 'such drinking (referring to non-Spartan parties) frees the tongue and leads to disgraceful stories, and weakens the body; dark mist sits in the eyes, and forgetfulness rots the memory, and the mind is befuddled. Servants cease to be obedient, and ruinous expense falls on the household. Spartan young men drink enough to bring joyful hope to the mind of all, and friendship and restrained gaiety to their conversation. Such drinking is good for the body, good for the mind, and not harmful to the purse; it is well suited for love and for sleep, the threshold of weariness, and also for Health, the sweetest of divinides to men, and for Self-control, the sister of Piety. ... The drinking of too many healths brings momentary pleasure but enduring pain. The Spartan way brings food and drink enough for thinking and working, but no excess; they have no day set aside for over-indulgence and drunkenness.' The excesses that often accompanied drinking parties are illustrated on a wide range of vases; one may naturally question the uniform sobriety with which the Spartans were credited—there was no check on what those over thirty did after they had gone home—but the whole Spartan system encouraged self-control. Xenophon realised that the theoretical ideal of equality of wealth was not a practical reality (see below), but, leaving this aside for the moment, it is probable that the *sussitia* did have many of the effects claimed for them; in particular, they would undoubtedly have fostered the comradely spirit which springs up in any similar military organisation, and would to that extent have been useful in the Spartan system. Equally, there was presumably a sound educational effect, as claimed, if the *sussition* was well conducted, though absence of wickedness and foul talk' would depend very much , on individual members. Restraint on excessive spending are more likely to have come from the various provisions and customs which restricted public display, discussed below.

V, 7–9 Sections 7 and 8 have something of the ring of afterthoughts to the main point. The matter of walking home at night only applied to those over thirty, since the others would be required to sleep where they were, and Xenophon's wording raises various other questions. The requirement to walk without a torch may make sense in preserving a soldier's night vision, but suggests dire possibilities if Aristophanes' description of the filth in the streets is anything to go by—as it presumably is in the absence of main drainage in Greek towns (*Wasps* 248,259). The phrase 'they must walk during the night as they do by day' is obscure: is one to take it as meaning with downcast eyes and without speech, with their hands within their cloaks (111, 4)? This could pose certain problems even if they were sober.

The relation of diet to exercise is fairly obvious (assuming the interpretation of the corrupt sentence to be approximately accurate), but adds little, and one might have expected the point at the end of §3.

Doubtless few would have quarrelled with the conclusion about Spartan physical health in §9 although it is somewhat exaggerated for effect, but it would have followed better from a full discussion of the training undertaken in the gymnasia. There is no clear indication why Spartan exercise was so much superior to that of other Greeks, though Oilier sees a possible hint in Xenophon's *Symposium*, 11, 17 and 1, 7, where it may be implied that there was some particular form of dance which was Spartan and particularly well designed to develop all parts of the body.

VI, 1–3 The exaggeration is manifest, not least in the last section; it is incredible that Sparta should have reached such a communistic- cum-utopian state that all goods were treated as common, and nobody minded if his neighbour helped himself at need. On the other hand, when one recognises the subjugation of the individual to the needs of the state which was normal in Greece, and reached its height in the Spartan tradition, it is possible to see this happening at times of crisis. Similarly, it is more credible to see the exercise of authority over another's children as being the exception rather than the rule. Yet here again, the necessity is more likely to have arisen at Sparta than elsewhere: they placed great stress on the training of boys by men, and yet the adults were so often absent on public service. There is practical sense behind the institution, but the moral value is presumably, as usual, deduced by Xenophon rather than the motive for introduction.

VI, 4–5 The danger of being caught out late must have been particularly relevant to the Spartan situation with the greater range of territory which could be covered and the difficulty of some of the terrain; it is noteworthy that the only reason which was normally accepted for absence from the evening meal in the *sussition* was that a man had been benighted while hunting. The exact nature of the caches of food referred to here is obscure, but it must be assumed that they were left in known spots for such an emergency, and regularly replenished; they presumably consisted of dried vegetables or some similar food which would last reasonably well. The accepted translation of this passage which implies that well equipped parties left behind what remained after they had eaten is scarcely tenable; there must have been more pattern than this, or the system would have been virtually useless.

The concluding sentence of the chapter implies that the arrangements of the *sussitia* and the provisions for hunting expeditions managed to level out inequalities of wealth in the society to an acceptable degree. Aristotle is definite that this was not so; there were Spartans who were so poor that they could not raise their contributions to their *sussition* without which they were expelled, and lost their status as full citizens (*Politics* 1271 a 3off), while others were very well off. Xenophon's rose- coloured spectacles are in evidence again.

VII If a system such as that at Sparta was to work effectively, it was essential that those who were to concentrate solely on military affairs had an assured source of income which would not be affected by their prolonged absence. Such a system would inevitably preclude normal competition for wealth; as Xenophon notes, the Spartiates were required to give their attention to other matters. Implicit behind this chapter is the thorny question of the 'lot' or parcel of land which it is said every Spartiate received, and from which he derived his necessary fixed income. If one could accept the evidence of Plutarch and other very late writers at face value, there would be no problem; unfortunately, as with so much relating to Lycurgus and early Sparta, the earlier the authority, the less clear the evidence. Xenophon says nothing of a Lycurgan land distribution or of a system of lots for every Spartiate, and Aristotle knew nothing of Lycurgan land reforms. Whatever be the exact truth in this vexed matter (which is not central to this chapter), it is certain that each Spartan had somehow a minimum land holding from which he derived income. In extreme cases his income was so low that he found it difficult to maintain his contributions to his *sussition* and keep up a family.

The 'Lycurgan' equality which is implicit in this chapter is certainly far from the truth at any period of Spartan history on which we have any information, and may always have been theoretical rather than real. At least some proportion of the land was the personal property of the family which held it, rather than state land allocated to them, and such land could be given away or left by will. Therefore, if a family only had daughters, the land would pass with them into families where the men already had holdings of their own; the inevitable result was inequalities of wealth which would increase with the passage of time. Aristotle says of his own day: 'Almost two-fifths of the whole country belongs to women because there are many heiresses and dowries are large' (*Politics* 1270 a 23).*   Note that at Sparta women could own property, while at Athens they could not.

Lycurgus cannot be credited with the decision to retain the primitive iron currency referred to in §5; no other currency was known in Greece until well after his death, whichever of the possible periods one accepts for his life. The owning of precious metals was restricted in some way in Classical Sparta, and the restriction was at least partly successful since writers so often ascribe many of the evils which later overtook her to its breakdown. Therefore, despite the implausible motives given, Xenophon must be on the right lines in his analysis. However, the ban on coinage was not total. The money contributions to the *sussitia* may have been made in the local iron currency, but visitors to Sparta presumably paid for accommodation and daily necessities in coin, and Spartan embassies abroad must have needed some money in coin to pay expenses; this may have been officially minted for the purpose. The Spartans offered the Messenians 'large sums of money' as a reward for smuggling food to Sphacteria in 425 (Thucydides iv,26,5). Then there are the vast fines imposed on some offenders, for example Agis 11, fined 100,000 drachmae (Thucydides v,63,2), and Pleistoanax 15 talents, which is 90,000 drachmae (Ephorus; Jacoby, *F Gr H* 11,70 F 193); there are other instances from the fourth century. Such fines may have been intended to force a man into exile rather than to be paid, but suggest at least the possibility of payment, whether in land, precious metal or coin. Perhaps the kings were exempt from the general prohibition on possessing precious metal; cf. below on xv. Further, it is never suggested that Spartiate families were totally self-sufficient; they had to acquire at least some of the necessities of

---

*   Plato, *Republic* viii,547 c 6-548 c 7, forms an instructive critical picture, which, for all its ostensibly theoretical nature, may plausibly be related to Sparta of the period.

life which they did not produce. Probably Sparta avoided coining money of her own for general use until late—the earliest extant Spartan coins date from about 300 BC—but enough coin found its way in from other states for some of their everyday purposes, and this circulated. The restriction on the acquiring of wealth, and therefore by extension on the regular use of coinage, only applies, of course, to the Spartiates; the *Perioikoi*, who often lived by trade and were vital to the existence of Sparta, used money as all other Greeks.

The rejection of commercial enterprise, necessary as it may have been to the military position of Sparta, probably did more harm than any other single factor to her cultural life, since it is a truism that all cultural pursuits are ultimately financed from the surplus of income over the expenditure needed for bare minimum survival; such a surplus was unlikely to appear without trade in ancient Greece.

VIII The logic of this chapter is not one of historical sequence; Xenophon is discussing the famous Spartan obedience, which leads him first to consider how Lycurgus secured the agreement of the people, though he disregards opposition which Plutarch says his measures met on their first introduction (*Lycurgus* 3 and 5); cf. below on xv. Then, although the powers he discusses are of much later origin, as he himself realised, he turns to the Ephors as clear examples of the obedience of Spartans even when holding magistracies; finally, he reverts to what he regards as Lycurgus' master stroke in securing obedience.

Like the last, this chapter raises problems of dating. First, it is not remotely likely that the whole of the *Eunomia* was brought in at one time, and it is therefore difficult to decide when the supposed consultation of the Delphic oracle took place. A document called the Great Rhetra is preserved in Plutarch, *Lycurgus* 6 (cf. Tyrtaeus frag. 3 Bergk), which is traditionally Lycurgan and sanctioned by Apollo, but must surely be dated to the seventh century, and probably not early in it either. Many of the other provisions, especially those which Xenophon has been discussing in the previous chapters, and which are therefore presumably referred to here, must be much earlier. However, it is not plausible to suggest that any legislator would have thought it worth while to get his proposals approved by Delphi much before 725, when the oracle first began to emerge as a political force. Delphic approval for one provision may have been extended in popular tradition to the whole system, much of which had been in existence for a long time in the late seventh century. The oracle may have been consulted about then in connection with a tightening up of the Spartan system which appears to have taken place then. It is worth noting that the approval of Delphi would have carried a good deal more weight with an average Greek than we might suppose from a modern standpoint; however, it is unlikely that even Delphic approval could have carried through reforms which were not basically acceptable to the Spartans and seen to be necessary.

The date of the institution of the Ephors is another insoluble conundrum. They held a position of power by the sixth century, and it is tempting to link this authority with the name of Chilon, who was Ephor in 556–5; however, Ephors probably existed well before this. By the fifth century their powers were very considerable, and Xenophon only touches on those which are germane to his theme. A frequently used analogy to the position of the Ephors is that of the Tribunes at Rome, but Tribunes had not the real powers of the Ephors, who also accompanied the kings on campaign after the beginning of the fifth century. Further, in many ways Ephors look like representatives of the aristocracy curbing the royal power; cf. xv,7.

The possibility of deposing magistrates in the course of their year of office was far from unique; as Xenophon well knew, all magistrates had to have their conduct approved once a month at Athens (to take only one example), and any complaint could lead to prosecution and deposition; equally, Athenian magistrates could be impeached at any time of the year for a sufficiently serious offence. The difference was that the Ephors apparently acted on their own authority (therefore 'like tyrants'), whereas at Athens or elsewhere a court decision was required. Xenophon's desire for the telling contrast has led him to obscure the precise point of difference.

IX It would indeed be a 'source of wonder' if one man had been able to establish the Spartan principle of bravery and their preference for death to dishonour. Such is the code of primitive, aristocratic and war-like societies, and it is not surprising to find such values elevated to the level of the greatest of virtues at Sparta. The Spartan scale of values was perhaps best expressed at an early date by Tyrtaeus, who, despite an anti-Spartan tradition that he was a lame Athenian summoned to Sparta to bolster morale at a time of difficulty during the second Messenian War of about 640-20, was probably himself a Spartan, and held command in the war:

'I would not remember nor include in my song any man for swiftness of foot or wrestling skill, not even if he had the strength and stature of the Cyclops and ran more swiftly than the north wind from Thrace, nor yet if he were more handsome than Tithonus or wealthier than Midas or Cinyras, nor again if he were more royal than Pelops the son of Tantalus or more sweet-tongued than Adrastus, nor even if he had every virtue other than might in war. A man is not good in war unless he has the courage to look on blood and slaughter and stand face to face with his foe and strike. This is virtue, this is the best and finest prize for a young man to win among men. It is a blessing common to the city and the whole people when a man stands firm in the front rank with determination, utterly forgetting the disgrace of flight, protected by his courage and endurance, steeling his neighbour by his words; this man is good in war. Swiftly he routs the savage ranks of the enemy, eagerly he stems the tide of battle. He who falls in the front rank and loses his dear life brings glory to his country, his people and his father; wounded many times in front through shield and breastplate, he is mourned by old and young alike, and the whole city grieves with bitter longing. His tomb, his children and his line are marked out among men; never will his glory and his fame perish; although he is in the tomb, he achieves immortality, for mighty Ares slew him at his moment of glory as he stood and fought for his children and his land. If he escapes the black fate of death and upholds the proud boast of his spear in victory, young and old alike honour him, and great are his joys before he dies; as he grows old he is outstanding among the citizens, and none would willingly deprive him of his honour or his rights; all yield place to him, the young, his contemporaries and his elders. This is the peak of virtue to which each should now aspire, never relaxing in war' (Diehl3 i, i, g).

The opposite point of view was expressed much more succinctly (and arguably more gracefully) at about the same time or a little earlier by Archilochus of Paros: 'Some Thracian now glories in the shield I dropped by a bush; there was nothing wrong with it, but I had no choice—and I saved my life. What do I care for that shield? To hell with it! I can get just as good a one again' (Diehl3 i, iii, 6). Plutarch (*Moralia* 239 B) records a story that as soon as Archilochus arrived in Sparta he was expelled for having written this epigram.

Whatever the truth of the story about Archilochus, it is surely true that not all Spartans naturally shared Tyrtaeus' approach to war, and this supposition is borne out by Xenophon and other sources, which list detailed penalties for those guilty of cowardice; even Spartans needed more than abstract ideals to encourage them to live up to the very high standards expected of them. In fact, if a Spartan deserted in the face of the enemy, the least penalty was to lose his citizenship; the penalties referred to here must therefore be for lesser forms of cowardice—it was not enough merely to do the minimum.

The whole discussion of penalties is obscure and rather unsatisfactory. The statement that cowards in other Greek cities suffer very little is demonstrably false, another rhetorical exaggeration designed to heighten the contrast. In Athens cowardice was a specific charge; those found guilty suffered partial loss of citizen rights, including exclusion from the market-place and state sacrifices—and here again for an offence less than actual desertion in the face of the enemy. Granted the military orientation of Spartan society, exclusion from the *sussitia* and social ostracism are penalties which are only to be expected; the others mentioned are less easy. The *sphairai* contests have already been noticed in passing in iv, 6. For long, scholars held that this was a form of ball game, but it seems more likely that it was a type of boxing match, particularly since the 'game' is said to be the nearest possible simulation of war. Obviously the branded coward could not be included in the group of 300 outstanding young men picked by the *Hippagretai*; it is not surprising that cowards were also left out of the less formal *sphairai* contests if they were some form of para-military exercise.

Plutarch (*Lycurgus* 21) refers to three choruses of differing age groups whose function was to sing of deeds of bravery, past, present and future; it is not surprising that the cowards did not play a major role, here, though Xenophon refers not merely to them, but to a wider field, including dancing. The reference to unmarried women is again presumably a matter of social ostracism, though this ostracism extended not merely to a coward's daughters but also to other girls whose guardian he might be. Spartans were unwilling to marry into such a family—for eugenic reasons? It is not surprising that it was difficult for a coward to find a wife, but the implication of this passage appears to be that a branded coward's wife might leave him, and despite this he would be subject to the penalties inflicted on bachelors. Plutarch describes the disabilities of the unmarried Spartiates (*Lycurgus* 15): 'They were excluded from watching the boys and girls at exercise. During the winter the magistrates ordered them to walk around the market-place without cloaks, and as they walked they had to sing a song against themselves stating the justice of their punishment for disobeying the laws; they were also deprived of the respect and service which the young showed to their elders.' Xenophon calls this *atimia*; while the primary meaning is 'disgrace' in this context, it is also used as the term for partial or total loss of citizen rights. Marriage was regarded as part of a man's duty to the state, and it was normal for the proposers of ideal constitutions, such as Plato, to include penalties for men not married by a certain age, usually the mid-thirties.

The final sentence is more of a comment on Xenophon than on Sparta.

X Xenophon here ends his discussion of the Spartan educational system, with all its pervasive and life-long control of what a man did; it has something of the feel of '1984' with 'every man's neighbour' taking the place of 'Big Brother'. The whole tone, particularly in § §4—7 is more theoretical, almost philosophical, than that of the previous nine chapters. He gives his approval to the core of Lycurgus' provisions, recognising their severity, but arguing their justice; finally he points to their antiquity, for him yet another proof of virtue. 'All praise' them is at least an exaggeration; the truth is betrayed by the remainder of Xenophon's concluding sentence.

On matters of detail, see the Introduction on the date of Lycurgus and on the *Homoioi*. The *Gerousia* was the main advisory council in Sparta, consisting of the kings and twenty-eight members who were all over the age of sixty. The method of election to this body is yet another 'primitive' survival, described in detail by Plutarch, *Lycurgus* 26. In brief, the candidates appeared before the assembly of Spartiates, who shouted their approval of each one. Men locked in a building near by where they could not see the Assembly, and therefore could not see which candidate appeared when, judged the loudness of each shout; the loudest won. Members of the Gerousia had a position of very great honour and probably considerable influence in day-to-day, informal discussions, though their political power 'on paper' was not very great. Xenophon approves, without apparently considering the dangers of a governing council many of whom must have been approaching senility, and the repressive effect its existence must have had on younger men with good ideas. Aristotle (*Politics* 1270 b 36–1271 a 13) is well aware of the disadvantages, and describes the method of election (not unjustifiably) as 'childish'.

XI The main aim, one might almost say the only aim, of the Lycurgan system was to produce the best possible military machine; it is therefore natural that Xenophon should turn now to a more detailed discussion of the Spartan army. He starts, as he did with the life of a Spartiate, from the very beginning, and it is interesting to see that the tradition on which he draws does not go back to a period earlier than that at which the Ephors established themselves as powerful magistrates; it cannot have been before the mid-sixth century at the earliest that they had control of the mobilisation of the army, and it is more likely to have been later. Similarly, the division of the army into regiments (*morai* §4) appears to have been a fairly recent innovation. Almost all Xenophon's military description relates to the Spartan army as he knew it himself in the early fourth century. He is presumably drawing on his extensive experience of fighting with Spartans, particularly in Asia Minor under Thibron and Dercylidas in 399–7, and under Agesilaus, to whom he became greatly devoted, in 396–4. For all this, there are numerous small details which cannot be made to tally with our knowledge of the actual Spartan field army of the period. This is the basis of one of Chrimes' main attacks on the authenticity of the work, but it seems more likely that here, as elsewhere, Xenophon sacrifices detailed precision to a generalised and idealised picture designed to support his main thesis of the excellence of Sparta.

XI, 2–3 It is difficult to judge how much superior the Spartan supporting forces were to those of the other Greeks. Xenophon was an experienced soldier, and his remarks in this section therefore merit great respect; note, however, that he merely comments on the efficiency of the system without specifically claiming superiority over others, although the properly organised baggage train *sounds* more efficient than the average administration of such things in Greece. Naturally, the artisans taken on campaign would have been *Perioikoi* or Helots; such occupations were not for the *Homoioi*. Despite the 300 so-called cavalry enlisted under the *Hippagretai*, Sparta did not have a regular cavalry force until 424; before this date the cavalry were a despised and unimportant arm of the forces, raised and equipped *ad hoc* for a particular job.

The red cloaks appear to have been worn in battle not merely because it was a colour which women in Greece did not wear, but also because blood would show up less on them if the soldiers were wounded (Aristotle, *Constitution of Sparta* fr. 86 = Müller *FHG* II, p. 130; Plutarch, *Moralia* 238 F). It is perhaps also relevant that red appears to have been associated throughout primitive Greece with amulets and other similar magical devices to ward off harm. Red cloaks are not exclusively Spartan. There are records of whole armies so dressed, of which only small sections were actually Spartans; had they been deliberately equipped in the Spartan fashion to produce a psychological effect on their enemies? The mention of bronze shields is more difficult in that they were standard throughout Greece at the time; it is possible that the Spartans had only recently abandoned the larger, leather shield of antiquity. If this were so, the comment would be explicable, even if grossly anachronistic, since Xenophon would be giving a reason for their adoption, and also incidentally commenting on Spartan turn-out—one can easily believe that they took more pride in the polish of their shields than the average Greek.

A fragment of Plato the comedian comments mockingly on the Spartans' long hair in wartime (Kock, 1,124); presumably it was archaic. To wear it was a considerable relaxation of the normal restrictions for those under thirty, as is shown by the passage in Plutarch where the bride has her hair cut short so that she shall look like a young man (see above on 1,5–6).

XI, 4–6 The division of the army into units is a subject on which ancient authorities conflict; in translating I have deliberately selected words to represent the various grades of officer and divisions of the army which carry as little overtone as possible from the modern world. Preconceptions should be totally eliminated from the reader's mind if possible, because in Sparta, as elsewhere in the ancient world, the whole officer structure and arrangement in tactical units was so different that terms are not transferable. The important aspect is that Sparta had a standard and highly organised officer structure, a feature missing from almost all contemporary Greek armies, who lacked more than anything the skill and steadiness in command best seen in the Roman centurion. Because of their command structure, the Spartans were able to carry out certain fairly basic manoeuvres on the battle-field which were beyond other Greek forces; normally, once a Greek army was committed there was little the general could do except join the ranks and hope to inspire those immediately around him by his example.

By Xenophon's day the *Perioikoi* were probably brigaded with the Spartiates in the hoplite army; he does not point this out because it would have been out of key with the whole passage which is dealing in wide generalisations, and to mention the essential contribution of the *Perioikoi* to the Spartan army would have lessened the impact of the picture he is painting. The exact numbers in each unit, and the total for the army are matters of deep controversy beyond the scope of this commentary; Thucydides (v, 68, 3) gives a slightly different picture. For a full discussion, see Gomme, Andrewes and Dover, *Commentary* Vol. iv, 110-7, and Wade-Gery, *Essays in Greek History*, 71ff.

XI, 7–10 The superior discipline of Spartan forces contributed enormously to their success, not least because of their steadiness (§7). For his security the Greek hoplite depended on the protection offered to his exposed right side by his neighbour's shield; thus any casualty or disruption of the line was potentially dangerous, and real discipline and automatic reactions were essential. The various manoeuvres mentioned in these sections are largely self-explanatory, though they must have depended on a detailed chain of command and precise reaction, for there is no question that Xenophon understates the difficulty of executing them in the face of the enemy. He was probably led to do so by the practical professional's contempt for the theorists (the 'instructors in tactics' of §8). When an enemy appeared in the rear the Spartans took up reverse order because the lines were normally drawn up with the most experienced men at the front; if they had not reversed their positions, the least experienced would have gone into battle in the front rank, and thus born the brunt of the fighting. The commander of a Greek army was normally stationed on the right, as was the commander of each individual unit in the line; this gave him greater control over the tendency of the hoplite to edge to the right to get more protection from his neighbour's shield. The claim that there is no disadvantage in having the commander on the left must assume the discipline of the Spartan army which would have minimised this tendency. The point about encircling is obscure; an attempt by the enemy to encircle the commander personally (rather than the whole formation) is probably meant, and, if so, then one can understand the benefit of having the shield on the outside.

XII It is surprising to find Xenophon even mentioning the shape of the Spartan camp, since Greek armies did not normally fortify their camps heavily, regarding them as places to be abandoned, not defended, if the enemy approached; the whole Greek fighting technique was geared to set-piece battles in the open. The reason for Xenophon's description may be a desire to give a context to his description of life inside the camp; he is the only authority for a circular camp.

The postings of sentries by day and by night show not merely military sense, but also that even on campaign the Spartans did not trust the Helots and other non-Spartans who accompanied them; this can be the only deduction from the central storage and guarding of arms, and one must assume that the arms dumps were guarded by night as well as by day, unless §7 is to be read as implying that all arms were drawn by their owners each night before they went to sleep. It is perhaps less than likely that the Helots would all be left armed during the night if such security precautions were taken during the day.

The Skiritai came from the northern end of Spartan territory, and were a hardy mountain people. It seems probable, though it is nowhere specifically stated, that they were light-armed specialists; cf. xiii, 6. Mercenaries were first used by the Spartans in the course of the Peloponnesian War (Thucydides III, 109, 2), and became a regular feature of the Spartan army, as of those of all other Greek states, in the fourth century. The tone of §4 is again defensive; probably many Greeks mocked the Spartans for their excessive caution even within their own camps, but again the passage is useful evidence of their attitude and position.

The daily routine in the camp is much what one would expect of Spartans, though a little more relaxed than their way of life in peacetime; such relaxation on campaign was unique in Greece (Plutarch, *Lycurgus* 22). Their efficiency and organisation contrast vividly with the laissez-faire apparent in the accounts of the encampments of some other Greek armies, for example that described in Demosthenes, *Against Conon*, 3f. To stress the piety of the Spartans in camp would be only natural for Xenophon, who throughout his life showed more than ordinary respect towards the traditional Greek religion.

XIII By a natural transition Xenophon now moves to a brief discussion of the kings; not merely were they in themselves a unique survival in Greece proper, but they commanded the army. It is with the latter aspect of their position that he is concerned, not with a general discussion of their role in the Spartan constitution. Xenophon assumes throughout that only one king was present on a campaign. The rule that only one king should accompany an army was established after the fiasco of Demaretus' disagreement with Cleomenes in 506, thus reversing earlier practice (Herodotus v, 75). Xenophon reflects the situation of his own day.

XIII, 1–5 It was normal for the king to be maintained at public expense at all times (Herodotus vi, 57), and Xenophon presumably comments because not merely he, but also his council were publicly maintained on campaign. The membership of the council is specified in §7; the most important members were the six regimental commanders. The list is not in order of importance; Xenophon appears to have listed first those who were almost always present—hence the high position of the *aulos*-players—and then those whose duties would often prevent their presence at meals. The 'volunteers' might be anyone invited, and in all probability it was in this capacity that Xenophon himself was a member of the entourage of Agesilaus.

The detailed description of sacrifices and the great importance attached to them are in tune with Xenophon's own interests, but are neither surprising nor a piece of archaism. One of the king's main functions was as an intermediary between men and gods; cf. xiii, ii. Modern readers tend to be misled by the 'advanced' and 'rationalist' tone of a few Athenian writers into thinking that official religion was not of any great importance in classical Greece; the reverse is true, as can be seen from a mass of evidence, not least the impiety trials in Athens towards the end of the fifth century. For the particular point of sacrifices at the border being taken seriously, see (e.g.) Thucydides v, 54,2. Quite incidentally, Xenophon shows up an important distinction: whereas in Sparta itself the Ephors had at least as much constitutional authority as the kings, on campaigns the authority of the king was much greater despite the restriction noted in §10 below—an exact parallel to the greatly increased power of a Roman magistrate in the field.

The sacrifice offered to Zeus the Leader is not merely a sacrifice to the father of the gods, but also to a god who was specifically a war god, under a name traditional at Sparta. 'The gods associated with him' are probably the Dioskouroi, Castor and Pollux, since they, and particularly Castor, were the tutelary war-gods of Sparta. Athena was associated with Zeus in at least one Spartan cult; the sacrifice mentioned by Xenophon was probably offered to her in her role as a tutelary divinity of Sparta called Athena of the Brazen House. To preserve the fire from a particular sacrifice for use on subsequent occasions was not solely a Spartan custom; such fire was regarded as peculiarly sacred and pure.

The hour of the day-to-day sacrifices is a little unusual; it was normal to sacrifice to the Olympian gods early in the day, but not as early as this. Xenophon's explanation, that the Spartans intended to preempt the favour of the gods before the enemy held their sacrifice, is possible, but it smacks of his personal combination of piety and practical utility, and may be his own guess at the explanation of an ancient custom. The list of those present at the sacrifice requires no comment except for the 'commanders of foreign detachments'. They may be the commanders of contingents from the Peloponnesian League, or of detachments of *Perioikoi*, although he does not use the normal term for the latter, and at the period referred to the *Perioikoi* were fully integrated in the Spartan army; it seems more likely that he is referring to Spartiates assigned to command mercenary troops.

XIII, 6–11 The fluent efficiency of the Spartan command structure was apparent *en passant* in §§i and 5—irrelevant and trivial matters are not allowed to distract the commander-in-chief, and once decisions are taken they are transmitted smoothly; cf. Thucydides v,66,3f. A similar theme runs through the rest of the chapter: the whole process is thorough and efficient because the arrangements have already been made, and each man knows his duties.

Before a battle, the king is said to take the *agema* of the first regiment. It is possible (though unlikely) that this just means 'takes command of'; it may alternatively be that the *agema* is a division of the regiment. However, Ollier has suggested attractively that, since the word came later to mean the royal bodyguard in the Macedonian army, *agema*, like other technical terms, was borrowed by the Macedonians from Sparta, and therefore the reference here is to a similar special corps, consisting of the 300 cavalry who were responsible for the king's safety. The translation 'the first company' is intended to give something of an 'élitist' feel without prejudicing the issue. The king's position towards the right wing was relatively well protected and secure, and from it he could exercise as much control as was practicable over the actual battle line. He was in no position to control the reserves, and Xenophon notes that this was the responsibility of the senior member of the king's council, who was presumably the senior regimental commander. It is symptomatic of the lack of sophistication of a hoplite battle that it was not felt necessary for the commander-in-chief to have personal control of the disposition of the reserves, nor, apparently, of where and when to commit them.

In §§8–9 Xenophon digresses to describe certain ceremonies at the beginning of an actual battle. The sacrifice of a year-old male goat, presumably to Artemis Agrotera, was a form of sympathetic magic designed to ensure that the same fate overtook their enemies. The musicians played the *aulos*, an instrument whose basic principle was not unlike that of our oboe, and their presence was designed to enhance the dignity of the occasion, and, combined with the dress of the army, was presumably intended to have an effect on the morale of the enemy. A noteworthy feature of a Spartan battle line was that it advanced in an organised and controlled way to the music of the *aulos*. Their soldiers had enough confidence and skill to do without the initial advantage which most Greek armies sought from the impact of as fast a charge as a hoplite could achieve, and they did not rely on shouting to encourage each other as they went into battle.

The discussion of 'words of encouragement' (§9) is extremely obscure. Perhaps Xenophon refers to the period immediately before the two sides actually met when general exhortations would be inaudible because of the *auloi* and general din. Even if this is so, it is suprising that the members of a single platoon, about thirty-two men, probably in four columns eight deep, could not hear their commanding officer; perhaps the whole process has been 'telescoped', and the point at issue is that the commander of the *next* platoon could not hear, and therefore the message had to be passed from the man on the nearest corner of the neighbouring platoon.

Xenophon returns in §§10–11 to the main theme of the chapter, the position of a king on campaign, and ends with some fairly random notes, together with an analysis of how he was relieved of unnecessary duties. The special officers mentioned handled some of the more delicate matters about which disputes might arise, particularly between the Spartiates and their allies. The functions of the king remain purely military and religious, which is not meant in any way to detract from his position, but rather to emphasize its dignity: all that really mattered at the time was entrusted to him.

XV After ascribing all the excellent aspects of the *Eunomia* to Lycurgus, the book not unnaturally concludes with a chapter on the method by which he ensured acceptance of his reforms. Despite the tendency of classical Sparta to ascribe almost everything to Lycurgus, nobody ever suggested that he was responsible for the double kingship; it was rightly recognised as being of much earlier origin. It was therefore necessary to posit some process whereby reform was accepted, and men realised that this reform involved some curtailment of the powers of the kings. Xenophon does not descend to the sort of folk-tales purveyed by Plutarch, who claims to have details of the strife which was the prelude to the reforms, and even to be able to give a significant number of names of those involved (*Lycurgus* 3 and 5), but concentrates on the firmer ground of the position which was established for the kings, implying that a reasonable compromise was reached. Accepted throughout the chapter is the belief, already mentioned in the Introduction, that the Spartan constitution remained unchanged from the time of Lycurgus until after the classical period; this is absurd, whatever the date assumed for Lycurgus, but does reflect the truth that Sparta received a stable constitution relatively early, and retained it for a long period with surprisingly little modification and an almost total lack of the violent change endemic in Greek politics. Chapter xv is the nearest the whole work comes to discussing the constitution in the modern sense, but there is no attempt at an exhaustive analysis. To take but two obvious examples, there is no discussion of the power to initiate legislation nor of the exact relative positions of kings and Ephors. Yet again, Xenophon is concerned with the actual situation rather than historical sequence or detailed precision. One point could be misleading: §§6–7 might be read as implying that Ephors were instituted, or more likely already important, at the time of Lycurgus; that this was not so is clear, and Xenophon himself implied as much in viii, 3.

The *Education of Cyrus* betrays in Xenophon a tendency to favour royalty, and he gives his preference full rein here. He restates the essence of the king's position: the leader of the state in matters of religion and war. This is, no doubt, a primitive survival, and the privileges which went with the position, and are listed here, were equally antique; the 'grant' by Lycurgus must in reality represent a moment of constitutional change when the kings were allowed to *retain* their ancestral privileges. On one point Xenophon is wide of the mark: Plato said: 'One must be quite sure that they (the Spartans) are the wealthiest of the Greeks in gold and silver, and the king is the wealthiest of them; the largest share of this income belongs to the kings, and the royal tribute which the Spartans pay to them is not insignificant' (*Alcibiades* i, 123 a–b). Despite all this income, the kings lived at public expense. There is no question that there were differentials of wealth, and that the 'inner group' of families were better off than most Spartiates; Xenophon's own discussion of the lending of hunting dogs (vi, 3) demonstrates that differences existed. Within the inner group, it would not be surprising if the two royal families were the most wealthy; they owned a considerable amount of land, and had large incomes and profitable privileges, including receiving the skins of sacrificial victims, mentioned here. Perhaps Xenophon is judging by the way of life of Agesilaus, which was notably modest.

The remaining details included by Xenophon are tantalisingly brief and disjointed, but together paint a picture of the high status of the king in society, while at the same time showing that he was not totally exempt from the ordinary duties of a Spartiate. The obligation of eating in the *sussitia* may have been waived relatively often, but it was there in theory, and it is recorded that Agis 11 was prevented from disregarding it when he returned from a successful foreign campaign (Plutarch, *Lycurgus* 12); equally, the king's arrival did not interrupt an Ephor engaged on public business. The exchange of oaths was a mark of the constitutional restraints on the king, and presumably dates from the time of their imposition. There was nothing unique about this *type* of oath being taken regularly by various organs of government in a Greek state.

Having chosen to focus so much attention on the regal aspect of the Spartan constitution, Xenophon tones down the unbalanced effect by his final remarks on the kings when alive, and perhaps it is not implausible to see the influence of Agesilaus here; if there was any question of the work being published, a king who wished to achieve his aims in Sparta by being modest could not have had his position jeopardised by Xenophon's fondness for royalty; their close association was too well known. The temporary lowering of the grandiose tone is more than compensated for by the stress laid on the semi-divine honours rendered to the kings after death; they included widespread and compulsory mourning, representatives to attend the funeral from all over Laconia, and the suspension of public business; the details are given by Herodotus (vi, 58).

XIV It is impossible to conceive that this chapter was originally designed to stand between xiii and xv as the manuscripts transmit it; its tone is altogether different, it refers to Sparta in decline, and is manifestly condemnatory, while the whole of the rest of the work is laudatory, and rather uncritically so. Assuming that xiv is genuine, which seems likely since a forger would hardly have inserted such a manifestly different piece so ineptly, one must fall back on some theory such as that propounded in the Introduction which assumes that Xenophon had written, but not 'published' the work fairly early in his life, and that xiv is a 'postscript' attempting to analyse briefly the cause of Sparta's later downfall.

Xenophon is by no means the only source for the fact that Spartans, once removed from the restraints inherent in life in Sparta, tended to fall away from 'Lycurgan' standards; Pausanias and Lysander were flagrant examples, and there were many more. In the years immediately following 404 so many Spartans had to go abroad, and even live abroad for long periods to administer Sparta's newly won dominion in Greece; worse, many of them were sent out as Harmosts, a position which made them virtual tyrant of a city; what could be more different from the restraints of everyday life at home? Equally, Sparta's position dictated that she must admit many more foreigners to Sparta itself, and therefore the ancient practice of expelling foreigners fell even more into abeyance. The practice was never rigid, but in times of tension had provided a way by which the leaders of the state could and did prevent the ordinary Spartiate from being exposed to seditious ideas; compare the story of Archilochus, above. At the time when xiv was written it was apparently these very leaders of the state who were most corrupted—perhaps understandably so if they had in any case been the wealthier members of society. The tragedy of the change is epitomised for Xenophon by the fact that, whereas formerly the Greeks in general looked to Sparta for moral leadership, now they were banding together to prevent a revival of her power. He can only comfort himself with the assertion that the fault lay not with the *Eunomia* which he admired so much, but with the men who rejected all that it stood for. However, such a disastrous collapse calls into question the whole of a system which cannot instil into those brought up under it sufficient strength of character and devotion to their professed ideals to stand up to any prolonged exposure to standards different from their own.

Select Bibliography

1. Ancient Sources

a.   The *Politeia of the Spartans*:

The present translation has been based on *Xenophontis Opera Omnia*, Vol. v; *Opuscula*, edited by E. C. Marchant, (Oxford, Oxford University Press, 1920) and also Marchant's edition in the Loeb Classical Library, *Xenophon* Vol. vii, *Scripta Minora*, (London, Heinemann, and Cambridge, Mass., Harvard University Press, 1925) and *Xenophontis Opuscula*, edited by G. Pierleoni, (Rome, Acad, dei Lyncei, 1954). There is no adequate commentary in English ; the standard work is *Xénophon, La République des Lacédémoniens*, text, translation and commentary by F. Ollier, (Lyon, Bos, 1934) a thorough and intelligent analysis to which I owe a good deal. I have also consulted Jenofonte, *La Republica de los Lacedemonios*, edited by M. R. Gomez, revised by M. F. Galiano, (Madrid, Instituto de Estudios Politicos, 1957) (in Spanish). K. M. T. Chrimes, *The Respublica Lacedaemonorium ascribed to Xenophon*, (Manchester, Manchester University Press, 1947) is ingenious, though I disagree with many of the conclusions reached there.

b.   Other works:

Plutarch's *Life of Lycurgus* is a mine of information, some reliable, some wildly anachronistic; other Plutarch lives of Spartans also contain useful material, his *Moralia* 208 B-242 B (*Sayings of Spartans, Ancient Customs of the Spartans and Sayings of Spartan Women*) must be treated with great caution. All are available in the Loeb Classical Library, *Lives*, edited by Bernadotte Perrin, xi Vols, 1914–26, *Moralia*, ed. F. C. Babbitt, Vol. m, 1931. For modern discussions of Plutarch, see: C. P. Jones, *Plutarch and Rome*, (Oxford, Clarendon Press, 1971) and D. A. Russell, Plutarch, (London, Duckworth, 1973).

Other information in classical authors tends to be scattered; some of the more obvious passages are referred to in the commentary. The majority of these works are available in Loeb or Penguin translations; for others, references are given to the standard collections. The ancient sources behind much of our knowledge of Sparta are fully listed in A. H. M. Jones, *Sparta*, (Oxford, Blackwell, 1967); this is much the most valuable aspect of this book.

2. General works on Sparta

Much the best general book is W. G. Forrest, *A History of Sparta 950–192 BC*, (London, Hutchinson; New York, Norton, 1968); mention may also be made of H. Mitchell, *Sparta*, (Cambridge, Cambridge University Press, 1952 (paperback edition 1964).) Three excellent constitutional essays on *Sparta* by A. Andrewes, A. H. M. Jones and F. W. Walbank are to be found in *Ancient Society and Institutions, Studies presented to Victor Ehrenberg*, (Oxford, Blackwell,

1966), pp. 1–20; 165–75; 303–12; compare the chapter on Sparta in A. Andrewes, *The Greek Tyrants*, (London, Hutchinson's University Library, 1956). Three important articles are: W. G. Forrest, 'The Lycourgan Reform', *Phoenix* xvii (1963), 157–79; Chester G. Starr, 'The Credibility of Early Spartan History', *Historia* xiv (1965), 257–72; M. I. Finley, 'Sparta', in *Problèmes de la Guerre en Grèce ancienne*, edited by J. P. Vernant, (Paris, Mouton, 1968) 143–160 (in English).

3. Other Works

Interesting material on Sparta and her influence may be found in E. Rawson, *The Spartan Tradition in European Thought*, (Oxford, Clarendon Press, 1969); E. N. Tigerstedt, *The Legend of Sparta in Classical Antiquity*, (Stockholm, Almqvist & Wiksell) Vol. 1, 1965. W. den Boer, *Laconian Studies*, (Amsterdam, N-Holland Publishing Company, 1954) centres his analysis in Part III on an anthropological approach, which on occasions leads to curious history; however, there are some thought-provoking ideas.

On the subject of education, the following books all contain useful analyses of Sparta in particular, and also of the systems of other Greek states: W. Jaeger, *Paideia* (trans, G. Highett), (4th edition, Oxford, Blackwell, 3 vols, 1954–61); F. A. G. Beck, *Greek Education*, 450–350 BC, (London, Methuen, 1964); H. I. Marrou, *A History of Education in Antiquity* (trans. George Lamb), (London, Sheed and Ward, 1956). On the family in general, and in particular on the problems of Spartan family life (if one may use the term at all), see W. K. Lacey, *The Family in Classical Greece*, (London, Thames and Hudson 1968). Finally, a great deal of excellent material and detailed critical discussion can be found by an intelligent use of the indices of A. W. Gomme, A. Andrewes, K. J. Dover, *A Historical Commentary on Thucydides*, (Oxford, Clarendon Press, 4 vols published, 1945–70).

The Constitution of Athens sections 42–69

FROM *Aristotle and Xenophon on Democracy and Oligarchy*

By Aristotle, translated by J.M. Moore

The Present Constitution

XLII The constitution of the present day is as follows. Full citizenship belongs to men both of whose parents were citizens, and they are inscribed on the list with their fellow demesmen when they are eighteen years old. When they are being registered, the members of the deme vote under oath first on whether they appear to have reached the legal age, and if they do not, they are returned to the status of children, and secondly on whether a man is free and born as the laws prescribe. If they decide that he is not free, he appeals to the *dikasterion*, while the demesmen select five of their number as accusers; if it is decided that he has no right to be registered as a citizen, the city sells him into slavery, but if he wins his case, the demesmen are required to

2 register him. Then the *Boule* reviews those who have been registered, and if it is decided that a man is younger than eighteen, the demesmen who registered him are fined. When the Ephebes have been approved, their fathers meet by tribes and choose under oath three members of the tribe over forty years old whom they consider best and most suitable to take charge of the Ephebes, and from them the people elect one for each tribe as guardian, and they elect a controller from the

3 rest of the citizen body for all of them. These men take the Ephebes, and after visiting the temples they go to the Peiraeus and take up guard duties, some at Munichia and others at Akte. The people also elect

two trainers for them, and two men to teach them to fight in armour, and to use the bow, the javelin and the catapult. The guardians receive a drachma each for their maintenance, and the Ephebes four obols. Each guardian receives the allowances for the members of his tribe and buys what is necessary for them all centrally (for they live together by tribes), and takes care of everything else for them.

4   This is how they spend the first year of their training. At the beginning of the second, at a meeting of the *Ekklesia* held in the theatre, they demonstrate to the people their knowledge of warfare, and receive a shield and spear from the city. For the year thereafter they patrol the

5   countryside and man the guard posts. For their two years service they wear the military cloak, and are exempt from all duties. They cannot prosecute or be prosecuted so that there may be no reason for their leaving their post; the only exception is to deal with matters of inheritance or an *epikleros*, or to take up a priesthood hereditary in a man's family. After this two years, they join the main citizen body.

XLIII   That is how citizens are registered and Ephebes trained. The holders of all routine offices in the state are selected by lot except for the treasurer of the military funds, the controllers of the Theoric Fund and the supervisor of the water supply. These are elected, and hold office from one Panathenaic festival to the next. All military officials are also elected.

2   The *Boule* of 500 members is selected by lot, 50 from each tribe. Each tribe acts as Prytany in an order decided by lot, the first four for thirty-six days each, the last six for thirty-five, for they

3   work by a lunar year. The Prytanies eat together in the Tholos at the city's expense, and summon meetings of the *Boule* and *Ekklesia*; the *Boule* meets every day except for holidays, the *Ekklesia*

4   four times in every prytany. They publish the agenda and place for each meeting of the *Boule*, and also draw up the agenda for the *Ekklesia*. In each prytany the *Ekklesia* meets for one plenary session, in which there must be a vote on whether all office-holders have performed their duties well; there must also be discussions of the corn supply and the safety of Attica; those who wish to bring impeachments do so at this meeting, lists of confiscated property are read out, and also

5   claims to inheritances and to marry *epikleroi*, so that nobody may be ignorant of any unclaimed estates. In the sixth prytany, in addition to the business already discussed, they put to the vote the question of whether an ostracism should be held, and hear accusations against informers, whether Athenians or metics (with a limit of three of each), and allegations against anyone who has

6   failed to fulfil an undertaking made to the city. The second meeting must hear petitioners, and any-one who wishes may appear as a suppliant on any subject he chooses, private or public, and address the people on it. The other two meetings deal with other matters, amongst which the law prescribes the consideration of three motions about sacred matters, three concerning heralds and embassies, and three about secular matters. On occasions they also consider matters without a preliminary vote. Heralds and ambassadors report to the Prytanies first, and despatches are delivered to them.

XLIV   One man is picked as chairman of the Prytanies by lot, and holds office for a night and a day; he cannot preside for longer, nor can the same man serve twice. He holds the keys of the sanctuaries where the treasure and the public records are kept; he holds the city's seal, and must remain in the

2   Tholos with one third of the Prytanies selected by him. When the Prytanies summon a meeting of the *Boule* or *Ekklesia*, he casts lots for nine chairmen, one from each tribe except the one supplying the Prytany; he casts lots again among the nine for the man who will actually preside, and he hands

3   over the agenda to them. The nine take over, and are responsible for good order, put forward topics for discussion, assess the voting, and control everything else. They also have the right to adjourn the meeting. An individual may not preside at a meeting more than once in a year, nor be one of the nine chairmen more than once in each prytany.

4   They elect *strategoi*, cavalry commanders and other military officers in the *Ekklesia* in accordance with the will of the people; the elections are held on the first meeting after the sixth prytany when the omens are favourable. There must also be a preliminary resolution to hold the elections.

XLV   In former times the *Boule* had powers of punishment by fine, imprisonment or execution. Once when the *Boule* had handed Lusimachos over to the public executioner and he was already sitting waiting for the sentence to be carried out, Eumelides of Alopeke saved him, saying that no citizen ought to be executed without a vote of the *dikasterion*. When the *dikasterion* heard the case, Lusimachos was acquitted and was nicknamed 'the man who escaped the rod'. The people deprived the *Boule* of all powers of fine, imprisonment or execution, and passed a law that if the *Boule* condemned a man or punished him, the *Thesmothetai* were to bring the condemnations or punishments before the *dikasterion* and their decision should be final.

2   The *Boule* conducts the investigations into the conduct of the great majority of the magistrates, particularly those who handle money; their decision is not final, but subject to appeal to the *dikasterion*. Private citizens too can bring a charge of acting illegally against any office holder they

2   wish; he has a right of appeal to the *dikasterion* if condemned by the *Boule*. It also considers the credentials of the following year's *Boule* and of the nine Archons; in the past, their decision was final, but now there is a right of appeal to the *dikasterion* for those disqualified.

4   In these matters, then, the *Boule* does not have the final decision, but it holds a preliminary discussion on everything that is to come before the people, nor can the people vote on anything that has not been previously discussed by them and put on the agenda by the Prytanies. Anyone who violates this law is liable to a prosecution for an illegal proposal.

XLVI   The *Boule* is in charge of the completed triremes, the tackle stores and the ship sheds, and builds new triremes or quadriremes, whichever the people vote to construct, and tackle and ship sheds for them, but the people elect the naval architects for the ships. If the *Boule* do not hand them over to the new *Boule* completed, they cannot receive the usual reward, for they receive the reward under

2 the next *Boule*. The triremes are constructed under the supervision of a board of ten members of the *Boule*. The *Boule* inspects all public buildings, and if it decides that someone has committed an offence, it reports him to the people, and hands him over to the *dikasterion* if they find him guilty.

XLVII The *Boule* also joins the other magistrates in most areas of the administration. First, there are ten Treasurers of Athena, one picked by lot from each tribe; in accordance with Solon's law (which is still in force) they must be *pentakosiomedimnoi*, but the man picked by lot holds office even if he is very poor. These officers take over in front of the *Boule* the image of Athena and the Victories,

2 and the other ceremonial equipment and the money. Then there are the ten *poletai* picked by lot, one from each tribe. They let out all the public contracts, sell the right to work the mines, and let the rights of collecting taxes with the treasurer of military affairs and those in charge of the Theoric Fund; this is done in front of the *Boule*. They confirm the position of anyone elected by the *Boule*, and matters concerning mining leases which have been sold, both those where rights of exploitation have been sold for a period of three years and those where special agreements cover a period of ten years. They sell the property of those exiled by the Areopagus and of other exiles before the *Boule*, and the nine Archons confirm the transaction. They list on whitened boards taxes sold for a

3 period of a year with the name of the buyer and the price. They hand the boards over to the *Boule*. They list separately on ten boards those who have to pay their instalments every prytany, on three boards those who have to pay three times a year, and on a separate list those who pay once a year in the ninth prytany. They also list the properties and houses confiscated and sold in the *dikasterion*, for they are responsible for their sale. The price of a house must be paid in five years, of land in ten;

4 these payments are made in the ninth prytany. The King Archon produces a list of the leases of the sacred estates on whitened boards; they are leased for a period of ten years, and the rent is payable

5 in the ninth prytany. For this reason a great deal of money is collected in this prytany. Lists of the payments due are deposited with the *Boule*, and the state secretary keeps them; when a payment is due, he takes from the pigeon holes the list of those whose payments are due on this particular day, and whose entry must be cancelled after payment, and hands it over to the Receivers; the other lists are stored separately so that nothing may be prematurely cancelled.

XLVIII There are ten Receivers, one picked by lot per tribe; they take the lists, and in front of the *Boule* in its chamber erase the record of the money that has been paid, and return the records to the state secretary. If anyone fails to pay an instalment, his name is recorded there, and he has to pay double

2 the arrears under penalty of imprisonment. The *Boule* has the legal right to exact the money or imprison the defaulter. On one day they receive all the payments and divide the money among the magistrates, and on the next they bring a record of their actions on a board and read it out in the chamber. They also pose the question in the *Boule* whether anyone knows of any malpractice by a magistrate or a private citizen in the division; if anyone is suspected, there is a vote on the case.

3   The members of the *Boule* select ten of their number by lot as auditors to check the accounts

4   of the magistrates every prytany. They also select by lot one man from each tribe for the *euthuna* and two assistants for each of them. They are required to sit each market-day* by the statue of the eponymous hero of their tribe, and if anyone wishes to bring a charge, whether of public misdemeanour or private malfeasance, against any of those who have undergone the *euthuna* in the *dikasterion* within three days of that hearing, he records on a whitened board the names of the

5   accuser and the defendant, the charge, and the fine which he considers suitable, and hands it to the representative of his tribe. The latter takes it and reads it, and if he considers the charge justified, he hands a private suit to the deme justices who prepare cases for the relevant tribe for the courts, while if it is a public offence, he reports the matter to the *Thesmothetai*. If the *Thesmothetai* take it over, they reopen the examination of this man before the *dikasterion*, and the decision of the jury is final.

XLIX   The *Boule* also reviews the horses, and if a man appears to have a good horse but to be maintaining it badly, deprives him of his maintenance allowance. Horses which cannot keep up, or will not remain in line but run away, are branded with a wheel on the jaw, and are disqualified. They also review the mounted skirmishers to find who seem to be suitable for this, and anyone they vote against loses his

2   horse. They also review the infantry attached to the cavalry, and anyone voted against loses his pay. The cavalry are enrolled by a board of ten elected by the people for this purpose; the names of those enrolled are handed to the cavalry commanders and the commanders of the tribal cavalry units who receive the list and bring it before the *Boule*. They open the sealed document in which the names of the cavalrymen are listed, and erase the names of those previously enrolled who swear that they are prevented by physical disability from serving as cavalry. Then they call those newly enrolled, and if anyone swears that he is physically or financially incapable of serving, they dismiss him. Those who do not take this oath are subject to a vote by the *Boule* as to their suitability for cavalry service; if they are approved, they are enrolled, if not they are dismissed.

3   The *Boule* used to take decisions about the models and the robe, but this is now done by a *dikasterion* selected by lot, for it was felt that the *Boule* was swayed by personal feelings. The *Boule* joins the treasurer of military affairs in supervising the making of the statues of Victory and the prizes for the Panathenaia.

4   The *Boule* also reviews the incapable; for there is a law that anyone with property of less than three minae who suffers from a physical disability which prevents his undertaking any employment should come before the *Boule*, and if his claim is approved he should receive two obols a day subsistence from public funds. There is a treasurer selected by lot to handle this.

5   The *Boule* also cooperates with the other magistrates in most of what they do.

L   Those then are the areas of administration handled by the *Boule*.

---

*   The word translated as 'market-day' may not be the correct restoration of a damaged part of the papyrus, but no convincing alternative has yet been suggested.

A board of ten are also selected by lot to take care of the sanctuaries; they are given thirty minae by the Receivers, and repair the temples most in need of attention. There are ten city commissioners, of whom five hold office in the Peiraeus and five in the city itself. They see that the girls who play the flute, the harp or the lyre are not hired for more than two drachmae; if more than one man wishes to hire the same performer, they cast lots, and allocate her to the winner. They ensure that the dung collectors do not deposit dung within ten stades of the walls, and see that no building either obstructs or has balconies overhanging the streets; they also prevent the construction of waste pipes with outfalls from above into the street, or windows with shutters opening into the road. With assistants provided by the state, they remove the corpses of those who die in the streets.

LI Ten superintendents of the markets are selected by lot, five for the Peiraeus and five for the city. They are required by law to supervise goods for sale to ensure that merchandise is pure and unadulterated. Ten inspectors of weights and measures are similarly selected, five for the city and five for the Peiraeus to ensure that honest weights and measures are used by those who are selling. There used to be ten commissioners in charge of the corn supply, picked by lot, of whom five were allocated to the Peiraeus and five to the city, but there are now twenty for the city and fifteen for the Peiraeus. They ensure first that there is no sharp practice in the selling of unground corn in the market, secondly that the millers should sell their barley flour at a price corresponding to that of unmilled barley, and thirdly that the bakers should sell loaves at a price corresponding to the price of wheat, and containing the full weight which the commissioners have laid down as the law requires them to do. They also pick by lot ten commissioners of trade to supervise trading and ensure that two-thirds of the corn imported is brought to the city.

LII The Eleven whose duty it is to take care of prisoners are selected by lot. They execute thieves, kidnappers and brigands who confess their guilt, while if they deny the charge, they bring them before the *dikasterion*, and if they are acquitted let them go, and if not put them to death after their trial. They report to the *dikasterion* land and houses listed as belonging to the city, and hand over to the *poletai* any that is judged to be public property. It is also part of their duties to bring summary indictments before the *dikasterion*, though the *Thesmothetai* also introduce some similar indictments.

2 Five men are picked by lot to introduce cases where proceedings may be instituted every month, each of whom covers two tribes. Gases falling in this category include failure to pay a dowry which is owed, failure to repay a loan made at an interest of a drachma per mina, or a loan of capital made to finance the opening of a business in the market; prosecutions for assault, cases involving friendly loans, cooperative ventures, slaves, animals, trierarchies and banking matters. These officials introduce and handle 'monthly' cases of these classes, while the Receivers handle cases

involving tax-farming, with the power to make a final decision in cases up to ten drachmae; they refer the remaining 'monthly' cases to the *dikasterion* for settlement.

LIII The Forty are picked by lot, four from each tribe, and other suits are brought before them. They used to be a board of thirty, and travel round the demes to try cases, but after the tyranny of the

2 Thirty their numbers were increased to forty. They can make the final decision in cases involving up to ten drachmae, but anything above that they hand over to the Arbitrators. These officials then take the case, and if they cannot bring about a settlement, give a decision; if the decision satisfies both sides and they accept it, the case is ended. If one party appeals to the *dikasterion*, the Arbitrators place the depositions, the challenges and the relevant laws in boxes, one for each side in the case, seal the boxes, add the decision of the Arbitrator written on a tablet, and hand every-

3 thing over to the four members of the Forty who handle the cases of the tribe of the defendant. They take them over, and bring the case before the *dikasterion*, cases of less than 1,000 drachmae before a jury of 201 members, those over 1,000 before 401 jurors. At the hearing it is forbidden to use laws, challenges or depositions other than those used in front of the Arbitrator and sealed

4 in the boxes. The Arbitrators are men in their sixtieth year; their age is known from the Archons and the eponymous heroes. There are ten eponymous heroes for the tribes, and forty-two for the age-groups; the Ephebes' names are recorded together with the Archon under whom they were enrolled and the eponymous hero of the previous year's Arbitrators; this used to be done on whitened boards, but they now use a bronze plaque which is set up in front of the chamber of

5 the *Boule* by the statues of the eponymous heroes. The Forty take the list under the name of the last of the eponymous heroes, and allot to those on the list the cases for arbitration and cast lots to decide which each will decide. The man selected is required to arbitrate as directed, for the law provides that if any man fails to serve as an Arbitrator when his age-group is performing this duty he shall lose his citizen rights, unless he happens to hold public office that year or to be abroad; only these categories are exempt.

6 Information can be laid before the Arbitrators as a body if anyone is wronged by an individual Arbitrator, and the penalty laid down by law for anyone condemned under this procedure is loss

7 of citizen rights; there is a right of appeal. They also use the names of the eponymous heroes for military service; when they send an age-group on campaign, they publish a notice saying that the groups from one Archon and eponymous hero to another are called up for service.

LIV The following offices are also filled by lot: five commissioners of roads, whose duty it is to employ

2 the slaves provided by the city to repair the roads. Ten Auditors and ten assistants for them, to whom all those who have held public office must submit their accounts; this is the only body which audits the accounts of those subject to the *euthuna* and submits the results to the *dikasterion*. If they detect anyone who has been guilty of embezzlement, the jury condemns him for theft of public

money, and he is sentenced to pay ten times the amount stolen; if they demonstrate that anyone has taken bribes and the jury convicts him, they assess the size of the bribe, and again he pays ten times this amount. If they condemn him for maladministration, they assess the amount, and this is what he pays as long as he pays up before the ninth prytany; if not, the sum is doubled. Fines of ten times the amount involved in the offence are not doubled.

3   They cast lots for the officer called Clerk to the Prytanies, who is in charge of the documents, keeps the decrees which have been passed, checks the transcription of everything else, and attends meetings of the *Boule*. In earlier days this official was elected, and they used to elect the most famous and reliable men; their names are recorded on the inscribed texts of alliances, and grants of

4   *proxenia* and citizenship; now they are selected by lot. They also pick another man by lot to look

5   after laws; he attends the *Boule* and also checks all transcriptions. The people elect the clerk whose duty it is to read out documents in the *Ekklesia* and *Boule*, and this is his only duty.

6   Ten sacred officials are elected who are called 'those in charge of expiation'; they make sacrifices

7   ordered by oracles, and if good *omens* are required they see to it with the prophets. Another ten religious officials are selected by lot, called 'those in charge of annual rites'; they offer certain sacrifices and are in charge of all four- yearly festibals except for the Panathenaia. The four- yearly festivals are: i. the mission to Delos (which is also celebrated every six years); 2. the Brauronia; 3. the Heracleia; 4. the Eleusinia; 5. the Panathenaia; none of these festivals occurs in the same place. The Hephaistia was added to the group in the Archonship of Kephisophon.

8   They appoint by lot an Archon for Salamis and a demarch for the Peiraeus; they celebrate the Dionysia in each place, and appoint the choregoi. In Salamis the name of the Archon is recorded.

LV   The holders of the above offices are selected by lot, and their duties are those listed above. As to the so-called nine Archons, I have already described their original ways of appointment; to-day, six *Thesmothetai* and their secretary and also the Archon, the King Archon and the Polemarch are

2   appointed by lot from each tribe in rotation. Their qualifications for office are checked first in the *Boule* of 500, except for the secretary, whose qualifications are checked only in the *dikasterion* as happens for other office holders—for all officials, whether selected by lot or elected, have their qualifications checked before they take up office; the nine Archons have to go before both the *Boule* and the *dikasterion*. In the past a man who was disqualified by the *Boule* could not hold office,

3   but now there is an appeal to the *dikasterion*, and the final decision is taken there. When they are checking qualifications, they ask first: 'Who is your father, and what is your deme? Who was your father's father, and who was your mother, and her father and his deme?' Then they ask whether the candidate is enrolled in a cult of Apollo Patroos and Zeus Herkeios, and where the shrines are, then whether he has family tombs and where they are; whether he treats his parents well, pays his taxes, and has gone on campaign when required. When these questions have been asked, the candidate

4   is required to call witnesses to his answers. When he has produced the witnesses, the question is

put: 'Does anyone wish to bring any charge against this man?' If an accuser appears, the accusation and defence are heard, and then the matter is put to the vote by a show of hands in the *Boule* or a ballot if the hearing is in the *dikasterion*. If no one wishes to bring an accusation, the vote is held immediately. In former times, only one ceremonial vote was cast,* but now everyone is required to vote on candidates, so that if a criminal has managed get rid of all his accusers it is still in the power

5   of the jurors to disqualify him. After this investigation, the candidates go to the stone on which are the parts of the sacrificial victim, and standing on it they swear to administer their office justly and in accordance with the laws, and not to take bribes in connection with their office, and if they do, to dedicate a golden statue. At this stone also the Arbitrators give their decisions on oath and witnesses swear† to their depositions. After taking the oath the candidates go to the Acropolis, and repeat the same oath there; after that they take up their office.

LVI   The Archon, the King Archon and the Polemarch each have two assessors of their own choice, and these men have their credentials checked in the *dikasterion* before they take up their positions, and are subject to the *euthuna* in respect of their tenure.

2   As soon as the Archon takes up office, he proclaims that every man shall hold and control
3   until the end of the year such property as he held before he took office. Then he appoints for the tragedians three *choregoi* who are the richest of all the Athenians; formerly he appointed five for the comedians, but now the tribes provide for them. Then he receives the *choregoi* appointed by the tribes, those for the men's and the boys' choruses and the comedies at the Dionysia, and for the men's and boys' choruses at the Thargelia; those for the Dionysia are each provided by one tribe, but two tribes combine for the Thargelia, each of the tribes serving in turn. The Archon then arranges exchanges of property, and presents any claims for exemption which may arise if a man claims either to have performed this liturgy before, or to be exempt on the grounds of having performed another liturgy after which his period of exemption has not yet passed, or not to be of the required age—for the choregos of the boys' chorus must be over forty years old. The Archon also appoints
4   *choregoi* for Delos and a chief of the sacred embassy to take the young people on the thirty-oared vessel. He is also in charge of the procession to Asclepius when the initiated hold a vigil, and the procession at the Great Dionysia. In arranging the latter he is aided by ten assistants who used to be elected by the people and meet the cost of the procession out of their own pockets, but now are
5   picked by lot, one from each tribe, and receive a hundred minae for their expenses. The Archon also organises the processions at the Thar- gelia and to Zeus Soter; he organises the contests at the
6   Dionysia and the Thargelia. These are the festivals which he organises. Some civil and criminal proceedings come before the Archon; he holds a preliminary hearing, and then introduces them

---

*   That is, where no charge was brought, a single, formal vote of acquittal was all that was required.

†   See note on this translation in the Commentary.

into the *dikasterion*. They include cases of illtreating parents, in which the prosecutor is immune from penalty; accusations of offences against orphans, which are brought against the guardians, and of offences against *epikleroi*, which are brought against the guardians and the people living with the *epikleroi*; accusations of mismanaging the estate of an orphan, which are also brought against the guardians; charges of insanity where it is alleged that a man is wasting his substance because he is of unsound mind, and requests for the appointment of officials to divide up property where a person is unwilling to share out what is held in common; requests to constitute or decide a wardship,

7   for production in court, for enrolment as a guardian, and claims to estates and *epikleroi*. He also looks after orphans, *epikleroi*, and widows who declare themselves pregnant after the death of their husbands. He has the power to fine offenders or bring them before the *dikasterion*. He rents out the houses of orphans and *epikleroi* until they are fourteen years old, and takes security for the leases; he exacts maintenance from guardians who do not provide it for children in their care.

LVII   These matters are the province of the Archon. The King Archon supervises the Mysteries together with assistants elected by the people, two of whom are elected from the whole citizen body, one from the family of the Eumolpidai, and one from the Kerukes. Secondly he has charge of the festival of Dionysus called the Lenaia, which involves a procession and contest. The King Archon and his assistants jointly arrange the procession, but the contest is in his hands alone. He also

2   arranges all torch-races and virtually all the traditional sacrifices. Cases of impiety come before him and disputes over priesthoods. He also decides all disputes about religious matters which arise between the clans or the priests; all cases of homicide come before him, and he it is who proclaims

3   the exclusion of an individual from the things specified in the laws. Charges of murder or wounding where a man deliberately kills or injures someone are heard before the Areopagus, as are cases of poisoning which result in death, and cases of arson; these are the only cases decided by that body. Charges of unintentional homicide, conspiracy to kill, and the killing of a slave, metic or foreigner are heard by the Court of the Palladion. Where a man admits to having killed someone but claims that his action was lawful, as for example if he caught an adulterer in the act, or killed unwittingly in war or in the course of the games, the case is heard in the Delphinion. If a man has retired into exile in a situation where reconciliation is possible and is then accused of killing or wounding

4   someone, his case is heard in the court of Phreatto, and he pleads his case from a boat anchored near the shore. Except for cases brought before the Areopagus, all these cases are tried by *Ephetai* selected by lot; the case is brought before the court by the King Archon, and the hearing is held in a sacred area out of doors; during the case the King Archon does not wear his crown. At all other times the defendant is excluded from all sanctuaries, and is even barred by law from the Agora, but for the trial he enters the sacred area and makes his defence. When the offender is not known, the proceedings are held against 'the guilty party'. The King Archon and the Tribal Kings also proceed against inanimate objects and animals.

LVIII   The Polemarch makes the sacrifices to Artemis the huntress and to Enualios, and arranges the

2   funeral games in honour of those who have fallen in war, and makes the offerings to Harmodius and Aristogeiton. He hears only private suits which involve metics, tax-exempt metics and *proxenoi*; it is his duty to take them and divide them into ten groups, and to assign by lot one group to

3   each of the ten tribes, and the jurors of the tribe must then bring them before the Arbitrators. The Polemarch himself introduces cases where a man is accused of disregarding his patron or not having one, and also cases involving inheritance and *epikleroi* of the metics; in other respects, the Polemarch performs for the metics the same duties as the Archon performs for citizens.

LIX   The *Thesmothetai* are responsible first for announcing the days on which the *dikasteria* will sit, and

2   then for allotting the magistrates to the courts; the latter bring cases to court as the *Thesmothetai* direct. They bring impeachments before the *Ekklesia*, and they introduce motions for the deposition of magistrates and all accusations brought in the *Ekklesia*, indictments for illegal proposals and accusations of having proposed laws against the interests of the state, indictments against the

3   chairmen or president, and the *euthunai* of the *strategoi*. They hear cases where the prosecutor has to make a deposit, including charges of wrongly claiming citizen rights, or using bribery to this end, which arises when a man uses bribery to escape a charge of wrongly claiming to be a citizen, charges of malicious prosecution, bribery, false entry in the lists of state debtors, falsely witnessing a summons, failure to erase the name of a debtor who has paid, non-registration of a debtor, and

4   adultery. They also introduce the investigations into the credentials of all candidates for office, the

5   appeals of those whose registration has been refused by their demes, and condemnations sent for confirmation by the *Boule*. They also introduce private suits involving trade or the mines, and cases where a slave is accused of slandering a free man. They allocate courts to the magistrates by lot for

6   public and private suits. They validate international agreements and introduce cases arising under them, and also charges of bearing false witness in the Areopagus.

7   The selection of the jurors by lot is done by all the nine Archons together with the secretary of the *Thesmothetai*, each handling his own tribe.

LX   Such then is the position of the nine Archons.

Ten commissioners are also selected by lot to run the games, one from each tribe. When they have passed the preliminary examination, they hold office for four years, and they organise the procession at the Panathenaia, the musical contest, the athletics and the horse races, and they arrange the

2   making of Athena's robe and the vases for prizes in conjunction with the *Boule*; they also give olive oil to the athletes. This oil comes from the sacred olives, and the Archon collects three-quarters of a pint per tree from the owners of the land in which they grow. In the past the city used to sell the fruit, and if anyone dug up or cut down one of the sacred olives, he was tried before the

Areopagus and the penalty for those found guilty was death. Ever since the owner of the land has paid the contribution of oil, the law has remained in force, but the penalty has been allowed to

3 lapse. The oil is now levied as a tax on the property, not collected from the trees themselves. The Archon collects the oil due in his year of office, and hands it over to the Treasurers for storage on the Acropolis; he is not allowed to take his seat in the Areopagus until he has handed over the full amount to the stewards. At other times the stewards keep the oil on the Acropolis, but at the time of the Panathenaia they measure it out to the commissioners of the games, who give it to the winning contestants. The prizes for those who win the musical contests are of silver and gold, for those who win the contests in manliness, shields, but for those who win the athletic events and the horse races, olive oil.

LXI All military offices are also filled by election. There are ten *strategoi*, who once were elected one from each tribe, but are now elected from the whole people. They are allocated by show of hands, one to the hoplites, to command on any expedition, and one to patrol Attica and to fight any enemy who invades the country; two are stationed in the Peiraeus, one in Munichia and one in Akte—their duty is to guard the Peiraeus; one is in charge of the symmories, and enrols the trierarchs, arranges any exchanges of property for them, and introduces cases where there are disputes to the *dikasteria*;

2 the remainder are despatched to deal with any situation that may arise. There is a vote in every prytany on their conduct of their office, and if the people vote against a man, he is tried in the *dikasterion*, and if condemned, the jury assesses the appropriate penalty or fine, while if he is acquitted he resumes his position. When in command of troops, they have the power to imprison anyone for insubordination, to discharge him, and to impose a fine, though this last is not usual.

3 Also elected are ten regimental commanders, one for each tribe; they lead their fellow tribesmen,

4 and appoint the subordinate officers. Two cavalry commanders are also elected from the whole citizen body; they lead the cavalry, divided into two units of five tribes each. They have the same authority

5 over their men as the *strategoi* have over the hoplites, and are likewise subject to a monthly vote on their conduct. They also elect ten tribal commanders, one per tribe, to command the cavalry just as

6 the regimental commanders command the hoplites. They elect a cavalry commander for Lemnos to

7 command the cavalry there, and a steward for the 'Paralos' and another for the 'Ammonis'.

LXII The magistrates chosen by lot were formerly divided into two groups, those who, with the nine Archons, were selected from whole tribes, and those who were selected from the demes in the Theseum. However, when corruption affected the choices of the demes, the selection of the latter officers was transferred to the whole tribe also, except that members of the *Boule* and the guards are still selected by demes.

2 The citizens receive the following fees for public services: at ordinary meetings of the *Ekklesia* a drachma, but nine obols for the plenary session; jurors receive three obols, while members of the

Boule receive five, and the Prytanies a sixth for their maintenance. The nine Archons receive four obols each for maintenance and have a herald and *aulor*-player to maintain, and the Archon of Salamis gets a drachma a day. The commissioners of the games receive their meals in the Prytaneion in the month of Hecatombaion during the Panathenaia, starting from the fourth day of the month. The sacred commissioners to Delos receive a drachma a day from Delos, and the officers sent out to Samos, Scyros, Lemnos or Imbros receive money for maintenance.

3   Military offices may be held repeatedly, but no other office may be held more than once, except that a man may sit in the *Boule* twice.

LXIII   The allocation of *dikastai* to the *dikasteria* is conducted by the nine Archons for their respective

2   tribes, and the secretary of the *Thesmothetai* handles the tenth tribe. There are ten entrances into the *dikasteria*, one for each tribe, twenty allotment machines, two for each tribe, one hundred boxes, ten for each tribe, and other boxes into which are thrown the tickets of the *dikastai* who have been successful in the ballot. There are two urns by the entrance to each court, and staves equal to the number of *dikastai* required; the same number of ballot balls are thrown into the urns as there are staves, and the balls have letters written on them starting with the eleventh of the alphabet, *A*, the

3   number of letters corresponding with the number of courts to be filled. Those over thirty years of age may sit as *dikastai* as long as they are not public debtors and have not lost their citizen rights. If a man who is disqualified sits, information is laid against him and he is brought before the *dikasterion*; if he is found guilty, the jury assess whatever penalty or fine seems to them appropriate, and if it is a fine, he must be imprisoned until he has paid the previous debt on the grounds of which he was

4   indicted and the additional fine imposed by the *dikasterion*. Each *dikastes* has a ticket of boxwood with his name, his father's name and his deme written on it, together with one of the first ten letters of the alphabet, those up to K; the *dikastai* of each tribe are divided into ten roughly equal sections

5   under the ten letters. The *Thesmothetes* draw lots for the letters which are to be placed by each court, and his servant puts the relevant letter up in each case.

LXIV   The ten boxes stand in front of the entrance for each tribe, and the letters up to K are inscribed on them. When the *dikastai* throw their tickets into the box which has the same letter on it as is on

2   their ticket, the servant shakes the boxes and the *Thesmothetes* draws one ticket from each. The man drawn is called the ticket-inserter, and inserts the tickets from the box into the column over which is the same letter as there is on the box. This man is selected by lot to prevent malpractice if the

3   same man should always make the draw. There are five columns of slots in each allotment machine. When the Archon has put the cubes into the machines, he draws lots for each tribe according to the allotment machines. The cubes are bronze, some white, some black; he puts in as many white cubes as *dikastai* are needed, one per five columns, and black cubes in the same proportion. When the Archon takes out the cubes, the herald calls the men who have been selected; the ticket-inserter

4   is included in their number. When a man has been called, he steps forward and draws a ball from

the urns, and holds it out with the letter upwards, and shows it first to the presiding Archon. The Archon then puts the man's ticket into the box on which is the letter which is on the ball, so that he shall go to the court which he has drawn by lot, not the one he wishes to sit in, and it may not

5 be possible for anyone to arrange to have the jury he wishes. There are beside the Archon as many boxes as there are courts to be manned, each with the letter on it which has been allocated to the relevant court,

LXV When the *dikastes* has shown his ball to the servant, he goes inside the inner door. The servant gives him a staff of the same colour as that of the court whose letter was the same as the one on his ball, so that he is compelled to sit in the court to which he has been allotted. If he goes into a different

2 court, the colour of the staff gives him away, for a colour is painted on the lintel of the entrance of each court. He takes his staff and goes into the court whose colour corresponds to his staff and whose letter is the same as that on his ball, and when he enters he receives an official token from

3 the man selected by lot to distribute them. The *dikastai* then take their seats with their ball and staff having got into court in the manner described above. The ticket-inserters return their tickets

4 to those who have been unsuccessful in the ballot. The public servants from each tribe hand over the boxes of each tribe, one for each court, in which are the names of the members of each tribe who are sitting in each court. They hand them over to those who have been selected by lot to return them to the *dikastai* in each court, so that they may summon them by using their tickets, and so give them their pay. There are five of these officials.*

LXVI When all the courts have their requisite juries, two allotment machines are set up in the first court, with bronze cubes on which are the colours of the courts and other cubes on which the names of the Archons are written. Two *Thesmothtai* picked by lot separately put the cubes in the machines, one putting the colours into one machine, the other the names of the Archons into the other. The herald announces whichever magistrate is picked first as allocated to the court which is drawn first, and the second to the second, and so on, so that no magistrate may know where he is to preside but each will preside over the one he draws by lot.

2 When the *dikastai* have arrived and been allocated to their courts, the presiding magistrate in each court draws one ticket from each box, so that he has ten, one from each tribe, and puts these tickets into an empty box, and draws five of these, and of the five drawn one supervises the water clock and the other four the voting, so that nobody may interfere either with the man in charge of the clock or

3 those in charge of the voting, and there may be no chicanery in these matters. The remaining five of the ten drawn receive instructions detailing how and where the jury will receive their pay in the court itself; this is done separately by tribes after they have fulfilled their duties, so that they may receive it in small groups and not cause trouble because there are a lot of people crowded together.

---

* The number is missing in the text; cf. LXVI,3 and Commentary.

LXVII   After these preparations, they call the cases. If they are dealing with private cases, they call four, one from each of the categories defined by law, and the litigants take an oath to speak to the point; when they deal with public cases, they summon the litigants, but deal with only one case.

2   There are water clocks with narrow tubes attached; they pour the prescribed amount of water into them, and this decides the length of time allowed for the speeches. They allow ten measures for cases involving over 5,000 drachmae, with three measures for the supporting speech, seven measures for those up to 5,000, with two for the supporting speech, and five and two for those under 1,000; six measures are allowed for the deciding of disputed claims, and second speeches are

3   not allowed. The man in charge of the water clock cuts off the flow of water when the clerk is going to read out a decree, law, piece of evidence or contract. If, however, parts of the day's hearing have

4   been allocated to each side, then he does not cut it off, but an equal period of time is allowed to the prosecutor and the defendant. The standard of division is the length of the day in the month of Poseideon

The following section of the papyrus is so badly mutilated that the text cannot be reconstructed; the only section of which something may be made is:

… The day is divided into proportionate parts … for contests where the penalty laid down on conviction is imprisonment, death, exile, loss of citizen rights or confiscation of property. …

There follows a further mutilated section of papyrus.

LXVIII   The majority of the juries are of five hundred members … but when it is necessary for public suits to

2   have a jury of 1,000, two juries are combined in the *Heliaia*. The votes are cast with tokens of bronze which have a pipe through the middle, half of them pierced and half blocked. At the conclusion of the speeches, those chosen to supervise the voting give each member of the jury two tokens, one pierced and one blocked, showing them clearly to the litigants so that the jury do not receive either two pierced tokens or two blocked ones. Then the designated official takes the staffs, in return for which each *dikastes* when he casts his vote receives a bronze tag with the number three on it, for when he hands it in he receives three obols; this is to ensure that all vote, for no one can receive a

3   tag without voting. There are two containers in the court, one of bronze and one of wood; they can be taken apart so that nobody can introduce votes into them fraudulently before the voting begins. The *dikastai* cast their votes in them, the bronze container counting while the wooden is for the vote which is not used. The bronze one has a lid with a hole in it through which only one token can pass,

4   so that the same man may not insert two tokens into it. When the jury are about to vote, the herald first asks whether the contestants wish to protest at any of the evidence, for protests cannot be lodged

after voting has commenced. Then he makes a second announcement: 'The pierced token for the first speaker, the solid for the second.' The *dikastes* takes the tokens from the stand, holding the pipe in the token so that he does not show the litigants which is pierced and which is not; he places the token that counts in the bronze container, and the other in the wooden one.

LXIX When the voting is complete, the servants take the container which counts and pour out the contents on to a reckoning frame which has as many holes in it as there are votes so that it may be easy to add up the tokens which count, both the pierced and solid ones. Those selected by lot for the task count them up on the board, separating the solid from the pierced, and the herald announces the number of votes cast, the pierced for the prosecutor and the solid for the defendant. Whichever gets

2 more votes wins, while if the votes are equal the verdict goes to the defendant. If it is necessary, they then assess a penalty by voting in the same way; for this the *dikastai* return their tags and take back their staffs. Each side is allowed half a measure of water for their speeches at this stage. When the *dikastai* have fulfilled their duties as required by law, they take their fees in the part of the building assigned to them.

Commentary: The Athenian Constitution of Aristotle's Own Day

Having described the historical development of the Athenian constitution, Aristotle turns to a detailed analysis of the various offices and institutions of his own day. The description is not fully applicable to the fifth-century democracy, but significant parts of it are, and they give us an invaluable insight into the details of government and administration which cannot emerge from the larger view of such historians as Thucydides and Xenophon. For them, the 'how' of political niceties is unimportant unless it had a direct bearing on the resultant action; we therefore get only a sporadic and fitful glimpse into procedure. Aristotle fills many of the gaps.

XLII Inclusion on the deme register was the basic proof of citizenship from the days of Cleisthenes, and enrolment took place before a man's fellow demesmen. Since 451/0 Pericles' citizenship law had required that both parents should be free and Athenian citizens, and the law had been reenacted after the fall of the oligarchy of 404/3. Nobody was admitted to full citizenship until he appeared to be eighteen; a man's age was the subject of investigation because there was no documentation of birth, and apparently many did not know their birthdays (cf. Plato *Lysis* 207 c). A man might produce evidence of the year of his presentation as an infant to the members of his father's phratry, or, if they could be found, witnesses to the Archonship in which he had been born. That disputes occurred shows that such evidence was not always available or decisive. That demesmen were fined for enrolling those who were judged to be under age (§2) will have ensured that they tried to avoid doing so.

There is no necessary contradiction between this passage and Aristophanes *Wasps* 578, where it is said that it is the privilege of the *dikastai* to decide on the maturity of the young men (and they much enjoyed their duty!); this would refer to the decision of disputed cases. Aristotle is, however, the only authority to assign the approval of the decision of the deme council on this to the *Boule*. The combination of passages implies that there was an appeal also from a decision that a man was too young; it would be surprisingly out of tune with normal Athenian practice if a relatively small body like the deme council could take such a decision without appeal being possible. If this deduction is correct, Aristotle's phrasing is less clear than it might be. Once enrolled in a deme, a man was officially of the age indicated by his enrolment class, and this dictated his military service and also when he would be eligible for positions like membership of the *Boule* which were restricted to those over thirty. Equally, the deme lists were used for selecting men to perform liturgies, to pay capital levies (*eisphorai*), and for other purposes.

An accusation that a man was not free born was serious. The Greek word for 'free' implied also the possibility of being accepted as a full member of the community; a man could be rejected either for being of slave parentage or for being a foreigner. If a man had applied to be enrolled on a deme list and failed this test, he was sold into slavery; the penalty was fitting for the son of slaves, who was a slave unless specifically freed, and it is this class which Aristotle has in mind in discussing the sale into slavery of those rejected. To treat the sons of foreigners in this way would have been monstrously unjust, particularly since they could not have been legally held responsible for starting what the *dikasteria* had judged to be a fraudulent attempt to obtain citizenship.*

The period of Ephebic training lasted for two years, and had been modified just before Aristotle wrote; exactly what it involved is controversial. From the age of eighteen, all Athenians were liable to military service, and it appears that from perhaps as early as the second quarter of the fifth century the first two years of this liability involved the young men in some form of service which included training to fit them to take a full place in the defence of their city thereafter. Aristotle describes the duties of the Ephebes as 'patrolling the countryside and manning the guard posts'; similarly, Thucydides says that the 'youngest' of the citizens were involved in defence against invasions (II,13,7). On the other hand, this training was not continuous, for we know of many young Athenians who continued their ordinary lives when they would have been Ephebes, for example Glaukon, who is recorded as having tried to speak in the *Ekklesia* when he was not yet twenty (Xenophon, *Memorabilia*, III,6,1). In other words, the liability of the Ephebes was very similar to, and perhaps identical with, that of every other adult male citizen:

---

* A. W. Gomme, *Essays in Greek History* 75ff; note that, apart from attempted false enrolment as a citizen, a man could also be sold into slavery for failure to repay a ransomer if he had been captured, enslaved and then redeemed as, for example, Plato was.

to serve in die armed forces when required. This had changed by Aristotle's own day, when the Ephebes were required to serve continuously for their two-year period of training; the change may have been instituted by a law of Epikrates in 336/5.*

Under the new system, the Ephebes during their training garrisoned the two forts mentioned in the text which protected the harbour of the Peiraeus (cf. LXI,i), and, after completing a year's basic instruction, other guard posts near the land frontiers of Attica. They learnt the basic skills necessary to make them useful members of the mainly hoplite army, though some will have started to acquire these skills earlier in the gymnasia. The whole process, and their way of life, is reminiscent of the training of the young Spartans, though, of course, it lasted for only a short period. The care with which they were relieved of all outside calls on their time indicates how important this period was felt to be. It should be noted that although technically all citizens, that is all adult males enrolled on the deme lists, were entitled to attend the *Ekklesia*, in practice the Ephebes were now not free to do so.

An exception to their concentration on military affairs was made in the case of lawsuits concerned with inheritance and *epikleroi*, as well as the obvious and expected case where a man had to take up a family priesthood. *Epikleroi* were daughters of a family where there were no male children; the family property passed through them, though they were not what we would describe as heiresses, for they could not dispose of the property in their own right—women in most states in Greece had no right to own property in the fullest sense, the most notable exception being Sparta. Property was vital, and had to stay within the family group if possible.† The laws about *epikleroi* were designed to ensure this, and also to protect a woman if her father died. In that case, the nearest male relative could claim the orphaned girl in marriage, and the property would pass to the offspring of the marriage; male relatives were required by law to provide a girl with a dowry if one of them did not marry her himself. A dowry was normal, and had to be repaid if there was a divorce; it was regarded as part of the father's estate set apart for the maintenance of the daughter, and it is important that Athenian law always required a man in possession of his wife's dowry to maintain her. It seems probable that more girls than boys survived infancy, and this combined with battle casualties must have ensured that there was some competition for girls to marry—hence the dowry became more important. In practice both divorce and remarriage were apparently quite common, and young widows were normally expected to marry a second time.

XLIII The standard democratic principle that officers responsible for administration should be selected by lot was not impractical because their duty was to carry out, or supervise the carrying out of, decisions made by the *Ekklesia*; they did not initiate policy themselves. The only deterrent which may have ensured a minimum degree of competence was that they had to undergo a euthuna at the end of their year of office; this was an investigation at which their accounts were checked and they were also

---

* See O. W. Reinmuth, 'The Ephebic Inscriptions of the Fourth Century B.C.', *Mnemosyne* Suppl. B. 14, 1971, 123–38.
† cf. W. K. Lacey, *The Family in Classical Greece*, 125ff on property, and 139–45 on *epikleroi*.

answerable for their official actions during their tenure of office (cf. LIV,2). It has been suggested that this was enough to stop the really incompetent from putting themselves forward.

On the other hand, even the most extreme democrats recognised that there were certain positions in which expertise was essential; the military officers mentioned here are the clearest case, for the lives of those under their command depended on their ability. These officials were always elected, and were also exempt from the normal rule which dictated that any particular office should only be held once by any one man; cf. LXII,3. Aristotle here lists some other exceptions. The treasurer of military funds (perhaps a fourth-century post) worked closely with the *strategoi*. The Theoric fund was established to supply Athenians who could not afford it with the two-obol entrance fee to the theatre of Dionysus. In the fourth century it became more important, since all surplus revenue of the state went into it. Separate magistrates in charge of the fund were probably instituted in the mid-fourth century, and were very important by Aristotle's day. Similarly, the chronic shortage of water in Athens made the supervisors of the water supply important. The phrase 'from one Panathenaic festival to the next' refers to the Great Panathenaia, celebrated once every four years; therefore these three groups of magistrates also went contrary to the usual principle that no office was held for more than a year. Meiggs/Lewis 72, lines 1–2 contains an exactly parallel period of office. The offices Aristotle lists required expertise, which explains why their holders were elected, and perhaps why they held office for four years rather than one.

A council of 500 such as the *Boule* could be democratic only if it were selected by lot; ideally, nobody would be a member more than once in his life, but in Athens it was found necessary to allow two terms in order to ensure enough qualified and willing candidates, though two consecutive terms were not allowed (cf. LXII,3).

The detailed analysis of the workings of the Prytany system is vital, for the Prytanies formed the only body that was more or less permanently on duty. Each tribe's members of the *Boule* formed the Prytany for one tenth of the year; in the fourth century the lunar year dictated that their periods of office should not be absolutely the same length, since it contained 354 days.* Before 407 the prytany year was distinct from the Archon's lunar year, and close to the solar year. The Prytanies ate together in the Tholos, a round building in the south-west corner of the Agora, next to the Bouleuterion where the *Boule* usually met. From the fifty members a chairman was selected each day by lot, and he was on duty for twenty-four hours, sleeping in the Tholos with one third of the Prytanies. They thus provided a standing committee who could at any time initiate action if necessary. In addition, they received messages as they arrived in the city, e.g. the embassies mentioned in §6. Details of the Prytanies' duties are given in XLIV, 1–3. There is an important distinction between the fourth century as Aristotle describes it and the fifth. In the fifth, the Prytanies, and in particular each chairman, presided over all meetings summoned during his day in office. This meant that there was a very reasonable chance of a

---

* Periods added to the calendar ensured that the lunar year was approximately harmonised with the solar year; see *OCD²* *s.v.* 'Calendars' with references.

man chairing a meeting of the *Boule*, for it met on every day except public holidays;* at a minimum there were four meetings of the *Ekklesia* in each prytany, and the chairman for the day presided there as well. Since there was a better than 70 per cent chance of each member of the *Boule* presiding over the Prytanies, there was a very real possibility of any member having to preside over a vital meeting of one of the other bodies. That they did so without disaster is a high tribute to the competence of the average members of the *Boule*. The above arrangements were changed in the fourth century to those described in xliv,2, but this is not an indication that the system had broken down; the aim seems to have been to divorce the presidents for the meetings where decisions were made from the Prytanies of the period, presumably because the Prytanies were deeply involved in the preliminary drafting of proposals, and it was therefore felt that they could be over-influential if they presided at the *Ekklesia* as well. The reform was aimed at even greater democratic equality, not at increased efficiency; it also gave all ten tribes a share in presiding throughout the year. The date when the system was changed is unknown, but may have been as late as 378/7.

Aristotle digresses from his discussion of the mechanics of the workings of the *Boule*, which leads into a full analysis of its duties, to outline the topics discussed obligatorily once a month by the *Ekklesia*; the transition is effected naturally from the point that it was the duty of the *Boule* to include these items on the agenda which it drew up. The list itself (§§4–6) requires little comment; most of the individual topics are discussed further below; for ostracism, see above on xxii. The list which Aristotle gives does not, of course, cover all the topics discussed by the *Ekklesia*, but only those which were mandatory at particular meetings. The main function of the *Ekklesia* is implicit rather than explicit throughout his discussion: it had to decide everything of moment in all aspects of government. Discussions had usually to be initiated on the basis of a preliminary motion from the *Boule* (*probouleuma*), though this might only amount to a proposal that a topic should be discussed, and on rare occasions a discussion might take place without a preliminary motion. There was apparently a preliminary show of hands as to whether the motion of the *Boule* should be put to the *Ekklesia*; cf. §6. It was also open to the *Ekklesia* to pass a motion requiring the *Boule* to put a particular matter on the agenda for the next meeting.

The *Ekklesia* met on the Pnyx, a hill near the Acropolis, and the speakers spoke from a platform which was eleven feet high, from which both the sea and the Acropolis were visible. Meetings were well attended in the fifth century, although they involved participants in losing a day's earnings—a sign of the healthy spirit of involvement of the community in the city's affairs. The introduction of a fee for attendance about the year 400 indicates a change of mood, and must suggest that attendances had been falling; further evidence was the use of a rope covered with red chalk to 'sweep' those in the agora into meetings (Scholiast on Aristophanes, *Acharnians* 22)—anyone whose clothes were marked with

---

* The apparently large number of festivals in the ancient world can be misleading; there was then no seven-day week with a rest day built into it. Our modern weekends give 104 days a year when public business is not normally conducted, and it is unlikely that the total of festival days was much higher in fifth- or fourth-century Athens, high though their total was; see Ps. Xenophon, *Constitution of the Athenians* iii,2.

the red who was not at the meeting was liable to a penalty; cf.XLI,3 and comment above. For a comic description of a meeting of the *Ekklesia* see Aristophanes, Acharnians 17–173.

Meetings were opened by priests purifying the assembly and reciting prayers, and the motions were then put forward, with the compulsory items listed by Aristotle coming first. The herald and the Scythian bowmen kept order, and speakers were required to keep to the point, speak on one subject at a time, and avoid scurrility, though one may legitimately doubt whether this regulation was observed meticulously. Anyone could speak, though members of the assembly were a critical audience quite prepared to shout down anyone they did not wish to listen to, or whom they regarded as incompetent. At the end of the speeches on a particular topic, a vote was if necessary taken on the motion put forward by the *Boule*; amendments were in order and could be voted on. Voting was normally by show of hands, though black and white pebbles were used for a form of secret ballot in important matters which affected individuals, particularly where loss of citizen rights or other severe punishment might result from the vote. The meeting was adjourned if any natural phenomenon occurred which could be interpreted as a bad omen, including rain, though this has an obvious practical reason for an assembly held in the open; for examples, see Aristophanes, *Acharnians* 171 (a joke?); Clouds 581–6; Thucydides V,45,4. If this happened, or if the business on the agenda was not completed, the meeting was reconvened the next day. Any emergency situation resulted in an immediate meeting of th *Ekklesia* outside the normal schedule.

One might easily overestimate the importance of the *Boule* and underestimate that of the *Ekklesia* from Aristotle's account; the impression is balanced by the works of the historians, who regularly talk of the *Ekklesia* and rarely of the *Boule*. The reason for this contrast is that Aristotle is concentrating on the mechanics of the constitution, and how proposals were formulated and came up for final decision, a process in which the *Boule* had a vital part to play; the historians are more interested in the actual decisions taken. One must always remember the detailed control exercised by the *Ekklesia*, not merely over major matters of policy, such as war and peace and alliances, but also over what we regard as administrative decisions. They appointed the generals for an expedition, fixed the size of the forces, and gave detailed instructions on the conduct of the campaign from which the commanders in the field diverged at their peril. For example, the generals sent to Sicily in 425–4 were convicted on their return; their offence was that they had made peace without the specific instructions of the *Ekklesia*—though they had been presented with a situation in which they had no other choice. No doubt, the political consequences for the individual *strategos* resulting from such use of initiative depended on the success or failure of the action in question. Equally, the internal control of the *Ekklesia* extended to such details as approving the designs for new temples. For a detailed discussion of the functions of the *Boule*, see the following pages.

The procedure for accusations described in §5 was used against those who had forced the illegal trial of the generals after the battle of Arginusae; cf. Xenophon, *History* I,VII,34. It is of interest that metics were entitled to lay information as well as citizens; presumably here, as in other official actions, the formalities were conducted through the Athenian citizen who looked after their interests; cf. below on LVIII. On informers see above on XXXV.

XLIV The first three sections are discussed above (see on XLIII); one small point remains. The main repository of the treasure of Athens was the 'rear room' (*Opisthodomos*) of the Parthenon; the text says 'sanctuaries', but the Greek need not imply more than one place, although it could; the public records were kept in the Bouleuterion, and later in the Metroon. Needless to say, custody of the keys does not imply that the chairman had any part in the administration of the treasure or records.

Elections were held in the seventh prytany, and, if they were not unduly delayed by bad omens, this would mean that the officers mentioned in §4 would be elected about four months before they took office. The interval was necessary for the investigation of their eligibility at the *dokimasia*, and for substitutions should any be rejected. To have a preliminary motion by the *Boule* for the elections when they came at a fixed point and were not amenable to a motion in the ordinary sense is at first sight odd, but is necessary in the light of the provision that nothing could normally be handled by the *Ekklesia* which was not the subject of a preliminary motion (XLV,4). On the individual officers mentioned, see below on LXI.

XLV The incident involving Lusimachos and Eumelides is otherwise unknown. The most plausible interpretation places it in the immediate aftermath of the overthrow of the oligarchy in 403, for in the later fifth century the *Boule* had certainly lost any powers of arbitrary arrest and execution they may have had at an earlier period; their summary jurisdiction was limited to a maximum fine of 500 drachmae, which, while not trivial, was not enormous. There were also limits on their powers of summary arrest; see the oath taken by members of the *Boule*, above on XXII. Demosthenes says that these limitations had been imposed by Solon (*against Timocrates* 148), but this cannot be so; he could not have reduced the powers of a body he created. In all probability the limitation was imposed at the time of the reforms of Ephialtes, and was included in the transference of all important judicial power to the *dikasteria*. Thereafter, if the *Boule* decided that the case demanded a more severe penalty than they were competent to inflict, they recommended accordingly, and passed the case to the *dikasteria* for a full trial and final decision. Apart from the fact that the powers of the *Boule* were probably greater before 462/1, the Areopagus certainly had wide-ranging authority at an early stage in Athenian history. It is therefore plausible to suggest that we have in the case of Lusimachos evidence that the oligarchs had revived some of these dormant powers in their recreation of the 'ancestral constitution'—witness also the 'trial' of Theramenes before the *Boule* under the Thirty—and that for a short while in a crisis situation the *Boule* of the restored democracy usurped similar powers until they were challenged and fifth-century democratic restrictions reimposed; cf. XL,2. The case of Lusimachos may well have been the moment when they were challenged. There is evidence that he had been involved with the Thirty (Xenophon, *History* ii,iv,8), and the form of penalty he escaped confirms that he had been accused of being involved in the execution of citizens without trial.*

Similar restrictions are also specifically mentioned as applying to the other judicial functions of the *Boule*: the reviewing of the conduct of magistrates, and the investigation of the credentials of the next year's *Boule* and Archons at the *dokimasia*. The procedure under the radical democracy was the result of historical development. At first, the *Boule* and Archons had wide judicial powers; then appeal was introduced in serious cases under Solon; appeal by one side or the other gradually became the regular practice, until in the later fifth century the hearings before magistrates and others with similar powers became in the main preliminary formalities. Those who presided over the hearings gave a decision, but it was not binding unless both sides accepted it voluntarily. The normal function of the hearing was parallel to that of our magistrates' courts: the pleadings were heard and recorded, but the real trial was before a jury in the *dikasteria*. The effect of the preliminary hearing was to limit the field that would be disputed at the main hearing, for it was not permitted to introduce at that stage considerations or testimony that had not been raised at the preliminary hearing; cf. LIII with Commentary.

In XLV-XLIX Aristode describes the functions of the *Boule* in administration and in relation to the other state officials. Individual points which need clarification will be discussed first, and the overall position of the *Boule* after the details have been clarified.

The investigation of the magistrates each prytany was conducted with the aid of auditors selected from the *Boule* (XLVIII,3) ; a good example of use by the people of the right of complaint against a magistrate and his subsequent deposition and fine is the case of Pericles in 430 (Thucydides 11,65,2-3. Antiphon (on the *Choreutes*, 49) gives examples of actions against a number of different officials before the *Boule* initiated in this way. There was apparently no appeal from an acquittal by the *Boule* under this procedure. The process of the *dokimasia* is described in detail in LV.

The provision that everything which went before the *Ekklesia* must do so after a preliminary discussion by the *Boule* was of key importance. It prevented 'snap' decisions since it imposed a certain period of time between the raising of a subject and the final vote (as also did the requirement that the agenda should be published in advance of the meeting), and it ensured that everything was discussed in a body whose size made proper consideration of technical and complicated issues easier than it would be in the *Ekklesia*, though even 500 must have been uncomfortably large for some discussions. In complex matters the proposal of the *Boule* was often accepted as drafted. The procedure was not rigid, as implied by Plutarch, Solon 19, but could be circumvented. Demosthenes (on the Crown 169) describes how, in the crisis after the capture of Elateia, the *Ekklesia* had assembled before the *Boule*

---

* The penalty was *apotumpanismos,* a cruel and lingering death by torture. Not all criminals were executed by the relatively humane cup of hemlock—indeed it is possible that hemlock did not come into use until the period of the Thirty right at the end of the fifth century; it was used in the fourth century, though by no means for all executions; cf. R. J. Bonner and G. Smith, *The Administration of Justice from Homer to Aristotle* ii, 279ff.

had had time to produce a proposal, and they therefore just introduced the subject for discussion; cf. above on XLIII.

The indictment for illegal proposals was introduced at some period in the fifth century as a check on the fully developed democracy. Those who argue that the Areopagus had extensive supervisory powers to preserve constitutionality before 462/1 frequently also argue that the indictment for illegal proposals was substituted at that date for the powers which had been abolished. However, the first definitely known cases are the prosecution of Speusippos by Leogoras in 415 and the prosecution of the general Demosthenes by Antiphon at about the same time. It seems unlikely that the statute was on the book for forty-five years without being used, or that it was used but we know nothing of the cases. It is more probable that it was introduced at a later date when the dangers of the unchecked democracy were becoming apparent. It covered illegality of drafting or a proposal which clashed with an existing law; the indictment could be brought against either a proposal or a motion already passed by the *Ekklesia*. The objector undertook to bring a prosecution under the statute, and the proposal was then 'frozen' until the case had been tried; the proposer of the indicted measure was only personally liable for punishment for a year, but the trial could be heard after any length of time. Thus it became a useful way of obstruction which need not involve a man in an actual penalty as long as the trial was suitably delayed. In the fourth century it was severely abused; Aristophon is said to have been acquitted seventy-five times! When properly used, it was a valuable constitutional safeguard; as abused it could be a menace.

XLVI Though, like everything else, under the general control of the *Ekklesia*, the supervision of the navy and everything to do with it was peculiarly the province of the *Boulé*; the details are given here. Diodorus (XI,43,3), dealing with the period about 477, refers to the *Boulé* having twenty new ships constructed, but there is no certainty that this was normal; *Anon. Argent.* 1,11 implies ten a year. Probably in Aristotle's day the vote of the *Ekklesia* (§1) specified how many were to be built. The election by the *Ekklesia* of the naval architects to build the ships is a good instance of the all-pervasive democratic control of what we should regard as technical matters. The members of a *Boulé* which was judged to have done its duty well were rewarded with crowns; Demosthenes (*against Androtion* 8) confirms this, and also supports the specific point that the *Boulé* were debarred from receiving the crowns unless they had had the requisite ships built. Aeschines (*against Ctesiphon* 30) implies that the board of ten who were responsible for the building of the triremes were picked by the tribes; perhaps the choice of the tribes was ratified by the *Boulé*, but the instance he mentions may have been an unusual burden on the tribes, not the normal procedure.

The mention of quadriremes in the passage is of interest; their construction is first recorded at Athens in 330/29, while quinqueremes first appear in the surviving records in 325/4. The Archonship of Kephisophon is mentioned in LIV,7, and gives a terminus post quem for the Constitution of Athens,

329/8. Combining the two pieces of information, one arrives at a tentative date of 328–5 for the composition of at least the later section of the book.

The inspection of public buildings presumably refers to new constructions, and was aimed to detect any faults or defalcations on the part of the builder. It is not easy to see how it could have been applied to already completed structures which were in use; any faults in the administration of them would be detected at the *euthuna* of the magistrate responsible at the end of his term of office. Note that offences of this class were reported to the *Ekklesia*, not to an official or the *dikasteria*.

XLVII The theme of the next section is the supervision exercised by the *Boule*; Aristotle lists a number of boards responsible for particular aspects of the administration, and includes them here because their important actions had to take place in front of the *Boule*. Thus the *Boule* acted as the City's witnesses of what happened, and ensured that duties were carried out properly.

Treasurers were originally selected from the richest class of citizens (cf. VIII,i) because it was felt that the temptation to petty embezzlement would be less; that the law was disregarded by the late fourth century is no surprise; compare the parallel case of the Thetes mentioned in VII,4. The Treasurers of Athena were responsible for the safe-keeping of large sums of money and very considerable treasures, but, as with the other offices filled by lot mentioned in this section of the work, they had no administrative responsibility which would have required expertise. All decisions were taken by the people; the responsibility of the officials was only to ensure the safety of what was in their charge, receive what was paid in, and pay out sums when instructed to do so by the people.

The 'image of Athena' is the famous statue by Pheidias; the value of the gold on the statue was given by Thucydides (11,13,5) as 40 talents of refined gold, while Philochorus (Jacoby, *F.Gr.H.* III B 323 F 121) gives 44 talents. This represents 560 or 616 talents of silver (the normal currency unit), since the ratio between gold and silver in the later fifth century was 14:1. Although it was removable, there is no evidence that the Athenians ever used any of this gold even in the darkest days of the Peloponnesian War, and it was therefore presumably still there in Aristotle's day. Gold statues of Victory were an accepted way of 'storing' surplus revenue. Ten are known in the late fifth century, of which eight were melted down to make gold coins in 407/6; others are mentioned in the fourth century, notably those in Plutarch, *Moralia* 841D: '(Lycurgus) constructed gold and silver ceremonial vessels for the city and gold Victories'; the date was 334. The ceremonial equipment would have been chariots, jewelry and many other things used in the major festival processions to the gods. For all of this, as well as the ordinary cash reserves of the city, the Treasurers were responsible, and the accounts were handed over from one board to the next in front of the *Boule*, and subject to the normal review at the end of a man's tenure of office.

The word '*poletai*' means literally 'sellers', though from the description of their duties they appear to have been rather controllers of public contracts. The post of treasurer of military affairs was established in 338, and replaced the officials called 'Treasurers of the Greeks' who had originally been established to handle the money of the Delian League, and come to be the treasurers of Athens' war effort when the League became effectively the Athenian Empire. On the Theoric Fund, see above on xliii; the officials of the Fund referred to here were established in the second half of the fourth century. Public contracts of whatever sort were the responsibility of the *poletai*, working in conjunction with the *Boule* and presumably also the *Ekklesia* where any policy decision had to be taken. Taxes were not collected directly by the Athenians, but the right to collect them was sold to private individuals who then recouped the price from what they collected, together with some profit, though there is no evidence of massive exploitation such as that practised at times by the Roman tax-farmers, presumably because they were collecting taxes from Athenians, not subject peoples; the collection of the tribute was never farmed out in this way.

The position about mines is obscure. They remained the property of the state, and what was sold was the right to work them for a period; the lessee had to pay a price and one twenty-fourth of the value of the precious metal mined. We do not know what lies behind the distinction between three- and ten-year contracts, but logic might suggest that the three-year contracts covered mines which were known to be profitable, while what I have translated as 'special agreements' covered the right to explore an unknown area and mine if any precious metal were discovered; the financial position in the latter case is unknown.*

In many cases those on capital charges were allowed to withdraw from Athens before the final stage was reached, and so avoid execution. Their property was forfeit and the procedure for its sale is described in §2; those exiled by the Areopagus were listed separately because they would have been guilty of crimes involving religious pollution; cf. LVII,3 with Commentary. At a time of general amnesty and recall of exiles, this class of offenders was specifically excluded. The whitened boards referred to were the normal vehicle for transitory public records, as here for lists of various forms of debts and payments which had to be recorded for a period, but did not require the permanence of a stone inscription. Lists of property sold by the state were inscribed on stone; see for example the fragmentary lists of the sale of the property of those involved in the mutilation of the Hermae (414), Meiggs/Lewis, 79.

The categories of debts which had to be repaid at various intervals are not known, though Aristotle sheds some light here. An interesting point is the arrangements for repayment of large capital sums over a period. The period allowed for the repayment of the price of a house may be compared with the statement by Isaeus (*on the Estate of Hagnias* 42) that property worth 35 minae brought in 3 minae per annum—i.e. one recovered the purchase price in under twelve years. In these terms, the period allowed for payment to the state was not ungenerous. It is not surprising that the King Archon was responsible for the collection of the rent from sacred property, for his particular preserve was the administration of religious affairs; see LVII and commentary. Again, the mechanics of all these payments were supervised by the *Boule*, and the system carefully devised to avoid anything being done in the wrong way or at the wrong time. The word translated as 'pigeon holes' is normally used of something resting on something else, for instance the architrave on the columns of a building; the exact connotation in the present passage is not certain, but the general meaning must be that given.

---

* On mining in Attica, see R. J. Hopper, 'The Laurion Mines; a reconsideration', in *BSA* 63 (1968) 293–326, with bibliography.

XLVIII The Receivers were officers instituted under Cleisthenes whose function was the corollary of the *poletai*; again, it is a typical democratic check that there were two boards of ten who effectively checked each other where a modern state might well employ the same people for both sides of the transaction. The penalties for defaulting on payment were severe; to the details given here should be added the statement of Demosthenes (*against Nikostratos* 27.) and Andocides (*on the Mysteries* 73) that the debtor's property was seized and sold to cover the amount due. Thus the *Boule* 'exacts the money', and imprisonment was presumably employed only if the sum realised did not cover the debt. The division of money referred to was the allocation to magistrates of funds needed for the performance of their duties. See also LII,3.

The auditors mentioned in §3 are not to be confused with those mentioned in LIV,2; the present body handled the month-to-month accounts of officials, while the latter investigated their accounts at the end of the year. The officials selected for the *euthuna* worked with the second group of auditors on the annual investigation of the magistrates, for which see LIV,2. The detail here that those whose investigation had been concluded in the *dikasteria* were still liable to be tried if a complaint was made within three days of the first hearing is interesting; everything possible was done to make it possible for a private citizen to get an airing for a grievance. It is probable that these accusations were made in the Athenian Agora, where statues of the eponymous heroes stood, but certainty is impossible in view of the state of the text; see note in the translation *ad loc*. The provision that the official must think the charge justified before the case can be reopened is a necessary check on totally frivolous accusations; hearings before the *dikasteria* were time-consuming and cost the city money in fees to the jurors. On the deme justices, see below on LIII.

XLIX The first two sections deal with elements of the armed forces where the state gave financial assistance to those enrolled in them; there was naturally a check on the recipients to make sure that money was not being spent to no purpose. The cavalry received a grant to cover the upkeep of horses, but there were other expenses on armour and equipment, and they had to maintain a mounted servant; hence it was not possible for a poor man to serve, and poverty was accepted as an excuse if a man had been summoned for cavalry service. The infantry attached to the cavalry worked closely with them on foot, and therefore had to be very fit to keep up; hence again it was essential to ensure that they were capable of fulfilling their duty.

The remainder of the chapter covers a few minor functions of the *Boule*. The Greek word translated as 'models' probably covers the plans for any major public undertaking, for example a temple, but would probably include also less important items such as the statues of Victory mentioned in §4 (cf. XLVII,i, with Commentary). The robe was woven for the statue of Athena, and taken up to the Acropolis during the Great Panathenaia; scenes in the design included the battle between Athena and the Giants. The date of the transference of the inspection of these things to the *dikasteria* is unknown.

The maintenance of the disabled at public expense started under Peisistratus, and was at first limited to those disabled by war wounds (Plutarch, *Solon* 31). Later anyone incapable of maintaining himself was included; the date of the change is unknown, but all were covered before the end of the fifth century when Lysias (*on the Refusal of a Disability Pension* 26) refers to a pension of this type which had been drawn for some years already; the speech was delivered shortly after 403. This rare example of 'social conscience' in the ancient world arose from the strong corporate sense of the city state: the first duty of every citizen was to do whatever the city required of him, and the corollary was to do whatever the city required of him, and the corollary was that he had a claim on the city for a minimum subsistence if he was absolutely incapable of maintaining himself by his own efforts through no fault of his own.

Thus, with the first sentence of chapter L, Aristotle concludes his analysis. The prominence of the *Boule* at Athens after 462/1 was the direct result of the triumph of radical democracy, and the body itself was symptomatic of it. The principle of selection by lot combined with rotation ensured that it consisted of a cross-section of the people, and that a large proportion of the citizens would be members at least once. In this way they had a say in the detailed planning of every aspect of government by the drafting of decrees and motions for the *Ekklesia*, and in the day-to-day supervision of all officials—an aspect of the duties of the *Boule* which Aristotle rightly stresses at the beginning and end of his discussion. Their control was the only thing which stood in the way of anarchy in the administration of finance, and the regular checks on all those handling public money ensured its proper use. The *Boule* apparently had little initiative, but its role was vital; the drafting of complex decrees is a difficult operation, and once drafted they were unlikely to be frequently or radically altered in the *Ekklesia* because of the sheer practical difficulties involved in doing so. The role of the *strategoi* in guiding these detailed discussions must have been important. From the details Aristotle gives it is easy to see why the *Boule* was permanently behind schedule; cf. *Constitution of the Athenians* III,1. Above all, one must remember the part it played in the political education of the average citizen; the fact that there would have been present at any meeting of the *Ekklesia* a significant number of people with personal experience of the functioning of the *Boule* and the day-to-day administration of government through the many administrative boards selected from its members must have contributed greatly to the wisdom and good sense of the decisions taken by the people as a whole.

L After discussing the *Boule*, Aristotle turns to other boards and officers selected by lot, most of whom had minor duties; it appears that these officials were not members of the *Boule*. From the small sum allocated to those in charge of the sanctuaries, they cannot have had any very important function to perform. The city commissioners are also mentioned in Aristotle's *Politics* (1321 b 18ff), where their duties are listed in similar terms, though there he adds that they are responsible for collapsed buildings (presumably to make sure that they are safe and do not obstruct the street), for the general safety and repair of the streets, and for boundaries between property. The entertainers referred to were hired for drinking-parties given by ordinary citizens—the price is not high (cf. Plato, *Protagoras* 347 d); the wealthy presumably had their own entertainers. Civic control of prices and the way in which 'double bookings' were fairly resolved are remarkable examples out of the many instances where the Athenian state intervened in what are normally thought to be private matters.

The disposal of refuse was a major problem since there was no sewage system; it is referred to not infrequently in the surviving literature. A decree of 320 affecting the Peiraeus also deals with the problem of rubbish, though there the duty of seeing that it is cleared up rests on the householder, with the superintendents of the market responsible for ensuring that it is done (Dittenberger *Syll.* i³, 313). The building regulations are all designed to ensure the safety of passers by; the reference to windows is a trifle obscure, since Greek houses normally did not have windows on the ground floor on the street, though this may have been because of the ban mentioned. If it was a well-known regulation, it is hard to see why anyone should have thought of breaking it. There is an interesting parallel from Rome, where Plutarch records (*Poplicola* 20) the practice in Greece of knocking on a door from the inside to warn passers-by before opening it on to the street; later, doors opening outwards were banned. The removal of corpses from the streets indicates a section of the population who were destitute and without any home to go to or anyone to look after them.

LI In the markets, also, the Athenians went to some trouble to ensure fair dealing and fair prices, even specifying the size of loaves. The increase of the numbers of commissioners of the corn supply may indicate that they found plenty to do; it was vital for the survival of Athens that enough should be brought into the city, and for the individual Athenian that it should be honestly sold.

LII The death penalty was mandatory for the offences listed, and was inflicted without trial on those who admitted their guilt. The main aim of kidnapping would have been to sell the victims into slavery—hence it was a serious offence. On the *poletai* see XLVII,2; the cooperation of the Eleven in the detection of houses and land alleged to be public property shows that the passage refers to a criminal offence, presumably an attempt to take private possession of public property. Among the indictments the Eleven were responsible for bringing was a particular technical charge, that of improperly usurping political rights ; the distinction between the cases brought by the Eleven and those brought by the *Thesmothetai* is unknown.

The procedure discussed in the second section ensured that certain classes of dispute received a speedy trial. The dowry was a part of the woman's family's property set aside for her maintenance; the payment referred to here was probably that required after divorce or the death of the husband, when the money would be vital for her. If it were not repaid, those who wrongfully retained it could be sued for its return together with interest at 18 per cent per annum—a fairly high rate which shows that the offence was regarded as serious. The interest rate of a drachma per mina represents i per cent per month or 12 per cent per annum; this was regarded as a moderate and reasonable rate (as opposed to the higher rates of 16, 18 or 36 per cent recorded in some cases), and therefore those who were wronged were entitled to get relief under the speedy procedure of cases to be settled within a month. Those aiming at higher returns had to wait longer if they needed to sue the debtor.

Demosthenes says that prosecutions for assault were heard before the Forty (cf. LIII) in his speech *against Pantainetos* 33; either the tribunal had changed by the time Aristotle wrote or there were different categories of assault heard by different bodies. Disputes about trierarchies arose in the fourth century much more than the fifth; in the former period an individual maintained a ship for the year, and the only usual cause for litigation was a charge that he had not taken up office on the proper day, not done his duty to the minimum standard prescribed by law, or handed over an unseaworthy vessel. In the fourth century the expense was divided amongst groups of men, and there was therefore a fruitful field for litigation arising from disputes about whether individuals had done their fair share, apart from the possible sources of dispute listed above. A good example of a case in the field of banking is Isocrates' *Trapezitikos*, where forgery and repudiation are the points at issue. That the Receivers should handle cases involving taxation is only natural; see XLVII,2 and XLVIII,i with Commentary.

LIII The Forty had by Aristotle's day taken over the functions of the deme justices established under Peisistratus (XVI,5) who had been revived under Pericles (XXVI,3). This is a rare occasion where Aristotle gives the date of a change between fifth- and fourth-century practice; one must not assume from this that there was no change where he does not mention one, for there are many cases already noted where the system he describes was not that of the fifth century. Very little is known of the Thirty in the fifth century, though it is probable that after a while they, like the Forty later, did not go on circuit as the original deme justices had. The Forty appear to have been mainly concerned with property disputes—hence the procedure involving arbitration below—and to have held the first hearing of private suits except those to be decided within the month; however, some private suits were heard in the first instance by the *Thesmothetai*; cf. LIX,5. It was sense that they should have the final word in really trivial cases, and not waste the time of a *dikasterion*; Aristotle (*Politics* 1300 b 33ff) approves of the principle of not having large juries for insignificant disputes.

The arbitration procedure is described in detail, and is interesting not least for the mechanism whereby an attempt was made to avoid prolonged litigation where a settlement could be arrived at without going to the *dikasteria*. If the case did go to the *dikasteria*, the hearings before the Arbitrators fulfilled the same functions of limiting the field for the final trial as were performed by the preliminary hearings before the *Boule* and the Archons discussed above; see on XLV. Voluntary arbitration seems to have existed in Athens for a long time; it perhaps became compulsory in private cases in the period 403–400; see Bonner and Smith, The *Administration of Justice* 1,346 if. Aristophanes (*Wasps* 962ff) implies that witnesses delivered their evidence in the *dikasteria* orally in the fifth century; this practice continued generally in the fourth, written depositions being used presumably to prevent witnesses changing their evidence.

The Arbitrators were those in their last year of the forty-two-year cycle of public service; from eighteen to fifty-eight men had to serve in the armed forces when required; then, when they were fifty-nine, they served as Arbitrators. Aristotle stresses that this service was as compulsory as any other part of their duties. Two distinct groups of eponymous heroes are mentioned here. First the ten of the ten tribes (XXI,6), and secondly the forty-two who gave their names to the age-groups in each year of the forty-two-year cycle. They were 'used' in rotation, so that the Ephebes of one year were enrolled under the eponymous hero of the Arbitrators of the previous year, who was 'available' since that year-group had finished their duties in this sense. Thus Athenians gave an absolute date by the Archon of the year, and placed a man in his age-group by the eponymous hero of his year.

An example of the actions against Arbitrators mentioned in §6 is referred to in Demosthenes *against Meidias* 86. Appeal from such a case lay naturally to the *dikasteria*.

LIV In this chapter Aristotle concludes the list of minor officials selected by lot. The commissioners of roads appear to overlap with the functions of the city commissioners as inferred from the *Politics* (see on L above); it may be that each body handled different roads—for example, the commissioners of roads may not have acted within the city—or it may be that the *Politics* and the *Constitution of Athens* cannot be conflated directly since the former is more theoretical. It is a minor point.

The Auditors are much the most important officials of those listed in liv; they are not the same body as that mentioned in XLVIII since the present group were responsible for the final investigation of accounts at the end of a year of office. The penalty for taking bribes could also be death, not merely ten times the bribe thought to have been taken. This paragraph makes it clear that all investigations under the *euthuna* had to go to the *dikasterion* before the final discharge of the official, not merely those where some crime was suspected.

'Clerk to the Prytanies' was another title for the Clerk to the *Boule*; he held an important post in which anyone bent on malpractice would have plenty of scope while checking and holding documents. It is therefore not surprising that by Aristotle's day the post was filled annually by lot; at what date this became the practice is not known, though it may have been between 367 and 363. The statement that before this the Athenians 'used to elect the most famous and reliable men' is a little puzzling since we know the names of at least sixty-six holders of the post in the fifth and fourth centuries, and hardly any of them are famous.

Proxenia was the status granted to Athenians who undertook to look after the interests of the nationals of other states resident in Athens; it was a position of considerable honour, and also involved duties, for foreigners were under certain disabilities; for example, they could go to law only with their *proxenos* bringing the case for them. The *Proxenoi* had a position in many respects parallel to modern consuls, but were always nationals of the state in which they lived. The term could also be used in an honorary sense, for example as a complement to foreign rulers and as a description of certain privileged metics, for whom see below LVIII,2 with Commentary. Grants of citizenship were rare but a field where dishonesty on the part of the Clerk would be very serious. The clerk whose duty it was to read out documents to the people and the *Boule* is mentioned (for example) in the account of Nicias' despatch from Sicily (Thucydides VII,10); later he apparently had the additional duty of reading out the official texts of tragedies to the actors (Plutarch *Moralia* 841 F).

The religious officials and their duties are largely self-explanatory. For the arrangements for the Panathenaia, see LX with Commentary; here the Great Panathenaia is referred to, not the Lesser, an annual celebration. The four-yearly mission to Delos had been revived in 425 (Thucydides III,104,2), and was different from the annual celebration; the six-year interval is obscure, but may have been introduced after 330. The Brauronia was a festival to Artemis at Brauron, while the Heracleia was celebrated at Marathon. The Eleusinia referred to are again not the regular yearly celebration, but a special festival. The archonship of Kephisophon is the latest date mentioned in the treatise—see above, Introduction and Commentary on XLVI.

Salamis was not an integral part of Attica, but partially populated by cleruchs, and was administered as a community dependent on Athens; hence the selection of an Archon. The Demarch was normally elected in each deme; the selection of the Demarch of the Peiraeus by lot probably indicates a feeling that it was too important a position to be filled by election since the holder might become too influential. It is alternatively possible that there was more than one deme in the Peiraeus area, and one of the elected Demarchs was chosen by lot to act in some sense as head of the local administration. The festivals of Dionysus referred to were 'Rural' Dionysia (as opposed to the 'City' Dionysia in Athens itself); they were celebrated in many places throughout Attica, and that at the Peiraeus was perhaps the grandest. On the *choregoi* (providers of choruses) see below, LVI, 3ff and *Commentary*.

LV Having discussed the *Ekklesia*, the *Boule*, the boards of administrative officials who were members of the *Boule*, and the other minor officials selected by lot, Aristotle now turns to the Archonship of his own day—an office also filled by lot, but very different in many ways from those which have been discussed up to now. The previous history of the office has been discussed already; see III,2–4; VIII,1; XXII,5; XXVI,2 with the Commentary on those passages. The first change from fifth-century practice noted is that the nine officials (the Archon, the King Archon, the Polemarch and the six *Thesmothetai*) together with their clerk were selected by lot in such a way that each tribe provided one member, and each tribe held each position in turn. Such democratic equality and rotation was applied much more rigidly in the fourth than the fifth century, though how early the principle of equal representation for all tribes was established is unknown.

Aristotle chooses the context of the Archons to give a general account of the process of the *dokimasia*, the preliminary investigation undergone by all office-holders before they could take up their position. The Archons, as opposed to other officials, had to go through the process twice, once before the *Boule* (cf. XLV,3) and again before the *dikasteria*. The questions asked appear to have been standard, and the aim was to test the basic qualifications of the office-holder elect; they established that he was a fully qualified citizen and had performed his basic civic and family duties. They did not in any sense test his capacity to perform the office for which he had been selected by lot. It may well be that the prospect of this examination was enough to deter some who would be hopelessly incompetent from standing, though the prospect of the *euthuna* at the end of their tenure and the monthly votes on their performance was more likely to do that.

The list of points investigated takes account of Pericles' citizenship law (xxvi,4), but omits the question of what class the candidate belonged to—cf. vii,4. Either this is just a slip, or the law excluding the Thetes from the Archonship had been a dead letter for so long that even the question had been dropped by Aristotle's day. The class question must have been asked for a few offices, notably the Treasurers who were nominally from the richest class—but see above xlvii,1. The cults mentioned were an essential part of Athenian life, and all citizens were enrolled; the gods mentioned had special care of the home and the hearth. Oral evidence was called to substantiate a man's answers; the Athenians used witnesses in a situation where modern society naturally turns to documentary evidence. Here, as everywhere else, the care taken to ensure that every citizen got a chance to lay any complaint he might have is manifest, and accentuated by the change noted by Aristotle, whereby the one formal vote of acquittal which had been traditional where no complaint had been offered against a magistrate elect was replaced by a full vote just in case bribery or intimidation had taken place before the hearing.

For the stone, and the golden statue to be dedicated for taking bribes, see vii,1 above with Commentary. The phrase translated as 'witnesses swear to their depositions' raises a problem in that the verb normally means 'foreswear' or 'deny on oath'. However, this seems a meaningless remark in the context, and it is more plausible to accept the meaning given in the text despite the fact that it is not paralleled in extant literature until much later.

LVI As a conclusion to his discussion of the Archons as a body and before turning to their individual functions, Aristotle notes the appointment of two assessors for each of the three senior Archons. There was presumably a survival of primitive practice in the procedure by which the Archons picked their own men for the job; however, once selected they were subject to all the usual democratic checks. Note that the traditional division into chapters does not go back to Aristotle; it is an eccentricity of renaissance texts that splits the first sentence of lvi from lv, where it clearly belongs, not a whim of the author.

The Archon was the official who gave his name to the year, and it was he who was the closest Athenian approximation to a modern Head of State; he had considerable ceremonial duties and some practical functions, but no real power after the reforms of the early fifth century. The oath he took on entering office must be a survival from the early period, for by it he guaranteed the population against disorder and any arbitrary action by the officers of the state; under the developed democracy his office gave him no powers by which he could take action against any who offended in this respect.

The *choregoi* were originally the men who trained and led the choruses for festivals; during the fifth century the position became one of the liturgies—a post where a wealthy man undertook a public duty at his own expense; see xxvii,3 and Commentary. The expense of the choruses lay in their costumes and training before the festival, and the Dionysia* (celebrated in Athens in late March) was a particularly fine opportunity for a wealthy man to spend heavily and thus earn prestige with his fellow citizens. Further expenditure could be incurred by hiring extras, and a generous *choregos* could make all the difference to the success of a play; it is said that Nicias never failed to win the prize when he was *choregos*. There were three groups of tragedies throughout the fifth and fourth centuries, perhaps five comedies before the Peloponnesian War, three during it as a measure of economy, and five again in the fourth century; the change of the method of appointing comic *choregoi* came in the middle of the fourth century.

Choruses were not restricted to those required for tragedies and comedies; there were choruses of men and boys for various dances and the dithyramb, which was the most expensive of all the liturgies, involving a chorus of fifty and the most expensive *aulos*-players. Five choruses of men and five of boys, each from one of the ten tribes, took part in the Dionysia as well as the choruses involved in the drama; the Thargelia, a festival to Apollo, was celebrated in late May. For a description of the duties of a *choregos* see Antiphon on the *Choreutes* 11–13.

When the Archon had appointed the *choregoi*, it was open to any of them either to claim that they were exempt or to challenge another wealthy Athenian to exchange property. The former claim was governed by complicated rules, the most important of which were that a man could not be required to perform more than one liturgy at the same time, and that the performance of a liturgy gave exemption for a fixed period of time; for example, a man could not be *choregos* until a full year had elapsed since he had completed his previous duties as *choregos*; allowing for the period of rehearsal, this meant that it was impossible to be *choregos* in consecutive years—unless, of course, a man volunteered for the job, which was not unheard of. The plea that a man had 'performed this liturgy before' is mystifying since it is known that men did on occasion perform the same liturgy more than once; perhaps a man could not be required to do so but might do it voluntarily, or perhaps this was a relatively recent change in the law in Aristotle's day. The restriction of age for the chorus leaders of boys' choruses was part of a general provision in Attic law which prevented younger men having charge of boys; cf. xLII,2.

The challenge to an exchange of property was a curious but in some ways highly egalitarian institution. It was open to somebody selected for a liturgy to allege that another citizen was wealthier and more able to bear the expense than he. He therefore challenged him to exchange property or accept the liturgy. The man challenged could either undertake the liturgy or exchange property, in which case the man originally selected had to undertake it; alternatively, an objection could be lodged to the challenge. In this case complete lists of property, except for holdings in the mines at Laurium which were exempt from assessment for the purposes of liturgies, had to be filed within three days of the challenge by both sides. Disputes, like claims for exemption, were reported to the *dikasteria* and decided there.

The *choregos* for Delos was in charge of the annual mission which happened to be absent at the time of the condemnation of Socrates, with the result that he was not executed until it returned, as the law

---

* The 'Great' or 'City' Dionysia, as opposed to the rural Dionysia celebrated in December; see above LIV, with Commentary.

provided; see Plato, *Phaedo* 58 a 7–c 3. This festival was different from the four- or six-yearly festival mentioned in LIV,7. The chorus taken may once have been of seven young men and seven girls, like the group which originally accompanied Theseus according to the myth, but it was presumably only young men in historical times. The vigil to Asclepius took place the night before the procession to Eleusis which fell in late September or October. The procession in honour of Zeus Soter ('the saviour') occurred in June/July, the last month of the Athenian year; there was also a sacrifice to Zeus Soter on the last day of the year, organised by the Archon. Little is known of the ten assistants of the Archon who helped to supervise these processions; selection of them by lot was a relatively recent innovation in Aristotle's day, and did not last long into the third century.

The cases coming under the Archon's preliminary jurisdiction were many, but the common element reflects his function as protector of the family in the widest sense and of those who could not look after them-themselves. The position of orphans and *epikleroi* has been discussed above, XLII, with Commentary. The immunity of prosecutors of those who illtreated their parents—that is failed to support them, were disobedient towards them, struck them, or failed to bury them—indicates how important it was to the Athenians that parents should be respected and properly treated. Normally a prosecutor who failed to get a proportion of the votes of the jury (usually a fifth) was fined, and could in certain circumstances lose the right to bring a similar case in the future. Actions for production in court arose where a man had control of property or documents which either belonged to another, or which the latter had the right to inspect; presumably here Aristotle is thinking of disputes involving inheritance, since this is the theme of the whole section. Similarly, the officials to divide up property probably dealt with inheritances in this instance, although they could also be appointed in business matters, for example on the break-up of a partnership.

Guardians for orphans were normally next of kin; if there were no directions in a will, the guardian was an adult male relative whose appointment had to be confirmed by the Archon; if there were no relatives, the Archon selected a suitable citizen. Disputes about inheritance or marrying *epikleroi* arose where more than one party laid claim; they had to be decided by the *dikasteria*, and the Archon was responsible for conducting the preliminary hearing and bringing the case to the *dikasteria*. The letting of properties belonging to minors or *epikleroi* was carefully controlled, and the Archon took securities for the property leased; the securities were valued by officials working under him. The limit of fourteen years old is restored in a damaged section of the papyrus; if the restoration is correct, the sentence may contain vital information not found elsewhere, the age at which Athenians came of age, at least in the sense of having some say over the handling of their property; alternatively, it may only be a carelessly phrased indication of the age at which an epikleros should be married. In all these cases the final power of the Archon was small, though he does seem from the text to have had some power of imposing fines and exacting payments which had been wrongly withheld. In most cases he initiated proceedings, held the preliminary hearing, and then introduced the case to the *dikasteria* for decision.

LVTI The King Archon was concerned primarily with religious matters. The unknown author of the speech *against Andocides* preserved among the works of Lysias summarises the position of the King Archon as follows (4): 'If (Andocides) becomes King Archon by lot, will he do anything other than make sacrifices and offer prayers on your behalf according to ancestral custom, some in the Eleusinion in Athens, some in the temple at Eleusis, and run the festival of the Mysteries?' That was, of course, not the sum total of his duties, but is the side with which Aristotle starts his account; the Eumolpidai and the Kerukes were two aristocratic families who were traditionally in charge of the cult at Eleusis; cf. xxxix,2. The Lenaia was celebrated about the end of January; many of the most successful comedies are known to have been produced in the contests there, including Aristophanes' *Acharnians*, *Knights*, *Wasps*, and *Frogs*. Torch-races figured in a number of Athenian festivals, including those to Theseus, Prometheus, Hephaestus and Pan, and also in the Panathenaia. The gymnasiarchs bore the expenses arising from the torch-races, and Demosthenes (*against Lakritos* 48) tells us that legal disputes between them came before the King Archon.

It would naturally be the function of the King Archon to initiate hearings concerning religious disputes and offences. Homicide also came within his province because it was regarded as a religious matter: the death brought a pollution on the state which required purification. The proclamation excluding the murderer (whether known or not) from all religious gatherings and from the Agora had the same motive—to prevent the spread of the pollution (cf. §4). The cases listed here were retained by the Areopagus at the time of the reforms of Ephialtes (xxv), together with damage to the sacred olives (lx,2). The element of pollution may explain why the democracy did not take them over, since religious conservatism was deeply ingrained, although the inclusion of arson is a little surprising. All homicide cases not tried by the Areopagus were brought by the King Archon before a jury of *Ephetai* who sat in different locations depending on the type of case they were trying. The origins of this archaic body are unknown, but by the fifth century they consisted of a jury of fifty-one persons, probably over fifty years of age; they did not apparently form a part of the ordinary *dikasteria* before which all other cases were brought by the magistrate or body which instituted the preliminary hearings. On the other hand, two cases mentioned by Isocrates and Demosthenes which were tried in the Palladion in the fourth century were both heard before juries of some hundreds. It may be that the *Ephetai* had been merged with the ordinary body of jurors, but it could equally be that the cases in question did not fall to the *Ephetai* to try, but were instances of ordinary actions before a *dikasterion* sitting in the Palladion.

Two unusual Athenian customs are noted here. First, the trials in the court of Phreatto; they arose when a man already in exile for one killing was charged with murder in respect of a second death. He was not allowed to set foot in Attica, but pleaded his case from a boat anchored just offshore before a jury seated near the water's edge. The taking of proceedings against 'the guilty party' is parallel to our coroner's verdict of 'murder by person or persons unknown', but takes the matter one step further in that a trial was actually held; again, the religious need for purification of the pollution was the motive. The same reason lay behind what seems to us the extraordinary practice of 'trying' animals or inanimate objects which had caused death; by doing so they had polluted the state, and it was necessary to remove them in full legal fashion. A passage in Plato's *Laws* (873 e-874 b) illustrates Athenian practice although it is theoretical, not written as history. 'If a baggage animal or any other beast kills someone, except if anything of this sort should happen to an athlete in the course of public contests, his relatives are to prosecute the killer for murder . . . and the animal when found guilty shall be killed and cast outside the borders of the land. If any inanimate object shall deprive a man of his life, unless it be a thunderbolt or some other stroke from the gods, and where a man is killed either by something falling on him or by his falling on it, the next of kin shall appoint his nearest neighbour as judge, and thus purify himself and his whole family. The guilty object shall be cast out of the land, as was laid down for the animals above. If a man is found dead, and the killer is unknown and cannot be found after careful search, the same proclamations shall be made as in other cases, and the same ban against the murderer. A trial shall be held, and proclamation made in the Agora that the murderer of so and so, having been found guilty, shall not enter the temples nor any part of the country of the victim on pain of death; if he does, and is recognised, his body is then to be thrown out of the country of the victim unburied.' The above passage also brings out the point that there was a legal obligation on the relatives to prosecute for murder; in other cases there was no such requirement, and prosecutions were brought only if the offended party wished to do so, or a public-spirited citizen was willing to bring the case, or an informer stepped in; cf. above on xxxv.

The crown mentioned in §4 is not peculiar to the King Archon, but was part of the official regalia of all Archons. Little is known of the functions of the Tribal Kings, but they had religious duties and some legal functions which were associated with the King Archon in the Prytaneion Court in the fourth century. Their position within the tribe appears to have been analogous to that of the King Archon within the whole state.

LVIII The Polemarch was originally the commander-in-chief, and concerned with military affairs. The sacrifices to Artemis in memory of the battle of Marathon, and to Enualios (Ares) were survivals from his military functions, as also was the organisation of funeral games, in which he was assisted by the *strategoi*. He had general control of all litigation which affected the numerous metics resident in Athens. They were allowed to live and work freely in the city, but were expected to undertake military service if required, and were subject to certain disabilities, such as special taxation, and restrictions, as for example not being allowed to own land. Tax-exempt metics were a privileged group free from the normal tax on metics and taxed as citizens; the *proxenoi* mentioned here are not the same group as the 'consuls' already discussed (above on LIV), but were metics granted exceptional privileges, such as the right to own land and to sit in the front seats in the theatre. Since the metics could not by definition be members of any deme or tribe, the Polemarch divided the cases in which they were involved into ten equal parts, and allocated them to the four members of the Forty in each tribe (cf. LIII, 1), who passed them to the Arbitrators; in this way the burden was evenly shared. It appears to have been a privilege to bring cases before the Polemarch; perhaps there were fewer of them, and the matter therefore came up for trial more speedily.

On Harmodius and Aristogeiton, see XVIII; on the Arbitrators, see liii; all metics were required to have a patron who acted for them in affairs which could be handled only by a citizen, in the same way as the *proxenoi* of LIV acted for Greeks from other cities who were temporarily in Athens.

LIX The *Thesmothetai*, the other six of the nine Archons, were probably introduced because of an increase of judicial business, and Aristotle gives here a long, though not exhaustive, list of the cases they handled. Most of the charges listed are self-explanatory; on motions for the deposition of magistrates and accusations in the *Ekklesia* (which were normally only a preliminary stage in the case) see XLIII; on the indictment for illegal proposals see on XLV, and on the chairmen and president see XLIV. The procedure for the collection of debts has been discussed above, XLVII–XLVIII, the *euthuna* of the *strategoi* at LIV, 2, and the investigation of credentials at LV. For appeals about citizenship see XLII, and judicial decisions of the *Boule* XLV, 1. The process whereby the *Thesmothetai* allotted courts (with the exception of cases of homicide), magistrates to individual cases, and the allocation of juries will be discussed below, lxi nff. See all these passages with the relevant sections of the Commentary.

The charge translated as 'malicious prosecution' has no exact equivalent in modern practice, and is frequently rendered (by transliterating the Greek) as sycophancy. As noted already, the Athenian had no public prosecutor, and relied on the injured party or public-spirited citizens to bring a prosecution where it was known or suspected that a crime had been committed, with the exception of cases of homicide where the family of the dead man were under a legal obligation to prosecute. Rewards had to be offered to successful prosecutors to make the system work; they received a large part of the property confiscated, the money recovered or the fine imposed as a result of conviction—often a half, sometimes even more. This naturally led to the appearance of informers and to some trumped up charges brought in the hope of personal profit; in these cases the prosecutors relied on extraneous circumstances or personal prejudices against the defendant to get convictions. There was some check on this inherent in the provision that a prosecutor who failed to receive a stated, small proportion of the votes of the jury, usually one fifth, or one who dropped a case before it came to court, faced significant penalties. They could be a fine of 1,000 drachmae, a fine of one obol per drachma of the claim (i.e. one sixth of the claim), or the loss of the right to bring a similar case in the future, depending on the circumstances of the particular case. This was some check, but not enough, since some cases were specifically excluded and the unsuccessful prosecutor suffered no penalty however badly he did. This was particularly serious since prosecution was a recognised and accepted way of attempting to revenge oneself on one's enemies, whether political or private; the threat of such charges could also be used to extort money as a blackmail 'pay-off'.

Sycophancy was widespread in the late fifth century, and is mentioned frequently in Aristophanes. The charge of sycophancy or malicious prosecution was used as a further way of checking abuse (though in itself it could become an abuse), and a charge of misleading the people could also be used, and could be effective, for the maximum penalty under it was death. Many prosecutors undoubtedly acted from the best motives, and without them the whole administration of justice in Athens would have been hamstrung; others misused the system severely, and no totally satisfactory solution was found. The appointment of a public prosecutor, which might or might not have solved the problem, would have been regarded as very undemocratic in the unlikely event of it ever occurring to the Athenians as a possibility.

The international agreements mentioned were ultimately ratified by the *dikasteria*. Where they existed, criminal and commercial cases between individuals of differing states were governed by their provisions, which included agreed laws which would govern any settlement. The plaintiff normally had the right to sue in whichever state he chose, but would usually bring the case in the defendant's state because he would be more likely to be able to execute judgment there if he won. Such suits were often commercial. If no such international agreement existed, the suit would be heard in the state where the contract had been made or the crime committed, and in accordance with its laws. Gases where perjury was alleged were normally handled by the court where it was said to have taken place; the procedure mentioned here for cases of perjury in the Areopagus was an exception.

LX The commissioners appointed to run the Panathenaic games are discussed separately because they held office for four years (cf. XLIII, 1), and this leads Aristotle naturally to reserve his discussion of the duties of the Archon in collecting the oil from the sacred olives for this section of the work. The musical contests were added to the Panathenaia by Pericles (Plutarch, *Pericles* 13); contests included singing and playing the *aulos* and *kithara* (wind and string instruments). The athletic contests were the usual ones—wrestling, running, boxing, the *pankration* and the pentathlon. On the robe for Athena see XLIV,3 with Commentary. The vases for prizes contained olive oil given to the athletes (§3). Many have been found in widely scattered places in the Mediterranean world; on one side is a representation of Athena, and on the other a picture of the event for which the prize was awarded. By Aristotle's day, the olive oil was not taken specifically from the trees dedicated to Athena, but was a general charge on the harvest from the estate on which the trees stood; the date of the change is unknown, but was later than 395. The speech of Lysias (about the Sacred Olive) also suggests that the penalty for destruction of the sacred trees had before that time ceased to be death and become exile with confiscation of property. The treasurers who received and stored the oil were the Treasurers of Athena (cf. XLVII,1). Prizes for all contests included a crown; the musical contests also carried a cash prize; the contests in manliness had carried a prize of an ox in the early fourth century—the date of the change to a shield is not known. The contest itself was a considerable test of physical fitness, involving running in full armour and horse-riding.

LXI The 'also' in the first sentence has nothing to refer to, and this has led scholars to suggest plausibly that some text is missing between chapters LX and LXI. The inference is supported by consideration of the content. Despite their importance, there is no detailed discussion of the treasurer of the military funds, the controllers of the Theoric Fund, or the supervisors of the water supply. All these offices were filled by election probably for a period of four years, and are mentioned in XLIII, 1 just before the *strategoi*; one might therefore expect some discussion of their duties precisely here, in between the commissioners of the games, who were also appointed for four years, and the *strategoi*.

Aristotle now turns his attention to military offices which were filled by election. The institution of the *strategoi* in 501/0 was described in XXII,2, and Aristotle now indicates an important change: instead of being elected one from each tribe, they were 'now' elected from the whole people; thus there were no longer necessarily representatives of all ten tribes among the ten *strategoi*. The date of the change is unknown; it was probably motivated by the realisation that, with the increasing importance of the post in every aspect of politics, it was vital to have able men filling it, and it would be foolish always to restrict each tribe to one member. This does not mean that one has to hypothesize any complicated system whereby only one tribe in any one year could have two members of the board, and no tribe was without a member for more than one year consecutively. We know that in 441 there were two *strategoi* from the tribe Akamantis, and in 432 there were two representatives of the tribe Akamantis and perhaps two from the tribe Kekropis; there are other similar examples. Thus from about the middle of the fifth century, the Athenians appear to have been able in certain circumstances not as yet fully understood to elect more than one man from a tribe; it should always be born in mind that tribal loyalty was by no means non-existent, and would have ensured a reasonable 'spread' of *strategoi* in normal circumstances.* Perhaps the most interesting single feature of the fully developed system of *strategoi* at Athens is the divorce of the individual *strategoi*, who were in origin commanders of their tribal contingents, from these units; this is a startling innovation, much more likely to belong to the fifth century than the period of the original institution of the office.

The allocation of *strategoi* to particular duties or particular areas for their year of office was not a fifth-century practice—then they were sent by the *Ekklesia* to deal with crises as they arose, as was done in Aristotle's day with the five who had no specific sphere allotted to them. The innovation appears to have been made very recently, probably between 334 and 325. For the garrisons in the Peiraeus, cf. XLII,3.

The symmories were a fourth-century institution replacing some of the liturgies undertaken by individuals in the fifth; instead of the burden falling on a single wealthy man, it fell on groups. Symmories were created in 378/7 in connection with the capital levy (*eisphora*), and henceforth almost all tax-paying Athenians were involved, as also were the metics in separate groups. In 357/6 symmories were set up to replace the trierarchy; the twelve hundred richest citizens were divided into twenty equal sections each responsible for the maintenance of a portion of the fleet. The reform was aimed at spreading the burden of taxation more fairly, and probably also reflected a reduction in the number of really wealthy men compared with the fifth century. It should be noted that the text makes it clear that

---

* This is a highly controversial topic, and space does not allow a lengthy discussion here; for an extreme thesis with excellent negative arguments but slightly more dubious positive points, see G. W. Fornara, *The Athenian Board of Generals from 501 to 404*.

men were still appointed as trierarchs even after the institution of the symmories of 357/6; exactly how the two systems interlocked is not clear. For exchanges of property, see above on LVI.

The vote on the conduct of the *strategoi* was part of the proceedings at the plenary session of the *Ekklesia* (XLIII,4) . It was of great importance for the democracy to keep a close check on their conduct, not merely for obvious wider reasons, but also because of the summary powers they had on campaign which are listed in the last sentence of §2. There is evidence that in the fifth century *strategoi* on campaign even inflicted the death penalty in extreme cases without trial. The importance of the check on the *strategoi* may be indicated by the detailed description given of the process; however, it would be unwise to read too much into it, since this is the only description which Aristotle gives of the procedure followed when an accusation was brought against a man in the course of his tenure of public office; he may have chosen this as the most appropriate place to include a description which he intended his readers to take as a type for all the other occasions when a similar procedure was appropriate.

The regimental commanders each had charge of one tribe's contingent of hoplites, usually his own. The post was instituted after 490, and it is tempting to associate its origin with the increasing importance of the ten *strategoi* after 487/6; perhaps their existence facilitated the development whereby the *strategoi* ceased to be tied to their own tribal units. It is of some interest that the subordinate officers were appointed by them, not by the *strategoi*—another sign of the divorce of the *strategoi* from their original function of tribal commanders. The two cavalry commanders held positions of considerable prestige—their post is linked with the office of *strategos* and ambassador as 'the greatest honours' by Lysias *on the* dokimasia *of Euandros* 20); the monthly vote on their conduct also shows that they were on a par with the *strategoi* at least in some respects. The position of the ten tribal cavalry commanders is strictly parallel to that of the ten regimental commanders. The cavalry commander in Lemnos commanded a detachment stationed there to protect the Athenian cleruchs on the island.

The 'Paralos' and the 'Ammonis' (or 'Ammonias') were the two state triremes which were used to send official despatches, carry ambassadors and for other public business; they were always manned by citizens, and were supposed to be the fastest ships of the fleet. In the fifth century the two state ships had been the 'Paralos' and the 'Salaminia'. The date when the 'Ammonis' was substituted for the 'Salaminia' as one of the two state vessels is unknown; interest in the oracle of Zeus Ammon may well have been increased by the visit of Alexander the Great in 331, but Athens is known to have consulted it as early as the late fifth century.

LXII The details lying behind the discussion of where and exactly how the selection for offices filled by lot took place are unknown; the text indicates that it was suspected or proved that the casting of lots for office in as small a group as those members of one deme who attended any particular election was open to abuse, and therefore most offices were allocated by tribe. It is a not unreasonable guess that at least all boards of ten were selected by lot by tribes, since one may presume that the existence of a board of ten implies one member from each tribe except where there is specific evidence to the contrary as in the case of the *strategoi*. The text is confirmed by the evidence of the inscriptions containing lists of the Prytanies of the fourth century: membership of the *Boule* was proportional to the size of the deme, and the preliminary selection must therefore have been made at the deme level. It is probable that each deme selected twice as many men as were required, half of whom were then selected as members, and half as reserves. The guards mentioned may have been the guards of the docks mentioned in xxiv,3 or may have been used abroad when required; see above on XXIV.

Pay for attendance at meetings of the *Ekklesia* was first introduced at the very beginning of the fourth century; see XLI,3 with Commentary. The highest fee mentioned in that passage is half a drachma; by Aristotle's day it had been doubled, and represents a fairly large sum, for the jurors still received only half a drachma—the level to which Cleon had raised the original two-obol fee which Pericles had introduced (XXVII,3). The nine-obol fee for the plenary sessions of the *Ekklesia* shows what fee was needed to encourage a good attendance at the most important meeting of each prytany rather than what the average citizen would lose by missing a day's earnings. Most of the rest of the officials mentioned have already been discussed: for the Prytanies, see XLIII–XLIV, for the Archons LV–LIX, and for the commissioners of the games LX, with the relevant section of the Commentary in each case. The sacred commissioners to Delos were in charge of the temple funds there, while the officials sent to Samos, Scyros, Lemnos and Imbros were all employed in government; one of them has already been mentioned, the cavalry commander for Lemnos in LXI,6. As already noted, fees were designed primarily as compensation for loss of earnings, with the purpose of enabling anyone to take an active part in politics; they were not intended to enable a man to make his living by doing his civic duty, and it is most unlikely that this would have been possible even with the higher fees paid in Aristotle's day; cf. above on XXIV.

The provision for repeated tenure of military positions is good sense; Pericles was *strategos* for some fifteen years, and Phocion held the position forty-five times. On the need for it to be possible to be a member of the *Boule* twice rather than once only (which was the rule for all other democratic offices) see above on XXXI.

LXIII–LXV Aristotle devotes the next three chapters to a very detailed account of the process of empanelling an Athenian jury. The highly complicated series of steps involved resulted from the passionate interest of the Athenians in ensuring that the system should be as fair as possible and that bribery or 'packing' of a jury should be prevented. The following discussion will first look at the process, and then deal with other details raised by Aristotle which have not been covered in the main discussion.

In the fifth century a body of 6,000 *dikastai* were selected each year by lot from those who put themselves forward; from this group juries were constituted each day as required. Up to ten courts might sit, and the juries might consist of any multiple of 100 members from 200 upwards (cf. LIII,3)! the largest might even include all the 6,000. In the fourth century there is something to suggest that odd numbers (e.g. 501) were used to avoid a tied vote, but this cannot have been universal since Aristotle mentions a specific provision for the acquittal of the defendant in the event of a tie (LXIX,1).

It was by no means certain that all the 6,000 would appear for service every day, especially since they tended to include a high proportion of the older members of the community—the fee was not as much as the average labourer would earn for a day's work, and was therefore more attractive to the infirm as 'pocket money' than to an able-bodied citizen. By Aristotle's day, the specific body of 6,000 had been discontinued, and the juries were drawn from all those who had put themselves forward for service that year; there might be as many as 10,000. However, the fact that the fee remained at 3 obols from at the latest 425 until Aristotle's day argues that there was no shortage for any sitting—otherwise it would have been necessary to raise the fee to make service more attractive.

Proceedings started early in the day; Aristophanes (*Wasps*) shows that the *dikastai* arrived so early that some at least had to leave home while it was still dark. Each man had a ticket with his name on it, and one of the first ten letters of the Greek alphabet, A-K; the *dikastai* from each tribe were divided into ten sections of roughly equal size (LXIII,4) . When the *dikastes* arrived at the place where the allotment was to take place, he went to whichever of the ten entrances corresponded to his tribe; there he placed his ticket in whichever of ten boxes corresponded to the letter on his ticket. The whole process of selection was presided over by the nine Archons with the secretary of the *Thesmothetai*, each presiding over one tribe at one entrance (LIX,7; LXIII,1). After the boxes containing the tickets had been shaken, the presiding magistrate drew out one from each box; the man so selected acted as 'ticket-inserter', and was automatically selected for jury service that day (LXIV,2–3). The next stage of the selection was conducted with the aid of an allotment machine, which was a tall block with five vertical rows of slots in it; there were two of these machines at each entrance, the rows of slots being labelled with the letters A-E and Z-K respectively.* The ticket-inserter drew the tickets of the *dikastai* from the box with the same letter as his own, and placed them in the column headed with this letter in the order in which they were drawn, starting at the top. The ticket-inserter was drawn each day, rather than being appointed for a period, because it must have been possible for him at least sometimes to see the names on the tickets he was drawing. It will be shown later that the last few drawn would on most days not serve on a jury, and it therefore follows that the ticket-inserter was potentially in a position where he could victimise some *dikastai*; hence, it would be wrong and dangerous for a man to hold this post for a period (LXIV,2).

Each presiding officer knew how many courts were to be filled and what size of jury was required for each; he therefore had to produce one-tenth of the total number of *dikastai* required from each tribe, and did this with the allotment machines. Naturally, not every column had the same number of slots filled, since the same number of men would not have appeared from each of the ten divisions of the tribe; he therefore automatically ruled out all those below the length of the shortest column. Assuming (purely as an illustrative example) that a total of 2,000 *dikastai* were required; 200 were therefore needed from each tribe, 100 from each of the allotment machines. *Dikastai* were accepted or rejected in horizontal rows of five; he therefore needed nineteen rows in addition to the ticket-inserters. The rows which were successful were decided by a device attached to the side of each allotment machine; this consisted of a long, narrow

---

*   Z is the sixth letter of the Greek alphabet, and K the tenth.

tube, into which cubes were placed, with a device to let them out one by one at the bottom. Assuming in the hypothetical example that there were 37 completed rows in a particular allotment machine, while 19 were needed to produce the hundred *dikastai* (allowing for the ticket-inserters), the presiding officer put 19 white cubes and 18 black cubes into a funnel at the top of the tube, and they fell into it in a random order. They were then released one at a time; if the first cube was white, the first horizontal row of five were selected for that day, if black they were rejected; the process decided the fate of each complete row (LXIV,3). Those unsuccessful in the ballot took their tickets and went home (LXV,3). This process was used for each machine of each tribe, the number of white cubes remaining constant, the number of black varying according to the length of the shortest column in each machine.

The juries having been selected, there was a second allotment which decided which court they sat in. Before the draw for seats on the juries had begun, one of the *Thesmothetai* had drawn lots which decided which letter (from A onwards) should be placed at the door of each court to be manned (LXIII,5). When the names of the successful *dikastai* were called by the herald, they stepped forward and drew a ball from an urn. This urn contained the same number of balls as there were *dikastai* required from that tribe, and each ball had a letter on it; the letters corresponded with those put up at the entrance of each court, and each tribe's urn contained one-tenth of the number of balls with each letter, the total number of balls with each letter corresponding to the size of the jury required in that court. Thus the jury contained an equal number of members of each tribe, and was of the requisite size. The letter was shown to the presiding magistrate, and the man's ticket was placed in a box with the same letter on it as was on the ball; since this ticket was returned to him at the end of the sitting when he drew his fee, this ensured that he sat in the right court, for he could not draw his fee unless he was sitting in the court to which his ticket was taken (LXIV,4–5).

The ball entitled the *dikastes* to pass through an inner door, presumably into a corridor off which the actual courts opened; at the same time, he received a staff with a colour on it which corresponded to a colour painted over the door of the court to which he had been allocated; this formed a further check to ensure that he went to the right court, for the colour would be plain for all to see. As he entered the court, the *dikastes* received an official token which entitled him to his fee at the end of the day; he handed this in when he received his fee, and received his original ticket back at the same time (LXV,1–3; LXVIII,2).

The system outlined above made it impossible for any man to know for which case he would be selected on any day, or even to know whether he would sit or not; thus it was out of the question for a litigant to ensure that his friends sat to hear his case, and almost equally difficult to bribe a jury. The case mentioned above (XXVII,5) shows that bribery was not totally impossible in the fifth century, though it appears to have been difficult. The system just described was the result of over a century's development, and it may well be that it was easier to know who would be on a jury in the fifth century, and that further precautions were taken as a result of such cases, with the near fool-proof system described by Aristotle as the end-product. The system was equally remarkable for its fairness. The one element in it

1. Voting tokens

2. Jurors' ticket

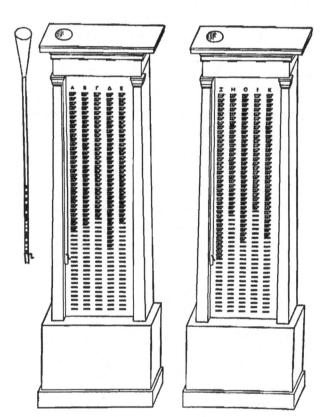

3. Reconstruction of an allotment machine

159

which was not totally equitable was the rejection of *dikastai* who were drawn in such a position that they occupied slots in the allotment machine lower than the last position filled in the shortest column. The most equitable form of draw would have involved using the black and white cubes in their tube to decide the representation of each column separately; thus the required number of *dikastai* would have been selected from those present in each letter-group of each tribe. However, this would have involved drawing ten times for each tribe; the process as described by Aristotle must have been time-consuming, and to draw ten times instead of twice for each tribe would probably have made it impossibly so. This consideration, in fact, explains the one odd feature not so far discussed: on the face of it, it seems strange that there were two allotment machines of five columns instead of one of ten, but this ensured that an unusually poor attendance by one section affected only four other sections of a tribe instead of nine. Thus the Athenians made an important step in the direction of total equity without going so far that they imperilled the working of the whole process.*

There remain some details which require comment. That the position of *dikastes* was regarded as a public office, not merely part of the everyday functions of citizenship, is proved both by the minimum age limit of thirty, which was normal for all public office, and also by the exclusion of public debtors; they were deprived of many active political rights until they had cleared the debt. The penalties for sitting when disqualified were severe; they were apparently assessed by the court where a man had wrongly sat (Demosthenes, against Meidias 182).

The exact geography of the courts is not known, and a final solution will have to wait on the excavation of the *dikasteria*. It is clear that there was a general assembly area with a separate entrance for each tribe; that there was an 'inner door' through which the *dikastes* passed on his way to the court which he had drawn; and that there was a further door at the entrance to the court itself, on the lintel of which a colour was permanently painted, and by which the letter drawn at the beginning of the day was hung. The exact shape and disposition of the courts is not certain. The name of one implies that it was triangular, which implies further that it had been fitted into an awkwardly shaped space at the time of its construction. The most economical theory would suggest a row of courts joined to each other, but this is not acceptable since the orators imply not merely that crowds could gather round the court and hear and see what was going on (which is easy enough), but that this crowd surrounded three sides of the place where the court sat. This in turn implies that the crowd could assemble between one court and the next, which poses difficulties for the supposed corridor down which the *dikastai* apparently passed from their tribe entrance to the entrance of the individual court in which they were to sit. All that one can be certain of is that the courts were surrounded only by low walls on one side at least, and perhaps on three; they may have been only partly roofed.

---

* The above note is deeply indebted to the definitive publication on the allotment machines: S. Dow, 'Aristotle, the Kleroteria and the Courts', *HSCP* L (1939) 1–34. A well-illustrated and brief summary may be found in the American School at Athens' Agora Picture Book no. 4, 'The Athenian Citizen'.

LXVI Once the juries had been allotted to their courts, the magistrates were allotted to the courts they would preside over; the allotment machines described here were very different from those used for the allotment of the juries, and probably consisted only of two of the tubes used to decide the fates of the rows of jurors whose tickets had already been inserted into the jury machines. Note that the element of lot went so far as to pick two of the *Thesmothetai* by lot to put the colours of the courts and the names of the magistrates into the machines; the Athenians were determined that it should not be at all possible for anyone to know in advance where he would be sitting.

When the presiding magistrate reached his court, he then drew one member of each tribe to serve as a court official; he drew the names from the boxes containing the original tickets of the *dikastai* which had been brought to the court where they were sitting. There was then a further draw to produce one of the ten to supervise the water clock which controlled the length of the speeches, four to supervise the voting procedure, and five to distribute fees to the jury at the end of the hearing. On the first five see further LXVII–LXIX with Commentary below; the fact that there were five distributing the fees suggests that the figure missing at LXV,4 was five.

LXVIII The papyrus of the *Constitution of Athens* is in reasonably good condition until the beginning of chapter LXIV, but from there on it becomes increasingly fragmentary. Towards the end of LXVII the papyrus is so mutilated that it is impossible to make anything very useful of it for a number of lines; the same is true of the opening of LXVIII. In the translation, I have used the text as restored by editors without indication of how much has been added by conjecture; to do that would produce a forest of brackets or italics in the worst areas. Restorations of LXIV and LXV are on the whole convincing, and confirmation can be drawn from the reconstruction of the processes involved in the allotting of jurors to courts, LXVI and LXVII are less certain, while LXVIII and LXIX are better preserved. Those who wish to study the exact authority behind the translation are referred to the Oxford Classical Text (Kenyon) or the standard editions; Von Fritz/Kapp also indicate restorations by italics and brackets in their translation.

The cases were called by the presiding magistrate in each court, though it should be stressed that his function bore almost no relation to that of a judge in a modern court; he was responsible for 'chairing the meeting' and preserving good order, not for expounding the law or giving any sort of judgement. The four types of private cases referred to in §i are probably those defined in §2, three being distinguished by the value of the property at issue; the 'disputed claims' would be to inheritances or wardships and the like.

The water clock was a standard way of measuring time in Greece. It consisted of two large jars; the upper one had a minute copper pipe at the bottom, and water ran from the upper through this pipe into the lower. The rate of flow was known, and the number of measures allowed for each type of case thus told the speaker how long he was allowed to speak for. In private cases the clock was stopped for the reading of evidence, laws and other relevant documents, which were read to the court by the clerk of the court, but in public cases, that is crimes alleged against the state, the whole day was allocated in equal sections to the litigants. In no circumstances did a case last more than one day. The fragments surviving from § §4–5 probably show that the public cases in which the day was divided into sections were the most serious cases, and that the division of the day did not mean precisely what it says. Poseideon fell in December—January, and the standard adopted was therefore that of the shortest days of the year. The text implies that the length of time that it was possible to allocate to each side during the period of daylight at this time of year was the length of time allocated to them at all times; it also must therefore have been measured by the water clock.

The primary speech on each side had to be delivered by the prosecutor and defendant respectively. They were allowed to employ professional orators to deliver the supporting speeches, and could also employ speech writers to compose what they delivered themselves. Thus the requirement for a man to deliver the main speech himself was not such a severe challenge as it sounds at first, but could still have been a major ordeal; it cannot have been without its effect on the outcome in some cases.

LXVIII The discussion of the size of juries (§1) is so fragmentary as to add very little to our knowledge; 'the majority' is, all but the last letter, a restoration, and must be treated with caution, plausible as it may be. *Heliaia* was originally used in Athens to mean the people sitting as a court as instituted by Solon (above, IX with Commentary); here the term appears to be used of any jury of over 500, though the text is too fragmentary to allow certainty.

Examples of the voting tokens used by *dikastai* have been found in Athens; they consist of a disc of bronze with a pipe or bar running through them, rather like a small wheel centrally placed on a short axle. Some are pierced, that is the 'axle' is hollow, others solid, that is the 'axle' is solid; pierced tokens were for the prosecution, solid for the defence (LXIX,1). Every man received one of each, and cast both, one into the container which would be counted, and one into the container for discards; thus the secrecy of the ballot was ensured, for by holding the 'axle' of the token between his finger and thumb (§4) and thus covering its ends, he could ensure that nobody knew which he put into which container. The fact that he voted in both rather than casting a vote either into a container for condemnation or a container for acquittal also ensured secrecy. Equally careful precautions were taken to ensure that the litigants saw that justice was done, to make certain that there had been no previous 'planting' of votes, and to make sure that the *dikastai* actually voted—otherwise they would not receive the tag which had to be handed in when they received their fee.

The exact significance of the process of protesting at evidence is not known; it may be that this was the moment at which allegations of perjury had to be made, though it seems unlikely that perjury could not be alleged and lead to prosecution at a later date. Perhaps this was the last moment at which protests could be made which would be discussed before the voting, and the proviso was solely aimed at preventing a man from disrupting proceedings by issuing a desperate challenge against some piece of evidence if he suspected half-way through the voting that he was losing. If this was so, logic would suggest that the procedure had arisen before the institution of quite such carefully devised secrecy for the ballot, so that it was possible for a man to know how the votes of the jury were being cast.

LXIX The procedure for counting votes is self-explanatory; the men in charge were the four picked by lot (LXVI,2). There was no parallel in Athens to the modern judge who assesses a penalty: either the penalty was prescribed in the statute under which the defendant was accused, or there was a second 'trial' in which each side proposed penalties. The defence naturally proposed a milder penalty than the prosecution; both sides were allowed to deliver brief speeches, and the *dikastai* then voted for the penalty they thought more suitable in exactly the same way as they had voted for the verdict. The most famous instance of this procedure is described in Plato's Apology, though there the alternative proposed by Socrates was manifestly too mild, and known to be so; hence the higher vote for the prosecution's penalty than was originally given for Socrates' condemnation.

The treatise ends very abruptly, but the lay-out of the last page of the papyrus shows that the scribe who copied it had copied all the text which he had in front of him, and it seems quite probable that the original did conclude at this point. It is by no means an unsuitable end; one would not expect a technical work of this sort necessarily to have a peroration or summing-up, and the detailed account of the many ways in which the Athenians attempted to ensure that the administration of justice was as fair and uncorruptible as possible makes a suitable end in view of the central and vital role which the Athenians always assigned to the *dikasteria* in the maintenance of the democracy.

Oedipus the King

By Sophocles, translated by David Greene

Scene: In front of the palace of Oedipus at Thebes. To the right of the stage near the altar stands the
Priest with a crowd of children. Oedipus emerges from the central door.

Oedipus

Children, young sons and daughters of old Cadmus,
why do you sit here with your suppliant crowns?
The town is heavy with a mingled burden
of sounds and smells, of groans and hymns and incense;   5
I did not think it fit that I should hear
of this from messengers but came myself,—
I Oedipus whom all men call the Great.

(*He turns to the Priest.*)

You're old and they are young; come, speak for them.
What do you fear or want, that you sit here   10
suppliant? Indeed I'm willing to give all
that you may need; I would be very hard
should I not pity suppliants like these.

Priest

O ruler of my country, Oedipus,
you see our company around the altar;   15

you see our ages; some of us, like these,
who cannot yet fly far, and some of us
heavy with age; these children are the chosen
among the young, and I the priest of Zeus.
Within the market place sit others crowned   20
with suppliant garlands, at the double shrine
of Pallas and the temple where Ismeus
gives oracles by fire. King, you yourself
have seen our city reeling like a wreck
already; it can scarcely lift its prow
out of the depths, out of the bloody surf.
A blight is on the fruitful plants of the earth,   25
A blight is on the cattle in the fields,
a blight is on our women that no children
are born to them; a God that carries fire,
a deadly pestilence, is on our town,
strikes us and spares not, and the house of Cadmus
is emptied of its people while black Death
grows rich in groaning and in lamentation.   30
We have not come as suppliants to this altar
because we thought of you as of a God,
but rather judging you the first of men
in all the chances of this life and when
we mortals have to do with more than man.
You came and by your coming saved our city,   35
freed us from tribute which we paid of old
to the Sphinx, cruel singer. This you did
in virtue of no knowledge we could give you,
in virtue of no teaching; it was God
that aided you, men say, and you are held
with God's assistance to have saved our lives.
Now Oedipus, Greatest in all men's eyes,   40
here falling at your feet we all entreat you,
find us some strength for rescue.
Perhaps you'll hear a wise word fro some God,
perhaps you will learn something from a man
(for I have seen that for the skilled of practice
the outcome of their counsels live the most).   45

Noblest of men, go, and raise up our city,
go,—and give heed. For now this land of ours
calls you its savior since you saved it once.
So, let us never speak about your reign
as of a time when first our feet were set
secure on high, but later fell to ruin.   50
Raise up our city, save it and raise it up.
Once you have brought us luck with happy omen;
be no less now in fortune.
If you will rule this land, as now you rule it,
better to rule it full of men than empty.   55
For neither tower nor ship is anything
when empty, and none live in it together.

Oedipus

I pity you, children. You have come full of longing,
but I have known the story before you told it
only too well. I know you are all sick,
yet there is not one of you, sick though you are,   60
that is as sick as I myself.
Your several sorrows each have single scope
and touch but one of you. My spirit groans
for city and myself and you at once.
You have not roused me like a man from sleep;   65
know that I have given many tears to this,
gone many ways wandering in thought,
but as I thought I found only one remedy
and that I took. I sent Menoeceus' son
Creon, Jocasta's brother, to Apollo,   70
to his Pythian temple,
that he might learn there by what act or word
I could save this city. As I count the days,
it vexes me what ails him; he is gone
far longer than he needed for the journey.   75
But when he comes, then, may I prove a villain,
if I shall not do all the God commands.

Priest

Thanks for your gracious words. Your servants here
signal that Creon is this moment coming.

Oedipus

His face is bright. O holy Lord Apollo,   80
grant that his news too may be bright for us
and bring us safety.

Priest

It is happy news,
I think, for else his head would not be crowned
with sprigs of fruitful laurel.

Oedipus

We will know soon,
he's within hail. Lord Creon, my good brother,   85
what is the word you bring us from the God?

(*Creon enters.*)

Creon

A good word,—for things hard to bear themselves
if in the final issue all is well
I count complete good fortune.

Oedipus

What do you mean?
What you have said so far
leaves me uncertain whether to trust or fear.   90

Creon

If you will hear my news before these others
I am ready to speak, or else to go within.

Oedipus

Speak it to all;
the grief I bear, I bear it more for these
than for my own heart.

Creon

I will tell you, then,   95
what I heard from the God.
King Phoebus in plain words commanded us
to drive out a pollution from our land,
pollution grown ingrained within the land;
drive it out, said the God, not cherish it,
till it's past cure.

Oedipus

    What is the rite

    of purification? How shall it be done?

Creon

    By banishing a man, or expiation   100

    of blood by blood, since it is murder guilt

    which holds our city in this destroying storm.

Oedipus

    Who is this man whose fate the God pronounces?

Creon

    My Lord, before you piloted the state

    we had a king called Laius.

Oedipus

    I know of him by hearsay. I have not seen him.   105

Creon

    The God commanded clearly: let some one

    punish with force this dead man's murderers.

Oedipus

    Where are they in the world? Where would a trace

    of this old crime be found? It would be hard

    to guess where.

Creon

    The clue is in this land;   110

    that which is sought is found;

    the unheeded thing escapes:

    so said the God.

Oedipus

    Was it at home,

    or in the country that death came upon him,

    or in another country travelling?

Creon

    He went, he said himself, upon an embassy,

    but never returned when he set out from home.   115

Oedipus

    Was there no messenger, no fellow traveller

    who knew what happened? Such a one might tell

    something of use.

Creon

> They were all killed save one. He fled in terror
> and he could tell us nothing in clear terms
> of what he knew, nothing, but one thing only.

Oedipus

> What was it? 120
> If we could even find a slim beginning
> in which to hope, we might discover much.

Creon

> This man said that the robbers they encountered
> were many and the hands that did the murder
> were many; it was no man's single power.

Oedipus

> How could a robber dare a deed like this
> were he not helped with money from the city,
> money and treachery? 125

Creon

> That indeed was thought.
> But Laius was dead and in our trouble
> there was none to help.

Oedipus

> What trouble was so great to hinder you
> inquiring out the murder of your king?

Creon

> The riddling Sphinx induced us to neglect 130
> mysterious crimes and rather seek solution
> of troubles at our feet.

Oedipus

> I will bring this to light again. King Phoebus
> fittingly took this care about the dead,
> and you too fittingly.
> And justly you will see in me an ally, 135
> a champion of my country and the God.
> For when I drive pollution from the land
> I will not serve a distant friend's advantage,
> but act in my own interest. Whoever
> he was that killed the king may readily

wish to dispatch me with his murderous hand;   140
so helping the dead king I help myself.

Come, children, take your suppliant boughs and go;
up from the altars now. Call the assembly
and let it meet upon the understanding
that I'll do everything. God will decide   145
whether we prosper or remain in sorrow.

Priest

Rise, children—it was this we came to seek,
which of himself the king now offers us.
May Phoebus who gave us the oracle
come to our rescue and stay the plague.   150

(Exeunt all but the Chorus.)

Chorus

Strophe

What is the sweet spoken word of God from the shrine of Pytho rich in gold
that has come to glorious Thebes?
I am stretched on the rack of doubt, and terror and trembling hold
my heart, O Delian Healer, and I worship full of fears
for what doom you will bring to pass, new or renewed in the revolving years.   155
Speak to me, immortal voice,
child of golden Hope.

Antistrophe

First I call on you, Athene, deathless daughter of Zeus,
and Artemis, Earth Upholder,   160
who sits in the midst of the market place in the throne which men call Fame,
and Phoebus, the Far Shooter, three averters of Fate,
come to us now, if ever before, when ruin rushed upon the state,   165
you drove destruction's flame away
out of our land.

Strophe

Our sorrows defy number;
all the ship's timbers are rotten;
taking of thought is no spear for the driving away of the plague.   170
There are no growing children in this famous land;
there are no women bearing the pangs of childbirth.

You may see them one with another, like birds swift on the wing, 175

quicker than fire unmastered,

speeding away to the coast of the Western God.

Antistrophe

In the unnumbered deaths

of its people the city dies;

those children that are born lie dead on the naked earth

unpitied, spreading contagion of death; and grey haired mothers and wives

everywhere stand at the altar's edge, suppliant, moaning; 182–85

the hymn to the healing God rings out but with it the wailing voices are blended.

From these our sufferings grant us, O golden Daughter of Zeus, glad-faced deliverance.

Strophe

There is no clash of brazen shields but our fight is with the War God,

a War God ringed with the cries of men, a savage God who burns us; 191

grant that he turn in racing course backwards out of our country's bounds

to the great palace of Amphitrite or where the waves of the Thracian sea 195

deny the stranger safe anchorage.

Whatsoever escapes the night

at last the light of day revisits;

so smite the War God, Father Zeus,

beneath your thunderbolt,

for you are the Lord of the lightning, the lightning that carries fire. 200

Antistrophe

And your unconquered arrow shafts, winged by the golden corded bow,

Lycean King, I beg to be at our side for help; 205

and the gleaming torches of Artemis with which she scours the Lycean hills,

and I call on the God with the turban of gold, who gave his name to this

country of ours, 210

the Bacchic God with the wind flushed face,

Evian One, who travel

with the Maenad company,

combat the God that burns us

with your torch of pine;

for the God that is our enemy is a God unhonoured among the Gods. 215

(*Oedipus returns.*)

Oedipus

    For what you ask me—if you will hear my words,
    and hearing welcome them and fight the plague,
    you will find strength and lightening of your load.

    Hark to me; what I say to you, I say
    as one that is a stranger to the story
    as stranger to the deed. For I would not   220
    be far upon the track if I alone
    were tracing it without a clue. But now,
    since after all was finished, I became
    a citizen among you, citizens—
    now I proclaim to all the men of Thebes:
    who so among you knows the murderer   225
    by whose hand Laius, son of Labdacus,
    died—I command him to tell everything
    to me,—yes, though he fears himself to take the blame
    on his own head; for bitter punishment
    he shall have none, but leave this land unharmed.
    Or if he knows the murderer, another,   230
    a foreigner, still let him speak the truth.
    For I will pay him and be grateful, too.
    But if you shall keep silence, if perhaps
    some one of you, to shield a guilty friend,
    or for his own sake shall reject my words—
    hear what I shall do then: 235
    I forbid that man, whoever he be, my land,
    my land where I hold sovereignty and throne;
    and I forbid any to welcome him
    or cry him greeting or make him a sharer   240
    in sacrifice or offering to the Gods,
    or give him water for his hands to wash.
    I command all to drive him from their homes,
    since he is our pollution, as the oracle
    of Pytho's God proclaimed him now to me.
    So I stand forth a champion of the God

and of the man who died.   245
Upon the murderer I invoke this curse—
whether he is one man and all unknown,
or one of many—may he wear out his life
in misery to miserable doom!
If with my knowledge he lives at my hearth   250
I pray that I myself may feel my curse.
On you I lay my charge to fulfill all this
for me, for the God, and for this land of ours
destroyed and blighted, by the God forsaken.

Even were this no matter of God's ordinance   255
it would not fit you so to leave it lie,
unpurified, since a good man is dead
and one that was a king. Search it out.
Since I am now the holder of his office,
and have his bed and wife that once was his,   260
and had his line not been unfortunate
we would have common children—(fortune leaped
upon his head)—because of all these things,
I fight in his defence as for my father,
and I shall try all means to take the murderer   265
of Laius the son of Labdacus
the son of Polydorus and before him
of Cadmus and before him of Agenor.
Those who do not obey me, may the Gods
grant no crops springing from the ground they plough   270
nor children to their women! May a fate
like this, or one still worse than this consume them!
For you whom these words please, the other Thebans,
may Justice as your ally and all the Gods
live with you, blessing you now and for ever!   275

Chorus

As you have held me to my oath, I speak:
I neither killed the king nor can declare
the killer; but since Phoebus set the quest
it is his part to tell who the man is.

Oedipus

    Right; but to put compulsion on the Gods   280

    against their will—no man can do that.

Chorus

    May I then say what I think second best?

Oedipus

    If there's a third best, too, spare not to tell it.

Chorus

    I know that what the Lord Teiresias

    sees, is most often what the Lord Apollo   285

    sees. If you should inquire of this from him

    you might find out most clearly.

Oedipus

    Even in this my actions have not been sluggard.

    On Creon's word I have sent two messengers

    and why the prophet is not here already I have been wondering.

Chorus

    His skill apart   290

    there is besides only an old faint story.

Oedipus

    What is it?

    I look at every story.

Chorus

    It was said

    that he was killed by certain wayfarers.

Oedipus

    I heard that, too, but no one saw the killer.

Chorus

    Yet if he has a share of fear at all,

    his courage will not stand firm, hearing your curse.   295

Oedipus

    The man who in the doing did not shrink

    will fear no word.

Chorus

    Here comes his prosecutor:

    led by your men the godly prophet comes

    in whom alone of mankind truth is native.

                    (*Enter Teiresias, led by a little boy.*)

Oedipus

    Teiresias, you are versed in everything,   300

    things teachable and things not to be spoken,

    things of the heaven and earth-creeping things.

    You have no eyes but in your mind you know

    with what a plague our city is afflicted.

    My lord, in you alone we find a champion,

    in you alone one that can rescue us.

    Perhaps you have not heard the messengers,   305

    but Phoebus sent in answer to our sending

    an oracle declaring that our freedom

    from this disease would only come when we

    should learn the names of those who killed King Laius,

    and kill them or expel from our country.

    Do not begrudge us oracles from birds,   310

    or any other way of prophecy

    within your skill; save yourself and the city,

    save me; redeem the debt of our pollution

    that lies on us because of this dead man.

    We are in your hands; pains are most nobly taken

    to help another when you have means and power.   315

Teiresias

    Alas, how terrible is wisdom when

    it brings no profit to the man that's wise!

    This I knew well, but had forgotten it,

    else I would not have come here.

Oedipus

    What is this?

    How sad you are now you have come!

Teiresias

    Let me

    go home. It will be easiest for us both   320

    to bear our several destinies to the end

    if you will follow my advice.

Oedipus

    You'd rob us

    of this your gift of prophecy? You talk

as one who had no care for law nor love
for Thebes who reared you.

Teiresias

Yes, but I see that even your own words
miss the mark; therefore I must fear for mine.   325

Oedipus

For God's sake if you know of anything,
do not turn from us; all of us kneel to you,
all of us here, your suppliants.

Teiresias

All of you here know nothing. I will not
bring to the light of day my troubles, mine—
rather than call them yours.

Oedipus

What do you mean?
You know of something but refuse to speak.   330
Would you betray us and destroy the city?

Teiresias

I will not bring this pain upon us both,
neither on you nor on myself. Why is it
you question me and waste your labour? I
will tell you nothing.

Oedipus

You would provoke a stone! Tell us, you villain,   335
tell us, and do not stand there quietly
unmoved and balking at the issue.

Teiresias

You blame my temper but you do not see
your own that lives within you; it is me
you chide.

Oedipus

Who would not feel his temper rise
at words like these with which you shame our city?   340

Teiresias

Of themselves things will come, although I hide them
and breathe no word of them.

Oedipus

Since they will come
tell them to me.

Teiresias

I will say nothing further.
Against this answer let your temper rage
as wildly as you will.

Oedipus

Indeed I am   345
so angry I shall not hold back a jot
of what I think. For I would have you know
I think you were complotter of the deed
and doer of the deed save in so far
as for the actual killing. Had you had eyes
I would have said alone you murdered him.

Teiresias

Yes? Then I warn you faithfully to keep   350
the letter of your proclamation and
from this day forth to speak no word of greeting
to these nor me; you are the land's pollution.

Oedipus

How shamelessly you started up this taunt!
How do you think you will escape?   355

Teiresias

I have.
I have escaped; the truth is what I cherish
and that's my strength.

Oedipus

And who has taught you truth?
Not your profession surely!

Teiresias

You have taught me,
for you have made me speak against my will.

Oedipus

Speak what? Tell me again that I may learn it better.

Teiresias

Did you not understand before or would you
provoke me into speaking?   360

Oedipus

> I did not grasp it,
> not so to call it known. Say it again.

Teiresias

> I say you are the murderer of the king
> whose murderer you seek.

Oedipus

> Not twice you shall
> say calumnies like this and stay unpunished.

Teiresias

> Shall I say more to tempt your anger more?

Oedipus

> As much as you desire; it will be said   365
> in vain.

Teiresias

> I say that with those you love best
> you live in foulest shame unconsciously
> and do not see where you are in calamity.

Oedipus

> Do you imagine you can always talk
> like this, and live to laugh at it hereafter?

Teiresias

> Yes, if the truth has anything of strength.

Oedipus

> It has, but not for you; it has no strength   370
> for you because you are blind in mind and ears
> as well as in your eyes.

Teiresias

> You are a poor wretch
> to taunt me with the very insults which
> every one soon will heap upon yourself.

Oedipus

> Your life is one long night so that you cannot
> hurt me or any other who sees the light.   375

Teiresias

> It is not fate that I should be your ruin,
> Apollo is enough; it is his care
> to work this out.

Oedipus

> Was this your own design
> or Creon's?

Teiresias

> Creon is no hurt to you,
> but you are to yourself.

Oedipus

> Wealth, sovereignty and skill outmatching skill   380
> for the contrivance of an envied life!
> Great store of jealousy fill your treasury chests,
> if my friend Creon, friend from the first and loyal,   385
> thus secretly attacks me, secretly
> desires to drive me out and secretly
> suborns this juggling, trick devising quack,
> this wily beggar who has only eyes
> for his own gains, but blindness in his skill.
> For, tell me, where have you seen clear, Teiresias,   390
> with your prophetic eyes? When the dark singer,
> the sphinx, was in your country, did you speak
> word of deliverance to its citizens?
> And yet the riddle's answer was not the province
> of a chance comer. It was a prophet's task
> and plainly you had no such gift of prophecy   395
> from birds nor otherwise from any God
> to glean a word of knowledge. But I came,
> Oedipus, who knew nothing, and I stopped her.
> I solved the riddle by my wit alone.
> Mine was no knowledge got from birds. And now
> you would expel me,
> because you think that you will find a place   400
> by Creon's throne. I think you will be sorry,
> both you and your accomplice, for your plot
> to drive me out. And did I not regard you
> as an old man, some suffering would have taught
> you that what was in your heart was treason.

Chorus

 We look at this man's words and yours, my king,

 and we find both have spoken them in anger.   405

 We need no angry words but only thought

 how we may best hit the God's meaning for us.

Teiresias

 If you are king, at least I have the right

 no less to speak in my defence against you.

 Of that much I am master. I am no slave   410

 of yours, but Loxias', and so I shall not

 enroll myself with Creon for my patron.

 Since you have taunted me with being blind,

 here is my word for you.

 You have your eyes but see not where you are

 in sin, nor where you live, nor whom you live with.

 Do you know who your parents are? Unknowing   415

 you are an enemy to kith and kin

 in death, beneath the earth, and in this life.

 A deadly footed, double striking curse,

 from father and mother both, shall drive you forth

 out of this land, with darkness on your eyes,

 that now have such straight vision. Shall there be

 a place will not be harbour to your cries,   420

 a corner of Cithaeron will not ring

 in echo to your cries, soon, soon,—

 when you shall learn the secret of your marriage,

 which steered you to a haven in this house,—

 haven no haven, after lucky voyage?

 And of the multitude of other evils

 establishing a grim equality

 between you and your children, you know nothing.   425

 So, muddy with contempt my words and Creon's!

 Misery shall grind no man as it will you.

Oedipus

 Is it endurable that I should hear

 such words from him? Go and a curse go with you!   430

 Quick, home with you! Out of my house at once!

Teiresias

    I would not have come either had you not called me.

Oedipus

    I did not know then you would talk like a fool—

    or it would have been long before I called you.

Teiresias

    I am a fool then, as it seems to you—   435

    but to the parents who have bred you, wise.

Oedipus

    What parents? Stop! Who are they of all the world?

Teiresias

    This day will show your birth and will destroy you.

Oedipus

    How needlessly your riddles darken everything.

Teiresias

    But it's in riddle answering you are strongest.   440

Oedipus

    Yes. Taunt me where you will find me great.

Teiresias

    It is this very luck that has destroyed you.

Oedipus

    I do not care, if it has saved this city.

Teiresias

    Well, I will go. Come, boy, lead me away.

Oedipus

    Yes, lead him off. So long as you are here,   445

    you'll be a stumbling block and a vexation;

    once gone, you will not trouble me again.

Teiresias

    I have said

    what I came here to say not fearing your

    countenance: there is no way you can hurt me.

    I tell you, king, this man, this murderer

    (whom you have long declared you are in search of,

    indicting him in threatening proclamation   450

    as murderer of Laius)—he is here.

    In name he is a stranger among citizens

but soon he will be shown to be a citizen
true native Theban, and he'll have no joy
of the discovery: blindness for sight
and beggary for riches his exchange,   455
he shall go journeying to a foreign country
tapping his way before him with a stick.
He shall be proved father and brother both
to his own children in his house; to her
that gave him birth, a son and husband both;
a fellow sower in his father's bed
with that same father that he murdered.
Go within, reckon that out, and if you find me   460
mistaken, say I have no skill in prophecy.

(Exeunt separately Teiresias and Oedipus.)

Chorus

Strophe

    Who is the man proclaimed
by Delphi's prophetic rock
as the bloody handed murderer,   465
the doer of deeds that none dare name?
Now is the time for him to run
with a stronger foot
than Pegasus
for the child of Zeus leaps in arms upon him   470
with fire and the lightning bolt,
and terribly close on his heels
are the Fates that never miss.

Antistrophe

    Lately from snowy Parnassus
clearly the voice flashed forth,
bidding each Theban track him down,   475
the unknown murderer.
In the savage forests he lurks and in
the caverns like
the mountain bull.
He is sad and lonely, and lonely his feet
that carry him far from the navel of earth;   480

but its prophecies, ever living,
flutter around his head.

Strophe

The augur has spread confusion,
terrible confusion;
I do not approve what was said   485
nor can I deny it.
I do not know what to say;
I am in a flutter of foreboding;
I never heard in the present
nor past of a quarrel between   490
the sons of Labdacus and Polybus,
that I might bring as proof
in attacking the popular fame
of Oedipus, seeking
to take vengeance for undiscovered
death in the line of Labdacus.   495

Antistrophe

Truly Zeus and Apollo are wise
and in human things all knowing;   500
but amongst men there is no
distinct judgment, between the prophet
and me—which of us is right.
One man may pass another in wisdom
but I would never agree
with those that find fault with the king
till I should see the word
proved right beyond doubt. For once
in visible form the Sphinx
came on him and all of us
saw his wisdom and in that test
he saved the city. So he will not be condemned by my mind.   512

(*Enter Creoti.*)

Creon

Citizens, I have come because I heard
deadly words spread about me, that the king
accuses me. I cannot take that from him.
If he believes that in these present troubles   515

184

he has been wronged by me in word or deed
I do not want to live on with the burden
of such a scandal on me. The report   520
injures me doubly and most vitally—
for I'll be called a traitor to my city
and traitor also to my friends and you.

Chorus

Perhaps it was a sudden gust of anger
that forced that insult from him, and no judgment.

Creon

But did he say that it was in compliance   525
with schemes of mine that the seer told him lies?

Chorus

Yes, he said that, but why, I do not know.

Creon

Were his eyes straight in his head? Was his mind right
when he accused me in this fashion?

Chorus

I do not know; I have no eyes to see   530
what princes do. Here comes the king himself.

(*Enter Oedipus.*)

Oedipus

You, sir, how is it you come here? Have you so much
brazen-faced daring that you venture in
my house although you are proved manifestly
the murderer of that man, and though you tried,
openly, highway robbery of my crown?   535
For God's sake, tell me what you saw in me,
what cowardice or what stupidity,
that made you lay a plot like this against me?
Did you imagine I should not observe
the crafty scheme that stole upon me or
seeing it, take no means to counter it?   540
Was it not stupid of you to make the attempt,
to try to hunt down royal power without
the people at your back or friends? For only
with the people at your back or money can
the hunt end in the capture of a crown.

185

Creon

Do you know what you're doing? Will you listen
to words to answer yours, and then pass judgment?

Oedipus

You're quick to speak, but I am slow to grasp you,   545
for I have found you dangerous,—and my foe.

Creon

First of all hear what I shall say to that.

Oedipus

At least don't tell me that you are not guilty.

Creon

If you think obstinacy without wisdom
a valuable possession, you are wrong.   550

Oedipus

And you are wrong if you believe that one,
a criminal, will not be punished only
because he is my kinsman.

Creon

This is but just—
but tell me, then, of what offense I'm guilty?

Oedipus

Did you or did you not urge me to send   455
to this prophetic mumbler?

Creon

I did indeed,
and I shall stand by what I told you.

Oedipus

How long ago is it since Laius … .

Creon

What about Laius? I don't understand.

Oedipus

Vanished—died—was murdered?

Creon

It is long,
a long, long time to reckon.

Oedipus

Was this prophet
in the profession then?

Creon

> He was, and honoured
> as highly as he is today.

Oedipus

> At that time did he say a word about me?

Creon

> Never, at least when I was near him. 465

Oedipus

> You never made a search for the dead man?

Creon

> We searched, indeed, but never learned of anything.

Oedipus

> Why did our wise old friend not say this then?

Creon

> I don't know; and when I know nothing, I
> usually hold my tongue.

Oedipus

> You know this much, 570
> and can declare this much if you are loyal.

Creon

> What is it? If I know, I'll not deny it.

Oedipus

> That he would not have said that I killed Laius
> had he not met you first.

Creon

> You know yourself
> whether he said this, but I demand that I 575
> should hear as much from you as you from me.

Oedipus

> Then hear,—I'll not be proved a murderer.

Creon

> Well, then. You're married to my sister.

Oedipus

> Yes,
> that I am not disposed to deny.

Creon

> You rule

this country giving her an equal share
in the government?

Oedipus

Yes, everything she wants   580
she has from me.

Creon

And I, as thirdsman to you,
am rated as the equal of you two?

Oedipus

Yes, and it's there you've proved yourself false friend.

Creon

Not if you will reflect on it as I do.
Consider, first, if you think any one
would choose to rule and fear rather than rule   585
and sleep untroubled by a fear if power
were equal in both cases. I, at least,
I was not born with such a frantic yearning
to be a king—but to do what kings do.
And so it is with every one who has learned
wisdom and self-control. As it stands now,
the prizes are all mine—and without fear.   590
But if I were the king myself, I must
do much that went against the grain.
How should despotic rule seem sweeter to me
than painless power and an assured authority?
I am not so besotted yet that I
want other honours than those that come with profit.   595
Now every man's my pleasure; every man greets me;
now those who are your suitors fawn on me,—
success for them depends upon my favour.
Why should I let all this go to win that?
My mind would not be traitor if it's wise;   600
I am no treason lover, of my nature,
nor would I ever dare to join a plot.
Prove what I say. Go to the oracle
at Pytho and inquire about the answers,
if they are as I told you. For the rest,   605

if you discover I laid any plot
together with the seer, kill me, I say,
not only by your vote but by my own.
But do not charge me on obscure opinion
without some proof to back it. It's not just
lightly to count your knaves as honest men,   610
nor honest men as knaves. To throw away
an honest friend is, as it were, to throw
your life away, which a man loves the best.
In time you will know all with certainty;
time is the only test of honest men,
one day is space enough to know a rogue.   615

Chorus

His words are wise, king, if one fears to fall.
Those who are quick of temper are not safe.

Oedipus

When he that plots against me secretly
moves quickly, I must quickly counterplot.
If I wait taking no decisive measure   620
his business will be done, and mine be spoiled.

Creon

What do you want to do then? Banish me?

Oedipus

No, certainly; kill you, not banish you.[1]

Creon

I do not think that you've your wits about you.   626

Oedipus

For my own interests, yes.

Creon

But for mine, too,
you should think equally.

Oedipus

You are a rogue.

---

1 Two lines omitted here owing to the confusion in the dialogue consequent on the loss of a third line. The lines as they stand in jebb's edition (1902) are:

Oed.: That you may show what manner of thing is envy.
Creon: You speak as one that will not yield or trust.
[Oed. lost line.]

Creon

    Suppose you do not understand?

Oedipus

    But yet

    I must be ruler.

Creon

    Not if you rule badly.

Oedipus

    O, city, city!

Creon

    I too have some share   630

    in the city; it is not yours alone.

Chorus

    Stop, my lords! Here—and in the nick of time

    I see Jocasta coming from the house;

    with her help lay the quarrel that now stirs you.

                                    (*Enter Jocasta.*)

Jocasta

    For shame! Why have you raised this foolish squabbling

    brawl? Are you not ashamed to air your private   635

    griefs when the country's sick? Go in, you, Oedipus,

    and you, too, Creon, into the house. Don't magnify

    your nothing troubles.

Creon

    Sister, Oedipus, your husband, thinks he has the right to do

    terrible wrongs—he has but to choose between   640

    two terrors: banishing or killing me.

Oedipus

    He's right, Jocasta; for I find him plotting

    with knavish tricks against my person.

Creon

    That God may never bless me! May I die

    accursed, if I have been guilty of   645

    one tittle of the charge you bring against me!

Jocasta

    I beg you, Oedipus, trust him in this,

    spare him for the sake of this his oath to God,

    for my sake, and the sake of those who stand here.

Chorus

649Be gracious, be merciful,
we beg of you.

Oedipus

In what would you have me yield?

Chorus

He has been no silly child in the past.
He is strong in his oath now.
Spare him.

Oedipus

Do you know what you ask?

Chorus

Yes.

Oedipus

Tell me then.

Chorus

He has been your friend before all men's eyes; do not cast him   656
away dishonoured on an obscure conjecture.

Oedipus

I would have you know that this request of yours
really requests my death or banishment.

Chorus

May the Sun God, king of Gods, forbid! May I die without God's   660
blessing, without friends' help, if I had any such thought. But my
spirit is broken by my unhappiness for my wasting country; and   665
this would but add troubles amongst ourselves to the other troubles.

Oedipus

Well, let him go then—if I must die ten times for it,   669
or be sent out dishonoured into exile.
It is your lips that prayed for him I pitied,
not his; wherever he is, I shall hate him.

Creon

I see you sulk in yielding and you're dangerous
when you are out of temper; natures like yours
are justly heaviest for themselves to bear.   675

Oedipus

Leave me alone! Take yourself off, I tell you.

Creon

    I'll go, you have not known me, but they have,

    and they have known my innocence.

                                                                (*Exit.*)

Chorus

    Won't you take him inside, lady?

Jocasta

    Yes, when I've found out what was the matter.   680

Chorus

    There was some misconceived suspicion of a story, and on the

    other side the sting of injustice.

Jocasta

    So, on both sides?

Chorus

    Yes.

Jocasta

    What was the story?

Chorus

    I think it best, in the interests of the country, to leave it where it ended.   685

Oedipus

    You see where you have ended, straight of judgment

    although you are, by softening my anger.

Chorus

    Sir, I have said before and I say again—be sure that I would have   689

    been proved a madman, bankrupt in sane council, if I should put

    you away, you who steered the country I love safely when she

    was crazed with troubles. God grant that now, too, you may   695

    prove a fortunate guide for us.

Jocasta

    Tell me, my lord, I beg of you, what was it

    that roused your anger so?

Oedipus

    Yes, I will tell you.   700

    I honour you more than I honour them.

    It was Creon and the plots he laid against me.

Jocasta

    Tell me—if you can clearly tell the quarrel—

Oedipus
> Creon says
> that I'm the murderer of Laius.

Jocasta
> Of his own knowledge or on information?

Oedipus
> He sent this rascal prophet to me, since   705
> he keeps his own mouth clean of any guilt.

Jocasta
> Do not concern yourself about this matter;
> listen to me and learn that human beings
> have no part in the craft of prophecy.
> Of that I'll show you a short proof.   710
> There was an oracle once that came to Laius,—
> I will not say that it was Phoebus' own,
> but it was from his servants—and it told him
> that it was fate that he should die a victim
> at the hands of his own son, a son to be born
> of Laius and me. But, see now, he,
> the king, was killed by foreign highway robbers   715
> at a place where three roads meet—so goes the story;
> and for the son—before three days were out
> after his birth King Laius pierced his ankles
> and by the hands of others cast him forth
> upon a pathless hillside. So Apollo   720
> failed to fulfill his oracle to the son,
> that he should kill his father, and to Laius
> also proved false in that the thing he feared,
> death at his son's hands, never came to pass.
> So clear in this case were the oracles,
> so clear and false. Give them no heed, I say;
> what God discovers need of, easily
> he shows to us himself.   725

Oedipus
> O dear Jocasta,
> as I hear this from you, there comes upon me
> a wandering of the soul—I could run mad.

Jocasta

    What trouble is it, that you turn again

    and speak like this?

Oedipus

    I thought I heard you say

    that Laius was killed at a crossroads.   730

Jocasta

    Yes, that was how the story went and still

    that word goes round.

Oedipus

    Where is this place, Jocasta,

    where he was murdered?

Jocasta

    Phocis is the country

    and the road splits there, one of two

    roads from Delphi,

    another comes from Daulia.

Oedipus

    How long ago is this?   735

Jocasta

    The news came to the city just before

    you became king and all men's eyes looked to you.

    What is it, Oedipus, that's in your mind?

Oedipus

    What have you designed, O Zeus, to do with me?

Jocasta

    What is the thought that troubles your heart?

Oedipus

    Don't ask me yet—tell me of Laius—   740

    How did he look? How old or young was he?

Jocasta

    He was a tall man and his hair was grizzled

    already—nearly white—and in his form

    not unlike you.

Oedipus

    O God, I think I have

    called curses on myself in ignorance.   745

Jocasta

    What do you mean? I am terrified

    when I look at you.

Oedipus

    I have a deadly

    fear that the old seer had eyes. You'll show me more

    if you can tell me one more thing.

Jocasta

    I will.

    I'm frightened,—but if I can understand,

    I'll tell you all you ask.

Oedipus

    How was his company? 750

    Had he few with him when he went this journey,

    or many servants, as would suit a prince?

jocasta

    In all there were but five, and among them

    a herald; and one carriage for the king.

Oedipus

    It's plain—its plain—who was it told you this? 755

Jocasta

    The only servant that escaped safe home.

Oedipus

    Is he at home now?

Jocasta

    No, when he came home again

    and saw you king and Laius was dead,

    he came to me and touched my hand and begged 760

    that I should send him to the fields to be

    my shepherd and so he might see the city

    as far off as he might. So I

    sent him away. He was an honest man,

    as slaves go, and was worthy of far more

    than what he asked of me.

Oedipus

    O, how I wish that he could come back quickly! 765

Jocasta

    He can. Why is your heart so set on this?

Oedipus

O dear Jocasta, I am full of fears
that I have spoken far too much; and therefore
I wish to see this shepherd.

Jocasta

He will come;
but, Oedipus, I think I'm worthy too
770to know what it is that disquiets you.

Oedipus

It shall not be kept from you, since my mind
has gone so far with its forebodings. Whom
should I confide in rather than you, who is there
of more importance to me who have passed
through such a fortune?
Polybus was my father, king of Corinth,
and Merope, the Dorian, my mother.   775
I was held greatest of the citizens
in Corinth till a curious chance befell me
as I shall tell you—curious, indeed,
but hardly worth the store I set upon it.
There was a dinner and at it a man,
a drunken man, accused me in his drink   780
of being bastard. I was furious
but held my temper under for that day.
Next day I went and taxed my parents with it;
they took the insult very ill
from him, the drunken fellow who had uttered it.
So I was comforted for their part, but   785
still this thing rankled always, for the story
crept about widely. And I went at last
to Pytho, though my parents did not know.
But Phoebus sent me home again unhonoured
in what I came to learn, but he foretold   790
other and desperate horrors to befall me,
that I was fated to lie with my mother,
and show to daylight an accursed breed
which men would not endure, and I was doomed

to be murderer of the father that begot me.
When I heard this I fled, and in the days
that followed I would measure from the stars   795
the whereabouts of Corinth—yes, I fled
to somewhere where I should not see fulfilled
the infamies told in that dreadful oracle.
And as I journeyed I came to the place
where, as you say, this king met with his death.
Jocasta, I will tell you the whole truth.   800
When I was near the branching of the crossroads,
going on foot, I was encountered by
a herald and a carriage with a man in it,
just as you tell me. He that led the way
and the old man himself wanted to thrust me   805
out of the road by force. I became angry
and struck the coachman who was pushing me.
When the old man saw this he watched his moment,
and as I passed he struck me from his carriage,
full on the head with his two pointed goad.
But he was paid in full and presently   810
my stick had struck him backwards from the car
and he rolled out of it. And then I killed them
all. If it happened there was any tie
of kinship twixt this man and Laius,
who is then now more miserable than I,   815
what man on earth so hated by the Gods,
since neither citizen nor foreigner
may welcome me at home or even greet me,
but drive me out of doors? And it is I,
and no other have so cursed myself.   820
And I pollute the bed of him I killed
by the hands that killed him. Was I not born evil?
Am I not utterly unclean? I had to fly
and in my banishment not even see
my kindred nor set foot in my own country,
or otherwise my fate was to be yoked   825
in marriage with my mother and kill my father,

Polybus who begot me and had reared me.
Would not one rightly judge and say that on me
these things were sent by some malignant God?
O no, no, no—O holy majesty   830
of God on high, may I not see that day!
May I be gone out of men's sight before
I see the deadly taint of this disaster come upon me.

Chorus

Sir, we too fear these things. But until you see this man face to
face and hear his story, hope.   835

Oedipus

Yes, I have just this much of hope—to wait until the herdsman comes.

Jocasta

And when he comes, what do you want with him?

Oedipus

I'll tell you; if I find that his story is the same as yours, I at least
will be clear of this guilt.   840

Jocasta

Why what so particularly did you learn from my story?

Oedipus

You said that he spoke of highway robbers who killed Laius. Now
if he uses the same number, it was not I who killed him. One man
cannot be the same as many. But if he speaks of a man travelling   845
alone, then clearly the burden of the guilt inclines towards me.

Jocasta

Be sure, at least, that this was how he told the story. He cannot
unsay it now, for every one in the city heard it—not I alone. But,   850
Oedipus, even if he diverges from what he said then, he shall
never prove that the murder of Laius squares rightly with the
prophecy—for Loxias declared that the king should be killed by
his own son. And that poor creature did not kill him surely,—
for he died himself first. So as far as prophecy goes, henceforward 855
I shall not look to the right hand or the left.

Oedipus

Right. But yet, send some one for the peasant to bring him here;   860
do not neglect it.

Jocasta

  I will send quickly. Now let me go indoors. I will do nothing
  except what pleases you.

(*Exeunt.*)

Chorus

Strophe

  May destiny ever find me
  pious in word and deed   865
  prescribed by the laws that live on high:
  laws begotten in the clear air of heaven,
  whose only father is Olympus;
  no mortal nature brought them to birth,
  no forgetfulness shall lull them to sleep;   870
  for God is great in them and grows not old.

Antistrophe

  Insolence breeds the tyrant, insolence
  if it is glutted with a surfeit, unseasonable, unprofitable,   875
  climbs to the roof-top and plunges
  sheer down to the ruin that must be,
  and there its feet are no service.
  But I pray that the God may never   880
  abolish the eager ambition that profits the state.
  For I shall never cease to hold the God as our protector.

Strophe

  If a man walks with haughtiness
  of hand or word and gives no heed   885
  to Justice and the shrines of Gods
  despises—may an evil doom
  smite him for his ill-starred pride of heart!—
  if he reaps gains without justice
  and will not hold from impiety   890
  and his fingers itch for untouchable things.
  When such things are done, what man shall contrive
  to shield his soul from the shafts of the God?
  When such deeds are held in honour,   895
  why should I honour the Gods in the dance?

Antistrophe

No longer to the holy place,
to the navel of earth I'll go
to worship, nor to Abae
nor to Olympia,   900
unless the oracles are proved to fit,
for all men's hands to point at.
O Zeus, if you are rightly called
the sovereign lord, all-mastering,
let this not escape you nor your ever-living power!   905
The oracles concerning Laius
are old and dim and men regard them not.
   Apollo is nowhere clear in honour; God's service perishes.   910

(Enter Jocasta, carrying garlands.)

Jocasta

Princes of the land, I have had the thought to go
to the Gods' temples, bringing in my hand
garlands and gifts of incense, as you see.
For Oedipus excites himself too much
at every sort of trouble, not conjecturing,   915
like a man of sense, what will be from what was,
but he is always at the speaker's mercy,
when he speaks terrors. I can do no good
by my advice, and so I came as suppliant
to you, Lycaean Apollo, who are nearest.
These are the symbols of my prayer and this   920
my prayer: grant us escape free of the curse.
Now when we look to him we are all afraid;
he's pilot of our ship and he is frightened.

(Enter Messenger.)

Messenger

Might I learn from you, sirs, where is the house of Oedipus? Or   925
best of all, if you know, where is the king himself?

Chorus

This is his house and he is within doors. This lady is his wife and
mother of his children.

Messenger

    God bless you, lady, and God bless your household! God bless   930
    Oedipus' noble wife!

Jocasta

    God bless you, sir, for your kind greeting! What do you want
    of us that you have come here? What have you to tell us?

Messenger

    Good news, lady. Good for your house and for your husband.

Jocasta

    What is your news? Who sent you to us?   935

Messenger

    I come from Corinth and the news I bring will give you pleasure.
    Perhaps a little pain too.

Jocasta

    What is this news of double meaning?

Messenger

    The people of the Isthmus will choose Oedipus to be their king.   940
    That is the rumour there.

Jocasta

    But isn't their king still old Polybus?

Messenger

    No. He is in his grave. Death has got him.

Jocasta

    Is that the truth? Is Oedipus' father dead?

Messenger

    May I die myself if it be otherwise!

Jocasta (to a servant)

    Be quick and run to the King with the news! O oracles of the   945
    Gods, where are you now? It was from this man Oedipus fled, lest
    he should be his murderer! And now he is dead, in the course of
    nature, and not killed by Oedipus.

                                                 (Enter Oedipus.)

Oedipus

    Dearest Jocasta, why have you sent for me?   950

Jocasta

    Listen to this man and when you hear reflect what is the outcome
    of the holy oracles of the Gods.

Oedipus
>Who is he? What is his message for me?

Jocasta
>He is from Corinth and he tells us that your father Polybus is
>dead and gone.

Oedipus
>What's this you say, sir? Tell me yourself.

Messenger
>Since this is the first matter you want clearly told: Poly bus has
>gone down to death. You may be sure of it.

Oedipus
>By treachery or sickness? 960

Messenger
>A small thing will put old bodies asleep.

Oedipus
>So he died of sickness, it seems,—poor old man!

Messenger
>Yes, and of age—the long years he had measured.

Oedipus
>Ha! Ha! O dear Jocasta, why should one
>look to the Pythian hearth? Why should one look 965
>to the birds screaming overhead? They prophesied
>that I should kill my father! But he's dead,
>and hidden deep in earth, and I stand here
>who never laid a hand on spear against him,—
>unless perhaps he died of longing for me,
>and thus I am his murderer. But they, 970
>the oracles, as they stand—he's taken them
>away with him, they're dead as he himself is,
>and worthless.

Jocasta
>That told you before now.

Oedipus
>You did, but I was misled by my fear.

Jocasta
>Then lay no more of them to heart, not one

Oedipus
>But surely I must fear my mother's bed?

Jocasta

    Why should man fear since chance is all in all

    for him, and he can clearly foreknow nothing?

    Best to live lightly, as one can, unthinkingly.

    As to your mother's marriage bed,—don't fear it.   980

    Before this, in dreams too, as well as oracles,

    many a man has lain with his own mother.

    But he to whom such things are nothing bears

    his life most easily.

Oedipus

    All that you say would be said perfectly

    if she were dead; but since she lives I must   985

    still fear, although you talk so well, Jocasta.

Jocasta

    Still in your father's death there's light of comfort?

Oedipus

    Great light of comfort; but I fear the living.

Messenger

    Who is the woman that makes you afraid?

Oedipus

    Merope, old man, Polybus' wife.   990

Messenger

    What about her frightens the queen and you?

Oedipus

    A terrible oracle, stranger, from the Gods.

Messenger

    Can it be told? Or does the sacred law

    orbid another to have knowledge of it?

Oedipus

    O no! Once on a time Loxias said

    that I should lie with my own mother and   995

    take on my hands the blood of my own father.

    And so for these long years I've lived away

    from Corinth; it has been to my great happiness;

    but yet it's sweet to see the face of parents.

Messenger

    This was the fear which drove you out of Corinth?   1000

Oedipus

Old man, I did not wish to kill my father.

Messenger

Why should I not free you from this fear, sir,

since I have come to you in all goodwill?

Oedipus

You would not find me thankless if you did.

Messenger

Why, it was just for this I brought the news,— 1005

to earn your thanks when you had come safe home.

Oedipus

No, I will never come near my parents.

Messenger

Son,

it's very plain you don't know what you're doing.

Oedipus

What do you mean, old man? For God's sake, tell me.

Messenger

If your homecoming is checked by fears like these. 1010

Oedipus

Yes, I'm afraid that Phoebus may prove right.

Messenger

The murder and the incest?

Oedipus

Yes, old man;

that is my constant terror.

Messenger

Do you know that all your fears are empty?

Oedipus

How is that, 1015

if they are father and mother and I their son?

Messenger

Because Polybus was no kin to you in blood.

Oedipus

What, was not Polybus my father?

Messenger

No more than I but just so much.

Oedipus

How can
my father be my father as much as one
that's nothing to me?

Messenger

Neither he nor I   1020
begat you.

Oedipus

Why then did he call me son?

Messenger

A gift he took you from these hands of mine.

Oedipus

Did he love so much what he took from another's hand?

Messenger

His childlessness before persuaded him.

Oedipus

Was I a child you bought or found when I   1025
was given to him?

Messenger

On Cithaeron's slopes
in the twisting thickets you were found.

Oedipus

And why
were you a traveller in those parts?

Messenger

I was
in charge of mountain flocks.

Oedipus

You were a shepherd?
A hireling vagrant?

Messenger

Yes, but at least at that time   1030
the man that saved your life, son.

Oedipus

What ailed me when you took me in your arms?

Messenger

In that your ankles should be witnesses.

Oedipus
    Why do you speak of that old pain?

Messenger
    I loosed you;
    the tendons of your feet were pierced and fettered,—

Oedipus
    My swaddling clothes brought me a rare disgrace.   1035

Messenger
    So that from this you're called your present name.

Oedipus
    Was this my father's doing or my mother's?
    For God's sake, tell me.

Messenger
    I don't know, but he
    who gave you to me has more knowledge than I.

Oedipus
    You yourself did not find me then? You took me
    from someone else?

Messenger
    Yes, from another shepherd.   1040

Oedipus
    Who was he? Do you know him well enough
    to tell?

Messenger
    He was called Laius' man.

Oedipus
    You mean the king who reigned here in the old days?

Messenger
    Yes, he was that man's shepherd.

Oedipus
    Is he alive
    still, so that I could see him?   1045

Messenger
    You who live here
    would know that best.

Oedipus
    Do any of you here
    know of this shepherd whom he speaks about

in town or in the fields? Tell me. It's time   1050
that this was found out once for all.

Chorus

I think he is none other than the peasant
whom you have sought to see already; but
Jocasta here can tell us best of that.

Oedipus

Jocasta, do you know about this man
whom we have sent for? Is he the man he mentions?   1055

Jocasta

Why ask of whom he spoke? Don't give it heed;
nor try to keep in mind what has been said.
It will be wasted labour.

Oedipus

With such clues
I could not fail to bring my birth to light.

Jocasta

I beg you—do not hunt this out—I beg you,   1060
if you have any care for your own life.
What I am suffering is enough.

Oedipus

Keep up
your heart, Jocasta. Though I'm proved a slave,
thrice slave, and though my mother is thrice slave,
you'll not be shown to be of lowly lineage.

Jocasta

O be persuaded by me, I entreat you;
do not do this.

Oedipus

I will not be persuaded to let be   1065
the chance of finding out the whole thing clearly.

Jocasta

It is because I wish you well that I
give you this counsel—and it's the best counsel.

Oedipus

Then the best counsel vexes me, and has
for some while since.

Jocasta

   O Oedipus, God help you!

   God keep you from the knowledge of who you are!

Oedipus

   Here, some one, go and fetch the shepherd for me;

   and let her find her joy in her rich family!   1070

Jocasta

   O Oedipus, unhappy Oedipus!

   that is all I can call you, and the last thing

   that I shall ever call you.

                                                                  (*Exit.*)

Chorus

   Why has the queen gone, Oedipus, in wild

   grief rushing from us? I am afraid that trouble   1075

   will break out of this silence.

Oedipus

   Break out what will! I at least shall be

   willing to see my ancestry, though humble.

   Perhaps she is ashamed of my low birth,

   for she has all a woman's high-flown pride.

   But I account myself a child of Fortune,   1080

   beneficent Fortune, and I shall not be

   dishonoured. She's the mother from whom I spring;

   the months, my brothers, marked me, now as small,

   and now again as mighty. Such is my breeding,

   and I shall never prove so false to it,   1085

   as not to find the secret of my birth.

Chorus

Strophe

   If I am a prophet and wise of heart

   you shall not fail, Cithaeron,   1090

   by the limitless sky, you shall not!—

   to know at tomorrow's full moon

   that Oedipus honours you,

   as native to him and mother and nurse at once;

   and that you are honoured in dancing by us, as finding favour in

   sight of our king.

   Apollo, to whom we cry, find these things pleasing!

Antistrophe

    Who was it bore you, child? One of   1098
    the long-lived nymphs who lay with Pan—
    the father who treads the hills?
    Or was she a bride of Loxias, your mother? The grassy slopes
    are all of them dear to him. Or perhaps Cyllene's king   1104
    or the Bacchants' God that lives on the tops
    of the hills received you a gift from some
    one of the Helicon Nymphs, with whom he mostly plays?

                        (Enter an old man, led by Oedipus' servants.)

Oedipus

    If some one like myself who never met him   1110
    may make a guess,—I think this is the herdsman,
    whom we were seeking. His old age is consonant
    with the other. And besides, the men who bring him
    I recognize as my own servants. You   1115
    perhaps may better me in knowledge since
    you've seen the man before.

Chorus

    You can be sure
    I recognize him. For if Laius
    had ever an honest shepherd, this was he.

Oedipus

    You, sir, from Corinth, I must ask you first,
    is this the man you spoke of?   1120

Messenger

    This is he
    before your eyes.

Oedipus

    Old man, look here at me
    and tell me what I ask you. Were you ever
    a servant of King Laius?

Herdsman

    I was,—
    no slave he bought but reared in his own house.

Oedipus

    What did you do as work? How did you live?

Herdsman

    Most of my life was spent among the flocks.   1125

Oedipus

    In what part of the country did you live?

Herdsman

    Cithaeron and the places near to it.

Oedipus

    And somewhere there perhaps you knew this man?

Herdsman

    What was his occupation? Who?

Oedipus

    This man here,   1130

    have you had any dealings with him?

Herdsman

    No—

    not such that I can quickly call to mind.

Messenger

    That is no wonder, master. But I'll make him remember what he

    does not know. For I know, that he well knows the country of

    Cithaeron, how he with two flocks, I with one kept company for   1135

    three years—each year half a year—from spring till autumn time

    and then when winter came I drove my flocks to our fold home

    again and he to Lams' steadings. Well—am I right or not in what   1140

    I said we did?

Herdsman

    You're right—although it's a long time ago.

Messenger

    Do you remember giving me a child

    to bring up as my foster child?

Herdsman

    What's this?

    Why do you ask this question?

Messenger

    Look old man,   1145

    here he is—here's the man who was that child!

Herdsman

    Death take you! Won't you hold your tongue?

Oedipus

No, no,

do not find fault with him, old man. Your words

are more at fault than his.

Herdsman

O best of masters,

how do I give offense?

Oedipus

When you refuse   1150

to speak about the child of whom he asks you.

Herdsman

He speaks out of his ignorance, without meaning.

Oedipus

If you'll not talk to gratify me, you

will talk with pain to urge you.

Herdsman

O please, sir,

don't hurt an old man, sir.

Oedipus

(to the servants)

Here, one of you,

twist his hands behind him.

Herdsman

Why, God help me, why?   1155

What do you want to know?

Oedipus

You gave a child

to him,—the child he asked you of?

Herdsman

I did.

I wish I'd died the day I did.

Oedipus

You will

unless you tell me truly.

Herdsman

And I'll die far worse if I should tell you.

Oedipus

    This fellow   1160

    is bent on more delays, as it would seem.

Herdsman

    O no, no! I have told you that I gave it.

Oedipus

    Where did you get this child from? Was it your own or did you

    get it from another?

Herdsman

    Not

    my own at all; I had it from some one.

Oedipus

    One of these citizens? or from what house?

Herdsman

    O master, please—I beg you, master, please   1165

    don't ask me more.

Oedipus

    You're a dead man if I

    ask you again.

Herdsman

    It was one of the children

    of Laius.

Oedipus

    A slave? Or born in wedlock?

Herdsman

    O God, I am on the brink of frightful speech.

Oedipus

    And I of frightful hearing. But I must hear.   1170

Herdsman

    The child was called his child; but she within,

    your wife would tell you best how all this was.

Oedipus

    She gave it to you?

Herdsman

    Yes, she did, my lord.

Oedipus

    To do what with it?

Herdsman

Make away with it.

Oedipus

She was so hard—its mother? 1175

Herdsman

Aye, through fear
of evil oracles.

Oedipus

Which?

Herdsman

They said that he
should kill his parents.

Oedipus

How was it that you gave it away to this old man?

Herdsman

O master,
pitied it, and thought that I could send it
off to another country and this man
was from another country. But he saved it 1180
for the most terrible troubles. If you are
the man he says you are, you're bred to misery.

Oedipus

O, O, O, they will all come,
all come out clearly! Light of the sun, let me
look upon you no more after today!
who first saw the light bred of a match
accursed, and accursed in my living
with them I lived with, cursed in my killing. 1185

(*Exeunt all but the Chorus.*)

Chorus

Strophe

O generations of men, how I
count you as equal with those who live not at all!
What man, what man on earth wins more 1190
of happiness than a seeming
and after that turning away?
Oedipus, you are my pattern of this,

Oedipus, you and your fate!
Luckless Oedipus, whom of all men   1196
I envy not at all.

Antistrophe

In as much as he shot his bolt
beyond the others and won the prize
of happiness complete—
O Zeus—and killed and reduced to nought
the hooked taloned maid of the riddling speech,
standing a tower against death for my land:
hence he was called my king and hence
was honoured the highest of all
honours; and hence he ruled
in the great city of Thebes.

Strophe

But now whose tale is more miserable?   1204
Who is there lives with a savager fate?
Whose troubles so reverse his life as his?
O Oedipus, the famous prince
for whom a great haven
the same both as father and son
sufficed for generation,
how, O how, have the furrows ploughed
by your father endured to bear you, poor wretch,
and hold their peace so long?

Antistrophe

Time who sees all has found you out   1213
against your will; judges your marriage accursed,
begetter and begot at one in it.
O child of Laius,
would I had never seen you.
I weep for you and cry
a dirge of lamentation.
To speak directly, I drew my breath
from you at the first and so now I lull
my mouth to sleep with your name.   1222

(*Enter a second messenger.*)

214

Second Messenger

    O Princes always honoured by our country,

    what deeds you'll hear of and what horrors see,

    what grief you'll feel, if you as true born Thebans

    care for the house of Labdacus's sons.

    Phasis nor Ister cannot purge this house,

    I think, with all their streams, such things

    it hides, such evils shortly will bring forth

    into the light, whether they will or not;

    and troubles hurt the most 1230

    when they prove self-inflicted.

Chorus

    What we had known before did not fall short

    of bitter groaning's worth; what's more to tell?

Second Messenger

    Shortest to hear and tell—our glorious queen 1235

    Jocasta's dead.

Chorus

    Unhappy woman! How?

Second Messenger

    By her own hand. The worst of what was done

    you cannot know. You did not see the sight.

    Yet in so far as I remember it

    you'll hear the end of our unlucky queen. 1240

    When she came raging into the house she went

    straight to her marriage bed, tearing her hair

    with both her hands, and crying upon Laius 1245

    long dead—Do you remember, Laius,

    that night long past which bred a child for us

    to send you to your death and leave

    a mother making children with her son?

    And then she groaned and cursed the bed in which

    she brought forth husband by her husband, children 1250

    by her own child, an infamous double bond.

    How after that she died I do not know,—

    for Oedipus distracted us from seeing.

    He burst upon us shouting and we looked

to him as he paced frantically around,
begging us always: Give me a sword, I say,   1255
to find this wife no wife, this mother's womb,
this field of double sowing whence I sprang
and where I sowed my children! As he raved
some god showed him the way—none of us there.
Bellowing terribly and led by some   1260
invisible guide he rushed on the two doors,—
wrenching the hollow bolts out of their sockets,
he charged inside. There, there, we saw his wife
hanging, the twisted rope around her neck.
When he saw her, he cried out fearfully   1265
and cut the dangling noose. Then, as she lay,
poor woman, on the ground, what happened after,
was terrible to see. He tore the brooches—
the gold chased brooches fastening her robe—
away from her and lifting them up high
dashed them on his own eyeballs, shrieking out   1270
such things as: they will never see the crime
have committed or had done upon me!
Dark eyes, now in the days to come look on
forbidden faces, do not recognize
those whom you long for—with such imprecations
he struck his eyes again and yet again   1275
with the brooches. And the bleeding eyeballs gushed
and stained his beard—no sluggish oozing drops
but a black rain and bloody hail poured down.

So it has broken—and not on one head   1280
but troubles mixed for husband and for wife.
The fortune of the days gone by was true
good fortune—but today groans and destruction
and death and shame—of all ills can be named   1285
not one is missing.

Chorus
Is he now in any ease from pain?

Second Messenger

He shouts

for some one to unbar the doors and show him

to all the men of Thebes, his father's killer,

his mother's—no I cannot say the word,

it is unholy—for he'll cast himself,

out of the land, he says, and not remain

to bring a curse upon his house, the curse   1290

he called upon it in his proclamation. But

he wants for strength, aye, and some one to guide him;

his sickness is too great to bear. You, too,

will be shown that. The bolts are opening.

Soon you will see a sight to waken pity

even in the horror of it.

(*Enter the blinded Oedipus.*)

Chorus

This is a terrible sight for men to see!

I never found a worse!

Poor wretch, what madness came upon you!   1300

What evil spirit leaped upon your life

to your ill-luck—a leap beyond man's strength!

Indeed I pity you, but I cannot

look at you, though there's much I want to ask

and much to learn and much to see.

I shudder at the sight of you.

Oedipus

O, O,

where am I going? Where is my voice

borne on the wind to and fro?

Spirit, how far have you sprung?

Chorus

To a terrible place whereof men's ears

may not hear, nor their eyes behold it.

Oedipus

Darkness!

Horror of darkness enfolding, resistless, unspeakable visitant sped by an ill

wind in haste!   1315

217

madness and stabbing pain and memory
of evil deeds I have done!

Chorus

In such misfortunes it's no wonder
if double weighs the burden of your grief.   1320

Oedipus

My friend,
you are the only one steadfast, the only one that attends on me;
you still stay nursing the blind man.
Your care is not unnoticed. I can know   1325
your voice, although this darkness is my world.

Chorus

Doer of dreadful deeds, how did you dare
so far to do despite to your own eyes?
what spirit urged you to it?

Oedipus

It was Apollo, friends, Apollo,
that brought this bitter bitterness, my sorrows to completion.   1330
But the hand that struck me
was none but my own.
Why should I see
whose vision showed me nothing sweet to see?   1335

Chorus

These things are as you say.

Oedipus

What can I see to love?
What greeting can touch my ears with joy?
Take me away, and haste—to a place out of the way!   1340
Take me away, my friends, the greatly miserable,
the most accursed, whom God too hates   1345
above all men on earth!

Chorus

Unhappy in your mind and your misfortune,
would I had never known you!

Oedipus

Curse on the man who took
the cruel bonds from off my legs, as I lay in the field.   1350

He stole me from death and saved me, no kindly service.
Had I died then
I would not be so burdensome to friends.   1355

Chorus

I, too, could have wished it had been so.

Oedipus

Then I would not have come
to kill my father and marry my mother infamously.
Now I am godless and child of impurity,   1360
begetter in the same seed that created my wretched self.
If there is any ill worse than ill,   1365
that is the lot of Oedipus.

Chorus

I cannot say your remedy was good;
you would be better dead than blind and living.

Oedipus

What I have done here was best done—don't tell me   1370
otherwise, do not give me further counsel.
I do not know with what eyes I could look
upon my father when I die and go
under the earth, nor yet my wretched mother—
those two to whom I have done things deserving
worse punishment than hanging. Would the sight
of children, bred as mine are, gladden me?   1375
No, not these eyes, never. And my city,
its towers and sacred places of the Gods,
of these I robbed my miserable self   1380
when I commanded all to drive *him* out,
the criminal since proved by God impure
and of the race of Laius.
To this guilt I bore witness against myself—
with what eyes shall I look upon my people?   1385
No. If there were a means to choke the fountain
of hearing I would not have stayed my hand
from locking up my miserable carcase,
seeing and hearing nothing; it is sweet   1390
to keep our thoughts out of the range of hurt.

Cithaeron, why did you receive me? why
having received me did you not kill me straight?
And so I had not shown to men my birth.

O Polybus and Corinth and the house,
the old house that I used to call my father's—   1395
what fairness you were nurse to, and what foulness
festered beneath! Now I am found to be
a sinner and a son of sinners. Crossroads,
and hidden glade, oak and the narrow way
at the crossroads, that drank my father's blood   1400
offered you by my hands, do you remember
still what I did as you looked on, and what
I did when I came here? O marriage, marriage!
you bred me and again when you had bred
bred children of your child and showed to men   1405
brides, wives and mothers and the foulest deeds
that can be in this world of ours.

Come—it's unfit to say what is unfit
to do.—I beg of you in God's name hide me   1410
somewhere outside your country, yes, or kill me,
or throw me into the sea, to be forever
out of your sight. Approach and deign to touch me
for all my wretchedness, and do not fear.
No man but I can bear my evil doom.   1415

Chorus

   Here Creon comes in fit time to perform
   or give advice in what you ask of us.
   Creon is left sole ruler in your stead.

Oedipus

   Creon! Creon! What shall I say to him?
   How can I justly hope that he will trust me?   1420
   In what is past I have been proved towards him
   an utter liar.

(*Enter Creon.*)

Creon

    Oedipus, I've come

    not so that I might laugh at you nor taunt you

    with evil of the past. But if you still

    are without shame before the face of men

    reverence at least the flame that gives all life,   1425

    our Lord the Sun, and do not show unveiled

    to him pollution such that neither land

    nor holy rain nor light of day can welcome.

                                   (*To a servant.*)

    Be quick and take him in. It is most decent   1430

    that only kin should see and hear the troubles

    of kin.

Oedipus

    I beg you, since you've torn me from

    my dreadful expectations and have come

    in a most noble spirit to a man

    that has used you vilely—do a thing for me.

    I shall speak for your own good, not for my own.

Creon

    What do you need that you would ask of me?   1435

Oedipus

    Drive me from here with all the speed you can

    to where I may not hear a human voice.

Creon

    Be sure, I would have done this had not I

    wished first of all to learn from the God the course

    of action I should follow.

Oedipus

    But his word   1440

    has been quite clear to let the parricide, the sinner, die.

Creon

    Yes, that indeed was said.

    But in the present need we had best discover

    what we should do.

Oedipus

    And will you ask about

    a man so wretched?

Creon

Now even you will trust   1445
the God.

Oedipus

So. I command you—and will beseech you—
to her that lies inside that house give burial
as you would have it; she is yours and rightly
you will perform the rites for her. For me—
never let this my father's city have me   1450
living a dweller in it. Leave me live
in the mountains where Cithaeron is, that's called
my mountain, which my mother and my father
while they were living would have made my tomb.
So I may die by their decree who sought
indeed to kill me. Yet I know this much: 1455
no sickness and no other thing will kill me.
I would not have been saved from death if not
for some strange evil fate. Well, let my fate go where it will.
Creon, you need not care   1460
about my sons; they're men and so wherever
they are, they will not lack a livelihood.
But my two girls—so sad and pitiful—
whose table never stood apart from mine,
and everything I touched they always shared—   1465
O Creon, have a thought for them! And most
I wish that you might suffer me to touch them and sorrow with them.

(Enter Antigone and Ismene, Oedipus' two daughters.)

O my lord! O true noble Creon! Can I   1470
really be touching them, as when I saw?
What shall I say?
Yes, I can hear them sobbing—my two darlings!
and Creon has had pity and has sent me
what I loved most?
Am I right?   1475

Creon

You're right: it was I gave you this
because I knew from old days how you loved them
as I see now.

Oedipus

    God bless you for it, Creon,
    and may God guard you better on your road
    than he did me!
    O children,   1480
    where are you? Come here, come to my hands,
    a brother's hands which turned your father's eyes,
    those bright eyes you knew once, to what you see,
    a father seeing nothing, knowing nothing,
    begetting you from his own source of life.   1485
    I weep for you—I cannot see your faces—
    I weep when I think of the bitterness
    there will be in your lives, how you must live
    before the world. At what assemblages
    of citizens will you make one? to what   1490
    gay company will you go and not come home
    in tears instead of sharing in the holiday?
    And when you're ripe for marriage, who will he be,
    the man who'll risk to take such infamy
    1495as shall cling to my children, to bring hurt
    on them and those that marry with them? What
    curse is not there? "Your father killed his father
    and sowed the seed where he had sprung himself
    and begot you out of the womb that held him."
    These insults you will hear. Then who will marry you?   1500
    No one, my children; clearly you are doomed
    to waste away in barrenness unmarried.
    Son of Menoeceus, since you are all the father
    left these two girls, and we, their parents, both   1505
    are dead to them—do not allow them wander
    like beggars, poor and husbandless.
    They are of your own blood.
    And do not make them equal with myself
    in wretchedness; for you can see them now
    so young, so utterly alone, save for you only.
    Touch my hand, noble Creon, and say yes.   1510
    If you were older, children, and were wiser,

there's much advice I'd give you. But as it is,
let this be what you pray: give me a life
wherever there is opportunity
to live, and better life than was my father's.

Creon

Your tears have had enough of scope; now go within the house. 1515

Oedipus

I must obey, though bitter of heart.

Creon

In season, all is good.

Oedipus

Do you know on what conditions I obey?

Creon

You tell me them,
and I shall know them when I hear.

Oedipus

That you shall send me out
to live away from Thebes.

Creon

That gift you must ask of the God.

Oedipus

But I'm now hated by the Gods.

Creon

So quickly you'll obtain your prayer.

Oedipus

You consent then? 1520

Creon

What I do not mean, I do not use to say.

Oedipus

Now lead me away from here.

Creon

Let go the children, then, and come.

Oedipus

Do not take them from me.

Creon

Do not seek to be master in everything,
for the things you mastered did not follow you throughout your life.

(As Creon and Oedipus go out.)

Chorus

    You that live in my ancestral Thebes, behold this Oedipus,—
    him who knew the famous riddles and was a man most masterful;   1525
    not a citizen who did not look with envy on his lot—
    see him now and see the breakers of misfortune swallow him!
    Look upon that last day always. Count no mortal happy till
    he has passed the final limit of his life secure from pain.   1530

Apology of Socrates[1], from Apologies by Plato and Xenophon

By Plato, translated by Mark Kremer

17a **SOCRATES**: In what way you, Athenian men, have been moved by my accusers, I do not know. As for myself, even I almost forgot myself on account of them, so persuasively did they speak. And yet, in a way, they said nothing true. I wondered, most of all, at one of the many falsehoods which they told–the one in which they said that you need to be on guard lest you should be deceived by me, as I am a clever

b speaker. That they are not ashamed that they will be immediately refuted by me in deed, when I appear in no way to be a clever speaker, seemed to me to be most shameful of them, unless of course they call the one who speaks the truth a clever speaker. For if this is what they are saying, then I would agree that I am an orator, though not of their sort. As I say, therefore, they have said little or nothing true, but from me you will hear the whole truth. By Zeus, Athenian men, neither

c speeches beautified like theirs with phrases and words, nor contrived, but rather you will hear what is spoken in words as they happen at random, since I trust the things I say to be just. And let none of you expect otherwise. For surely, it is not fitting, men, for someone of my age to come before you like a youth making up speeches. And above everything, Athenian

---

1   The word for apology is *apologia* and can be used to mean legal defense, but is used by both Plato and Xenophon to mean something deeper, as in the accounting or justification for one's very existence, which can be justified by nature as opposed to law or *nomos*. The defense speech to the jury is almost equivalent to defending oneself in assembly or before the city as a whole. There is no judge and instruction in law, and one can bring in personal matters such as the suffering of one's family. Socrates' defense speech is really a defense to the city and not just to a judge, jury, and law in our sense.

men, I beg and implore this of you. If you hear me defend myself with the very speeches I am accustomed to speak both in the marketplace at the counters, where many of you have

d   heard me, and elsewhere, neither be amazed nor clamor[1] because of this. For it holds thus: for the first time, before a court of justice I come, at the age of seventy. Therefore, I am simply foreign to the ways of speaking here. If I happened to be a foreigner, you would surely sympathize with me if I spoke in the dialect and way in which I was

18a raised, likewise I also beg it of you now, and it is just as it appears to me. Disregard my way of speaking, for perhaps it is worse, perhaps better, but rather consider this alone and apply your mind to it: whether or not the things I say are just. For this is the virtue[2] of a judge, that of an orator, to speak the truth.

First, then, I am right to defend myself, Athenian men, against the first false accusations and

b   my first accusers, and then next against the later accusations and the later accusers. To you, many have accused me from long ago and already for many years, yet they say nothing true. Of them, I am more afraid than of Anytus[3] and those among him, though they too are dangerous. But those are more dangerous, men, the one's laying hold of many of you since childhood, who persuaded you and accused me of nothing true: that there is a Socrates, a wise man, a ponderer on the things above, and one who has investigated all the things under the earth and makes the weaker speech stronger.[4]

c   Those ones, Athenian men, who have spread this report are my dangerous accusers, since the ones who listen think that those who investigate these things do not believe in the gods. Furthermore, these accusers are many and have accused me for a long time and, moreover, said these things to you in those years in which you are most trusting, some of you being children and some youths,

d   and they accused me in a case that was entirely by default, there being no one to defend. And, the thing most unaccountable of all is that it is impossible to know and to say their names, unless one should be a comic poet.[5] They persuaded you using envy and slander and the ones having been

---

1   The verb to clamor is *thorubein*. It is an insult that characterizes the indignation of the jury as noisy and pointless. Since we do not hear the jury speak, their decision appears in the light of Socrates' characterization of them.

2   The word for virtue is *aretē* and it means excellence. The excellence of a thing need not be moral. The word for truth is *alētheia*. Socrates emphasizes the intellect by distinguishing virtue and truth from passion and prejudice.

3   Anytus was a tanner, who became wealthy and eventually held a leading political position in the democracy. In Xenophon's *Apology*, Socrates suggests that Anytus' hatred was the real animus for the trial. Socrates blames Anytus for ruining his own son, who had a noble soul requiring a noble activity and object, but who was ruined by sensual passions because his father provided for him coarse and plebian duties. Socrates suggests that participation in politics is for coarse souls.

4   The accusation of being a wise man is related to both the formal charges and to Aristophanes' play the *Clouds*, where Socrates is shown studying natural science and teaching rhetoric. The study of natural science threatens the belief in the gods by giving natural explanations to heavenly movements and occurrences. By looking beneath the earth, Socrates threatens the beliefs in Hades in addition to the cosmic gods. The accusation of making the weaker speech the stronger suggests that he disrupts the divine order by assisting injustice to triumph over justice through the art of rhetoric.

5   Aristophanes, who parodied Socrates' wisdom in the *Clouds*.

persuaded themselves, persuaded others. All of these are most difficult to deal with, for to bring any of them forward here is not possible, nor to refute any of them, but it is simply necessary, as if fighting shadows, to speak in my defense and to refute with no one to respond. You too consider it to be exactly as I say—that there are two groups of accusers, the ones accusing me now and the 18e ones long ago of whom I speak. And, consider it necessary as well to first defend myself against these first, because both earlier and much more than the later ones did you hear them accusing me.

Well then, a defense speech is necessary, O Athenian men, as well as an attempt to remove from 19a you, in the little time here, the slander that you acquired over much time.[6] I would wish things might be like that, were it in any way better for both you and me, and that I, in making a defense speech, might accomplish something. I consider this to be hard and I am not entirely forgetful of it. Nonetheless, let it be in whatever way is dear to the god, though it is necessary to obey the law and to make a defense speech.

Let us take up, therefore, from the beginning what the accusation is from which the slander b against me has arisen—and in which Meletus trusted when he wrote the indictment against me. Well then, whatever did the slanderers say in their slanders? Just like accusers, their charge must be read: "Socrates does injustice and is a busybody, investigating the things beneath the earth and in the heavens and making the weaker speech the stronger, and teaching these things to others."

c It is like this. You yourselves have also seen such things in the comedy of Aristophanes, a Socrates paraded about claiming to walk on air and spouting much other nonsense about which I have no knowledge, neither much nor little. I do not say this in order to dishonor this kind of knowledge, if anyone is wise in such subjects, only let me not be prosecuted by Meletus on such charges, for, in d fact, Athenian men, I have no share in these matters. As witnesses, I offer once more yourselves, and I deem it well that you teach and also tell one another—the ones of you who at anytime heard me conversing, and many are such ones among you, if ever, either little or great, anyone of you heard me conversing about such things, and from this you will see that it is likewise for the other things that the many say concerning me.

e But, in fact, neither are these things so, and if you have heard from anyone that I attempt to educate human beings and take money, neither is that true either. Though this too seems to me to be noble,[7] if one should be able to educate human beings just as Gorgias the Leontine, and Prodicus the Ceon, and Hippias the Elean.[8] For of these, each, men, is able, going into each of the

---

6 A trial for a capital offense was circumscribed by a very limited amount of time, indicating little concern with the truth.

7 The word for noble is *kalon*, which also means beautiful. The use of the same word for noble and for beautiful is indicative of how the Greeks understood the relation of soul to appearance. The beauty of the outer appearance is meant to reflect the soul or the capacity for noble activity. For example, the beauty of Achilles' body contains the expectation of the soul capable of his noble deeds. Socrates reforms the Greek understanding of the noble, since he is famously ugly but claims to have true beauty of soul.

8 These men are sophists. Aristophanes taught that Socrates had an affinity to them. Socrates, however, emphasizes his differences and especially his purer soul (he does not take money), and he does not make unfounded and proud claims to

20a cities, to persuade the young, who can be with, for free, any of their own citizens whom they wish, to abandon being with these ones and to be with themselves and to give them money and to show thanks besides.

And there is another wise man from Parios here, who I thought was residing in town, for I chanced to encounter a Callias,[9] son of Hipponicus, who has paid out more money to sophists than all others taken together. Therefore, I questioned him, for he had two sons—"Callias," I said, "if your sons were born colts or calves, then we could get and hire for them an overseer, who would
b   make both of them noble and good in the virtue belonging to them, he being someone from either horsemen or farmers. But now, since they are human beings, who do you have in mind to get to oversee them? Who is a knower of such virtue—that of a human being and also of a citizen? For I suppose you have carefully considered it, on account of your having two sons. Is there someone," I said, "or not."

"Very much so" he said.

"Who" I said, "and where and for how much does he teach?"

"Evenus" he said, "Socrates, from Paros, five minae."

c   And I deemed blessed Evenus, if truly he possessed this art and teaches at so modest a price. I, at any rate, would be preening myself on it, if I knew these things. But I do not know, Athenian men.

Now, one of you might object: "But, Socrates, what is your affair?[10] From where did these slanders against you come? For surely if you were not engaging in anything any more than others, then such a rumor and account would not have been born, unless you were practicing something
d   other than the many. Therefore, tell us what it is, lest we treat you rashly."

These things, it seems to me, are just—those the speaker says. And I shall attempt to show from whence this came, which brought to me this name and slander. Listen. Perhaps I will seem to some of you to be joking, but be assured, I will tell you the whole truth. For I, Athenian men, have received this name on account of nothing but a certain wisdom. What kind of wisdom is this?
e   Perhaps that wisdom belonging to a human being. With respect to that, I probably really have this wisdom. Whereas, those of whom I just spoke, are by chance wise in either some wisdom greater than human wisdom, or some I don't know what. For I do not know it, and whoever says I do lies, and speaks in order to slander me. And, Athenian men, do not clamor against me, not even if I

---

knowledge. One of Plato's many poetic achievements is to sublimate the art of rhetoric and sophistry towards philosophy through the art of the dialogue.

9   Callias was a wealthy Athenian famous for his support of the sophists, as well as for his dissolute desires. His house is the scene for both the *Protagoras* and Xenophon's *Banquet*.

10   The word for affair is *pragma* and can also mean trouble or problem. In discussing Socrates, Nietzsche referred to the "Problem of Socrates".

appear to you[11] to speak somewhat boastfully. For "not mine is the story"[12] which I will tell but I will attribute it to a speaker, an authority for you. For with respect to me, if I have any wisdom and of what sort, I will provide as witness to you the god in Delphi. You know Charephon,[13] surely.

21a He was my companion from youth and a fellow to many of you, and he shared your late exile and returned with you. And you know what type Charephon was, so fervent in what he would undertake. And once, indeed, having gone into Delphi, he ventured to ask this of the oracle, and again I say—do not clamor, men, for he asked if anyone was wiser than me. Then the Pythia[14] answered that no one was wiser. And about these things his brother here will give testimony to you, since the other has himself reached his end.

b   Now consider the reasons for what I say, for I intend to teach you from where the slander against me has come. For I, learning these things, pondered thus: "Whatever is the god saying, and what riddle is he speaking? As I, in fact, am conscious that I am not wise, either much or little. Whatever, then, does he say when asserting that I am wisest? For certainly, at the least, he is not speaking falsely, for that is not decreed for him." And for a long time, I was at a loss about what he even meant, then, very reluctantly, I turned to an investigation of it something like this: I went to those opined to be

c   wise, as there, if anywhere, I would refute the divination and show to the oracle "that this man is wiser than me, but you said I was wisest." Considering this man, therefore, for it is not necessary to speak his name, he was, however, one of the politicians, and considering him and speaking with him, men of Athens, I received an impression something like the following: it seemed to me that this man seemed to be wise to many human beings and most of all to himself, yet he was not. Then I attempted to show him that he thought he was wise but was not. From this I became hated by him

d   and by many of those present. When I went away, I reasoned with respect to myself: "I am wiser than this human being for it is likely that neither of us know anything noble and good, but this one thinks he knows something while not knowing, whereas I, as I do not know, do not think to know. At any rate, I am likely to be a bit wiser than this one with respect to this peculiar thing—that which I do not know, I do not think to know."

      From there, I went to another, one opined to be wiser than him, and these things seemed to me

e   the same. And from that point, I incurred the hatred of both him and many others.

      After this, I went from one to another, perceiving, distressed, and fearing that I was incurring hatred. Nonetheless, it seemed to be necessary to hold the matter of the god as most important.

---

11   The god in Delphi, Apollo, spoke in riddles about the destinies of men. The most famous pronouncement from the god was that Oedipus would kill his father and marry his mother. Oedipus tried to avoid his destiny and prove himself wiser than the Oracle by answering the riddle of the Sphinx, which is the riddle of man. He could not live with his knowledge, whereas Socrates' destiny constitutes his happiness.

12   Socrates uses the word logos for story, replacing Euripides' use of *mythos*. See *Symposium* 177a.

13   Charephon is Socrates' companion and admirer. In the *Clouds*, Charephon introduces Strepsiades to Socrates. The match ends with the destruction of both. Here we also see that Charephon is an eager admirer of Socrates who creates a bridge between Socrates and the *demos*.

14   The Pythia delivers Apollo's oracles.

22a Therefore, to consider what the oracle meant, I had to go to all those reputed to know something. And by the dog, Athenian men, as it is necessary to speak the truth to you, I really underwent something like the following: the ones with the best reputations appeared to me to be nearly most deficient in my investigation in accord with the god, whereas others with paltrier reputations appeared to be men more suited to having prudence.

In fact, it is necessary to present to you my wandering as the doing of certain labors,[15] for the sake of the oracle becoming irrefutable. After the politicians, I went to the poets, the ones of

b tragedies and the ones of dithyrambs,[16] and the others, so that there I would lay hold of myself in the act of being more ignorant than them. Therefore, I took up their poems that seemed to me they had worked on most, and questioned them about what they said, in order that at the same time I might also learn something from them. I am ashamed to tell you, men, the truth, nonetheless, it must be spoken. For so to speak, nearly all of those present could have spoken better about the poems than the ones who made them. Thus again with respect to the poets as well, I soon realized

c that they do not make what they make by wisdom but by some kind of nature and inspiration[17] like the diviners and deliverers of oracles. For these also say many noble things, but they understand nothing of what they say. It was clear to me that the poets too are affected in the same manner. And at the same time, I perceived that they thought, because of their poetry, that they were the wisest of men in other things as well, in which they were not. Thus I left there too, thinking that in the end I was superior to them in like manner as I was to the politicians.

d Finally, I went to the manual artisans, for I was conscious that I had knowledge, so to say, of nothing but surely I would discover that they knew many noble things. And I was not deceived in this, for they knew of things of which I did not know, and in this respect were wiser than me. Yet, Athenian men, it seemed to me that the good craftsmen had failed in the very same manner as the poets. Since each one executed his own art nobly, he thought himself wisest and worthy of other things—the greatest things, and this erroneous note of theirs hid their wisdom. Thus I asked myself

e for the sake of the oracle whether I would prefer to be just as I am, neither being wise at all in their wisdom, nor ignorant in their ignorance, or to possess both things they have. I answered to myself, and to the oracle, that it pays me to be just as I am.

From this investigation, Athenian men, much hatred has come, the most grievous and serious

23a kind, so that many slanders have arisen from them, and I received this appellation of being "wise", for those present at each occasion think that I am wise in those things about which I refute others, whereas it is likely, men, that the god is wise, and that the oracle meant that human wisdom is worth

b little or nothing. And he appears to say this of Socrates and to have made use of my name for the

---

15   Socrates here compares himself to Hercules whose labors were those of strength rather than of intellect.

16   A song in honor of the god of poetry Dionysus.

17   In Greek the word for enthusiasm literally means a god within. The poets were thought to have been inspired by the gods. The Muses are the daughters of Zeus.

sake of making of me a pattern, as if to say, "the one of you, human beings, is wisest, who, just like Socrates, realizes that in truth, he is worth nothing in regard to wisdom."

Thus, up until now, I continue seeking and investigating, in accord with the god, any townsmen or foreigner I think to be wise. And whenever he appears to me not to be, I show that he is not and come to the assistance of the god. And as the result of this occupation, I have no leisure either to

c   attend in a way worthy of speaking about the affairs of the city or the affairs of my family. Rather, I am in ten-thousand-fold poverty on account of my devotion to the god.

In addition to this, the young who voluntarily follow me, the ones who have the most leisure— the sons of the wealthiest—delight in hearing human beings questioned and often imitate me, and themselves attempt to question others.[18] And, then, I think they find a great many human beings who think they know something, yet know little or nothing. Thence, the ones questioned by them are

d   angry at me, not themselves, and say that Socrates is someone most vile and corrupts the young. And whenever someone asks them, "By doing what and teaching what?" they have nothing to say but are ignorant, and not to appear at a loss, they assert the things ready at hand against all philosophers: "the things above and the things below the earth" and "not believing in the gods" and "making the weaker speech the stronger."[19] For I don't think, they would wish to speak the truth, that in the end it is clear that they pretend to know while knowing nothing. Therefore, as they are, I think, ambitious and

e   vehement and numerous, and as they have spoken of me in an orderly and persuasive manner for a long time, they have filled your ears.

From among these men, Meletus, Anytus, and Lycon attacked me. Meletus being angry on

24a   behalf of the poets, Anytus on behalf of the craftsmen and the politicians, and Lycon on behalf of the orators. Thus, as I said in the beginning, it would be a wonder to me, should I be able in so short a time to remove from you this slander which has grown to be so great. Athenian men, this is the truth for you. I am concealing from you nothing in my speech, either great or small, nor am I holding anything back, though I know well that I exact hatred from these very things, which is also proof that I speak the truth and that this is the slander against me and that these are its causes.

b   And if you should investigate these things now or later, you will find it thus.

So with respect to the things of which my first accusers accused me, let this be a sufficient apology to you. Against Meletus, however, the good and patriotic,[20] as he says, and the later accusers, I will attempt next to give a defense. Here again, as if they were any other accuser, let us take up their sworn statement. It is like this: Socrates, it says, does injustice by corrupting the young, and

---

18   In the *Clouds*, Socrates educates Pheidippides, who believes philosophy is a kind of authority. He demands obedience to wisdom and is willing to claim the right to punish his mother and father.

19   Aristophanes makes use of these prejudices to caricature Socrates.

20   Socrates here implies that Meletus is more imbued with hatred than with love and goodness.

c not believing in the gods in which the city believes, but rather in other, strange *daimonia*.[21] Such are the charges. Let us examine the charge in each of its particulars.

He says I do injustice by corrupting the youth, but, Athenian men, I say Meletus does, because he jokes with respect to a serious matter, readily bringing human beings to trial, pretending to be serious and earnest about matters for which he cared nothing at all. That it is thus, I will attempt to show you.

d Now, come then, Meletus, and tell me: do you not consider how the youth will be the best possible as most important?

Meletus: I do

Soc: Come then, tell those men, who is it that makes them better. For it is clear that you know, since you care. For having discovered the one who corrupts them, as you say, namely myself, you bring me before these men and accuse me. Come then, tell them and inform them who it is. Do you see, Meletus, that you are silent and have nothing to say? And does it not seem to you to be disgraceful and a sufficient proof of the very thing I say—that you never cared? Tell me, my good man, who makes them better?

Mel: The laws.

e **Soc:** But that is not what I am asking, best of men, but rather what human being is it who first of all knows this very thing—the laws.

Mel: These ones, Socrates, the judges.

Soc: How do you mean, Meletus? Are these ones here able to educate the young and make them better?

Mel: Most definitely.

Soc: All of them, or some of them and some not?

Mel: All.

Soc: You speak well, by Hera, and of a great abundance of benefactors. What then? The ones listening, do they make them better or not?

25a **Mel:** Them also.

Soc: What about the councilmen?

Mel: The councilmen too.

Soc: Then, Meletus, the ones in the Assembly, the Assemblymen, they do not corrupt the young? Or do they also make them better?

Mel: Those as well.

Soc: Then it seems that all the Athenians make them noble and good except me; I alone corrupt them. Is this what you are asserting?

---

21 *Daimonia* are certain bastard children of the gods, and, therefore, are appropriate go-betweens joining Socrates and the divine.

Mel: I do assert this most emphatically.

b **Soc:** You charge me with a great misfortune. Now, answer me. Does it also seem to be the same to you with respect to horses? Do all human beings make them better, but one particular one is the corrupter? Or is it wholly contrary to this, that one particular one is able to make them better—or the very few who are skilled with horses, whereas the many, if they ever have to do with horses and use them, make them worse? Is it not thus, Meletus, with respect to both horses and all other animals?

c It certainly is, whether you or Anytus deny it or affirm it. For it would be a great happiness for the young if one alone corrupts, and many other confer benefits. However, Meletus, you have sufficiently shown that you have never given any thought to the young, and you make clear your own lack of concern, as you care nothing for the things for which you have brought me to court.

But continue to tell us, Meletus, by Zeus, whether it is better to live with decent citizens or knaves. Answer sir, for I am asking of you nothing difficult. Do not knaves do something bad to those who are always near them, whereas the good something good?

Mel: Very much so.

d **Soc:** Is there anyone, then, who wishes to be harmed by those he is with rather than to be benefited? Answer, good man, for the law commands you to answer. Is there anyone who wishes to be harmed?

Mel: Surely not.

Soc: Come then, do you bring me here asserting that I corrupt the young voluntarily and make them more knavish, or involuntarily?

Mel: Voluntarily, I say.

Soc: What, then, Meletus, are you so much wiser at your time of life than me at mine, so that you know that the bad always do something bad to those nearest them, and the good something e good, while I have come into so much ignorance as not to know that if ever I do something vile to one of my companions, I will risk receiving in return something bad from him? And, yet, I do so much bad voluntarily, as you say? Of this I am not persuaded by you, Meletus, nor do I think is any other human being. But either I do not corrupt, or if I do corrupt, I do 26a it involuntarily, so that in both cases what you say is false.

And if I corrupt involuntarily, it is not the law to bring me here for such involuntary offenses but rather for you, in private, to take me aside and teach me and admonish me. For it is evident that if I learn, I will at least cease what I do involuntarily. But you fled being with me and teaching me, and were not willing, but you brought me here, where the law is to bring those who need punishment, but not learning.[22]

---

22 Socrates here alludes to his belief that virtue is knowledge and vice is ignorance, or that punishment is against nature because it places blame where there is none.

26b Thus, then, Athenian men, what I was saying is already evident—that Meletus never cared either much or little about these matters. Nonetheless, tell us, Meletus, how do you mean that I corrupt the youth? Is it not clear from the indictment which you brought, that it is by teaching them not to believe in the gods in whom the city believes, but in other *daimonia* that are novel? Do you not say that by teaching these things, I corrupt them?

Mel: Certainly, I most emphatically do say so.

c **Soc:** By these very gods, then, Meletus, of whom our discussion now is, speak to me and these men more clearly. For I cannot understand if you mean that I teach them to believe that there are some kind of gods—and thus that I myself believe that there are gods and am not myself completely without god,[23] nor do injustice in this respect, but that I do not believe in those in which the city believes, but in others, and this is your charge against me, that I believe in others. Or do you mean that I do not believe in any gods and that I teach this to others?

Mel: I say that you do not believe in gods at all.

d **Soc:** O wondrous Meletus, on account of what do you say this? Do I not, then, as other human beings, even believe that the sun and moon are gods?

Mel: No by Zeus, judges, as he asserts that the sun is stone and the moon is earth.

Soc: Do you think you are accusing Anaxagoras, dear Meletus? And do you thus despise these men and suppose them to be so inexperienced in letters as not to know that the book of Anaxagoras of Clazomene is full of these accounts.[24] And, moreover, that the young learn these things from me, which they can purchase at times in the orchestra for a drachma at most; and, then, to mock Socrates if he were to pretend they were his own, especially since they are so atypical. But, before Zeus, is it thus I appear to you? That I believe there is no god?

Mel: Absolutely not, by Zeus, in no way at all do you believe.

Soc: You are unbelievable, Meletus, even to yourself, as it seems to me. For this man, Athenian men, appears to me to be very hubristic and unrestrained and simply to have brought this indictment with some sort of hubris, intemperance, and youthful rashness. He seems like

27a someone testing me by composing a riddle: "Will Socrates the wise know that I am jesting and that I contradict myself, or will I deceive him and the rest of the audience?" For he seems to me to contradict himself in the indictment, as if he should say, Socrates does injustice

---

23 The English word atheist comes from the Greek which literally means without God.

24 Anaxagoras was a natural scientist who was also the teacher of Pericles. When Socrates abandons his earlier way of looking at the world, he says that he was rejecting the thought of Anaxagoras (Phaedo 97b8-99d2). The fact that Anaxagoras' books are readily available suggests that Athens was more tolerant of science than Socrates suggests. According to Plutarch, Anaxagoras was charged with impiety and fled the city, but the charge was perhaps more the result of his relation to Pericles than of Anaxagoras' philosophy. Perhaps the charges against Socrates were more the result of his relations to Charmides and Critias than to his philosophizing.

in not believing that there are gods and believing that there are gods. And surely this is the conduct of one who jests.[25]

Consider with me now, men, how he appears to me to assert this. And you answer us, Meletus. And you others, as I begged you at the outset, do not clamor if I speak in my accustomed way.

Is there any human being, Meletus, who believes that there are human affairs but does not believe that there are human beings?

Let him answer, men, and do not clamor incessantly. Is there anyone who does not believe that there are horses, but believes that there are affairs related to horses? Or anyone who does not believe in flute-players, but believes in matters related to flutes? There is not, O best of men. Lest you do not wish to answer, I speak to you and these others. But at least answer to this: "Is there anyone who believes in affairs related to *daimonia* but does does not believe in *daimons*?

Mel: There is not.

Soc: How helpful of you to answer reluctantly when compelled by these men. Now then, you assert that I believe in and teach things related to *daimons*. Therefore, whether old or new, according to your account, I do believe in things related to *daimons* and this you swore to in the indictment. But if I believe in things related to *daimons*, surely there is also much necessity for me to believe in *daimons*. Is it not thus? It sure is. I put you down as agreeing since you do not answer. But with respect to *daimons*, do we not believe they are gods or children of gods? Do you assert or not?

Mel: Much indeed.

Soc: Thus, then, I do believe in *daimons*, as you say, and if *daimons* are some kind of god, then it is this about which I say you riddle and jest: asserting that I do not believe in gods, though I believe in *daimons*.

But if *daimons* are certain bastard children of gods, either from nymphs or from some other of whom it is said, what human being believes in children of gods, but not in gods? For it would be strange, just as if someone believed in mules, children of horses or asses, but did not believe that there are horses or asses.

But Meletus, it cannot be other than that you brought this indictment either to try us in these things or because you were at a loss at what true injustice to allege against me. That you could persuade any human being, even one of little intelligence, that the same man believes there are things related to *daimons* and gods, and again that this same man believes in neither *daimons*, gods, nor heroes, there is no device.

---

25 Socrates believes that it is ridiculous for someone to believe in gods and not to believe in gods at the same time, which means that the gods exist or they do not exist. All thought that is theistic and atheistic is contradictory. Agnosticism appears problematic in this light.

But in fact, Athenian men, that I do not do injustice according to the indictment of Meletus does not seem to me to need much of an apology, but sufficient even is this. And with respect to what I said earlier, that I have incurred much hatred and from many men, be assured this is true. This is what will convict me, if I am convicted, not Meletus, nor Anytus, but the slander and envy of the multitude. It has convicted many other good men already, and I think it will convict me as well. And there is no danger that it will stop with me.

28b

Perhaps, then, someone might say, "Are you not ashamed, Socrates, for having engaged in the sort of pursuit from which you are now in danger of dying?" To that someone, with just words I would answer: "What you say is ignoble, fellow, if you think that a man, who is of even little use, ought to take into account the risk of living or dying, but ought to consider this alone when he acts: whether he is acting justly or unjustly and whether his deeds are of a good man or a bad. For according to your account, those who met their end at Troy would be contemptible, especially the son of Thetis. Instead of enduring anything shameful, he held danger in so much contempt that his mother, a goddess, spoke to him, something like this, I think, when he was ardent upon killing Hector; she says: "Son, if you revenge the death of your comrade Patroclus by killing Hector, thereupon, you yourself will die after Hector, destiny is upon you." He, on hearing this, made light of death and danger, dreading much more to live as a bad man and not avenge his friends. "Thereupon may I die," he says, "after I inflict punishment on the doer of injustice, so that I may not remain here ridiculous beside the curved ships, a burden to the ground."[26] Certainly you do not think he gave any thought to death and danger?

c

d

Thus, in truth, it is, men of Athens. Wherever anyone stations himself, holding that it is best, or has been stationed by a ruler, there he must remain and face the danger, as it appears to me, and not take into consideration death or anything else in comparison to what is disgraceful. Thus I should have performed dreadful acts, men of Athens, if, when the rulers whom you elected to govern me stationed me in Potidaiea and Amphipolis and at Delium,[27] I remained where they stationed me and faced the danger of dying like everyone else, yet when the god stationed me, as I thought and assumed, ordering me to live the life of philosophy and to examine myself and others, I should then leave my station because I feared death and anything else whatsoever.

e

29a

Dire indeed that would be, and then in truth someone might justly bring me to trial, asserting that I do not believe in the gods, as I would be disobeying the oracle, fearing death and thinking that I am wise when I am not. For to fear death, men, is in fact nothing other than to appear to be wise, while not being so. For it is to appear to know what one does not know; no one knows if death happens to be the greatest of all goods for a human being,

---

26   See *Iliad* Book XVIII, l.95–104.

27   In the *Symposium* (220d–221b), we are told that Socrates was courageous in retreat.

29b but the multitude fear it as if they know well that it is the greatest evil. How is this not that reprehensible ignorance, that of thinking that one knows what one does not know? But I, men, in this perhaps am also different from most human beings, and if I should assert that I am wiser than everyone in anything, it would be this: that as I do not know sufficiently about the things of Hades, I, therefore, also think that I do not know. But to do injustice and to disobey someone better than oneself, whether god or human being, I know is bad and shameful. Therefore, compared to the bad things which I know are bad, I will never fear to flee things that I do not know, which may even happen to be good, compared to the things I know are bad.

c Thus, not even if you dismiss me now and disobey Anytus, who claimed that either I should not have been brought here at all, or, since I was brought here, that it is impossible not to kill me, asserting to you that if I am acquitted, soon your sons will be completely corrupted from pusuing the things Socrates teaches, and if you should say to me with respect to this: "Socrates, now we will not obey Anytus; we will allow you to leave, but on this condition—that you no longer pursue this investigation or philosophize, and if you are

d found still doing this, you shall die." If you should allow me to leave, as I said, on these conditions, then I would say to you, "men of Athens, I welcome you and love you, but I will obey the god rather than you, and for so long as I breathe and am capable of it, I will surely not stop philosophizing, and I will exhort you and point out to any of you I happen to meet, saying the sorts of things I am accustomed to: "best of men, you are an Athenian from a city that is greatest and most renowned for wisdom and strength, are you not ashamed for being concerned with having as much as possible, as well as renown and honor, yet you have no

e concern for and give no thought to prudence and truth, and how your soul will be the best possible?" And if any of you debate it and say that he is concerned, I shall then not let him go and I will not depart, but will speak to him and question him and test him. And if he should appear to me not to possess virtue, but only says he does, I shall reproach him, saying that he

30a holds the things worth the most as least important, and the pettier things as more important. I will act thus to anyone I meet, younger or older and both foreigner and townsman, but especially the townsmen as you are closer to me in kin.

Let it be known that god commands this. And I think that until now no greater good has befallen the city than my service to the god. For I go about doing nothing other than

b persuading you, both young and old, not to care for bodies and money as earnestly as how your soul will be the best possible. I say, "Virtue does not come from money, but from virtue comes money and all the other good things for human beings both private and public."[28] If by saying these things I corrupt the youth, then it might be harmful. But if anyone says

---

28 Socrates thought that only the philosopher loved virtue, whereas others need to be taught that money will come from virtue. The idea is paradoxical since Socrates is poor.

that what I speak is other than this, he speaks without sense. With respect to these things, Athenian men, I would say, either obey Anytus or not, and either let me go or not, since I will not do otherwise, even if I were to die many times.

30c   Do not clamor, Athenian men, but stick to what I asked you and do not clamor at the things I say, but listen. For, as I think, you will benefit from listening, as I am going to tell you other things at which, perhaps, you will clamor, but do not do so on any account. Rest assured that if you kill me, being the man that I say I am, you will not harm me more than yourselves. For neither will Meletus nor Anytus harm me, he would not even be able to, for I

d do not think it is possible for a better man to be harmed by a worse. Perhaps he may kill, or banish, or dishonor me, and this man no doubt, and others as well, think that these are great evils, whereas I do not think so, but much rather to do what this man is now doing—trying to kill a man unjustly.

    Thus, I, Athenian men, am far from making an apology on my behalf, as one might think, but I do it on your behalf, lest by condemning me, you do something wrong with

e respect to the gift the god has given to you. For if you kill me, you will not easily find another of my kind, who, though it may sound absurd to say, has simply been set upon the city by the god, as upon a great and well-born horse that is somewhat slow, because of its great size, and needs to be awakened by a gadfly, so the god seems to have set me upon the city as such

31a a one. I awaken and persuade and reprove every one of you, and I do not cease besetting you the whole day. Men, another of this kind will surely not arise easily for you. Thus, if you obey me, you will spare me. But perhaps being irritated like the drowsy when they are awakened, you might obey Anytus and slap me, easily killing me. Then you would live the rest of your life in sleep, unless the god, in his care for you, sends you someone else.

b   That I happen to be someone of this kind, given by the god to the city, you may discern hence: it does not appear to be human to have neglected all my own things and to have endured that the affairs of my family be neglected for so many years now, whereas I always attend to your business, going to each of you in private, like a father or older brother might, persuading you to the concern for virtue. If I was benefiting from this, and receiving pay for my exhortations to these things, there would be some explanation, but it is the case, you yourselves see, that even the accusers, who shamelessly accused me in all other things, have

c not been able to become so completely shameless as to bring in a witness to testify that I ever took money or asked for it. For that I speak the truth, I think I offer a sufficient witness: my poverty.

    Perhaps, however, it might seem to be strange that, going around being a busybody in private, I give this counsel, but do not dare go before your multitudes to counsel in public.

d The reason for this is the one you have heard me tell many times and in many places, that something divine and daemonic comes to me, a voice that Meletus, making a comedy of it, mentioned in the indictment. This began with me in childhood, a sort of voice comes, and whenever it does, it keeps me from whatever I am about to do, but never urges me on.

This is what opposes my participation in politics, and this opposition appears to me to be entirely noble. For be assured, men of Athens, that if long ago, I had attempted to be politically active I would long ago have perished, and would have benefited neither you nor myself. Do not be angry with me for speaking the truth. For there is no human being who will be spared from either you or any other multitude, should he be single-mindedly

32a   opposed to and prevent many unjust and illegal things from taking place in the city, but it is necessary for one who really fights for the just to lead a private, rather than a public life, in order to preserve himself even for a brief time.

I will offer to you great proofs of this, not speeches but what you honor, deeds. Listen, then, to what has happened to me, that you may see that I would not yield to one man against the just on account of fear of death, though I would perish for not yielding. I will

b   tell you vulgar things, common to the law courts, yet true. For I, Athenian men, never held any office in the city but that of Councilman. And it happened that my tribe Antiochus constituted the prytany[29] when you wanted to judge as a group the ten generals, the ones who did not rescue the men from the naval battle, against the law as it appeared afterward to all of you.[30] Then, I alone of all the prytanes opposed you doing anything against the laws and I voted against you. And though the orators were ready to indict me and arrest me, and

c   you were ordering and urging them on, I thought that I should face danger with the law and the just on my side rather than like you, who on account of fear of prison or death, were counseling unjust things.

And this was when the city was still ruled democratically. But when it became an oligarchy, the Thirty[31] sent for five of us to the Tholos,[32] and ordered us to arrest Leon the Salaminian and bring him from Salamis for execution.[33] And they ordered many others to do many

---

29   A prytany is an administrative period. There were ten a year corresponding to each of the tribes, whose councilmen, selected by lot, served as prytanes.

30   The generals abandoned the dead and left some of the living for dead. According to Homeric poetry, these men were lost souls because they were never put to rest. The demagogue Theramenes aroused religious fear and indignation, as well as democratic jealousy against the generals, who were put on trial together, convicted, and executed. See Xenophon, *Hellenica*, I 7.

31   "The Thirty" refers to the oligarchs instituted by the Spartans at the end of the war. Among these were Critias and Charmides, with whom Socrates had some relation. His association with them, as well as with Alcibiades, might have encouraged the charges and indictment. Anytus, who Xenophon presents as the most vengeful of the accusers, was exiled during the brief reign of the Thirty, only to return as one of the leaders of the democracy. Xenophon suggests that Socrates' association with Alcibiades and Critias was the reason for the charge of corrupting the youth (*Memorabilia* I.2. 12–48).

32   The meeting place of the prytanes under the democracy.

33   Leon of Salamis was reputed for his justice, which no doubt stood as a reproach to the Thirty. They hoped to implicate as many as possible in his murder in order to spread the blame and soften the outrage. Socrates uses the example of Leon to shed some light on his own trial and conviction.

32d things of this kind, wishing that as many as possible would be implicated in the criminal charge. Then, however, I showed once more, not in speech but in deed, that I do not care about death, if it is not too rude to say, in the slightest way, but that all my care was to do no unjust or impious deed. For that government, as strong as it was, did not terrify me into doing anything unjust, but upon coming out of the Tholos, the four went to Salamis and arrested Leon, but I went home. And I might have died because of this, if that government e had not soon been destroyed. And of these things you will have many witnesses.

Do you think, then, that I would have survived so many years, if I had been in public affairs and had acted in a way befitting a good man, aiding the just things, and as one ought, considering this as most important? Far from it, Athenian men, nor would any other human being.

33a But I, throughout my entire life, if I was ever publicly active, it is apparent that I was the kind of man, and I was the same in private, who never conceded anything to anyone contrary to justice—neither to those my slanderers say are my students, nor to anybody else. I have never been the teacher of anyone, but if anyone desired to hear me speaking and going b about my business, whether young or old, I never refused it to him. Nor do I converse only when I receive money, and not when I do not receive any, but to rich and poor alike I give myself to questioning, and if anyone wishes to hear what I say, he can respond to me. And with respect to these, if any one of them becomes an upright man or not, I cannot be justly held responsible, because I have neither promised them any instruction nor taught them any. If anyone ever says that he learned from me or heard in private anything that anyone else had not, be sure that he does not speak the truth.

c But why do some delight in spending so much time with me? You have heard it, Athenian men! I have told you the whole truth—that they delight to hear those examined who think they are wise but are not, as it is not unpleasant. I have been commanded to practice this by the god, as I say, by divinations, and by dreams, and by every means that any divine decree ever commanded a human being to do anything at all. These things, Athenian men, are both true and easily tested. For if I am corrupting the youth now, and have already corrupted others, and if any of them, having become older, recognized that I even advised them badly in anything when they were young, then now, surely, they should have stood up to accuse me and take revenge for themselves. If they themselves were unwilling to do it, some of their families (fathers and brothers, and other relatives) should now have recalled it and taken revenge, if their families had suffered anything bad from me.

e However, there are present here many of them whom I see: first Crito here, my contemporary and my deme, the father of Critobulus here; then Lysanius the Sphettian, the father of Aeschines here; then there is Antiphon the Cephisean, the father of Eigenes. In addition, here are others, whose brothers have kept time in this manner: Theozotides' son Nicostratus,

34a the brother of Theodotus—Theodotus has died so he could not beg him to stop, and the son of Demodocus Paralus, whose brother was Theages. And here Adeimantus son of Ariston, whose brother is Plato here, and Aeantodorus whose brother is Apollodorus here.

I could mention many others to you, some of whom Meletus particularly ought to have offered as a witness in the course of his own speech. If he forgot, let him now offer one, I will give way to him and let him speak if he has anyone of the kind. But totally to the contrary of this, you will find, men, that everyone is ready to assist me, the corrupter, who does evil to their families as Meletus and Anytus say. Those who have themselves been corrupted might

b have a reason to come to my assistance, but those who have not been corrupted, the relatives, men of older years, what other reason can they have to assist me except the correct and just one, that they know Meletus speaks falsely whereas I am being truthful?

Well then, men, these and perhaps other things are pretty much the things I have to say in my defense. Perhaps some among you may be indignant upon recollecting himself, if he

c should have, in contesting a trial even smaller than this trial, begged and supplicated the judges with many tears, bringing forward his children and many other of his relatives and friends, in order to be pitied as much as possible, whereas I will do none of this, despite that in this as well, I might appear to be risking the greatest danger. Perhaps someone thinking about this may become rather set against me, and being angered by this very thing, he might

d set his vote down in anger, should there be anyone of you like this. I, however, do not think that there is, but if there is, it seems to me decent to say to him, "I, best of men, do indeed have some relatives", for it is just as Homer says: "not even have I sprung from an oak or a rock but from human beings,"[34] so that I have a family and sons too, three of them, Athenian men, one now a youth and two still children. I will, nonetheless, not bring them forward to beg you to vote to acquit me.

e Why, then, will I not do this? Not because I am stubborn, Athenian men, nor because I disrespect you. Whether or not I am undaunted by death is another matter, but with respect to reputation, mine and yours, and the whole city's, it does not appear to me noble for me to do any of these things as I am old and have this name, whether true or false, it is repeated at

35a least that Socrates is different from the generality of human beings in some manner.

If those among you who are reputed to excel, whether in wisdom or courage or any other virtue whatsoever, should act in such a manner, then it would be shameful. I have often seen some who, when brought to judgment, though reputed to be something, do wondrous deeds, as thinking they will suffer something dreadful if they die, and as if they would be immortal if you did not kill them. They seem to me to disgrace the city,

---

34 In *Odyssey* XIX. 163 and *Iliad* XXII. 126 this phrase is used by Penelope and Hector, respectively, to connect our identities and emotions to our origins. Socrates' Delphic mission, to the contrary, encourages an attachment to truth and reputation contrary to sentimentality. His care for his sons is to make sure that they are stung with questions like every other citizen.

35b so that a foreigner might suppose that those Athenians who excel in virtue, whom they choose from among themselves for their own public offices and other honors, are no better than women. For those of you, Athenian men, who are reputed to be something in like manner, you should neither do these things, nor, whenever we do them, should you allow it. But you should make manifest that you would much rather vote to convict him who introduces these piteous dramas and makes the city look ridiculous, than him who stays silent.

c Reputation aside, men, it does not seem to me to be just to beg the judge, or to be acquitted through begging, but rather to teach and to persuade, for a judge does not sit to hand out justice as a favor, but to judge, as he has not sworn to favor whoever seems likeable to him, but to judge according to the laws. Therefore, we should not accustom you, and you should not be accustomed, to making false oaths, as neither of us would be pious.

d So do not think that I, Athenian men, ought to practice such things toward you which I consider to be neither noble, nor just, nor pious, as well, by Zeus, certainly not when I am being accused of impiety by Meletus here. For clearly, if I should persuade you and force you through begging, having sworn an oath, I would be teaching you that there are no gods, and while making my defense speech, would accuse myself of not believing in gods. But that is far from being so, for I believe, men of Athens, as none of my accusers do, and I give it to you and the god to judge me in the manner that is best both for me and for you.

[*A vote is taken and the majority finds him guilty. Meletus proposes the death penalty and Socrates offers a counter proposal.*]

36a There are many concurrences, men of Athens, that keep me from being indignant at this outcome, that you voted to condemn me, and one of them is that the outcome was not unexpected by me. I, however, wonder at the number of votes on either side, as I did not think that [the vote] would be by a few but by many. But now it appears that if only thirty votes had fallen otherwise, I would have been acquitted. So far as Meletus is concerned, it seems to me that I have already been acquitted; and not only have I been acquitted but it is

b clear to all that, had not Anytus and Lycon come forward to accuse me, he would have to pay a fine of a thousand drachmas, as he would not have obtained a fifth of the votes.

As is the case, the man proposes for me the penalty of death. Well now. What shall I in return propose to you, men of Athens? Is it not clear that it should be that for which I am worthy? What is it, then? What do I deserve to suffer or pay because during my life I remained quiet and did not care about the things for which the many care—money and the household, and military command and popular oration, as well as the other offices, and the

c conspiracies and factions that grow in the city—as I considered myself too decent to survive if I took part in these things? I did not enter into affairs where, if I entered, I would be of no benefit to either you or to myself, but to each of you I went in private to do the greatest benefaction, I affirm, and I endeavored to persuade each of you not to care for anything

36d of his own before having cared for himself—how he will be the best and most prudent possible, and not to care for the things of the city before having cared for the city itself, and to care for other things in the same manner. What penalty, then, do I deserve, being as I am? Something good, men of Athens, at least if you give me what I deserve according to my true worth—and, moreover, a good of a kind that would be fitting for me. What then is fitting for a man of poverty, a benefactor, and one who needs leisure to exhort you? There is nothing more fitting, Athenian men, than that such a man be given his meals in the Prytaneum,[35]

e and much more fitting than if any one of you won a victory at Olympia with a horse or a chariot, either two or four horse. For such a one makes you seem to be happy, whereas I make you so; and he does not need sustenance, but I am in need. Therefore, it is necessary for me to propose what I deserve consistent with justice. I propose then to be awarded my meals in the Prytaneum.

37a Perhaps, however, in proposing this, I seem to you to speak in almost the same proud manner as I spoke about lament and supplication. But it is not the case, Athenian men, but rather that I am convinced that I do not voluntarily do injustice to any human being, though I have not persuaded you, as we have conversed with each other for but a short time. You would be persuaded, as I suppose, if you had a law like other human beings, not to try

b someone in a matter of death in one day alone, but over many. But as things stand, it is not easy to erase great slanders in a short time.

Being convinced, then, that I do not do injustice to anyone, I am far from doing injustice to myself by declaiming against myself, that I myself deserve something bad, and by proposing this sort of thing as my desert. What should I fear? That I might suffer what Meletus proposes for me, to which I say that I do not know whether it is good or bad. Instead of this, should I choose something of the things I know well to be bad, and propose that? Should I

c propose prison? And why should I live imprisoned, a slave to the authority that is regularly established there, the Eleven?[36] Or should I propose money and imprisonment until I pay? But for me this is the same penalty of which I just spoke, as I have no money to pay.

Should I then propose exile? For perhaps you would allow me this as my desert. I should indeed have much love of soul, men of Athens, if I were so unreasonable as not to be able

d to see that you, who are my fellow-citizens, have been unable to endure my way of life and speeches, but rather that they have become burdensome and hateful to you, so that you now seek to be free of them—will others then easily bear them? Far from it, Athenian men. Fine indeed would life be for me, a human being of my age to be exiled going from city to city,

---

35 Meals at the Prytaneum were reserved for the greatest benefactors of the city.
36 Socrates is speaking of the eleven prison authorities, chosen by lot from the citizenry.

always being driven out. For I know well that wherever I might go, the youth will listen to me when I speak, as they do here. And if I repel them, they will themselves drive me out, persuading their elders. But if I do not repel them, then their fathers and families will drive me out on account of these same youths.

37e

Yet, perhaps someone will say: "Socrates, can you not live in exile from us, by being silent and keeping quiet?" This is the hardest thing of all of which to persuade some of you. For if I say that it would be to disobey the god, and on this account it is impossible to keep quiet, you will not be persuaded by me, supposing that I am being ironic. If, on the other hand, I say that this is a very great good for a human being—to make speeches every day about virtue and other things of which you have heard me speak when examining myself and others, and that for a human being the unexamined life is not worth living, still less, when I say these things, will you be persuaded by me. Yet, such is the case, as I affirm, men, however to persuade you is not easy.

38a

b

And at the same time I am not accustomed to think of myself as deserving something bad. If I had money, I would have proposed as much as I could afford to pay, since that would do me no harm. But it is the case that I do not have any money—unless of course you want me to pay what I am able. Perhaps, then, I could pay you a minae of silver. So I propose that amount.

But, Plato here, Athenian men, and Crito, Critobulus, and Appolodorus urge me to propose thirty minae and they will guarantee it. So I propose that amount and they will be sufficient guarantors of the money for you.

[*The jury votes to condemn Socrates to death*]

c

You, in order to save a little time, men of Athens, will get a reputation and be charged with the guilt of having killed Socrates, a wise man, by those wishing to defame the city. For those who wish to defame will assert that I am wise even if I am not. In any case, if you would have waited a short time, this would have taken place on its own. You surely see my age, that it is far advanced in life and close to death. I do not say this to all of you, but to those who voted to condemn me to death.

d

And I say this as well to these same persons. Perhaps you think, men of Athens, that I have been convicted for want of the kinds of speeches that would have persuaded you, as if I had thought that I should do or say anything to escape the penalty. Far from it. I have been convicted for a want, not of speeches, but of boldness and shamelessness, and willingness to

e

say the kinds of things to you that would have pleased you most to hear—to have me wail and lament and do and say many other things unworthy of me, as I affirm, but such as you have been accustomed to hear from others. But neither then did I think that I ought to do anything, in order to avoid danger, unworthy of a free man, nor do I regret having defended myself as I did. I would much prefer to die defending myself like this than to live like that.

39a For neither in a trial nor in a war should I or anybody else plan to escape death by doing anything possible. In battle it is frequently evident that one might escape death by laying down one's arms and turning to supplicate one's pursuers. And, there are many other devices in every danger to avoid death, if one dares to do and to say anything. But I suspect this is not difficult, men, to avoid death, but that it is much more difficult to avoid wickedness,

b for it runs faster than death. And now I, being slow and old, am taken by the slower of the two, but my accusers being clever and agile, are taken by the faster—wickedness. And now I leave, condemned by you to death, but they are by the truth convicted of wretchedness and injustice. And I abide by my sentence, as do they. These things, perhaps, must be as they are, and I suppose there is just measure in them.

c Next, I desire to prophesize to you, O you who voted to condemn me. For now I am where human beings are apt to prophesize, when they are about to die. I say to you who have condemned me to death, that vengeance will come to you straight away after my death, and far more severe by Zeus, than the kind you have given me by killing me. For you have done this thinking you will be freed from giving an account of your life, but rather quite the

d contrary will happen to you, as I affirm. There will be more who will confound you, whom I have been restraining though you did not notice them. And they will be more severe in so far as they are younger, and you will be angrier. For if you think that by killing human beings you will keep someone from reproaching you for not living correctly, then you do not think finely. For that kind of escape is neither at all possible nor noble. But rather the noblest and easiest kind is not to restrain others, and to prepare oneself to be the best possible. Having foretold these things to you who voted to condemn me, I am set free.

e But with you who voted for me, I would gladly converse about what has taken place, while the officials are busy and I do not yet go to the place where, when I do go, I must die.

40a Stay with me, men, for this time. Nothing keeps us from telling stories to one another for as long as possible. For I am willing to show you, as to friends, the meaning of whatever it is that has just occurred to me. To me, at least, judges, and by calling you judges I address you correctly, something wondrous has happened. For my customary prophesy from the daimonion was always very frequent on all other former occasions, opposing me even in trifling matters if I was about to do something wrong. But now you yourselves behold what has happened to me, which anyone might think to be, and which is believed to be, the

b ultimate evil. Yet, when I departed from my home this morning, the sign of the god did not oppose me, nor when I came up here to the trial, nor anywhere in my speech when I was about to say anything, despite that in other speeches it has frequently restrained me while I was talking. But now, with respect to this proceeding, it has not opposed me, in either deed or speech. What, then, do I think is the cause of this? I will tell you. It is likely that what

c has befallen to me is good and that it is not possible that those think correctly who think being dead is bad. To me, a great proof of this has occurred, for it is not possible that the accustomed sign should not have opposed me, unless I were about to do some good.

But let us keep in mind the following possibility in which there is a great hope that it is good. For being dead is either of two things. It is either like being annihilated and the dead man has no perception of anything, or as it is said, it is a kind of change and passage of the soul from here to another place.

40d   And if there is no perception, but it is like a sleep in which the sleeper has no dream whatsoever, death would be a wondrous gain. For I think that if someone had to pick the night in which he slept so soundly that he did not even dream, and had to compare the other nights and days of his life to that one, and then upon reflection had to compare how many days and nights in his own life he had lived better and more pleasantly than that one, then I

e   think that, not just a private man, but the Great King himself would find them easy to count compared to the other days and nights. Now, if death is something like that, I at least say it is a gain, as in this manner, all time seems to be nothing more than a single night.

On the other hand, if death is like a journey from here to another place, and if what is said is true, that all the dead are indeed there, what greater good could there be than that,

41a   judges? For if arriving in Hades,[37] released from those here who claim to be judges, discovering judges in truth—the very ones who are said to judge there—Minos and Rhadamanthys, and Aeacus and Triptolemus, and those other of the demi-gods, who were just during their own lives, would this be a paltry journey? Or again, how much would any of you give to be with Orpheus and Musaeus and Hesiod and Homer? I, indeed, am willing to die often,

b   if these things are true, as for me in particular, passing time there would be wondrous. I would compare my own experiences with theirs when chancing upon Palamedes,[38] or Telemonian Ajax,[39] or anyone else of the ancients who died on account of an unjust verdict. And I think it would not be unpleasant.

And in particular the greatest thing, to spend time examining and discovering those there, as I do to the ones here, whoever of them is wise and whoever thinks he is but is not.

---

37   Socrates is taking issue with the account of Hades given by Odysseus (*Odyssey*, Book XI). A comparison between these two accounts provides insight into Plato's intention.

38   Palamedes, whose name means literally a "handy or contriving man," was one of the Greek heroes in the Trojan war depicted in the tales after Homer. His tragedy was treated also in plays by Aeschylus, Sophocles, and Euripides, all now lost. The myth about him varies, although it runs generally as follows. Odysseus had feigned madness to avoid joining the Greeks in the Trojan war, but the clever Palamedes disclosed his ruse by means of a test: he either placed Odysseus' infant son (Telemachus) in Odysseus' path while he was pretending to plow his field dementedly, or he threatened to kill the infant with a sword. Odysseus saved his son, thereby revealing his sanity. Odysseus then contrived a plot to murder him in revenge: he forged a letter from Priam to Palamedes that promised a payoff in gold if he were to betray the Greeks; he then buried the identical amount in Palamedes' place at camp. After reading the letter, Agamemnon discovered the gold and delivered Palamedes into the hands of the army, who stoned him to death (cf. Apollodorus, *Epitome* 3.7–8; Hyginus, *Fabulae* 95.2, 105). He is mentioned especially for his proverbial cleverness. (See in particular Euripides, Orestes 432; Aristophanes, Frogs 1448–52.)

39   Ajax committed suicide.

41c What would one give, men of the jury, to examine the one who led the great army against Troy, or Odysseus, or Sisyphus, or the thousand others whom one could mention, both men and women, with whom to converse and to be with and to examine would be inconceivable happiness? Certainly those there do not kill for that. For they are happier than those here, in other things as well as being deathless for the rest of time, provided the things said are true.

d But you, men of the jury, should also be of good hope toward death and to hold in mind this certain thing as true—that for a good man there is nothing bad, whether alive or dead, neither are the gods without care for that one's troubles, nor have my current troubles come from themselves, but it is clear to me that it is now better for me to be dead and to have been freed from my troubles. On account of this, the sign did not turn me aside, and I am neither in any way angry at those who voted to condemn me, nor my accusers. Though it was not

e with this in mind that they voted to condemn me and accused me, rather they thought to harm me. For this, they deserve to be blamed.

This much, however, I beg of them. Punish my sons when they grow up, men, paining them as I have pained you, should they appear to you to care for money or anything else more than virtue. And if they are reputed to be something, though being nothing, reproach them as I have you—that they do not care for the things they should and that they think they

42a are something when they are worth-nothing. And if you do these things, we will have been treated justly by you, I myself and also my sons.

But now it is time to depart—I to die and you to live. Which of us takes a better path is unclear to everyone except the god.

Clouds

By Aristophanes, translated by Ian Johnston

DRAMATIS PERSONAE

STREPSIADES: a middle-aged Athenian
PHEIDIPPIDES: a young Athenian, son of Strepsiades
XANTHIAS: a slave serving Strepsiades
STUDENT: one of Socrates' pupils in the Thinkery
SOCRATES: chief teacher in the Thinkery
CHORUS OF CLOUDS
THE BETTER ARGUMENT: an older man
THE WORSE ARGUMENT: a young man
PASIAS: one of Strepsiades' creditors
WITNESS: a friend of Pasias
AMYNIAS: one of Strepsiades' creditors
STUDENTS OF SOCRATES

[Scene: In the centre of the stage area is a house with a door to Socrates' educational establishment, the Thinkery.* On one side of the stage is Strepsiades' house, in front of which are two beds. Outside the Thinkery there is a small clay statue of a round goblet, and outside Strepsiades' house there is a small clay statue of Hermes. It is just before dawn. Strepsiades and Pheidippides are lying asleep in the two beds. Strepsiades tosses and turns restlessly. Pheidippides lets a very loud fart in his sleep. Strepsiades sits up wide awake]

STREPSIADES

    Damn! Lord Zeus, how this night drags on and on!
    It's endless. Won't daylight ever come?
    I heard a cock crowing a while ago,
    but my slaves kept snoring. In the old days,
    they wouldn't have dared. Oh, damn and blast this war—
    so many problems. Now I'm not allowed
    to punish my own slaves.* And then there's him—
    this fine young man, who never once wakes up,
    but farts the night away, all snug in bed,
        wrapped up in five wool coverlets. Ah well,   10

[10]

    I guess I should snuggle down and snore away.

[Strepsiades lies down again and tries to sleep. Pheidippides farts again. Strepsiades finally gives up trying to sleep]

STREPSIADES

    I can't sleep. I'm just too miserable,
    what with being eaten up by all this debt—
    thanks to this son of mine, his expenses,
    his racing stables. He keeps his hair long
    and rides his horses—he's obsessed with it—
    his chariot and pair. He dreams of horses.*
    And I'm dead when I see the month go by—
    with the moon's cycle now at twenty days,

---

*   *Thinkery:* The Greek word *phrontisterion* (meaning school or academy) is translated here as Thinkery, a term borrowed from William Arrowsmith's translation of *The Clouds.*

*   During the war it was easy for slaves to run away into enemy territory, so their owners had to treat them with much more care.

*   Wearing one's hair long and keeping race horses were characteristics of the sons of very rich families.

as interest payments keep on piling up.*   20

[Calling to a slave]

Hey, boy! Light the lamp. Bring me my accounts.

[Enter the slave Xanthias with light and tablets]

Let me take these and check my creditors.
How many are there? And then the interest—   [20]
I'll have to work that out. Let me see now . . .
What do I owe? "Twelve minai to Pasias?"
Twelve minai to Pasias! What's that for?
O yes, I know—that's when I bought that horse,
the pedigree nag. What a fool I am!
I'd sooner have a stone knock out my eye.*

PHEIDIPPIDES [talking in his sleep]
Philon, that's unfair! Drive your chariot straight.   30

STREPSIADES
That there's my problem—that's what's killing me.
Even fast asleep he dreams of horses!

PHEIDIPPIDES [in his sleep]
In this war-chariot race how many times
do we drive round the track?

STREPSIADES
                                        You're driving me,
your father, too far round the bend. Let's see,
after Pasias, what's the next debt I owe?   [30]
"Three minai to Amynias." For what?
A small chariot board and pair of wheels?

---

*   The interest on Strepsiades' loans would increase once the lunar month came to an end.
*   *twelve minai* is 100 drachmas, a considerable sum. The Greek reads "the horse branded with a *koppa* mark." That brand was a guarantee of its breeding.

PHEIDIPPIDES [in his sleep]
>Let the horse have a roll. Then take him home.

STREPSIADES
>You, my lad, have been rolling in my cash.   40
>Now I've lost in court, and other creditors
>are going to take out liens on all my stuff
>to get their interest.

PHEIDIPPIDES [waking up]
>What's the matter, dad?
>You've been grumbling and tossing around there
>all night long.

STREPSIADES
>I keep getting bitten—
>some bum bailiff in the bedding.

PHEIDIPPIDES
>   Ease off, dad.
>Let me get some sleep.

STREPSIADES
>   All right, keep sleeping.
>Just bear in mind that one fine day these debts   [40]
>will all be your concern.

[Pheidippides rolls over and goes back to sleep]

>Damn it, anyway.
>I wish that matchmaker had died in pain—   50
>the one who hooked me and your mother up.
>I'd had a lovely time up to that point,
>a crude, uncomplicated, country life,
>lying around just as I pleased, with honey bees,

and sheep and olives, too. Then I married—
the niece of Megacles—who was the son
of Megacles. I was a country man,
and she came from the town—a real snob,
extravagant, just like Coesyra.*
When I married her and we both went to bed,   60
I stunk of fresh wine, drying figs, sheep's wool—   [50]
an abundance of good things. As for her,
she smelled of perfume, saffron, long kisses,
greed, extravagance, lots and lots of sex.*
Now, I'm not saying she was a lazy bones.
She used to weave, but used up too much wool.
To make a point I'd show this cloak to her
and say, "Woman, your weaving's far too thick."*

[The lamp goes out]

XANTHIAS
    We've got no oil left in the lamp.

STREPSIADES
    Damn it!
    Why'd you light such a thirsty lamp? Come here.   70
    I need to thump you.

XANTHIAS
    Why should you hit me?

STREPSIADES
    Because you stuck too thick a wick inside.

[The slave ignores Strepsiades and walks off into the house]

---

* *Megacles* was a common name in a very prominent aristocratic family in Athens. *Coesyra* was the mother of a Megacles from this family, a woman well known for her wasteful expenditures and pride.
* The Greek has "of Colias and Genetyllis" names associated with festivals celebrating women's sexual and procreative powers.
* Packing the wool tight in weaving uses up more wool and therefore costs more. Strepsiades holds up his cloak which is by now full of holes.

After that, when this son was born to us— [60]
I'm talking about me and my good wife—
we argued over what his name should be.
She was keen to add -hippos to his name,
like Xanthippos, Callipedes, or Chaerippos.*
Me, I wanted the name Pheidonides,
his grandpa's name. Well, we fought about it,
and then, after a while, at last agreed. 80
And so we called the boy Pheidippides.
She used to cradle the young lad and say,
"When you're grown up, you'll drive your chariot
to the Acropolis, like Megacles,
in a full-length robe . . ." I'd say, "No— [70]
you'll drive your goat herd back from Phelleus,
like your father, dressed in leather hides . . ."
He never listened to a thing I said.
And now he's making my finances sick—
a racing fever. But I've spent all night 90
thinking of a way to deal with this whole mess,
and I've found one route, something really good—
it could work wonders. If I could succeed,
if I could convince him, I'd be all right.
Well, first I'd better wake him up. But how?
What would be the gentlest way to do it?

[Strepsiades leans over and gently nudges Pheidippides]

Pheidippides . . . my little Pheidippides . . .

PHEIDIPPIDES [very sleepily]
    What is it, father? [80]

STREPSIADES

                    Give me a kiss—
then give me your right hand.

_____

* -*hippos* means "horse." The mother presumably wanted her son to have the marks of the aristocratic classes. Xanthippos was the name of Pericles' father and his son. The other names are less obviously aristocratic or uncommon.

[Pheidippides sits up, leans over, and does what his father has asked]

PHEIDIPPIDES

                    All right. There.

What's going on?

STREPSIADES

                Tell me this—do you love me?   100

PHEIDIPPIDES

Yes, I do, by Poseidon, lord of horses.

STREPSIADES

Don't give me that lord of horses stuff—
he's the god who's causing all my troubles.
But now, my son, if you really love me,
with your whole heart, then follow what I say.

PHEIDIPPIDES

What do you want to tell me I should do?

STREPSIADES

Change your life style as quickly as you can,
then go and learn the stuff I recommend.

PHEIDIPPIDES

So tell me—what are you asking me?

STREPSIADES: You'll do just what I say?

PHEIDIPPIDES

                    Yes, I'll do it—   110   [90]

I swear by Dionysus.

STREPSIADES

                    All right then.

Look over there—you see that little door,
there on that little house?

PHEIDIPPIDES

                              Yes, I see it.
What are you really on about, father?

STREPSIADES

That's the Thinkery—for clever minds.
In there live men who argue and persuade.
They say that heaven's an oven damper—
it's all around us—we're the charcoal.
If someone gives them cash, they'll teach him
how to win an argument on any cause,   120
just or unjust.

PHEIDIPPIDES

Who are these men?

STREPSIADES

I'm not sure   [100]
just what they call themselves, but they're good men,
fine, deep-thinking intellectual types.

PHEIDIPPIDES

Nonsense! They're a worthless bunch. I know them—
you're talking about pale-faced charlatans,
who haven't any shoes, like those rascals
Socrates and Chaerephon.*

STREPSIADES

                              Shush, be quiet.
Don't prattle on such childish rubbish.
If you care about your father's daily food,
give up racing horses and, for my sake,   130
join their company.

---

* *Chaerephon*: a well-known associate of Socrates.

PHEIDIPPIDES

    By Dionysus, no!
    Not even if you give me as a gift
    pheasants raised by Leogoras.*

STREPSIADES

                    Come on, son—   [110]
    you're the dearest person in the world to me.
    I'm begging you. Go there and learn something.

PHEIDIPPIDES

    What is it you want me to learn?

STREPSIADES

                    They say
    that those men have two kinds of arguments—
    the Better, whatever that may mean,
    and the Worse. Now, of these two arguments,
    the Worse can make an unjust case and win.   140
    So if, for me, you'll learn to speak like this,
    to make an unjust argument, well then,
    all those debts I now owe because of you
    I wouldn't have to pay—no need to give
    an obol's worth to anyone.*

PHEIDIPPIDES

                  No way.
    I can't do that. With no colour in my cheeks
    I wouldn't dare to face those rich young Knights.*   [120]

STREPSIADES

    Then, by Demeter, you won't be eating
    any of my food—not you, not your yoke horse,

---

*   *pheasants* were a rich rarity in Athens. *Leogoras* was a very wealthy Athenian.
*   *an obol* was a relatively small amount, about a third of a day's pay for a jury member.
*   *Knights* is a term used to describe the affluent young men who made up the cavalry. Pheidippides has been mixing with people far beyond his father's means.

nor your branded thoroughbred. To hell with you— 150
I'll toss you right out of this house.*

PHEIDIPPIDES

All right—
but Uncle Megacles won't let me live
without my horses. I'm going in the house.
I don't really care what you're going to do.

[Pheidippides stands up and goes inside the house. Strepsiades gets out of bed]

STREPSIADES
Well, I'll not take this set back lying down.
I'll pray to the gods and then go there myself—
I'll get myself taught in that Thinkery.
Still, I'm old and slow—my memory's shot.
How'm I going to learn hair-splitting arguments, [130]
all that fancy stuff? But I have to go. 160
Why do I keep hanging back like this?
I should be knocking on the door.

[Strepsiades marches up to the door of the Thinkery and knocks]

Hey, boy . . . little boy.

STUDENT [from inside]
Go to Hell!

[The door opens and the student appears]

Who's been knocking on the door?

STREPSIADES
I'm Strepsiades, the son of Pheidon,
from Cicynna.

---

* A *yoke horse* was part of the four-horse team which was harnessed to a yoke on the inside.

STUDENT

> By god, what a stupid man,
> to kick the door so hard. You just don't think.
> You made a newly found idea miscarry!

STREPSIADES

> I'm sorry. But I live in the country,
> far away from here. Tell me what's happened.
> What's miscarried?

STUDENT

> It's not right to mention it,   170   [140]
> except to students.

STREPSIADES

> You needn't be concerned—
> you can tell me. I've come here as a student,
> to study at the Thinkery.

STUDENT

> I'll tell you, then.
> But you have to think of these as secrets,
> our holy mysteries. A while ago,
> a flea bit Chaerephon right on the eye brow,
> and then jumped onto Socrates' head.
> So Socrates then questioned Chaerephon
> about how many lengths of its own feet
> a flea could jump.

STREPSIADES

> How'd he measure that?   180

STUDENT

> Most ingeniously. He melted down some wax,
> then took the flea and dipped two feet in it.
> He took those off and measured out the space.

STREPSIADES

By Lord Zeus, what intellectual brilliance!

STUDENT

Would you like to hear more of Socrates,
another one of his ideas? What do you say?

STREPSIADES

Which one? Tell me . . .

[The student pretends to be reluctant]

I'm begging you.

STUDENT

All right.

Chaerephon of Sphettus once asked Socrates
whether, in his opinion, a gnat buzzed   190
through its mouth or through its anal sphincter.

STREPSIADES

What did Socrates say about the gnat?

STUDENT

He said that the gnat's intestinal tract   [160]
was narrow—therefore air passing through it,
because of the constriction, was pushed with force
towards the rear. So then that orifice,
being a hollow space beside a narrow tube,
transmits the noise caused by the force of air.

STREPSIADES

So a gnat's arse hole is a giant trumpet!
O triply blessed man who could do this,   200
anatomize the anus of a gnat!
A man who knows a gnat's guts inside out
would have no trouble winning law suits.

STUDENT

    Just recently he lost a great idea—
    a lizard stole it!

STREPSIADES

    How'd that happen? Tell me.   [170]

STUDENT

    He was studying movements of the moon—
    its trajectory and revolutions.
    One night, as he was gazing up, open mouthed,
    staring skyward, a lizard on the roof
    relieved itself on him.

STREPSIADES

    A lizard crapped on Socrates!   210
    That's good!

STUDENT

    Then, last night we had no dinner.

STREPSIADES

    Well, well. What did Socrates come up with,
    to get you all some food to eat?

STUDENT

    He spread some ashes thinly on the table,
    then seized a spit, went to the wrestling school,
    picked up a queer, and robbed him of his cloak,
    then sold the cloak to purchase dinner.*

STREPSIADES

    And we still admire Thales after that?*   [180]

---

* I adopt Sommerstein's useful reading of this very elliptical passage, which interprets the Greek word *diabetes* as meaning a passive homosexual (rather than its usual meaning, "a pair of compasses"—both senses deriving from the idea of spreading legs apart). The line about selling the cloak is added to clarify the sense.

* *Thales* was a very famous thinker from the sixth century BC.

Come on, now, open up the Thinkery—
let me see Socrates without delay.   220
I'm dying to learn. So open up the door.

[The doors of the Thinkery slide open to reveal Socrates' students studying on a porch (not inside a room). They are in variously absurd positions and are all very thin and pale]

By Hercules, who are all these creatures!
What country are they from?

STUDENT

You look surprised.
What do they look like to you?

STREPSIADES

Like prisoners—
those Spartan ones from Pylos.* But tell me—
Why do these ones keep staring at the earth?

STUDENT

They're searching out what lies beneath the ground.

STREPSIADES

Ah, they're looking for some bulbs. Well now,
you don't need to worry any longer,
not about that. I know where bulbs are found,   230   [190]
lovely big ones, too. What about them?
What are they doing like that, all doubled up?

STUDENT

They're sounding out the depths of Tartarus.

STREPSIADES

Why are their arse holes gazing up to heaven?

---

* The Athenians had captured a number of Spartans at Pylos in 425 and brought them to Athens where they remained in captivity.

STUDENT
Directed studies in astronomy.

[The Student addresses the other students in the room]

Go inside. We don't want Socrates
to find you all in here.

STREPSIADES
Not yet, not yet.
Let them stay like this, so I can tell them
what my little problem is.

STUDENT
It's not allowed.
They can't spend too much time outside,   240
not in the open air.

[The students get up from their studying positions and disappear into the interior of the Thinkery.
Strepsiades starts inspecting the equipment on the walls and on the tables]

STREPSIADES
My goodness,
what is this thing? Explain it to me.   [200]

STUDENT
That there's astronomy.

STREPSIADES
And what's this?

STUDENT
That's geometry.

STREPSIADES
What use is that?

STUDENT

It's used to measure land.

STREPSIADES

You mean those lands
handed out by lottery.*

STUDENT

Not just that—
it's for land in general.

STREPSIADES

A fine idea—
useful . . . democratic, too.

STUDENT

Look over here—
here's a map of the entire world. See?
Right there, that's Athens.

STREPSIADES

What do you mean?   250
I don't believe you. There are no jury men—
I don't see them sitting on their benches.

STUDENT

No, no—this space is really Attica.*

STREPSIADES

Where are the citizens of Cicynna,   [210]
the people in my deme?*

STUDENT

They're right here.

---

* Athenians sometimes apportioned land by lot outside the state which they had appropriated from other people.
* Attica is the territory surrounded by and belonging to Athens.
* A deme was a political unit in Athens. Membership in a particular deme was a matter of inheritance from one's father.

This is Euboea, as you can see,
beside us, really stretched a long way out.

STREPSIADES

I know—we pulled it apart, with Pericles.*
Where abouts is Sparta?

v
STUDENT

Where is it? Here.

STREPSIADES

It's close to us. You must rethink the place—   260
shift it—put it far away from us.

STUDENT

Can't do that.

STREPSIADES [threatening]

Do it, by god, or I'll make you cry!

[Strepsiades notices Socrates descending from above in a basket suspended from a rope]

Hey, who's the man in the basket—up there?

STUDENT

The man himself.

STREPSIADES

Who's that?

STUDENT

Socrates.

STREPSIADES

Socrates! Hey, call out to him for me—   [220]
make it loud.

_____

*   In 446 BC the Athenians under Pericles put down a revolt in Euboea, a large island just off the coast of Attica.

STUDENT

    You'll have to call to him yourself.
    I'm too busy now.

[The Student exits into the interior of the house]

STREPSIADES

    O Socrates . . .
    my dear little Socrates . . . hello . . .

SOCRATES

    Why call on me, you creature of a day?

STREPSIADES

    Well, first of all, tell me what you're doing.   270

SOCRATES

    I tread the air, as I contemplate the sun.

STREPSIADES

    You're looking down upon the gods up there,
    in that basket? Why not do it from the ground,
    if that's what you're doing?

SOCRATES

                  Impossible!
    I'd never come up with a single thing
    about celestial phenomena,
    if I did not suspend my mind up high,
    to mix my subtle thoughts with what's like them—   [230]
    the air. If I turned my mind to lofty things,
    but stayed there on the ground, I'd never make   280
    the least discovery. For the earth, you see,
    draws moist thoughts down by force into itself—
    the same process takes place with water cress.

STREPSIADES

    What are you talking about? Does the mind
    draw moisture into water cress? Come down,
    my dear little Socrates, down here to me,
    so you can teach me what I've come to learn.

[Socrates' basket slowly descends]

SOCRATES

    Why have you come?

STREPSIADES

            I want to learn to argue.
    I'm being pillaged—ruined by interest   [240]
    and by creditors I can't pay off—   290
    they're slapping liens on all my property.

SOCRATES

    How come you got in such a pile of debt
    without your knowledge?

STREPSIADES

    I've been ravaged
    by disease—I'm horse sick. It's draining me
    in the most dreadful way. But please teach me
    one of your two styles of arguing, the one
    which never has to discharge any debt.
    Whatever payment you want me to make,
    I promise you I'll pay—by all the gods.

SOCRATES

    What gods do you intend to swear by?   300
    To start with, the gods hold no currency with us.

STREPSIADES

    Then, what currency do you use to swear?
    Is it iron coin, like in Byzantium?

SOCRATES

Do you want to know the truth of things divine,   [250]
the way they really are?

STREPSIADES

Yes, by god, I do,
if that's possible.

SOCRATES

And to commune and talk
with our own deities the Clouds?

STREPSIADES

Yes, I do.

SOCRATES

Then sit down on the sacred couch.

STREPSIADES

All right.
I'm sitting down.

SOCRATES

Take this wreath.

STREPSIADES

Why a wreath?
Oh dear, Socrates, don't offer me up   310
in sacrifice, like Athamas.*

SOCRATES

No, no.
We go through all this for everyone—
it's their initiation.

---

* *Athamas*, a character in one of Sophocles' lost plays who was prepared for sacrifice. He was rescued by Hercules.

STREPSIADES

    What do I get?

SOCRATES

    You'll learn to be a clever talker,   [260]
    to rattle off a speech, to strain your words
    like flour. Just keep still.

[Socrates sprinkles flour all over Strepsiades]

STREPSIADES

    By god, that's no lie!
    I'll turn into flour if you keep sprinkling me.

SOCRATES

    Old man, be quiet. Listen to the prayer.

[Socrates shuts his eyes to recite his prayer]

    O Sovereign Lord, O Boundless Air,
    who keeps the earth suspended here in space,   320
    O Bright Sky, O Sacred Goddesses—
    the Thunder-bearing Clouds—arise,
    you holy ladies, issue forth on high,
    before the man who holds you in his mind.

STREPSIADES [lifting his cloak to cover his head]

    Not yet, not yet. Not 'til I wrap this cloak
    like this so I don't get soaked. What bad luck,
    to leave my home without a cap on.

SOCRATES [ignoring Strepsiades]

    Come now, you highly honoured Clouds, come—
    manifest yourselves to this man here—
    whether you now sit atop Olympus,   330   [270]
    on those sacred snow-bound mountain peaks,
    or form the holy choruses with nymphs

in gardens of their father Ocean,
or gather up the waters of the Nile
in golden flagons at the river's mouths,
or dwell beside the marsh of Maeotis
or snowy rocks of Mimas—hear my call,
accept my sacrifice, and then rejoice
in this holy offering I make.

CHORUS [heard offstage]
    Everlasting Clouds—   340
let us arise, let us reveal
our moist and natural radiance—
moving from the roaring deep
of father Ocean to the tops
    of tree-lined mountain peaks,   [280]
where we see from far away
the lofty heights, the sacred earth,
whose fruits we feed with water,
the murmuring of sacred rivers,
    the roaring of the deep-resounding sea.   350
For the unwearied eye of heaven
blazes forth its glittering beams.
Shake off this misty shapelessness
from our immortal form and gaze upon
    the earth with our far-reaching eyes.   [290]

SOCRATES
O you magnificent and holy Clouds,
you've clearly heard my call.

[To Strepsiades]

Did you hear that voice
intermingled with the awesome growl of thunder?

STREPSIADES
O you most honoured sacred goddesses,

in answer to your thunder call I'd like to fart—   360
it's made me so afraid—if that's all right . . .

[Strepsiades pull down his pants and farts loudly in the direction of the offstage Chorus]

Oh, oh, whether right nor not, I need to shit.

SOCRATES
Stop being so idiotic, acting like
a stupid damn comedian. Keep quiet.
A great host of deities is coming here—
they're going to sing.

CHORUS [still offstage]
O you maidens bringing rain—
let's move on to that brilliant place,   [300]
to gaze upon the land of Pallas,
where such noble men inhabit   370
Cecrops' lovely native home,*
where they hold those sacred rites
no one may speak about,
where the temple of the mysteries
is opened up in holy festivals,*
with gifts for deities in heaven,
what lofty temples, holy statues,
most sacred supplication to the gods,
with garlands for each holy sacrifice,
and festivals of every kind   380   [310]
in every season of the year,
including, when the spring arrives,
that joyful Dionysian time,
with rousing choruses of song,
resounding music of the pipes.

---

* *Cecrops*: a legendary king of Athens. Pallas is Pallas Athena, patron goddess of Athens.
* *holy festivals*: the Eleusinian mysteries, a traditionally secret and sacred festival for those initiated into the band of cult worshippers.

STREPSIADES

By god, Socrates, tell me, I beg you,
who these women are who sing so solemnly.
Are they some special kind of heroines?

SOCRATES

No—they're heavenly Clouds, great goddesses
for lazy men—from them we get our thoughts,   390
our powers of speech, our comprehension,
our gift for fantasy and endless talk,
our power to strike responsive chords in speech
and then rebut opponents' arguments.

STREPSIADES

Ah, that must be why, as I heard their voice,
my soul took wing, and now I'm really keen
to babble on of trivialities,
to argue smoke and mirrors, to deflate   [320]
opinions with a small opinion of my own,
to answer someone's reasoned argument   400
with my own counter-argument. So now,
I'd love to see them here in front of me,
if that's possible.

SOCRATES

Just look over there—
towards Mount Parnes. I see them coming,
slowly moving over here.*

STREPSIADES

Where? Point them out.

SOCRATES

They're coming down here through the valleys—
a whole crowd of them—there in the thickets,
right beside you.

---

*   *Mount Parnes*: a mountain range to the north of Athens.

STREPSIADES
    This is weird. I don't see them.

SOCRATES [pointing into the wings of the theatre]
    There—in the entrance way.

STREPSIADES
    Ah, now I see—
    but I can barely make them out.

[The Clouds enter from the wings]

SOCRATES
    There—   410
    surely you can see them now, unless your eyes
    are swollen up like pumpkins.

STREPSIADES
    I see them.
    My god, what worthy noble presences!
    They're taking over the entire space.

SOCRATES
    You weren't aware that they are goddesses?
    You had no faith in them?

STREPSIADES
    I'd no idea.
    I thought clouds were mist and dew and vapour.   [330]

SOCRATES
    You didn't realize these goddesses
    support a multitude of charlatans—
    prophetic seers from Thurium, quacks   420
    who specialize in books on medicine,
    lazy long-haired types with onyx signet rings,
    poets who produce the twisted choral music
    for dithyrambic songs, those with airy minds—

all such men so active doing nothing
the Clouds support, since in their poetry
these people celebrate the Clouds.

STREPSIADES

Ah ha, so that's why they poeticize
"the whirling radiance of watery clouds
as they advance so ominously,"   430
"waving hairs of hundred-headed Typho,"*
with "roaring tempests," and then "liquid breeze,"
or "crook-taloned, sky-floating birds of prey,"
"showers of rain from dewy clouds"—and then,
as a reward for this, they stuff themselves
on slices carved from some huge tasty fish
or from a thrush.*

SOCRATES

  Yes, thanks to these Clouds.   [340]
Is that not truly just?

STREPSIADES

All right, tell me this—
if they're really clouds, what's happened to them?
They look just like mortal human women.   440
The clouds up there are not the least like that.

SOCRATES

What are they like?

STREPSIADES

I don't know exactly.
They look like wool once it's been pulled apart—
not like women, by god, not in the least.
These ones here have noses.

---

* *Typho*: a monster with a hundred heads, father of the storm winds (hence, our word *typhoon*).

* *thrush*: meat from a thrush was considered a delicacy, something that might be given to the winner of a public competition. These lines are mocking the dithyrambic poets (perhaps in comparison with the writers of comic drama).

SOCRATES

Let me ask you something.
Will you answer me?

STREPSIADES

Ask me what you want.
Fire away.

SOCRATES

Have you ever gazed up there
and seen a cloud shaped like a centaur,
or a leopard, wolf, or bull?

STREPSIADES

Yes, I have.
So what?

SOCRATES

They become anything they want.   450
So if they see some hairy savage type,
one of those really wild and wooly men,
like Xenophantes' son, they mock his moods,
transforming their appearance into centaurs.*   [350]

STREPSIADES

What if they glimpse a thief of public funds,
like Simon? What do they do then?*

SOCRATES

They expose
just what he's truly like—they change at once,
transform themselves to wolves.

---

* *Xenophantes' son*: a reference to Hieronymos, a dithyrambic and tragic poet. A centaur was known for its savage temper
and wild appearance.
* *Simon*: an allegedly corrupt Athenian public official.

STREPSIADES

Ah ha, I see.
So that's why yesterday they changed to deer.
They must have caught sight of Cleonymos—   460
the man who threw away his battle shield—
they knew he was fearful coward.*

SOCRATES

And now it's clear they've seen Cleisthenes—
that's why, as you can see, they've changed to women.*

STREPSIADES [to the Chorus of Clouds]

All hail to you, lady goddesses.
And now, if you have ever spoken out
to other men, let me hear your voice,
you queenly powers.

CHORUS LEADER

Greetings to you, old man born long ago,
hunter in love with arts of argument—   470
you, too, high priest of subtlest nonsense,
tell us what you want. Of all the experts   [360]
in celestial matters at the present time,
we take note of no one else but you—
and Prodicus*—because he's sharp and wise,
while you go swaggering along the street,
in bare feet, shifting both eyes back and forth.
You keep moving on through many troubles,
looking proud of your relationship with us.

STREPSIADES

By the Earth, what voices these Clouds have—   480
so holy, reverent, and marvelous!

---

*   *Cleonymos*: an Athenian accused of dropping his shield and running away from a battle.

*   *Cleisthenes*: a notorious homosexual whom Aristophanes never tires of holding up to ridicule.

*   *Prodicus*: a well-known Athenian intellectual, who wrote on a wide variety of subjects. Linking Socrates and Prodicus as intellectual equals would strike many Athenians as quite absurd.

SOCRATES

Well, they're the only deities we have—
the rest are just so much hocus pocus.

STREPSIADES

Hang on—by the Earth, isn't Zeus a god,
the one up there on Mount Olympus?

SOCRATES

What sort of god is Zeus? Why spout such rubbish?
There's no such being as Zeus.

STREPSIADES

What do you mean?
Then who brings on the rain? First answer that.

SOCRATES

Why, these women do. I'll prove that to you
with persuasive evidence. Just tell me—   490   [370]
where have you ever seen the rain come down
without the Clouds being there? If Zeus brings rain,
then he should do so when the sky is clear,
when there are no Clouds in view.

STREPSIADES

By Apollo, you've made a good point there—
it helps your argument. I used to think
rain was really Zeus pissing through a sieve.
Tell me who causes thunder? That scares me.

SOCRATES

These Clouds do, as they roll around.

STREPSIADES

But how?
Explain that, you who dares to know it all.   500

SOCRATES

When they are filled with water to the brim
and then, suspended there with all that rain,
are forced to move, they bump into each other.
They're so big, they burst with a great boom.

STREPSIADES

But what's forcing them to move at all?
Doesn't Zeus do that?

SOCRATES

No—that's the aerial Vortex.*

STREPSIADES

Vortex? Well, that's something I didn't know.   [380]
So Zeus is now no more, and Vortex rules
instead of him. But you still have not explained
a thing about those claps of thunder.   510

SOCRATES

Weren't you listening to me? I tell you,
when the Clouds are full of water and collide,
they're so thickly packed they make a noise.

STREPSIADES

Come on now—who'd ever believe that stuff?

SOCRATES

I'll explain, using you as a test case.
Have you ever gorged yourself on stew
at the Panathenaea and later
had an upset stomach—then suddenly
some violent movement made it rumble?*

---

*   *Vortex*: the Greek word is *dinos* meaning a *whirl* or *eddy*. I adopt Sommerstein's suggestion for this word here.
*   *Panathenaea*: a major annual festival in Athens.

STREPSIADES

    Yes, by Apollo! It does weird things—   520
    I feel unsettled. That small bit of stew
    rumbles around and makes strange noises,
    just like thunder. At first it's quite quiet—   [390]
    "pappax pappax"—then it starts getting louder—
    "papapappax"—and when I take a shit,
    it really thunders "papapappax"—
    just like these Clouds.

SOCRATES

    So think about it—
    if your small gut can make a fart like that,
    why can't the air, which goes on for ever,
    produce tremendous thunder. Then there's this—   530
    consider how alike these phrases sound,
    "thunder clap" and "fart and crap."

STREPSIADES

    All right, but then explain this to me—
    Where does lightning come from, that fiery blaze,
    which, when it hits, sometimes burns us up,
    sometimes just singes us and lets us live?
    Clearly Zeus is hurling that at perjurers.

SOCRATES

    You stupid driveling idiot, you stink
    of olden times, the age of Cronos!* If Zeus
    is really striking at the perjurers,   540
    how come he's not burned Simon down to ash,
    or else Cleonymos or Theorus?
    They perjure themselves more than anyone.   [400]
    No. Instead he strikes at his own temple
    at Sunium, our Athenian headland,
    and at his massive oak trees there. Why?
    What's his plan? Oak trees can't be perjured.

---

*   *Cronos*: the divine father of Zeus, the age of Cronos is part of the mythic past.

STREPSIADES

    I don't know. But that argument of yours
    seems good. All right, then, what's a lightning bolt?

SOCRATES

    When a dry wind blows up into the Clouds   550
    and gets caught in there, it makes them inflate,
    like the inside of a bladder. And then
    it has to burst them all apart and vent,
    rushing out with violence brought on
    by dense compression—its force and friction
    cause it to consume itself in fire.

STREPSIADES

    By god, I went through that very thing myself—
    at the feast for Zeus. I was cooking food,
    a pig's belly, for my family. I forgot
    to slit it open. It began to swell—   560   [410]
    then suddenly blew up, splattering blood
    in both my eyes and burning my whole face.

CHORUS LEADER

    O you who seeks from us great wisdom,
    how happy you will be among Athenians,
    among the Greeks, if you have memory,
    if you can think, if in that soul of yours
    you've got the power to persevere,
    and don't get tired standing still or walking,
    nor suffer too much from the freezing cold,
    with no desire for breakfast, if you abstain   570
    from wine, from exercise, and other foolishness,
    if you believe, as all clever people should,
    the highest good is victory in action,
    in deliberation and in verbal wars.

STREPSIADES

    Well, as for a stubborn soul and a mind   [420]
    thinking in a restless bed, while my stomach,

lean and mean, feeds on bitter herbs, don't worry.
I'm confident about all that—I'm ready
to be hammered on your anvil into shape.

SOCRATES

    So now you won't acknowledge any gods   580
    except the ones we do—Chaos, the Clouds,
    the Tongue—just these three?

STREPSIADES

                  Absolutely—
    I'd refuse to talk to any other gods,
    if I ran into them—and I decline
    to sacrifice or pour libations to them.
    I'll not provide them any incense.

CHORUS LEADER

    Tell us then what we can do for you.
    Be brave—for if you treat us with respect,
    if you admire us, and if you're keen
    to be a clever man, you won't go wrong.   590

STREPSIADES

    O you sovereign queens,
    from you I ask one really tiny favour—
    to be the finest speaker in all Greece,   [430]
    within a hundred miles.

CHORUS LEADER

    You'll get that from us.
    From now on, in time to come, no one will win
    more votes among the populace than you.

STREPSIADES

    No speaking on important votes for me!
    That's not what I'm after. No, no. I want
    to twist all legal verdicts in my favour,
    to evade my creditors.

CHORUS LEADER

> You'll get that,   600
> just what you desire. For what you want
> is nothing special. So be confident—
> give yourself over to our agents here.

STREPSIADES

> I'll do that—I'll place my trust in you.
> Necessity is weighing me down—the horses,
> those thoroughbreds, my marriage—all that
> has worn me out. So now, this body of mine   [440]
> I'll give to them, with no strings attached,
> to do with as they like—to suffer blows,
> go without food and drink, live like a pig,   610
> to freeze or have my skin flayed for a pouch—
> if I can just get out of all my debt
> and make men think of me as bold and glib,
> as fearless, impudent, detestable,
> one who cobbles lies together, makes up words,
> a practised legal rogue, a statute book,
> a chattering fox, sly and needle sharp,
> a slippery fraud, a sticky rascal,
> foul whipping boy or twisted villain,   [450]
> troublemaker, or idly prattling fool.   620
> If they can make those who run into me
> call me these names, they can do what they want—
> no questions asked. If, by Demeter, they're keen,
> they can convert me into sausages
> and serve me up to men who think deep thoughts.

CHORUS

> Here's a man whose mind's now smart,
> no holding back—prepared to start
> When you have learned all this from me   [460]
> you know your glory will arise
> among all men to heaven's skies.   630

STREPSIADES

    What must I undergo?

CHORUS

    For all time, you'll live with me
    a life most people truly envy.

STREPSIADES

    You mean I'll really see that one day?

CHORUS

    Hordes will sit outside your door
    wanting your advice and more—   [470]
    to talk, to place their trust in you
    for their affairs and lawsuits, too,
    things which merit your great mind.
    They'll leave you lots of cash behind.   640

CHORUS LEADER [to Socrates]

    So get started with this old man's lessons,
    what you intend to teach him first of all—
    rouse his mind, test his intellectual powers.

SOCRATES

    Come on then, tell me the sort of man you are—
    once I know that, I can bring to bear on you
    my latest batteries with full effect.   [480]

STREPSIADES

    What's that? By god, are you assaulting me?

SOCRATES

    No—I want to learn some things from you.
    What about your memory?

STREPSIADES

    To tell the truth
    it works two ways. If someone owes me something,   650

I remember really well. But if it's poor me
that owes the money, I forget a lot.

SOCRATES

Do you have any natural gift for speech?

STREPSIADES

Not for speaking—only for evading debt.

SOCRATES

So how will you be capable of learning?

STREPSIADES

Easily—that shouldn't be your worry.

SOCRATES

All right. When I throw out something wise
about celestial matters, you make sure
you snatch it right away.   [490]

STREPSIADES

What's that about?
Am I to eat up wisdom like a dog?   660

SOCRATES [aside]

This man's an ignorant barbarian!
Old man, I fear you may need a beating.

[to Strepsiades]

Now, what do you do if someone hits you?

STREPSIADES

If I get hit, I wait around a while,
then find witnesses, hang around some more,
then go to court.

SOCRATES

    All right, take off your cloak.

STREPSIADES

    Have I done something wrong?

SOCRATES

    No. It's our custom
    to go inside without a cloak.

STREPSIADES

    But I don't want
    to search your house for stolen stuff.*

SOCRATES

    What are you going on about? Take it off.   670

STREPSIADES [removing his cloak and his shoes]

    So tell me this—if I pay attention   [500]
    and put some effort into learning,
    which of your students will I look like?

SOCRATES

    In appearance there'll be no difference
    between yourself and Chaerephon.

STREPSIADES

    Oh, that's bad.
    You mean I'll be only half alive?

SOCRATES

    Don't talk such rubbish! Get a move on
    and follow me inside. Hurry up!

STREPSIADES

---

* Legally an Athenian who believed someone had stolen his property could enter the suspect's house to search. But he first had to remove any garments in which he might conceal something which he might plant in the house.

First, put a honey cake here in my hands.   680
I'm scared of going down in there. It's like
going in Trophonios' cave.*

SOCRATES
Go inside.
Why keep hanging round this doorway?

[Socrates picks up Strepsiades' cloak and shoes. Then Strepsiades and Socrates exit into the interior of the Thinkery]

CHORUS LEADER
Go. And may you enjoy good fortune,   [510]
a fit reward for all your bravery.

CHORUS
We hope this man
thrives in his plan.
For at his stage
of great old age   690
he'll take a dip
in new affairs
to act the sage.

CHORUS LEADER [stepping forward to address the audience directly]
You spectators, I'll talk frankly to you now,
and speak the truth, in the name of Dionysus,
who has cared for me ever since I was a child.
So may I win and be considered a wise man.*   [520]
For I thought you were a discerning audience
and this comedy the most intelligent
of all my plays. Thus, I believed it worth my while   700
to produce it first for you, a work which cost me

---

* *Trophonios' cave* was a place people went to get prophecies. A suppliant carried a honey cake as an offering to the snakes in the cave.
* *win*: this is a reference to the fact that the play is part of a competition. The speech obviously is part of the revisions made after the play failed to win first prize in its initial production. The speaker may have been Aristophanes himself or the Chorus Leader speaking on his behalf.

a great deal of effort. But I left defeated,
beaten out by vulgar men—which I did not deserve.
I place the blame for this on you intellectuals,
on whose behalf I went to all that trouble.
But still I won't ever willingly abandon
the discriminating ones among you all,
not since that time when my play about two men—
one was virtuous, the other one depraved—
was really well received by certain people here,   710
whom it pleases me to mention now. As for me,
I was still unmarried, not yet fully qualified   [530]
to produce that child. But I exposed my offspring,
and another woman carried it away.
In your generosity you raised and trained it.*
Since then I've had sworn testimony from you
that you have faith in me. So now, like old Electra,
this comedy has come, hoping she can find,
somewhere in here, spectators as intelligent.
If she sees her brother's hair, she'll recognize it.*   720
Consider how my play shows natural restraint.
First, she doesn't have stitched leather dangling down,
with a thick red knob, to make the children giggle.*
She hasn't mocked bald men or danced some drunken reel.   [540]
There's no old man who talks and beats those present
with a stick to hide bad jokes. She doesn't rush on stage
with torches or raise the cry "Alas!" or "Woe is me!"
No—she's come trusting in herself and in the script.
And I'm a poet like that. I don't preen myself.
I don't seek to cheat you by re-presenting here   730
the same material two or three times over.

---

* *trained it*: This passage is a reference to Aristophanes' first play, *The Banqueters*, and to those who helped him get the work produced. The child mentioned is a metaphorical reference to that work or to his artistic talent generally. The other woman is a metaphorical reference to Callistratos, who produced *The Banqueters*.

* *Electra* was the sister of Orestes and spent a long time waiting to be reunited with him. That hope kept her going. When she saw her brother's lock of hair on their father's tomb, she was overjoyed that he had come back. The adjective "old" refers to the story, which was very well known to the audience.

* These lines may indicate that in *The Clouds* the male characters did not wear the traditional phalluses or that the phalluses they did wear were not of a particular kind.

Instead I base my art on framing new ideas,
all different from the rest, and each one very deft.
When Cleon was all-powerful, I went for him.
I hit him in the gut. But once he was destroyed,
I didn't have the heart to kick at him again.   [550]
Yet once Hyperbolos let others seize on him,
they've not ceased stomping on the miserable man—
and on his mother, too.* The first was Eupolis—
he dredged up his Maricas, a wretched rehash   740
of my play The Knights—he's such a worthless poet—
adding an aging female drunk in that stupid dance,
a woman Phrynichos invented years ago,
the one that ocean monster tried to gobble up.*
Then Hermippos wrote again about Hyperbolos,
Now all the rest are savaging the man once more,
copying my images of eels. If anyone
  laughs at those plays, I hope mine don't amuse him.   [560]
But if you enjoy me and my inventiveness,
then future ages will commend your worthy taste.   750

CHORUS
    For my dance I first here call
    on Zeus, high-ruling king of all
    among the gods—and on Poseidon,
    so great and powerful—the one
    who with his trident wildly heaves
    the earth and all the brine-filled seas,
    and on our famous father Sky,
  the most revered, who can supply   [570]
    all things with life. And I invite
    the Charioteer whose dazzling light   760
    fills this wide world so mightily
    for every man and deity.

---

* *Cleon* was a very powerful Athenian politician after Pericles. Aristophanes savagely attacked him in *Knights*. Cleon was killed in battle (in 422). Hyperbolos became a very influential politician after Cleon's death.

* Eupolis, Phrynichos, and Hermippos were comic playwrights, rivals of Aristophanes.

CHORUS LEADER

    The wisest in this audience should here take note—
    you've done us wrong, and we confront you with the blame.
    We confer more benefits than any other god
    upon your city, yet we're the only ones
    to whom you do not sacrifice or pour libations,
    though we're the gods who keep protecting you.
If there's some senseless army expedition,   [580]
    then we respond by thundering or bringing rain.   770
    And when you were selecting as your general
    that Paphlagonian tanner hated by the gods,*
    we frowned and then complained aloud—our thunder pealed
    among the lightning bursts, the moon moved off her course,
    the sun at once pulled his wick back inside himself,
    and said if Cleon was to be your general
    then he'd give you no light. Nonetheless, you chose him.
    They say this city likes to make disastrous choices,
    but that the gods, no matter what mistakes you make,
    convert them into something better. If you want   780
    your recent choice to turn into a benefit,
    I can tell you how—it's easy. Condemn the man—   [590]
    that seagull Cleon—for bribery and theft.*
    Set him in the stocks, a wooden yoke around his neck.
    Then, even if you've made a really big mistake,
    for you things will be as they were before your vote,
    and for the city this affair will turn out well.

CHORUS

        Phoebus Apollo, stay close by,
        lord of Delos, who sits on high,
        by lofty Cynthos mountain sides;   790
        and holy lady, who resides
        in Ephesus, in your gold shrine,

---

* *Paphlagonian tanner* is a reference to Cleon, who earned his money from tanneries. Paphlagonia is an area in Asia Minor. The word here implies that Cleon was not a true Athenian.

* *seagull* was a bird symbolic of thievery and greed. The contradiction in these speeches in the attitude to Cleon (who died the year following the original production) may be accounted for by the incomplete revision of the script.

where Lydian girls pray all the time;   [600]
Athena, too, who guards our home,
her aegis raised above her own,
and he who holds Parnassus peaks
and shakes his torches as he leaps,
lord Dionysus, whose shouts call
amid the Delphic bacchanal.*

CHORUS LEADER

When we were getting ready to move over here,   800
Moon met us and told us, first of all, to greet,
on her behalf, the Athenians and their allies.
Then she said she was upset—the way you treat her   [610]
is disgraceful, though she brings you all benefits—
not just in words but in her deeds. To start with,
she saves you at least one drachma every month
for torchlight— in the evening, when you go outside,
you all can say, "No need to buy a torch, my boy,
Moon's light will do just fine." She claims she helps you all
in other ways, as well, but you don't calculate   810
your calendar the way you should—no, instead
you make it all confused, and that's why, she says,
the gods are always making threats against her,
when they are cheated of a meal and go back home
because their celebration has not taken place
according to a proper count of all the days.*
And then, when you should be making sacrifice,   [620]
you're torturing someone or have a man on trial.
And many times, when we gods undertake a fast,
because we're mourning Memnon or Sarpedon,*   820
you're pouring out libations, having a good laugh.

---

* *holy lady* is a reference to the goddess Artemis. The *aegis* is a divine cloak which has invincible powers to strike fear into the god's enemies. Here it is invoked as a protection for Athens, Athena's city. *Dionysus* lived in Delphi when Apollo was absent from the shrine during the winter.

* Athenians followed a lunar calendar, but there were important discrepancies due to a very careless control over inserting extra days.

* *Memnon or Sarpedon*: Memnon, the son of Dawn, was killed at Troy, as was Sarpedon, a son of Zeus, and leader of the Lycian allies of the Trojans.

That's the reason, after his choice by lot this year
to sit on the religious council, Hyperbolos
had his wreath of office snatched off by the gods.
That should make him better understand the need
to count the days of life according to the moon.*

[Enter Socrates from the interior of the Thinkery]

SOCRATES

By Respiration, Chaos, and the Air,
I've never seen a man so crude, stupid,
clumsy, and forgetful. He tries to learn
the tiny trifles, but then he forgets   830   [630]
before he's even learned them. Nonetheless,
I'll call him outside here into the light.

[Socrates calls back into the interior of the Thinkery]

Strepsiades, where are you? Come on out—
and bring your bed.

STREPSIADES [from inside]

                                    I can't carry it out—
the bugs won't let me.

SOCRATES

                                    Get a move on. Now!

[Strepsiades enters carrying his bedding]

SOCRATES

Put it there. And pay attention.

---

*   *religious council*: the Amphictyonic Council, which controlled some important religious shrines, was made up of delegates
from different city states. In Athens the delegate was chosen by lot. It's not clear how the gods could have removed the wreath
in question.

STREPSIADES [putting the bed down]

                                        There!

SOCRATES

    Come now, of all the things you never learned
    what to you want to study first? Tell me.

[Strepsiades is very puzzled by the question]

SOCRATES

    Poetic measures? Diction? Rhythmic verse?

STREPSIADES

    I'll take measures. Just the other day   840
     the man who deals in barley cheated me—   [640]
    about two quarts.

SOCRATES

    That's not what I mean.
    Which music measure is most beautiful—
    the triple measure or quadruple measure?

STREPSIADES

    As a measure nothing beats a gallon.

SOCRATES

    My dear man, you're just talking nonsense.

STREPSIADES

    Then make me a bet—I say a gallon
    is made up of quadruple measures.

SOCRATES

    O damn you—you're such a country bumpkin—
     so slow! Maybe you can learn more quickly   850
    if we deal with rhythm.

STREPSIADES
>Will these rhythms
>help to get me food?

SOCRATES
>Well, to begin with,
>they'll make you elegant in company—
>and you'll recognize the different rhythms,   [650]
>the enoplian and the dactylic,
>which is like a digit.*

STREPSIADES
>Like a digit!
>By god, that's something I do know!

SOCRATES
>Then tell me.

STREPSIADES
>When I was a lad a digit meant this!

[Strepsiades sticks his middle finger straight up under Socrates' nose]

SOCRATES
>You're just a crude buffoon!

STREPSIADES
>No, you're a fool—
>I don't want to learn any of that stuff.   860

SOCRATES
>Well then, what?

STREPSIADES
>You know, that other thing—
>how to argue the most unjust cause.

---

* the *dactyl* is named from the Greek word for finger because it consists of one long stress followed by two short stresses, like the structure of bones in a finger. The phrase "which is like a digit" has been added to make the point clearer.

SOCRATES

But you need to learn these other matters
before all that. Now, of the quadrupeds
which one can we correctly label male?

STREPSIADES

Well, I know the males, if I'm not witless—   [660]
the ram, billy goat, bull, dog, and fowl.

SOCRATES

And the females?

STREPSIADES

The ewe, nanny goat,
cow, bitch and fowl.*

SOCRATES

You see what you're doing?
You're using that word "fowl" for both of them,   870
Calling males what people use for females.

STREPSIADES

What's that? I don't get it.

SOCRATES

What's not to get?
"Fowl" and "Fowl" . . .

STREPSIADES

By Poseidon, I see your point.
All right, what should I call them?

---

* I adopt Sommerstein's suggested insertion of this line and a half in order to clarify what now follows in the conversation, which hinges on the gender of words (masculine, feminine, or neuter) and the proper ascription of a specific gender to words which describe male and female objects. The word "fowl" applies to both male and females and therefore is not, strictly speaking masculine. This whole section is a satire on the "nitpicking" attention to language attributed to the sophists.

SOCRATES
Call the male a "fowl"—
and call the other one "fowlette."

STREPSIADES
"Fowlette?"
By the Air, that's good! Just for teaching that
I'll fill your kneading basin up with flour,
right to the brim.*

SOCRATES
Once again, another error!   [670]
You called it basin—a masculine word—
when it's feminine.

STREPSIADES
How so? Do I call   880
the basin masculine?

SOCRATES
Indeed you do.
It's just like Cleonymos.*

STREPSIADES
How's that?
Tell me.

SOCRATES
You treated the word basin
just as you would treat Cleonymos.

STREPSIADES [totally bewildered by the conversation]
But my dear man, he didn't have a basin—
not Cleonymos—not for kneading flour.
His round mortar was his prick—the wanker—

---

*   *kneading basin*: a trough for making bread.
*   *Cleonymos* was an Athenian politician who allegedly ran away from the battle field, leaving his shield behind.

he kneaded that to masturbate.*
But what should I call a basin from now on?

SOCRATES

Call it a basinette, just as you'd say   890
the word Sostratette.

STREPSIADES

Basinette—it's feminine?

SOCRATES

It is indeed.

STREPSIADES

All right, then, I should say
Cleonymette and basinette.*   [680]

SOCRATES

You've still got to learn about people's names—
which ones are male and which are female.

STREPSIADES

I know which ones are feminine.

SOCRATES

Go on.

STREPSIADES

Lysilla, Philinna, Cleitagora,
Demetria . . .

SOCRATES

---

* *to masturbate*: the Greek here says literally "Cleonymos didn't have a kneading basin but kneaded himself with a round mortar [i.e., masturbated]."
* The point of this very laboured joke seems to be making Cleonymos feminine, presumably because of his cowardice (running away in battle).

Which names are masculine?

STREPSIADES

There are thousands of them—Philoxenos,
Melesias, Amynias . . .

SOCRATES

You fool,   900
those names are not all masculine.*

STREPSIADES

What?
You don't think of them as men?

SOCRATES

Indeed I don't.
If you met Amynias, how would you greet him?

STREPSIADES

How? Like this, "Here, Amynia, come here."*   [690]

SOCRATES

You see? You said "Amynia," a woman's name.

STREPSIADES

And that's fair enough, since she's unwilling
to do army service. But what's the point?
Why do I need to learn what we all know?

---

* The three names mentioned belong to well known Athenians, who may have all been famous for their dissolute life style. Socrates is taking issue with the spelling of the last two names which (in some forms) look like feminine names. Strepsiades, of course, thinks Socrates is talking about the sexuality of the people.

* *Amynia*: in Greek (as in Latin) the name changes when it is used as a direct form of address—in this case the last letter is dropped, leaving a name ending in -*a*, normally a feminine ending.

SOCRATES

    That's irrelevant, by god. Now lie down—

[indicating the bed]

    right here.

STREPSIADES

    And do what?

SOCRATES

    You should contemplate—   910
    think one of your own problems through.

STREPSIADES

    Not here,
    I beg you—no. If I have to do it,
    let me do my contemplating on the ground.

SOCRATES

    No—you've got no choice.

STREPSIADES [crawling very reluctantly into the bedding]
                              Now I'm done for—
    these bugs are going to punish me today.

[Socrates exits back into the Thinkery]

CHORUS

    Now ponder and think,   [700]
    focus this way and that.
    Your mind turn and toss.
    And if you're at a loss,
    then quickly go find   920
    a new thought in your mind.
    From your eyes you must keep
    all soul-soothing sleep.

STREPSIADES

O god . . . ahhhhh . . .

CHORUS

What's wrong with you? Why so distressed?

STREPSIADES

I'm dying a miserable death in here!
 These Corinthian crawlers keep biting me.*   [710]
gnawing on my ribs,
slurping up my blood,
yanking off my balls,   930
tunneling up my arse hole—
they're killing me!

CHORUS

Don't complain so much.

STREPSIADES

Why not? When I've lost my goods,
lost the colour in my cheeks, lost my blood,
 lost my shoes, and, on top of all these troubles,   [720]
I'm here like some night watchman singing out—
it won't be long before I'm done for.

{Enter Socrates from inside the Thinkery]

SOCRATES

What are you doing? Aren't you thinking something?

STREPSIADES

Me? Yes I am, by Poseidon.

SOCRATES

What about?   940

---

*   *Corinthian* is obviously a reference to bed bugs, but the link with Corinth is unclear (perhaps it was a slang expression).

STREPSIADES

Whether there's going to be any of me left
once these bugs have finished.

SOCRATES

You imbecile,
why don't you drop dead!

[Socrates exits back into the Thinkery]

STREPSIADES

But my dear man,
I'm dying right now.

CHORUS LEADER

Don't get soft. Cover up—
get your whole body underneath the blanket.
You need to find a good idea for fraud,
a sexy way to cheat.

STREPSIADES

Damn it all—
instead of these lambskins here, why won't someone
throw over me a lovely larcenous scheme?   [730]

[Strepsiades covers his head with the wool blankets. Enter Socrates from the Thinkery and looks around thinking what to do]

SOCRATES

First, I'd better check on what he's doing.   950
You in there, are you asleep?

STREPSIADES [uncovering his head]

No, I'm not.

SOCRATES

Have you grasped anything?

STREPSIADES

    No, by god, I haven't.

SOCRATES

    Nothing at all?

STREPSIADES

    I haven't grasped a thing—
    except my right hand's wrapped around my cock.

SOCRATES

    Then cover your head and think up something—
    get a move on!

STREPSIADES

    What should I think about?
    Tell me that, Socrates.

SOCRATES

    First you must formulate
    what it is you want. Then tell me.

STREPSIADES

    You've heard
    what I want a thousand times—I want to know
    about interest, so I'll not have to pay   960
    a single creditor.

SOCRATES

    Come along now,
    cover up.

[Strepsiades covers his head again, and Socrates speaks to him through the blanket]

                Now, carve your slender thinking   [740]
    into tiny bits, and think the matter through,
    with proper probing and analysis.

STREPSIADES

    Ahhh . . . bloody hell!

SOCRATES

    Don't shift around.
    If one of your ideas is going nowhere,
    let it go, leave it alone. Later on,
    start it again and weigh it one more time.

STREPSIADES

    My dear little Socrates . . .

SOCRATES

    Yes, old man,
    what is it?

STREPSIADES

    I've got a lovely scheme   970
    to avoid paying interest.

SOCRATES

    Lay it out.

STREPSIADES

    All right. Tell me now . . .

SOCRATES

    What is it?

STREPSIADES

    What if I purchased a Thessalian witch
    and in the night had her haul down the moon—   [750]
    then shut it up in a circular box,
    just like a mirror, and kept watch on it.

SOCRATES

    How would that provide you any help?

STREPSIADES

    Well, if no moon ever rose up anywhere,
    I'd pay no interest.

SOCRATES

    And why is that?

STREPSIADES

    Because they lend out money by the month.   980

SOCRATES

    That's good. I'll give you another problem—
    it's tricky. If in court someone sued you
    to pay five talents, what would you do
    to get the case discharged.

STREPSIADES

    How? I don't know.
     I'll have to think   [760]

SOCRATES

    These ideas of yours—
    don't keep them wound up all the time inside you.
    Let your thinking loose—out into the air—
    with thread around its foot, just like a bug.*

STREPSIADES

    Hey, I've devised a really clever way
    to make that lawsuit disappear—it's so good,   990
    you'll agree with me.

SOCRATES

    What's your way?

STREPSIADES

    At the drug seller's shop have you seen

---

*   *bug*: children sometimes tied a thread around the foot of a large flying bug and played with it.

that beautiful stone you can see right through,
the one they use to start a fire?

SOCRATES

You mean glass?

STREPSIADES

Yes.

SOCRATES

So what?

STREPSIADES

What if I took that glass,
and when the scribe was writing out the charge,   [770]
I stood between him and the sun—like this—
some distance off, and made his writing melt,
just the part about my case?*

SOCRATES

By the Graces,
that's a smart idea!

STREPSIADES

Hey, I'm happy—   1000
I've erased my law suit for five talents.

SOCRATES

So hurry up and tackle this next problem.

STREPSIADES

What is it?

SOCRATES

How would you evade a charge

---

* The scribe would be writing on a wax tablet which the heat would melt.

and launch a counter-suit in a hearing
you're about to lose without a witness?

STREPSIADES

No problem there—it's easy.

SOCRATES: So tell me.

STREPSIADES: I will. If there was a case still pending,
    another one before my case was called,
    I'd run off and hang myself.   [780]

SOCRATES

                    That's nonsense.

STREPSIADES

    No, by the gods, it's not. If I were dead,   1010
    no one could bring a suit against me.

SOCRATES

    That's rubbish. Just get away from here.
    I'll not instruct you any more.

STREPSIADES

    Why not?
    Come on, Socrates, in god's name.

SOCRATES

    There's no point—
    as soon as you learn anything, it's gone,
    you forget it right away. Look, just now,
    what was the very first thing you were taught?

STREPSIADES

    Well, let's see . . . The first thing—what was it?
    What was that thing we knead the flour in?
    Damn it all, what was it?

SOCRATES

To hell with you!   1020
    You're the most forgetful, stupidest old man . . .   [790]
    Get lost!

STREPSIADES

    Oh dear! Now I'm in for it.
    What going to happen to me? I'm done for,
    if I don't learn to twist my words around.
    Come on, Clouds, give me some good advice.

CHORUS LEADER

    Old man, here's our advice: if you've a son
    and he's full grown, send him in there to learn—
    he'll take your place.

STREPSIADES

    Well, I do have a son—
    a really good and fine one, too—trouble is
    he doesn't want to learn. What should I do?   1030

CHORUS LEADER

    You just let him do that?

STREPSIADES

    He's a big lad—
    and strong and proud—his mother's family
    are all high-flying women like Coesyra.   [800]
    But I'll take him in hand. If he says no,
    then I'll evict him from my house for sure.

[to Socrates]

    Go inside and wait for me a while.

[Strepsiades moves back across the stage to his own house]

CHORUS [to Socrates]
> Don't you see you'll quickly get
> from us all sorts of lovely things
> since we're your only god?
> This man here is now all set   1040
> to follow you in anything,
> you simply have to prod.

> You know the man is in a daze.
> He's clearly keen his son should learn.
> So lap it up—make haste—
> get everything that you can raise.   [810]
> Such chances tend to change and turn
> into a different case.

[Socrates exits into the Thinkery. Strepsiades and Pheidippides come out of their house. Strepsiades is pushing his son in front of him]

STREPSIADES
> By the foggy air, you can't stay here—
> not one moment longer! Off with you—   1050
> go eat Megacles out of house and home!

PHEIDIPPIDES
> Hey, father—you poor man, what's wrong with you?
> By Olympian Zeus, you're not thinking straight.

STREPSIADES
> See that—"Olympian Zeus"! Ridiculous—
> to believe in Zeus—and at your age!

PHEIDIPPIDES
> Why laugh at that?

STREPSIADES
> To think you're such a child—
> and your views so out of date. Still, come here,

so you can learn a bit. I'll tell you things.
When you understand all this, you'll be a man.
But you mustn't mention this to anyone.   1060

PHEIDIPPIDES
    All right, what is it?

STREPSIADES
    You just swore by Zeus.

PHEIDIPPIDES
    That's right. I did.

STREPSIADES
    You see how useful learning is?
    Pheidippides, there's no such thing as Zeus.

PHEIDIPPIDES
    Then what is there?

STREPSIADES
    Vortex now is king—
    he's pushed out Zeus.

PHEIDIPPIDES
    Bah, that's nonsense!

STREPSIADES
    You should know that's how things are right now.

PHEIDIPPIDES
    Who says that?

STREPSIADES

Socrates of Melos*   [830]
and Chaerephon—they know about fleas' footprints.

PHEIDIPPIDES

Have you become so crazy you believe
these fellows? They're disgusting!

STREPSIADES

Watch your tongue.   1070
Don't say nasty things about such clever men—
men with brains, who like to save their money.
That's why not one of them has ever shaved,
or oiled his skin, or visited the baths
to wash himself. You, on the other hand,
keep on bathing in my livelihood,
as if I'd died.* So now get over there,
as quickly as you can. Take my place and learn.

PHEIDIPPIDES

But what could anyone learn from those men

that's   any   use   at   all?
[840]

STREPSIADES

You have to ask?   1080
Why, wise things—the full extent of human thought.
You'll see how thick you are, how stupid.
Just wait a moment here for me.

[Strepsiades goes into his house]

PHEIDIPPIDES

O dear,
What will I do? My father's lost his wits.

---

* *Melos*: Strepsiades presumably is confusing Socrates with Diagoras, a well known materialistic atheist, who came from Melos (whereas Socrates did not).
* *died*: part of the funeral rituals in a family required each member to bathe thoroughly.

Do I haul him off to get committed,
on the ground that he's a lunatic,
or tell the coffin-makers he's gone nuts.

[Strepsiades returns with two birds, one in each hand. He holds out one of them]

STREPSIADES
Come on now, what do you call this? Tell me.

PHEIDIPPIDES
It's a fowl.

STREPSIADES
        That's good. What's this?

PHEIDIPPIDES
                That's a fowl.

STREPSIADES
   They're both the same? You're being ridiculous.   1090
From now on, don't do that. Call this one "fowl,"   [850]
and this one here "fowlette."

PHEIDIPPIDES
"Fowlette"? That's it?
That's the sort of clever stuff you learned in there,
by going in with these Sons of Earth?*

STREPSIADES
Yes, it is—
and lots more, too. But everything I learned,
I right away forgot, because I'm old.

PHEIDIPPIDES
That why you lost your cloak?

---

*   *Sons of Earth*: a phrase usually referring to the Titans who warred against the Olympian gods. Here it also evokes a sense of the materialism of Socrates' doctrine in the play and, of course, ironically ridicules the Thinkery.

STREPSIADES

    I didn't lose it—
    I gave it to knowledge—a donation.

PHEIDIPPIDES

    And your sandals—what you do with them,
    you deluded man?

STREPSIADES

     Just like Pericles,   1100
    I lost them as a "necessary expense."*
    But come on, let's go. Move it. If your dad   [860]
    asks you to do wrong, you must obey him.
    I know I did just what you wanted long ago,
    when you were six years old and had a lisp—
    with the first obol I got for jury work,
    at the feast of Zeus I got you a toy cart.

PHEIDIPPIDES

    You're going to regret this one fine day.

STREPSIADES

    Good—you're doing what I ask.

[Strepsiades calls inside the Thinkery]

    Socrates,
    come out here . . .

[Enter Socrates from inside the Thinkery]

    Here—I've brought my son to you.   1110
    He wasn't keen, but I persuaded him.

---

*   "*necessary expense*": refers to the well-known story of Pericles who in 445 BC used this phrase in official state accounts to refer to an expensive but secret bribe he paid to a Spartan general to withdraw his armies from Athenian territories around Athens. No one asked any embarrassing questions about the entry.

SOCRATES

He's still a child—he doesn't know the ropes.

PHEIDIPPIDES

Go hang yourself up on some rope,   [870]
and get beaten like a worn-out cloak.

STREPSIADES

Damn you! Why insult your teacher?

SOCRATES

Look how he says "hang yourself"—it sounds
like baby talk. No crispness in his speech.*
With such a feeble tone how will he learn
to answer to a charge or summons
or speak persuasively? And yet it's true   1120
Hyperbolos could learn to master that—
it cost him one talent.*

STREPSIADES

                        Don't be concerned.
Teach him. He's naturally intelligent.
When he was a little boy—just that tall—
even then at home he built small houses,
carved out ships, made chariots from leather,   [880]
and fashioned frogs from pomegranate peel.
You can't imagine! Get him to learn
those two forms of argument—the Better,
whatever that may be, and the Worse.   1130
If not both, then at least the unjust one—
every trick you've got.

SOCRATES

                        He'll learn on his own
from the two styles of reasoning. I'll be gone.

---

* *speech*: the Greek says "with his lips sagging [or loosely apart]." Socrates is criticizing Pheidippides' untrained voice.
* *talent*: an enormous fee to pay for lessons in rhetoric. Socrates is, of course, getting Strepsiades ready to pay a lot for his son's education.

STREPSIADES
    But remember this—he must be able
    to speak against all just arguments.

[Enter the Better Argument from inside the Thinkery, talking to the Worse Argument who is still inside]

BETTER ARGUMENT
    Come on. Show yourself to the people here—
    I guess you're bold enough for that.   [890]

[The Worse Argument emerges from the Thinkery]

WORSE ARGUMENT
                Go where you please.
    The odds are greater I can wipe you out
    with lots of people there to watch us argue.

BETTER ARGUMENT
    You'll wipe me out? Who'd you think you are?   1140

WORSE ARGUMENT
    An argument.

BETTER ARGUMENT
    Yes, but second rate.

WORSE ARGUMENT
    You claim that you're more powerful than me,
    but I'll still conquer you.

BETTER ARGUMENT
    What clever tricks
    do you intend to use?

WORSE ARGUMENT
    I'll formulate

new principles.

BETTER ARGUMENT [indicating the audience]
  Yes, that's in fashion now,
  thanks to these idiots.

WORSE ARGUMENT
  No, no. They're smart.

BETTER ARGUMENT
  I'll destroy you utterly.

WORSE ARGUMENT
  And how?
  Tell me that.

BETTER ARGUMENT
  By arguing what's just.   [900]

WORSE ARGUMENT
  That I can overturn in my response,
  by arguing there's no such thing as Justice.   1150

BETTER ARGUMENT
  It doesn't exist? That's what you maintain?

WORSE ARGUMENT
  Well, if it does, where is it?

BETTER ARGUMENT
  With the gods.

WORSE ARGUMENT
  Well, if Justice does exist, how come Zeus
  hasn't been destroyed for chaining up his dad.*

---

*   Zeus overthrew his father, Cronos, and the Titans and imprisoned them deep inside the earth.

BETTER ARGUMENT
>This is going from bad to worse. I feel sick.
>Fetch me a basin.

WORSE ARGUMENT
>You silly old man—
>you're so ridiculous.

BETTER ARGUMENT
>And you're quite shameless,
>you bum fucker.

WORSE ARGUMENT
>Those words you speak—like roses!

BETTER ARGUMENT

Buffoon!

[910]

WORSE ARGUMENT
>You adorn my head with lilies.

BETTER ARGUMENT
>You destroyed your father!

WORSE ARGUMENT
>You don't mean to,   1160
>but you're showering me with gold.

BETTER ARGUMENT
>No, not gold—
>before this age, those names were lead.

WORSE ARGUMENT
>But now,
>your insults are a credit to me.

BETTER ARGUMENT
     You're too obstreperous.

WORSE ARGUMENT
     You're archaic.

BETTER ARGUMENT
     It's thanks to you that none of our young men
     is keen to go to school. The day will come
     when the Athenians will all realize
     how you teach these silly fools.

WORSE ARGUMENT
     You're dirty—
     it's disgusting.

BETTER ARGUMENT
     But you're doing very well—   [920]
     although in earlier days you were a beggar,   1170
     claiming to be Telephos from Mysia,
     eating off some views of Pandeletos,
     which you kept in your wallet.*

WORSE ARGUMENT
     That was brilliant—
     you just reminded me . . .

BETTER ARGUMENT
     It was lunacy!
     Your own craziness—the city's, too.
     It fosters you while you corrupt the young.

WORSE ARGUMENT
     You can't teach this boy—you're old as Cronos.

---

* *Telephos from Mysia* was a hero in a play by Euripides in which a king was portrayed as a beggar. Pandeletos was an Athenian politician. The imputation here is that the Worse Argument once did very badly, barely surviving on his wits and borrowed ideas.

BETTER ARGUMENT
> Yes, I must—if he's going to be redeemed [930]
> and not just prattle empty verbiage.

WORSE ARGUMENT [to Pheidippides]
> Come over here—leave him to his foolishness. 1180

BETTER ARGUMENT
> You'll regret it, if you lay a hand on him.

CHORUS LEADER
> Stop this fighting, all these abusive words.

[addressing first the Better Argument and then the Worse Argument]

> Instead, explain the things you used to teach
> to young men long ago—then you lay out
> what's new in training now. He can listen
> as you present opposing arguments
> and then decide which school he should attend.

BETTER ARGUMENT
> I'm willing to do that.

WORSE ARGUMENT
> All right with me.

CHORUS LEADER
> Come on then, which one of you goes first? [940]

WORSE ARGUMENT
> I'll grant him that right. Once he's said his piece, 1190
> I'll shoot it down with brand-new expressions
> and some fresh ideas. By the time I'm done,
> if he so much as mutters, he'll get stung
> by my opinions on his face and eyes—
> like so many hornets—he'll be destroyed.

CHORUS

 Trusting their skill in argument,

 their phrase-making propensity,   [950]

 these two men here are now intent

 to show which one will prove to be

  the better man in oratory.   1200

 For wisdom now is being hard pressed—

 my friends, this is the crucial test.

CHORUS LEADER [addressing the Better Argument]

 First, you who crowned our men in days gone by

 with so much virtue in their characters,

 let's hear that voice which brings you such delight—

 explain to us what makes you what you are.   [960]

BETTER ARGUMENT

 All right, I'll set out how we organized

 our education in the olden days,

 when I talked about what's just and prospered,

 when people wished to practise self-restraint.   1210

 First, there was a rule—children made no noise,

 no muttering. Then, when they went outside,

 walking the streets to the music master's house,

 groups of youngsters from the same part of town

 went in straight lines and never wore a cloak,

 not even when the snow fell thick as flour.

 There he taught them to sing with thighs apart.*

 They had memorize their songs—such as,

 "Dreadful Pallas Who Destroys Whole Cities,"

 and "A Cry From Far Away." These they sang   1220

 in the same style their fathers had passed down.

 If any young lad fooled around or tried

 to innovate with some new flourishes,

 like the contorted sounds we have today

 from those who carry on the Phrynis style,*   [970]

---

*   *thighs apart*: keeping the thighs together was supposed to enable boys to stimulate themselves sexually.

*   *Phrynis style*: Phrynis was a musician who introduced certain innovations in music around 450 BC.

he was beaten, soundly thrashed, his punishment
for tarnishing the Muse. At the trainer's house,
when the boys sat down, they had to keep
their thighs stretched out, so they would not expose
a thing which might excite erotic torments   1230
in those looking on. And when they stood up,
they smoothed the sand, being careful not to leave
imprints of their manhood there for lovers.
Using oil, no young lad rubbed his body
underneath his navel—thus on his sexual parts
there was a dewy fuzz, like on a peach.
He didn't make his voice all soft and sweet
to talk to lovers as he walked along,
or with his glances coyly act the pimp.   [980]
When he was eating, he would not just grab   1240
a radish head, or take from older men
some dill or parsley, or eat dainty food.
He wasn't allowed to giggle, or sit there
with his legs crossed.

WORSE ARGUMENT
    Antiquated rubbish!
    Filled with festivals for Zeus Polieus,
    cicadas, slaughtered bulls, and Cedeides.*

BETTER ARGUMENT
    But the point is this—these very features
    in my education brought up those men
    who fought at Marathon. But look at you—
    you teach these young men now right from the start   1250
    to wrap themselves in cloaks. It enrages me
    when the time comes for them to do their dance
    at the Panathenaea festival
    and one of them holds his shield low down,

---

*   *Cedeides*: a dithyrambic poet well known for his old-fashioned style. The other references are all too ancient customs and rituals (like the old tradition of wearing a cicada broach or the ritual killing of oxen).

over his balls, insulting Tritogeneia.*

   And so, young man, that's why you should choose me,   [990]
the Better Argument. Be resolute.
You'll find out how to hate the market place,
to shun the public baths, to feel ashamed
of shameful things, to fire up your heart   1260
when someone mocks you, to give up your chair
when older men come near, not to insult
your parents, nor act in any other way
which brings disgrace or which could mutilate
your image as an honourable man.
You'll learn not to run off to dancing girls,
in case, while gaping at them, you get hit
with an apple thrown by some little slut,
and your fine reputation's done for,
and not to contradict your father,   1270
or remind him of his age by calling him
Iapetus—not when he spent his years
in raising you from infancy.*

WORSE ARGUMENT

   My boy, if you're persuaded by this man,   [1000]
then by Dionysus, you'll finish up
just like Hippocrates' sons—and then
they'll all call you a sucker of the tit.*

BETTER ARGUMENT

   You'll spend your time in the gymnasium—
your body will be sleek, in fine condition.
You won't be hanging round the market place,   1280
chattering filth, as boys do nowadays.
You won't keep on being hauled away to court
over some damned sticky fierce dispute

---

* *Marathon*: a battle in 490 BC in which a small band of Greeks, mainly Athenians, defeated the Persian armies which had landed near Athens. The Panathenaea was a major religious festival in Athens. Tritogeneia was one of Athena's titles.

* *Iapetus* was a Titan, a brother of Cronos, and hence very ancient.

* Hippocrates was an Athenian, a relative of Pericles. He had three sons who had a reputation for childishness.

about some triviality. No, no.
Instead you'll go to the Academy,*
to race under the sacred olive trees,
with a decent friend the same age as you,
wearing a white reed garland, with no cares.
You'll smell yew trees, quivering poplar leaves,   1290
as plane trees whisper softly to the elms,
rejoicing in the spring. I tell you this—
if you carry out these things I mention,
if you concentrate your mind on them,   [1010]
you'll always have a gleaming chest, bright skin,
broad shoulders, tiny tongue, strong buttocks,
and a little prick. But if you take up
what's in fashion nowadays, you'll have,
for starters, feeble shoulders, a pale skin,
a narrow chest, huge tongue, a tiny bum,
and a large skill in framing long decrees.*   1300
And that man there will have you believing
what's bad is good and what's good is bad.   [1020]
Then he'll give you Antimachos' disease—
you'll be infected with his buggery.*

CHORUS

O you whose wisdom stands so tall,
the most illustrious of all.
The odour of your words is sweet,
the flowering bloom of modest ways—
happy who lived in olden days!

[to the Worse Argument]

Your rival's made his case extremely well,   1310
so you who have such nice artistic skill.

---

* *Academy*: this word refers, not to Plato's school (which was not in existence yet) but to a public park and gymnasium in Athens.
* *long decrees*: The Greek says "and a long decree," which makes little sense in English. The point of the joke is to set the audience up to expect "and a long prick" (which was considered a characteristic of barbarians).
* Antimachos was satirized in comedy as a particularly effeminate man.

must in reply give some new frill.   [1030]

CHORUS LEADER

 If you want to overcome this man
 it looks as if you'll need to bring at him
 some clever stratagems —unless you want
 to look ridiculous.

WORSE ARGUMENT

 It's about time!
 My guts have long been churning with desire
 to rip in fragments all those things he said,
 with counter-arguments. That's why I'm called
 Worse Argument among all thinking men,   1320
 because I was the very first of them
 to think of coming up with reasoning
 against our normal ways and just decrees.   [1040]
 And it's worth lots of money—more, in fact,
 than drachmas in six figures*—to select
 the weaker argument and yet still win.
 Now just see how I'll pull his system down,
 that style of education which he trusts.
 First, he says he won't let you have hot water
 when you take a bath. What's the idea here?   1330
 Why object to having a warm bath?

BETTER ARGUMENT

 The effect they have is very harmful—
 they turn men into cowards.

WORSE ARGUMENT

       Wait a minute!
 The first thing you say I've caught you out.
 I've got you round the waist. You can't escape.
 Tell me this—of all of Zeus' children

---

* *drachmas*: the Greek has "more than ten thousand staters." A stater was a general term for non-Athenian coins, usually of high value. The idea, of course, is equivalent to "a ton of money."

which man, in your view, had the greatest heart
and carried out the hardest tasks? Tell me.

BETTER ARGUMENT

In my view, no one was a better man   [1050]
than Hercules.

WORSE ARGUMENT

  And where'd you ever see   1340
cold water in a bath of Hercules? But who
was a more manly man than him?*

BETTER ARGUMENT

That's it, the very things which our young men
are always babbling on about these days—
crowding in the bath house, leaving empty
all the wrestling schools.

WORSE ARGUMENT

Next, you're not happy
when they hang around the market place—
but I think that's good. If it were shameful,
Homer would not have labelled Nestor—
and all his clever men—great public speakers.*   1350
Now, I'll move on to their tongues, which this man
says the young lads should not train. I say they should.
He also claims they should be self-restrained.
These two things injure them in major ways.   [1060]
Where have you ever witnessed self-restraint
bring any benefit to anyone?
Tell me. Speak up. Refute my reasoning.

---

*   *bath of Hercules* was a term commonly applied to thermal hot springs.

*   This part of the argument is impossible to render quickly in English. Homer's word is *agoretes*, meaning "speaking in the assembly." The Worse Argument is implying that, since the word *agora* means market place, Homer is commending these men for "talking in the market place."

BETTER ARGUMENT

> There are lots of people. For example,
> Peleus won a sword for his restraint.*

WORSE ARGUMENT

> A sword! What a magnificent reward   1360
> the poor wretch received! While Hyperbolos,
> who sells lamps in the market, is corrupt
> and brings in lots of money, but, god knows,
> he's never won a sword.

BETTER ARGUMENT

> But his virtue
> enabled Peleus to marry Thetis.*

WORSE ARGUMENT

> Then she ran off, abandoning the man,
> because he didn't want to spend all night
> having hard sweet sex between the sheets—
> that rough-and-tumble love that women like.
> You're just a crude old-fashioned Cronos.   1370

[1070]

> Now, my boy, just think off all those things
> that self-restraint requires—you'll go without
> all sorts of pleasures—boys and women,
> drunken games and tasty delicacies,
> drink and riotous laughter. What's life worth
> if you're deprived of these? So much for that.
> I'll now move on to physical desires.
> You've strayed and fallen in love—had an affair
> with someone else's wife. And then you're caught.
> You're dead, because you don't know how to speak.   1380
> But if you hang around with those like me,

---

* Peleus once refused the sexual advances of the wife of his host. She accused him of immoral activity, and her husband set Peleus unarmed on a mountain. The gods admired Peleus' chastity and provided him a sword so he could defend himself against the wild animals.

* *Peleus*, a mortal king, married Thetis, a sea goddess, with the blessing of the gods. Their child was the hero Achilles. She later left him to return to her father (but not for the reason given in the lines following).

you can follow what your nature urges.
You can leap and laugh and never think
of anything as shameful. If, by chance,
you're discovered screwing a man's wife,
just tell the husband you've done nothing wrong.
Blame Zeus—alleging even he's someone   [1080]
who can't resist his urge for sex and women.
And how can you be stronger than a god?
You're just a mortal man.

BETTER ARGUMENT

    All right—but suppose   1390
he trusts in your advice and gets a radish
rammed right up his arse, and his pubic hairs
are burned with red-hot cinders. Will he have
some reasoned argument to demonstrate
he's not a loose-arsed bugger?*

WORSE ARGUMENT

    So his asshole's large—
why should that in any way upset him?

BETTER ARGUMENT

    Can one suffer any greater harm
than having a loose asshole?

WORSE ARGUMENT

    What will you say
if I defeat you on this point?

BETTER ARGUMENT

                 I'll shut up.
What more could a man say?

---

*   *asshole*: Someone caught in the act of adultery was punished by having a radish shoved up his anus and his pubic hair singed with hot ash. The various insults here ("loose-arsed bugger," "gigantic asshole," and so on) stand for the Greek perjorative phrase "wide arsed," which, in addition to meaning "lewd" or "disgusting," also carries the connotation of passive homosexuality, something considered ridiculous in mature men. Terms like "bum fucker" are too active to capture this sense of the insult.

WORSE ARGUMENT
    Come on, then—   1400
    Tell me about our legal advocates.
    Where are they from?

BETTER ARGUMENT
    They come from loose-arsed buggers.

WORSE ARGUMENT
  I grant you that. What's next? Our tragic poets,   [1090]
    where they from?

BETTER ARGUMENT
              They come from major assholes.

WORSE ARGUMENT
    That's right. What about our politicians—
    where do they come from?

BETTER ARGUMENT
               From gigantic assholes!

WORSE ARGUMENT
    All right then—surely you can recognize
    how you've been spouting rubbish? Look out there—
    at this audience—what sort of people
    are most of them?

BETTER ARGUMENT
            All right, I'm looking at them.   1410

WORSE ARGUMENT
    Well, what do you see?

BETTER ARGUMENT
               By all the gods,
    almost all of them are men who spread their cheeks.

It's true of that one there, I know for sure . . .
and that one . . . and the one there with long hair.   [1100]

WORSE ARGUMENT
    So what do you say now?

BETTER ARGUMENT
                 We've been defeated.
    O you fuckers, for gods' sake take my cloak—
    I'm defecting to your ranks.

[The Better Argument takes off his cloak and exits into the Thinkery]

WORSE ARGUMENT [to Strepsiades]
                 What now?
    Do you want to take your son away?
    Or, to help you out, am I to teach him
    how to argue?

STREPSIADES
           Teach him—whip him into shape.   1420
    Don't forget to sharpen him for me,
    one side ready to tackle legal quibbles.
    On the other side, give his jaw an edge
    for more important matters.   [1110]

WORSE ARGUMENT
               Don't worry.
    You'll get back a person skilled in sophistry.

PHEIDIPPIDES
    Someone miserably pale, I figure.

CHORUS LEADER
            All right. Go in.
    I think you may regret this later on.

[Worse Argument and Pheidippides go into the Thinkery, while Strepsiades returns into his own house]

CHORUS LEADER

> We'd like to tell the judges here the benefits
> they'll get, if they help this chorus, as by right they should.
> First, if you want to plough your lands in season,   1430
> we'll rain first on you and on the others later.
> Then we'll protect your fruit, your growing vines,
> so neither drought nor too much rain will damage them.   [1120]
> But any mortal who dishonours us as gods
> should bear in mind the evils we will bring him.
> From his land he'll get no wine or other harvest.
> When his olive trees and fresh young vines are budding,
> we'll let fire with our sling shots, to smash and break them.
> If we see him making bricks, we'll send down rain,
> we'll shatter roofing tiles with our round hailstones.   1440
> If ever there's a wedding for his relatives,
> or friends, or for himself, we'll rain all through the night,
> so he'd rather live in Egypt than judge this wrong.   [1130]

[Strepsiades comes out of his house, with a small sack in his hand]

STREPSIADES

> Five more days, then four, three, two—and then
> the day comes I dread more than all the rest.
> It makes me shake with fear—the day that stands
> between the Old Moon and the New—the day
> when any man I happen to owe money to
> swears on oath he'll put down his deposit,
> take me to court.* He says he'll finish me,   1450
> do me in. When I make a modest plea
> for something fair, "My dear man, don't demand
> this payment now, postpone this one for me,
> discharge that one," they say the way things are
> they'll never be repaid—then they go at me,   [1140]

---

* The person making the charge in court had to make a cash deposit which was forfeit if he lost the case.

330

abuse me as unfair and say they'll sue.
Well, let them go to court. I just don't care,
not if Pheidippides has learned to argue.
I'll find out soon enough. Let's knock here,
at the thinking school.

[Strepsiades knocks on the door of the Thinkery]

Boy . . . Hey, boy . . . boy!   1460

[Socrates comes to the door]

SOCRATES
Hello there, Strepsiades.

STREPSIADES
                                    Hello to you.
First of all, you must accept this present.

[Strepsiades hands Socrates the small sack]

It's proper for a man show respect
to his son's teacher in some way. Tell me—
has the boy learned that style of argument
you brought out here just now?

SOCRATES
                                    Yes, he has.

STREPSIADES
In the name of Fraud, queen of everything,
that's splendid news!

SOCRATES
You can defend yourself
in any suit you like—and win.

STREPSIADES
    I can?
    Even if there were witnesses around   1470
    when I took out the loan?

SOCRATES
    The more the better—
    even if they number in the thousands.

STREPSIADES [in a parody of tragic style]
    Then I will roar aloud a mighty shout—
    Ah ha, weep now you petty money men,
    wail for yourselves, wail for your principal,
    wail for your compound interest. No more
    will you afflict me with your evil ways.
    On my behalf there's growing in these halls
    a son who's got a gleaming two-edged tongue—   [1160]
    he's my protector, saviour of my home,   1480
    a menace to my foes. He will remove
    the mighty tribulations of his sire.
    Run off inside and summon him to me.

[Socrates goes back into the Thinkery]

    My son, my boy, now issue from the house—
    and hearken to your father's words.

[Socrates and Pheidippides come out of the Thinkery. Pheidippides has been transformed in appearance, so that he now looks, moves, and talks like the other students in the Thinkery]

SOCRATES
    Here's your young man.

STREPSIADES
    Ah, my dear, dear boy.

SOCRATES

    Take him and go away.

[Socrates exits back into the Thinkery]

STREPSIADES

    Ah ha, my lad—

    what joy. What sheer delight for me to gaze,   [1170]

    first, upon your colourless complexion,

    to see how right away you're well prepared   1490

    to deny and contradict—with that look

    which indicates our national character

    so clearly planted on your countenance—

    the look which says, "What do you mean?"—the look

    which makes you seem a victim, even though

    you're the one at fault, the criminal.

    I know that Attic stare stamped on your face.

    Now you must rescue me—since you're the one

    who's done me in.

PHEIDIPPIDES

    What are you scared about?

STREPSIADES

    The day of the Old Moon and the New.   1500

PHEIDIPPIDES

    You mean there's a day that's old and new?

STREPSIADES

    The day they say they'll make deposits

    to charge me in the courts!   [1180]

PHEIDIPPIDES

    Then those who do that

    will lose their cash. There's simply no way

    one day can be two days.

STREPSIADES

It can't?

PHEIDIPPIDES:

How?
Unless it's possible a single woman
can at the same time be both old and young.

STREPSIADES

Yet that seems to be what our laws dictate.

PHEIDIPPIDES

In my view they just don't know the law—
not what it really means.

STREPSIADES

What does it mean?   1510

PHEIDIPPIDES

Old Solon by his nature loved the people.*

STREPSIADES

But that's got no bearing on the Old Day—
or the New.

PHEIDIPPIDES

Well, Solon set up two days   [1190]
for summonses—the Old Day and the New,
so deposits could be made with the New Moon.*

STREPSIADES

Then why did he include Old Day as well?

---

*   *Solon*: was a very famous Athenian law maker. In the early sixth century he laid down the basis for Athenian laws.

*   Pheidippides' hair-splitting argument which follows supposedly establishes that the law suits against Strepsiades are illegal and should be tossed out because (in brief) the court had taken the deposit, which the creditor had to make to launch the suit, on the wrong day (the last day of the month instead of the first day of the new month). The case rests on a misinterpretation of the meaning of the term Old and New Day—which was single day between the old and the new moon. The passage is, of course, a satire on sophistic reasoning and legal quibbling for self-interest.

PHEIDIPPIDES

    So the defendants, my dear fellow,
    could show up one day early, to settle
    by mutual agreement, and, if not,
    they should be very worried the next day   1520
    was the start of a New Moon.

STREPSIADES

    In that case,
    why do judges not accept deposits
    once the New Moon comes but only on the day
    between the Old and New?

PHEIDIPPIDES

    It seems to me
    they have to act like those who check the food—   [1200]
    they want to grab as fast as possible
    at those deposits, so they can nibble them
    a day ahead of time.

STREPSIADES

    That's wonderful!

[to the audience]

    You helpless fools! Why do you sit there—   1530
    so idiotically, for us wise types
    to take advantage of? Are you just stones,
    ciphers, merely sheep or stacked-up pots?
    This calls for a song to me and my son here,
    to celebrate good luck and victory.

[He sings]

    O Strepsiades is truly blessed
    for cleverness the very best,
    what a brainy son he's raised.

So friends and townsfolk sing his praise.
Each time you win they'll envy me—   1540   [1210]
you'll plead my case to victory.
So let's go in—I want to treat,
and first give you something to eat.

[Strepsiades and Pheidippides go together into their house. Enter one of Strepsiades' creditors, Pasias, with a friend as his witness]

PASIAS
Should a man throw away his money?
Never! But it would have been much better,
back then at the start, to forget the loan
and the embarrassment than go through this—
to drag you as a witness here today
in this matter of my money. I'll make
this man from my own deme my enemy.*   1550
But I'll not let my country down—never—   [1220]
not as long as I'm alive. And so . . .

[raising his voice]

I'm summoning Strepsiades . . .

[Enter Strepsiades]

STREPSIADES
Who is it?

PASIAS
. . . on this Old Day and the New.

STREPSIADES
I ask you here
to witness that he's called me for two days.
What's the matter?

---

*   *my own deme*: the deme was the basic political unit in Athens. Membership in it passed down from one's father.

PASIAS

    The loan you got, twelve minai,
    when you bought that horse—the dapple grey.

STREPSIADES

    A horse? Don't listen to him. You all know
    how I hate horses.

PASIAS

    What's more, by Zeus,
    you swore on all the gods you'd pay me back.   1560

STREPSIADES

    Yes, by god, but Pheidippides back then
    did not yet know the iron-clad argument
    on my behalf.

PASIAS

    So now, because of that,
    you're intending to deny the debt?   [1230]

STREPSIADES

    If I don't, what advantage do I gain
    from everything he's learned?

PASIAS

    Are you prepared
    to swear you owe me nothing—by the gods—
    in any place I tell you?

STREPSIADES

    Which gods?

PASIAS

    By Zeus, by Hermes, by Poseidon.

STREPSIADES

    Yes, indeed, by Zeus—and to take that oath   1570
    I'd even pay three extra obols.*

PASIAS

    You're shameless—may that ruin you some day!

STREPSIADES [patting Pasias on the belly]
    This wine skin here would much better off
    if you rubbed it down with salt.*

PASIAS

    Damn you—
     you're ridiculing me!

STREPSIADES [still patting Pasias' paunch]
    About four gallons,
     that's what it should hold.

PASIAS

    By mighty Zeus,
     by all the gods, you'll not make fun of me
    and get away with it!

STREPSIADES

    Ah, you and your gods—   [1240]
    that's so incredibly funny. And Zeus—
    to swear on him is quite ridiculous   1580
    to those who understand.

PASIAS

    Some day, I swear,
     you're going to have to pay for all of this.
     Will you or will you not pay me my money?
     Give me an answer, and I'll leave.

---

*   *three extra obols*: Strepsiades means here that swearing the oath will be such fun he's prepared to pay for the pleasure—an obvious insult to Pasias.

*   *salt*: leather was rubbed down as part of the tanning process. The phrase "wine skin" has been added to clarify the sense.

STREPSIADES

    Calm down—

    I'll give you a clear answer right away.

[Strepsiades goes into his house, leaving Pasias and the Witness by themselves]

PASIAS

    Well, what do you think he's going to do?

    Does it strike you he's going to pay?

[Enter Strepsiades carrying a kneading basin]

STREPSIADES

    Where's the man who's asking me for money?

    Tell me—what's this?

PASIAS

    What's that? A kneading basin.

STREPSIADES

    You're demanding money when you're such a fool?   1590

    I wouldn't pay an obol back to anyone   [1250]

    who called a basinette a basin.

PASIAS

    So you won't repay me?

STREPSIADES

    As far as I know,

    I won't. So why don't you just hurry up

    and quickly scuttle from my door.

PASIAS

    I'm off.

    Let me tell you—I'll be making my deposit.

    If not, may I not live another day!

[Pasias exits with the Witness]

STREPSIADES [calling after them]
>   That'll be more money thrown away—
>   on top of the twelve minai. I don't want
>   you going thorough that just because you're foolish   1600
>   and talk about a kneading basin.

[Enter Amynias, another creditor, limping He has obviously been hurt in some way]

AMYNIAS
>   Oh, it's bad. Poor me!

STREPSIADES
>   Hold on. Who's this
>   who's chanting a lament? Is that the cry   [1260]
>   of some god perhaps—one from Carcinus?*

AMYNIAS
>   What's that? You wish to know who I am?
>   I'm a man with a miserable fate!

STREPSIADES
>   Then go off on your own.

AMYNIAS [in a grand tragic manner]
>   "O cruel god,
>   O fortune fracturing my chariot wheels,
>   O Pallas, how you've annihilated me!"*

STREPSIADES
>   How's Tlepolemos done nasty things to you?*   1610

AMYNIAS
>   Don't laugh at me, my man—but tell your son
>   to pay me back the money he received,
>   especially when I'm going through all this pain.

---

*   *Carcinus*: an Athenian writer of tragic drama.
*   Amynias is here quoting from a tragedy written by Carcinus' son Xenocles.
*   *Tlepolemos* is a character in the tragedy mentioned in the previous note.

STREPSIADES

    What money are you talking about?

AMYNIAS

    The loan he got from me.   [1270]

STREPSIADES

    It seems to me
    you're having a bad time.

AMYNIAS

    By god, that's true—
    I was driving in my chariot and fell out.

STREPSIADES

    Why then babble on such utter nonsense,
    as if you'd just fallen off a donkey?

AMYNIAS

    If I want him to pay my money back   1620
    am I talking nonsense?

STREPSIADES

    I think it's clear
    your mind's not thinking straight.

AMYNIAS

    Why's that?

STREPSIADES

    From your behaviour here, it looks to me
    as if your brain's been shaken up.

AMYNIAS

    Well, as for you,
    by Hermes, I'll be suing you in court,
    if you don't pay the money.

STREPSIADES

Tell me this—
do you think Zeus always sends fresh water
each time the rain comes down, or does the sun   [1280]
suck the same water up from down below
for when it rains again?

AMYNIAS

I don't know which—   1630
and I don't care.

STREPSIADES

Then how can it be just
for you to get your money reimbursed,
when you know nothing of celestial things?

AMYNIAS

Look, if you haven't got the money now,
at least repay the interest.

STREPSIADES

This "interest"—
What sort of creature is it?

AMYNIAS

Don't you know?
It's nothing but the way that money grows,
always getting larger day by day
month by month, as time goes by.

STREPSIADES

That's right.
What about the sea? In your opinion,   1640
[1290]
is it more full of water than before?

AMYNIAS

No, by Zeus— it's still the same. If it grew,
that would violate all natural order.

STREPSIADES

In that case then, you miserable rascal,
if the sea shows no increase in volume
with so many rivers flowing into it,
why are you so keen to have your money grow?
Now, why not chase yourself away from here?

[calling inside the house]

Bring me the cattle prod!

AMYNIAS

I have witnesses!

[The slave comes out of the house and gives Strepsiades a cattle prod. Strepsiades starts poking Amynias with it]

STREPSIADES

Come on! What you waiting for? Move it,   1650
you pedigree nag!

AMYNIAS

This is outrageous!

STREPSIADES [continuing to poke Amynias away]
Get a move on—or I'll shove this prod   [1300]
all the way up your horse-racing rectum!

[Amynias runs off stage]

You running off? That's what I meant to do,
get the wheels on that chariot of yours

343

really moving fast.

[Strepsiades goes back into his house]

CHORUS

    Oh, it's so nice
    to worship vice.
    This old man here
    adores it so   1660
    he will not clear
    the debts he owes.
    But there's no way
    he will not fall
    some time today,
    done in by all
    his trickeries,
    he'll quickly fear
    depravities
    he's started here.   1670

    It seems to me
    he'll soon will see
    his clever son
    put on the show
    he wanted done
    so long ago—
    present a case
    against what's true
    and beat all those
    he runs into   1680
    with sophistry.
    He'll want his son
    (it may well be)
    to be struck dumb.   [1320]

[Enter Strepsiades running out of his house with Pheidippides close behind him hitting him over the head]

STREPSIADES

>Help! Help! You neighbours, relatives,
>fellow citizens, help me—I'm begging you!
>I'm being beaten up! Owww, I'm in such pain—
>my head . . . my jaw.

[To Pheidippides]

>You good for nothing,
>are you hitting your own father?

PHEIDIPPIDES

>Yes, dad, I am.

STREPSIADES

>See that! He admits he's beating me.   1690

PHEIDIPPIDES

>I do indeed.

STREPSIADES

>You scoundrel, criminal—
>a man who abuses his own father!

PHEIDIPPIDES

>Go on—keep calling me those very names—
>the same ones many times. Don't you realize
>I just love hearing streams of such abuse?

STREPSIADES

>You perverted asshole!

PHEIDIPPIDES

>Ah, some roses!   [1330]
>Keep pelting me with roses!!

STREPSIADES

    You'd hit your father?

PHEIDIPPIDES

    Yes, and by the gods I'll now demonstrate
    how I was right to hit you.

STREPSIADES

    You total wretch,
    how can it be right to strike one's father?   1700

PHEIDIPPIDES

    I'll prove that to you—and win the argument.

STREPSIADES

    You'll beat me on this point?

PHEIDIPPIDES

    Indeed, I will.
    It's easy. So of the two arguments
    choose which one you want.

STREPSIADES

    What two arguments?

PHEIDIPPIDES

    The Better or the Worse.

STREPSIADES

    By god, my lad,
    I really did have you taught to argue
    against what's just, if you succeed in this—
    and make the case it's fine and justified
    for a father to be beaten by his son.

PHEIDIPPIDES

Well, I think I'll manage to convince you,   1710
so that once you've heard my arguments,
you won't say a word.

STREPSIADES

Well, to tell the truth,
I do want to hear what you have to say.

CHORUS

You've some work to do, old man.
Think how to get the upper hand.
He's got something he thinks will work,
or he'd not act like such a jerk.
There's something makes him confident—
his arrogance is evident.   [1350]

CHORUS LEADER [addressing Strepsiades]

But first you need to tell the Chorus here   1720
how your fight originally started.
That's something you should do in any case.

STREPSIADES

Yes, I'll tell you how our quarrel first began.
As you know, we were having a fine meal.
I first asked him to take up his lyre
and sing a lyric by Simonides*—
the one about the ram being shorn.
But he immediately refused—saying
that playing the lyre while we were drinking
was out of date, like some woman singing   1730
while grinding barley.

PHEIDIPPIDES

Well, at that point,
you should have been ground up and trampled on—

---

*   *Simonides*: was a well-known lyric poet of the previous century.

asking for a song, as if you were feasting [1360]
with cicadas.

STREPSIADES
    The way he's talking now—
    that's just how he was talking there before.
    He said Simonides was a bad poet.
    I could hardly stand it, but at first I did.
    Then I asked him to pick up a myrtle branch
    and at least recite some Aeschylus for me.*
    He replied at once, "In my opinion,   1740
    Aeschylus is first among the poets
    for lots of noise, unevenness, and bombast—
    he piles up words like mountains." Do you know
    how hard my heart was pounding after that?
    But I clenched my teeth and kept my rage inside,
    and said, "Then recite me something recent,
    from the newer poets, some witty verse."   [1370]
    So he then right off started to declaim
    some passage from Euripides in which,
    spare me this, a brother was enjoying sex   1750
    with his own sister— from a common mother.
    I couldn't keep my temper any more—
    so on the spot I verbally attacked
    with all sorts of nasty, shameful language.
    Then, as one might predict, we went at it—
    hurling insults at each other back and forth.
    But then he jumped up, pushed me, thumped me,
    choked me, and started killing me.

PHEIDIPPIDES
    Surely I was entitled to do that
    to a man who will not praise Euripides,   1760
    the cleverest of all.

---

*   *myrtle branch*: traditionally a person singing at a drinking party held a myrtle branch unless he was playing a musical instrument.

STREPSIADES

    Him? The cleverest? Ha!
     What do I call you? No, I won't say—
    I'd just get beaten one more time.

PHEIDIPPIDES

     Yes, by Zeus,
    you would—and with justice, too.

STREPSIADES

    How would that be just? You shameless man,
    I brought you up. When you lisped your words,
    I listened 'til I recognized each one.
    If you said "waa," I understood the word
    and brought a drink; if you asked for "foo foo,"
    I'd bring you bread. And if you said "poo poo"   1770
    I'd pick you up and carry you outside,
    and hold you up. But when you strangled me
    just now, I screamed and yelled I had to shit—
    but you didn't dare to carry me outside,
    you nasty brute, you kept on throttling me,
    until I crapped myself right where I was.   [1390]

CHORUS

    I think the hearts of younger spry
    are pounding now for his reply—
    for if he acts in just this way
    and yet his logic wins the day   1780
    I'll not value at a pin
    any older person's skin.

CHORUS LEADER

    Now down to work, you spinner of words,
    you explorer of brand new expressions.
    Seek some way to persuade us, so it will appear
    that what you've been saying is right.

PHEIDIPPIDES

    How sweet it is to be conversant with

    things which are new and clever, capable   [1400]

    of treating with contempt established ways.

    When I was only focused on my horses,   1790

    I couldn't say three words without going wrong.

    But now this man has made me stop all that,

    I'm well acquainted with the subtlest views,

    and arguments and frames of mind. And so,

    I do believe I'll show how just it is

    to punish one's own father.

STREPSIADES

    By the gods,

    keep on with your horses then—for me

    caring for a four-horse team is better

    than being beaten to a pulp.

PHEIDIPPIDES

    I'll go back

    to where I was in my argument,   1800

    when you interrupted me. First, tell me this—

    Did you hit me when I was a child?

STREPSIADES

    Yes.

    But I was doing it out of care for you.

PHEIDIPPIDES

    Then tell me this: Is it not right for me

    to care for you in the same way—to beat you—

    since that's what caring means—a beating?

    Why must your body be except from blows,

    while mine is not? I was born a free man, too.

    "The children howl—you think the father

    should not howl as well?" You're going to claim   1810

    the laws permit this practice on our children.

    To that I would reply that older men

are in their second childhood. More than that—
it makes sense that older men should howl
before the young, because there's far less chance
their natures lead them into errors.

STREPSIADES

    There's no law that fathers have to suffer this.   [1420]

PHEIDIPPIDES

    But surely some man first brought in the law,
    someone like you and me? And way back then
    people found his arguments convincing.   1820
    Why should I have less right to make new laws
    for future sons, so they can take their turn
    and beat their fathers? All the blows we got
    before the law was brought in we'll erase,
    and we'll demand no payback for our beatings.
    Consider cocks and other animals—
    they avenge themselves against their fathers.
    And yet how are we different from them,
    except they don't propose decrees?

STREPSIADES

    Well then,   [1430]
    since you want to be like cocks in all you do,   1830
    why not sleep on a perch and feed on shit?

PHEIDIPPIDES

    My dear man, that's not the same at all—
    not according to what Socrates would think.

STREPSIADES

    Even so, don't beat me. For if you do,
    you'll have yourself to blame.

PHEIDIPPIDES

    Why's that?

STREPSIADES

    Because I have the right to chastise you,
    if you have a son, you'll have that right with him.

PHEIDIPPIDES

    If I don't have one, I'll have cried for nothing,
    and you'll be laughing in your grave.

STREPSIADES [addressing the audience]

    All you men out there my age, it seems to me   1840
    he's arguing what's right. And in my view,
    we should concede to these young sons what's fair.
    It's only right that we should cry in pain
    when we do something wrong.

PHEIDIPPIDES

    Consider now another point.

STREPSIADES

    No, no.

                              It'll   finish   me!

[1440]

PHEIDIPPIDES

    But then again
    perhaps you won't feel so miserable
    at going through what you've suffered.

STREPSIADES

    What's that?
    Explain to me how I benefit from this.

PHEIDIPPIDES

    I'll thump my mother, just as I hit you.   1850

STREPSIADES

    What's did you just say? What are you claiming?
    This second point is even more disgraceful.

PHEIDIPPIDES

    But what if, using the Worse Argument,
    I beat you arguing this proposition—
    that it's only right to hit one's mother?

STREPSIADES

    What else but this—if you do a thing like that,
    then why stop there? Why not throw yourself
    and Socrates and the Worse Argument   [1450]
    into the execution pit?

[Strepsiades turns towards the Chorus]

    It's your fault,
    you Clouds, that I have to endure all this.   1860
    I entrusted my affairs to you.

CHORUS LEADER

    No.
    You're the one responsible for this.
    You turned yourself toward these felonies.

STREPSIADES

    Why didn't you inform me at the time,
    instead of luring on an old country man?

CHORUS

    That's what we do each time we see someone
    who falls in love with evil strategies,
    until we hurl him into misery,   [1460]
    so he may learn to fear the gods.

STREPSIADES

    O dear. That's harsh, you Clouds, but fair enough.   1870
    I shouldn't have kept trying not to pay
    that cash I borrowed. Now, my dearest lad,
    come with me—let's exterminate those men,

the scoundrel Chaerephon and Socrates,
the ones who played their tricks on you and me.

PHEIDIPPIDES

But I couldn't harm the ones who taught me.

STREPSIADES

Yes, you must. Revere Paternal Zeus.*

PHEIDIPPIDES

Just listen to that—Paternal Zeus.
How out of date you are! Does Zeus exist?

STREPSIADES

He does.

PHEIDIPPIDES

  No, no, he doesn't—there's no way,   1880   [1470]
for Vortex has now done away with Zeus
and rules in everything.

STREPSIADES

He hasn't killed him.

[He points to a small statue of a round goblet which stands outside Thinkery]

I thought he had because that statue there,
the cup, is called a vortex.* What a fool
to think this piece of clay could be a god!

PHEIDIPPIDES

Stay here and babble nonsense to yourself.

---

* *Paternal Zeus*: This seems to be an appeal to Zeus as the guardian of the father's rights and thus a way or urging Pheidippides to go along with what his father wants. The line may be a quote from a lost tragedy.

* *Vortex*: the Greek word *dinos*, meaning "whirl," "eddy," or "vortex," also means a round goblet. The statue of such a goblet outside the Thinkery represents the presiding deity of the house.

[Pheidippides exits]*

STREPSIADES
    My god, what lunacy. I was insane
    to cast aside the gods for Socrates.

[Strepsiades goes up and talks to the small statue of Hermes outside his house]

    But, dear Hermes, don't vent your rage on me,
    don't grind me down. Be merciful to me.   1890
    Their empty babbling made me lose my mind.   [1480]
    Give me your advice. Shall I lay a charge,
    go after them in court. What seems right to you?

[He looks for a moment at the statue]

    You counsel well. I won't launch a law suit.
    I'll burn their house as quickly as I can,
    these babbling fools.

[Strepsiades calls into his house]

    Xanthias, come here.
    Come outside—bring a ladder—a mattock, too.
    then climb up on top of that Thinkery
    and, if you love your master, smash the roof,
    until the house collapses in on them.   1900

[Xanthias comes out with ladder and mattock, climbs up onto the Thinkery and starts demolishing the roof]

    Someone fetch me a flaming torch out here.
    They may brag all they like, but here today   [1490]

---

*   It's not clear whether Pheidippides goes back into his house or back into the school. If he does the latter, then the comic violence at the end of the play takes on a much darker tone, since Strepsiades' murderous anger includes his son. In fact, the loss of his son might be the key event which triggers the intensity of the final destruction.

I'll make somebody pay the penalty
for what they did to me.

[Another slave comes out and hands Strepsiades a torch. He joins Xanthias on the roof and tries to burn down the inside of the Thinkery]

STUDENT [from inside the Thinkery]

Help! Help!

STREPSIADES

Come on, Torch, put your flames to work.

[Strepsiades sets fire to the roof of the Thinkery. A student rushes outside and looks at Strepsiades and Xanthias on the roof]

STUDENT

You there, what are you doing?

STREPSIADES

What am I doing?
What else but picking a good argument
with the roof beams of your house?

[A second student appears at a window as smoke starts coming out of the house]

STUDENT

Help! Who's setting fire to the house?

STREPSIADES

It's the man
whose cloak you stole.

STUDENT

We'll die. You'll kill us all!   1910

STREPSIADES

That's what I want—unless this mattock

disappoints my hopes or I fall through somehow   [1500]
   and break my neck.

[Socrates comes out of the house in a cloud of smoke. He is coughing badly]

SOCRATES
   What are you doing up on the roof?

STREPSIADES
   I walk on air and contemplate the sun.

SOCRATES [coughing]
   This is bad—I'm going to suffocate.

STUDENT [still at the window]
   What about poor me? I'll be burned up.

[Strepsiades and Xanthias come down from the roof]

STREPSIADES [to Socrates]
   Why were you so insolent with gods
   in what you studied and when you explored
   the moon's abode? Chase them off, hit them,
   throw things at them—for all sorts of reasons,
   but most of all for their impiety.   1920

[Strepsiades and Xanthias chase Socrates and the students off the stage and exit after them]

CHORUS LEADER
   Lead us on out of here. Away!
   We've had enough of song and dance today.

[The Chorus exits]

Aeneid

Book 2

FROM *The Essential Aenid Virgil*

translated by Stanley Lombardo

The room fell silent, all eyes on Aeneas,
Who from his high couch now began to speak:

"My Queen, you are asking me to relive
Unspeakable sorrow, to recall how the Greeks
Pulled down Troy, that tragic realm   5
With all its riches. I saw those horrors myself
And played no small part in them. What Myrmidon
Or Dolopian, what brutal soldier of Ulysses
Could tell such a tale and refrain from tears?
And now dewy night is rushing from the sky,   10
And the setting stars make sleep seem sweet.
But if you are so passionate to learn
Of our misfortunes, to hear a brief account
Of Troy's last struggle—although my mind
Shudders to remember and recoils in pain,   15
I will begin.

Broken by war and rebuffed by the Fates
For so many years, the Greek warlords
Built a horse, aided by the divine art
Of Pallas, a horse the size of a mountain,   20
Weaving its ribs out of beams of fir.
They pretended it was a votive offering
For their safe return home. So the story went.
But deep within the Horse's cavernous dark
They concealed an elite band, all their best,   25
Stuffing its huge womb with men at arms.

Within sight of Troy lies a famous island,
Tenedos, prosperous while Priam's kingdom stood,
Now just a bay with poor anchorage for ships.
The Greeks sailed there and hid on the desolate shore;   30
They were gone, we thought, sailed off to Mycenae.
And so all of Troy shook off its long sorrow.
The gates were opened. It was a joy to visit
The Doric camp, the abandoned beachhead,
The deserted sites. Here the Dolopians   35
Pitched their tents, here fierce Achilles,
Here lay the ships, here were the battle-lines.
Some of us gaped at the virgin Minerva's
Fatal gift, amazed at the massive Horse.
Thymoetes wanted it dragged inside the walls   40
And installed in the citadel. Treason perhaps.
Or Troy's doom was already in motion.
But Capys, and other wiser heads, urged us
To either pitch this insidious Greek gift
Into the sea, or burn it on the spot, or else   45
Pierce and probe the belly's hidden hollows.
The crowd took sides, uncertain what to do.

And now Laocoön comes running down
From the citadel at the head of a great throng
And in his burning haste he cries from afar: 50

'Are you out of your minds, you poor fools?
Are you so easily convinced that the enemy
Has sailed away? Do you honestly think
That any Greek gift comes without treachery?
What is Ulysses known for? Either this lumber   55
Is hiding Achaeans inside, or it has been built
As an engine of war to attack our walls.
To spy on our homes and come down on the city
From above. Or some other evil lurks inside.
Do not trust the Horse, Trojans! Whatever it is,   60
I fear the Greeks, even when they bring gifts.'

With that, he hurled his spear with enormous force
Into the vaulting belly of the beast. The shaft
Stood quivering, and the hollow insides
Reverberated with a cavernous moan.   65
If we had not been on the gods' wrong side,
If we had been thinking right, Laocoön
Would have driven us to hack our way into
The Greek lair, and Troy would still stand,
And you, high rock of Priam, would remain.   70

But at that moment a band of Dardan shepherds
Came up with loud shouts, dragging to the king
A prisoner with his hands bound behind his back.
This man had deliberately gotten himself captured
With one purpose in mind, to open Troy to the Greeks,   75
Ready to either work his deceits or face certain death.
The Trojan youths streamed in from all sides
To see the captive and jeer at him.
                              Hear now
The treachery of the Greeks, and from one offense
Learn all their evil.
                    The man stood in full sight   80
Of the crowd, dismayed, unarmed, and
glancing Around at the ranks of men he cried
out:

'Ah, what land, what sea, can receive me now,
What will be my final wretched fate?
I have no place among the Greeks,   85
And the Trojans are clamoring for my blood.'

At this our mood changed, and we prodded him
To tell us what he meant. Who were his people,
And what was he counting on to save him
Now that he was our prisoner? Finally,   90
He stopped trembling and began to speak:

'Come what may, King, I will tell you all
And not deny, first, that I am a Danaan.
Fortune may have damned Sinon to misery,
But she will not make him a liar as well.   95
You may have heard the name Palamedes,
Belus' glorious son, whom the Greeks
Condemned to death, under false charges,
Because he opposed the war. He was innocent.
Now they mourn him, now that he is dead.   100
He was my kinsman, and my father,
A poor man, sent me here in his company
When I was just a boy. While Palamedes
Was still in good standing, still thrived in council,
I too had somewhat of a name, some honor.   105
But when through the malice of cunning Ulysses
(Everyone knows this) he passed from this world,
I was a ruined man and dragged on my life
In darkness and grief, eating my heart out
Over the fate of my innocent friend.   110
Nor was I silent, but I raved
That if I ever had the chance, ever returned
As victor to Argos, I would have my vengeance.
My words aroused resentment, and my life
Was now infected. Ulysses made it his mission   115
To terrorize me with countless new charges.
Sowing rumors in everyone's ears, searching

In his guilt for weapons against me. In the end
He found Fortune's tool, Calchas the soothsayer—
But you don't want to hear all this. And why   120
Should I stall? If you paint all Greeks
With the same stripe, if "he's Achaean"
Is all you need to hear, take your vengeance
At once. This is what the Ithacan would want.
And what Atreus' sons would, pay dearly for.'   125

Now indeed we burned to know more,
Strangers as we were to infamy so great
And to Greek guile. Trembling, he went
on:

'Weary with the long war, the Greeks
Often wanted to quit Troy and sail home.   130
If only they had! But stormy weather
And rough seas would scare them from leaving.
And when they'd hammered together
The maple horse, the sky rumbled even more.
Anxious, we sent Eurypylus to consult   135
The oracle of Phoebus Apollo,
And he brought back these dismal words:
You placated the winds with a virgin's blood
To come, O Danaans, to the shores of Troy.
Your return must be won with an Argive life.   *140*
When the god's words reached the army's ears
Everyone was dazed, and an icy fear
Seeped into their bones. Which man was doomed,
Whom would Apollo claim? The Ithacan.
Dragged Calchas out into the roaring crowd   145
And demanded to know what heaven portended.
Many divined that this despicable ploy
Was aimed at me and saw what was coming.
Five days and five more the seer sat in his hut,
Silent, refusing to sentence anyone to death.   150
Finally, forced by the Ithacan's cries,

Calchas broke his silence and, as agreed.
Doomed me to the altar. Everyone approved,
And the ruin each had feared for himself
They bore well when it devolved upon one.   155

'And now the dark day dawned. The salted grain.
The sacral headbands were being prepared
For my ritual slaughter, when, I confess,
I broke my bonds and snatched myself from death.
I skulked all night in a muddy swamp,   160
Hidden in the sedge, holding my breath
Until they sailed. Now I have no hope
Of seeing my homeland, my sweet children.
The father I long for. And the Greeks
May make them pay for my escape, poor things,   165
And by their death expiate my sin.
And so I pray, by whatever powers above
Still witness Truth, and by any Faith we men
Still have uncorrupted, show mercy
To a suffering soul, guiltless and wronged.'   170
We spared him for his tears and pitied him
Of our own accord. Priam himself ordered
His shackles removed and spoke to him kindly:

'Whoever you are, take no further thought
Of the Greeks. You are one of us now.   175
But tell me, and speak the whole truth:
Why did they erect this monstrous horse?
Who devised it, and to what purpose?
Is it a religious offering or an. engine of war?'

Thus Priam. And Sinon, the consummate liar,   180
Lifting his unchained hands to the stars:

'Eternal fires of heaven, I summon you
And your inviolable Power to witness,
And you altars and nefarious blades

Which I escaped, and you consecrated fillets   185
Which as victim I wore: it is just for me
To break the sacred oaths of the Greeks,
Just to abhor those men, and to lay bare to the sky
Every secret they would conceal. I am bound
By no law of my country. But you, Troy,   190
Stand by your word and keep your faith,

If what I say proves to be your salvation.
'From the war's beginning, Pallas Athena
Was the Greeks' entire hope. But when
Wicked Diomedes and Ulysses,   195
With his criminal mind, entered
Her high temple, murdered the guards,
And stole the fateful Palladium,
Daring to handle her virgin fillets
With bloodstained fingers—then   200
The Danaans' fortunes began to falter,
Their strength was broken, and the goddess
Turned her back on them. Tritonia
Gave us clear portents of her displeasure.
As soon as her statue was set up in camp,   205
Flames glittered from her upturned eyes,
Sweat poured down her limbs, and three times
She flashed up from the ground, miraculous,
Holding her shield and quivering spear.
Calchas at once began to prophesy: 210

"The Greeks must attempt a retreat by sea.
Troy cannot be taken by Argive weapons
Until they seek new omens in Argos
And return the godhead carried away

In curved keels over open water."   215
'They are sailing over to Mycenae now.
And when they have recruited soldiers and gods
They will recross the water all unforeseen.

So Calchas sifted the omens and counseled the Greeks
To erect this Horse, in expiation   220
Of the Palladium's theft and the godhead wronged.
And he ordered them to build its oaken bulk
Up to the sky, so it could not be brought
Through the city's gates or walls and there protect
The Trojan people under the old religion.   225
For if you lay violent hands
Upon this offering to Minerva,
Destruction will fall—may the gods turn this omen
Against the Greeks—upon Priam's realm.
But if your hands bring it into the city,   230
Asia will wage war upon Pelops' walls,
And this fate awaits our children's children.'

And so through Sinon's treacherous art
His story was believed, and we were taken
With cunning, captured with forced tears,   235
We whom neither great Diomedes
Nor Achilles of Larissa could subdue.
Nor ten years of war, nor a thousand ships.

What happened next was more horrible still
And threw us into deepening chaos.   240
Laocoön, serving by lot as Neptune's priest,
Was sacrificing a great bull at the god's altar,
When we saw, coming from Tenedos
Over the calm water, a pair of serpents—
I shudder to recall them—making for shore.   245
Trailing huge coils they sheared through the sea,
And their bloody crests arched over the waves
As they writhed and twisted in the seething surf.
They were almost ashore. Their eyes
Were shot with blood and fire, and their tongues   250
Hissed and flickered in their open mouths.
We scattered, pale with fear, as the sea-snakes
Glided through the sand straight for Laocoön.

First, they entwined the priest's two sons
In great looping spirals, and then they sank their fangs 255
Into the boys' wretched bodies and began to feed.
Then they seized Laocoön as he ran to their aid,
Weapon in hand, and lashed their scaly bodies
Twice around his waist and twice around his neck,
Their heads reared high. As the priest struggled 260
To wrench himself free from the knotted coils,
His headbands were soaked with venom, and gore,
And his horrible cries reached up to the stars.

Wounded by an ill-aimed blow, a bull will bellow
As it flees the altar and shakes the axe from his neck. 265

So too Laocoön. But the twin serpents
Slithered off to the high temple of Pallas
And took refuge at the grim goddess's feet,
Vanished behind the disk of her shield.
An inhuman terror coiled through our hearts. 270
Shuddering with horror, everyone said Laocoön
Had received the punishment he deserved
For wounding the sacred wood of the Horse
With his accursed spear. All proclaimed
The Horse should be drawn to Minerva's temple 275
And her godhead appeased. We breached the walls,
Everyone girding themselves for the work.
And set wheels beneath the feet of the Horse.
A noose was made taut around its neck
And the fateful contraption inched up the battlements, 280
Pregnant with arms. Boys and unwed girls
Circled around it, singing hymns
And touching the rope with glee. On it moved.
Gliding like a threat into the city.
O my country! O Ilium, home of the gods! 285
O walls of Troy famed in war! Four times
At the very threshold of the city gate
The Horse halted, and four times

Weapons clattered in its belly. Yet we pressed on
Mindlessly, blind with passion, and installed 290
The ill-starred monster on our high holy rock.
Even then Cassandra opened her lips
Against the coming doom, lips cursed by a god
Never to be believed by the Teucrians,
And we pitiful Trojans, on our last day, 295
Wreathed the shrines of the gods with flowers.

The sky turned, and night swept up from Ocean,
Enfolding in its great shadow earth and heaven—
And the Myrmidons' treachery. The Trojans
Spread out along the wall were dead silent now, 300
Slumber entwining their weary limbs,
And the Argive fleet started to sail from Tenedos
Through the silent, complicit moonlight,
Making for the shore they knew all too well.
The flagship raised a beacon, and at this signal 305
Sinon, cloaked by the gods' unjust decrees,
Stealthily unlocked the pine trapdoor,
And the Horse released from its open womb
The enclosed Danaans, glad to push themselves out
Of the hollow oak into the cool night air, 310
Thessandrus and Sthenelus and grim Ulysses—
Sliding down the rope—Acamas and Thoas,
Achilles' son, Neoptolemus, great Machaon,
Menelaus, and Epeos himself,
The fabricator of the insidious horse. 315
They fanned out through a city drowned in sleep,
Slit the guards' throats, opened all the gates,
And joined as planned the invading Greeks.

At that late hour, when sleep begins to drift
Upon fretful humanity as grace from the gods, 320
Hector appeared to me in my dreams,
Pitiful spirit, weeping, black with blood
And dust from the ruts of Achilles' chariot,

Thongs piercing his swollen ankles. Ah,
How he looked, how different from that Hector   325
Who returned to Troy wearing Achilles' armor,
The Hector who threw fire on the Danaan ships!
His beard was matted, his hair clotted with gore,
And he bore all the wounds he had received
Fighting before his country's walls. In my dream   330
I blurted out to him these tearful words:

'Light of Dardania, Troy's finest hope,
What has delayed you? From what shores have you come
To answer our prayers? We have suffered
Many losses since you left us, Hector.   335
Yet, we have labored on, and now we see you
At the end of our strength. Why has your face
Been defiled, and what are these wounds I see?'

My empty questions meant nothing to him.
With a heavy sigh from deep within, he said: 340

'Run, child of the goddess, save yourself
From these flames! The enemy holds the walls.
Great Troy is falling. Enough has been given
To Priam and his country. If Pergamum's height
Could be defended by a hero's hand,   345
Its defense would have been this hand of mine.
Troy commends to you the gods of the city.
Accept them as companions of your destiny
And seek for them the great walls you will found
After you have wandered across the sea.'   350

He spoke, and brought out from the sanctuary
Great Vesta, her chaplets, and her eternal, fire.

By now the lamentation in the city
Had grown to such proportions that it reached
My father Anchises' house, secluded though it was   355

Among the pines. The sickening sound of battle
Startled me from sleep, and I climbed to the roof
And stood at the very top, upright and listening.

It was as if the South Wind were fanning fire
Through the fields, or a mountain torrent had leveled   360
The farmlands and swept away the oxen's tillage,
Flattening the hedgerows, and I was a shepherd
Listening in the dark from some towering rock.

Then the truth was revealed. The Danaans' treachery
Lay open before me. Deiphobus' great house   365
Was collapsing in flames, as was Ucalegon's
Next door. The Sigean straits burned
With the inferno's reflected light.
Men's shouts rose with the shrill sound of horns.
Out of my mind, I took up arms—no battle plan,   370
But my soul burned to gather a war party
And storm the citadel. Rage and fury
Sent my mind reeling, and my only thought
Was how glorious it is to die in combat.

At that moment Panthus, priest of Apollo,   375
Ran up to my door, dragging his grandson
Away from Greek swords, the sacred images
Of our vanquished gods clutched in his arms.
'Where is the fighting thickest, Panthus?
What position should we try to hold?'

My words   380
Were scarcely out when he answered, groaning:

'Troy's last day and final hour have come.
We are Trojans no more. Ilium is no more.
The great glory of the Teucrians is gone.
Jupiter in his rage has given all to Argos,   385
And Greeks are lords of our burning city.

High stands the Horse, pouring forth armed men,
And Sinon, insolent in victory,
Sets fires everywhere. Thousands of troops.
As many as ever came from Mycenae,   390
Are at the wide-open gates. Others patrol the streets.
A line of unsheathed, glistening steel
Stands ready for slaughter. Our night guard
Is barely resisting and fighting blind.'

Panthus' words and will of the gods   395
Drove me through the inferno of battle
Wherever the grim Fury called, wherever
The roars and shouts rose to the sky.
Falling in with me in the moonlight
Were Rhipeus and Epytus, one of Troy's best,   400
Hypanis and Dymas, a little throng now,
And young Coroebus, son of Mygdon.
He had come to Troy in those last days,
Madly in love with Cassandra, and brought
Aid to Priam, a sturdy son-in-law. Poor boy,   405
If only he had listened to the warnings
Of his raving bride.
When I saw them close ranks, eager for battle,
I began:

'Brave hearts—brave in vain
If you are committed to follow me to the end—   410
You see how we stand. All the gods
Who sustained this realm are gone, leaving
Altar and shrine. You are fighting to save
A city in flames. All that is left for us
Is to rush onto swords and die. The only chance   415
For the conquered is to hope for none.'

This added fury to the young men's courage.
Like wolves in a black mist, blind with hunger.
Their whelps waiting with dry throats, we passed

Through the enemy's swords to certain death   420
And held our course to the city's center.
Ebony night swirled around us. Who could tell
That night's carnage, or match it with tears?
The ancient city fell, that had for many years
Been queen. Corpses lay piled everywhere,   425
In the streets, the houses, the hallowed thresholds
Of the temples. And it was not only Trojans
Who paid in blood. At times the vanquished
Felt their valor pulse through their hearts,
And the conquering Greeks fell. Raw fear   430
Was everywhere, grief was everywhere,
Everywhere the many masks of death.

Androgeos offered himself to us first.
Heading up a large company of Greeks,
He mistook us for an allied band and called: 435

'On the double, men! What took you so long?
We're burning and looting Pergamum here,
And you're just arriving from, the ships?'

He realized at once from our tentative reply
That we were the enemy. He froze, choked   440
On his own words, and then tried to backpedal,

   Like a man who has stepped on a snake
   Hidden in briars and in sudden terror cringes
   When it rears and puffs out its purple hood.

Androgeos was shaking and backing away   445
When we charged and hedged them in.
Unfamiliar with the terrain, they panicked.
And we cut them down, Fortune smiling
On our first effort. Flushed with success,
Coroebus cried:

Aeneid

'Let's follow Fortune's lead   450
And exchange our armor for Danaan
gear. Who cares if this is deceit or
valor?
The enemy will supply us with
weapons.'

With that he put on Androgeos' plumed helmet.
Hefted his emblazoned shield, and hung   455
An Argive sword by his side. So too Rhipeus,
Dymas, and my other boys, their spirits high
As they armed themselves in new-won spoils.
We moved out, mingling with the Greeks
And with gods not ours. In the blind night   460

We engaged in many skirmishes, and sent
Many a Greek into the jaws of Orcus.
Some scattered to the safety of the shore
And the ships. Others, like terrified children,
Climbed back up into the belly of the Horse.   465

Never rely on the gods for anything
Against their will. The next thing we saw
Was Cassandra, Priam's daughter,
Being dragged, hair streaming, from the shrine
Of Minerva's temple, lifting to heaven   470

Her burning eyes—her eyes only,
For her tender hands were bound. Coroebus
Could not endure this. He threw himself
Into the midst of the band, determined to die.
We closed ranks and charged, but were overwhelmed.   475

First, our countrymen targeted our uniforms.
The misleading crests on our Greek helmets.
hen the Greeks themselves, grunting with anger

APicking us off from the roof, a piteous slaughter.
Tt the attempted rescue of Cassandra,   480

Came at us from all sides, Ajax most viciously.
Then the two sons of Atreus and Ulysses' men.

> It was like a hurricane when winds clash
> Front every direction, Winds West and South
> And the East proud with his colts of Dawn.   485
> The forests groan, and Nereus foams with rage
> As he stirs with his trident the lowest depths.

The men we had routed with our stratagem
In the dim of night rematerialized, the first
To recognize our mendacious shields   490
And discordant accents. We were outnumbered.
Coroebus fell first, killed by Peneleos
At the war goddess's altar. Then Rhipeus,
Of all Teucrians the most righteous (but the gods
Saw otherwise) went down. Hypanis   495
And Dymas were run through by friends;
And you, Panthus, neither your piety
Nor Apollo's fillet protected you
When you fell. O ashes of Ilium!
Olast flames of my people! Be witness   500
That in your fall I shunned neither fight nor chance,
And had my fate been to die by Greek hands
Ihad earned that fate. We were torn from there,
Iphitus, Pelias, and myself, we three,
Iphitus heavy with years, Pelias slowed   505
By a wound from Ulysses. Without pause
We were called by the clamor to Priam's house.

Here was an enormous battle, so intense
It was as if there was no one fought anywhere else,
And men were not dying throughout the city.   510
Here we saw the War God unchained. Greeks
Scrambled to the roof, and the threshold

Was besieged by a bulge of shields. Ladders
Hugged the walls, and men inched their way
Upward on the rungs, left hands holding up shields 515
Against projectiles, right hands clutching
Posts and battlements. Above, the Trojans
Tore down the towers and all the rooftop
To use as missiles—they saw the end was near—
Defending themselves to the death, rolling down 520
Gilded rafters, their fathers' splendors of old.
Other troops, swords drawn, massed around the doors,
Blocking the entrances. Our pulses quickened
With new energy to protect the palace
And come to the aid of our vanquished men. 525
There was a secret entry in the rear,
A passageway through Priam's palace
By which Andromache, poor soul,
Would come unattended to her husband's parents
While Troy still stood and lead her boy, 530
Astyanax, to see his grandfather.
I scaled the roof, where the Teucrians
Were lobbing their useless missiles to little effect.
Rising to the sky from the roof's sheer edge
Stood a tower from which all Troy 535
Could once be seen, and in the distance
A thousand Greek ships and their beachhead camp.
We pried at its upper stories with our swords
Until the joints gave way, wrenched it loose,
And sent it crashing down like rolling thunder 540
Onto the ranks of the Greeks. But more Greeks
Kept coming, and more stones kept falling.

Framed by the portal to the entrance court
Pyrrhus stood in his glory, haloed in bronze,

As *a snake raised on poison basks in the light* 545
After a cold winter has kept him underground,
Venomous and swollen. Now, having sloughed
His old skin, glistening with youth, he puffs out

His breast and slides his lubricious coils
Toward, the sun, flicking his three-forked tongue.   *550*

At his side loomed Periphas, and Automedon,
Once Achilles' charioteer, now the armor-bearer
Of Achilles' son. Massed around them
Were all the tough troops from Scyros,
Hurling torches onto the roof as they closed in   555
On Priam's palace. Pyrrhus led the charge,
Cleaving through the solid threshold
With a battle-axe, tearing the brass-bound doors
From their hinges, and hatcheting a hole
The size of a window in a huge oaken panel,   560
Revealing all the house in a grim tableau.
Open to view were the long halls; laid bare
Was the inner sanctum of Priam
And the kings of old, who now saw

Armed men standing on their very threshold.   565
A tumultuous roar tore through the house;
Its vaulted halls echoed with women's wails,
And the din reverberated to the golden stars.
Trembling matrons roamed lost through the rooms.
Clinging to the doors, lips pressed against them.   570
Pyrrhus moved on with all his father's might.
And nothing could stop him. The gate gave way
Before the battering ram, and the doors,
Wrenched from their sockets, fell to the floor.
The Greeks forced their way in, butchered   575
The Trojans who stood up against them,
And filled the whole space with their soldiery,

Worse than a river bursting through its banks,
The water churning in overwhelming fury,
Flooding the fields and. sweeping herds and folds   *580*
Over the plain.

I saw with my own eyes
Neoptolemus, lusting for slaughter,
And Atreus' two sons, there on the threshold.
I saw Hecuba, with her hundred daughters,
And Priam, polluting with his blood   585
The very altars he had consecrated himself.
Those fifty bedchambers, that promise of offspring, The
doorposts proud with barbarian gold—
All lost. The Greeks held what the fire spared.
And what, you may ask, was Priam's fate?   590

When he saw that his city had fallen,
The doors of his palace shattered,
And the enemy at his very hearth,
The old man slung his long-unused armor
Over his trembling shoulders, strapped on   595
His useless sword, and, bound to die,
Charged the enemy.

In the middle of the palace,
Under heaven's naked wheel, an enormous altar
Lay beneath the branches of an ancient laurel
Whose shade embraced the household gods.   600
In this sacred place Hecuba and her daughters
Huddled like doves driven by a black storm,
Clutching the gods' images. But when she saw
Priam, himself clad in the armor of his youth.
She cried out:

'My poor husband,   605
What insanity has driven you
To take up these weapons? Where
Are you rushing to? The hour is past
For defense like this, even if my Hector
Were still here. Come to this altar, please,   610
It will protect us all, or you will die with us.'

Hecuba said these things, took the aged man
In her arms, and placed him on the holy seat.

And now Polites, one of Priam's sons,
Pursued by Pyrrhus, came running   615
Through the colonnades, wounded.
When he reached the vast atrium
Pyrrhus was breathing down his neck.
And yet he slipped away to face his parents' eyes.

There he fell, Pyrrhus' spear in his back,   620
And poured out his life in a pool of blood.
Then Priam, in death's grip as he was,
Did not hold back his anger or spare his voice.

'For this heinous crime,' he cried, 'this outrage,
May the gods in heaven—if there is in heaven   625
Any spirit that cares for what is just and good—
May the gods treat you as you deserve
For making me watch my own son's murder
And defiling with death a father's face.
Not so was Achilles, whom you falsely claim   630
To be your father, in the face of Priam his foe,
But honored a suppliant's rights and trust,
And allowed the bloodless corpse of Hector
Burial, and. sent me back to my own realm.'

And the old man threw his feeble spear. Its tip   635
Clanged against the bronze of Pyrrhus' shield
And dangled uselessly from its boss. And Pyrrhus:

'Then you can take this news to my father,
The son of Peleus. Be sure to tell him
About my sad behavior and how degenerate   640
His son has become. Now die.'

So saying,
He dragged Priam, trembling and slipping

In his son's blood, up to the altar. Winding
His left hand in the old man's hair, with his right
He lifted his flashing sword and buried it   645
Up to its hilt in his side. So ended Priam,
Such was his fated doom, as Troy burned
Before his eyes and ergamum fell.
Once the lord of so many peoples,
The sovereign of Asia, he lies now   650
A huge trunk upon the shore, head
severed From his neck, a corpse without a
name.

Then an awful sense of dread enveloped me.
I stood in a daze, and there rose before me
The image of my dear father, the same age   655
As the wounded king whom. I was watching
Gasp out his life. Before me rose Creüsa,
Abandoned, the pillaged house, and the plight
Of little lülus. I looked around
For my troops. They had all deserted me.   660
Too fatigued to fight, they had either jumped
To a welcome death or dropped limply into the flames.

Now I alone was left, when I saw,
Hiding in the shadows of Vesta's shrine,
Helen, daughter of Tyndareus. The bright fires   665
Gave me light as I wandered here and there
Casting my eyes over everything.
Fearing the Trojans' anger for Troy's fall,
The vengeance of the Greeks, and the wrath
Of her deserted husband, Helen, destroyer   670
Alike of her own country and ours,
This detestable woman, crouched by the altars.
My soul flared with a burning desire
To avenge Troy and make her pay for her sins.
'So she will look upon Sparta unscathed   675
And enter Mycenae as a triumphant queen?

She will get to see her husband and home,
Her parents and children, attended
By Trojan women and Phrygian slaves?
Was it for this that Priam was slaughtered,   680
Ilium burned, and our shore soaked with blood?
Never! Although there is no heroic name
In killing a woman, no victory,
I will be praised for snuffing out evil
And meting out justice. And it will be sweet   685
To quench my soul with vengeful fire
And satisfy my people's ashes.'

I was carried away by this frenzy, when,
Shining through the dark in a halo of light.
My mother appeared before my eyes, more clearly   690
Than ever before, revealing herself
As a radiant goddess, just as the great ones
In heaven see her, so beautiful, so tall.
She caught me by the hand and, in grace,
Spoke these words from her pale-rose lips: 695

'What anguish is behind this uncontrollable rage?
Why so angry, my son? And where has your love
For our family gone? Will you not first see
Where you left your father, Anchises,
Feeble with age, or whether Creüsa   700
And your child, Ascanius, are still alive?
They are surrounded by Greek soldiers
And but for my loving care would have died
In the flames by now, or the swords of the enemy
Would have tasted their blood. It is not   705
The detestable beauty of Tyndarean Helen
Or sinful Paris that is to blame. No, it is the gods,
The remorseless gods, who have ruined Troy
And burnt the topless towers of Ilium.
See for yourself. I will dispel the mist   710
That enshrouds you and dulls your mortal vision.

You might not trust your mother otherwise,
And disregard her kind instructions.

Here,
Where you see piles of rubble, stones
Wrenched from stones, and plumes of smoke and dust,   715
Is Neptune, shaking the walls he has pried up
With his great trident and uprooting the city
From its foundations. Over here, Juno,
Ferocious in her iron vest, first to hold
The Western Gates, summons with her usual   720
Fury reinforcements from the ships.
And now look up. Tritonian Pallas
Is already seated on the highest
towers, Glowing from a thunderhead,
grim
With her Gorgon. The Father himself   725
Gives the Greeks courage and strength
And incites the gods to oppose the Trojans.
Hurry away, my son, and end your struggle.
I will bring you safely to your father's door.'

And she plunged into night's shadows.
Dire faces,   730
Numinous presences hostile to Troy, now loomed
In the darkness visible.

To my eyes it seemed that all Ilium
Was sinking in flames, and Neptune's Troy
Was being overturned from its base.   735

> It was just like an ancient mountain ash
> That woodsmen are straining to fell Iron axes
> Ring thick and fast on its trunk, hacking it through,
> And it threatens to fall, nodding front its crest,
> Its foliage trembling, until, bit by bit,   740
> Overcome with wounds, it gives one last groan
> And torn from the hillside comes crashing down.

I descended and, guided by a god,
Somehow got through fire and foe.
Weapons gave way; the flames receded.   745

When I reached the doors of my father's house,
My old home, I sought him first and wanted
More than anything to lift him up

Into the mountains—but he refused
To draw out his life and suffer exile   750
With Troy in ashes.

'You are young,'
He cried, 'and still strong; you must take flight.
If the gods wanted to prolong ray life
They would have preserved this home of mine.
It is enough and more that I have seen   755
Such destruction once before and have survived
One capture of my city. Say farewell
To my body lying just as it is
And depart. I shall die by my own hand.
The Greeks will pick over my spoils and pity me.   760
Loss of burial is light. Despised by heaven
And useless, I have lived too many years
Since the Lord of Gods and Men breathed winds
Of lightning upon me and touched me with fire.'

He kept repeating words such as these   765
And would not move. We were all in tears,
My wife, Creüsa, Ascanius, all our household,
Pleading with my father not to compound
Our desperate plight and destroy us with him.
He refused, and remained just as he was.   770
I reached for my gear, wanting only to die.
What hope was there for deliverance now?

'Did you think I could leave without you, Father?
How could such a thing come out of your mouth?

If it pleases the gods that nothing be left   775
Of this great city, and if you are determined,
If it is your pleasure, to throw yourself
And all of us into Troy's holocaust—
The door to that fate is wide open. Pyrrhus,
Grimed with Priam's gore, will be here soon;   780
Pyrrhus, who mutilates the son
Before the father's eyes, butchers the father
Like a beast at the altar. O my merciful mother,
Was it for this you saved me from the enemy,
So I could see the enemy in my own home   785
And Ascanius, and my father, and Creüsa
Slaughtered In each other's blood?

                              To anus, men!
The last light calls the vanquished. Take me back
To the Greeks. Let me start the battle again.
Never this day shall we all die unavenged!'   790

Once more I strapped on my sword, gripped my
shield In my left hand, and was hurrying out of the door,
When Creüsa embraced my feet at the threshold
And held up little Iulus to his father, saying:

'If you go to die, take us with you,   795
To whatever fate. But if experience has taught you
To rely on your weapons, guard first this house.
To whom do you leave us, little Iülus,
Your father, and me, once called your wife?'

Her voice filled the house with moaning,   800
And then, without warning, a strange portent
Flickered between the faces and hands
Of Iülus' anxious parents: a light tongue of flame
Glearning above his head. Harmless to the touch,
It licked his soft locks and grazed his temples.   805
Trembling with fear, we shook the fire from his hair
Quickly and doused the holy flames with water.

But my father, Anchises, enraptured,
Raised his eyes to the stars above
And lifted his hands and his voice to heaven: 810

'Almighty Jupiter, if you are moved
By any prayers, only look upon us,
And if by our piety we have earned it,
Give us your aid and confirm this omen.'

His aged words had just finished, when suddenly   815
Thunder crashed on our left, and a star
Shot down from the sky, sliding through the dark
And trailing a luminous flood of sparks.
We watched it glide over the palace roof
And bury its splendor in Ida's forest,   820
Leaving a shining furrow in its wake.
The air reeked with sulfur all around.

Overwhelmed, my father lifted himself up
In adoration of the star and spoke to heaven:

'No more delay. I follow, and where yon lead,   825
There I am. Gods of our fathers, save this house,
Save my grandson. Yours is this omen,
In your power is Troy. And now, my son,
I am ready to go as your companion.'

He spoke, and now the sound of the fire   830
Could be heard more clearly, and the inferno
Rolled its seething heat ever closer.

'Come, dear Father, onto my shoulders now.
You will not weigh me down, and come what may
We will face it together, peril or salvation.   835
Little Iulus will walk beside me, and my wife
Will walk in my footsteps some distance behind.
Now listen to me, all of my household:

Just outside the city there is a mound,

And a temple of Ceres, long deserted.   840
Beside these stands an ancient cypress
Worshiped by my ancestors for many years.
There, by our separate ways, we will meet.
Take into your hands, Father, the sacred gods
Of our country. It would be a sacrilege   845
If I touched them before I washed away
The bloody filth of battle in a living river.'

This said, I spread upon my shoulders
A golden lionskin and bent to my burden.
Little Iulus held my hand and kept up,   850
Although his stride could not match his father's,
And my wife followed behind.

We kept
To the shadows and I undisturbed before
By any number of weapons thrust my way
And whole platoons of Greeks, now was frightened   855
By every breeze and startled by every sound,
Afraid for my companion and my burden.

We were nearing the gates, and it looked like

We had made it through, when suddenly
The sound of marching feet drifted on the wind.   860
Squinting through the gloom, my father cried:

'Run for it, Son! They're getting close.
I can see the bronze glitter of their shields.'

I panicked. Some malignant spirit
Robbed me of my wits, for while I ran   865
Down back alleys, leaving the familiar streets,
My wife, Creüsa, was taken from me

By some evil fortune. Had she stopped,
Or got lost and sat down exhausted?
I never saw her again, didn't even look back   870
Or think of her behind me until we arrived
At the mound by Ceres' ancient temple.
When finally we were all gathered there,
She alone was missing. No one had seen her,
Not her husband, not her son, no one.   875
What man or god did I not accuse
In my delirium? What cruder thing
Had I seen in our overturned city?
I entrusted Ascanius, Anchises,
And the gods of Troy to my companions   880
And hid them in a bend of the valley.
Myself, I strapped on my glittering armor
And went back to the city, hell-bent
On running every risk again,
Combing through all of Troy,   885
And putting my life on the line once more.

I started at the walls and the dark gate
Where I had escaped and retraced my steps
Through the night, looking everywhere by torchlight.
Everywhere there was fear. The very silence   890
Was terrifying. Then I turned homeward,
In case, just in case, she had gone there.
The Greeks were there in force, and the house
Consumed with fire. Fanned by the wind,
It spiraled up past the eaves and gnawed at the roof,   895
Blasting the sky with its heat. I moved on
And saw once more the palace of Priam.

On the citadel. There, in the empty court
Of Juno's sanctuary, stood Phoenix
And dire Ulysses, chosen to guard the spoils,   900
Treasures from, every part of Troy, ripped
Out of burning temples—tables of the gods,
Solid gold bowls, and plundered robes—

All in a heap. Boys and trembling matrons
Stood around in long rows. 905

I even risked casting my voice into the night
And filled the streets with shouts, calling
'Creüsa' over and over again
In my misery, all in vain.

But as I rushed
Through the empty shells of buildings, frantic 910
To find her, there rose before my eyes
The sad ghost of Creüsa herself, an image
Larger than life. I was transfixed,
My hair stood on end, and my voice choked.
Then she spoke to me and calmed my fears: 915

'What good does it do, my sweet husband,
To indulge in such mad grief? These things
Do not happen without the will of the gods.
You may not take your Creüsa with you;
The Lord of Olympus does not allow it. 920
Long exile is yours, plowing a vast stretch
Of sea. Then you will come to Hesperia,
Where the Lydian Tiber runs gently
Through fertile fields. There, happy times.
Kingship, and a royal wife shall be yours. 925
Dry your tears for your beloved Creüsa.
I shall not look upon the proud domains
Of the Myrmidons or Dolopians,
Nor go to be a slave for Greek matrons,
I, a Trojan woman, and wife of the son 930
Of the goddess Venus. No,
The Great Mother keeps me on these shores.
Farewell, and keep well your love for our child.'

Creüsa spoke, and then left me there, 935
Weeping, with many things yet to say.

She vanished into thin air. Three times
I tried to put my arms around her; three times
Her wraith slipped through my hands,
Soft as a breeze, like a vanishing dream.

The long night was spent, and at last   940
I went back to rejoin my people.
I was surprised by the great number
Of new arrivals I found, women and men,
Youth gathered for exile, a wretched band
Of refugees who had poured in from all over,   945
Prepared to journey across the sea
To whatever lands I might lead them.
The brilliant morning star was rising
Over Ida's ridges, ushering in the day.
The Greeks held all the city gates.   950
There was no hope of help. I yielded
And, lifting up my father, sought the mountains."

The Life of Nero

By Suetonius, translated by J.C. Rolfe

1 Of the Domitian family two branches have acquired distinction, the Calvini and the Ahenobarbi. The latter have as the founder of their race and the origin of their surname Lucius Domitius, to whom, as he was returning from the country, there once appeared twin youths of more than mortal majesty, so it is said, and bade him carry to the senate and people the news of a victory,[1] which was as yet unknown. And as a token of their divinity it is said that they stroked his cheeks and turned his black beard to a ruddy hue, like that of bronze. This sign was perpetuated in his descendants, a great part of whom had red beards. 2 After they had attained seven consulships, a triumph, and two censorships, and were enrolled among the patricians, they all continued to use the same surname. They confined their forenames to Gnaeus and Lucius, and used even these with a noteworthy variation, now conferring each one on three members of the family in succession, and now giving them to individual members in turn. Thus the first, second, and third of the Ahenobarbi, we are told, were called Lucius, the next three in order Gnaeus, while all those that followed were called in turn first Lucius and then Gnaeus. It seems to me worth while to give an account of several members of this family, to show more clearly that though Nero degenerated from the good qualities of his ancestors, he yet reproduced the vices of each of them, as if transmitted to him by natural inheritance.

2 1 To begin then somewhat far back, his great-grandfather's grandfather, Gnaeus Domitius, when tribune of the commons, was enraged at the pontiffs for choosing another than himself in his father's place among them, and transferred the right of filling vacancies in the priesthoods from the colleges themselves to the people. Then having vanquished the Allobroges and the Arverni in his consulship, he rode through the province on an elephant, attended by a throng of soldiers, in a kind of triumphal procession.[2] 2 He it was of whom the orator Licinius Crassus said that it was not surprising that he had a brazen beard, since he had a face[3] of iron and a heart of lead. His son, who was praetor at the time, summoned Gaius Caesar to an investigation before the senate at the close of his consulship, because it was thought that his administration had been in violation of the auspices and the laws. Afterwards in his own consulship he tried to deprive Caesar of the command of the armies in Gaul, and being named Caesar's successor by his party, was taken prisoner at Corfinium at the beginning of the civil war.[4] 3 Granted his freedom, he at first gave courage by his presence to the people of Massilia, who were hard pressed by their besiegers, but suddenly abandoned them and at last fell in the battle at Pharsalus. He was a man of no great resolution, though he had a violent temper, and when he once attempted to kill himself in a fit of despair and terror, he so shrank from the thought of death that he changed his mind and vomited up the poison, conferring freedom on his physician, since, knowing his master, he had purposely given him what was not a fatal dose. When Gnaeus Pompeius brought forward the question of the treatment of those who were neutral and sided with neither party, he alone was for regarding them as hostile.

3 1 He left a son, who was beyond all question better than the rest of the family. He was condemned to death by the Pedian law[5] among those implicated in Caesar's death, though he was guiltless, and accordingly joined Brutus and Cassius, who were his near relatives. After the death of both leaders he retained the fleet of which he had previously been made commander, and even added to it, and it was not until his party had been everywhere routed that he surrendered it to Mark Antony, of his own free will and as if it were a great favour. 2 He too was the only one of those who were condemned by that same law[6] who was allowed to return to his native land, where he successively held all the highest offices. When the civil strife was subsequently renewed, and he was appointed one of Antony's lieutenants, he did not venture, owing to a sudden attack of illness, to accept the chief command when it was offered by those who were ashamed of Cleopatra, nor yet positively to decline it; but he went over to Augustus and a few days later died. Even he did not escape with an unblemished reputation, for Antony openly declared that he had changed sides from desire for the company of his mistress, Servilia Nais.

4 1 He was the father of the Domitius who was later well known from being named in Augustus' will as the purchaser of his goods and chattels,[7] a man no less famous in his youth for his skill in driving than he was later for winning the insignia of a triumph in the war in Germany. But he was haughty, extravagant, and cruel, and when he was only an aedile, forced the censor Lucius Plancus to make way for him on the street. While holding the offices of praetor and consul, he brought Roman knights and matrons on the stage to act a farce. He gave beast-baitings both in the

Circus and in all the regions of the city; also a gladiatorial show, but with such inhuman cruelty that Augustus, after his private warning was disregarded, was forced to restrain him by an edict.

5 1 He had by the elder Antonia a son Domitius who became the father of Nero, a man hateful in every walk of life; for when he had gone to the East on the staff of the young Gaius Caesar,[8] he slew one of his own freedmen for refusing to drink as much as he ordered, and when he was in consequence dismissed from the number of Gaius' friends, he lived not a whit less lawlessly. On the contrary, in a village on the Appian Way, suddenly whipping up his team, he purposely ran over and killed a boy; and right in the Roman Forum he gouged out the eye[9] of a Roman knight for being too outspoken in chiding him. 2 He was moreover so dishonest that he not only cheated some bankers of the prices of wares which he had bought,[10] but in his praetorship he even defrauded the victors in the chariot races of the amount of their prizes. When for this reason he was held up to scorn by the jests of his own sister, and the managers of the troupes made complaint, he issued an edict[11] that the prizes should thereafter be paid on the spot. Just before the death of Tiberius he was also charged with treason, as well as with acts of adultery and incest with his sister Lepida, but escaped owing to the change of rulers and died of dropsy at Pyrgi, after acknowledging[12] Nero son of Agrippina, the daughter of Germanicus.

6 1 Nero was born at Antium nine months after the death of Tiberius, on the eighteenth day before the Kalends of January, just as the sun rose, so that he was touched by its rays almost before he could be laid upon the ground.[13] Many people at once made many direful predictions from his horoscope,[a] and a remark of his father Domitius was also regarded as an omen; for while receiving the congratulations of his friends, he said that "nothing that was not abominable and a public bane could be born of Agrippina and himself." 2 Another manifest indication of Nero's future unhappiness occurred on the day of his purification;[14] for when Gaius Caesar was asked by his sister to give the child whatever name he liked, he looked at his uncle Claudius, who later became emperor and adopted Nero, and said that he gave him his name. This he did, not seriously, but in jest, and Agrippina scorned the proposal, because at that time Claudius was one of the laughing-stocks of the court.

3 At the age of three he lost his father, being left heir to a third of his estate; but even this he did not receive in full, since his fellow heir Gaius seized all the property. Then his mother was banished too, and he was brought up at the house of his aunt Lepida almost in actual want, under two tutors, a dancer and a barber. But when Claudius became emperor, Nero not only recovered his father's property, but was also enriched by an inheritance from his stepfather, Passienus Crispus. 4 When his mother was recalled from banishment and reinstated, he became so prominent through her influence that it leaked out that Messalina, wife of Claudius, had sent emissaries to strangle him as he was taking his noonday nap, regarding him as a rival of Britannicus. An addition to this bit of gossip is, that the would-be assassins were frightened away by a snake which darted out from under

his pillow. The only foundation for this tale was, that there was found in his bed near the pillow the slough of a serpent; but nevertheless[15] at his mother's desire he had the skin enclosed in a golden bracelet, and wore it for a long time on his right arm. But when at last the memory of his mother grew hateful to him, he threw it away, and afterwards in the time of his extremity sought it again in vain.

7 1 While he was still a young, half-grown boy he took part in the game of Troy at a performance in the Circus with great self-possession and success. In the eleventh[16] year of his age he was adopted by Claudius and consigned to the training of Annaeus Seneca, who was then already a senator. They say that on the following night Seneca dreamed that he was teaching Gaius Caesar, and Nero soon proved the dream prophetic by revealing the cruelty of his disposition at the earliest possible opportunity. For merely because his brother Britannicus had, after his adoption, greeted him as usual as Ahenobarbus, he tried to convince his father[17] that Britannicus was a changeling. Also when his aunt Lepida was accused, he publicly gave testimony against her, to gratify his mother, who was using every effort to ruin Lepida.

2 At his formal introduction into public life he announced a largess to the people and a gift of money to the soldiers, ordered a drill[18] of the praetorians and headed them shield in hand; and thereafter returned thanks to his father in the senate. In the latter's consulship he pleaded the cause of the people of Bononia before him in Latin, and of those of Rhodes and Ilium in Greek. His first appearance as judge was when he was prefect of the city during the Latin Festival, when the most celebrated pleaders vied with one another in bringing before him, not trifling and brief cases according to the usual custom, but many of the highest importance, though this had been forbidden by Claudius. Shortly afterwards he took Octavia to wife and gave games and a beast-baiting in the Circus, that health might be vouchsafed Claudius.

8 1 When the death of Claudius was made public, Nero, who was seventeen years old, went forth to the watch[19] between the sixth and the seventh hour, since no earlier time for the formal beginning of his reign seemed suitable because of bad omens throughout the day.[20] Hailed emperor on the steps of the Palace, he was carried in a litter to the praetorian camp, and after a brief address to the soldiers was taken from there to the House, which he did not leave until evening, of the unbounded honours that were heaped upon him refusing but one, the title of father of his country, and that because of his youth.

9 1 Then beginning with a display of filial piety, he gave Claudius a magnificent funeral, spoke his eulogy, and deified him. He paid the highest honours to the memory of his father Domitius. He left to his mother the management of all public and private business. Indeed, on the first day of his rule he gave to the tribune on guard the watchword "The Best of Mothers," and afterwards he often rode with her through the streets in her litter. He established a colony at Antium, enrolling the veterans of the praetorian guard and joining with them the wealthiest of the chief centurions, whom he compelled to change their residence; and he also made a harbour there at great expense.

10 1 To make his good intentions still more evident, he declared that he would rule according to the principles of Augustus, and he let slip no opportunity for acts of generosity and mercy, or even for displaying his affability. The more oppressive sources of revenue he either abolished or moderated. He reduced the rewards paid to informers against violators of the Papian law[21] to one fourth of the former amount. He distributed four hundred sesterces to each man of the people, and granted to the most distinguished of the senators who were without means an annual salary,[22] to some as much as five hundred thousand sesterces; and to the praetorian cohorts he gave a monthly allowance of grain free of cost. 2 When he was asked according to custom to sign the warrant for the execution of a man who had been condemned to death, he said: "How I wish I had never learned to write!" He greeted men of all orders off-hand and from memory.[23] When the senate returned thanks to him, he replied, "When I shall have deserved them." He admitted even the commons to witness his exercises in the Campus, and often declaimed in public. He read his poems too, not only at home but in the theatre as well, so greatly to the delight of all that a thanksgiving[24] was voted because of his recital, while that part[25] of his poems was inscribed in letters of gold and dedicated to Jupiter of the Capitol.

11 1 He gave many entertainments of different kinds: the Juvenales,[26] chariot races in the Circus, stage-plays, and a gladiatorial show. At the first mentioned he had even old men of consular rank and aged matrons take part. For the games in the Circus he assigned places to the knights apart from the rest,[27] and even matched chariots drawn by four camels. 2 At the plays which he gave for the "Eternity of the Empire," which by his order were called the Ludi Maximi, parts were taken by several men and women of both the orders; a well known Roman knight mounted an elephant and rode down a rope;[28] a Roman play of Afranius, too, was staged, entitled "The Fire," and the actors were allowed to carry off the furniture of the burning house and keep it. Every day all kinds of presents were thrown to the people; these included a thousand birds of every kind each day, various kinds of food, •tickets for grain, clothing, gold, silver, precious stones, pearls, paintings, slaves, beasts of burden, and even trained wild animals; finally, ships, blocks of houses, and farms.

12 1 These plays he viewed from the top of the proscenium. At the gladiatorial show, which he gave in a wooden amphitheatre, erected in the district of the Campus Martius within the space of a single year, he had no one put to death, not even criminals. But he compelled four hundred senators and six hundred Roman knights, some of whom were well to do and of unblemished reputation, to fight in the arena. Even those who fought with the wild beasts and performed the various services in the arena[29] were of the same orders. He also exhibited a naval battle in salt water with sea monsters swimming about in it; besides pyrrhic dances[30] by some Greek youths,[31] handing each of them certificates of Roman citizenship at the close of his performance. 2 The pyrrhic dances represented various scenes. In one a bull mounted Pasiphae, who was concealed in a wooden image of a heifer; at least many of the spectators thought so. Icarus at his very first attempt fell close by the imperial couch and bespattered the emperor with his blood; for Nero very seldom presided at the games, but used to view them while reclining on a couch, at first through small openings, and then with the entire balcony[32] uncovered.

3 He was likewise the first to establish at Rome a quinquennial[b] contest in three parts, after the Greek fashion, that is in music,[33] gymnastics, and riding, which he called the Neronia; at the same time he dedicated his baths and gymnasium,[34] supplying every member of the senatorial and equestrian orders with oil. To preside over[35] the whole contest he appointed ex-consuls, chosen by lot, who occupied the seats of the praetors. Then he went down into the orchestra among the senators and accepted the prize for Latin oratory and verse, for which all the most eminent men had contended but which was given to him with their unanimous consent; but when that for lyre-playing was also offered him by the judges, he knelt before it and ordered that it be laid at the feet of Augustus' statue. 4 At the gymnastic contest, which he gave in the •Saepta, he shaved his first beard to the accompaniment of a splendid sacrifice of bullocks, put it in a golden box adorned with pearls of great price, and dedicated it in the Capitol. He invited the Vestal virgins also to witness the contests of the athletes,[36] because at Olympia the priestesses of Ceres were allowed the same privilege.

13 1 I may fairly include among his shows the entrance of Tiridates into the city. He was a king of Armenia, whom Nero induced by great promises to come to Rome; and since he was prevented by bad weather from exhibiting him to the people on the day appointed by proclamation, he produced him at the first favourable opportunity, with the praetorian cohorts drawn up in full armour about the temples in the Forum, while he himself sat in a curule chair on the rostra in the attire of a triumphing general, surrounded by military ensigns and standards. 2 As the king approached along a sloping platform, the emperor at first let him fall at his feet, but raised him with his right hand and kissed him. Then, while the king made supplication, Nero took the turban from his head and replaced it with a diadem, while a man of praetorian rank translated the words of the suppliant and proclaimed them to the throng. From there the king was taken to the theatre,[37] and when he had again done obeisance, Nero gave him a seat at his right hand. Because of all this Nero was hailed as Imperator,[38] and after depositing a laurel wreath in the Capitol,[39] he closed the two doors of the temple of Janus,[40] as a sign that no war was left anywhere.

14 1 He held four consulships, the first for two months, the second and the last for six months each, the third for four months. The second and third were in successive years, while a year intervened between these and each of the others.[41]

15 1 In the administration of justice he was reluctant to render a decision to those who presented cases, except on the following day and in writing. The procedure was, instead of continuous pleadings, to have each point presented separately by the parties in turn. Furthermore, whenever he withdrew for consultation, he did not discuss any matter with all his advisers in a body, but had each of them give his opinion in written form; these he read silently and in private and then gave a verdict according to his own inclination, as if it were the view of the majority.

2 For a long time he would not admit the sons of freedmen to the senate and he refused office to those who had been admitted by his predecessors. Candidates who were in excess of the number of vacancies received the command of a legion as compensation for the postponement and delay. He commonly appointed consuls for a period of six months. When one of them died just before the Kalends of January, he appointed no one in his place, expressing his disapproval of the old-time case of Caninius Rebilus, the twenty-four hour consul.[42] He conferred the triumphal regalia even on men of the rank of quaestor, as well as on some of the knights, and sometimes for other than military services. As regards the speeches which he sent to the senate on various matters, he passed over the quaestors, whose duty it was to read them,[43] and usually had them presented by one of the consuls.

16 1 He devised a new form for the buildings of the city and in front of the houses and apartments he erected porches, from the flat roofs of which fires could be fought;[44] and these he put up at his own cost. He had also planned to extend the walls as far as Ostia and to bring the sea from there to Rome by a canal.

2 During his reign many abuses were severely punished and put down, and no fewer new laws were made: a limit was set to expenditures; the public banquets were confined to a distribution of food; the sale of any kind of cooked viands in the taverns was forbidden, with the exception of pulse and vegetables, whereas before every sort of dainty was exposed for sale.[45] Punishment was inflicted on the Christians, a class of men given to a new and mischievous superstition. He put an end to the diversions of the chariot drivers, who from immunity of long standing claimed the right of ranging at large and amusing themselves by cheating and robbing the people. The pantomimic actors and their partisans were banished from the city.[46]

17 1 It was in his reign that a protection against forgers was first devised, by having no tablets signed that were not bored with holes through which a cord was thrice passed.[47] In the case of wills it was provided that the first two leaves should be presented to the signatories[48] with only the name of the testator written upon them, and that no one who wrote a will for another should put down a legacy for himself; further, that clients should pay a fixed and reasonable fee for the services of their advocates,[49] but nothing at all for benches, which were to be furnished free of charge by the public treasury; finally as regarded the pleading of cases, that those connected with the treasury should be transferred to the Forum[50] and a board of arbiters, and that any appeal from the juries should be made to the senate.

18 1 So far from being actuated by any wish or hope of increasing or extending the empire, he even thought of withdrawing the army from Britain and changed his purpose only because he was ashamed to seem to belittle the glory of his father.[51] He increased the provinces only by the realm of Pontus, when it was given up by Polemon, and that of Cottius in the Alps on the latter's death.

19 1 He planned but two foreign tours, to Alexandria and Achaia; and he gave up the former on the very day when he was to have started, disturbed by a threatening portent. For as he was making the round of the temples and had sat down in the shrine of Vesta, first the fringe of his garment caught when he attempted to get up, and then such darkness overspread his eyes that he could see nothing. 2 In Achaia he attempted to cut through the Isthmus[52] and called together the praetorians and urged them to begin the work; then at a signal given on a trumpet he was first to break ground with a mattock and to carry off a basketful of earth upon his shoulders. He also prepared for an expedition to the Caspian Gates, after enrolling a new legion of raw recruits of Italian birth, each •six feet tall,[53] which he called the "phalanx of Alexander the Great."

3 I have brought together these acts of his, some of which are beyond criticism, while others are even deserving of no slight praise, to separate them from his shameful and criminal deeds, of which I shall proceed now to give an account.

20 1 Having gained some knowledge of music in addition to the rest of his early education, as soon as he became emperor he sent for Terpnus, the greatest master of the lyre in those days, and after listening to him sing after dinner for many successive days until late at night, he little by little began to practise himself, neglecting none of the exercises which artists of that kind are in the habit of following, to preserve or strengthen their voices. For he used to lie upon his back and hold a leaden plate on his chest, purge himself by the syringe and by vomiting, and deny himself fruits and all foods injurious to the voice. Finally encouraged by his progress, although his voice was weak and husky, he began to long to appear on the stage, and every now and then in the presence of his intimate friends he would quote a Greek proverb meaning "Hidden music counts for nothing."[54] 2 And he made his début at Naples, where he did not cease singing until he had finished the number which he had begun, even though the theatre was shaken by a sudden earthquake shock.[55] In the same city he sang frequently and for several days. Even when he took a short time to rest his voice, he could not keep out of sight but went to the theatre after bathing and dined in the orchestra with the people all about him, promising them in Greek, that when he had wetted his whistle a bit, he would ring out something good and loud.[56] 3 He was greatly taken too with the rhythmic applause of some Alexandrians, who had flocked to Naples from a fleet that had lately arrived, and summoned more men from Alexandria. Not content with that, he selected some young men of the order of knights and more than five thousand sturdy young commoners, to be divided into groups and learn the Alexandrian styles of applause (they called them "the bees," "the roof-tiles," and "the bricks"),[57] and to ply them vigorously whenever he sang. These men were noticeable for their thick hair and fine apparel; their left hands were bare and without rings, and the leaders were paid four hundred thousand sesterces each.

21 1 Considering it of great importance to appear in Rome as well, he repeated the contest of the Neronia[58] before the appointed time, and when there was a general call for his "divine voice," he replied that if any wished to hear him, he would favour them in the gardens; but when the guard of soldiers which was then on duty seconded the entreaties of the people, he gladly agreed to appear at once. So without delay he had his name added to the list of the lyre-players who entered the contest, and casting his own lot into the urn with the rest, he came forward in his turn, attended by the prefects of the Guard carrying his lyre, and followed by the tribunes of the soldiers and his intimate friends. 2 Having taken his place and finished his preliminary speech,[59] he announced through the ex-consul Cluvius Rufus that "he would sing Niobe"; and he kept at it until late in the afternoon, putting off the award of the prize for that event and postponing the rest of the contest to the next year, to have an excuse for singing oftener. But since even that seemed too long to wait, he did not cease to appear in public from time to time. He even thought of taking part in private performances[60] among the professional actors, when one of the praetors offered him a million sesterces. 3 He also put on the mask and sang tragedies representing gods and heroes and even heroines and goddesses, having the masks fashioned in the likeness of his own features or those of the women of whom he chanced to be enamoured. Among other themes he sang "Canace in Labor," "Orestes the Matricide," "The Blinding of Oedipus" and the "Frenzy of Hercules." At the last named performance they say that a young recruit, seeing the emperor in mean attire and bound with chains, as the subject required, rushed forward to lend him aid.

22 1 From his earliest years he had a special passion for horses and talked constantly about the games in the Circus, though he was forbidden to do so.[61] Once when he was lamenting with his fellow pupils the fate of a charioteer of the "Greens,"[62] who was dragged by his horses, and his preceptor scolded him, he told a lie and pretended that he was talking of Hector. At the beginning of his reign he used to play every day with ivory chariots on a board, and he came from the country to all the games, even the most insignificant, at first secretly, and then so openly that no one doubted that he would be in Rome on that particular day. 2 He made no secret of his wish to have the number of prizes increased, and in consequence more races were added and the performance was continued to a late hour, while the managers of the troupes no longer thought it worth while to produce their drivers at all except for a full day's racing. He soon longed to drive a chariot himself and even to show himself frequently to the public; so after a trial exhibition in his gardens before his slaves and the dregs of the populace, he gave all an opportunity of seeing him in the Circus Maximus, one of his freedmen dropping the napkin[63] from the place usually occupied by the magistrates.

3 Not content with showing his proficiency in these arts at Rome, he went to Achaia, as I have said,[64] influenced especially by the following consideration. The cities in which it was the custom to

hold contests in music had adopted the rule of sending all the lyric prizes to him. These he received with the greatest delight, not only giving audience before all others to the envoys who brought them, but even inviting them to his private table. When some of them begged him to sing after dinner and greeted his performance with extravagant applause, he declared that "the Greeks were the only ones who had an ear for music and that they alone were worthy of his efforts." So he took ship without delay and immediately on arriving at Cassiope made a preliminary appearance as a singer at the altar of Jupiter Cassius, and then went the round of all the contests.[65]

23 1 To make this possible, he gave orders that even those which were widely separated in time should be brought together in a single year, so that some had even to be given twice, and he introduced a musical competition at Olympia also, contrary to custom. To avoid being distracted or hindered in any way while busy with these contests, he replied to his freedman Helius, who reminded him that the affairs of the city required his presence, in these words: "However much it may be your advice and your wish that I should return speedily, yet you ought rather to counsel me and to hope that I may return worthy of Nero."

2 While he was singing no one was allowed to leave the theatre even for the most urgent reasons. And so it is said that some women gave birth to children there, while many who were worn out with listening and applauding, secretly leaped from the wall,[66] since the gates at the entrance[67] were closed, or feigned death and were carried out as if for burial. The trepidation and anxiety with which he took part in the contests, his keen rivalry of his opponents and his awe of the judges, can hardly be credited. As if his rivals were of quite the same station as himself, he used to show respect to them and try to gain their favour, while he slandered them behind their backs, sometimes assailed them with abuse when he met them, and even bribed those who were especially proficient.

3 Before beginning, he would address the judges in the most deferential terms, saying that he had done all that could be done, but the issue was in the hands of Fortune; they however, being men of wisdom and experience, ought to exclude what was fortuitous. When they bade him take heart, he withdrew with greater confidence, but not even then without anxiety, interpreting the silence and modesty of some as sullenness and ill-nature, and declaring that he had his suspicions of them.

24 1 In competition he observed the rules most scrupulously, never daring to clear his throat and even wiping the sweat from his brow with his arm.[68] Once indeed, during the performance of a tragedy, when he had dropped his sceptre but quickly recovered it, he was terribly afraid that he might be excluded from the competition because of his slip, and his confidence was restored only when his accompanist[69] swore that it had passed unnoticed amid the delight and applause of the people. When the victory was won, he made the announcement himself; and for that reason he always took part in the contests of the heralds.[70] To obliterate the memory of all other victors in games[71] and leave no trace of them, their statues and busts were all thrown down by his order, dragged off with hooks, and cast into privies.

2 He also drove a chariot in many places, at Olympia even a ten-horse team, although in one of his own poems he had criticised Mithridates for just that thing. But after he had been thrown from the car and put back in it, he was unable to hold out and gave up before the end of the course; but he received the crown just the same. On his departure he presented the entire province with freedom[72] and at the same time gave the judges Roman citizenship and a large sum of money. These favours he announced in person on the day of the Isthmian Games, standing in the middle of the stadium.

25 1 Returning from Greece, since it was at Naples that he had made his first appearance, he entered that city with white horses through a part of the wall which had been thrown down, as is customary with victors in the sacred games.[73] In like manner he entered Antium, then Albanum, and finally Rome; but at Rome he rode in the chariot which Augustus had used in his triumphs in days gone by, and wore a purple robe and a Greek cloak adorned with stars of gold, bearing on his head the Olympic crown and in his right hand the Pythian, while the rest were carried before him with inscriptions telling where he had won them and against what competitors, and giving the titles of the songs or of the subject of the plays. His car was followed by his claque[74] as by the escort of a triumphal procession, who shouted that they were the attendants of Augustus and the soldiers of his triumph. 2 Then through the arch of the Circus Maximus, which was thrown down,[75] he made his way across the Velabrum and the Forum to the Palatine and the temple of Apollo. All along the route victims were slain, the streets were sprinkled from time to time with perfume, while birds,[76] ribbons, and sweetmeats were showered upon him. He placed the sacred crowns in his bed-chambers around the couches, as well as statues representing him in the guise of a lyre-player; and he had a coin too struck with the same device. 3 So far from neglecting or relaxing his practice of the art after this, he never addressed the soldiers except by letter or in a speech delivered by another, to save his voice; and he never did anything for amusement or in earnest without an elocutionist[77] by his side, to warn him to spare his vocal organs and hold a handkerchief to his mouth. To many men he offered his friendship or announced his hostility, according as they had applauded him lavishly or grudgingly.

26 1 Although at first his acts of wantonness, lust, extravagance, avarice and cruelty were gradual and secret, and might be condoned as follies of youth, yet even then their nature was such that no one doubted that they were defects of his character and not due to his time of life. No sooner was twilight over than he would catch up a cap or a wig and go to the taverns or range about the streets playing pranks, which however were very far from harmless; for he used to beat men as they came home from dinner, stabbing any who resisted him and throwing them into the sewers. He would even break into shops and rob them, setting up a market[78] in the Palace, where he divided the booty which he took, sold it at auction, and then squandered the proceeds. 2 In the strife which resulted he often ran the risk of losing his eyes[79] or even his life, for he was beaten almost to death by a man of the senatorial order,[80] whose wife he had maltreated. Warned by this, he never afterwards ventured to appear in public at that hour without having tribunes follow him at a distance and unobserved. Even in the daytime he would be carried privately to the theatre in a sedan, and from the upper part of the proscenium would watch the brawls of the pantomimic actors[81] and egg them on; and when they came to blows and fought with stones and broken benches, he himself threw many missiles at the people and even broke a praetor's head.

27 1 Little by little, however, as his vices grew stronger, he dropped jesting and secrecy and with no attempt at disguise openly broke out into worse crime. 2 He prolonged his revels from midday to midnight, often livening himself by a warm plunge, or, if it were summer, into water cooled with snow. Sometimes too he closed the inlets and banqueted in public in the great tank,[82] in the Campus Martius, or in the Circus Maximus, waited on by harlots and dancing girls from all over the city. 3 Whenever he drifted down the Tiber to Ostia, or sailed about the Gulf of Baiae, booths were set up at intervals along the banks and shores, fitted out for debauchery, while bartering matrons played the part of inn-keepers and from every hand solicited him to come ashore. He also levied dinners on his friends, one of whom spent four million sesterces for a banquet at which turbans were distributed, and another a considerably larger sum for a rose dinner.[83]

28 1 Besides abusing freeborn boys and seducing married women, he debauched the vestal virgin Rubria. The freedwoman Acte he all but made his lawful wife, after bribing some ex-consuls to perjure themselves by swearing that she was of royal birth. He castrated the boy Sporus and actually tried to make a woman of him; and he married him with all the usual ceremonies, including a dowry and a bridal veil, took him to his house attended by a great throng, and treated him as his wife. And the witty jest that someone made is still current, that it would have been well for the world if Nero's father Domitius had had that kind of wife. 2 This Sporus, decked out with the finery of the empresses and riding in a litter, he took with him to the assizes and marts of Greece, and later at Rome through the Street of the Images,[84] fondly kissing him from time to time. That he even desired illicit relations with his own mother, and was kept from it by her enemies, who feared that such a help might give the reckless and insolent woman too great influence, was notorious, especially after he added to his concubines a courtesan who was said to look very like Agrippina. Even before that, so they say, whenever he rode in a litter with his mother, he had incestuous relations with her, which were betrayed by the stains on his clothing.

29 1 He so prostituted his own chastity that after defiling almost every part of his body, he at last devised a kind of game, in which, covered with the skin of some wild animal, he was let loose from a cage and attacked the private parts of men and women, who were bound to stakes, and when he had sated his mad lust, was dispatched[85] by his freedman Doryphorus; for he was even married to this man in the same way that he himself had married Sporus, going so far as to imitate the cries and lamentations of a maiden being deflowered. I have heard from some men that it was his unshaken conviction that no man was chaste or pure in any part of his body, but that most of them concealed their vices and cleverly drew a veil over them; and that therefore he pardoned all other faults in those who confessed to him their lewdness.

30 1 He thought that there was no other way of enjoying riches and money than by riotous extravagance, declaring that only stingy and niggardly fellows kept a correct account of what they spent,[86] while fine and genuinely magnificent gentlemen wasted and squandered. Nothing in his uncle Gaius so excited his envy and admiration as the fact that he had in so short a time run through the vast wealth which Tiberius had left him. 2 Accordingly he made presents and wasted money without stint. On Tiridates,[87] though it would seem hardly within belief, he spent eight hundred thousand sesterces a day, and on his departure presented him with more than a hundred millions. He gave the lyre-player Menecrates and the gladiator Spiculus properties and residences equal to those of men who had celebrated triumphs. He enriched the monkey-faced usurer Paneros with estates in the country and in the city and had him buried with almost regal splendour. 3 He never wore the same garment twice. He played at dice for four hundred thousand sesterces a point.[88] He fished with a golden net drawn by cords woven of purple and scarlet threads. It is said that he never made a journey with less than a thousand carriages, his mules shod with silver and their drivers clad in wool of Canusium, attended by a train of Mazaces[89] and couriers with bracelets and trappings.[90]

31 1 There was nothing however in which he was more ruinously prodigal than in building. He made a palace extending all the way from the Palatine to the Esquiline, which at first he called the House of Passage, but when it was burned shortly after its completion and rebuilt, the Golden House. Its size and splendour will be sufficiently indicated by the following details. Its vestibule was large enough to contain a colossal statue of the emperor •a hundred and twenty feet high; and it was so extensive that it had a triple colonnade[91] •a mile long. There was a pond too, like a sea, surrounded with buildings to represent cities,[92] besides tracts of country, varied by tilled fields, vineyards, pastures and woods, with great numbers of wild and domestic animals. 2 In the rest of the house all parts were overlaid with gold and adorned with gems and mother-of-pearl. There were dining-rooms with fretted ceils of ivory, whose panels could turn and shower down flowers and were fitted with pipes for sprinkling the guests with perfumes. The main banquet hall was circular and constantly revolved day and night, like the heavens.[93] He had baths supplied with sea water and sulphur water. When the edifice was finished in this style and he dedicated it, he deigned to say nothing more in the way of approval than that he was at last beginning to be housed like a human being.

3 He also began a pool, extending from Misenum to the lake of Avernus, roofed over and enclosed in colonnades, into which he planned to turn all the hot springs in every part of Baiae; a canal from

Avernus all the way to Ostia, to enable the journey to be made by ship yet not by sea; its length was to be •a hundred and sixty miles and its breadth sufficient to allows ships with five banks of oars to pass each other. For the execution of these projects he had given orders that the prisoners all over the empire should be transported to Italy, and that those who were convicted even of capital crimes should be punished in no other way than by sentence to this work.

4 He was led to such mad extravagance, in addition to his confidence in the resources of the empire, by the hope of a vast hidden treasure, suddenly inspired by the assurance of a Roman knight, who declared positively that the enormous wealth which queen Dido had taken with her of old in her flight from Tyre was hidden away in huge caves in Africa and could be recovered with but trifling labour.[c]

32 1 When this hope proved false, he resorted to false accusations and robbery, being at the end of his resources and so utterly impoverished that he was obliged to postpone and defer even the pay of the soldiers and the rewards due to the veterans.

2 First of all he made a law, that instead of one-half, five-sixths of the property of deceased freedmen should be made over to him, if without good and sufficient reason they bore the name of any family with which he himself was connected; further, that the estates of those who were ungrateful to their emperor[94] should belong to the privy purse, and that the advocates who had written or dictated such wills should not go unpunished. Finally, that any word or deed on which an informer could base an action should be liable to the law against lese-majesty. 3 He demanded the return of the rewards[95] which he had given in recognition of the prizes conferred on him by any city in competition. Having forbidden the use of amethystine or Tyrian purple dyes, he secretly sent a man to sell a few ounces on a market day and then closed the shops of all the dealers.[96] It is even said that when he saw a matron in the audience at one of his recitals clad in the forbidden colour he pointed her out to his agents, who dragged her out and stripped her on the spot, not only of her garment, but also of her property.

4 He never appointed anyone to an office without adding: "You know what my needs are," and "Let us see to it that no one possess anything." At last he stripped many temples of their gifts and melted down the images of gold and silver, including those of the Penates, which however Galba soon afterwards restored.

33 1 He began his career of parricide and murder with Claudius, for even if he was not the instigator of the emperor's death, he was at least privy to it, as he openly admitted; for he used afterwards to laud mushrooms, the vehicle in which the poison was administered to Claudius, as "the food of the gods," as the Greek proverb has it.[97] At any rate, after Claudius's death he vented on him every kind of insult, in act and word,[98] charging him now with folly and now with cruelty; for it was a favourite joke of his to say that Claudius had ceased "to play the fool"[99] among mortals, lengthening the first syllable of the word morari, and he disregarded many of his decrees and acts as the work of a madman and a dotard. Finally, he neglected to enclose the place where his body was burned except with a low and mean wall.

2 He attempted the life of Britannicus by poison, not less from jealousy of his voice (for it was more agreeable than his own) than from fear that he might sometime win a higher place than himself in the people's regard because of the memory of his father. He procured the potion from an archpoisoner, one Locusta, and when the effect was slower than he anticipated, merely physicing Britannicus, he called the woman to him and flogged her with his own hand, charging that she had administered a medicine instead of a poison; and when she said in excuse that she had given a smaller dose to shield him from the odium of the crime, he replied: "It's likely that I am afraid of the Julian law;"[100] and he forced her to mix as swift and instant a potion as she knew how in his own room before his very eyes. 3 Then he tried it on a kid, and as the animal lingered for five hours, had the mixture steeped again and again and threw some of it before a pig. The beast instantly fell dead, whereupon he ordered that the poison be taken to the dining-room and given to Britannicus. The boy dropped dead at the very first taste, but Nero lied to his guests and declared that he was seized with the falling sickness, to which he was subject, and the next day had him hastily and unceremoniously buried in a pouring rain. He rewarded Locusta for her eminent services with a full pardon[101] and large estates in the country, and actually sent her pupils.[102]

34 1 His mother offended him by too strict surveillance and criticism of his words and acts, but at first he confined his resentment to frequent endeavours to bring upon her a burden of unpopularity by pretending that he would abdicate the throne and go off to Rhodes. Then depriving her of all her honours and of her guard of Roman and German soldiers, he even forbade her to live with him and drove her from the Palace. After that he passed all bounds in harrying her, bribing men to annoy her with lawsuits while she remained in the city, and after she had retired to the country, to pass her house by land and sea and break her rest with abuse and mockery. 2 At last terrified by her violence and threats, he determined to have her life, and after thrice attempting it by poison and finding that she had made herself immune by antidotes, he tampered with the ceiling of her bedroom, contriving a mechanical device for loosening its panels and dropping them upon her while she slept. When this leaked out through some of those connected with the plot, he devised a collapsible boat,[103] to destroy her by shipwreck or by the falling in of its cabin. Then he pretended a reconciliation and invited her in a most cordial letter to come to Baiae and celebrate the feast of Minerva[104] with him. On her arrival, instructing his captains to wreck the galley in which she had come, by running into it as if by accident, he detained her at a banquet,[105] and when she would return to Bauli, offered her his contrivance in place of the craft which had been damaged, escorting her to it in high spirits and even kissing her breasts as they parted." 3 The rest of the night he passed sleepless in intense anxiety, awaiting the outcome of his design. On learning that everything had gone wrong and that she had escaped by swimming, driven to desperation he secretly had a dagger thrown down beside her freedman Lucius Agermus, when he joyfully brought word that she was safe and sound, and then ordered that the freedman be seized and bound, on the charge of being hired to kill the emperor; that his mother be put to death, and the pretence made that she had escaped the consequences of her detected guilt by suicide. 4 Trustworthy authorities[106] add still more gruesome details: that he hurried off to view the corpse, handled her limbs, criticising some and commending others, and that becoming thirsty meanwhile, he took a drink. Yet he could not either then or ever afterwards endure the stings of conscience, though soldiers, senate and people tried to hearten him with their congratulations; for he often owned that he was hounded by his mother's ghost and by the whips and blazing torches of the Furies. He even had rites performed by the Magi, in the effort to summon her shade and entreat it for forgiveness. Moreover, in his journey through Greece he did not venture to take part in the Eleusinian mysteries, since at the beginning the godless and wicked are warned by the herald's proclamation to go hence.

5 To matricide he added the murder of his aunt. When he once visited her as she was confined to her bed from costiveness, and she, as old ladies will, stroking his downy beard (for he was already well grown) happened to say fondly: "As soon as I receive this,[107] I shall gladly die," he turned to those with him and said as if in jest: "I'll take it off at once." Then he bade the doctors give the sick woman an overdose of physic and seized her property before she was cold, suppressing her will, that nothing might escape him.

35 1 Besides Octavia he later took two wives, Poppaea Sabina, daughter of an ex-quaestor and previously married to a Roman knight, and then Statilia Messalina, daughter of the great-granddaughter of Taurus, who had been twice consul and awarded a triumph. To possess the latter he slew her husband Atticus Vestinus while he held the office of consul. He soon grew tired of living with Octavia, and when his friends took him to task, replied that "she ought to be content with the insignia of wifehood."[108]

2 Presently after several vain attempts to strangle her, he divorced her on the ground of barrenness, and when the people took it ill and openly reproached him, he banished her besides; and finally he had her put to death on a charge of adultery that was so shameless and unfounded, that when all who were put to the torture maintained her innocence, he bribed his former preceptor Anicetus[109] to make a pretended confession that he had violated her chastity by a stratagem. 3 He dearly loved Poppaea, whom he married twelve days after his divorce from Octavia, yet he caused her death too by kicking her when she was pregnant and ill, because she had scolded him for coming home late from the races. By her he had a daughter, Claudia Augusta, but lost her when she was still an infant.

4 Indeed there is no kind of relationship that he did not violate in his career of crime. He put to death Antonia, daughter of Claudius,[110] for refusing to marry him after Poppaea's death, charging her with an attempt at revolution; and he treated in the same way all others who were in any way connected with him by blood or by marriage. Among these was the young Aulus Plautius, whom he forcibly defiled before his death, saying "Let my mother come now and kiss my successor,"

openly charging that Agrippina had loved Plautius and that this had roused him to hopes of the throne.

5 Rufrius Crispinus, a mere boy, his stepson and the child of Poppaea, he ordered to be drowned by the child's own slaves while he was fishing, but it was said that he used to play at being a general and an emperor. He banished his nurse's son Tuscus, because when procurator in Egypt, he had bathed in some baths which were built for a visit of Nero's. He drove his tutor Seneca to suicide, although when the old man often pleaded to be allowed to retire and offered to give up his estates,[111] he had sworn most solemnly that he did wrong to suspect him and that he would rather die than harm him. He sent poison to Burrus, prefect of the Guard, in place of a throat medicine which he had promised him. The old and wealthy freedmen who had helped him first to his adoption and later to the throne, and aided him by their advice,[112] he killed by poison, administered partly in their food and partly in their drink.

36 1 Those outside his family he assailed with no less cruelty. It chanced that a comet[113] had begun to appear on several successive nights, a thing which is commonly believed to portend the death of great rulers. Worried by this, and learning from the astrologer Balbillus that kings usually averted such omens by the death of some distinguished man, thus turning them from themselves upon the heads of the nobles, he resolved on the death of all the eminent men of the State; but the more firmly, and with some semblance of justice, after the discovery of two conspiracies. The earlier and more dangerous of these was that of Piso at Rome; the other was set on foot by Vinicius at Beneventum and detected there. 2 The conspirators made their defence in triple sets of fetters, some voluntarily admitting their guilt, some even making a favour of it, saying that there was no way except by death that they could help a man disgraced by every kind of wickedness.[114] The children of those who were condemned were banished or put to death by poison or starvation; a number are known to have been slain all together at a single meal along with their preceptors and attendants,[115] while others were prevented from earning their daily bread.

37 1 After this he showed neither discrimination nor moderation in putting to death whomsoever he pleased on any pretext whatever. To mention but a few instances, Salvidienus Orfitus was charged with having let to certain states as headquarters three shops which formed part of his house near the Forum; Cassius Longinus, a blind jurist, with retaining in the old family tree of his house the mask of Gaius Cassius, the assassin of Julius Caesar; Paetus Thrasea with having a sullen mien, like that of a preceptor. 2 To those who were bidden to die he never granted more than an hour's respite, and to avoid any delay, he brought physicians who were at once to "attend to" such as lingered; for that was the term he used for killing them by opening their veins. It is even believed that it was his wish to throw living men to be torn to pieces and devoured by a monster[116] of Egyptian birth, who would crunch raw flesh and anything else that was given him. 3 Transported and puffed up by such successes, as he considered them, he boasted that no prince had ever known what power he really had, and he often threw out unmistakable hints that he would not spare even those of the senate who survived, but would one day blot out the whole order from the State and hand over the rule of the provinces and the command of the armies to the Roman knights and to his freedmen. Certain it is that neither on beginning a journey nor on returning did he kiss any member[117] or even return his greeting; and at the formal opening of the work at the Isthmus the prayer which he uttered in a loud voice before a great throng was, that the event might result favourably "for himself and the people of Rome," thus suppressing any mention of the senate.

38 1 But he showed no greater mercy to the people or the walls of his capital. When someone in a general conversation said:

"When I am dead, be earth consumed by fire,"[118]

he rejoined "Nay, rather while I live," and his action was wholly in accord. For under cover of displeasure at the ugliness of the old buildings and the narrow, crooked streets, he set fire to the city[119] so openly that several ex-consuls did not venture to lay hands on his chamberlains although they caught them on their estates with tow and fire-brands, while some granaries near the Golden House, whose room he particularly desired, were demolished by engines of war and then set on fire, because their walls were of stone. 2 For six days and seven nights destruction raged, while the people were driven for shelter to monuments and tombs. At that time, besides an immense number of dwellings,[120] the houses of leaders of old were burned, still adorned with trophies of victory, and the temples of the gods vowed and dedicated by the kings and later in the Punic and Gallic wars, and whatever else interesting and noteworthy had survived from antiquity. Viewing the conflagration from the tower of Maecenas[121] and exulting, as he said, in "the beauty of the flames," he sang the whole of the "Sack of Ilium,"[122] in his regular stage costume. 3 Furthermore, to gain from this calamity too all the spoil and booty possible, while promising the removal of the debris and dead bodies free of cost he allowed no one to approach the ruins of his own property; and from the contributions which he not only received, but even demanded, he nearly bankrupted the provinces and exhausted the resources of individuals.

39 1 To all the disasters and abuses thus caused by the prince there were added certain accidents of fortune; a plague which in a single autumn entered thirty thousand deaths in the accounts of Libitina;[123] a disaster in Britain, where two important towns were sacked[124] and great numbers of citizens and allies were butchered; a shameful defeat in the Orient, in consequence of which the legions in Armenia were •sent under the yoke and Syria was all but lost. It is surprising and of special note that all this time he bore nothing with more patience than the curses and abuse of the people, and was particularly lenient towards those who assailed him with gibes and lampoons. 2 Of these many were posted or circulated both in Greek and Latin, for example the following:

"Nero, Orestes, Alcmeon their mothers slew."

"A calculation new. Nero his mother slew."[125]

"Who can deny the descent from Aeneas' great line of our Nero?
One his mother took off, the other one took off his sire."

"While our ruler his lyre doth twang and the Parthian his bowstring, Paean-singer our
prince shall be, and Far-darter our foe."

"Rome is becoming one house; off with you to Veii, Quirites!
If that house does not soon seize upon Veii as well."

He made no effort, however, to find the authors; in fact, when some of them were reported to the
senate by an informer, he forbade their being very severely punished.
3 As he was passing along a public street, the Cynic Isidorus loudly taunted him, "because he was
a good singer of the ills of Nauplius, but made ill use of his own goods." Datus also, an actor of
Atellan farces, in a song beginning:

"Farewell to thee, father; farewell to thee, mother,"

represented drinking and swimming in pantomime, referring of course to the death of Claudius
and Agrippina; and in the final tag,

"Orcus guides your steps,"

he indicated the senate by a gesture.[126] Nero contented himself with banishing the actor and
the philosopher from the city, either because he was impervious to all insults, or to avoid sharpen-
ing men's wits by showing his vexation.

40 1 After the world had put up with such a ruler for nearly fourteen years, it at last cast him
off, and the Gauls took the first step under the lead of Julius Vindex, who at that time governed
their province as propraetor.
2 Astrologers had predicted to Nero that he would one day be repudiated, which was the occasion of that well known saying of his: "A humble art affords us daily bread,"[127] doubtless uttered
to justify him in practising the art of lyre-playing, as an amusement while emperor, but a necessity
for a private citizen. Some of them, however, had promised him the rule of the East, when he was
cast off, a few expressly naming the sovereignty of Jerusalem, and several the restitution of all his

former fortunes. Inclining rather to this last hope, after losing Armenia and Britain and recovering both, he began to think that he had suffered the misfortunes which fate had in store. 3 And after consulting the oracle at Delphi and being told that he must look out for the seventy-third year, assuming that he would die only at that period, and taking no account of Galba's years, he felt so confident not only of old age, but also of unbroken and unusual good fortune, that when he had lost some articles of great value by shipwreck, he did not hesitate to say among his intimate friends that the fish would bring them back to him.

4 He was at Naples when he learned of the uprising of the Gallic provinces, on the anniversary of his mother's murder, and received the news with such calmness and indifference that he incurred the suspicion of actually rejoicing in it, because it gave him an excuse for pillaging those wealthy provinces according to the laws of war. And he at once proceeded to the gymnasium, where he watched the contests of the athletes with rapt interest. At dinner too when interrupted by a more disturbing letter, he fired up only so far as to threaten vengeance on the rebels. In short for eight whole days making no attempt to write a reply to anyone, nor even to give any commission or command, he blotted out the affair with silence.

41 1 At last he was driven by numerous insulting edicts of Vindex, to urge the senate in a letter to avenge him and the state, alleging a throat trouble as his excuse for not appearing in person. Yet there was nothing which he so much resented as the taunt that he was a wretched lyre-player and that he was addressed as Ahenobarbus instead of Nero.[128] With regard to his family name, which was cast in his teeth as an insult, he declared that he would resume it and give up that of his adoption. He used no other arguments to show the falsity of the rest of the reproaches than that he was actually taunted with being unskilled in an art to which he had devoted so much attention and in which he had so perfected himself, and he asked various individuals from time to time whether they knew of any artist who was his superior. 2 Finally, beset by message after message, he returned to Rome in a panic; but on the way, when but slightly encouraged by an insignificant omen, for he noticed a monument on which was sculptured the overthrow of a Gallic soldier by a Roman horseman, who was dragging him along by the hair, he leaped for joy at the sight and lifted up his hands to heaven.[129] Not even on his arrival did he personally address the senate or people, but called some of the leading men to his house and after a hasty consultation spent the rest of the day in exhibiting some water-organs of a new and hitherto unknown form, explaining their several features and lecturing on the theory and complexity of each of them; and he even declared that he would presently produce them all in the theatre "with the kind permission of Vindex."

42 1 Thereafter, having learned that Galba also and the Spanish provinces had revolted, he fainted and lay for a long time insensible, without a word and all but dead. When he came to himself, he rent his robe and beat his brow, declaring that it was all over with him; and when his old nurse tried to comfort him by reminding him that similar evils had befallen other princes before him, he declared that unlike all others he was suffering the unheard of and unparalleled fate of losing the supreme power while he still lived. 2 Nevertheless he did not abandon or amend his slothful and luxurious habits; on the contrary, whenever any good news came from the provinces, he not only gave lavish feasts, but even ridiculed the leaders of the revolt in verses set to wanton music, which have since become public, and accompanied them with gestures; then secretly entering the audience room of the theatre, he sent word to an actor who was making a hit that he was taking advantage of the emperor's busy days.[130]

43 1 At the very beginning of the revolt it is believed that he formed many plans of monstrous wickedness, but in no way inconsistent with his character: to depose and assassinate the commanders of the armies and the governors of the provinces, on the ground that they were all united in a conspiracy against him; to massacre all the exiles everywhere and all men of Gallic birth in the city: the former, to prevent them from joining the rebels; the latter, as sharing and abetting the designs of their countrymen; to turn over the Gallic provinces to his armies to ravage; to poison the entire senate at banquets; to set fire to the city, first letting the wild beasts loose, that it might be harder for the people to protect themselves. 2 But he was deterred from these designs, not so much by any compunction, as because he despaired of being able to carry them out, and feeling obliged to take the field, he deposed the consuls before the end of their term and assumed the office alone in place of both of them, alleging that it was fated that Gallic provinces could not be subdued except by a consul.[131] Having assumed the fasces, he declared as he was leaving the dining-room after a banquet, leaning on the shoulders of his comrades, that immediately on setting foot in the province he would go before the soldiers unarmed and do nothing but weep; and having thus led the rebels to change their purpose, he would next days rejoice among his rejoicing subjects and sing paeans of victory, which he ought at that very moment to be composing.

44 1 In preparing for his campaign his first care was to select wagons to carry his theatrical instruments, to have the hair of his concubines, whom he planned to take with him, trimmed man-fashion, and to equip them with Amazonian axes and shields. Next he summoned the city tribes to enlist, and when no eligible person responded, he levied on their masters a stated number of slaves, accepting only the choicest from each household and not even exempting paymasters and secretaries. 2 He also required all classes to contribute a part of their incomes, and all tenants of private houses and apartments to pay a year's rent at once to the privy purse.[132] With great fastidiousness and rigour he demanded newly minted coin, refined silver, and pure gold,[133] so that many openly refused to make any contribution at all, unanimously demanding that he should rather compel the informers to give up whatever rewards had been paid them.

45 1 The bitter feeling against him was increased because he also turned the high cost of grain to his profit;[134] for indeed, it so fell out that while the people were suffering from hunger it was reported that a ship had arrived from Alexandria, bringing sand for the court wrestlers.

2 When he had thus aroused the hatred of all, there was no form of insult to which he was not subjected. A curl[135] was placed on the head of his statue with the inscription in Greek: "Now there is a real contest[136] and you must at last surrender." To the neck of another statue a sack was tied and with it the words: "I have done what I could, but you have earned the sack."[137] People wrote on the columns that he had stirred up even the Gauls[138] by his singing. When night came on, many men pretended to be wrangling with their slaves and kept calling out for a defender.[139]

46 1 In addition he was frightened by manifest portents from dreams, auspices and omens, both old and new. Although he had never before been in the habit of dreaming, after he had killed his mother it seemed to him that he was steering a ship in his sleep and that the helm was wrenched from his hands; that he was dragged by his wife Octavia into thickest darkness, and that he was now covered with a swarm of winged ants, and now was surrounded by the statues of the nations which had been dedicated in Pompey's theatre and stopped in his tracks. A Spanish steed of which he was very fond was changed into the form of an ape in the hinder parts of its body, and its head, which alone remained unaltered, gave forth tuneful neighs. 2 The doors of the Mausoleum flew open of their own accord, and a voice was heard from within summoning him by name. After the Lares had been adorned on the Kalends of January, they fell to the ground in the midst of the preparations for the sacrifice. As he was taking the auspices, Sporus made him a present of a ring with a stone on which was engraved the rape of Proserpina. When the vows were to be taken[140] and a great throng of all classes had assembled, the keys of the Capitol could not be found for a long time. 3 When a speech of his in which he assailed Vindex was being read in the senate, at the words "the wretches will suffer punishment and will shortly meet the end which they deserve," all who were present cried out with one voice: "You will do it, Augustus."[141] It also had not failed of notice that the last piece which he sang in public was "Oedipus in Exile," and that he ended with the line:

"Wife, father, mother drive me to my death."

47 1 When meanwhile word came that the other armies had revolted, he tore to pieces the dispatches which were handed to him as he was dining, tipped over the table, and dashed to the ground two favourite drinking cups, which he called "Homeric," because they were carved with scenes from Homer's poems.[142] Then taking some poison from Locusta and putting it into a golden box, he crossed over into the Servilian gardens, where he tried to induce the tribunes and centurions of the Guard to accompany him in his flight, first sending his most trustworthy freedmen to Ostia, to get a fleet ready. 2 But when some gave evasive answers and some openly refused, one even cried:

"Is it so dreadful a thing then to die?"[143]

Whereupon he turned over various plans in his mind, whether to go as a suppliant to the Parthians or Galba, or to appear to the people on the rostra, dressed in black, and beg as pathetically as he could for pardon for his past offences; and if he could not soften their hearts, to entreat them at least to allow him the prefecture of Egypt. Afterwards a speech composed for this purpose was found in his writing desk; but it is thought that he did not dare to deliver it for fear of being torn to pieces before he could reach the Forum.

3 Having therefore put off further consideration to the following day, he awoke about midnight and finding that the guard of soldiers had left, he sprang from his bed and sent for all his friends. Since no reply came back from anyone, he went himself to their rooms[144] with a few followers. But finding that all the doors were closed and that no one replied to him, he returned to his own chamber, from which now the very caretakers had fled, taking with them even the bed-clothing and the box of poison. Then he at once called for the gladiator Spiculus[145] or any other adept[146] at whose hand he might find death, and when no one appeared, he cried "Have I then neither friend nor foe?" and ran out as if to throw himself into the Tiber.

48 1 Changing his purpose again,[d] he sought for some retired place, where he could hide and collect his thoughts; and when his freedman Phaon offered his villa in the suburbs between the Via Nomentana and the Via Salaria near the fourth milestone, just as he was, barefooted and in his tunic, he put on a faded cloak, covered his head, and holding a handkerchief before his eyes, mounted a horse with only four attendants, one of whom was Sporus. 2 At once he was startled by a shock of earthquake and a flash of lightning full in his face, and he heard the shouts of the soldiers from the camp hard by, as they prophesied destruction for him and success for Galba. He also heard one of the wayfarers whom he met say: "These men are after Nero," and another ask: "Is there anything new in the city about Nero?" Then his horse took fright at the smell of a corpse which had been thrown out into the road, his face was exposed, and a retired soldier of the Guard recognised him and saluted him. 3 When they came to a by-path leading to the villa, they turned the horses loose and he made his way amid bushes and brambles and along a path through a thicket of reeds to the back wall of the house, with great difficulty and only when a robe was thrown down for him to walk on. Here the aforesaid Phaon urged him to hide for a time in a pit, from which sand had been dug, but he declared that he would not go under ground while still alive, and after waiting for a while until a secret entrance into the villa could be made, he scooped up in his hand some water to drink from a pool close by, saying: "This is Nero's distilled water."[147] 4 Then, as his cloak had been torn by the thorns, he pulled out the twigs which had pierced it, and crawling on all fours through a narrow passage that had been dug, he entered the villa and lay down in the first room[148] he came to, on a couch with a common mattress, over which an old cloak had been thrown. Though suffering from hunger and renewed thirst, he refused some coarse bread which was offered him, but drank a little lukewarm water.

49 1 At last, while his companions one and all urged him to save himself as soon as possible from the indignities that threatened him, he bade them dig a grave in his presence, proportioned to the size of his own person, and at the same time bring water and wood for presently disposing of his body.[149] As each of these things was done, he wept and said again and again: "What an artist the world is losing!"

2 While he hesitated, a letter was brought to Phaon by one of his couriers. Nero snatching it from his hand read that he had been pronounced a public enemy by the senate, and that they were seeking him to punish in the ancient fashion;[150] and he asked what manner of punishment that was. When he learned that the criminal was stripped, fastened by the neck in a fork[151] and then beaten to death with rods, in mortal terror he seized two daggers which he had brought with him, and then, after trying the point of each, put them up again, pleading that the fatal hour had not yet come. 3 Now he would beg Sporus to begin to lament and wail, and now entreat someone to help him take his life by setting him the example; anon he reproached himself for his cowardice in such words as these: "To live is a scandal and a shame—this does not become Nero, does not become him—one should be resolute at such times—come, rouse thyself!" And now the horsemen were at hand who had orders to take him off alive. When he heard them, he quavered:

"Hark, now strikes on my ear the trampling of swift-footed coursers!"[152]

and drove a dagger into his throat, aided by Epaphroditus, his private secretary.[153] 4 He was all but dead when a centurion rushed in, and as he placed a cloak to the wound, pretending that he had come to aid him, Nero merely gasped: "Too late!" and "This is fidelity!" With these words he was gone, with eyes so set and starting from their sockets that all who saw him shuddered with horror. First and beyond all else he had forced from his companions a promise to let no one have his head, but to contrive in some way that he be buried unmutilated. And this was granted by Icelus, Galba's freedman,[154] who had shortly before been released from the bondage to which he was consigned at the beginning of the revolt.

50 1 He was buried at a cost of two hundred thousand sesterces and laid out in white robes embroidered with gold, which he had worn on the Kalends of January. His ashes were deposited by his nurses, Egloge and Alexandria, accompanied by his mistress Acte, in the family tomb of the Domitii on the summit of the Hill of Gardens,[155] which is visible from the Campus Martius. In that monument his sarcophagus of porphyry, with an altar of Luna marble standing above it, is enclosed by a balustrade of Thasian stone.

51 1 He was about the average height, his body marked with spots and malodorous, his hair light blond, his features regular rather than attractive, his eyes blue and somewhat weak, his neck over thick, his belly prominent, and his legs very slender. His health was good, for though indulging in every kind of riotous excess, he was ill but three times in all during the fourteen years of his reign, and even then not enough to give up wine or any of his usual habits. He was utterly shameless in the care of his person and in his dress, always having his hair arranged in tiers of curls, and during the trip to Greece also letting it grow long and hang down behind; and he often appeared in public in a dining-robe,[156] with a handkerchief bound about his neck, ungirt and unshod.[157]

52 1 When a boy he took up almost all the liberal arts; but his mother turned him from philosophy, warning him that it was a drawback to one who was going to rule, while Seneca kept him from reading the early orators, to make his admiration for his teacher endure the longer. Turning therefore to poetry, he wrote verses with eagerness and without labour, and did not, as some think, publish the work of others as his own. I have had in my possession note-books and papers with some well-known verses of his, written with his own hand and in such wise that it was perfectly evident that they were not copied or taken down from dictation, but worked out exactly as one writes when thinking and creating; so many instances were there of words erased or struck through and written above the lines. He likewise had no slight interest in painting and sculpture.

53 1 But above all he was carried away by a craze for popularity and he was jealous of all who in any way stirred the feeling of the mob. It was the general belief that after his victories on the stage he would at the next lustrum[158] have competed with the athletes at Olympia; for he practised wrestling constantly, and all over Greece he had always viewed the gymnastic contests after the fashion of the judges, sitting on the ground in the stadium; and if any pairs of contestants withdrew too far from their positions, he would force them forward with his own hand. Since he was acclaimed as the equal of Apollo in music and of the Sun in driving a chariot, he had planned to emulate the exploits of Hercules as well; and they say that a lion had been specially trained for him to kill naked in the arena of the amphitheatre before all the people, with a club or by the clasp of his arms.

54 1 Towards the end of his life, in fact, he had publicly vowed that if he retained his power, he would at the games in celebration of his victory give a performance on the water-organ, the flute, and the bagpipes, and that on the last day he would appear as an actor and dance "Vergil's Turnus." Some even assert that he put the actor Paris to death as a dangerous rival.

55 1 He had a longing for immortality and undying fame, though it was ill-regulated. With this in view he took their former appellations from many things and numerous places and gave them new ones from his own name. He also called the month of April Neroneus and was minded to name Rome Neropolis.

56 1 He utterly despised all cults, with the sole exception of that of the Syrian God,[159] and even acquired such a contempt for her that he made water on her image, after he was enamoured of another superstition, which was the only one to which he constantly clung. For he had received as a gift from some unknown man of the commons, as a protection against plots, a little image of a girl; and since a conspiracy at once came to light, he continued to venerate it as a powerful divinity and to offer three sacrifices to it every day, encouraging the belief that through its communication he had knowledge of the future. A few months before his death he did attend an inspection of victims, but could not get a favourable omen.

57 1 He met his death in the thirty-second year of his age, on the anniversary of the murder of Octavia, and such was the public rejoicing that the people put on liberty-caps[160] and ran about all over the city. Yet there were some who for a long time decorated his tomb with spring and summer flowers, and now produced his statues on the rostra in the fringed toga, and now his edicts, as if he were still alive and would shortly return and deal destruction to his enemies. 2 Nay more, Vologaesus, king of the Parthians, when he sent envoys to the senate to renew his alliance, earnestly begged this too, that honour be paid to the memory of Nero. In fact, twenty years later, when I was a young man, a person of obscure origin appeared, who gave out that he was Nero,[161] and the name was still in such favour with the Parthians that they supported him vigorously and surrendered him with great reluctance.

The Editor's Notes:

1 The youths were Castor and Pollux, and the victory that at Lake Regillus, in 498 B.C., according to the traditional chronology.

2 Suetonius is in error here; it was the father of the tribune who defeated the Allobroges.

3 Os has about the force of "cheek" in colloquial English.

4 See *Jul.* xxxiv.1.

5 Proposed by Q. Pedius, Caesar's colleague in the consulship.

6 The Pedian law.

7 That is, as his executor. The maker of a will chose a man to whom he made a symbolic sale (per aes et librum; see *Aug.* lxiv.1) of all his goods in the presence of witnesses. The purchaser then made the designated payments to the heirs and legatees.

8 *Aug.* lxiv and lxv.°

9 Gouging out the eyes seems to have been a favourite mode of attack among the Italians; cf. *Aug.* xxvii.4, *Nero* xxvi.2, and the frequent allusions in comedy.

10 And paid for through the bankers; *cf.* perscriptum fuisset, *Jul.* xlii.2.

11 In his capacity as praetor; this was adding insult to injury, since the edict did not affect the present case.

12 See note on *Tib.* vii.2.

13 See note on *Tib.* vii.2 and *cf. Aug.* v.

14 Boys on the ninth day after birth, and girls on the eighth,° were purified by a sacrifice and given a name; the ceremony was called lustratio.

15 That is, as if the story had a better foundation, and the serpent had really saved his life through divine agency.

16 So the mss., but it should be the twelfth (*Lipsius*) or thirteenth (*Oudendorp*).

17 That is, his adoptive father Claudius.

18 See note ⁷ on *Claud.* i.3.

19 See note ¹⁰⁷ on *Claud.* xlii.1.

20 *Cf.* Tac. *Ann.* 12.68.

21 See *Claud.* xix.

22 *Cf. Vesp.* xvii.

23 *Cf. Aug.* liii.3, nullo submonente.

24 An honour previously conferred only on generals after a great victory; *cf. Jul.* xxiv.3, at the end.

25 That is, the part which he had read.

26 In commemoration of the first shaving of his beard; see chap. xii.4, below.

27 This had previously been done only at the theatre (see note on *Jul.* xxxix.2); senators were first given special seats at the Circus by Claudius; See *Claud.* xxi.3.

28 A tight-rope, sloping downwards across the arena; *cf. Galba*, vi.

29 The musicians, machinists, etc.; *cf. Claud.* xxxiv.2.

30 *Cf. Jul.* xxxix.1. Originally war dances, their scope was extended to pantomime of all kinds, as appears from what follows.

31 See note on *Aug.* xcviii.3.

32 The podium in the amphitheatre was a raised platform, close to the arena, on which the imperial family, the curule magistrates, and the Vestal virgins sat on curule chairs. Nero reclined there on a couch.

33 In the broad sense, including poetry and oratory.

34 The baths, the Thermae Neronianae, were in the Campus Martius, near the Pantheon. The gymnasium, the first permanent building of the kind at Rome, was attached to the baths.

35 And to act as judges.

36 *Cf. Aug.* xliv.3.

37 Of Pompey.

38 See note on *Aug.* xiii.2.

39 This was usual only when a triumph was celebrated.

40 See note on *Aug.* xxii.

41 He assumed a fifth consulship in 68; see chap. xliii below.

42 See *Jul.* lxxvi.2, where, however, the man's name is not mentioned.

43 See *Aug.* lxv.2.

44 This was undoubtedly after the great fire; see chap. xxxviii.

45 Various attempts had however been made to check this form of luxury; see *Claud.* xl.1.°

46 Because of their disorderly conduct; see chap. xxvi.2, and Tac. *Ann.* 13.25.

47 The tablets consisted of three leaves, two of which were bound together and sealed. The contract was written twice, on the open leaf and on the closed ones. In cases of dispute the seals were broken in the presence of the signers and the two versions compared.

48 As witnesses. The testator afterwards wrote the names of the heirs on these leaves.

49 The Cincian law of 204 B.C. forbade fees. Augustus renewed the law in 17 B.C. (Dio, 54.18). Claudius limited fees to 10,000 sesterces (Tac. *Ann.* 11.5–6). The senate again abolished fees at the beginning of Nero's reign (Tac. *Ann.* 13.5), but Nero apparently revived the law of Claudius, with a provision against the addition of "costs."

50 Instead of coming before the prefects of the treasury; *cf. Claud.* ix.2.

51 That is, his adoptive father Claudius.

52 Of Corinth; *cf. Jul.* xliv.3.

53 Roman measure; •a little under 5ft. 10in. English.

54 *Cf. Gell.* 13.31.3.

55 It collapsed in consequence, but not until the audience had dispersed; see Tac. *Ann.* 15.34.

56 Literally, "full-packed," *i.e.* full of sound, sonorous.

57 The first seems to have derived its name from the sound, which was like the humming of bees, the second and third from clapping with the hands rounded or hollowed, like roof-tiles, or flat, like bricks or flat tiles.

58 See chap xii.3.

59 Probably asking for the favourable attention of the audience; *cf.* Dio, 61.20 and chap. xxiii.3.

60 That is, those given by the magistrates; under the Empire all but the emperor were privati, regardless of their official positions.

61 By his guardian and teachers.

62 See note on *Calig.* lv.2.

63 The signal for the start.

64 Chap. xix.1.

65 *Cf.* Juv. VIII.224 ff.

66 Of the theatre; for a similar use of murus see chap. xxxviii.1.

67 Oppida, the term applied to the towers and other structures at the entrance to the Circus, seems to be used here of the corresponding part of the theatre.

68 The use of a handkerchief was not allowed; see also Tac. *Ann.* 16.4.

69 The hypocrites (hypocrita) made the gestures and accompanied the tragic actor on the flute, as he spoke his lines.

70 The heralds for the great festivals were selected by competition among the rival candidates.

71 The Greek term hieronices, "victor in the sacred games," indicates the religious nature of the festivals.

72 That is, with local self-government, not with actual independence.

73 See note ⁷⁵ on chap. xxv.°

74 See chap. xx.3.

75 To make more room for the procession, which passed through the Circus (Dio, 63.20). The reference is probably to the gateway at the eastern end, through which the procession entered and passed out again, after marching around the spina (see note on *Claud.* xxi.3). Suetonius mentions only the exit from the Circus. In his time the gateway was formed by the Arch of Vespasian and Titus, erected by Domitian in 81 A.D.

76 That is, song-birds, as a compliments to Nero's voice; the other offerings were also typical of his art and his triumph.

77 *Cf. Aug.* lxxxiv.2.

78 Quintana is really the market of a camp, named from the Quintana via, one of the streets of a Roman camp, on which the market was regularly placed.

79 See note on chap. v.1.

80 Julius Montanus; see Tac. *Ann.* 13.25.

81 And their bands of partisans; see chap. xvi.2.

82 Made for sea-fights; see *Aug.* xliii.1; *Tib.* lxxii.1.

83 With mitellita and rosaria we may supply cena; the former means a banquet at which silken turbans were a distinguishing feature.

84 *Cf. Claud.* xvi.4.

85 Used in a double sense.

86 That is, could balance the account of their expenditures.

87 See chap. xiii.

88 That is, for each pip of the winning throw.

89 Celebrated horsemen° of Mauretania.

90 See note on *Aug.* xxv.3.

91 That is, with three parallel rows of columns.

92 One may compare Hadrian's villa at Tibur (Tivoli) with its Canopus, its Vale of Tempe, and the like.

93 Suetonius' brevity is here inexact; it was evidently the spherical ceiling which revolved.

94 That is, had left him nothing in their wills, or an insufficient amount.

95 See chap. xxiv.2.

96 Of course confiscating their property.

97 According to Dio, 60.35 (at the end) the saying was original with Nero; but as Dio calls it "a remark not unworthy of record," it perhaps became proverbial among the Greeks.

98 But. *cf.* chap. ix.

99 The pun on morari, "to linger, remain" and mōrari, "to play the fool," seems untranslatable.

100 Against assassination (*De sicariis*), including poisoning, passed by Sulla and renewed by Julius Caesar.

101 For her past offences; see Tac. *Ann.* 12.66.

102 See Juv. I.71 f.

103 The inventor was his freedman Anicetus; Tac. *Ann.* 14.3.

104 *See Aug.* lxxi.3.

105 Given by the future emperor Otho; see *Otho*, iii.

106 Tacitus tells us that some denied this; *Ann.* 14.9.

107 That is, "when I see you arrived at man's estate." The first shaving of the beard by a young Roman was a symbolic act, usually performed at the age of twenty-one with due ceremony; see chap. xii.3, above. According to Tac. *Ann.* 14.15, and Dio, 61.19, Nero first shaved his beard in 59 A.D. at the age of twenty-one and commemorated the event by establishing the Juvenales ludi or Juvenalia (chap. xi.1).

108 A brutal pun. Just as the consular insignia or ornamenta were given in place of the regular office (See *Claud.* v), and the triumphal insignia in place of a triumph, so Octavia ought to be content with being the emperor's wife in name only.

109 Anicetus was at the time prefect of the praetorian fleet at Misenum; see Tac. *Ann.* 14.62.

110 See *Claud.* xxvii.1.

111 Seneca's speech and Nero's reply are preserved by Tacitus (*Ann.* 14.53–56).

112 Pallas and Doryphorus; see Tac. *Ann.* 14.65.

113 Tacitus mentions two comets, one in 60 and the other in 64; see *Ann.* 14.22; 15.47.

114 As Dio says (62.24) "they desired at the same time to be rid of these evils *and to give Nero his release from them.*" Death with the only remedy for one as far gone in wickedness; hence in attempting to apply this remedy, they were doing him a favour. Cf. also Tac. *Ann.* 15.68.

115 The capsarii carried the children's books and writing materials in a box (capsa).

116 The Greek word means "a glutton," or something stronger.

117 Such a salutation was usual; see Plin. *Paneg.* xxiii.

118 A line put by Dio, 58.23, into the mouth of Tiberius. It is believed to be from the *Bellerophon*, a lost play of Euripides.

119 But *cf.* Tac. *Ann.* 15.38.

120 Insulae here refers to blocks of houses, or tenements, in which rooms were rented to the poorer classes; domus to detached houses or mansions.

121 A tower connected with the house and gardens of Maecenas on the Esquiline; see Hor. *Odes*, 3.29.10, molem propinquam nubibus arduis. It was probably connected with the Palatine by the domus transitoria; see chap. xxi.2 and Tac. *Ann.* 15.39, whose account, as well as that of Dio, 62.18, differs from that of Suetonius.

122 Probably a composition of his own; *cf.* Juv. 8.221 and *Vitell.* xi.2.

123 Venus Libitina, in whose temple funeral outfits and a register of deaths were kept; *cf.* Hor. *Serm.* II.6, 19.

124 Camulodunum (Meldon) and Verulamium (St. Albans); according to Xiphilinus (61.1) 80,000 perished.

125 See the reference to the *Rh. Mus.* in the textual note. The numerical value of the Greek letters in Nero's name (1005) is the same as that of the rest of the sentence; hence we have an equation, Nero = the slayer of one's own mother.

126 Referring to Nero's design mentioned in chap. xxxvii.3.

127 If the text is right, the remark must be of a general nature ("us" = mankind). Dio, 63.27, who reads διαθρε'ψει, says that Nero when planning to kill the senators, burn Rome, and sail to Alexandria, said: "Even though we be driven from our empire, yet this little artistic gift of ours shall support us there"; *i.e.* at Alexandria.

128 *Cf.* chap. vii.1.

129 This and the following sentences show Nero's utter failure to realize the real gravity of the situation and his fluctuation between panic fear and fatuous confidence.

130 Implying that Nero would have been the centre of attraction, if he were not otherwise engaged.

131 Since Nero commanded the army, the consul in question must be himself; hence the se of ς is unnecessary.

132 Instead of to their landlords. These people had no rating on the census list and their contribution took this form.

133 That is, tested by fire; see Plin. *N. H.* 33.59.

134 By using, for his own purposes, ships which would of which have been loaded with grain; but the text and the meaning are uncertain.

135 Doubtless an allusion to the long hair which he wore during his Greek trip; see chap. li.

136 In contrast with those of the stage.

137 The one in which parricides were put; see *Aug.* xxxiii.1. But the text and the meaning are uncertain. *Cf.* Juv. 8.213.

138 There is obviously a pun on Galli, "Gauls," and galli, "cocks," and on cantare in the sense of "sing" and of "crow."

139 Punning of course on Vindex, the leader of the revolt.

140 On the first of January, for the prosperity of the emperor and the State.

141 Of course used in a double sense.

142 Plin. *H. N.* 37.29, tells us that the cups were of crystal.

143 Verg. *Aen.* 12.646.

144 In the Palace.

145 See chap. xxx.2.

146 The word percussor implies experience in dealing death. Nero wished to be killed swiftly and painlessly.

147 Referring to a drink of his own contrivance, distilled water cooled in snow; *cf.* Plin. *H. N.* 31.40.

148 Cella implies a small room, for the use of slaves.

149 The water was for washing the corpse and the fire for burning it.

150 *Cf. Claud.* xxxiv.1.

151 Two pieces of wood, fastened together in the form of a **V**.

152 *Iliad*, 10.535.

153 See *Domit.* xiv.4.

154 See *Galba*, xiv.2.

155 The modern Pincio.

156 This synthesina (sc. vestis), or synthesis, was a loose robe of bright-coloured silk, worn at dinner, during the Saturnalia, and by women at other times. Nero's is described by Dio, 63.13, as "a short, flowered tunic with a muslin collar."

157 Probably meaning "in slippers."

158 See note on *Aug.* xcvii.1. Here lustrum is applied to the five-year period of the Olympic games.

159 Atargatis, the principal deity of Northern Syria, identified with Magna Mater and Caelestis; often mentioned in inscriptions and called by Apul. *Metam.* 8.25, omnipotens et omniparens.

160 See note on *Tib.* iv.2.

161 In 88, Terentius Maximus by name; another pseudo-Nero had appeared in 70; see Tac. *Hist.* 2.8.

The Art of Love, Book 1

FROM *The Love Books of Ovid*

By Ovid, translated by J. Lewis Mary

IF there be anyone among you who is ignorant of the art of loving, let him read this poem and, having read it and acquired the knowledge it contains, let him address himself to Love.

By art the swift ships are propelled with sail and oar; there is art in driving the fleet chariots, and Love should by art be guided. Automedon was a skilled charioteer and knew how to handle the flowing reins; Tiphys was the pilot of the good ship Argo. I have been appointed by Venus as tutor to tender Love. I shall be known as the Tiphys and Automedon of Love. Love is somewhat recalcitrant and ofttimes refuses to do my bidding; but 'tis a boy, and boys are easily moulded. Chiron brought up the boy Achilles to the music of the lyre, and by that peaceful art softened his wild nature; he, before whom his enemies were destined so oft to tremble, who many a time struck terror even into his own companions was, so 'tis said, timid and submissive in the presence of a feeble old man, obedient to his master's voice, and held out to him for chastisement those hands whereof Hector was one day destined to feel the weight. Chiron was tutor to Achilles; I am tutor to Love; both of them formidable youngsters, both of them goddess-born. But the fiery bull has to submit to the yoke; the mettled steed vainly champs at the curb that masters him. I, too, will bring Love to heel, even though his arrows pierce my breast and he brandish over my head his flaming torch. The keener his arrows, the fiercer his fires, the more they stir me to avenge my wounds.

I shall not try, O Apollo, to convey the notion that it was from thee I learned the art which I impart; no birds came and sang it in my ear. Clio and her sisters appeared not to me, grazing my herds, O Ascra, in thy vales. Experience is my guide; give ear to the adept; true are the things I sing. Mother of Love, smile on my undertaking.

Hence, ye narrow frontlets, insignia of chastity, and ye trailing robes that half conceal the feet. I sing of love where danger is not; I sing permitted pilferings; free of all offence my verses are.

You, who for the first time are taking up arms beneath the standard of Venus, find out, in the first place, the woman you are fain to love. Your next task will be to bend her to your will; your third to safeguard that your love shall endure. This is my plan, my syllabus. This is the course my chariot will pursue; such is the goal that it will endeavour to attain.

Now, that you still are fancy-free, now is the time for you to choose a woman and say to her: "You are the only woman that I care for." She's not going to be wafted down to you from heaven on the wings of the wind. You must use your own-eyes to discover the girl that suits you. The hunter knows where to spread his nets in order to snare the stag; he knows the valley where the wild boar has his lair. The birdcatcher knows where he should spread his lime; and the fisherman, what waters most abound in fish. And thou who seekest out the object of a lasting love, learn to know the places which the fair ones most do haunt. You won't have to put to sea in order to do that, or to undertake any distant journeys. Perseus may bring home his Andromeda from sun-scorched India, and the Phrygian swain may go to Greece to bear away his bride; Rome alone will give you a choice of such lovely women, and so many of them, that you will be forced to confess that she

gathers within her own bosom all the treasures that the world can show. As numerous as the ears of corn on Gargarus, grapes in Methymna, fish in the ocean, birds in the thickets, stars in the heavens, so numerous are the beautiful girls you'll find in Rome: Venus has made her seat of empire the city of her beloved Æneas.

If your tastes incline to a young beauty, in the very flower of girlhood, a really inexperienced girl will offer herself to your gaze; if you prefer one rather more mature, there are hundreds of young women who will take your fancy: 'twill be a veritable *embarras de richesses*. But perhaps you would rather have someone still older, still more experienced. In that case you've got a yet larger number to choose from. When the sun begins to enter the sign of the Lion, you've only got to take a stroll beneath the cool shade of Pompey's portico, or near that building adorned with foreign marbles erected by a loving mother who united her offerings to those of a dutiful son.

Omit not to visit that portico which, adorned with ancient pictures, is called the portico of Livia, after its foundress. There you will see the Danaides plotting the death of their unhappy kinswomen, and their fell sire grasping in his hand a naked sword. And do not miss the festival of Adonis, mourned of Venus, and the rites celebrated every seventh day by the Syrian Jews.

Shun not the Temple of the Cow of Memphis, who persuades so many women to play the part she played to Jupiter. Even the Forum, strange though it sound, is propitious to love-making. Lawyers are by no means proof against the fiery shafts of Love. Hard by the marble temple sacred to Venus, where play the waters of the Appian fount, many an advocate has fallen a victim to the snares of Love; for the man who defends his client cannot always defend himself. In such a pass, words sometimes fail even the most learned orator. The tables are turned and he finds himself obliged to plead his own
cause. From her temple close at hand, Venus laughs to see him in such a quandary. A patron but a little while ago, he would now rejoice to be a client.

But it is especially at the theatre you should lay your snares; that is where you may hope to have your desires fulfilled. Here you will find women to your taste: one for a moment's dalliance, another to fondle and caress, another to have all for your own. Even as the ants that come and go in long battalions with their stores of food, or as the bees, when they have found plants to plunder of their honey, hover hither and thither among the thyme and the flowers, so, and no less numerous, you may see crowds of lovely women, gaily dressed, hastening away to the theatre. I have often found it difficult to choose from such a galaxy. They come to see and, more important still, to be seen! The theatre's the place where modesty acts a fall.

It was you, Romulus, who first mingled the cares of love with public games, that far-off day when the rape of the Sabine women gave wives to your warriors who had waited for them so long. No curtains then hung in the marble theatre, nor was the stage made red with liquid saffron. In those days branches from the woods of the Palatine were the only adornment of our simple stage. The people sat on seats of turf, their heads canopied with boughs.

As soon as he had sat him down, each Roman looked about, marking the woman whom he most desired, giving free play to the thoughts that surged within him. Whilst to the sound of a rustic pipe an actor strikes his foot three times upon the levelled earth, amid the unforced applause of the expectant throng (for in those days applause was neither bought nor sold), Romulus signed to his men to seize upon their prey. In a trice, with shouts that made their object clear, they laid their eager hands upon the cowering women. Even as the weak and timid doves flee

before an eagle, even as a young lamb quails at the sight of a wolf, so shuddered the Sabine women when they beheld these fierce warriors making towards them. Every one turned pale, terror spread throughout the throng, but it showed itself in different ways. Some tore their hair; some swooned away; some wept in silence; some called vainly for their mothers; some sobbed aloud; others seemed stupefied with fear; some stood transfixed; others tried to flee. Nevertheless, the Romans carry off the women, sweet booty for their beds, and to many of them, terror lends an added charm.

If one shows herself too rebellious and refuses to follow her ravisher, he picks her up and, pressing her lovingly to his bosom, exclaims, "Why with tears do you thus dim the lovely radiance of your eyes? What your father is to your mother, that will I be to you." O Romulus, you are the only one who has ever known how to reward his soldiers; for such pay, I would willingly enrol myself beneath your banners. Ever since those days, the theatres, faithful to this ancient custom, have always been a dangerous lure to loveliness.

Forget not the arena where mettled steeds strive for the palm of Victory. This circus, where an immense concourse of people is gathered, is very favourable to Love. There, if you would express the secret promptings of your heart, there is no need for you to talk upon your fingers, or to watch for signs to tell you what is in your fair one's mind. Sit close beside her, as close as you are able; there's nothing to prevent. The narrowness of the space compels you to press against her and, fortunately for you, compels her to acquiesce. Then, of course, you must think of some means of starting the conversation. Begin by saying the sort of thing people generally do say on such occasions. Some horses are seen entering the stadium; ask her the name of their owner; and whoever she favours, you should follow suit. And when the solemn procession of the country's gods and goddesses

passes along, be sure and give a rousing cheer for Venus, your protectress. If, as not infrequently befalls, a speck of dust lights on your fair one's breast, flick it off with an airy finger; and if there's nothing there, flick it off just the same; anything is good enough to serve as a pretext for paying her attention. Is her dress dragging on the ground? Gather it up, and take special care that nothing soils it. Perchance, to reward you for your kindness, she'll grant you the favour of letting you see her leg. And then again, you must keep an eye on the people seated in the row behind and see that no one thrusts his knee into her soft shoulders.

The merest trifle is enough to win these butterfly ladies. Why, hosts of men have succeeded with a woman merely by the attentive manner in which they have arranged a cushion for her, or fanned her with a fan, or put a stool beneath her dainty feet. Both the circus and the forum afford opportunities for a love-affair. Love often delights to try his strength there, and many a man, who came to see another wounded, finds that he has been pinked himself. While he is talking and stroking her hand, asking for the race-card and, having put his money on, is inquiring what has won, an arrow pierces him before he knows where he is; he heaves a sigh and, instead of being a mere spectator of the combat, he finds himself a victim.

Did we not see this happen quite recently, when Caesar offered us the spectacle of a sea-fight showing the Persian and the Athenian ships in action. Then indeed, from both seas, youths and maidens flocked to see the show and the whole world was gathered within the City. Which of us, in that vast throng, found not a woman worthy of his love; and, alas, how many were tortured by a foreign flame.

But lo, Caesar makes ready to complete the conquest of the world! Ye far-off countries of the East, to our laws shall ye submit; and you, ye arrogant Parthians, shall be punished as ye deserve. Rejoice, shades of Crassus, and

you, ye Roman Eagles, ashamed at your long sojourn in barbarian hands, be of good cheer, your avenger is at hand. Scarce has he essayed to wield his arms, and yet he proves himself a skilful leader. Though he himself is but a boy, he wages a war unsuited to his boyish years. O, ye of little faith, vex not your souls about the age of the gods! Courage in a Caesar does not wait upon the years. Genius divine outpaces time and brooks not the tedium of tardy growth. Hercules was still no more than a child when he 'crushed the serpents in his baby hands. Even in the cradle he proved himself a worthy son of Jove. And you, Bacchus, still glowing with youthful radiance, how mighty wast thou when India trembled at thy conquering Thyrsi! With the auspices and with the courage of thy sire shalt thou wield thine arms, young Caesar; with the courage and with the auspices of thy sire shalt thou overthrow thine enemies. Such a beginning becomes the name thou bearest. To-day thou art Prince of the Youths; one day thou shalt be Prince of the Elders. Since thou hast brothers, avenge thy slaughtered brethren; and since thou hast a sire, defend thy father's rights. It is thy father, thy country's father, who hath armed thee, what time the foe is violently wrestling the sceptre from a parent's struggling hand. Thy sacred cause shall triumph o'er the perjured foe; justice and piety shall march beneath thy standards. The righteousness of our cause shall overcome the Parthians; arms shall drive the victory home, and so to Latium's riches, the wealth of the Orient shall my young hero add. Mars, his sire, and thou

Caesar, his sire too, a god the one, the other soon a god to be, watch over him and keep him from all harm. I can read the hidden secrets of the future. Aye, thou wilt conquer. I will sing thy glory in verses consecrate to thee; with a loud voice I will sound thy praise. Standing erect will I depict thee, and urging thy warriors to the combat. Grant that my song be not unworthy of the prowess that it celebrates! I

will sing of the Parthian turning to flee, and of the Roman facing the arrows aimed at him by the flying foe. What, Parthian, dost thou leave to the conquered, who seekest victory in flight? Henceforth, for thee Mars forebodeth nought but ill.

That day shall dawn, O fairest of mankind, when, resplendent with gold, by four white horses drawn, thou shalt pass within the City walls. Before thee, laden with chains, shall walk the conquered leaders; nor shall they then, as erst they did, seek safety in flight. Young men and maidens shall with joy behold the sight, and with gladness shall all hearts be filled. Then if some fair one shall ask of thee the name of this or that defeated monarch, what all these emblems mean, what country this, what mountain that, or what that river yonder represents, answer at once, anticipate her questions, speak up with confidence, and even when your mind's a blank, speak up as if you had the knowledge pat. " Here's the Euphrates, with his sedgy crown; and that old fellow there, with sky-blue hair, why, he's the Tigris; and those? . . hum! . . . well, they're Armenians. That woman yonder? She is Persia, where the son of Danaë was born. That town till lately rose up amid the vales of Achæmenes. That prisoner there, or that other one yonder? Oh., they are captured generals." And if you know them, give their names. If you don't, invent them.

Dinners and banquets offer easy access to women's favour, and the pleasures of the grape are not the only entertainment you may find there; Love, with rosy cheeks, often presses in her frail hands the amphora of Bacchus. As soon as his wings are drenched with wine, Cupid grows drowsy and stirs not from his place. But anon he'll be up and shaking the moisture from his wings, and woe betide the man or woman who receives a sprinkling of this burning dew. Wine fills the heart with thoughts of love and makes it prompt to catch on fire. All troubles vanish, put to flight by copious draughts.

Then is the time for laughter, the poor man plucks up courage and imagines he's a millionaire. To the deuce with worries and troubles! Brows unpucker and hearts expand; every tongue's inspired by frankness, and calls a spade a spade. We've often lost our heart to a pretty girl at dinner. Bringing love and wine together is adding fuel to fire indeed. Don't judge a woman by candle-light, it's deceptive. If you really want to know what she's like, look at her by daylight, and when you're sober. It was broad daylight, and under the open sky, that Paris looked upon the three goddesses and said to Venus, "You are lovelier than your two rivals." Night covers a multitude of blemishes and imperfections. At night there is no such thing as an ugly woman! If you want to look at precious stones, or coloured cloth, you take them out into the light of day; and it's by daylight you should judge a woman's face and figure.

But if I'm to mention all the places favourable to woman-hunting, I might as well attempt to number the sands of the seashore. Of course, there's Baiæ, with white sails gleaming out in the bay, and its hot sulphur spring. Many a bather, who has gone there for his health, comes away saying, "Those precious baths are not such healthy things as people make out." Not far from the gates of Rome, behold the temple of Diana shaded by trees, the scene of many a hard-fought contest for the prize of Love. Because she's a virgin and hates the darts of Love, Diana has inflicted many a wound there, and will inflict many more.

Thus far my Muse, borne in her chariot with wheels of different height, has, told you, would-be lover, where to seek your prey, and how to lay your snares. Now I'll teach you how to captivate and hold the woman of your choice. This is the most important part of all my lessons. Lovers of every land, lend an attentive ear to my discourse; let goodwill warm your hearts, for I am going to fulfil the promises I made you.

First of all, be quite sure that there isn't a woman who cannot be won, and make up your mind that you will win her. Only you must prepare the ground. Sooner would the birds cease their song in the springtime, or the grasshopper be silent in the summer, or the hare turn and give chase to a hound of Mænalus, than a woman resist the tender wooing of a youthful lover. Perhaps you think she doesn't want to yield. You're wrong.

She wants to in her heart of hearts. Stolen love is just as sweet to women as it is to us. Man is a poor dissembler; woman is much more skilful in concealing her desire. If all the men agreed that they would never more make the first advance, the women would soon be fawning at our feet. Out in the springy meadow the heifer lows with longing for the bull; the mare neighs at the approach of the stallion. With men and women love is more restrained, and passion is less fierce. They keep within bounds. Need I mention Byblis, who burned for her brother with an incestuous flame, and hanged herself to expiate her crime? Or Myrrha, who loved her father, but not as a father should be loved, and now her shame is hidden by the bark of the tree that covered her. O sweetly scented tree, the tears which she distils, to us give perfume and recall the ill-fated maid's unhappy name.

One day in wood-crowned Ida's shady vale, a white bull went wandering by. The pride of all the herd was he. Between his horns was just a single spot of black; save for that mark, his body was as white as milk; and all the heifers of Gnossus and of Cydonia sighed for the joy of his caress. Pasiphaë conceived a passion for him and viewed with jealous eye the loveliest among the heifers. There's no gainsaying it, Crete with her hundred cities, Crete, liar though she be, cannot deny it. 'Tis said that Pasiphaë, with hands unused to undertake such toil, tore from the trees their tenderest shoots, culled from the meadows bunches of sweet grass and hastened to offer them to her beloved bull. Whithersoever he went, she followed him;

nothing would stay her. She recked not of her spouse; the bull had conquered Minos. "What avails it, Pasiphaë, to deck yourself in costly raiment? How can your lover of such riches judge? Wherefore, mirror in hand, dost thou follow the wandering herd up to the mountain top? Wherefore dost thou for ever range thy hair? Look in thy mirror: 'twill tell thee thou art no meet mistress for a bull. Ah, what wouldst thou not have given if Nature had but armed thy brow with horns! If Minos still doth hold a corner in thy heart, cease this adulterous love; or if thou must deceive thy spouse, at least deceive him with a man." She hearkens not, but, fleeing from his royal couch, she ranges ever on and on, through forest after forest, like to a Bacchante full of the spirit that unceasingly torments her. How often, looking with jealous anger on a heifer, did she exclaim) "How then can she find favour in his sight? See how she prances before him on the green. Fool, she doubtless deems that thus she is lovelier in his eyes." Then, at her command, the hapless beast is taken from the herd and sent to bow her head beneath the yoke; or else, pretending to offer sacrifice to the gods, she orders her to be slain; at the altar; and then with joy fingers o'er the entrails of her rival. How often, under the guise of one who offers sacrifice, hath she appeased the alleged displeasure of the gods, and waving the bleeding trophies in her hand exclaimed, "Go, get thee to my lover, please him now!" Now she would be Europa; now she would be Io; the one because she was a heifer, the other because a bull bore her on his back. Howbeit, deceived by the image of a cow of maple wood, the king of the herd performed with her the act of love, and by the offspring was the sire betrayed.
Had that other Cretan girl been able to forego her passion for Thyestes (but how hard it is for a woman to love one man alone), Phœbus would not have been compelled to stay his steeds in mid-career, and to have

driven his chariot back again towards the Dawn. The daughter of Nisus, because she had stolen from the father's head the fatal lock of hair, is evermore beset by ravening dogs. The son of Atreus, though he escaped the perils of the battlefield and the ocean, died beneath the dagger of his cruel spouse. Who has listened to the love story of Creusa? Who has not hated the mad fury of Medea, a mother stained with her children's blood? Phoenix, the son of Amyntor, wept with his sightless orbs. You, ye steeds, in your terror, tore Hippolytus in pieces. Wherefore, Phineus, didst thou put out the eyes of thy innocent sons? Upon thine own head will that punishment return.

Such are the consequences of woman's unbridled passion. Fiercer it is than ours, with more of frenzy in it.

Be, then, of good cheer, and never doubt that you will conquer. Not one woman in a thousand will seriously resist. Whether a pretty woman grants or withholds her favours, she always likes to be asked for them. Even if you are repulsed, you don't run any danger. But why should a woman refuse? People don't resist the temptation of new delights. We always deem that other people are more fortunate than ourselves. The crop is always better in our neighbour's field; his cows more rich in milk.

Now the first thing you have to do is to get on good terms with the fair one's maid. She can make things easy for you. Find out whether she is fully in her mistress's confidence, and if she knows all about her secret dissipations. Leave no stone unturned to win her over. Once you have her on your side, the rest is easy. Let her watch for a favourable time (that's a precaution that doctors do not neglect); let her take advantage of the moment when her mistress may more easily be persuaded, when she is more likely to surrender to a lover's solicitations. At such times, the whole world seems *couleur de rose* to her; gaiety dances in her eyes as the golden wheat-ears dance in a fertile field. When the heart is glad, when it is not gripped by sorrow, it opens and expands. Then it is that Love slips gently into its inmost folds. So long as Ilion was plunged in mourning, her warriors kept the Greeks at bay; it was when she was rejoicing and making merry that she received within her walls the fatal horse with its armèd freight. Choose, too, the moment when your charmer is smarting from the insult of a rival; make her see in you a means of wiping off the score. When, in the morning, she is doing her mistress's hair, let the maid foment her anger, let her press on with sail and oar and, sighing, murmur, "Why not, Madam, pay him out in his own coin?" Then let her talk of you; let her adroitly sing your praises and swear that you, poor fellow, are wildly in love with her. But don't lose any time, for fear the wind should drop and the sails hang limp. Fragile as ice, a woman's anger is a transient thing.

"What about the maid herself?" you ask. "Is it well to win her favours first?" Now that's a ticklish business. Sometimes it stimulates their zeal; sometimes the opposite's the case. One girl will do her utmost for her mistress, another will want to keep you for herself. The only thing is just to try, and see how it turns out. On the whole, my advice to you is "Don't." I shouldn't risk these steep and dangerous by-ways myself. If you keep with me, you'll be on the right road. If, however, you are taken with the servant's charms, if you find her as pretty as she's zealous, win the mistress first, and afterwards turn your attention to the maid; but don't begin with her. Only I warn you, if you have any faith in my teaching, if my words are not dispersed by the winds over the seas, don't make the attempt at all unless you carry it right through. Once she herself is well involved, she won't give *you* away. The bird, with its wings well limed, won't fly far; the boar can't escape from the nets; once a fish is on the hook, he can't get away. So my

advice to you is, push your attack well home, and don't be in a hurry to withdraw your forces when the victory's won. Thus she'll be your companion in crime, and she'll never betray you; she'll tell you everything you want to know about her mistress. The great thing is to be careful. If you keep your goings-on with the maid quite dark, you'll hear about everything her mistress does.

Some people think that time and the seasons only concern farmers and seafaring men. They're wrong. just as there's a time to sow, and a time to sail, so there's a time to begin on a pretty girl. Success often depends on your seizing the right moment to open the attack. Keep clear of her birthday, for example, and shun the Kalends of March. Don't begin when there's a big show on at the circus. That would prove the winter of your discontent, when the stormy winds would blow, and you'd do well to hold off. If you launch the ship then, you'll be lucky if you're washed ashore clinging to a spar. If you want a really good opportunity, wait for the anniversary of the fatal day when Roman blood incarnadined the waters of the Allia, or for that one day out of the seven on which the Syrian Jew will do no manner of work. Above all, don't go near her on her birthday; or indeed on any day when you're expected to give a present. However much you try to wriggle out of it, she'll make you buy her something. A woman always knows how to exploit an ardent lover. Some pedlar fellow will be sure to turn up, and since buying's a mania with them all, she'll be sure to find the very things she wants. She'll ask you to look at 'em; then she'll kiss you, and say, "Oh, do buy me that. It'll last for years; it's just the very thing I want, and you couldn't buy me anything I should like more." It's no good saying you haven't got the money on you; she'll ask you to draw a cheque, and then you'll curse the day you learned to write. And how many times you'll have to give her something for her birthday! Every time she wants anything very special, she'll have a

birthday. And then she'll come grieving some pretended loss; she'll come to you with eyes all red with weeping and tell you she's lost one of her precious ear-rings. That's the little game they play. Then they'll keep on asking you to lend them money; and once they've got it, I wouldn't give much for your chances of getting it back. You can look on that as gone, and

430

they won't give you so much as a "thank you." Why, if I'd got ten mouths and ten tongues, I couldn't tell you all the tricks our ladies of the *demi-monde* get up to.

In the first place, it's best to send her a letter, just to pave the way. In it you should tell her how you dote on her; pay her pretty compliments and say all the nice things lovers always say. Achilles gave way to Priam's supplications. Even the gods are moved by the voice of entreaty. And promise, promise, promise. Promises will cost you nothing. Everyone's a millionaire where promises are concerned. Hope, if only she is duly fostered, holds out a long time. She's a deceitful goddess, but a very useful one. If you give your mistress something, she may give you your *congé*. She will have had her *quid pro quo*. Always make her think you're just about to give, but never really do so. Thus your farmer will keep on manuring a barren field, hoping it will produce a crop some day. Your gambler will keep throwing good money after bad, in hopes of redeeming all his losses; and thus his greed falls a victim to his hope of gain. The really great problem, the problem that takes all a man's skill to solve, is to win a woman's favours without making her a present. If you succeed in that, she will go on giving, so as not to lose the guerdon of the favours she has already bestowed. So send off your letter and couch it in the sweetest terms; it should be a sort of preliminary reconnaissance and pave the way to her heart. A few characters written on an apple led the young Cydippe astray and, when she had read them, the rash girl found she was ensnared by her own words.

Take my advice, my youthful fellow-citizens, and study the fine arts, not only that you may champion the cause of some trembling dependent. The common herd, the austere judge, and those superior people, the senators, are not the only people who are moved by eloquence. But don't show your hand, and don't be in too much of a hurry to display your powers of speech. And don't put on the professorial style. Who but an idiot would write to his mistress as though he were addressing a meeting. A show-off letter will often turn a woman against you. Be quite natural, quite simple, but engaging. In a word, say just what you would say if you were speaking to her. If she refuses your letter and sends it back unread, don't give up; hope for the best and try again. The unruly bull bows to the yoke in time, and, in time, the most obstreperous colt gets broken in. You can wear through an iron ring by continuous friction; the ploughshare wears away every day against the soil it cleaves. What could you have harder than a rock, or less hard than water? Nevertheless, water will wear away the hardest rock. So keep pegging away, and, given time, you'll get your way with Penelope herself. Troy held out a long time, but it fell at last. Suppose she reads your letter but doesn't answer. So be it. Only keep her busy reading. Since she has condescended to read, she'll answer some fine day. Everything comes gradually and at its appointed hour. Peradventure she'll write in a huff and tell you to cease annoying her. If she does, she's trembling lest you take her at her word. She wants you to go on, although she tells you not to. So go on, and soon you'll have your heart's desire.

If you see your mistress being borne along on her litter, go up to her as if by accident, and say what you've got to say in vague ambiguous language, for fear some busybody should be listening. If you see her hanging about under some portico, as if she didn't know what to do with herself, go and walk there too. Sometimes get

in front of her, and sometimes drop behind. Don't be bashful about getting clear of the crowd and crossing over to her side. Don't, on any account, let her go to the theatre, looking her loveliest, without your being there to see. Her bare shoulders will give you something charming to contemplate. And you can look at her and admire her at your leisure; and speak to her with eyes and gestures. Applaud the actor that plays the girl's part; applaud still more the man that plays the lover. If she stands up, stand up too; and while she is sitting, keep your seat; don't worry about the time, squander it as your mistress may require.

And don't, for heaven's sake, have your hair waved, or use powder on your skin. Leave such foppishness as that to the effeminate priests who wail their Phrygian chants in honour of Cybele. Simplicity in dress is what best befits a man. Theseus conquered Ariadne without troubling about the way his hair was done. Phædra fell in love with Hippolytus, who certainly was not a dandy. Adonis, a simple woodlander, was the idol of a goddess. Study to be clean, let your skin be tanned in the open air, wear well-cut clothes, and see there are no spots on them. Have a clean tongue, and let your teeth be free from tartar; and don't slop about in boots that are two or three sizes too big for you.

Don't let your hair stick up in tufts on your head; see that your hair and your beard are decently trimmed. See also that your nails are clean and nicely filed; don't have any hair growing out of your nostrils; take care that your breath is sweet, and don't go about reeking like a billy-goat. All other toilet refinements leave to the women or to perverts.

But lo, Bacchus is summoning his bard; propitious to lovers, he fosters the fires with which he is consumed himself. Ariadne was wandering distraught along the lonely wave-beaten shores of Naxos. Scarce had sleep departed from her eyes, and she wore but an airy shift;

her feet were bare and her fair tresses were blowing about her shoulders. To the heedless billows she was crying wildly for her Theseus, and tears flowed in torrents down her cheeks. She cried aloud and wept at the same time. But both enhanced her beauty. "Oh, the faithless one," she cried, beating her tender bosom again and again, "he has abandoned me. Oh, what will become of me! What will be my fate!" She spake. And on a sudden, drums and cymbals beaten and tossed by frenzied hands resounded along the shore. Stricken with terror, she fell gasping out a few broken words, and the blood faded from her lifeless corpse. But lo, the Mænads, with their hair floating wildly out behind them, and the light-footed Satyrs, the rout that leads the procession of Apollo, came upon the scene. Behold, old Silenus, reeling-ripe as usual, who can scarce keep his seat on the ass that staggers beneath the heavy burden. He pursues the Mænads, who flee from him and mock him as they flee, and as he belabours his long-eared beast with his staff, the unskilful cavalier tumbles head-foremost from his steed. And all the Satyrs shout, "Up with you, old man Silenus, up with you again!"

Meanwhile from his lofty chariot with vine branches all bedecked, the god, handling the golden reins, drives on his team of tigers. The girl, in losing Theseus, had lost her colour and her voice. Thrice she attempted flight, thrice did fear paralyse her steps; she shuddered, she trembled like the tapering stem or the slender reed that sways at the slightest breath. "Banish all thy fears," cried the god. "In me thou findest a tenderer, more faithful lover than Theseus. Daughter of Minos, thou shalt be the bride of Bacchus. Thy guerdon shall be a dwelling in the sky; thou shalt be a new star and thy bright diadem shall be a guide to the pilot uncertain of his course." So saying he leapt from his chariot lest his tigers should affright her. The sand yielded beneath his feet. Clasping to his breast the swooning, unresisting

girl, he bore her away. For a god may do as he wills, and who shall say him nay. Then some sang *Hymenæe!* and some *Evion Evoë!* and to these strains the god and his bride consummated their spousals on the sacred couch.

When, then, you find yourself at a feast where the wine is flowing freely, and where a woman shares the same couch with you, pray to that god whose mysteries are celebrated during the night, that the wine may not overcloud thy brain. 'Tis then thou mayest easily hold converse with thy mistress in hidden words whereof she will easily divine the meaning. A drop of wine will enable you to draw sweet emblems on the table wherein she will read the proof of the love you have for her. Fix well thine eyes on her and so confirm the message of thy love. Ofttimes, without a word being spoken, the eyes can tell a wondrous tale. When she has drunk, be thou the first to seize the cup, and where her lips have touched, there press thine own and drink. Choose thou the dainties that her fingers have lightly touched, and as thou reachest for them, let thy hand softly encounter hers.

Be courteous to her husband too. Nothing could better serve your plans than to be in his good graces. If, when the dice are thrown, chance crowns thee king of the feast, yield him the honour; take off thy wreath and place it on his brow. Whether he be thy equal or inferior matters not. Let him be served the first, and flatter him in everything you say. The surest and most common means to success is to deceive him under the cloak of friendship. But though 'tis sure and common, 'tis none the less a crime. Sometimes in love the ambassador goes too far and doth exceed the terms of his mandate.

Now I will lay down the limits thou shouldst observe in drinking: never drink enough to cloud your brain or make your gait unsteady; avoid the quarrels that are born of wine and be not prompt to take offence. Follow

not the example of Eurytion, who, like a fool, gave up the ghost because he had drunk too much. The food and the wine should inspire a gentle gaiety. If you have a voice, sing; and if your limbs are supple, dance; in short, do everything you can to make a good impression. Downright drunkenness is a loathsome thing; simulated inebriety may serve a useful purpose. Let your tongue falter with a cunning stammer; pretend it's difficult for you to pronounce your words, so that whatever you do or say a little on the risky side may be put down to the fact that you've had too much liquor. Drink to your mistress, and do it openly, and drink to the man that shares her bed-and, under your breath, curse her lawful spouse. When the guests rise up to go, you'll have a good chance to get very close to your lady. Mingle in the crowd, contrive to get near her, press her side with your fingers and rub your foot against hers.

And now, we'll say, you've got her to yourself. Now you can talk to her. Avaunt then, rustic modesty! Fortune and Venus favour the brave. Don't ask me to tell you what to say. just take and begin, the words will come fast enough without your having to search for them. You must play the lover for all you're worth. Tell her how you are pining for her; do everything you know to win her over. She will believe you fast enough. Every woman thinks herself attractive; even the plainest is satisfied with the charms she deems that she possesses. And, then, how often it has happened that the man who begins by feigning love ends by falling in love in real earnest. Ali, my fair ones, look with indulgent eye on those that give themselves a lover's airs; the love, now feigned, will soon be love indeed.

By subtle flatteries you may be able to steal into her heart, even as the river insensibly o'erflows the banks which fringe it. Never cease to sing the praises of her face, her hair, her taper fingers and her dainty foot. The coldest beauty is moved by praises of her charms, and

even the innocent and greenest girl takes pride and pleasure in the care of her good looks. If it were not so, wherefore should Juno and Minerva blush even now to have failed to carry off the prize for loveliness, in the woods of Ida? See that peacock there; if you belaud his plumage, he'll spread his tail with pride; but if in silence you look at him, he'll never show his treasures. The courser, in the chariot race, is proud of the admiration bestowed on his well-groomed mane and his proudly arched neck. Be not backward in your promises; women are drawn on by promises; and swear by all the gods that you'll be as good as your word. Jove, from his high abode, looks down and laughs on lovers' perfidies, and gives them to Æolus for the winds to sport with. Often he swore to Juno by the Styx that he'd be faithful, and he broke his vows. His example should lend us courage.

'Tis well that the gods should exist and well that we should believe in them. Let us bring offerings of wine and frankincense to their immemorial altars. They are not sunk in indolent repose and slothful ease. Live then in innocence, for the gods are omnipresent. Fulfil the trust that has been reposed in you; observe the precepts of religion; have nought to do with fraud; stain not your hands with blood. If you are wise, practise deceit on women alone, for that you may do with impunity; but in all other matters let your word be your bond. Deceive them that are deceivers; women for the most part are a perfidious race; let them fall into the snares which they themselves have prepared. Egypt, so they tell, being deprived of the rains which fertilise its soil, had suffered nine years of continuous drought when Thrasius came to Busiris and announced that Jove could be propitiated by the shedding of a stranger's blood. "Then," said Busiris, "thou shalt be the first victim offered to the god; thou shalt be that stranger-guest to whom Egypt shall owe the rain from heaven." Phalaris, too, caused the ferocious

Perillus to be burnt within the brazen bull which he had fashioned, and the ill-fated craftsman was the first to put his handiwork to the proof Both penalties were just; and indeed there is no law more righteous than that the contrivens of death should perish by their own inventions. Wherefore, since a lie should pay for a lie, let woman be deceived and let her blame no one but herself for the treachery whereof she set the example.

Tears, too, are a mighty useful resource in the matter of love. They would melt a diamond. Make a point, therefore, of letting your mistress see your face all wet with tears. Howbeit, if you cannot manage to squeeze out any tears--and they won't always flow just when you want them to--put your finger in your eyes. What lover of experience does not know how greatly kisses add. cogency to tender speeches? If she refuse to be kissed, kiss her all the same. She may struggle to begin with. "Horrid man!" she'll say; but if she fights, 'twill be a losing battle. Nevertheless, don't be too rough with her and hurt her dainty mouth. Don't give her cause to say that you're a brute. And if, after you've kissed her, you fail to take the rest, you don't deserve even what you've won. What more did you want to come to the fulfilment of your desires? Oh, shame on you! It was not your modesty, it was your stupid clownishness.

You would have hurt her in the struggle, you say? But women like being hurt. What they like to give, they love to be robbed of. Every woman taken by force in a hurricane of passion is transported with delight; nothing you could give her pleases her like that. But when she comes forth scathless from a combat in which she might have been taken by assault, however pleased she may try to look, she is sorry in her heart. Phoebe was raped, and so, too, was her sister Elaira; and yet they loved their ravishers not a whit the less.

A well-known story, but one that may well be told again, is that of Achilles and the maid of Scyros. Venus

had rewarded Paris for the homage he had paid to her beauty when at the foot of Mount Ida she triumphed over her two rivals. From a far-off country a new daughter-in-law has come to Priam, and within the walls of Ilion there dwells an Argive bride. The Greeks swore to avenge the outraged husband; for an affront to one was an affront to all. Howbeit, Achilles (shame on him if he had not yielded to a mother's prayers) had disguised his manhood beneath the garments of a girl. "What dost thou there, descendant of Æacus? Dost thou busy thyself with carding wool? Is that a task for a man? It is by other arts of Pallas that thou shouldst seek for fame. What hast thou to do with work-baskets? Thine arm is made to bear the shield. How comes this distaff in the hand that should lay Hector low? Cast from thee these spindles, and let thy doughty hand brandish a spear from Pelion." Once chance brought Achilles and the royal maiden together in the same bedchamber, and then the onslaught she underwent swiftly revealed to her the sex of her companion. Doubtless she yielded only to superior force; so we must of course believe; but at least she was not angry that force gained the day. "Stay yet awhile," she said entreatingly, when Achilles, eager to be gone, had laid aside the distaff to seize his valiant arms. What then has become of this alleged violence? Wherefore, Deidamia, wilt thou retain with pleading tones the author of thy downfall?

True, if modesty does not permit a woman to make the first advance, it nevertheless delights her to yield when her lover takes the initiative. In truth a lover reposes too much confidence in his good looks if he thinks that a woman will be the first to ask. 'Tis for him to begin, for him to entreat her; and to his supplications she will incline her ear. Ask and thou shalt receive; she only waits to be implored. Tell her the cause and origin of your desire. Jove bent the knee to the heroines of old times, and for all his greatness, none ever came of her

own accord to entreat him. If, however, you only get disdain for all your pains, draw back and press your suit no farther. Many women long for what eludes them, and like not what is offered them. Cool off; don't let her think you too importunate. Do not betray the hope of too swift a victory; let Love steal in disguised as Friendship. I've often seen a woman thus disarmed, and friendship ripen into love.

A pale complexion ill becomes a sailor. The rays of the sun and the salt spray should have tanned his features; nor does it suit the husbandman who, with plough or heavy rakes, is for ever turning up the soil in the open air; and ye who strive for the athlete's crown of olive, it would ill beseem you to have too white a skin. But every lover should be pale; pallor is the symptom of Love, it is the hue appropriate to Love. So, deceived by your paleness, let your mistress be tenderly solicitous for your health. Orion was pale with love when he wandered after Lyrice in the woods of Dirce. Pale, too, was Daphnis for the Naiad that disdained him. Thinness, too, is an index to the feelings; and be not ashamed to veil your shining hair beneath the hood. Sleepless nights make thin a young man's body. So that thou mayest come to the fruition of your desires, shrink not from exciting pity, that all who behold you may exclaim, "Why, poor wretch, you are in love!"

Shall I complain aloud or only whisper it, how virtue is on every side confounded with vice? Friendship and constancy are both but empty names. You cannot with safety tell your friend all the charms of the woman you adore; if he believed what you said of her, he would straightway become your rival. But, you will argue, the grandson of Actor stained not the couch of Achilles; Phædra erred not, at least, not in favour of Pirithoüs; Pylades loved Hermione with a love as chaste as that which Phoebus bore for Pallas, or as the love of Castor and Pollux for their sister Helen. But if you count on miracles like that, you

might as well expect to cull apples from the tamarisk, or to gather honey in the middle of a river. Vice is so inviting, and each man seeks but to gratify his own pleasure. And pleasure is sweetest when 'tis paid for by another's pain. Shun those men you think you can rely on, and you'll be safe. Beware alike of kinsman, brother, and dear friend. They are the people who generally make the trouble.

I was on the point of ending here; but let me add that women are things of many moods. You must adapt your treatment to the special case. The same soil is not equally good for everything. This land is good for the vine, and this for olives; and here's the place for corn. You'll find as many dispositions in the world as you meet with different figures and faces. A clever man will know how to adapt himself to this diversity of temper and disposition, and suit his conversation to the needs of the hour, even as Proteus, who is now a graceful wave, now a lion, now a tree, and now a boar with bristling hide. It's the same with fish; some you spear, others you take with the line, and others again in the encircling net. Different methods suit different people. You must vary them according to the age of your mistresses.

An old hind will descry your machinations from afar. If you display too much skill to the novice, and too much enterprise to the bashful, you'll frighten her and put her on her guard. Thus it sometimes happens that a woman, who has feared to yield to the caresses of a man of breeding, will fall into the arms of a worthless knave.

A part of my enterprise is now achieved, though more remains behind. Here then let us heave the anchor and give ourselves a little rest.

On the Spectacles

(Epigrams, Book 1)

FROM *Epigrams: Spectacles, Books 1–5*

By Martial, translated by D.R. Shackleton-Bailey

Martial on Gladiatorial Spectacles

1. Let barbarous Memphis speak no more of the wonder of her pyramids, nor Assyrian toil boast of Babylon; nor let the soft Ionians be extolled for Trivia's temple; let the altar of many horns say naught of Delos; nor let the Carians exalt to the skies with extravagant praises the Mausoleum poised in empty air. All labour yields to Caesar's Amphitheatre; Fame shall tell of one work in lieu of all.

2. Where the starry colossus sees the constellations at close range and lofty scaffolding rises in the middle of the road, once gleamed the odious halls of a cruel monarch, and in all Rome there stood a single house. Where rises before our eyes the august pile of the Amphitheatre, was once Nero's lake. Where we admire the warm baths, a speedy gift, a haughty tract of land had robbed the poor of their dwellings. Where the Claudian colonnade unfolds its wide-spread shade, was the outermost part of the palace's end. Rome has been restored to herself, and under your rule Caesar, the pleasances that belonged to a master now belong to the people.

3. What race is so remote, so barbarous, Caesar, that no spectator from it is in your city? That farmer of Rhodope has come from Orphic Haemus, the Samaritan fed on draughts of horses' blood has come, and he who drinks discovered-Nile's first stream, and he on whom beats the wave of farthest Tethys. The Arab has sped hither, the Sabaeans too, and Cilicians have here been sprayed with their own showers. Sygambrians have come with hair curled in a knot and Ethiopians with hair curled otherwise. Diverse sounds the speech of the peoples, and yet it is one, when you are called true father of the fatherland.

4. A company dangerous to peace and inimical to placid tranquillity, ever harrying hapless wealth, was led in parade, and the vast arena did not have room enough for the guilty. The informer has the exile he used to give.

5. The informer is a fugitive in exile from the Ausonian city. This you may reckon among our prince's expenses.

6. Believe that Pasiphae was mated to the Dictaean bull; we have seen it, the old legend has won credence. And let not hoary antiquity plume itself, Caesar: whatever Fame sings of, the arena affords you.

7. It is not enough that warrior Mars serves you in unconquered arms, Caesar. Venus herself serves you too.

8. Illustrious Fame used to sing of the lion laid low in Nemea's spacious vale, Hercules' work. Let ancient testimony be silent, for after your shows, Caesar, we have now seen such things done by women's valour.

9. As Prometheus, bound on Scythian crag, fed the tireless bird with his too abundant breast, so did Laureolus, hanging on no sham cross, give his naked flesh to a Caledonian boar. His lacerated limbs live on, dripping gore, and in all his body, body there was none. Finally he met with the punishment he deserved; the guilty wretch had plunged a sword into his father's throat or his master's, or in his madness had robbed a temple of its secret gold, or laid a cruel torch to Rome. The criminal had outdone the misdeeds of ancient story; in him, what had been a play became an execution.

10. Daedalus, when you are being thus torn by a Lucanian bear, how you wish you now had your wings!

11. The rhinoceros, displayed all over the arena, performed for you, Caesar, battles that he did not promise. How he lowered his head and flamed into a fearful rage! How mighty a bull was he, to whom a bull was as a dummy!

12. A treacherous lion had harmed his master with his ingrate mouth, daring to violate the hands he knew so well; but he paid a fitting penalty for such a crime, and suffered weapons who had not suffered stripes. What should be the manners of men under such a prince, who commands wild beasts to be of a milder nature?

13. A bear, whirling headlong in the bloody arena, got entangled in birdlime and lost his escape. Now let shining spears lie idle with covered points, and let not the lance fly, launched by extended arm. Let the hunter catch his quarry in the empty air, if it pleases us to hunt wild beasts with the fowler's art.

14. Amid the cruel perils of Caesar's hunt a light spear had pierced a pregnant sow. One of her litter leapt out of the hapless mother's wound. Savage Lucina, was this a delivery? She would have wished to die wounded by further weapons, so that the sad path might open for all her brood. Who denies that Bacchus sprang from his mother's death? Believe that a deity was so given birth: so born was a beast.

15. A mother sow, struck by a heavy weapon and laid open by the wound, lost life and gave it at one and the same time. How sure was the hand that poised the steel! I believe this hand was Lucina's. Dying, the creature sampled the divine power of either Diana. By one the parent was delivered, by the other the beast was slain.

16. A wild sow, now pregnant, sent forth her progeny, pledge of her ripe womb, made parent by a wound. Nor did the offspring lie on the ground, but ran as the mother fell. How ingenious are sudden chances!

17. That which was the topmost glory of your renown, Meleager, how small a portion is it of Carpophorus's, a felled boar! He plunged his spear in a charging bear, once prime in the peak of the Arctic pole; he laid low a lion of unprecedented size, a sight to see, who might have done honour to Hercules' hands; he stretched dead a fleet leopard with a wound dealt from afar . . . since one bore off glory as his reward, the other a dish.

18. The bull was snatched up in the midst of the arena and departed for the sky. The was the work, not of art, but of devotion.

19. A bull carried Europa through his brother's sea; but now a bull has borne Alcides to the stars. Compare now, Fame, the steers of Caesar and of Jove; even though they bore an equal load, this one bore his load higher.

20. Devoted and suppliant the elephant adores you, Caesar, he who but lately was so formidable to the bull. He does it unbidden, no master teaches him. Believe me, he too feels our god.

21. A tigress, wont to lick the hand of the fearless trainer, rare Hyrcanian mountains, fiercely tore a wild lion with rabid tooth; unknown in any times. She dared do no such thing while she lived forests, but since she had been among us she has gained ferocity.

22. The bull, that goaded with fire through the whole arena had just snatched up dummies and tossed them to the stars, at length met his death, trampled by a horned mouth. He thought it would be easy to toss an elephant so.

23. One party wanted Myrinus, the other Triumphus. Caesar with either hand promised both alike. There was no better way for him to end the merry dispute. Oh pleasant device of our unconquered prince!

24. Whatever Rhodope is said to have watched on Orpheus' stage, the arena, Caesar, displayed to you. Rocks crept and a wondrous forest ran, such as the grove of the Hesperides is believed to have been. Every kind of wild beast was present, mingling with the tame, and many a bird hovered above the bard. But himself lay torn by an ungrateful bear. This thing alone was done contrary to the legend.

25. Earth through a sudden opening sent a bear to attack Orpheus. She came from Eurydice.

26. While the trembling trainers were goading the rhinoceros and the great beast's anger was long a-gathering, men were giving up hope of the combats of promised warfare; but at length the fury we earlier knew returned. For with his double horn he tossed a heavy bear as a bull tosses dummies from his head to the stars. With how sure a stroke does the strong hand of Carpophorus, still a youth, aim Norican spears! He lifted two steers with his mobile neck, to him yielded the fierce buffalo and the bison. A lion fleeing before him ran headlong upon the spears. Go now, you crowd, complain of tedious delays!

27. If you are here from distant land, a late spectator for whom this was the first day of the sacred show, let not the naval warfare deceive you with its ships, and the water like to a sea: here but lately was land. You don't believe it? Watch while the waters weary Mars. But a short while hence you will be saying: "Here but lately was sea."

28. Cease to wonder, Leander, that the night wave spared you. 'Twas Caesar's wave.

29. When bold Leander was seeking his sweetheart and the swollen waters were already overwhelming his weary body, he is said, poor fellow, to have addressed the surging waves in these words: "Spare me as I hasten, down me as I return."

30. The well-trained bevy of Nereids sported all over the surface and in various conformations decorated the yielding waters. The trident menaced with upright tooth, the anchor with curved. We thought we saw an oar, we thought we saw a boat, and the Laconians' star shining, welcome to seamen, and broad sails bellying in conspicuous folds. Who invented such devices in the clear water? Thetis either taught these games or learned them.

31. As Priscus and Verus each drew out the contest and the struggle between the pair long stood equal, shouts loud and often sought discharge for the combatants. But Caesar obeyed his own law (the law was that the bout go on without shield until a finger be raised). What he could do, he did, often giving dishes and presents. But an equal end to the even strife was found: equal they fought, equal they yielded. To both Caesar sent wooden swords and to both palms. Thus valour and skill had their reward. This has happened under no prince but you, Caesar: two fought and both won.

32. If the ages of old, Caesar, In which a barbarous earth brought forth wild monsters, had produced Carpophorus, Marathon would not have feared her bull, nor leafy Nemea her lion, nor Arcadians the boar of Maenalus. When he armed his hands, the Hydra would have met a single death, one stroke of his would have sufficed for the entire Chimaera. He could yoke the fire-bearing bulls without the Colchian, he could conquer both the beasts of Pasiphae. If the ancient tale of the sea monster is recalled, he would release Hesione and Andromeda single-handed. Let the glory of Hercules' achievement be numbered: it is more to have subdued twice ten wild beasts at one time.

33. As the startled hind fled the swift Molossians and with various cunning spun lingering delays, suppliant and like to one begging she halted at Caesar's feet; and the hounds did not touch their prey . . . such was the boon she won from knowing her prince. Caesar has divine power; sacred, sacred is this potency, believe it. Wild beasts never learned to lie.

34. It had been Augustus' labour to pit fleets against each other here and rouse the waters with naval clarion. How small a part is this of our Caesar! Thetis and Galatea saw in the waves beasts they never knew. Triton saw chariots in hot career in the sea's dust and thought his master's horses had passed by. As Nereus prepared fierce battle for ferocious ships, he was startled to find himself walking on foot in the liquid expanse. Whatever is viewed in the Circus and the Amphitheatre, that, Caesar, the wealth of your water has afforded you. So no more of Fucinus and the lake of direful Nero; let this be the only sea fight known to posterity.

Letters

(Book 10)

FROM *Pliny the Younger: Correspondence with Trajan from Bithynia*

By Pliny, translated by Wynne Williams

EPISTLES X

15. *C. Plinius to Traianus Imperator*

Because I feel sure, sir, that you are interested, I am reporting to you that, together with all my people, I have reached Ephesus by sea, after "rounding Males", despite being held up by opposing winds. Now I intend to set out for the province, by coastal vessels for part of the way, by carriages for the rest. For, just as oppressive heat is an obstacle to travel by land, so are the Etesian winds to an unbroken voyage by sea.

16. *Traianus to Plinius*

You were right to report to me, my dearest Secundus. For I do feel concern about what kind of journey you are having on the way to the province. It is a wise decision of yours to use ships for part of the time, and carriages for part of the time, according to what local conditions require.

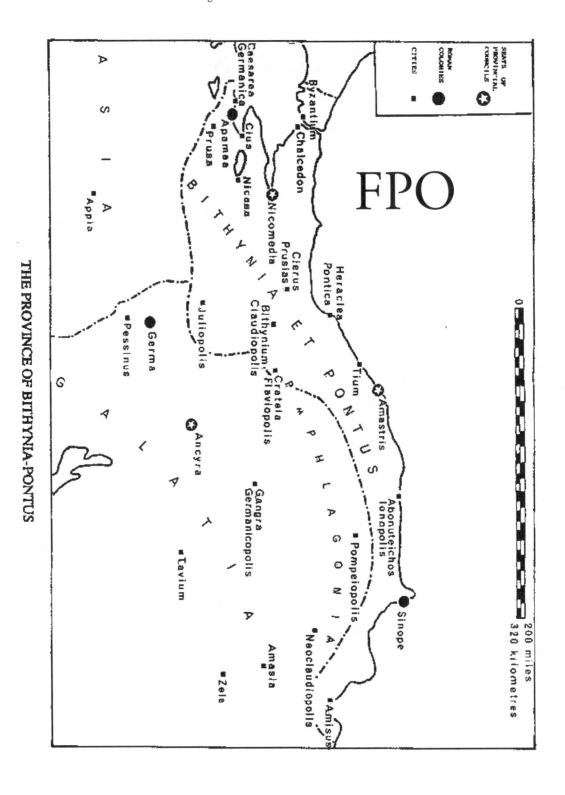

THE PROVINCE OF BITHYNIA-PONTUS

17A. C. Plinius to Traianus Imperator

(1) Although I had a very healthy voyage, as far as Ephesus, sir, yet thereafter, when I had begun to pursue my journey by carriage, I was troubled by the most oppressive heat and also by slight attacks of fever, and I halted at Pergamum. (2) Subsequently, when I had shifted to coastal vessels, I was held back by opposing winds, and I entered Bithynia rather later than I had hoped, that is on September 17th. I cannot, however, complain about this delay, since it was my good fortune to celebrate your birthday in the province, which was a very good omen. (3) At the moment I am examining the expenditures, revenues and debtors of the state of Prusa; from the very process of investigation I am learning more and more that this is necessary. For many sums of money are being kept in their possession by private persons under different pretexts; moreover some sums are being paid out on wholly unlawful outlays. (4) I have written to you about this, sir, at the very moment of my arrival.

17B. C. Plinius to Traianus Imperator

(1) On September 17th, sir, I entered the province, which I found in that state of reverence and of loyalty to yourself which you deserve from the human race. (2) Consider, sir, whether you think it necessary to send a surveyor here. For it appears that considerable sums of money could be recovered from the administrators of public works if measurements were carried out honestly. Such at any rate is my estimate on the basis of the balance-sheet of Prusa with which I am dealing at this very moment.

18. Traianus to Plinius

(1) I could wish that you had been able to reach Bithynia without any complaint about your own physical condition or that of your people, and that your journey from Ephesus had been similar to your experience of the voyage as far as there. (2) The date of your arrival in Bithynia I learnt from your letter, my dearest Secundus. The provincials, I believe, will understand that I have taken thought for their interests. For you in your turn will see to it that it is evident to them that you have been picked out to be sent to them in my place. (3) Moreover, you must above all examine the accounts of the communities: for it is an established fact that they have been in confusion. I have scarcely enough surveyors for those works which are in progress at Rome or nearby; but men who can be trusted are to be found in every province, and therefore you will have no lack of them, if only you are willing to search for them diligently.

19. C. Plinius to Traianus Imperator

(1) I ask you, sir, to guide me with your advice in my doubts about whether I ought to have prisoners guarded by public slaves owned by the cities, which has hitherto been the practice, or by soldiers.

For I fear both that an insufficiently reliable watch will be kept by the public slaves and also that this responsibility will call a considerable number of soldiers away from their duties. (2) For the time being I have included a few soldiers among the public slaves. However, I see that there is a risk that this may itself be a reason for neglect of duty by both groups, as the former feel certain that they can throw the burden of their shared guilt upon die latter, and the latter upon the former.

20. *Traianus to Plinius*

(1) There should be no necessity, my dearest Secundus, for more of my fellow-soldiers to be transferred to guarding prisoners. Let us persist with what is the custom in that province, to have prisoners guarded by public slaves. (2) And in fact it is up to you by your strictness and thoroughness to see that they do it conscientiously. For, as you say in your letter, what is to be feared above all is that, if soldiers were to be mixed in with public slaves, they would become more negligent as a result of either group relying upon the other; but let us also stick to this rule, that as few of them as possible should be called away from their units.

21. *C. Plinius to Traianus Imperator*

Gavius Bassus, the Prefect of the Pontic shore, has come to me, sir, showing me the greatest respect and attention, and has been with me for several days, a worthy man, so far as I have been able to judge, and one deserving of your generosity, I informed him that you had given instructions that he should be satisfied with 10 privileged men, two cavalrymen and one centurion, drawn from the cohorts which you wanted me to have under my command. (2) He replied that this number was not enough for him, and that he would write to you to this effect. It was for this reason that I decided that the soldiers he has in excess of the total should not be recalled at once.

22. *Traianus to Plinius*

Gavius Bassus has also written to me that the number of soldiers which I laid down in my instructions should be given to him was not large enough for him. I have ordered a copy of what I wrote back to him to be appended to this letter, for your information. It makes a great difference whether the situation requires it or whether he wants to make wider use of them on this pretext. (2) But we should consider only what is useful, and, as far as possible, ensure that soldiers are not absent from their units.

23. *C. Plinius to Traianus Imperator*

(1) The people of Prusa, sir, have a bath-house: it is squalid and old. They therefore regard it as of great importance to have a new one built; it seems to me that you can grant their request in this matter.

(2) For there will be the money for it to be built: in the first place that which I have already begun to recover and to exact from private persons; in the second place they are ready to transfer to the building of the bath-house the money which they have themselves been in the practice of spending on olive-oil; besides it is something which both the standing of the city and the splendour of your age requires.

24. Traianus to Plinius

If the building of a bath-house is not going to put a burden on the resources of the people of Prusa, we can grant their request, provided that no special tax is imposed for that purpose and that they do not have less available for necessary expenditures in the future.

25. C. Plinius to Traianus Imperator

Servilius Pudens, my deputy, came to me at Nicomedia on November 24th, sir, and freed me from the anxiety caused by a long period of waiting.

26. C. Plinius to Traianus Imperator

(1) Your kindnesses to me have bound Rosianus Geminus to me by the closest of links, sir: for I had him as quaestor in my consulship. I have found him to be most attentive to me: so great is the respect he shows me since my consulship, and he heaps personal services on top of the tokens of our official relationship. (2) So I ask that you yourself in response to my prayers show him on your side the favour appropriate to his rank. You will also, if you have any trust in my judgment, show him your generosity; he himself will devote his efforts in those tasks which you will have entrusted to him to show he deserves greater honours. What makes me more sparing in my praise is the fact that I hope his integrity and honesty and diligence are very well known to you, as a result not only of the offices which he has filled in the city under your own eyes, but also from his military service with you. (3) This one request I keep making again and again, something which, because of my affection for him, I cannot convince myself that I have yet done in full measure, and I beg you, sir, to allow me as soon as possible to rejoice in the enhanced standing of my quaestor, and so, through him, in my own.

27. C. Plinius to Traianus Imperator

Your freedman and procurator Maximus, sir, asserts that he too needs six soldiers apart from the ten privileged soldiers whom you ordered to be allocated by me to that excellent man Gemellinus. For the time being I have decided that these men should be left in attendance upon him, just as I had found them, especially since he was setting off for Paphlagonia to collect grain. In fact I even added two cavalrymen to guard him, since he requested it. I ask you to write back about the rule you wish to have followed in future.

28. *Traianus to Plinius*

Since he was in fact at that moment setting off to collect grain you were right to supply my freedman Maximus with soldiers. For he too was undertaking a special duly. When he has returned to his old post, two soldiers supplied by you and the same number by my procurator Virdius Gemellinus, whose assistant he is, will be enough for him.

29. *C. Plinius to Traianus Imperator*

(1) Sempronius Caelianus, an excellent young man, has sent two slaves who had been discovered among the recruits to me. I postponed their sentence until I could ask your advice as the founder and upholder of military discipline about the manner of their punishment. (2) For I am myself in doubt principally because of the fact that, while they had already sworn the oath, they had not yet been enrolled in the ranks. So I ask you, sir, to write to me about what course I should follow, especially since this would set a precedent.

30. *Traianus to Plinius*

(1) Sempronius Caelianus acted in obedience to my instructions in sending to you those persons who will need to be the subject of a hearing to decide whether they should be held to have deserved the capital penalty. Now it makes a difference whether they put themselves forward as volunteers or were conscripted or even offered as substitutes. (2) If they are conscripts, it is the examination which was at fault; if they were offered as substitutes, blame lies at the door of those who offered them; if they came forward on their own initiative, when they had full knowledge of their status, they will deserve execution. For the fact that they have not yet been enrolled in the ranks is of no great importance. For that day on which they were first approved demanded that they tell the truth about their origin.

31. *C. Plinius to Traianus Imperator*

(1) You can condescend to attend to my worries, sir, without injury to your dignity, since you have given me the privilege of placing before you matters about which I am in doubt. (2) In very many of the cities, and at Nicomedia and Nicaea in particular, individuals who were sentenced to forced labour or to appearing at the games and similar kinds of penalties to these are carrying out the functions and duties of public slaves, and even receiving a yearly allowance as public slaves. When I had learned of this, I was for a long time in great uncertainty about what I ought to do. (3) For I both considered it excessively harsh to

send back to finish their sentences after a long interval a considerable number of men who are now old and who, so it is claimed, lead a simple and respectable life, and I also thought it quite improper to continue to use convicts in official posts; again I reflected that it was inexpedient to have these same men supported in idleness at public expense, but also dangerous not to have them supported at alL (4) Of necessity, therefore, I left the whole matter undecided, until I could take your advice. You will perhaps enquire how it came about that they were released from the penalties to which they had been sentenced; I too enquired, but I found out nothing which I could tell you for certain. Although the judgments in which they had been sentenced were produced, yet there were no documents in which they could be shown to have been set free. (5) There were, however, some who claimed that, upon appealing for mercy, they had been released at the orders of proconsuls or legates. What made this more convincing was the fact that it was unbelievable that anyone should have ventured to do this without authority.

32. Traianus to Plinius

(1) Let us remember that it was for this reason that you were sent to that province, because many things in it evidently stood in need of correction. Now this will especially need to be put right, that men sentenced to punishment have not only been released from it without authority, as you say in your letter, but are also restored to the position of respectable officials. (2) So it will be necessary for those who were sentenced within these last ten years, and were released without any proper authorisation, to be sent back to their punishment; if any shall be found to be convicts of longer standing and old men sentenced more than ten years ago, we should assign them to those functions which would not be very different from a punishment They are usually allocated to the public baths, to cleaning sewers, likewise to the repair of roads and streets.

33. C. Plinius to Traianus Imperator

(1) While I was travelling through a distant part of the province, a very extensive fire in Nicomedia destroyed many houses belonging to private persons and two public buildings, the Gerusia and the temple of Isis, even though there was a road separating them. (2) It spread quite widely, in the first place because there was a strong wind, in the second place because of the inactivity of the people: it is generally agreed that they stood around, idle and motionless spectators of so great a disaster; besides, nowhere was there publicly available any pump, any bucket, indeed any apparatus at all for fighting fires. These things too will in fact be supplied in accordance with instructions I have already given; (3) pray consider, sir, whether you think an association of firemen should be set up, provided that it has only 150 members, I shall myself see to it that no one except a fireman is admitted and that they do not use the permission they have been granted for any other purpose; and it will not be hard to keep watch over so few.

34. *Traianus to Plinius*

You are in fact following the example set by very many people in conceiving a plan that an association of firemen could be established at Nicomedia. But let us recall that that province and especially those cities have been troubled by cliques of that kind. Whatever name we may give, for whatever reason, to those who gather together for a common purpose, they will turn into political clubs, and that in a short time. (2) It is therefore more appropriate to have those things which can be of use in checking fires made available, and to urge the owners of properties both themselves to make use of them, and, if the situation requires it, to use for this purpose the crowd which gathers.

35. *C. Plinius to Traianus Imperator*

The customary vows for your preservation, upon which the safely of the state depends, we have both undertaken, sir, and at the same time fulfilled, praying to the gods that they be willing for these vows to be perpetually fulfilled and perpetually sealed.

36. *Traianus to Plinius*

I learnt with pleasure from your letter, my dearest Secundus, that you along with the provincials had both fulfilled and pronounced vows to the immortal gods for my safety and preservation.

37. *C. Plinius to Traianus Imperator*

(1) The people of Nicomedia, sir, have spent 3,318,000 sesterces on an aqueduct, which was abandoned while still unfinished, and was also demolished; subsequently 200,000 were laid out on another aqueduct. Since this too was abandoned, fresh expenditure is required in order that those who have wasted so much money may get their water. (2) I have myself visited a very pure spring, from which it appears that the water must be brought, as was attempted on the first occasion, on an arched structure, so that it may not reach just the flat and low-lying parts of the city. A very few arches are still standing: some can also be built up from the dressed stone which was pulled down from the earlier structure; some part of it, in my judgment, should be made of brickwork, for this would be both easier and cheaper. (3) But what is needed above all is for you to send out a water engineer or an architect, in order that what has happened may not occur again. This one thing I assert, that both the usefulness and the beauty of the work are fully worthy of your age.

38. *Traianus to Plinius*

The effort must be made to bring water to the city of Nicomedia. I am truly confident that you will approach this task with the diligence which you ought to show. But, by heaven, it is also your duty diligently to investigate whose fault it is that the people of Nicomedia have until now wasted so much money, in case it was in the course of doing each other favours that they began and abandoned aqueducts. What you thus discover, bring to my attention.

39. C. Plinius to Traianus Imperator

A theatre at Nicaea, sir, most of which has already been built, though it is still incomplete, has swallowed up more than ten million sesterces (so I am informed; for the balance-sheet for the project has not been examined); I fear it may have been in vain. (2) For it is sinking and it gapes with huge cracks, either because the soil is wet and spongy, or because the stone itself is soft and crumbling; at all events it is worth considering whether it should be finished or abandoned or even demolished. For the supports and substructures, on which it is held up from below, appear to me not to be as strong as they are expensive. (3) Many embellishments for this theatre were promised by private persons and are still owed, for example halls around it, and a colonnade above the auditorium. All these are postponed now that the building which needs to be finished first is at a stop. (4) These same people of Nicaea began, before my arrival, to restore a gymnasium which had been destroyed in a fire, on a much more lavish and extensive scale than before, and they have already spent a considerable sum; the danger is that it will have been to little practical purpose; for it is ill-planned and rambling. Moreover, an architect, admittedly a rival of the one by whom the building was started, claims that the walls, despite being twenty-two feet thick, cannot support the load put upon them, because they are made up of a core of rubble and are not encased in brickwork.

(5) The people of Claudiopolis too are excavating rather than building a huge bath-house on a low-lying site which also has a mountain hanging over it, and indeed they are using that money which those members who were added to their council through your act of favour either have already paid upon their admission, or will contribute when we extract it from them. (6) Therefore, since I fear that in the former case the city's money, in the latter your gift, which is more valuable than any money, is being ill-spent, I am forced to ask you to send out an architect, not only on account of the theatre, but also of this bath-house, to consider whether it will be more expedient, after the expenditure which has already been made, to finish by some means or other the buildings in the form in which they have been started, or to put right what it appears can be corrected, and to change the sites where it appears they can be changed, in case we waste additional expenditure in our anxiety to save what has been spent.

40. Traianus to Plinius

(1) As the man on the spot you will be the best person to consider and decide what ought to be done with the theatre which has been begun at Nicaea. It will be enough for me to be informed of the decision you arrive at. After that make the private individuals add the embellishments, when the theatre in connection with which those embellishments were promised has been finished, (2) The Greeklings do

enjoy their gymnasia; perhaps it was for that reason that the people of Nicaea set about building one in an over-ambitious spirit: but they must be content with the kind which can meet their needs. (3) You shall decide what advice should be given to the people of Claudiopolis about the bath-house they have begun to build on a site which, as you say in your letter, is quite unsuitable. You cannot be short of architects. There is no province which does not have men who are both expert and skilful; only do not suppose that it is quicker to have them sent from the capital, when they are actually accustomed to come from Greece to us.

41. C. Plinius to Traianus Imperator

When I reflect on the greatness of both your station and your character, it seems to me most appropriate that projects should be brought to your notice which are as worthy of your eternal fame as of your glory and will have as much utility as beauty. (2) There is a very large lake in the territory of the people of Nicomedia. Across it marble, grain, firewood and timber are carried by boat as far as the road with little expense and effort, but by cart from there to the sea with great effort and at even greater cost... [Probable lacuna in the text]. This project calls for many hands. But those are readily available. For there is both a plentiful supply of men in the countryside and a very plentiful one in the town, and the sure prospect that they will all most gladly take part in a project which is of advantage to all. (3) It remains for you, if you see fit, to send a surveyor or an architect, to make a thorough investigation to see whether the lake is at a higher level than the sea; the experts in this district claim that it is forty cubits higher. (4) I myself learn that a ditch was cut through the same area by one of the kings, but it is uncertain whether it was done to drain off water from the surrounding fields or to link the lake to the river, for it is incomplete. It is also a matter of doubt whether the king was cut off by sudden death or whether the success of the enterprise was despaired of. (5) But what spurs me on and inspires me (you will bear with my aspirations to advance your glory) is my desire to see what the kings had merely begun completed by your agency.

42. Traianus to Plinius

That lake of yours can incite us to wish to link it to the sea; but clearly there must be a thorough investigation to find out how much water it collects and from what sources in case, if let out into the sea, it would drain away entirely. You will be able to apply to Calpurnius Macer for a surveyor, and I shall send from here someone skilled in projects of this kind.

43. C. Plinius to Traianus Imperator

(1) When I was examining the very heavy expenditures which the state of the Byzantines has been making, it was pointed out to me, sir, that an envoy is sent every year with a resolution to bring you greetings, and that he is given twelve thousand sesterces. (2) Mindful, therefore, of your policy. I have

decided that the envoy should be kept at home, but that the resolution should be sent on, in order that the expense may be lightened and the city's act of loyalty may at the same time be carried out (3) Sums of three thousand sesterces have been charged to the account of the same city, which were being paid every year under the heading of travelling expenses to an envoy who went to bring the city's greetings to the person who is governor of Moesia. I thought this should be cut back for the future. (4) I ask you, sir, to write back what you think and to deign either to confirm my decision or to correct my mistake.

44. Traianus to Plinius

You acted quite correctly, dearest Secundus, in remitting to the Byzantines those twelve thousand sesterces which were being spent on an envoy to bring me greetings. They will be carrying out this duty even if the resolution on its own is sent or through you. The governor of Moesia also will excuse them if they pay their respects to him in a less expensive way.

45. C. Plinius to Traianus Imperator

I ask you to write, sir, and free me from my uncertainty about whether you would want passes which have reached their expiry date to be respected at all, and for how long. For I am concerned not to err in either direction through ignorance or to sanction what is unlawful or to stand in the way of essential business.

46. Traianus to Plinius

Passes which have reached their expiry date ought not to be in use. It is for that reason that I lay it upon myself as one of my first duties to send new passes out through all the provinces before they can be required.

47. C. Plinius to Traianus Imperator

(1) When I wanted, sir, to investigate the public debtors and revenue and expenditures at Apamea, the answer given to me was that the whole citizen-body was in fact anxious to have the colony's accounts examined by me, but that they had never been examined by any of the proconsuls; that they had had the privilege and long-established custom of running their community according to their own judgment (2) I required them to include the statements they were making and the precedents they were quoting in a memorandum; this I have sent to you in the form in which I had received it, although I was aware that a great deal in it was not relevant to the issue which is in dispute. (3) I ask you to deign to guide me about the principle which you think I ought to follow. For I am concerned not to be thought either to have exceeded the bounds of my duty or not to have fulfilled it.

48. *Traianus to Plinius*

The memorandum of the people of Apamea, which you had attached to your letter, has relieved me of the need to weigh the kind of reasons they had for wishing it to be seen that the proconsuls who ruled this province had refrained from an examination of their accounts, since they have not refused to let you examine them. (2) Their honesty should therefore be rewarded, so that they should now know that by my wish you will be carrying out this inspection which you are going to make without prejudice to the privileges which they now possess.

49. *C. Plinius to Traianus Imperator*

Before my arrival, sir, the people of Nicomedia began to add a new forum to their old one; in a corner of it there is a very ancient temple of the Great Mother which needs either to be rebuilt or moved to another site, principally for the reason that it is at a considerably lower level than the buildings which are going up at this very moment. (2) When I enquired whether the temple had any foundation chapter, I discovered that the practice of consecration here is different from ours. Consider therefore, sir, whether you think that a temple without any foundation charter can be moved to another site without any breach of religious law: apart from that, if religious law is not an obstacle, this is the most suitable course.

50. *Traianus to Plinius*

You can, my dearest Secundus, without anxiety about religious law, move the temple of the Mother of the Gods, if the situation of its site seems to require it, to that site which is more convenient; and do not let the fact that no foundation charter is to be found trouble you, since land in a foreign state is incapable of undergoing the consecration which takes place under our law.

51. *C. Plinius to Traianus Imperator*

(1) It is hard, sir, to put into words how much joy I felt because you granted both myself and my mother-in-law the favour of transferring her kinsman Caelius Clemens to this province. (2) For, from this, I also comprehend profoundly the scope of your kindness, when, along with my whole family, I experience generosity so full that I do not even venture to respond with equal gratitude, however much it may be in my power to do so. Accordingly I resort to prayers and I beg the gods that I may not be considered unworthy of those favours which you are constantly bestowing upon me.

52. *C. Plinius to Traianus Imperator*

The day, sir, upon which you saved the empire by taking it over, we have celebrated with as great a joy as you deserve, praying to the gods to bestow upon the human race, whose protection and safety have depended upon your well-being, the favour of keeping you unharmed and prosperous. We have also administered the oath to our fellow-soldiers in the customary manner, while the provincials vied with them in swearing the oath with the same loyalty.

53. *Traianus to Plinius*

With how much devotion and joy my fellow-soldiers, along with the provincials, celebrated the day of my accession under your guidance, I learnt with pleasure from your letter, my dearest Secundus.

54. *C. Plinius to Traianus Imperator*

(1) The moneys of the cities, sir, by your foresight and my efforts have already been and are still being recovered; I am concerned that they do not lie idle. For there is no opportunity, or only a very rare one, of buying estates, and men who would be willing to become debtors to the community are not to be found, especially at a rate of twelve asses, the rate at which they borrow from private persons. (2) Consider, therefore, sir, whether you think the rate of interest should be lowered and suitable borrowers should be attracted by this means, and whether, if they are not forthcoming even on these terms, the money should be allocated among the decurions, on condition that they provide their community with adequate security; although they may be unwilling and refuse, this step will be less harsh if a lighter rate of interest is fixed.

55. *Traianus to Plinius*

I myself also see no other remedy, my dearest Secundus, than to reduce the amount of interest in order that the moneys of the cities may the more easily be put out on loan. Its level you shall determine in accordance with the numbers of those who will take up loans. To force men to accept against their will that which may perhaps lie idle on their hands is not in accordance with the justice of our age.

56. *C. Plinius to Traianus Imperator*

(1) I offer you my most profound thanks, sir, because in the midst of your most pressing duties you have deigned to guide me also on those points on which I have consulted you: which is what I ask you to do on this occasion as well. (2) For a man has come to me and informed me that his opponents, who had been banished for three years by that most distinguished man Servilius Calvus, were still residing in the province; they asserted in rebuttal that they had their status restored by the same governor and they read out his edict. For this reason I believed it necessary to refer the case to you as it stands. (3) For, while it is laid down in your instructions that I should not restore the status of men banished by another person or by myself, yet no provision is made for those whom another

person has both banished and restored to their former status. So you had to be consulted, sir, about what rule you wish me to follow, as well, of course, as about those who, having been banished in perpetuity and not having had their status restored, are apprehended in the province. (4) For this category also has come before me for judgment. For a man who had been banished in perpetuity by the proconsul Iulius Bassus was brought before me. Because I was aware that Bassus' decisions had been revoked and that the right had been granted by the Senate to all those who had been involved in cases decided by him to plead their cases afresh, provided that they applied within two years, I asked this man whom he (Bassus) had banished whether he had approached a proconsul and informed him. He said he had not. (5) It was this which led me to consult you about whether you think he should be sent back to serve out his sentence or whether a heavier sentence should be imposed, and which sentence in particular, both on this man and on any others who may by chance be found to be in a similar position. I have appended to this letter Calvus' judgment and edict, and likewise Bassus' judgment.

57. Traianus to Plinius

I shall write back to you presently about what decision should be taken about the status of those who had been banished for three years by the proconsul Publius Servilius Calvus and afterwards had their status restored by an edict of the same person, and have stayed on in the province, after I have ascertained from Calvus the reasons for this action. (2) The man who was banished in perpetuity by Iulius Bassus, since he had for two years the opportunity of going to law if he thought he had been banished wrongfully, and since he did not do this and persisted in staying on in the province, ought to be sent in chains to the Prefects of my Praetorian Guard. For it is not enough for him to be sent back to serve out his sentence which he insolently evaded.

58. C. Plinius to Traianus Imperator

(1) While I was calling out the names of jurymen, sir, as I was about to begin the assizes, Flavius Archippus started to apply for exemption as a philosopher. (2) Some people said he should not be freed from the obligation of jury service, but removed entirely from the ranks of jury-men, and sent back to suffer the punishment from which he had escaped by breaking out of his fetters. (3) A judgment of the proconsul Velius Paulus was read out, from which it was demonstrated that Archippus had been condemned to the mines on a charge of forgery: he was unable to produce anything by which he could show that his status had been restored; however, he advanced as evidence of his restoration both a petition submitted by himself to Domitian and epistles of the latter which had a bearing upon his reputation, as well as a resolution of the people of Prusa. To these he also added letters which you had written to him, he added both an edict and an epistle of your father's, in which he had confirmed the favours bestowed by Domitian. (4) Accordingly, although such serious

charges were laid against this man, I thought no judgment should be reached until I consulted you about this matter, which seemed to me to be worthy of your decision. I have appended to this letter the documents which were read out on either side.

(5) *Epistle of Domitian to Terentius Maximus*

Flavius Archippus the philosopher has prevailed upon me to give instructions for the purchase of an estate worth up to 100,000 sesterces for him in the area of Prusa, his native city, on the income from which he can support his dependents. I wish this to be bestowed upon him. You will charge the full cost to my generosity.

(6) *Of the same person to Lappius Maximus*

I should wish you, Maximus my friend, to treat the philosopher Archippus, a good man whose character lives up to his profession, as a man recommended by me, and to show him your full kindness in those requests he may respectfully make of you.

(7) *Edict of the deified Nerva*

Some things, citizens, the very happiness of our age proclaims for certain by edict, nor does a good emperor need to be waited for in matters where it is enough for him to be understood, since the confidence of my fellow-citizens can be assured, even without being explicitly told, of this fact, that I have placed the safety of all before my own tranquillity, in order that I might both grant new favours and confirm those conceded before my reign. (8) In order, however, that neither the uncertainty of those who obtained favours nor the reputation of him who conferred them should introduce any element of hesitation into the public rejoicing, I have judged it alike necessary and delightful to anticipate their doubts by my generosity. (9) I wish no man to suppose that what he has obtained in the reign of another emperor, whether as an individual or as a member of a community, would be revoked by me, for this reason at any rate, that he should be indebted for it to me instead. Let these favours be confirmed and secure, nor should the joy of anyone on whom the good fortune of the empire has looked with a kind face require renewed prayers. Let them permit me to keep my time free for new favours, and let them know that only those things which they do not possess need to be asked for.

(10) *Epistle of the same person to Tullius Iustus*

Since the arrangement of all matters which have been begun and completed in earlier times is to be respected, then one must also abide by the epistles of Domitian.

59. C. Plinius to Traianus Imperator

Flavius Archippus begs me in the name of your well-being and eternal fame to send you the memorandum which he has given to me. I decided that, since he has asked in this way, this request must be granted, on condition, however, that I made it known to the woman who is his accuser that I was going to send it. A memorandum which I have received from her in her turn I have attached to these epistles, that you may the more easily, having as it were listened to both parties, consider what you think should be decided.

60. Traianus to Plinius

(1) Domitian could, it is true, have been unaware of what the status of Archippus was at the time when he wrote so much that had a bearing upon his reputation; but it is more in accordance with my character to believe that support-was given to his status by the emperor's intervention, especially since the honour of having his statue put up was voted to him on so many occasions by those who were not unaware of the judgment which the proconsul Paulus had delivered against him. (2) This, however, my dearest Secundus, does not imply that, if anything in the way of a fresh accusation is laid against him, you should suppose that less notice is to be taken of it. I have read the memoranda from his accuser Furia Prima, and also from Archippus himself, which you had attached to your second letter.

61. C. Plinius to Traianus Imperator

(1) You are indeed most far-sighted, sir, in your anxiety in case the lake, if linked to the river and so to the sea, drains away; I, however, believe that, being on the spot, I have found a means of forestalling this danger. (2) For the lake can be brought as far as the river by means of a canal, yet not be let out into the river, but, by leaving a bank as it were, it can be at the same time both brought together and kept separate. In this way we shall ensure that it is not deprived of its water by being mingled with the river, yet that it should be in the same position as if it were mingled. For it will be easy to transport to the river loads brought down on the canal across the very narrow strip of land which will lie in between. (3) It will be carried out in this way, if necessity forces us, and (I hope) it will not force us. For the lake is both deep enough in itself and at present pours a river out in the opposite direction. If the outlet is closed off on that side and turned aside in the direction we wish, it will only discharge the amount of water it carries at present, without any loss to the lake. Moreover streams run across the tract through which the canal will have to be dug; if these are carefully collected together, they will increase the supply of water which the lake will have provided. (4) Again, if it is decided to extend the canal further and, by cutting it deeper, to bring it to the level of the sea, and to let it out, not into the river, but into the sea itself, the counter-pressure of the sea will protect and push back whatever comes out of the lake. If the nature of the ground did not permit us any of these schemes, yet it would be practicable to restrain the flow of the water by means of sluice-gates. (5) However, a surveyor, whom you certainly should send out, sir, as you promise, will investigate and assess these and other schemes with far more skill. For the

project is one worthy both of your greatness and your concern, I in the meantime have written, on your authority, to that most distinguished man Calpurnius Macer, to send as capable a surveyor as possible.

62. Traianus to Plinius

It is evident, my dearest Secundus, that you have spared neither forethought nor effort in the matter of that lake of yours, seeing that you have worked out so many devices to ensure that it would not be in danger of being drained and would be of greater use to us for the future. Choose therefore the scheme which the actual situation especially recommends. I believe that Calpurnius Macer will see to it that he supplies you with a surveyor, and those provinces of yours are not lacking in these experts.

63. C. Plinius to Traianus Imperator

Your freedman Lycormas has written to me, sir, to detain until his arrival any embassy which might have come from the Bosporus in order to make its way to the city. And in fact no embassy has yet come, at any rate to the city where I am myself staying, but a letter-carrier from king Sauromates has come. I decided to take advantage of the opportunity which chance had offered me and to send him along with the letter-carrier who arrived in advance of Lycormas on his journey, in order that you should be able to learn at the same moment from Lycormas' and the king's epistles news about which you should perhaps be informed at the same moment.

64. C. Plinius to Traianus Imperator

King Sauromates has written to me that there are some matters about which you ought to be informed as soon as possible. For this reason I have assisted with a pass the speedy journey of a letter-carrier whom he has sent to you with epistles.

65. C. Plinius to Traianus Imperator

(1) Sir, there is an important dispute, and one which affects the whole province, concerning the status and the costs of rearing of those whom they call "foster-children". (2) I myself, after having heard decisions of emperors on this matter read to me, because I could not find any local rule or any general one which should be applied to the Bithynians, decided that I must consult you about what rule you wish to have followed; and I did not think that, on a matter which called for your authority, I could be satisfied with precedents. (3) In fact there was read out in my presence an edict relating to Achaia which was said to be one of the deified Augustus; there were also read out epistles of the deified Vespasian to the Spartans, and of the deified Titus to the same people and to the Achaeans, and of Domitian to the proconsuls Avidius Nigrinos and Armenius Brocchus, and likewise to the Spartans. I have not sent these texts to you for this

reason, because they seemed to me to be both inadequately corrected and, in some cases, of doubtful authenticity, and because I believed that the genuine and corrected texts were in your archives.

66. *Traianus to Plinius*

(1) That dispute, which is concerned with those persons who, born free, have been put out to die and then rescued by certain individuals and reared in slavery, has often been discussed, and there is no rule to be found in the registers of those who were emperors before me which was laid down for all the provinces. (2) There are, it is true, epistles of Domitian to Avidius Nigrinus and Armenius Brocchus, which ought perhaps to be respected; but Bithynia is not among those provinces about which he wrote in reply; and for that reason I do not think that the right to free status should be refused to those who will be proved to be entitled to freedom on grounds of this kind, nor should they have to buy back their actual freedom by paying for the costs of their rearing.

67. *C. Plinius to Traianus Imperator*

(1) When the ambassador of king Sauromates had waited of his own accord for two days at Nicaea, where he had found me, I did not think, sir, that he ought to experience a longer delay, in the first place because it was still uncertain when your freedman Lycormas was going to arrive, in the second because I was myself on the point of setting out for a distant part of the province at the pressing call of my duties. (2) I considered that I must bring these facts to your attention, because I had only just written that Lycormas had asked me to detain any embassy which might have come from the Bosporus until his arrival. No satisfactory reason has presented itself to me for doing so any longer, especially since it seemed likely that Lycormas' epistles, which, as I told you earlier, I did not want to hold back, would arrive from here several days in advance of the ambassador.

68. *C. Plinius to Traianus Imperator*

Certain persons have asked me to allow them, in accordance with the precedent set by the proconsuls, to transfer the remains of their relatives to some site or other either because of damage caused by the passage of time or because of the flooding of a river and other reasons similar to these. Because I knew that in our city it is the custom for application to be made to the college of pontiffs in a case of this kind, I decided that I must consult you, sir,. as supreme pontiff, about what course you wish me to follow.

69. *Traianus to Plinius*

It is harsh to enforce upon provincials an obligation to apply to the pontiffs, should they wish to move the remains of their relatives from one site to another for some proper reasons. It is therefore the precedents set by those who have governed that province before you which ought rather to be followed by you, and permission ought to be granted or refused in accordance with the reason each person gives.

70. C. Plinius to Traianus Imperator

(1) When I was investigating whereabouts in Prusa the bath-house for which you had given permission could be built, the best site seemed to be one on which there was once a house, a beautiful one, so I am told, but which is now unsigthly with ruins. For by this means we shall ensure that a most foul blot upon the city is beautified and that at the same time the city itself is enhanced without any buildings being demolished, but that those which have crumbled away with age are enlarged and improved. (2) Now the circumstances of this house are as follows: Claudius Polyaenus had bequeathed it to Claudius Caesar and directed that a temple to him should be built in the courtyard, while the rest of the house was to be let. For a while the city collected income from it; then, little by little, in part through being looted, in part through being neglected, the whole house along with the courtyard fell into ruin, and by now almost nothing of it is left except the ground. Whether you, sir, make a gift of it to the city or give orders for it to be sold, the city will consider it a very great service because of the convenience of the site. (3) I myself, if you give your permission, am thinking of siting the bath-house on the unoccupied ground, but of enclosing the actual place where the buildings stood with a recess and colonnades and dedicating them to you, through whose favour a handsome building, and one worthy of your name, will be put up. (4) I have sent you a copy of the will, although it is defective: from it you will learn that Polyaenus bequeathed many items for the embellishment of the same house, which, like the house itself, have disappeared, but which will be hunted out by me as far as will be possible.

71. Traianus to Plinius

We can use that ground at Prusa with the ruined house, which you say in your letter is unoccupied, for the building of the bath-house. You did not however make this quite clear, whether a temple was put up to Claudius in the courtyard. For, if it was put up, even though it may have fallen down, its religious influence has filled the site.

72. C. Plinius to Traianus Imperator

Certain persons are requesting that I should myself exercise jurisdiction in cases of children being acknowledged and having their freeborn status restored, in accordance with an epistle of Domitian written to Minicius Rufus and with the precedents set by the proconsuls. I have looked at the resolution of the Senate relating to the same kinds of cases, which talks only about those provinces which have proconsuls as governors; and for that reason I have left the matter undecided until you, sir, direct me about the principle you wish me to follow.

73. *Traianus to Plinius*

If you send me the resolution of the Senate which has given you pause, I shall judge whether you ought to exercise jurisdiction in cases of children being acknowledged and having their true birth-status restored.

74. *C. Plinius to Traianus Imperator*

(1) Appuleius, sir, the soldier who is stationed at the military post in Nicomedia, wrote to me that an individual named Callidromus, when he was being kept under duress by Maximus and Dionysius, bakers to whom he had hired out his services, had taken refuge at your statue, and that, when he was brought before the magistrates, he had revealed that he had at one time been the slave of Laberius Maximus and been taken prisoner by Susagus in Moesia and sent by Decibalus as a gift to Pacorus the king of Parthia, and that he had been in his service for many years, and then escaped, and so had come to Nicomedia. (2) I had him brought before me; when he had told the same story, I decided that he should be sent to you; I have done so somewhat belatedly, while I sought to find a jewel bearing a likeness of Paconis and the things which he was wearing, which he claimed had been taken away from him, (3) For I wished to send this also at the same time, if it could be found, just as I have sent the small lump of ore which he said he had brought from a Parthian mine. It has been sealed with my ring, the device on which is a four-horse chariot.

75. *C. Plinius to Traianus Imperator*

(1) Iulius Largus, sir, from Pontus, a man I had never seen and not even heard of (no doubt he put his faith in your good judgment) has entrusted me with the disposal and management of an act of devotion towards you. (2) For in his will he has asked me to accept and enter upon his estate, and then, after fifty thousand sesterces have been set aside as a prior legacy, to hand over all the residue to the cities of Heraclea and Tium, with the provision that it should be in my power to decide whether I thought buildings should be put up which would be dedicated in your honour or quinquennial competitions should be founded which would be known as the Trajanic. I decided that this should be brought to your attention, mainly for this purpose, that you may consider which I ought to choose.

76. *Traianus to Plinius*

Iulius Largus settled upon your good faith as if he had known you well. So choose for yourself what will particularly conduce to the perpetuation of his memory, in accordance with the circumstances of each place, and follow the course which you decide is the best.

77. C. Plinius to Traianus Imperator

(1) You acted with the greatest forethought, sir, in that you instructed that most distinguished man Calpurnius Macer to send a legionary centurion to Byzantium. (2) Consider whether you think the interests of the people of Iuliopolis should also be provided for by a similar plan. Their city, although it is very small, bears very heavy burdens and suffers injuries which are the more serious by reason of its greater weakness. (3) Moreover, whatever help you give to the people of Iuliopolis will also be of advantage to the entire province. For they lie at the edge of Bithynia, and provide passage for very many persons who travel through it.

78. Traianus to Plinius

(1) The situation of the city of the Byzantines, with a throng of travellers flooding into it from every direction, is such that we thought it right, following the practice of earlier periods, that its magistrates should be supported by the protection of a legionary centurion. (2) If we decide that the people of Iuliopolis should be helped in the same way, we shall be burdening ourselves with a precedent: for more cities will seek the same help to the extent that they are weaker ones. I have such confidence in your con- scientiousness that I feel sure you will employ every means to ensure that they are not exposed to injuries. (3) If any individuals conduct themselves in violation of my discipline, let them be punished at once; or, if they commit acts too serious for it to be enough for them to be punished summarily, if they are soldiers, you shall make it known to their commanding officers that you have arrested them, or, if they are persons on their way back to the city, you shall write to me.

79. C. Plinius to Traianus Imperator

(1) It is prescribed, sir, in the Pompeian law which was laid down for the Bithynians, that no one should hold a magistracy or be a member of a senate who was under thirty years of age. In the same law it was provided that those who had held a magistracy should be members of a senate. (2) Next there followed an edict of the deified Augustus in which he allowed men to hold lesser magistracies from the age of twenty-two. (3) The question is therefore raised whether a man under thirty years of age who has held a magistracy can be enrolled in a senate by the censors, and, if he can, whether those who have not held a magistracy can also, under the same construction be enrolled as senators from that age at which they have been allowed to hold a magistracy; furthermore this is asserted to have been the practice hitherto and to be necessary, because it is far better that the sons of honourable men should be admitted to the senate-house than that commoners should be. (4) I myself, when asked what my opinion was by the censors-elect, thought that men under thirty years of age who had held a magistracy could indeed be enrolled in a senate both according to the edict of Augustus and according to the Pompeian law, since Augustus had allowed men under thirty years of age to hold a magistracy and the law had wanted anyone

who had held a magistracy to be a senator. (5) But about those who had not held one, although they were of the same age as those who had been allowed to hold one, I was in doubt. Hence I have been led to consult you, sir, about what principle you wish to have followed. I have appended to this letter the chapters of the law, and the edict of Augustus.

80. *Traianus to Plinius*

I agree with your construction, my dearest Secundus: that the Pompeian law was amended to this extent by the edict of the deified Augustus, that men who were not younger than twenty-two years of age could indeed hold a magistracy and that those who had held one might enter the senate of each city. However, I do not think that those who are under thirty years of age can be enrolled in the senate of each place without having held a magistracy, just because they can hold a magistracy.

81. *C. Plinius to Traianus Imperator*

(1) While I was attending to official business, sir, in my lodgings at Prusa by Olympus, on the same day that I was intending to leave, the magistrate Asclepiades reported that an appeal had been made to me by Claudius Eumolpus. When Cocceianus Dion at a session of the council requested that a building, the supervision of which he had undertaken, should be handed over to the city, at that moment Eumolpus, acting as counsel for Flavius Archippus, said that the accounts of the building should be demanded from Dion before it was transferred to the community, because he had behaved otherwise than he ought to have done. (2) He further added that your statue had been placed in the same building as well as the bodies of persons who had been buried, the wife and the son of Dion, and he requested that I should hear the case in open court. (3) When I had said that I would do this at once and that I would postpone my departure, he asked me to give him a longer period to put his case together, and to hold the hearing in another city. I answered that I would hear the case at Nicaea, (4) When I had taken my place on the bench there in order to hold the hearing, this same Eumolpus began to apply for an adjournment on the grounds that he was not fully prepared, while Dion in response demanded that the case should be heard. Many things were said on either side, some of them also about the case. (5) When I had decided that an adjournment should be granted and that you must be consulted on a matter which involved a precedent, I told both sides to supply memoranda of their pleadings. For I wanted you to learn the arguments which had been advanced as far as possible from their own words. (6) And Dion in fact said that he would supply this. Eumolpus replied that he would include in a memorandum the claims he was making for the community, but that, as far as the buried bodies were concerned, he was not the plaintiff but counsel for Flavius Archippus whose instructions he had been carrying out, Archippus, for whom Eumolpus was acting as counsel just as he had at Prusa, said that he would supply a memorandum. However, neither Eumolpus nor Archippus, despite being waited for for very many days, has yet supplied me with the memoranda; Dion has supplied one which I have attached to this epistle. (7) I have been to the spot myself and seen your statue also which

has been placed in the library, and the site where Dion's son and wife are said to be buried, which lies in open ground which is enclosed by colonnades. (8) I ask you, sir, to deign to guide me especially in this kind of case, since there is in addition great public interest, as is inevitable with an issue which is both not contested and is defended by precedents.

82. Traianus to Plinius

(1) You could have been in no uncertainty, my dearest Secundus, about that matter on which you decided that I should be consulted, since you were very well aware of my determination not to obtain respect for my name through inspiring men with fear or terror or through charges of treason. (2) Accordingly that charge which I should not allow even if it were supported by the precedents should be dropped; rather let the accounts of the building carried out under the supervision of Cocceianus Dion be examined, since the interest of the city requires it and Dion does not object, nor ought he to object.

83. C. Plinius to Traianus Imperator

Having been requested, sir, by the people of Nicaea as a community, in the name of those things which are and ought to be most sacred to me, that is in the name of your eternal fame and your well-being, to pass on to you their petition, I did not think it light to refuse and I have attached to this letter the memorandum which I have received from them.

84. Traianus to Plinius

You will be obliged to give a hearing to the people of Nicaea who maintain that the right to claim the property of their fellow-citizens who die intestate was conceded to them by the deified Augustus. Collect together all the persons involved in this same business and summon as your advisers the procurators Virdius Gemellinus and Epimachus my freedman, in order that, after also assessing the arguments which are maintained on the opposite side, you may jointly reach the decision which you will jointly believe to be the best.

85. C. Plinius to Traianus Imperator

Having found by experience, sir, that your freedman and procurator Maximus, during the whole period we have been together, is upright, hardworking and conscientious, and as completely devoted to your interests as he is faithful in observing your discipline, I am very pleased to send him on his way with my recommendation to you, in that good faith which I owe to you.

86A. C. Plinius to Traianus Imperator

Having found by experience, sir, that Gavius Bassus the prefect of the Pontic shore is honourable, upright, hardworking, and besides this most respectful towards myself, I send him on his way with my prayers as well as my support, in that good faith which I owe to you.

86B. (C. Plinius to Traianus Imperator)

. . . a man trained by his military service in your company, to whose discipline he is indebted for the fact that he is deserving of your generosity. Both soldiers and civilians, by whom his fairness and his kindness have been closely examined, have vied with each other in bearing witness to him before me, both as individuals and as communities. I bring this fact to your attention, in that good faith which I owe to you.

87. C. Plinius to Traianus Imperator

(1) I had Nymphidius Lupus, the former chief centurion, as a comrade in arms, sir, when I was a tribune and he a prefect: then I began to feel a close affection for him. Later these feelings strengthened with the long duration of our mutual friendship. (2) Therefore I made my claim on his retirement and required him to help me with his advice in Bithynia. This he in a most friendly way has already done and will continue to do, having set aside the usual consideration of leisure and old age. (3) For these reasons I count his relatives as my own, especially his son, Nymphidius Lupus, an upright, hard-working young man, and most worthy of an excellent father. He will be well qualified to receive your generosity, as you can learn from the first trials you have made of him, since he has earned as prefect of a cohort the fullest commendation of those most distinguished men Iulius Ferox and Fuscus Salinator. You will crown my happiness and my satisfaction, sir, by conferring an honour on the son.

88. C. Plinius to Traianus Imperator

I pray, sir, that you may celebrate both this and very many other birthdays in as much happiness as possible and that with eternal fame . . . the flourishing glory of your merit . . . [probable lacuna] which, safe and strong, you will increase by achievements upon achievements.

89. Traianus to Plinius

I acknowledge your prayers, my dearest Secundus, in which you beg that I may celebrate very many most happy birthdays with our commonwealth in a prosperous condition.

90.   C. Plinius to Traianus Imperator

(1) The people of Sinope, sir, are short of water, this, it appears, both good and plentiful, can be brought to them from the sixteenth milestone. However, there is ground which is suspect and soft, just by the source, a little more than a mile away. In the meantime I have given orders for it to be investigated, at little expense, to see whether it can take and support a structure. (2) Money, collected under our supervision, will not be wanting, if you, sir, permit this kind of building which will contribute both to the health and the attractiveness of a very thirsty colony.

91.   Traianus to Plinius

Investigate thoroughly, dearest Secundus, just as you have begun to do, whether the ground which you consider suspect can support the structure of an aqueduct. And I do not think there should be any hesitation about bringing water to the colony of Sinope, provided only that it can in fact carry the work through out of its own resources, seeing that this project will contribute very greatly both to its health and its pleasure.

92.   C. Plinius to Traianus

The free and allied city of the Amiseni employs its own laws through the benefit of your generosity. I have appended to this letter a memorandum concerning *eranoi* which was handed to me in this city, in order that you, sir, may consider what you think should be forbidden and to what extent they should be allowed.

93.   Traianus to Plinius

If the Amiseni, whose memorandum you had attached to your epistle, are permitted by their own laws, which they employ through the benefit of a treaty, to have an eranus, we cannot stand in the way of their having one, all the more readily if they use contributions of this land not on crowds and unlawful assemblies, but to support the poverty of the humbler people. In the other cities, which are bound by our law, anything of this kind is forbidden.

94.   C. Plinius to Traianus Imperator

(1) I have long, sir, included that most upright, honourable and learned man, Suetonius Tranquillus, among my friends, having admired both his character and his learning, and I have begun to love him all the more now that I have had a closer insight into his character. (2) Two reasons make it necessary for him to be awarded the rights of a parent of three children; for he both earns the good opinion of his friends and has had rather an unfortunate experience of marriage, and he must obtain from your kindness through our agency that which the hostility of fortune has denied him. (3) I know, sir, how

great is the favour for which I apply, but I am applying to you, and I have experience of your generosity in all my requests. For you can infer how greatly I want this from the fact that I should not be asking for it when not face to face with you if I only wanted it to a moderate degree.

95. *Traianus to Plinius*

You are certainly aware, my dearest Secundus, of how sparing I am in granting these favours, since I am in the practice of stating in the Senate itself that I have not exceeded the number which I declared in the presence of that most noble order would be large enough for me. However, I have agreed to your request and have given orders for an entry to be made in my registers that I have given Suetonius Tranquillus the rights of a parent of three children, subject to that proviso which I have been in the habit of making.

96. *C. Plinius to Traianus Imperator*

(1) It is my custom, sir, to bring before you everything about which I am in doubt. For who can better guide my uncertainty or inform my ignorance? I have never been present at trials of Christians; for that reason I do not know what the charge usually is and to what extent it is usually punished, (2) I have been in no little uncertainty about whether any distinction should be made between different ages or whether, however young they may be, they should be treated no differently from the more mature ones; whether pardon should be granted for repentance or whether it is of no help to the man who has been a Christian at all to have given it up; whether it is the name itself, if it is free from crimes, or the crimes associated with the name which are being punished. Meanwhile, in the case of those who were prosecuted before me on the charge of being Christians, I followed this procedure. (3) I asked the people themselves whether they were Christians. Those who admitted that they were I asked a second and a third time, warning them of the punishment; those who persisted I ordered to be executed. For I was in no doubt that, whatever it might be that they were admitting to, their stubbornness and unyielding obstinacy certainly ought to be punished. (4) There were others of a similar madness whom I have listed as due to be sent on to the city, because they were Roman citizens.

Subsequently, through the very course of dealing with the matter, as usually happens, the charge spread widely and more forms of it turned up. (5) An anonymous pamphlet containing the names of many persons was posted up. Those who denied that they were or had been Christians, after they had called upon the gods when I dictated the formula, and after they had made offerings of incense and wine to your statue which I had ordered to be brought in along with the cult-images of the gods for this purpose, and had in addition cursed Christ, none of which acts, it is said, those who are truly Christians can be compelled to perform, I decided should be discharged. (6) Others, named by an informer, said that they were Christians and then denied it; they said that they had in fact been Christians but had given it up, some three years before, some more years earlier than that, and a few even twenty years ago. All these also both paid homage to your statue and to the cult-images of the gods and cursed Christ, (7) Moreover they maintained that this had been the sum of their guilt or error, that they had been in the habit of gathering together before dawn on a fixed day, and of singing antiphonally a hymn to Christ as if to a god, and of binding themselves by oath, not to some wickedness, but not to commit acts of theft or robbery or adultery, not to break faith, not to refuse to return money placed in their keeping when called upon to do so. When these ceremonies had been completed, they said it had been their custom to disperse and to meet again to take food, but food that was ordinary and harmless; they said that they had given up doing even this after my edict, in which, in accordance with your instructions, I had banned secret societies. (8) So I believed it to be all the more necessary to ascertain what the truth was from two slave women, who were called deaconesses, and under torture. I found nothing other than a depraved and extravagant superstition.

(9) Accordingly I postponed the hearing and hastened to consult you. For the matter seemed to me to be worthy of your consideration, especially on account of the number of people who are endangered. For many persons of every age, of every rank, of both sexes, are being brought and will be brought into danger. The infection of this superstition has spread, not only through the towns, but also through the villages and the countryside; it seems possible for it to be checked and put right (10) At any rate it is well established that temples which just now were almost abandoned have begun to be thronged, and customary rites which had long been suspended to be renewed, and the flesh of sacrificial victims, for which until recently very few buyers were to be found to be sold far and wide. From this it is easy to conjecture what a host of people could be reformed, if room were given for repentance.

97. Traianus to Plinius

You followed the procedure which you ought to have followed, my dear Secundus, in examining the cases of those who were being prosecuted before you as Christians. For no rule with a universal application, such as would have, as it were, a fixed form, can be laid down. (2) They should not be sought out; if they are prosecuted and proved to be guilty, they should be punished, provided, however, that the man who denies that he is a Christian and makes this evident by his action, that is by offering prayers to our gods, shall obtain pardon for his repentance, however suspect he may be with regard to the past. However, pamphlets posted up without an author's name ought to have no place in any criminal charge. For they both set the worst precedent and are not in keeping with the spirit of our age.

98. C. Plinius to Traianus Imperator

(1) The elegant and finely built city of the Amastrians, sir, has among its outstanding structures a most beautiful and also very long street; by the side of this, along its entire length, there stretches, what is by name a stream, but in reality a most foul sewer, and, Just as it is disgusting in its most filthy appearance, so it is injurious to health in its most revolting stench. (2) For these reasons it is just as much in the interest of health as of beauty that it should be covered over, this will be done, if you permit it, and we will ensure that money also is not lacking for a project both grand and necessary.

99. *Traianus to Plinius*

There is good reason, my dearest Secundus, for that stream which flows through the city of the Amastrians to be covered over, if, left uncovered, it is a danger to health. I feel certain that with your usual diligence you will ensure that money is not lacking for this project.

100. *C. Plinius to Traianus Imperator*

The vows, sir, undertaken last year, we have eagerly and joyfully fulfilled and we have again undertaken new ones, with my fellow-soldiers and the provincials vying with each other in devotion. We prayed to the gods that they would keep you and the commonwealth prosperous and safe with that kindness which you have earned, apart from your great and numerous merits, by your outstanding purity and reverence and honour to the gods.

101. *Traianus to Plinius*

I was delighted to learn from your letter, my dearest Secundus, that my fellow-soldiers in most joyful unanimity with the provincials have fulfilled, with you dictating the formula to them, the vows to the immortal gods for my preservation, and renewed them for the future.

102. *C. Plinius to Traianus Imperator*

We have celebrated with due observance the day on which guardianship of the human race was passed on to you in a most happy succession, recommending both our public vows and our rejoicings to the gods who are the authors of your rule.

103. *Traianus to Plinius*

I was delighted to learn from your letter that the day of my accession was celebrated with due joy and observance by my fellow-soldiers and the provincials, with you dictating the formula to them.

104. *C. Plinius to Traianus Imperator*

Valerius Paulinus, sir, having excluded Paulinus, has bequeathed to me his rights over his Latin freedmen; for the time being I ask you to grant three of these the rights of Roman citizens. For I fear that it may be presumptuous to appeal on behalf of all of them at once to your generosity which I am obliged to use the more sparingly, the fuller my experience of it is. Those for whom I am making the request are in fact C. Valerius Astraeus, C. Valerius Dionysius, C. Valerius Aper.

105. *Traianus to Plinius*

Since you most honourably wish to make prudent provision through me for the interests of those who were entrusted to your good faith by Valerius Paulinus, I have in the mean time given orders for an entry to be made in my registers that I have granted the rights of Roman citizens to those on whose behalf you have made a request this time, and I shall do the same in the case of all the others on whose behalf you make a request.

106. *C. Plinius to Traianus Imperator*

Having being asked, sir, by P. Accius Aquila, centurion of the sixth mounted cohort, to send on to you a petition in which he appeals to your generosity on behalf of the status of his daughter, I thought it harsh to refuse, since I knew how much patience and kindness you were in the habit of showing to the appeals of soldiers.

107. *Traianus to Plinius*

I have read the petition of P. Accius Aquila, centurion of the sixth mounted cohort, which you sent on to me; moved by his appeal, I have granted Roman citizenship to his daughter. I have sent you the petition with its rescript, for you to hand over to him.

108. *C. Plinius to Traianus Imperator*

(1) I ask, sir, that you write back about what rights you wish the cities both of Bithynia and of Pontus to have in recovering sums of money which are owed to them from leases or from sales or for other reasons. I have discovered that the right of prior claim was granted to them by very many of the proconsuls, and that this has come to have the force of law. (2) I think, however, that by your forethought some rule ought to be decided upon and laid down through which their interests may be safeguarded for ever. For the practices which have been introduced by them, even though they may have been wisely conceded, are nevertheless short-lived and precarious, if your authority does not uphold them.

109. *Traianus to Plinius*

What rights the cities of Bithynia or Pontus ought to exercise in respect of those sums of money which, for whatever reason, will be owed to the community, must be determined in accordance with the law of each city. For, if they have a privilege by which they take priority over all the other creditors, it should be protected, but if they do not have one, it will not be appropriate for this to be granted by me to the detriment of private persons.

110. C. Plinius to Traianus Imperator

(1) The public advocate of the city of the Amiseni, sir, was suing Iulius Piso before me for around forty thousand denarii which had been granted to him from public funds twenty years ago with the agreement of the Council and the Assembly, and he cited in support your instructions in which grants of this kind are forbidden. (2) Piso in response said he had made very many gifts to the community and had nearly spent his entire fortune. He also pointed out the lapse of time and begged that he should not be compelled to repay what he had received in return for many gifts and a long lime ago, to the ruin of what was left of his standing. For these reasons I thought that the case should be left undecided, in order that I might ask your advice, sir, about what course you think should be followed.

111. Traianus to Plinius

Although the instructions do forbid gifts to be made from public funds, yet, in order that the security of many persons may not be undermined, those that were made some time ago must not be reconsidered or claimed to be invalid. Let us therefore disregard whatever was done for this reason twenty years ago. For I wish the interests of individuals in each place to be safeguarded, no less than those of public funds.

112. C. Plinius to Traianus Imperator

(1) The Pompeian law, sir, which the people of Bithynia and Pontus observe, does not order those who are enrolled in a council by censors to pay money; but those whom your generosity has allowed some of the cities to add over and above the lawful number have paid one or two thousand denarii each. (2) Later the proconsul Anicius Maximus Ordered those who were enrolled by censors to pay as well, but only in a very few cities, and different sums in different cities. (3) So it remains for you yourself to consider whether in all the cities all those who will henceforward be enrolled as councillors ought to pay some fixed sum for their admission. For it is fitting that that which will remain permanently in force should be determined by you to whose deeds and words eternal fame is due.

113. Traianus to Plinius

No general rule can be laid down by me about whether or not all those who become decurions in every city in Bithynia should pay a fee for their decurionate. So I think that the law of each city should be followed, something which is always the safest course, but indeed I am sure that those who become decurions by invitation will so act that they oututstrip all the rest in generosity.

114. C. Plinius to Traianus Imperator

(1) Under the Pompeian law, sir, the Bythinian cities are allowed to enrol any persons they choose as honorary citizens, provided that none of them come from those cities which are in Bythinia. In the same law it is laid down for what reasons men may be expelled from a senate by censors. (2) And so some of the censors decided that they should consult me about whether they ought to expel a man who came from another city. (3) I myself, because the law, although it forbade a foreigner to be enrolled as a citizen, yet did not order a man to be expelled from a senate for that reason, and because, moreover, I was assured that in every city there were very many councillors from other cities and that the result would be that many men and many cities would be thrown into confusion by that part of the law which had long since become a dead letter by a kind of general agreement, thought it necessary to consult you about what course you think should be followed. I have appended the chapters of the law to this letter.

115. Traianus to Plinius

You had good reason to be uncertain, dearest Secundus, about what you ought to write in response to the censors who consulted you about whether those who were citizens of other cities, but came from the same province, ought to remain in a senate. For the authority of the law and a custom which had been long established in violation of the law could have pulled you in different directions. I have decided on the following resolution of this issue, that we should make no change in respect of what was done in the past, but that citizens of whatever cities, although they were enrolled in violation of the law, should remain; for the future, however, the Pompeian law should be observed. Should we wish do maintain the force of the law retrospectively as well, it is inevitable that many things would be thrown into confusion.

116. C. Plinius to Traianus Imperator

(1) Those who put on the toga of manhood or celebrate a wedding or enter upon a magistracy or dedicate a public building are in the habit of inviting the whole council and no small number from the commons as well and to give them two denarii or a single denarius apiece. I ask you to write to say whether you think this celebration should be held and on what scale. (2) For my own part, while I believe that this kind of right of invitation should be allowed, especially for the customary reasons, yet I am afraid that those who invite a thousand people, and sometimes even more, may be thought to be going beyond the bounds and to fall into a type of bribery.

117. Traianus to Plinius

You have good reason to fear that an invitation would turn into a type of bribery, if it is one which goes beyond the bounds in the matter of numbers and gathers people together for customary gifts in organised bodies, as it were, not as separate individuals on the basis of personal acquaintance. But it was to this purpose that I chose a man of your wisdom, that you might exercise control over shaping the habits of that province and lay down those rules which would be of benefit for the permanent tranquillity of the province.

118. C. Plinius to Traianus Imperator

(1) The athletes, sir, think that the rewards which you established for triumphal games are due to them from the very day on which they were crowned; for, they say, it is not the date on which they made a triumphal entry into their native city which matters, but the date when they were victorious in the games, as a result of which they can make a triumphal entry. I myself, on the other hand, seriously doubt whether it should not rather be the time at which they made their entry which ought to be observed. (2) These same men are applying for allowances in respect of that contest which was made triumphal by you, although they won their victories before it was so made. For they say that it is fitting that, just as allowances are not paid to them in respect of those games which ceased to be triumphal after they won their victories, they should likewise be paid in respect of those which began to be triumphal (after they won their victories). (3) On this point also I have the gravest doubts, whether consideration should be given to anyone retrospectively and whether that which was not due to them when they won their victories should be paid to them. So I ask you to deign to guide my uncertainty yourself, that is to clarify your own benefactions.

119. Traianus to Plinius

It seems to me that a triumphal reward first begins to be due at that time when any man himself has made his entry into his own city. The allowances in respect of those games which I have decided are to be triumphal are not due retrospectively, if they were not triumphal previously. Nor does the fact that they have ceased to receive allowances in respect of those games which I decided should not be triumphal after they won their victories support the claim of the athletes. For, although the status of the games has been changed, the allowances which they had collected before that are nevertheless not being reclaimed.

120. C. Plinius to Traianus Imperator

(1) Up to this time, sir, I have not provided anyone with passes nor have I sent anyone off on any business but yours. A kind of necessity has broken down this permanent rule of mine. (2) For I thought it harsh to deny the use of these passes to my wife who, after hearing of her grandfather's death, was anxious to hasten to her aunt's side, since the value of a service of this kind depends

on speed, and I knew that you would approve of the reason for a journey the motive for which was family affection. I have written to you about this, because I considered that I should be quite ungrateful, if I had concealed the fact that, in addition to your other kindnesses, I was also indebted to your generosity for this particular fact, that I did not hesitate, in my confidence in that generosity, to take action as if I had consulted you, since, if I had consulted you, I should have acted too late.

121. *Traianus to Plinius*

You were right lo feel confidence in my attitude, dearest Secundus, nor should there have been any doubt whether you should have wailed until you could consult me about whether your wife's journey ought to be expedited by the passes which I provided for your official dudes, seeing that your wife was under an obligation to enhance the gratitude felt by her aunt for her arrival by its promptness as well.

Alexander the Oracle-Monger

FROM *Lucian of Samosata*

By Lucian, translated by H. W. Fowler and F. G. Fowler

You, my dear Celsus, possibly suppose yourself to be laying upon me quite a trifling task: *Write me down in a book and send me the life and adventures, the tricks and frauds, of the impostor Alexander of Abonutichus*. In fact, however, it would take as long to do this in full detail as to reduce to writing the achievements of Alexander of Macedon; the one is among villains what the other is among heroes. Nevertheless, if you will promise to read with indulgence, and fill up the gaps in my tale from your imagination, I will essay the task. I may not cleanse that Augean stable completely, but I will do my best, and fetch you out a few loads as samples of the unspeakable filth that three thousand oxen could produce in many years.

2 I confess to being a little ashamed both on your account and my own. There are you asking that the memory of an arch-scoundrel should be perpetuated in writing; here am I going seriously into an investigation of this sort--the doings of a person whose deserts entitled him not to be read about by the cultivated, but to be torn to pieces in the amphitheatre by apes

or foxes, with a vast audience looking on. Well, well, if any one does cast reflections of that sort upon us, we shall at least have a precedent to plead. Arrian himself, disciple of Epictetus, distinguished Roman, and product of lifelong culture as he was, had just our experience, and shall make our defence. He condescended, that is, to put on record the life of the robber

Tilliborus. The robber we propose to immortalize was of a far more pestilent kind, following his profession not in the forests and mountains, but in cities; *he* was not content to overrun a Mysia or an Ida; *his* booty came not from a few scantily populated districts of Asia; one may say that the scene of his depredations was the whole Roman Empire.

3   I will begin with a picture of the man himself, as lifelike (though I am not great at description) as I can make it with nothing better than words. In person—not to forget that part of him—he was a fine handsome man with a real touch of divinity about him, white-skinned, moderately bearded; he wore besides his own hair artificial additions which matched it so cunningly that they were not generally detected. His eyes were piercing, and suggested inspiration, his voice at once sweet and sonorous. In fact there was no fault to be found with him in these respects.

4   So much for externals. As for his mind and spirit--well, if all the kind Gods who avert disaster will grant a prayer, it shall be that they bring me not within reach of such a one as he; sooner will I face my bitterest enemies, my country's foes. In understanding, resource, acuteness, he was far above other men; curiosity, receptiveness, memory, scientific ability--all these were his in overflowing measure. But he used them for the worst purposes. Endowed with all these instruments of good, he very soon reached a proud pre-eminence among all who have been famous for evil; the Cercopes, Eurybatus, Phrynondas, Aristodemus, Sostratus--all thrown into the shade. In a letter to his father-in-law Rutilianus, which puts his own pretensions

in a truly modest light, he compares himself to Pythagoras. Well, I should not like to offend the wise, the divine Pythagoras; but if he had been Alexander's contemporary, I am quite sure he would have been a mere child to him. Now by all that is admirable, do not take that for an insult to Pythagoras, nor suppose I would draw a parallel between their achievements. What I mean is: if any one would make a collection of all the vilest and most damaging slanders ever vented against Pythagoras--things whose truth I would not accept for a moment--, the sum of them would not come within measurable distance of Alexander's cleverness. You are to set your imagination to work and conceive a temperament curiously compounded of falsehood, trickery, perjury, cunning; it is versatile, audacious, adventurous, yet dogged in execution; it is plausible enough to inspire confidence; it can assume the mask of virtue, and seem to eschew what it most desires. I suppose no one ever left him after a first interview without the impression that this was the best and kindest of men, ay, and the simplest and most unsophisticated. Add to all this a certain greatness in his objects; he never made a small plan; his ideas were always large.

5   While in the bloom of his youthful beauty, which we may assume to have been great both from its later remains and from the report of those who saw it, he traded quite shamelessly upon it.

Among his other patrons was one of the charlatans who deal in magic and mystic incantations; they will smooth your course of love, confound your enemies, find you treasure, or secure you an inheritance. This person was struck with the lad's natural qualifications for apprenticeship to his trade, and finding him as much attracted by rascality as attractive in appearance, gave him a regular training as accomplice, satellite, and attendant. His own ostensible profession was medicine, and his knowledge included, like that of Thoon the Egyptian's wife,

> Many a virtuous herb, and many a bane;

to all which inheritance our friend succeeded. This teacher and lover of his was a native of Tyana, an associate of the great Apollonius, and acquainted with all his heroics. And now you know the atmosphere in which Alexander lived.

6   By the time his beard had come, the Tyanean was dead, and he found himself in straits; for the personal attractions which might once have been a resource were diminished. He now formed great designs, which he imparted to a Byzantine chronicler of the strolling competitive order, a man of still worse character than himself, called, I believe, Cocconas. The pair went about living on occult pretensions, shearing 'fat-heads,' as they describe ordinary people in the native Magian lingo. Among these they got hold of a rich Macedonian woman; her youth was past, but not her desire for admiration; they got sufficient supplies out of her, and accompanied her from Bithynia to Macedonia. She came from Pella, which had been a flourishing place under the Macedonian kingdom, but has now a poor and much reduced population.

7   There is here a breed of large serpents, so tame and gentle that women make pets of them, children take them to bed, they will let you tread on them, have no objection to being squeezed, and will draw milk from the breast like infants. To these facts is probably to be referred the common story about Olympias when she was with child of Alexander; it was doubtless one of these that was her bedfellow. Well, the two saw these creatures, and bought the finest they could get for a few pence.

8   And from this point, as Thucydides might say, the war takes its beginning. These ambitious scoundrels were quite devoid of scruples, and they had now joined forces; it could not escape their penetration that human life is under the absolute dominion of two mighty principles, fear and hope, and that any one who can make these serve his ends may be sure of a rapid fortune.

They realized that, whether a man is most swayed by the one or by the other, what he must most depend upon and desire is a knowledge of futurity. So were to be explained the ancient wealth and fame of Delphi, Delos, Clarus, Branchidae; it was at the bidding of the two tyrants aforesaid that men thronged the temples, longed for fore-knowledge, and to attain it sacrificed their hecatombs or dedicated their golden ingots. All this they turned over and debated, and it issued in the resolve to establish an oracle. If it were successful, they looked for immediate wealth and prosperity; the result surpassed their most sanguine expectations.

9   The next things to be settled were, first the theatre of operations, and secondly the plan of campaign. Cocconas favoured Chalcedon, as a mercantile centre convenient both for Thrace and Bithynia, and accessible enough for the province of Asia, Galatia, and tribes still further east. Alexander, on the other hand, preferred his native place, urging very truly that an enterprise like theirs required congenial soil to give it a start, in the shape of 'fat-heads' and simpletons; that was a fair description, he said, of the Paphlagonians beyond Abonutichus; they were mostly superstitious and well-to-do; one had only to go there with some one to play the flute, the tambourine, or the cymbals, set the proverbial mantic sieve[1] a-spinning, and there they would all be gaping as if he were a God from heaven.

10   This difference of opinion did not last long, and Alexander prevailed. Discovering, however, that a use might after all be made of Chalcedon, they went there first, and in the temple

of Apollo, the oldest in the place, they buried some brazen tablets, on which was the statement that very shortly Asclepius, with his father Apollo, would pay a visit to Pontus, and take up his abode at Abonutichus. The discovery of the tablets took place as arranged, and the news flew through Bithynia and Pontus, first of all, naturally, to Abonutichus. The people of that place at once resolved to raise a temple, and lost no time in digging the foundations. Cocconas was now left at Chalcedon, engaged in composing certain ambiguous crabbed oracles. He shortly afterwards died, I believe, of a viper's bite.

11   Alexander meanwhile went on in advance; he had now grown his hair and wore it in long curls; his doublet was white and purple striped, his cloak pure white; he carried a scimetar in imitation of Perseus, from whom he now claimed descent through his mother. The wretched Paphlagonians, who knew perfectly well that his parentage was obscure and mean on both sides, nevertheless gave credence to the oracle, which ran:

> Lo, sprung from Perseus, and to Phoebus dear,
> High Alexander, Podalirius' son!

Podalirius, it seems, was of so highly amorous a complexion that the distance between Tricca and Paphlagonia was no bar to his union with Alexander's mother. A Sibylline prophecy had also been found:

> Hard by Sinope on the Euxine shore
> Th' Italic age a fortress prophet sees.
> To the first monad let thrice ten be added,
> Five monads yet, and then a triple score:
> Such the quaternion of th' alexic name[1].

12   This heroic entry into his long-left home placed Alexander conspicuously before the public; he affected madness, and frequently foamed at the mouth—a manifestation easily produced by chewing the herb soap-wort, used by dyers; but it brought him reverence and awe. The two had long ago manufactured and fitted up a serpent's head of linen; they had given it a more or less human expression, and painted it very like the real article; by a contrivance of horsehair, the mouth could be opened and shut, and a forked black serpent tongue protruded, working on the same system. The serpent from Pella was also kept ready in the house, to be produced at the right moment and take its part in the drama--the leading part, indeed.

13   In the fullness of time, his plan took shape. He went one night to the temple foundations, still in process of digging, and with standing water in them which had collected from the rainfall or otherwise; here he deposited a goose egg, into which, after blowing it, he had inserted some new-born reptile. He made a resting-place deep down in the mud for this, and departed. Early next morning he rushed into the market-place, naked except for a gold-spangled loin-cloth; with nothing but this and his scimetar, and shaking his long loose hair, like the fanatics who collect money in the name of Cybele, he climbed on to a lofty altar and delivered a harangue, felicitating the city upon the advent of the God now to bless them with his presence. In a few minutes nearly the whole population was on the spot, women, old men, and children included; all was awe, prayer, and adoration. He uttered some unintelligible sounds, which might have been Hebrew or Phoenician, but completed his victory over his audience, who could make nothing of what he said, beyond the constant repetition of the names Apollo and Asclepius.

14   He then set off at a run for the future temple. Arrived at

the excavation and the already completed sacred fount, he got down into the water, chanted in a loud voice hymns to Asclepius and Apollo, and invited the God to come, a welcome guest, to the city. He next demanded a bowl, and when this was handed to him, had no difficulty in putting it down at the right place and scooping up, besides water and mud, the egg in which the God had been enclosed; the edges of the aperture had been joined with wax and white lead. He took the egg in his hand and announced that here he held Asclepius. The people, who had been sufficiently astonished by the discovery of the egg in the water, were now all eyes for what was to come. He broke it, and received in his hollowed palm the hardly developed reptile; the crowd could see it stirring and winding about his fingers; they raised a shout, hailed the God, blessed the city, and every mouth was full of prayers--for treasure and wealth and health and all the other good things that he might give. Our hero now departed homewards, still running, with the new-born Asclepius in his hands--the twice-born, too, whereas ordinary men can be born but once, and born moreover not of Coronis 1 nor even of her namesake the crow, but of a goose! After him streamed the whole people, in all the madness of fanatic hopes.

15   He now kept the house for some days, in hopes that the Paphlagonians would soon be drawn in crowds by the news. He was not disappointed; the city was filled to overflowing with persons who had neither brains nor individuality, who bore no resemblance to men that live by bread, and had only their outward shape to distinguish them from sheep. In a small room he took his seat, very imposingly attired, upon a couch. He took into his bosom our Asclepius of Pella (a very fine and large one, as I observed), wound its body round his neck, and let its tail hang down; there was enough of this not

only to fill his lap, but to trail on the ground also; the patient creature's head he kept hidden in his armpit, showing the linen head on one side of his beard exactly as if it belonged to the visible body.

16   Picture to yourself a little chamber into which no very brilliant light was admitted, with a crowd of people from all quarters, excited, carefully worked up, all a-flutter with expectation. As they came in, they might naturally find a miracle in the development of that little crawling thing of a few days ago into this great, tame, human-looking serpent. Then they had to get on at once towards the exit, being pressed forward by the new arrivals before they could have a good look. An exit had been specially made just opposite the entrance, for all the world like the Macedonian device at Babylon when Alexander was ill; he was *in extremis*, you remember, and the crowd round the palace were eager to take their last look and give their last greeting. Our scoundrel's exhibition, though, is said to have been given not once, but many times, especially for the benefit of any wealthy newcomers.

17   And at this point, my dear Celsus, we may, if we will be candid, make some allowance for these Paphlagonians and Pontics; the poor uneducated 'fat-heads' might well be taken in when they handled the serpent--a privilege conceded to all who choose--and saw in that dim light its

head with the mouth that opened and shut. It was an occasion for a Democritus, nay, for an Epicurus or a Metrodorus, perhaps, a man whose intelligence was steeled against such assaults by scepticism and insight, one who, if he could not detect the precise imposture, would at any rate have been perfectly certain that, though this escaped him, the whole thing was a lie and an impossibility.

18   By degrees Bithynia, Galatia, Thrace, came flocking in, every one who had been present doubtless reporting that he had

beheld the birth of the God, and had touched him after his marvellous development in size and in expression. Next came pictures and models, bronze or silver images, and the God acquired a name. By divine command, metrically expressed, he was to be known as Glycon. For Alexander had delivered the line:

> Glycon my name, man's light, son's son to Zeus.

19   And now at last the object to which all this had led up, the giving of oracular answers to all applicants, could be attained. The cue was taken from Amphilochus in Cilicia. After the death and disappearance at Thebes of his father Amphiaraus, Amphilochus, driven from his home, made his way to Cilicia, and there did not at all badly by prophesying to the Cilicians at the rate of threepence an oracle. After this precedent, Alexander proclaimed that on a stated day the God would give answers to all comers. Each person was to write down his wish and the object of his curiosity, fasten the packet with thread, and seal it with wax, clay, or other such substance. He would receive these, and enter the holy place (by this time the temple was complete, and the scene all ready), whither the givers should be summoned in order by a herald and an acolyte; he would learn the God's mind upon each, and return the packets with their seals intact and the answers attached, the God being ready to give a definite answer to any question that might be put.

20   The trick here was one which would be seen through easily enough by a person of your intelligence (or, if I may say so without violating modesty, of my own), but which to the ordinary imbecile would have the persuasiveness of what is marvellous and incredible. He contrived various methods of undoing the seals, read the questions, answered them as seemed good, and then folded, sealed, and returned them, to the great astonishment

of the recipients. And then it was, 'How could he possibly know what I gave him carefully secured under a seal that defies imitation, unless he were a true God, with a God's omniscience?'

21 Perhaps you will ask what these contrivances were; well, then--the information may be useful another time. One of them was this. He would heat a needle, melt with it the under part of the wax, lift the seal off, and after reading warm the wax once more with the needle--both that below the thread and that which formed the actual seal--and re-unite the two without difficulty. Another method employed the substance called collyrium; this is a preparation of Bruttian pitch, bitumen, pounded glass, wax, and mastich. He kneaded the whole into collyrium, heated it, placed it on the seal, previously moistened with his tongue, and so took a mould. This soon hardened; he simply opened, read, replaced the wax, and reproduced an excellent imitation of the original seal as from an engraved stone. One more I will give you. Adding some gypsum to the glue used in book-binding he produced a sort of wax, which was applied still wet to the seal, and on being taken off solidified at once and provided a matrix harder than horn, or even iron. There are plenty of other devices for the purpose, to rehearse which would seem like airing one's knowledge. Moreover, in your excellent pamphlets against the magians (most useful and instructive reading they are) you have yourself collected enough of them--many more than those I have mentioned.

22 So oracles and divine utterances were the order of the day, and much shrewdness he displayed, eking out mechanical ingenuity with obscurity, his answers to some being crabbed and ambiguous, and to others absolutely unintelligible. He did however distribute warning and encouragement according to his lights, and recommend treatments and diets; for he

had, as I originally stated, a wide and serviceable acquaintance with drugs; he was particularly given to prescribing 'cytmides,' which were a salve prepared from goat's fat, the name being of his own invention. For the realization of ambitions, advancement, or successions, he took care never to assign early dates; the formula was, 'All this shall come to pass when it is my will, and when my prophet Alexander shall make prayer and entreaty on your behalf.'

23 There was a fixed charge of a shilling the oracle. And, my friend, do not suppose that this would not come to much; he made something like £3,000 *per annum*; people were insatiable--would take from ten to fifteen oracles at a time. What he got he did not keep to himself, nor put it by for the future; what with accomplices, attendants, inquiry agents, oracle writers and keepers, amanuenses, seal-forgers, and interpreters, he had now a host of claimants to satisfy.

24 He had begun sending emissaries abroad to make the shrine known in foreign lands; his prophecies, discovery of runaways, conviction of thieves and robbers, revelations of hidden treasure, cures of the sick, restoration of the dead to life--all these were to be advertised. This brought them running and crowding from all points of the compass; victims bled, gifts were

presented, and the prophet and disciple came off better than the God; for had not the oracle spoken?--

> Give what ye give to my attendant priest;
> My care is not for gifts, but for my priest.

25   A time came when a number of sensible people began to shake off their intoxication and combine against him, chief among them the numerous Epicureans; in the cities, the imposture with all its theatrical accessories began to be seen through. It was now that he resorted to a measure of intimidation; he proclaimed that Pontus was overrun with

atheists and Christians, who presumed to spread the most scandalous reports concerning him; he exhorted Pontus, as it valued the God's favour, to stone these men. Touching Epicurus, he gave the following response. An inquirer had asked how Epicurus fared in Hades, and was told:

> Of slime is his bed,
> And his fetters of lead.

The prosperity of the oracle is perhaps not so wonderful, when one learns what sensible, intelligent questions were in fashion with its votaries. Well, it was war to the knife between him and Epicurus, and no wonder. What fitter enemy for a charlatan who patronized miracles and hated truth, than the thinker who had grasped the nature of things and was in solitary possession of that truth? As for the Platonists, Stoics, Pythagoreans, they were his good friends; he had no quarrel with them. But the unmitigated Epicurus, as he used to call him, could not but be hateful to him, treating all such pretensions as absurd and puerile. Alexander consequently loathed Amastris beyond all the cities of Pontus, knowing what a number of Lepidus's friends and others like-minded it contained. He would not give oracles to Amastrians; when he once did, to a senator's brother, he made himself ridiculous, neither hitting upon a presentable oracle for himself, nor finding a deputy equal to the occasion. The man had complained of colic, and what he meant to prescribe was pig's foot dressed with mallow. The shape it took was:

> In basin hallowed
> Be pigments mallowed.

26   I have mentioned that the serpent was often exhibited by request; he was not completely visible, but the tail and body were exposed, while the head was concealed under the prophet's dress. By way of impressing the people still more, he

announced that he would induce the God to speak, and give his responses without an interme-diary. His simple device to this end was a tube of cranes' windpipes, which he passed, with due regard to its matching, through the artificial head, and, having an assistant speaking into the end outside, whose voice issued through the linen Asclepius, thus answered questions. These oracles were called *autophones*, and were not vouchsafed casually to any one, but reserved for officials, the rich, and the lavish.

27   It was an autophone which was given to Severian regarding the invasion of Armenia. He encouraged him with these lines:

> Armenia, Parthia, cowed by thy fierce spear,
> To Rome, and Tiber's shining waves, thou com'st,
> Thy brow with leaves and radiant gold encircled.

Then when the foolish Gaul took his advice and invaded, to the total destruction of himself and his army by Othryades, the adviser expunged that oracle from his archives and substituted the following:

> Vex not th' Armenian land; it shall not thrive;
> One in soft raiment clad shall from his bow
> Launch death, and cut thee off from life and light.

28   For it was one of his happy thoughts to issue prophecies after the event as antidotes to those premature utterances which had not gone right. Frequently he promised recovery to a sick man before his death, and after it was at no loss for second thoughts:

> No longer seek to arrest thy fell disease;
> Thy fate is manifest, inevitable.

29   Knowing the fame of Clarus, Didymus, and Mallus for sooth-saying

much like his own, he struck up an alliance with them, sending on many of his clients to those places. So

> Hie thee to Clarus now, and hear my sire.

And again,

Draw near to Branchidae and counsel take.

Or

Seek Mallus; be Amphilochus thy counsellor.

30   So things went within the borders of Ionia, Cilicia, Paphlagonia, and Galatia. When the fame of the oracle travelled to Italy and entered Rome, the only question was, who should be first; those who did not come in person sent messages, the powerful and respected being the keenest of all. First and foremost among these was Rutilianus; he was in most respects an excellent person, and had filled many high offices in Rome; but he suffered from religious mania, holding the most extraordinary beliefs on that matter; show him a bit of stone smeared with unguents or crowned with flowers, and he would incontinently fall down and worship, and linger about it praying and asking for blessings. The reports about our oracle nearly induced him to throw up the appointment he then held, and fly to Abonutichus; he actually did send messenger upon messenger. His envoys were ignorant servants, easily taken in. They came back having really seen certain things, relating others which they probably thought they had seen and heard, and yet others which they deliberately invented to curry favour with their master. So they inflamed the poor old man and drove him into confirmed madness.

31   He had a wide circle of influential friends, to whom he communicated the news brought by his successive messengers, not without additional touches of his own. All Rome was full of his tales; there was quite a commotion, the gentlemen of the Court being much fluttered, and at once taking measures to

learn something of their own fate. The prophet gave all who came a hearty welcome, gained their goodwill by hospitality and costly gifts, and sent them off ready not merely to report his answers, but to sing the praises of the God and invent miraculous tales of the shrine and its guardian.

32   This triple rogue now hit upon an idea which would have been too clever for the ordinary robber. Opening and reading the packets which reached him, whenever he came upon an equivocal, compromising question, he omitted to return the packet; the sender was to be under his thumb, bound to his service by the terrifying recollection of the question he had written down. You know the sort of things that wealthy and powerful personages would be likely to ask. This blackmail brought him in a good income.

33   I should like to quote you one or two of the answers given to Rutilianus. He had a son by a former wife, just old enough for advanced teaching. The father asked who should be his tutor, and was told,

> Pythagoras, and the mighty battle-bard.

When the child died a few days after, the prophet was abashed, and quite unable to account for this summary confutation. However, dear good Rutilianus very soon restored the oracle's credit by discovering that this was the very thing the God had foreshown; he had not directed him to choose a living teacher; Pythagoras and Homer were long dead, and doubtless the boy was now enjoying their instructions in Hades. Small blame to Alexander if he had a taste for dealings with such specimens of humanity as this.

34   Another of Rutilianus's questions was, Whose soul he had succeeded to, and the answer:

> First thou wast Peleus' son, and next Menander;
> Then thine own self; next, a sunbeam shalt be;
> And nine score annual rounds thy life shall measure.

At seventy, he died of melancholy, not waiting for the God to pay in full.

35   That was an autophone too. Another time Rutilianus consulted the oracle on the choice of a wife. The answer was express:

> Wed Alexander's daughter and Selene's.

He had long ago spread the report that the daughter he had had was by Selene: she had once seen him asleep, and fallen in love, as is her way with handsome sleepers. The sensible Rutilianus lost no time, but sent for the maiden at once, celebrated the nuptials, a sexagenarian bridegroom, and lived with her, propitiating his divine mother-in-law with whole hecatombs, and reckoning himself now one of the heavenly company.

35   His finger once in the Italian pie, Alexander devoted himself to getting further. Sacred envoys were sent all over the Roman Empire, warning the various cities to be on their guard against pestilence and conflagrations, with the prophet's offers of security against them. One oracle in particular, an autophone again, he distributed broadcast at a time of pestilence. It was a single line:

> Phoebus long-tressed the plague-cloud shall dispel.

This was everywhere to be seen written up on doors as a prophylactic. Its effect was generally disappointing; for it somehow happened that the protected houses were just the ones to be desolated. Not that I would suggest for a moment that the line was their destruction; but, accidentally no doubt, it did so fall out. Possibly common people put too much confidence in the verse, and lived carelessly without troubling to help the oracle against its foe; were there not the words fighting their battle, and long-tressed Phoebus discharging his arrows at the pestilence?

37   In Rome itself he established an intelligence bureau well manned with his accomplices. They sent him people's characters, forecasts of their questions, and hints of their ambitions, so that he had his answers ready before the messengers reached him.

38   It was with his eye on this Italian propaganda, too, that he took a further step. This was the institution of mysteries, with hierophants and torch-bearers complete. The ceremonies occupied three successive days. On the first, proclamation was made on the Athenian model to this effect: 'If there be any atheist or Christian or Epicurean here spying upon our rites, let him depart in haste; and let all such as have faith in the God be initiated and all blessing attend them.' He led the litany with, 'Christians, avaunt!' and the crowd responded, 'Epicureans, avaunt!' Then was presented the child-bed of Leto and birth of Apollo, the bridal of Coronis, Asclepius born. The second day, the epiphany and nativity of the God Glycon.

39   On the third came the wedding of Podalirius and Alexander's mother; this was called Torch-day, and torches were used. The finale was the loves of Selene and Alexander, and the birth of Rutilianus's wife. The torch-bearer and hierophant was Endymion-Alexander. He was discovered lying asleep; to him from heaven, represented by the ceiling, enter as Selene one Rutilia, a great beauty, and wife of one of the Imperial procurators. She and Alexander were lovers off the stage too, and the wretched husband had to look on at their public kissing and embracing; if there had not been a good supply of torches, things might possibly have gone even further. Shortly after, he reappeared amidst a profound hush, attired as hierophant; in a loud voice he called, 'Hail, Glycon!', whereto the Eumolpidae and Ceryces of Paphlagonia, with their clod-hopping shoes and their garlic breath, made sonorous response, 'Hail, Alexander!'

40   The torch ceremony with its ritual skippings often enabled

him to bestow a glimpse of his thigh, which was thus discovered to be of gold; it was presumably enveloped in cloth of gold, which glittered in the lamp-light. This gave rise to a debate between two wiseacres, whether the golden thigh meant that he had inherited Pythagoras's soul, or merely that their two souls were alike; the question was referred to Alexander himself, and King Glycon relieved their perplexity with an oracle:

Waxes and wanes Pythagoras' soul: the seer's
Is from the mind of Zeus an emanation.
His Father sent him, virtuous men to aid,
And with his bolt one day shall call him home.

43   I will now give you a conversation between Glycon and one Sacerdos of Tius; the intelligence of the latter you may gauge from his questions. I read it inscribed in golden letters in Sacerdos's house at Tius. 'Tell me, lord Glycon,' said he, 'who you are.' 'The new Asclepius.' 'Another, different from the former one? Is that the meaning?' 'That it is not lawful for you to learn.' 'And how many years will you sojourn and prophesy among us?' 'A thousand and three.' 'And after that, whither will you go?' 'To Bactria; for the barbarians too must be blessed with my presence.' 'The other oracles, at Didymus and Clarus and Delphi, have they still the spirit of your grandsire Apollo, or are the answers that now come from them forgeries?' 'That, too, desire not to know; it is not lawful.' 'What shall I be after this life?' 'A camel; then a horse; then a wise man, no less a prophet than Alexander.' Such was the conversation. There was added to it an oracle in verse, inspired by the fact that Sacerdos was an associate of Lepidus:

Shun Lepidus; an evil fate awaits him.

As I have said, Alexander was much afraid of Epicurus, and the solvent action of his logic on imposture.

44   On one occasion, indeed, an Epicurean got himself into great

trouble by daring to expose him before a great gathering. He came up and addressed him in a loud voice. 'Alexander, it was you who induced So-and-so the Paphlagonian to bring his slaves before the governor of Galatia, charged with the murder of his son who was being educated in Alexandria. Well, the young man is alive, and has come back, to find that the slaves had been cast to the beasts by your machinations.' What had happened was this. The lad had sailed up the Nile, gone on to a Red Sea port, found a vessel starting for India, and been persuaded to make the voyage. He being long overdue, the unfortunate slaves supposed that he had either perished in the Nile or fallen a victim to some of the pirates who infested it at that time; so they came home to report his disappearance. Then followed the oracle, the sentence, and finally the young man's return with the story of his absence.

45   All this the Epicurean recounted. Alexander was much annoyed by the exposure, and could not stomach so well deserved an affront; he directed the company to stone the man, on pain of being involved in his impiety and called Epicureans. However, when they set to work, a distinguished Pontic called Demostratus, who was staying there, rescued him by interposing his own body; the man had the narrowest possible escape from being stoned to death--as he richly deserved to be; what business had he to be the only sane man in a crowd of madmen, and needlessly make himself the butt of Paphlagonian infatuation?

46   This was a special case; but it was the practice for the names of applicants to be read out the day before answers were given; the herald asked whether each was to receive his oracle; and sometimes the reply came from within, To perdition! One so repulsed could get shelter, fire or water, from no man; he must be driven from land to land as a blasphemer, an atheist, and--lowest depth of all--an Epicurean.

47   In this connexion Alexander once made himself supremely ridiculous. Coming across Epicurus's *Accepted Maxims*, the most admirable of his books, as you know, with its terse presentment of his wise conclusions, he brought it into the middle of the market-place, there burned it on a fig-wood fire for the sins of its author, and cast its ashes into the sea. He issued an oracle on the occasion:

      The dotard's maxims to the flames be given.

The fellow had no conception of the blessings conferred by that book upon its readers, of the peace, tranquillity, and independence of mind it produces, of the protection it gives against terrors, phantoms, and marvels, vain hopes and inordinate desires, of the judgement and candour that it fosters, or of its true purging of the spirit, not with torches and squills and such rubbish, but with right reason, truth, and frankness.

48   Perhaps the greatest example of our rogue's audacity is what I now come to. Having easy access to Palace and Court by Rutilianus's influence, he sent an oracle just at the crisis of the German war, when M. Aurelius was on the point of engaging the Marcomanni and Quadi. The oracle required that two lions should be flung alive into the Danube, with quantities of sacred herbs and magnificent sacrifices. I had better give the words:

To rolling Ister, swoln with Heaven's rain,
Of Cybelean thralls, those mountain beasts,
Fling ye a pair; therewith all flowers and herbs
Of savour sweet that Indian air doth breed.
Hence victory, and fame, and lovely peace.

These directions were precisely followed; the lions swam across to the enemy's bank, where they were clubbed to death by the barbarians, who took them for dogs or a new kind of wolves; and our forces immediately after met with a severe defeat, losing some twenty thousand men in one engagement. This

was followed by the Aquileian incident, in the course of which that city was nearly lost. In view of these results, Alexander warmed up that stale Delphian defence of the Croesus oracle: the God had foretold a victory, forsooth, but had not stated whether Romans or barbarians should have it.

49　The constant increase in the number of visitors, the inadequacy of accommodation in the city, and the difficulty of finding provisions for consultants, led to his introducing what he called *night oracles*. He received the packets, slept upon them, in his own phrase, and gave answers which the God was supposed to send him in dreams. These were generally not lucid, but ambiguous and confused, especially when he came to packets sealed with exceptional care. He did not risk tampering with these, but wrote down any words that came into his head, the results obtained corresponding well enough to his conception of the oracular. There were regular interpreters in attendance, who made considerable sums out of the recipients by expounding and unriddling these oracles. This office contributed to his revenue, the interpreters paying him £250 each.

50　Sometimes he stirred the wonder of the silly by answers to persons who had neither brought nor sent questions, and in fact did not exist. Here is a specimen:

> Who is 't, thou askst, that with Calligenia
> All secretly defiles thy nuptial bed?
> The slave Protogenes, whom most thou trustest.
> Him thou enjoyedst: he thy wife enjoys--
> The fit return for that thine outrage done.
> And know that baleful drugs for thee are brewed,
> Lest thou or see or hear their evil deeds.
> Close by the wall, at thy bed's head, make search.
> Thy maid Calypso to their plot is privy.

The names and circumstantial details might stagger a Democritus, till a moment's thought showed him the despicable trick.

51 He often gave answers in Syriac or Celtic to barbarians who questioned him in their own tongue, though he had difficulty in finding compatriots of theirs in the city. In these cases there was a long interval between application and response, during which the packet might be securely opened at leisure, and somebody found capable of translating the question. The following is an answer given to a Scythian:

> Morphi ebargulis for night
> Chnenchicrank shall leave the light.

52 Another oracle to some one who neither came nor existed was in prose. 'Return the way thou earnest,' it ran; 'for he that sent thee hath this day been slain by his neighbour Diocles, with aid of the robbers Magnus, Celer, and Bubalus, who are taken and in chains.'

53 I must give you one or two of the answers that fell to my share. I asked whether Alexander was bald, and having sealed it publicly with great care, got a night oracle in reply:

> Sabardalachu malach Attis was not he.

Another time I did up the same question--What was Homer's birthplace?--in two packets given in under different names. My servant misled him by saying, when asked what he came for, a cure for lung trouble; so the answer to one packet was:

> Cytmide and foam of steed the liniment give.

As for the other packet, he got the information that the sender was inquiring whether the land or the sea route to Italy was preferable. So he answered, without much reference to Homer:

> Fare not by sea; land-travel meets thy need.

54 I laid a good many traps of this kind for him; here is another. I asked only one question, but wrote outside the packet in the usual form, So-and-so's eight Queries, giving a fictitious name

and sending the eight shillings. Satisfied with the payment of the money and the inscription on the packet, he gave me eight answers to my one question. This was, When will Alexander's imposture be detected? The answers concerned nothing in heaven or earth, but were all silly and meaningless together. He afterwards found out about this, and also that I had tried to dissuade Rutilianus both from the marriage and from putting any confidence in the oracle; so he naturally conceived a violent dislike for me. When Rutilianus once put a question to him about me, the answer was:

Night-haunts and foul debauch are all his joy.

55   It is true his dislike was quite justified. On a certain occasion I was passing through Abonutichus, with a spearman and a pikeman whom my friend the governor of Cappadocia had lent me as an escort on my way to the sea. Ascertaining that I was the Lucian he knew of, he sent me a very polite and hospitable invitation. I found him with a numerous company; by good luck I had brought my escort. He gave me his hand to kiss according to his usual custom. I took hold of it as if to kiss, but instead bestowed on it a sound bite that must have come near disabling it. The company, who were already offended at my calling him Alexander instead of Prophet, were inclined to throttle and beat me for sacrilege. But he endured the pain like a man, checked their violence, and assured them that he would easily tame me, and illustrate Glycon's greatness in converting his bitterest foes to friends. He then dismissed them all, and argued the matter with me: he was perfectly aware of my advice to Rutilianus; why had I treated him so, when I might have been preferred by him to great influence in that quarter? By this time I had realized my dangerous position, and was only too glad to welcome these advances; I presently went my way in all friendship with

him. The rapid change wrought in me greatly impressed the observers.

56   When I intended to sail, he sent me many parting gifts, and offered to find us (Xenophon and me, that is; I had sent my father and family on to Amastris) a ship and crew--which offer I accepted in all confidence. When the passage was half over, I observed the master in tears arguing with his men, which made me very uneasy. It turned out that Alexander's orders were to seize and fling us overboard; in that case his war with me would have been lightly won. But the crew were prevailed upon by the master's tears to do us no harm. 'I am sixty years old, as you can see,' he said to me; 'I have lived an honest blameless life so far, and I should not like at my time of life, with a wife and children too, to stain my hands with blood.' And with that preface he informed us what we were there for, and what Alexander had told him to do.

57   He landed us at Aegiali, of Homeric fame, and thence sailed home. Some Bosphoran envoys happened to be passing, on their way to Bithynia with the annual tribute from their king Eupator. They listened kindly to my account of our dangerous situation, I was taken on board, and reached Amastris safely after my narrow escape. From that time it was war between

Alexander and me, and I left no stone unturned to get my revenge. Even before his plot I had hated him, revolted by his abominable practices, and I now busied myself with the attempt to expose him; I found plenty of allies, especially in the circle of Timocrates the Heracleot philosopher. But Avitus, the then governor of Bithynia and Pontus, restrained me, I may almost say with prayers and entreaties. He could not possibly spoil his relations with Rutilianus, he said, by punishing the man, even if he could get clear evidence against him. Thus arrested in my course, I did not persist in what must have been, considering the disposition of the judge, a fruitless prosecution.

58   Among instances of Alexander's presumption, a high place must be given to his petition to the Emperor: the name of Abonutichus was to be changed to Ionopolis; and a new coin was to be struck, with a representation on the obverse of Glycon, and, on the reverse, Alexander bearing the garlands proper to his paternal grandfather Asclepius, and the famous scimetar of his maternal ancestor Perseus.

59   He had stated in an oracle that he was destined to live to a hundred and fifty, and then die by a thunderbolt; he had in fact, before he reached seventy, an end very sad for a son of Podalirius, his leg mortifying from foot to groin and being eaten of worms; it then proved that he was bald, as he was forced by pain to let the doctors make cooling applications to his head, which they could not do without removing his wig.

60   So ended Alexander's heroics; such was the catastrophe of his tragedy; one would like to find a special providence in it, though doubtless chance must have the credit. The funeral celebration was to be worthy of his life, taking the form of a contest--for possession of the oracle. The most prominent of the impostors his accomplices referred it to Rutilianus's arbitration which of them should be selected to succeed to the prophetic office and wear the hierophantic oracular garland. Among these was numbered the grey-haired physician Paetus, dishonouring equally his grey hairs and his profession. But Steward-of-the-Games Rutilianus sent them about their business ungarlanded, and continued the defunct in possession of his holy office.

61   My object, dear friend, in making this small selection from a great mass of material has been twofold. First, I was willing to oblige a friend and comrade who is for me the pattern of wisdom, sincerity, good humour, justice, tranquillity, and geniality. But secondly I was still more concerned (a preference

which you will be very far from resenting) to strike a blow for Epicurus, that great man whose holiness and divinity of nature were not shams, who alone had and imparted true insight into the good, and who brought deliverance to all that consorted with him. Yet I think casual readers too may find my essay not unserviceable, since it is not only destructive, but, for men of sense, constructive also.

H.

Endnotes

216:1   I have no information on Coscinomancy or sieve-divination.

'This kind of divination was generally practised to discover thieves . . . They tied a thread to the sieve, by which it was upheld, then prayed to the Gods to direct and assist them. After which they repeated the names of the person suspected, and he at whose name the sieve whirled round or moved was thought to have committed the fact' *Francklin's Lucian.*

217:1   In 1. 2 of the oracle, the Italic age is the Roman Empire; the fortress prophet is one who belongs to a place ending in -tichus (fort). ll. 3–5 mean: Take 1, 30, 5, 60 (the Greek symbols for which are the letters of the alphabet A, L, E, X), and you will have four letters of the name of your coming protector (alexic).

219:1   Coronis was the mother of Asclepius; 'corone' is Greek for a crow.

Book 11 of The Golden Ass

By Apuleius, translated by Jack Lindsay

BOOK THE ELEVENTH

About the first watch of the night I was aroused by sudden panic. Looking up I saw the full orb of the Moon shining with peculiar lustre and that very moment emerging from the waves of the sea. Then the thought came to me that this was the hour of silence and loneliness when my prayers might avail. For I knew that the Moon was the primal Goddess of supreme sway; that all human beings are the creatures of her providence; that not only cattle and wild beasts but even inorganic objects are vitalized by the divine influence of her light; that all the bodies which are on earth, or in the heavens, or in the sea, increase when she waxes, and decline when she wanes. Considering this, therefore, and feeling that Fate was now satiated with my endless miseries and at last licensed a hope of salvation, I determined to implore the august image of the risen Goddess.

So, shaking off my tiredness, I scrambled to my feet and walked straight into the sea in order to purify myself. I immersed my head seven times because (according to the divine Pythagoras) that number is specially suited for all ritual acts; and then, speaking with lively joy, I lifted my tear-wet face in supplication to the irresistible Goddess:

Queen of Heaven, whether you are fostering Ceres the motherly nurse of all growth, who (gladdened at the discovery of your lost daughter) abolished the brutish nutriment of the primitive acorn and pointed the way to gentler food (as is yet shown in the tilling of the fields of Eleusis); or whether you are celestial Venus who in the first moment of Creation mingled the opposing sexes in the generation of mutual desires, and who (after sowing in humanity the seeds of indestructible continuing life) are now worshipped in the wave-washed shrine of Paphos; or whether you are the sister of Phoebus, who by relieving the pangs of childbirth travail with soothing remedies have brought safe into the world lives innumerable, and who are now venerated in the thronged sanctuary of Ephesus; or whether you are Proserpine, terrible with the howls of midnight, whose triple face has power to ward off all the assaults of ghosts and to close the cracks in the earth, and who wander through many a grove, propitiated in divers manners, illuminating the walls of all cities with beams of female light, nurturing the glad seeds in the earth with your damp heat, and dispensing abroad your dim radiance when the sun has abandoned us—O by whatever name, and by whatever rites, and in whatever form, it is permitted to invoke you, come now and succour me in the hour of my calamity. Support my broken life, and give me rest and peace after the tribulations of my lot. Let there be an end to the toils that weary me, and an end to the snares that beset me. Remove from me the hateful shape of a beast, and restore me to the sight of those that love me. Restore me to Lucius, my lost self. But if an offended god pursues me implacably, then grant me death at least since life is denied me.'

Having thus poured forth my prayer and given an account of my bitter sufferings, I drowsed and fell asleep on the same sand-couch as before. But scarcely had I closed my eyes before a god-like face emerged from the midst of the sea with lineaments that gods themselves would revere. Then gradually I saw the whole body (resplendent image that it was) rise out of the scattered deep and stand beside me.

I shall not be so brave as to attempt a description of this marvellous form, if the poverty of human language will not altogether distort what I have to say, or if the divinity herself will deign to lend me a rich enough stock of eloquent phrase. First, then, she had an abundance of hair that fell gently in dispersed ringlets upon the divine neck. A crown of interlaced wreaths and varying flowers rested upon her head; and in its midst, just over the brow, there hung a plain circlet resembling a mirror or rather a miniature moon—for it emitted a soft clear light. This ornament was supported on either side by vipers that rose from the furrows of the earth; and above it blades of corn were disposed. Her garment, dyed many colours, was woven of fine ax. One part was glearning white; another was yellow as the crocus; another was flamboyant with the red of roses. But what obsessed my gazing eyes by far the most was her pitch-black cloak that shone with a dark glow. It was wrapped round her, passing from under the right arm over the left shoulder and fastened with a knot like the boss of a shield. Part of it fell down in pleated folds and swayed gracefully with a knotted fringe along the hem. Upon the embroidered edges and over the whole surface sprinkled stars were burning; and in the centre a mid-month moon breathed forth her floating beams. Lastly, a garland wholly composed of every kind of fruit and flower clung of its own accord to the fluttering border of that splendid robe.

500

Many strange things were among her accoutrements. In her right hand she held a brazen sistrum, a flat piece of metal curved like a girdle, through which there passed some little rods—and when with her arm she vibrated these triple chords they produced a shrill sharp cry. In her left hand she bore an oblong golden vessel shaped like a boat, on the handle of which (set at the most conspicuous angle) there coiled an asp raising its head and puffing out its throat. The shoes that covered her ambrosial feet were plaited from the palm, emblem of victory.

Such was the goddess as breathing forth the spices of pleasant Arabia she condescended with her divine voice to address me.

'Behold, Lucius,' she said, 'moved by your prayer I come to you—I, the natural mother of all life, the mistress of the elements, the first child of time, the supreme divinity, the queen of those in hell, the first among those in heaven, the uniform manifestation of all the gods and goddesses—I, who govern by my nod the crests of light in the sky, the purifying wafts of the ocean, and the lamentable silences of hell—I, whose single godhead is venerated all over the earth under manifold forms, varying rites, and changing names. Thus, the Phrygians that are the oldest human stock call me Pessinuntia, Mother of the Gods. The aboriginal races of Attica call me Cecropian Minerva. The Cyprians in their island-home call me Paphian Venus. The archer Cretans call me Diana Dictynna. The three-tongued Sicilians[1] call me Stygian Proserpine. The Eleusinians call me the ancient goddess Ceres. Some call me Juno. Some call me Bellona. Some call me Hecate. Some call me Rhamnusia. But those who are enlightened by the earliest rays of that divinity the sun, the Ethiopians, the Arii, and the Egyptians who excel in antique lore, all worship me with their ancestral ceremonies and call me by my true name, Queen Isis.

'Behold, I am come to you in your calamity. I am come with solace and aid. Away then with tears. Cease to moan. Send sorrow packing. Soon through my providence shall the sun of your salvation arise. Hearken therefore with care unto what I bid. Eternal religion has dedicated to me the day which will be born from the womb of this present darkness. Tomorrow my priests will offer to me the first fruits of the year's navigation. They will consecrate in my name a new-built ship. For now the tempests of the winter are lulled; the roaring waves of the sea are quieted; and the waters are again navigable. You must await this ceremony, without anxiety and without wandering thoughts. For the priest at my suggestion will carry in the procession a crown of roses attached to the sistrum in his right hand; and you must unhesitatingly push your way through the crowd, join the procession, and trust in my good will. Approach close to the priest as if you meant to kiss his hand, and gently crop the roses. Instantly you will slough the hide of this beast on which I have long looked with abhorrence.

'Fear for no detail of the work to which I once put my hand. Even at this moment of time in which I appear before you, I am also in another place instructing my priest in a vision what is to be brought to pass. By my command the crush of people will open to give you way; and despite all the gay rites and ferial revelries not one of my worshippers will feel disgust because of the unseemly shape in which you

---

1 'Three-tongued Sicilians': The islanders changed from Sicilian to Greek to Latin. The Arii are of Parthian Aria.

are incarcerated. Neither will any one of them misinterpret your sudden metamorphosis or rancorously use it against you.

'Only remember, and keep the remembrance fast in your heart's deep core, that all the remaining days of your life must be dedicated to me, and that nothing can release you from this service but death. Neither is it aught but just that you should devote your life to her who redeems you back into humanity. You shall live blessed. You shall live glorious under my guidance; and when you have travelled your full length of time and you go down into death, there also (on that hidden side of earth) you shall dwell in the Elysian Fields and frequently adore me for my favours. For you will see me shining on amid the darkness of Acheron and reigning in the Stygian depths.

'More, if you are found to merit my love by your dedicated obedience, religious devotion, and constant chastity, you will discover that it is within my power to prolong your life beyond the limits set to it by Fate.'

At last the end of this venerable oracle was reached, and the invincible Goddess ebbed back into her own essence. No time was lost. Immediately snapping the threads of sleep, and wrung with a sweat of joy and terror, I wakened. Wondering deeply at so direct a manifestation of the Goddess's power, I sprinkled myself with salt water; and eager to obey her in every particular, I repeated over to myself the exact words in which she had framed her instructions. Soon the sun of gold arose and sent the clouds of thick night flying; and lo, a crowd of people replenished the streets, filing in triumphal religious procession. It seemed to me that the whole world, independent of my own high spirits, was happy. Cattle of every kind, the houses, the very day, all seemed to lift serene faces brimful with jollity. For sunny and placid weather had suddenly come upon us after a frosty yesterday; and the tuneful birdlets, coaxed out by the warmths of the Spring, were softly singing sweet hymns of blandishment to the Mother of the Stars, the Producer of the Seasons, the Mistress of the Universe. The trees also, both those that blossomed into fruit and those that were content to yield only sterile shade, were loosed by the southerly breezes; and glistening gaily with their budded leaves, they swished their branches gently in sibilant sighs. The crash of storm was over; and the waves, no longer mountainous with swirling foam, lapped quietly upon the shore. The dusky clouds were routed; and the heavens shone with clear sheer splendour of their native light.

By this time the forerunners of the main procession were gradually appearing, every man richly decked as his votive fancy suggested. One fellow was girded about the middle like a soldier; another was scarfed like a huntsman with hunting-knife and shoes; another, wearing gilt sandals, silken gown, and costly ornaments, walked with a woman's mincing gait; another with his leg-harness, targe, helm, and sword, looked as if he had come straight from gladiatorial games. Then, sure enough, there passed by a man assuming the magistrate with fasces and purple robe, and a man playing the philosopher with cloak, staff, wooden clogs, and goat's beard; a fowler with bird-lime elbowing a fisherman with hooks. I saw also a tame she-bear dressed as a matron and carried in a sedon-chair; an ape with bonnet of plaited straw and saffron-hued garment, holding in his hand a golden cup and representing Phrygian Ganymede the shepherd; and lastly, an ass with wings glued on his back ambling after an old man—so that you could at once have exclaimed that one was Pegasus and the other Bellerophon, and would have laughed at the pair in the same breath.

Into this playful masquerade of the overflowing populace the procession proper now marched its way. Women glowing in their white vestments moved with symbolic gestures of delight. Blossomy with the chaplets of the Spring, they scattered flowerets out of the aprons of their dresses all along the course of the holy pageant. Others, who bore polished mirrors on their backs, walked before the Goddess and reflected all the people coming-after as if they were advancing towards the Image. Others, again, carrying combs of ivory, went through the various caressive motions of combing and dressing the queenly tresses of their Lady; or they sprinkled the street with drops of unguent and genial balm.

There was a further host of men and women who followed with lanterns, torches, waxtapers, and every other kind of illumination in honour of Her who was begotten of the Stars of Heaven. Next came the musicians, interweaving in sweetest measures the notes of pipe and flute; and then a supple choir of chosen youths, clad in snow-white holiday tunics, came singing a delightful song which an expert poet (by grace of the Muses) had composed for music, and which explained the antique origins of this day of worship. Pipers also, consecrated to mighty Serapis, played the tunes annexed to the god's cult on pipes with transverse-mouthpieces and reeds held sidelong towards the right ear; and a number of officials kept calling out, 'Make way for the Goddess!'

Then there came walking a great band of men and women of all classes and ages, who had been initiated into the Mysteries of the Goddess and who were all clad in linen garments of the purest white. The women had their hair anointed and hooded in limpid silk; but the men had shaven shining polls. Terrene stars of mighty deity were these men and women; and they kept up a shrill continuous tingle upon sistra of brass and silver and even gold. The chief ministers of the ceremony, dressed in surplices of white linen tightly drawn across the breast and hanging loose to the feet, bore the relics of the mighty gods exposed to view. The first priest held on high a blazing lamp—not at all like the lamps that illumine our evening suppers; for its long bowl was gold, and it thrust up from an aperture in the middle a fat flame. The second priest was similarly vestured, but he carried in both hands model altars to which the auxiliary love of the supreme Goddess has given the fitting title of Auxilia. The third priest grasped a palmtree with all its leaves subtly wrought in gold, and the wand of Mercury. The fourth priest displayed the Symbol of Equity; a left hand moulded with open palm (since the left hand seemed to be more adapted to administer equity than the busier, craftier right hand). The same man also bore a vessel of gold rounded into the shape of a woman's breast, from which he let milk trickle to the ground. The fifth priest had a winnowing-fan constructed with thickset sprigs of gold; and the sixth priest had an amphora.

After these came the Gods themselves (deigning to walk before our eyes on the feet of men). First we saw the dreadful messenger of the gods of heaven and hell, Anubis, with his face blackened on one side and painted gold on the other, lifting on high his dog's head and bearing his rod in his left hand. Close upon his heels followed a Cow (emblem of the Goddess that is fruitful mother of all) sitting upright upon the proud shoulders of her blessed worshipper. Another man carried the chest that contained the Secret Things of her unutterable mystery. Another bore in his beatified bosom a venerable effigy of Supreme Deity, which showed no likeness to any bird or beast (wild or tame) or even to man, but which was worthy of reverence because of its exquisite invention and originality: a symbol inexpressible of the true religion that should be veiled in Deep Silence. This effigy was of burnished gold, made as follows: a small urn was delicately hollowed out with a round bottom: the strange hieroglyphs of the Egyptians covered its outside; the spout was shaped rather low but jutting out like a funnel; the handle on the other side projected with a wide sweep; and on this stood an asp, stretching up his scaly, wrinkled, swollen throat and twining round the whole length.

At last the glorious moment which the presiding Goddess had promised me was at hand. For the priest, adorned exactly as she had described, neared with the instrument of my salvation. In his right hand he carried the Goddess's sistrum and a crown of roses. Ah, by Hercules, a crown indeed it was for me, since by the providence of the overmastering gods, after so many toils of experience, I was now to find my efforts crowned with victory over Fortune, my cruel foe.

However, though shaken with up-bubbling joy, I did not dash immediately forwards; for I did not want the peaceful order of the holy procession to be disturbed by an unruly beast. Instead, I nosed through the crowd with a polite all-but-human tread and a sidelong twist of my body; and, as the people (clearly by the Goddess's dispensation) disparted to let me through, I slowly approached the flowers. But the priest (as was obvious to me) recollected his admonitory vision of the night. He at once stopped stockstill; and spontaneously raising his right hand, he held the bunch up to my mouth. Trembling, with a thudding heart, I seized the crown in which some fine rose blooms were brightly woven; and greedily I masticated the whole lot.

Nor did the heavenly promise fail. At once my ugly and beastly form left me. My rugged hair thinned and fell; my huge belly sank in; my hooves separated out into fingers and toes; my hands ceased to be feet and adapted themselves to the offices of my erected state; my long neck telescoped itself; my face and head became round; my flapping ears shrank to their old size; my stony molars waned into human teeth; and my tail (the worst cross of my ass-days) simply disappeared.

The populace stood in blinking wonder; and the devotees adored the Goddess for the miraculous revelation of her power in a metamorphosis which partook of the shifting pageantry of a dream. Lifting their hands to heaven, with one voice the beholders rendered testimony to the lovingkindness of the Goddess thus signally declared. As for me, I remained nailed to the spot in mute stupefaction; for my wits were scattered by the shock of joy, and I was quite at a loss. What was the right utterance with which to begin my new life? Where was my voice to come from? How was I most auspiciously to employ my newborn tongue? What phrases could I choose to express my gratitude to so great a Goddess?

But the priest (who by advertisement knew the whole tale of my misfortunes) though wonderstruck at the miracle recovered himself so far as to signify with gestures that I should be handed a linen garment. For from the moment that the ass stripped me of his wretched skin I had been doing my naked best to hide my privities with the sole naturally-supplied veil (the hand), while compressing my thighs. At once one of the initiated pulled off his upper tunic and wrapped me in it; and then the priest, smiling kindly but still staring at my quite-human countenance, thus addressed me:

'At last, Lucius, after the long days of disaster and the heavy storms of fortune you have reached the haven of peace and the altar of mercy. Neither your high lineage, nor your pride of place, nor your learning, profited you one jot. You gave yourself to the slavery of pleasure in the lewdness of hot-blooded youth; and you have reaped the reward of your unprospering curiosity. Nevertheless, blind Fortune, persecuting you with horrors and snares, has led you in her shortsighted malice to this beatitude of release. Let her go now and rage as madly as she will; but let her seek another object for her hate. For terror and calamity have no power over him whose life the majesty of our Goddess has claimed for her service.

'What benefit has furying Fortune gained from the robbers, from the wild beasts, from the servitude, from the unending hardships of the way, from the daily fears of death? You are now received into the protection of Fortune, but of Fortune who is open-eyed and who lightens even the other gods with the splendours of her light. Let your face be joyous therefore. Let it be such a face as accords with that white gown you wear. Follow in the train of the Goddess your Saviour with steps of triumph. Let the scoffer behold. Let him behold and be shamed, saying in his heart:

'"Lo, here is Lucius who rejoices in the providence of mighty Isis. Lo, he is loosed from the bonds of misery and victorious over his fate."

'Yet, that you may be the safer and the surer, enrol your name in this army of holiness, to which you were but a short time past pledged by oath. Dedicate yourself to the service of true religion, and voluntarily bend your neck to the yoke of this ministry. For when you have begun to serve the Goddess you will feel the full fruitfulness of your liberty.'

When the worthy priest, labouring hard to breathe under the pressure of inspiration, had concluded this speech, I joined the ranks of the religious and followed the procession. All pointed or nodded at me, and cried aloud: 'This day has the august power of Almighty Goddess restored him that you see there to human form. Happy, by Hercules, thrice blessed is he who by the purity and faith of his past life has merited such particular patronage from above! For it is as though he had been set apart from the moment of his second birth for the ministry of heaven.'

Among these ejaculations and the hum of happy prayers, we moved slowly on till we approached the sea. The spot chosen was the very beach where on the preceding day (while yet an ass) I had stabled myself. First, the images of the gods were orderly disposed; and then the high priest dedicated and consecrated to the Goddess a nobly built boat (scribbled all over with the peculiar Egyptian marks) after purifying its torch, flame, egg, and sulphur, and pouring solemn prayers from his sanctified lips.

The shining-white sail of this blessed ship bore a broidered inscription repeating the words of the prayer for this year's prosperous navigation. The mast, when raised, was seen to be a rounded pine-tree of great height with a glittering top that drew all eyes. The prow was curved to represent a goose-neck[2] and covered with flaming gold-plates, while the whole of the polished keel consisted of rich citronwood.

All the people (initiate or lay) zealously piled up winnowing-fans with aromatic scents and other such offerings, and threw libations of milk mixed with crumbs into the sea, until the ship, cargoed with plentiful gifts and auspicious devotions, was let slip from her anchoring ropes. She put out to sea with a mild breeze; all her own; and after she had sailed out of sight into the distance on her course, the bearers of the holy things reassumed their burdens and began a lively return journey to the temple in the same order and propriety as they had come.

On arrival at the temple, the high priest, those who bore the divine figures, and those who had been admitted into the inner light of the cult, collected in the sanctuary of the Goddess. First they put back the breathing images into their right places; then a man (whom all entitled the scribe) took his stand in a high pulpit before the doors, and the Society of the Pastophori[3] (such is the name of the sacred college) was convoked. The scribe thereupon read out of a book a set of patriotic prayers for 'the great Prince, the Senate, the Equestrian Order, the Roman people, and all sailors and ships which come under the jurisdiction of Rome'. After that he pronounced in the Greek tongue and manner the words '*Laois aphesis*'. The people were dismissed.

The shout that followed showed the popular approval of the day's proceedings; and the congregation began to file out, beaming with joy, carrying boughs of olive and other votive wreaths, and garlanded with flowers. As they left the precincts, they one and all stopped to kiss the feet of a silver image of the Goddess that stood on the steps. But my emotions would not allow me to stir a single inch away from the place. With my eyes fixed upon the image I brooded over my past miseries.

Winging rumour, however, let no moss grow on her feathers. The tale of the Goddess's adorable goodness and of my curious adventures very soon had reached my native city; and my servants, friends, and those near to me in blood, at once discarded the sorrow into which the false tidings of my death had plunged them. Overjoyed and surprised, they hastened to visit me with various gifts, looking upon me as a man divinely raised up out of death. I who had shared their grief now shared their pleasure but gratefully refused their gifts, particularly as my servants had luckily taken care to bring me more than enough of clothes and money. Therefore, after I had met these acquaintances politely and told them the full story of my past pains and present prospects, I once more returned to what had become my chief source of delight: the contemplation of the Goddess. Renting a temporary apartment within the temple enclosure I took part in all the services, frequenting the company of the priests and becoming a constant worshipper at the shrine. Nor did a single night pass without some vision visiting my sleep and commanding me to be initiated into the priesthood, to which vocation I had long since been destined.

---

2 'Goose-neck': The goose was sacred to Isis.
3 'Pastophori': The priests that carried the shrines of the gods.

But though I profoundly desired to take this step, yet a religious qualm held me back. For after careful inquiry I had learned that a consecrated life was full of snags, that the requisite chastity was difficult to observe, and that only the most unrelenting discipline could save the priest from casual pollutions. Turning these doubts over and over in my mind, I kept delaying my initiation, though every day brought me closer to the final decision.

One night I had a dream. I thought that the high priest came to me with his bosom full of something or other. I asked him what he was offering me, and he answered, 'presents from Thessaly, for that Snowy Servant of yours has arrived from that province.'

When I awoke I pondered over the meaning of this vision, especially as I was sure that I had never had a servant of that name. However, I concluded that something to my advantage was portended by the priest offering me presents. Thus, worried and yet hopeful, I awaited the opening of the temple in the morning. At last the white curtains were drawn, and we offered up our prayers before the holy face of the Goddess. The priest went the round of the altars, performed the sacred ceremonial with solemn supplications, and poured out libations of water from the sanctuary-spring. When all these rites were completed, the worshippers saluted the rays of dawn and announced in clear voices that the day had begun.

Then lo, some men who had been in my employ arrived from Hypata, where I had left them on the day when Fotis by her wicked error fitted me for a halter. Accosting them I found that they had brought back my old horse, which had been recovered after changing hands several times and which I indentified by a mark on his back. At once I realized how admirably prophetic was my dream; for not only had it foretold gain in a general way but it had actually described the recovery of the horse, my snowy servant.

After this I applied myself even more diligently to attendance on the temple-services; for I considered that the Goddess had vouchsafed sure token of future blessings by her present benignity. Besides, my desire to enter the priesthood increased by bounds every day. Accordingly I had frequent interviews with the high priest, during which I earnestly besought him to initiate me into the mysteries of the Holy Night. But he, a serious-minded man who was noted for his strict observance of his unevangelical religion, checked my implorations with gentle friendliness, as parents get rid of children who come bothering at the wrong moment. At the same time he was careful to soothe me with hopes for the future.

For (he said) the initiation date for each aspirant was given by direct sign from the Goddess; and the officiating priest was selected by the same process—as also the precise sum to be expended on the ceremony. All these details must be awaited with uncomplaining patience, since it was necessary on every count to avoid either forwardness or contumacy, and neither to be slothful when called nor precipitate when not called. Not indeed that there was a single man among them who was so lost to common sense or so foolhardy that he would dare in rank blasphemy to undertake the ministries of the Goddess, which without her consent would be an invocation of destruction. For the gates of shadow as well as the bulwarks of life were under the Goddess's control; and the act of initiation had been compared to a voluntary death with a slight chance of redemption. Therefore the divine will of the Goddess was wont to choose men who had lived their life to the full, who were coming near to the limits of waning light, and who yet could be safely trusted with the mighty secrets of her religion. These men by her divine providence she regenerated and restored to strength sufficient for their new career. Conseauently I must await the celestial token, although I had already been manifestly indicated as destined for the blessed ministry. Meanwhile I should abstain from all profane or forbidden foods like the other devotees, that I might hasten the more uprightly into the secret bosom of the faith.

Thus spoke the priest; nor did impatience fret my obedient days. For I ambitiously performed the daily tasks of the ministry, intent upon preserving a serenity of soul and a laudable silence. Nor did the mindful love of the Goddess desert me or nail me on a cross of long delay; for there was no darkness in the visions that admonished the darkness of my sleep. She appeared and told me that the day of my desire had arrived, the day which would fulfil my dearest wishes. She also stated the sum of money to be spent on the ceremonial, and appointed the high priest Mithras to preside over my initiation; for (she said) he and I had our destinies mingled by a conjunction of our stars.

Elated by these and other divine commandments of the supreme Goddess, I threw off the coverlet of my sleep, although light was just greying. Hastening straightway to the retreat of the high priest I greeted him just as he was leaving his bedchamber. I had resolved to press my initiation as a thing now due; but the moment that he saw me he began speaking:

'O Lucius, what a happy and blessed man are you, whom the august deity has selected for such direct honours. O why,' he cried, 'do you stand there idle? Why do you delay a moment? The day that you have so constantly desired is come. You are to be initiated into the holy mysteries by these hands of mine in accordance with the divine mandate of the many-titled Goddess.'

Thereupon the old man took me by the hand and led me towards the spacious temple; and after he had duly performed the rituals of opening the doors and of making the morning-sacrifice, he produced from the secret recesses of the shrine certain books written in unknown characters. The meaning of these characters was concealed, at times by the concentrated expression of hieroglyphically painted animals, at times by wreathed and twisted letters with tails that twirled like wheels or spiralled together like vine- tendrils—so that it was altogether impossible for any peeping profane to comprehend. From these book? the high priest interpreted to me the matters necessary for my mystic preparation.

That done, I set about purchasing, partly at my own cost and partly with the aid of friends, all the required commodities. This I did on a larger scale than I had been bidden; and then, at the time that the priest had appointed as most suitable, I was led to the Baths, surrounded by a crowd of devotees. There, after I had taken the usual bath, Mithras himself washed and sprinkled me with pure water, invoking first the pardon of the gods.

Then he led me back once more into the temple and sat me down at the very feet of the Goddess. Two parts of the day had now gone; and after giving me some secret charges (too holy to be uttered) he bade me aloud to fast for the next ten days, eating no flesh and drinking no wine. This fast I reverently observed; and then at last the day arrived when I was to pledge myself to heaven. The sun swung down and drew the evening on; and lo, hosts of people came eagerly from every direction, each man honouring me with various gifts according to the ancient rite. Then, after the uninitiated had withdrawn to a distance and I had donned a new linen gown, the priest grasped my hand and conducted me into the Holy of Holies.

Perhaps, curious reader, you are keen to know what was said and done. I would tell you if it were permitted to tell. But both the ears that heard such things and the tongue that told them would reap a heavy penalty for such rashness. However, I shall not keep you any longer on the cross of your anxiety, distracted as you doubtless are with religious yearning. Hear therefore and believe what I say to be truth.

I approached the confines of death. I trod the threshold of Proserpine; and borne through the elements I returned. At midnight I saw the Sun shining in all his glory. I approached the gods below and the gods above, and I stood beside them, and I worshipped them. Behold, I have told my experience, and yet what you hear can mean nothing to you. I shall therefore keep to the facts which can be declared to the profane without offence.

Morning arrived; and after the due solemnities I came forth sanctified with twelve stoles, an habiliment of deep religious import, but which the bonds of my obligation do not keep me from mentioning, as I was seen by many bystanders. For, by order of the priest, I climbed a wooden pulpit which stood in the middle of the temple before the image of the Goddess. I wore a vestment of linen embroidered with a flower-pattern; a costly cope hung down from my shoulders to my ankles; and from whatever angle you inspected me you saw interesting new animal-shapes among the decorations—here Indian serpents, there Hyperborean griffins (which the Antipodes incubate like birds). This latter garment was what the priests commonly call an Olympic Stole. In my right hand I held a lighted torch; and a comely chaplet was wound round my head, from which the palm-tree leaves jetted like rays of the sun.

Thus decorated like the sun and draped like a statue (the curtains being whisked away) I was suddenly revealed to the gaze of the multitude. After this I celebrated the festal day of initiation (as if it were a birthday) with a sumptuous feasting and merry converse; and the third day was taken up with similar ceremonies, with a ritual-breakfast and the consummation of my priesthood.

Lingering about the temple for several more days, I was granted the delight of viewing the Holy Face: a benefit that no grateful services can ever repay—till at length, after humbly thanking the Goddess (not as she deserved but as I was able), I received her admonition to depart home; and I reluctantly made my preparations. But I could hardly bear to break the ties of intense affection that bound me to the place. Prostrating myself before the Goddess and watering her feet with my tears, I addressed her, gulping back the sobs that disturbed my articulation:

'Most holy and everlasting Redeemer of the human race, you munificently cherish our lives and bestow the consoling smiles of a Mother upon our tribulations. There is no day or night, not so much as the minutest fraction of time, that is not stuffed with the eternity of your mercy. You protect men on land and sea. You chase the storms of life and stretch out the hand of succour to the dejected. You can untwine the hopelessly tangled threads of the Fates. You can mitigate the tempests of Fortune and check the stars in the courses of their malice. The gods of heaven worship you. The gods of hell bow before you. You rotate the globe. You light the sun. You govern space. You trample hell. The stars move to your orders, the sea-sons return, the gods rejoice, the elements combine. At your nod the breezes blow, clouds collect, seeds sprout, blossoms increase. The birds that fly in the air, the beasts that roam on the hills, the serpents that hide in the earth, the monsters that swim in the ocean, tremble before your majesty.

'O my spirit is not able to give you sufficient praises, nor have I the means to make acceptable sacrifice. My voice has no power to utter what I think of you. Not a thousand mouths with a thousand tongues, not an eternal flow of unwearied declaration, could utter it.

'Howbeit, poor as I am, I shall do all that a truly religious man may do. I shall conjure up your divine countenance within my breast, and there in the secret depths I shall keep divinity for ever guarded.'

I thus offered my prayer to the supreme Goddess. Then I embraced the priest Mithras (my father in Her); and clinging upon his neck and kissing him oft, I begged his forgiveness that I could not recompense him adequately for the benefits he had heaped upon me. After expressing my sense of obligation at full length, I left him and prepared to revisit my ancestral home from which I had been so long absent.

So, a few days later (as the Goddess admonished), after hastily packing my luggage I went on shipboard and set sail for Rome. Safely and swiftly carried by a favouring breeze, we soon reached the port of Augustus. There I disembarked; and travelling by post-chariot I arrived at the Holy City on the evening of the day before the Ides of December. Nothing now mattered to me so much as to supplicate daily the supreme godhead of Queen Isis (who is propitiated in this city with the deepest veneration as Campensis:[4] a name derived from the site of her temple). In short, I became an unslackening worshipper, a newcomer to this church of hers, but indigenous to her religion.

Now the strong-thewed Sun had passed through all the signs of the circling zodiac, and the year was ended. But the loving insistence of the Goddess once more broke in upon my sleep, once more strongly speaking of mysteries and holy rites. I wondered what was the meaning of this, and what even was foreshadowed. How should I not? For I had thought myself fully initiated already.

After I had re-examined all my religious doubts in the privacy of my own conscience, I consulted a priest. I then learned a new and disturbing thing: that I was initiated into the mysteries of the Goddess, but that I knew nothing of the rites of the mighty God, the supreme Father of the Gods, unconquerable Osiris.

For though there is amity and even unity to be found between the two essences and their religious statement, yet the approach to knowledge of them is by different tracks. So now what I had to do was to await a summons from the great God to his service. Nor was I left long in doubt. During the next night I saw in a dream one of his devotees clad in linen and bearing ivied thyrsi and other objects (which I may not name). He placed his load before my Household Gods; and then, seating himself in my chair, he recited to me the articles necessary for a splendid religious feast—and, in order that I might know

---

4 'Campensis': In-the-Fields—the Campus Martius.

him again, he showed me how the heel of his left foot was somewhat hurt, giving him a slight hobble. All the mists of my doubt were cleared away by such a manifest sign of the will of the gods.

Therefore, as soon as my matins were finished, I carefully noted the priests, to see if any of them walked like the man in my dream. There he was, the very man. One of the Pastophori closely resembled my midnight visitor in stature and looks as well as in gait. His name, I later found, was Asinius Marcellus (a name asininely suggestive of my late plight). I at once approached the priest, who was not at all surprised at what he heard me say; for he had been similarly admonished as to my initiation into the mysteries of Osiris. On the preceding night, while dressing the garlands on the statue of the Great God, he imagined that the Mouth (which pronounced the dooms of all mankind) spoke to him. The message said that a native of Madaura was being sent to him and that he must impart to this man, poor as he was, the sacraments of the God—whereby through the God's providence the one would be glorified for his religious exercises and the other greatly profited.

Thus affianced to religion I was yet held back from the full consummation of my desire through the slenderness of my means. For the travel expenses had wasted the remnant of my estate; and the cost of living in Rome was far ahead of that in the provinces. My poverty thus kept interfering with my plans; and I was left stranded (as the saying goes) between the altar and the block.

Yet the mandates from the God did not weaken their pressure. They continued to goad me till I became very troubled; and then as the commands grew more incisive, I sold the clothes off my back and scraped up enough to carry on. This indeed was the course prescribed; for the God said to me: 'If you were hot after some trifle of pleasure, would you hesitate to throw your clothes away? And now, on the brink of initiation, do you shrink from a poverty that can bring no repentance?'

Everything was thus fully prepared; and now once more I abstained for ten days from eating flesh. Then, admitted with shaven head to the nocturnal orgies of the Lord of Gods, I resorted to the ceremonies with the full confidence that knowledge of a kindred ritual evoked. This occurrence consoled me for my sojourn in a foreign city and also gave me a better chance of earning my livelihood. For, favoured by the god Good-Luck, I managed to subsist on the small fees I gained in the Forum pleading causes in the Latin tongue.

But shortly afterwards I was once more molested by unexpected visionary commands; and a third time[5] I found myself yearning towards a mystery. This left me in an oppressively shaken and perplexed state of mind, uncertain what could be the significance of this new and peculiar expression of celestial will and what could remain incomplete in my dual initiation. Surely (thought I) the instructions given me by the two priests must have been either incorrect or fragmentary; and, by Hercules, I began to suspect them of bad faith. While, however, I was drifting on these stormy tides of doubt and driven to the verge of distraction, the benign figure of the God appeared in dream once more.

'To no end,' said he, 'are you frightened by the continued series of religious rites, as if something had been previously omitted. Rather, you should take heart because the deities repeat the tokens of their

---

5 'Third time': This initiation was into the mysteries of the Roman Isis—the first having been into those of the Athaian Isis.

love for you. You should exult that you will thrice achieve that which is scarcely even once given to others. And you may rightly conjecture from the number Three that you will remain eternally blessed. Moreover, you will find the ceremony indispensable if you will but realize that the stole of the Goddess with which you were invested in the province is still kept in the temple there. You are thus unable to supplicate at Rome in your stole or to be distinguished by that auspicious garment when you are bidden to don it. Therefore let my command be as glory, happiness, and health to you. Once more joyously become initiated, with the mighty gods for your sponsors.'

Thus far did the persuasive majesty of the divine vision announce what I must profitably do. So I did not neglect or weakly postpone the matter. At once I related to a priest what I had seen; and I not only submitted to the yoke of abstinence from meat but voluntarily extended the period beyond the ten days ordained by everlasting law. Then I bought all the necessary articles, considering more the measure of my piety than the narrowness of the regulations. Nor, by Hercules, was I ever sorry for my trouble and expense. And why should I? For now by the generous aid of the gods I was being decently repaid for my forensic labours.

At length, after the lapse of a few days, the Lord Osiris, the most powerful of the great gods, the highest of the greater, the greatest of the highest, and the ruler of the greatest, appeared to me in the night, now no longer disguised by deigning to speak to me in his own person and with his own divine voice. He declared that I should rapidly come to the forefront of the legal profession at Rome and that I should not fear the slanders of the malevolent who naturally disliked me on account of the learning I had studiously acquired.

In addition, to enable me to mingle with the throng of devotees and duly serve his mysteries, he appointed me a member of the College of Pastophori—and more, one of the five-yearly decurions; and so, with tonsured crown, I set about joyfully executing my duties in that most ancient society (which had been founded in the period of Sylla), not shading or hiding my baldness but freely exposing it where- ever I went.

Book 1 of the Ten Books on Architecture

By Vitruvius, translated by Morris Hicky Morgan

Preface

1. While your divine intelligence and will, Imperator Caesar, were engaged in acquiring the right to command the world, and while your fellow citizens, when all their enemies had been laid low by your invincible valour, were glorying in your triumph and victory,--while all foreign nations were in subjection awaiting your beck and call, and the Roman people and senate, released from their alarm, were beginning to be guided by your most noble conceptions and policies, I hardly dared, in view of your serious employments, to publish my writings and long considered ideas on architecture, for fear of subjecting myself to your displeasure by an unseasonable interruption.

2. But when I saw that you were giving your attention not only to the welfare of society in general and to the establishment of public order, but also to the providing of public buildings intended for utilitarian purposes, so that not only should the State have been enriched with provinces by your means, but that the greatness of its power might likewise be attended with distinguished authority in its public buildings, I thought that I ought to take the first opportunity to lay before you my writings on this theme. For in the first place it was this subject which made me known to your father, to whom I was devoted on account of his great qualities. After the council of heaven gave him a place in the dwellings of immortal life and transferred your father's power to your hands, my devotion continuing unchanged

as I remembered him inclined me to support you. And so with Marcus Aurelius, Publius Minidius, and Gnaeus Cornelius, I was ready to supply and repair ballistae, scorpiones, and other artillery, and I have received rewards for good service with them. After your first bestowal of these upon me, you continued to renew them on the recommendation of your sister.

3. Owing to this favour I need have no fear of want to the end of my life, and being thus laid under obligation I began to write this work for you, because I saw that you have built and are now building extensively, and that in future also you will take care that our public and private buildings shall be worthy to go down to posterity by the side of your other splendid achievements. I have drawn up definite rules to enable you, by observing them, to have personal knowledge of the quality both of existing buildings and of those which are yet to be constructed. For in the following books I have disclosed all the principles of the art.

Chapter I

The Education Of The Architect

1. The architect should be equipped with knowledge of many branches of study and varied kinds of learning, for it is by his judgement that all work done by the other arts is put to test. This knowledge is the child of practice and theory. Practice is the continuous and regular exercise of employment where manual work is done with any necessary material according to the design of a drawing. Theory, on the other hand, is the ability to demonstrate and explain the productions of dexterity on the principles of proportion.

2. It follows, therefore, that architects who have aimed at acquiring manual skill without scholarship have never been able to reach a position of authority to correspond to their pains, while those who relied only upon theories and scholarship were obviously hunting the shadow, not the substance. But those who have a thorough knowledge of both, like men armed at all points, have the sooner attained their object and carried authority with them.

3. In all matters, but particularly in architecture, there are these two points:--the thing signified, and that which gives it its significance. That which is signified is the subject of which we may be speaking; and that which gives significance is a demonstration on scientific principles. It appears, then, that one who professes himself an architect should be well versed in both directions. He ought, therefore, to be both naturally gifted and amenable to instruction. Neither natural ability without instruction nor instruction without natural ability can make the perfect artist. Let him be educated, skilful with the pencil, instructed in geometry, know much history, have followed the philosophers with attention, understand

music, have some knowledge of medicine, know the opinions of the jurists, and be acquainted with astronomy and the theory of the heavens.

4. The reasons for all this are as follows. An architect ought to be an educated man so as to leave a more lasting remembrance in his treatises. Secondly, he must have a knowledge of drawing so that he can readily make sketches to show the appearance of the work which he proposes. Geometry, also, is of much assistance in architecture, and in particular it teaches us the use of the rule and compasses, by which especially we acquire readiness in making plans for buildings in their grounds, and rightly apply the square, the level, and the plummet. By means of optics, again, the light in buildings can be drawn from fixed quarters of the sky. It is true that it is by arithmetic that the total cost of buildings is calculated and measurements are computed, but difficult questions involving symmetry are solved by means of geometrical theories and methods.

5. A wide knowledge of history is requisite because, among the ornamental parts of an architect's design for a work, there are many the underlying idea of whose employment he should be able to explain to inquirers. For instance, suppose him to set up the marble statues of women in long robes, called Caryatides, to take the place of columns, with the mutules and coronas placed directly above their heads, he will give the following explanation to his questioners. Caryae, a state in Peloponnesus, sided with the Persian enemies against Greece; later the Greeks, having gloriously won their freedom by victory in the war, made common cause and declared war against the people of Caryae. They took the town, killed the men, abandoned the State to desolation, and carried off their wives into slavery, without permitting them, however, to lay aside the long robes and other marks of their rank as married women, so that they might be obliged not only to march in the triumph but to appear forever after as a type of slavery, burdened with the weight of their shame and so making atonement for their State. Hence, the architects of the time designed for public buildings statues of these women, placed so as to carry a load, in order that the sin and the punishment of the people of Caryae might be known and handed down even to posterity.

6. Likewise the Lacedaemonians under the leadership of Pausanias, son of Agesipolis, after conquering the Persian armies, infinite in number, with a small force at the battle of Plataea, celebrated a glorious triumph with the spoils and booty, and with the money obtained from the sale thereof built the Persian Porch, to be a monument to the renown and valour of the people and a trophy of victory for posterity. And there they set effigies of the prisoners arrayed in barbarian costume and holding up the roof, their pride punished by this deserved affront, that enemies might tremble for fear of the effects of their courage, and that their own people, looking upon this ensample of their valour and encouraged by the glory of it, might be ready to defend their independence. So from that time on, many have put up statues of Persians supporting entablatures and their ornaments, and thus from that motive have greatly enriched the diversity of their works. There are other stories of the same kind which architects ought to know.

7. As for philosophy, it makes an architect high-minded and not self-assuming, but rather renders him courteous, just, and honest without avariciousness. This is very important, for no work can be rightly done without honesty and incorruptibility. Let him not be grasping nor have his mind preoccupied with the idea of receiving perquisites, but let him with dignity keep up his position by cherishing a good reputation. These are among the precepts of philosophy. Furthermore philosophy treats of physics (in Greek [Greek: physiologia]) where a more careful knowledge is required because the problems which come under this head are numerous and of very different kinds; as, for example, in the case of the conducting of water. For at points of intake and at curves, and at places where it is raised to a level, currents of air naturally form in one way or another; and nobody who has not learned the fundamental principles of physics from philosophy will be able to provide against the damage which they do. So the reader of Ctesibius or Archimedes and the other writers of treatises of the same class will not be able to appreciate them unless he has been trained in these subjects by the philosophers.

8. Music, also, the architect ought to understand so that he may have knowledge of the canonical and mathematical theory, and besides be able to tune ballistae, catapultae, and scorpiones to the proper key. For to the right and left in the beams are the holes in the frames through which the strings of twisted sinew are stretched by means of windlasses and bars, and these strings must not be clamped and made fast until they give the same correct note to the ear of the skilled workman. For the arms thrust through those stretched strings must, on being let go, strike their blow together at the same moment; but if they are not in unison, they will prevent the course of projectiles from being straight.

9. In theatres, likewise, there are the bronze vessels (in Greek [Greek: êcheia]) which are placed in niches under the seats in accordance with the musical intervals on mathematical principles. These vessels are arranged with a view to musical concords or harmony, and apportioned in the compass of the fourth, the fifth, and the octave, and so on up to the double octave, in such a way that when the voice of an actor falls in unison with any of them its power is increased, and it reaches the ears of the audience with greater clearness and sweetness. Water organs, too, and the other instruments which resemble them cannot be made by one who is without the principles of music.

10. The architect should also have a knowledge of the study of medicine on account of the questions of climates (in Greek [Greek: klimata]), air, the healthiness and unhealthiness of sites, and the use of different waters. For without these considerations, the healthiness of a dwelling cannot be assured. And as for principles of law, he should know those which are necessary in the case of buildings having party walls, with regard to water dripping from the eaves, and also the laws about drains, windows, and water supply. And other things of this sort should be known to architects, so that, before they begin upon buildings, they may be careful not to leave disputed points for the householders to settle after the works are finished, and so that in drawing up contracts the interests of both employer and contractor may be wisely safe-guarded. For if a contract is skilfully drawn, each may obtain a release from the other without disadvantage. From astronomy we find the east, west, south, and north, as well as the theory of the heavens, the equinox, solstice, and courses of the stars.

If one has no knowledge of these matters, he will not be able to have any comprehension of the theory of sundials.

11. Consequently, since this study is so vast in extent, embellished and enriched as it is with many different kinds of learning, I think that men have no right to profess themselves architects hastily, without having climbed from boyhood the steps of these studies and thus, nursed by the knowledge of many arts and sciences, having reached the heights of the holy ground of architecture.

12. But perhaps to the inexperienced it will seem a marvel that human nature can comprehend such a great number of studies and keep them in the memory. Still, the observation that all studies have a common bond of union and intercourse with one another, will lead to the belief that this can easily be realized. For a liberal education forms, as it were, a single body made up of these members. Those, therefore, who from tender years receive instruction in the various forms of learning, recognize the same stamp on all the arts, and an intercourse between all studies, and so they more readily comprehend them all. This is what led one of the ancient architects, Pytheos, the celebrated builder of the temple of Minerva at Priene, to say in his Commentaries that an architect ought to be able to accomplish much more in all the arts and sciences than the men who, by their own particular kinds of work and the practice of it, have brought each a single subject to the highest perfection. But this is in point of fact not realized.

13. For an architect ought not to be and cannot be such a philologian as was Aristarchus, although not illiterate; nor a musician like Aristoxenus, though not absolutely ignorant of music; nor a painter like Apelles, though not unskilful in drawing; nor a sculptor such as was Myron or Polyclitus, though not unacquainted with the plastic art; nor again a physician like Hippocrates, though not ignorant of medicine; nor in the other sciences need he excel in each, though he should not be unskilful in them. For, in the midst of all this great variety of subjects, an individual cannot attain to perfection in each, because it is scarcely in his power to take in and comprehend the general theories of them.

14. Still, it is not architects alone that cannot in all matters reach perfection, but even men who individually practise specialties in the arts do not all attain to the highest point of merit. Therefore, if among artists working each in a single field not all, but only a few in an entire generation acquire fame, and that with difficulty, how can an architect, who has to be skilful in many arts, accomplish not merely the feat--in itself a great marvel--of being deficient in none of them, but also that of surpassing all those artists who have devoted themselves with unremitting industry to single fields?

15. It appears, then, that Pytheos made a mistake by not observing that the arts are each composed of two things, the actual work and the theory of it. One of these, the doing of the work, is proper to men trained in the individual subject, while the other, the theory, is common to all scholars: for example, to physicians and musicians the rhythmical beat of the pulse and its metrical movement. But if there is a wound to be healed or a sick man to be saved from danger, the musician will not call, for the business will be appropriate to the physician. So in the case of a musical instrument, not the physician but the musician will be the man to tune it so that the ears may find their due pleasure in its strains.

16. Astronomers likewise have a common ground for discussion with musicians in the harmony of the stars and musical concords in tetrads and triads of the fourth and the fifth, and with geometricians in the subject of vision (in Greek [Greek: logos optikos]); and in all other sciences many points, perhaps all, are common so far as the discussion of them is concerned. But the actual undertaking of works which are brought to perfection by the hand and its manipulation is the function of those who have been specially trained to deal with a single art. It appears, therefore, that he has done enough and to spare who in each subject possesses a fairly good knowledge of those parts, with their principles, which are indispensable for architecture, so that if he is required to pass judgement and to express approval in the case of those things or arts, he may not be found wanting. As for men upon whom nature has bestowed so much ingenuity, acuteness, and memory that they are able to have a thorough knowledge of geometry, astronomy, music, and the other arts, they go beyond the functions of architects and become pure mathematicians. Hence they can readily take up positions against those arts because many are the artistic weapons with which they are armed. Such men, however, are rarely found, but there have been such at times; for example, Aristarchus of Samos, Philolaus and Archytas of Tarentum, Apollonius of Perga, Eratosthenes of Cyrene, and among Syracusans Archimedes and Scopinas, who through mathematics and natural philosophy discovered, expounded, and left to posterity many things in connexion with mechanics and with sundials.

17. Since, therefore, the possession of such talents due to natural capacity is not vouchsafed at random to entire nations, but only to a few great men; since, moreover, the function of the architect requires a training in all the departments of learning; and finally, since reason, on account of the wide extent of the subject, concedes that he may possess not the highest but not even necessarily a moderate knowledge of the subjects of study, I request, Caesar, both of you and of those who may read the said books, that if anything is set forth with too little regard for grammatical rule, it may be pardoned. For it is not as a very great philosopher, nor as an eloquent rhetorician, nor as a grammarian trained in the highest principles of his art, that I have striven to write this work, but as an architect who has had only a dip into those studies. Still, as regards the efficacy of the art and the theories of it, I promise and expect that in these volumes I shall undoubtedly show myself of very considerable importance not only to builders but also to all scholars.

Chapter II

The Fundamental Principles Of Architecture

1. Architecture depends on Order (in Greek [Greek: taxis]), Arrangement (in Greek [Greek: diathesis]), Eurythmy, Symmetry, Propriety, and Economy (in Greek [Greek: oikonomia]).

2. Order gives due measure to the members of a work considered separately, and symmetrical agreement to the proportions of the whole. It is an adjustment according to quantity (in Greek [Greek: posotês]). By this I mean the selection of modules from the members of the work itself and, starting from these individual parts of members, constructing the whole work to correspond. Arrangement includes the putting of things in their proper places and the elegance of effect which is due to adjustments appropriate to the character of the work. Its forms of expression (Greek [Greek: ideai]) are these: groundplan, elevation, and perspective. A groundplan is made by the proper successive use of compasses and rule, through which we get outlines for the plane surfaces of buildings. An elevation is a picture of the front of a building, set upright and properly drawn in the proportions of the contemplated work. Perspective is the method of sketching a front with the sides withdrawing into the background, the lines all meeting in the centre of a circle. All three come of reflexion and invention. Reflexion is careful and laborious thought, and watchful attention directed to the agreeable effect of one›s plan. Invention, on the other hand, is the solving of intricate problems and the discovery of new principles by means of brilliancy and versatility. These are the departments belonging under Arrangement.

3. Eurythmy is beauty and fitness in the adjustments of the members. This is found when the members of a work are of a height suited to their breadth, of a breadth suited to their length, and, in a word, when they all correspond symmetrically.

4. Symmetry is a proper agreement between the members of the work itself, and relation between the different parts and the whole general scheme, in accordance with a certain part selected as standard. Thus in the human body there is a kind of symmetrical harmony between forearm, foot, palm, finger, and other small parts; and so it is with perfect buildings. In the case of temples, symmetry may be calculated from the thickness of a column, from a triglyph, or even from a module; in the ballista, from the hole or from what the Greeks call the [Greek: peritrêtos]; in a ship, from the space between the tholepins [Greek: (diapêgma)]; and in other things, from various members.

5. Propriety is that perfection of style which comes when a work is authoritatively constructed on approved principles. It arises from prescription [Greek: (thematismô)], from usage, or from nature. From prescription, in the case of hypaethral edifices, open to the sky, in honour of Jupiter Lightning, the Heaven, the Sun, or the Moon: for these are gods whose semblances and manifestations we behold before our very eyes in the sky when it is cloudless and bright. The temples of Minerva, Mars, and Hercules, will be Doric, since the virile strength of these gods makes daintiness entirely

inappropriate to their houses. In temples to Venus, Flora, Proserpine, Spring-Water, and the Nymphs, the Corinthian order will be found to have peculiar significance, because these are delicate divinities and so its rather slender outlines, its flowers, leaves, and ornamental volutes will lend propriety where it is due. The construction of temples of the Ionic order to Juno, Diana, Father Bacchus, and the other gods of that kind, will be in keeping with the middle position which they hold; for the building of such will be an appropriate combination of the severity of the Doric and the delicacy of the Corinthian.

6. Propriety arises from usage when buildings having magnificent interiors are provided with elegant entrance-courts to correspond; for there will be no propriety in the spectacle of an elegant interior approached by a low, mean entrance. Or, if dentils be carved in the cornice of the Doric entablature or triglyphs represented in the Ionic entablature over the cushion-shaped capitals of the columns, the effect will be spoilt by the transfer of the peculiarities of the one order of building to the other, the usage in each class having been fixed long ago.

7. Finally, propriety will be due to natural causes if, for example, in the case of all sacred precincts we select very healthy neighbourhoods with suitable springs of water in the places where the fanes are to be built, particularly in the case of those to Aesculapius and to Health, gods by whose healing powers great numbers of the sick are apparently cured. For when their diseased bodies are transferred from an unhealthy to a healthy spot, and treated with waters from health-giving springs, they will the more speedily grow well. The result will be that the divinity will stand in higher esteem and find his dignity increased, all owing to the nature of his site. There will also be natural propriety in using an eastern light for bedrooms and libraries, a western light in winter for baths and winter apartments, and a northern light for picture galleries and other places in which a steady light is needed; for that quarter of the sky grows neither light nor dark with the course of the sun, but remains steady and unshifting all day long.

8. Economy denotes the proper management of materials and of site, as well as a thrifty balancing of cost and common sense in the construction of works. This will be observed if, in the first place, the architect does not demand things which cannot be found or made ready without great expense. For example: it is not everywhere that there is plenty of pitsand, rubble, fir, clear fir, and marble, since they are produced in different places and to assemble them is difficult and costly. Where there is no pitsand, we must use the kinds washed up by rivers or by the sea; the lack of fir and clear fir may be evaded by using cypress, poplar, elm, or pine; and other problems we must solve in similar ways.

9. A second stage in Economy is reached when we have to plan the different kinds of dwellings suitable for ordinary householders, for great wealth, or for the high position of the statesman. A house in town obviously calls for one form of construction; that into which stream the products of country estates requires another; this will not be the same in the case of money-lenders and still different for the opulent and luxurious; for the powers under whose deliberations the commonwealth is guided dwellings are to be provided according to their special needs: and, in a word, the proper form of economy must be observed in building houses for each and every class.

Chapter III

The Departments Of Architecture

1. There are three departments of architecture: the art of building, the making of timepieces, and the construction of machinery. Building is, in its turn, divided into two parts, of which the first is the construction of fortified towns and of works for general use in public places, and the second is the putting up of structures for private individuals. There are three classes of public buildings: the first for defensive, the second for religious, and the third for utilitarian purposes. Under defence comes the planning of walls, towers, and gates, permanent devices for resistance against hostile attacks; under religion, the erection of fanes and temples to the immortal gods; under utility, the provision of meeting places for public use, such as harbours, markets, colonnades, baths, theatres, promenades, and all other similar arrangements in public places.

2. All these must be built with due reference to durability, convenience, and beauty. Durability will be assured when foundations are carried down to the solid ground and materials wisely and liberally selected; convenience, when the arrangement of the apartments is faultless and presents no hindrance to use, and when each class of building is assigned to its suitable and appropriate exposure; and beauty, when the appearance of the work is pleasing and in good taste, and when its members are in due proportion according to correct principles of symmetry.

Chapter IV

The Site of A City

1. For fortified towns the following general principles are to be observed. First comes the choice of a very healthy site. Such a site will be high, neither misty nor frosty, and in a climate neither hot nor cold, but temperate; further, without marshes in the neighbourhood. For when the morning breezes blow toward the town at sunrise, if they bring with them mists from marshes and, mingled with the mist, the poisonous breath of the creatures of the marshes to be wafted into the bodies of the inhabitants, they will make the site unhealthy. Again, if the town is on the coast with a southern or western exposure, it will not be healthy, because in summer the southern sky grows hot at sunrise and is fiery at noon, while a western exposure grows warm after sunrise, is hot at noon, and at evening all aglow.

2. These variations in heat and the subsequent cooling off are harmful to the people living on such sites. The same conclusion may be reached in the case of inanimate things. For instance, nobody draws the light for covered wine rooms from the south or west, but rather from the north, since that quarter is never subject to change but is always constant and unshifting. So it is with granaries: grain exposed to the sun›s course soon loses its good quality, and provisions and fruit, unless stored in a place unexposed to the sun›s course, do not keep long.

3. For heat is a universal solvent, melting out of things their power of resistance, and sucking away and removing their natural strength with its fiery exhalations so that they grow soft, and hence weak, under its glow. We see this in the case of iron which, however hard it may naturally be, yet when heated thoroughly in a furnace fire can be easily worked into any kind of shape, and still, if cooled while it is soft and white hot, it hardens again with a mere dip into cold water and takes on its former quality.

4. We may also recognize the truth of this from the fact that in summer the heat makes everybody weak, not only in unhealthy but even in healthy places, and that in winter even the most unhealthy districts are much healthier because they are given a solidity by the cooling off. Similarly, persons removed from cold countries to hot cannot endure it but waste away; whereas those who pass from hot places to the cold regions of the north, not only do not suffer in health from the change of residence but even gain by it.

5. It appears, then, that in founding towns we must beware of districts from which hot winds can spread abroad over the inhabitants. For while all bodies are composed of the four elements (in Greek [Greek: stoicheia]), that is, of heat, moisture, the earthy, and air, yet there are mixtures according to natural temperament which make up the natures of all the different animals of the world, each after its kind.

6. Therefore, if one of these elements, heat, becomes predominant in any body whatsoever, it destroys and dissolves all the others with its violence. This defect may be due to violent heat from certain quarters of the sky, pouring into the open pores in too great proportion to admit of a mixture suited to the natural temperament of the body in question. Again, if too much moisture enters the channels of a body, and thus introduces disproportion, the other elements, adulterated by the liquid, are impaired, and the virtues of the mixture dissolved. This defect, in turn, may arise from the cooling properties of moist winds and breezes blowing upon the body. In the same way, increase or diminution of the proportion of air or of the earthy which is natural to the body may enfeeble the other elements; the predominance of the earthy being due to overmuch food, that of air to a heavy atmosphere.

7. If one wishes a more accurate understanding of all this, he need only consider and observe the natures of birds, fishes, and land animals, and he will thus come to reflect upon distinctions of temperament. One form of mixture is proper to birds, another to fishes, and a far different form to land animals. Winged creatures have less of the earthy, less moisture, heat in moderation, air in large amount. Being made up, therefore, of the lighter elements, they can more readily soar away into the air. Fish, with their aquatic nature, being moderately supplied with heat and made up in great part of air and the earthy, with as little of moisture as possible, can more easily exist in moisture for the very reason that they have less of it than of the other elements in their bodies; and so, when they are drawn to land, they leave life and water at the same moment. Similarly, the land animals, being moderately supplied with

the elements of air and heat, and having less of the earthy and a great deal of moisture, cannot long continue alive in the water, because their portion of moisture is already abundant.

8. Therefore, if all this is as we have explained, our reason showing us that the bodies of animals are made up of the elements, and these bodies, as we believe, giving way and breaking up as a result of excess or deficiency in this or that element, we cannot but believe that we must take great care to select a very temperate climate for the site of our city, since healthfulness is, as we have said, the first requisite.

9. I cannot too strongly insist upon the need of a return to the method of old times. Our ancestors, when about to build a town or an army post, sacrificed some of the cattle that were wont to feed on the site proposed and examined their livers. If the livers of the first victims were dark-coloured or abnormal, they sacrificed others, to see whether the fault was due to disease or their food. They never began to build defensive works in a place until after they had made many such trials and satisfied themselves that good water and food had made the liver sound and firm. If they continued to find it abnormal, they argued from this that the food and water supply found in such a place would be just as unhealthy for man, and so they moved away and changed to another neighbourhood, healthfulness being their chief object.

10. That pasturage and food may indicate the healthful qualities of a site is a fact which can be observed and investigated in the case of certain pastures in Crete, on each side of the river Pothereus, which separates the two Cretan states of Gnosus and Gortyna. There are cattle at pasture on the right and left banks of that river, but while the cattle that feed near Gnosus have the usual spleen, those on the other side near Gortyna have no perceptible spleen. On investigating the subject, physicians discovered on this side a kind of herb which the cattle chew and thus make their spleen small. The herb is therefore gathered and used as a medicine for the cure of splenetic people. The Cretans call it [Greek: hasplênon]. From food and water, then, we may learn whether sites are naturally unhealthy or healthy.

11. If the walled town is built among the marshes themselves, provided they are by the sea, with a northern or north-eastern exposure, and are above the level of the seashore, the site will be reasonable enough. For ditches can be dug to let out the water to the shore, and also in times of storms the sea swells and comes backing up into the marshes, where its bitter blend prevents the reproductions of the usual marsh creatures, while any that swim down from the higher levels to the shore are killed at once by the saltness to which they are unused. An instance of this may be found in the Gallic marshes surrounding Altino, Ravenna, Aquileia, and other towns in places of the kind, close by marshes. They are marvellously healthy, for the reasons which I have given.

12. But marshes that are stagnant and have no outlets either by rivers or ditches, like the Pomptine marshes, merely putrefy as they stand, emitting heavy, unhealthy vapours. A case of a town built in such a spot was Old Salpia in Apulia, founded by Diomede on his way back from Troy, or, according to some writers, by Elpias of Rhodes. Year after year there was sickness, until finally the suffering inhabitants came with a public petition to Marcus Hostilius and got him to agree to seek and find them a proper place to which to remove their city. Without delay he made the most skilful investigations, and at once purchased an estate near the sea in a healthy place, and asked the Senate and Roman people for

permission to remove the town. He constructed the walls and laid out the house lots, granting one to each citizen for a mere trifle. This done, he cut an opening from a lake into the sea, and thus made of the lake a harbour for the town. The result is that now the people of Salpia live on a healthy site and at a distance of only four miles from the old town.

Chapter V

The City Walls

1. After insuring on these principles the healthfulness of the future city, and selecting a neighbourhood that can supply plenty of food stuffs to maintain the community, with good roads or else convenient rivers or seaports affording easy means of transport to the city, the next thing to do is to lay the foundations for the towers and walls. Dig down to solid bottom, if it can be found, and lay them therein, going as deep as the magnitude of the proposed work seems to require. They should be much thicker than the part of the walls that will appear above ground, and their structure should be as solid as it can possibly be laid.

2. The towers must be projected beyond the line of wall, so that an enemy wishing to approach the wall to carry it by assault may be exposed to the fire of missiles on his open flank from the towers on his right and left. Special pains should be taken that there be no easy avenue by which to storm the wall. The roads should be encompassed at steep points, and planned so as to approach the gates, not in a straight line, but from the right to the left; for as a result of this, the right hand side of the assailants, unprotected by their shields, will be next the wall. Towns should be laid out not as an exact square nor with salient angles, but in circular form, to give a view of the enemy from many points. Defence is difficult where there are salient angles, because the angle protects the enemy rather than the inhabitants.

3. The thickness of the wall should, in my opinion, be such that armed men meeting on top of it may pass one another without interference. In the thickness there should be set a very close succession of ties made of charred olive wood, binding the two faces of the wall together like pins, to give it lasting endurance. For that is a material which neither decay, nor the weather, nor time can harm, but even though buried in the earth or set in the water it keeps sound and useful forever. And so not only city walls but substructures in general and all walls that require a thickness like that of a city wall, will be long in falling to decay if tied in this manner.

4. The towers should be set at intervals of not more than a bowshot apart, so that in case of an assault upon any one of them, the enemy may be repulsed with scorpiones and other means of hurling missiles from the

towers to the right and left. Opposite the inner side of every tower the wall should be interrupted for a space the width of the tower, and have only a wooden flooring across, leading to the interior of the tower but not firmly nailed. This is to be cut away by the defenders in case the enemy gets possession of any portion of the wall; and if the work is quickly done, the enemy will not be able to make his way to the other towers and the rest of the wall unless he is ready to face a fall.

5. The towers themselves must be either round or polygonal. Square towers are sooner shattered by military engines, for the battering rams pound their angles to pieces; but in the case of round towers they can do no harm, being engaged, as it were, in driving wedges to their centre. The system of fortification by wall and towers may be made safest by the addition of earthen ramparts, for neither rams, nor mining, nor other engineering devices can do them any harm.

6. The rampart form of defence, however, is not required in all places, but only where outside the wall there is high ground from which an assault on the fortifications may be made over a level space lying between. In places of this kind we must first make very wide, deep ditches; next sink foundations for a wall in the bed of the ditch and build them thick enough to support an earth-work with ease.

7. Then within this substructure lay a second foundation, far enough inside the first to leave ample room for cohorts in line of battle to take position on the broad top of the rampart for its defence. Having laid these two foundations at this distance from one another, build cross walls between them, uniting the outer and inner foundation, in a comb-like arrangement, set like the teeth of a saw. With this form of construction, the enormous burden of earth will be distributed into small bodies, and will not lie with all its weight in one crushing mass so as to thrust out the substructures.

8. With regard to the material of which the actual wall should be constructed or finished, there can be no definite prescription, because we cannot obtain in all places the supplies that we desire. Dimension stone, flint, rubble, burnt or unburnt brick,--use them as you find them. For it is not every neighbourhood or particular locality that can have a wall built of burnt brick like that at Babylon, where there was plenty of asphalt to take the place of lime and sand, and yet possibly each may be provided with materials of equal usefulness so that out of them a faultless wall may be built to last forever.

Chapter VI

The Directions Of The Streets; With Remarks On The Winds

1. The town being fortified, the next step is the apportionment of house lots within the wall and the laying out of streets and alleys with regard to climatic conditions. They will be properly laid out if foresight is employed to exclude the winds from the alleys. Cold winds are disagreeable, hot winds enervating, moist winds unhealthy. We must, therefore, avoid mistakes in this matter and beware of the common experience of many communities. For example, Mytilene in the island of Lesbos is a town built with magnificence and good taste, but its position shows a lack of foresight. In that community when the wind is south, the people fall ill; when it is northwest, it sets them coughing; with a north wind they do indeed recover but cannot stand about in the alleys and streets, owing to the severe cold.

2. Wind is a flowing wave of air, moving hither and thither indefinitely. It is produced when heat meets moisture, the rush of heat generating a mighty current of air. That this is the fact we may learn from bronze eolipiles, and thus by means of a scientific invention discover a divine truth lurking in the laws of the heavens. Eolipiles are hollow bronze balls, with a very small opening through which water is poured into them. Set before a fire, not a breath issues from them before they get warm; but as soon as they begin to boil, out comes a strong blast due to the fire. Thus from this slight and very short experiment we may understand and judge of the mighty and wonderful laws of the heavens and the nature of winds.

3. By shutting out the winds from our dwellings, therefore, we shall not only make the place healthful for people who are well, but also in the case of diseases due perhaps to unfavourable situations elsewhere, the patients, who in other healthy places might be cured by a different form of treatment, will here be more quickly cured by the mildness that comes from the shutting out of the winds. The diseases which are hard to cure in neighbourhoods such as those to which I have referred above are catarrh, hoarseness, coughs, pleurisy, consumption, spitting of blood, and all others that are cured not by lowering the system but by building it up. They are hard to cure, first, because they are originally due to chills; secondly, because the patient's system being already exhausted by disease, the air there, which is in constant agitation owing to winds and therefore deteriorated, takes all the sap of life out of their diseased bodies and leaves them more meagre every day. On the other hand, a mild, thick air, without draughts and not constantly blowing back and forth, builds up their frames by its unwavering steadiness, and so strengthens and restores people who are afflicted with these diseases.

4. Some have held that there are only four winds: Solanus from due east; Auster from the south; Favonius from due west; Septentrio from the north. But more careful investigators tell us that there are eight. Chief among such was Andronicus of Cyrrhus who in proof built the marble octagonal tower in Athens. On the several sides of the octagon he executed reliefs representing the several winds, each facing the point from which it blows; and on top of the tower he set a conical shaped piece of marble and on this a bronze Triton with a rod outstretched in its right hand. It was so contrived as to go round with the wind, always stopping to face the breeze and holding its rod as a pointer directly over the representation of the wind that was blowing.

5. Thus Eurus is placed to the southeast between Solanus and Auster: Africus to the southwest between Auster and Favonius; Caurus, or, as many call it, Corus, between Favonius and Septentrio; and Aquilo between Septentrio and Solanus. Such, then, appears to have been his device, including the numbers and names of the wind and indicating the directions from which particular winds blow. These facts being thus determined, to find the directions and quarters of the winds your method of procedure should be as follows.

6. In the middle of the city place a marble amussium, laying it true by the level, or else let the spot be made so true by means of rule and level that no amussium is necessary. In the very centre of that spot set up a bronze gnomon or "shadow tracker" (in Greek [Greek: skiathêras]). At about the fifth hour in the morning, take the end of the shadow cast by this gnomon, and mark it with a point. Then, opening your compasses to this point which marks the length of the gnomon›s shadow, describe a circle from the centre. In the afternoon watch the shadow of your gnomon as it lengthens, and when it once more touches the circumference of this circle and the shadow in the afternoon is equal in length to that of the morning, mark it with a point.

7. From these two points describe with your compasses intersecting arcs, and through their intersection and the centre let a line be drawn to the circumference of the circle to give us the quarters of south and north. Then, using a sixteenth part of the entire circumference of the circle as a diameter, describe a circle with its centre on the line to the south, at the point where it crosses the circumference, and put points to the right and left on the circumference on the south side, repeating the process on the north side. From the four points thus obtained draw lines intersecting the centre from one side of the circumference to the other. Thus we shall have an eighth part of the circumference set out for Auster and another for Septentrio. The rest of the entire circumference is then to be divided into three equal parts on each side, and thus we have designed a figure equally apportioned among the eight winds. Then let the directions of your streets and alleys be laid down on the lines of division between the quarters of two winds.

8. On this principle of arrangement the disagreeable force of the winds will be shut out from dwellings and lines of houses. For if the streets run full in the face of the winds, their constant blasts rushing in from the open country, and then confined by narrow alleys, will sweep through them with great violence. The lines of houses must therefore be directed away from the quarters from which the winds blow, so that as they come in they may strike against the angles of the blocks and their force thus be broken and dispersed.

9. Those who know names for very many winds will perhaps be surprised at our setting forth that there are only eight. Remembering, however, that Eratosthenes of Cyrene, employing mathematical theories and geometrical methods, discovered from the course of the sun, the shadows cast by an equinoctial gnomon, and the inclination of the heaven that the circumference of the earth is two hundred and fifty-two thousand stadia, that is, thirty-one one million five hundred thousand paces, and observing that an eighth part of this, occupied by a wind, is three million nine hundred and thirty-seven thousand five hundred paces, they should not be surprised to find that a single wind, ranging over so wide a field, is subject to shifts this way and that, leading to a variety of breezes.

10. So we often have Leuconotus and Altanus blowing respectively to the right and left of Auster; Libonotus and Subvesperus to the right and left of Africus; Argestes, and at certain periods the Etesiae, on either side of Favonius; Circias and Corus on the sides of Caurus; Thracias and Gallicus on either side of Septentrio; Supernas and Caecias to the right and left of Aquilo; Carbas, and at a certain period the Ornithiae, on either side of Solanus; while Eurocircias and Volturnus blow on the flanks of Eurus which is between them. There are also many other names for winds derived from localities or from the squalls which sweep from rivers or down mountains.

11. Then, too, there are the breezes of early morning; for the sun on emerging from beneath the earth strikes humid air as he returns, and as he goes climbing up the sky he spreads it out before him, extracting breezes from the vapour that was there before the dawn. Those that still blow on after sunrise are classed with Eurus, and hence appears to come the Greek name [Greek: euros] as the child of the breezes, and the word for "to-morrow," [Greek: aurion], named from the early morning breezes. Some people do indeed say that Eratosthenes could not have inferred the true measure of the earth. Whether true or untrue, it cannot affect the truth of what I have written on the fixing of the quarters from which the different winds blow.

12. If he was wrong, the only result will be that the individual winds may blow, not with the scope expected from his measurement, but with powers either more or less widely extended. For the readier understanding of these topics, since I have treated them with brevity, it has seemed best to me to give two figures, or, as the Greeks say, [Greek: schêmata], at the end of this book: one designed to show the precise quarters from which the winds arise; the other, how by turning the directions of the rows of houses and the streets away from their full force, we may avoid unhealthy blasts. Let A be the centre of a plane surface, and B the point to which the shadow of the gnomon reaches in the morning. Taking A as the centre, open the compasses to the point B, which marks the shadow, and describe a circle. Put the gnomon back where it was before and wait for the shadow to lessen and grow again until in the afternoon it is equal to its length in the morning, touching the circumference at the point C. Then from the points B and C describe with the compasses two arcs intersecting at D. Next draw a line from the point of intersection D through the centre of the circle to the circumference and call it E F. This line will show where the south and north lie.

13. Then find with the compasses a sixteenth part of the entire circumference; then centre the compasses on the point E where the line to the south touches the circumference, and set off the points G and H to the right and left of E. Likewise on the north side, centre the compasses on the circumference at the point F on the line to the north, and set off the points I and K to the right and left; then draw lines through the centre from G to K and from H to I. Thus the space from G to H will belong to Auster and the south, and the space from I to K will be that of Septentrio. The rest of the circumference is to be divided equally into three parts on the right and three on the left, those to the east at the points L and M, those to the west at the points N and O. Finally, intersecting lines are to be drawn from M to O and from L to N. Thus we shall have the circumference divided into eight equal spaces for the winds. The figure being finished, we shall have at the eight different divisions, beginning at the south, the letter G between Eurus and Auster, H between Auster and Africus, N between Africus and Favonius, O between Favonius and Caurus, K between Caurus and Septentrio, I between Septentrio and Aquilo, L between Aquilo and Solanus, and M between Solanus and Eurus. This done, apply a gnomon to these eight divisions and thus fix the directions of the different alleys.

Chapter VII

The Sites For Public Buildings

1. Having laid out the alleys and determined the streets, we have next to treat of the choice of building sites for temples, the forum, and all other public places, with a view to general convenience and utility. If the city is on the sea, we should choose ground close to the harbour as the place where the forum is to be built; but if inland, in the middle of the town. For the temples, the sites for those of the gods under whose particular protection the state is thought to rest and for Jupiter, Juno, and Minerva, should be on the very highest point commanding a view of the greater part of the city. Mercury should be in the forum, or, like Isis and Serapis, in the emporium: Apollo and Father Bacchus near the theatre: Hercules at the circus in communities which have no gymnasia nor amphitheatres; Mars outside the city but at the training ground, and so Venus, but at the harbour. It is moreover shown by the Etruscan diviners in treatises on their science that the fanes of Venus, Vulcan, and Mars should be situated outside the walls, in order that the young men and married women may not become habituated in the city to the temptations incident to the worship of Venus, and that buildings may be free from the terror of fires through the religious rites and sacrifices which call the power of Vulcan beyond

the walls. As for Mars, when that divinity is enshrined outside the walls, the citizens will never take up arms against each other, and he will defend the city from its enemies and save it from danger in war. 2. Ceres also should be outside the city in a place to which people need never go except for the purpose of sacrifice. That place should be under the protection of religion, purity, and good morals. Proper sites should be set apart for the precincts of the other gods according to the nature of the sacrifices offered to them.

The principle governing the actual construction of temples and their symmetry I shall explain in my third and fourth books. In the second I have thought it best to give an account of the materials used in buildings with their good qualities and advantages, and then in the succeeding books to describe and explain the proportions of buildings, their arrangements, and the different forms of symmetry.

Book 1 of On the Nature of Things: De Rerum Natura

By Lucretius, translated by Walter Englert

Mother of the descendants of Aeneas,[1] pleasure of humans and gods,
lifegiving Venus, it is you who beneath the gliding signs
of heaven makes the ship-bearing sea and the fruitful earth
teem with life, since through you the whole race of living creatures
5   is conceived, born, and gazes on the light of the sun.
You, goddess, you the winds flee, you the clouds
of the sky flee at your coming, for you earth the artificer
sends up her sweet flowers, for you the expanses of the sea smile,
and the heavens, now peaceful, shine with diffused light.
10   For as soon as the sight of a spring day is revealed,
and the life-bringing breeze of the west wind is released and blows,
the birds of the air are the first to announce you and your arrival,
o goddess, overpowered in their hearts by your force.
Next wild beasts and flocks prance about their glad pastures

---

1   The "descendants of Aeneas" are the Romans. According to legend, Aeneas was a Trojan hero who, after the fall of Troy to the Greeks, led a group of Trojans to Italy and founded a city. His descendants eventually founded the city of Rome. The story of Aeneas' journey to Italy and actions there are told in Virgil's *Aeneid*, written thirty to forty years after Lucretius' poem.

15 and swim across rushing streams. So taken by delight
each follows you eagerly wherever you proceed to lead them.
Then through the seas and mountains and fast-clutching rivers,
through the leaf-thronged home of birds and the verdant plains,
you strike, injecting sweet love into the hearts of all,

20 and make them eagerly create their off spring, each according to kind.
Since you alone guide the nature of things
and without you nothing emerges into the sunlit shores
of light, nothing glad or lovely comes into being,
I am eagerly striving for you to be my ally in writing these verses

25 that I am trying to set out about the nature of things
for our illustrious son of the Memmii,[2] whom you, goddess, on every
occasion have wished to be preeminent, adorned with every blessing.
All the more endow these words with everlasting charm, goddess.
Meanwhile, make it so that the savage claims of war

30 are put to sleep and lie quiet throughout every sea and land.
For you alone have the power to bring aid to mortals
with tranquil peace, since Mars, strong in arms, rules
the savage claims of war, and he often lets himself sink
into your lap, completely overcome by the unceasing wound of love.

35 And so gazing upwards, bending back his smooth neck,
he gapes at you, goddess, and feeds his hungry eyes with love.
And as he lies there, his breath hangs on your lips.
Goddess, with your blessed body flow down around him
as he reclines, and pour forth sweet words from your mouth,

40 o glorious one, seeking gentle peace for the Romans.
For neither can I perform my task with a tranquil mind
when our country is in trouble, nor can the shining offspring of the Memmii
fail to attend to the safety of the state at such times.
For it must be that the entire nature of the gods

45 spends everlasting time enjoying perfect peace,
far removed and long separated from our concerns.
For free from all anxiety, free from dangers,
powerful in its own resources, having no need of us,
it is not won over by the good things we do nor touched by anger.[3]

---

2 The poem is addressed to a Roman named Memmius, probably Gaius Memmius, the patron of the Roman poet Catullus.
3 1.44–49 = 2.646–651.

50   For the rest, turn open ears and a sharp mind

set free from cares to the true system of philosophy,

so that you do not despise and abandon my gifts to you,

set out with constant eagerness, before they are understood.

For I am beginning to set out for you the deepest workings

55   of the heavens and the gods, and to reveal the first beginnings[4] of things

out of which nature creates all things, and increases and maintains them,

and into which nature dissolves them again once they have perished.

These we are accustomed, in setting forth our account, to call "matter" and "the generating

bodies of things" and to name them

"the seeds of things," and to use the term

60   "first bodies" for them,

because all things exist from these first beginnings.[5]

It used to be that human life, polluted, was lying

in the dirt before our eyes, crushed by the weight of religion,

which stretched out its head on display from the regions of heaven, threatening mortals from above with

65   its horrible-looking face.

It was a Greek man[6] who first dared to raise his mortal eyes

against religion, and who first fought back against it.

Neither the stories about the gods, nor thunderbolts, nor the sky with its threatening rumbles

held him back, but provoked

all the more the fierce sharpness of his

70   mind, so that he desired

to be the first to shatter the imprisoning bolts of the gates of nature. As a result the vital force

of his mind was victorious,

and he traveled far beyond the flaming walls of the world

and trekked throughout the measureless universe in mind and spirit. As victor he brings back from there the

75   knowledge of what can come to be,

what cannot, in short, by what process each thing

has its power limited, and its deep-set boundary stone.

And so the tables are turned. Religion lies crushed

---

4   "The first beginnings" = *primordia*, one of the Latin terms Lucretius uses for "atoms." Lucretius never uses the Greek term *atomoi* ("atoms") in the poem.

5   As just noted, Lucretius does not transliterate Epicurus' Greek term for atom (*atomos*, literally "unable to be cut") into Latin, but instead uses a number of different Latin terms to get at the idea.

6   Epicurus (341–271 BC), the founder of Epicureanism and the philosophical hero of Lucretius' poem.

beneath our feet, and his victory raises us to the sky.

I am afraid of one thing in all this: that

80   you might think

that you are starting on the first steps of an unholy system of thought, and are walking the path of crime. On the contrary, it has happened too often

that this so-called religion has produced criminal and unholy actions. Thus was the case at Aulis when the chosen leaders of

85   the Greeks, the first among men, foully defiled the altar

of the virgin goddess of the crossroads[7] with the blood of Iphianassa.[8] As soon as the sacrificial headband was wreathed about her virgin locks

with its streamers flowing down equally from both her cheeks,

and as soon as she saw her father standing in mourning before the altar,

90   with his attendants beside him concealing the iron blade,

and the citizens pouring forth tears at the sight of her,

speechless with fear she sank in her knees and fell to the ground. Nor was it a help to the wretched girl at such a moment

that she had been the first child to call the king "father."

95   She was lifted up by men's hands and led trembling

to the altar, not so that she might be greeted by the loud-ringing marriage hymn when the solemn wedding rite was finished,

but that the chaste girl might be slaughtered unchastely at the very point

of marriage, a grieving victim, by the sacrificial stroke of her father.

100   All this so that a happy and auspicious departure might be granted to the fleet.

Such great evils could religion make seem advisable.

Even you today at some time or other will be overcome

by the fearful words of seers and try to desert us.

Why not, since so many are the dreams they can now

105   invent for you which can overturn the guiding principles of your life and throw all your fortunes into complete confusion with fear!

And deservedly so. For if people saw that there is a fixed limit

to oppressive cares, with some reason they would be strong enough to fight back against religious beliefs and the threats of seers.

---

7   "Virgin goddess of the crossroads" = Diana (Artemis in Greek).

8   Iphianassa is the name Homer used for Iphigenia, the daughter of Agamemnon and Clytemnestra. Artemis forced Agamemnon and the Greeks to sacrifice Iphigenia before the Greeks could sail to Troy at the beginning of the Trojan War. The story of her sacrifice was retold in many 5th c. BC Greek tragedies, including Euripides' *Iphigenia at Aulis*, and Aeschylus' *Agamemnon*.

110 As it is, there is no means of resisting, no power,
   since death must bring with it the fear of eternal punishment.
   For people do not know what the nature of the soul is.
   Is it born, or does it work its way into us as we are being born?
   Does it perish when we do, torn apart by death,

115 or does it go to see the shades of Orcus[9] and its desolate pits?
   Or does it work its way by divine aid into other creatures,
   as our Ennius[10] proclaimed? He was the first to bring down
   a crown of everlasting foliage from lovely Mount Helicon[11]
   to become famous throughout the Italian tribes of people.

120 And yet moreover Ennius still sets forth
   in his everlasting verses that there really are regions of Acheron, where neither our souls nor
   our bodies remain,
   but certain kinds of shades pale in wondrous ways.
   He recalls how from that region the shade of Homer, forever

125 blooming, rose before him and began to shed salty
   tears, setting out in words the nature of things.
   Therefore we must not only give a correct account of celestial matters, explaining in what way
   the wanderings of the sun
   and moon occur and by what power things happen on earth.
   We must also take special care and

130 employ keen reasoning
   to see where the soul and the nature of the mind come from,
   and what it is that meets our minds and terrifies us when
   we are awake and suffering from disease, and when we are buried in sleep,
   so that we seem to hear and see face to face people

135 who have already met death and whose bones the earth embraces. Nor does it escape my
   thought that it is difficult to throw light
   upon the obscure discoveries of the Greeks in Latin verses, especially since we must use new
   words for many things
   because of the poverty of our language and the newness of the subject matter.

140 But still it is your excellence and the pleasure of the sweet friendship I hope to have with you
   that urges me to undergo hardship however great and to keep my watch in the quiet of the
   night

---

9 "The shades of Orcus" = the underworld.
10 Ennius (239–169 BC) was one of the greatest early Roman poets. For Ennius, see Introduction p. xix.
11 Mt. Helicon, located in Boeotia in Greece, was the home of the Muses.

as I try to find the right words and poem with which at last
I might be able to hold a clear light up to your mind
145 that will allow you to see deeply into obscure matters.
Therefore this fear and darkness of the mind must be shattered
apart not by the rays of the sun and the clear shafts
of the day but by the external appearance and inner law of nature.[12] Its first principle will take
its starting point for us as follows:
150 nothing ever comes to be from nothing through divine intervention.[13]
The reason that fear so dominates all mortals is
because they see many things happen on earth and in the heavens the causes of whose
activities they are able in no way
to understand, and they imagine they take place through divine power.
155 For which reason, when we see that nothing can be created from nothing,
then we will more correctly perceive what we are after:
the source from which each thing is created, and the way
each thing happens without divine intervention.
For if things came to be from nothing, every kind of thing
160 could be born from all things, and nothing would need a seed.
Men might sprout from the sea and the scaly race
of fishes from the earth, and birds might hatch from the sky.
Cattle and other livestock, and every kind of beast,
with uncertain birth would inhabit farms and wilderness alike.
165 Trees would not consistently produce the same fruit,
but they would change, and all trees could bear all fruit.
Since there would not be generating bodies for each thing,
how could there be a fixed and constant mother for things?
But now, since all things are created from fixed seeds,
170 each thing is born and emerges into the shores of light
from the source of the matter and first bodies of each thing.
And thus all things are unable to be born from all things,
because there is a separate power present in fixed things.
And why do we see roses in the spring, grain in the heat,
175 or vines bursting forth in response to autumn's call?

---

12 1.146–148 = 3.91–93.

13 This is the first major law of Epicurean physics: Nothing can come to be out of nothing. Cf. Epicurus' *Letter to Herodotus* 38 ("First, nothing comes into being out of what does not exist"). Lucretius' words in 150, "through divine intervention," appear to be his own addition.

Is it not because whatever is created becomes visible

in its own time when fixed seeds have flowed together,

while favorable seasons are at hand and the lively earth safely brings forth tender things into the shores of light?

180 But if they came to be from nothing, they would suddenly spring forth at random periods of time and during unsuitable parts of the year, seeing that there would be no first beginnings which would be able to be kept apart from generating union at an unfavorable time.

Nor further, in order for things to increase, would there need to be time

185 for seeds to come together, if they were able to grow from nothing.

For tiny babies would suddenly become young adults,

and trees would rise up and leap from the earth in an instant.

It is obvious that none of these things happens, since everything increases little by little, as is fitting for fixed seed,

190 and preserves their kind as they increase. Thus you can recognize that each thing grows and is nourished from its own matter.

In addition, without dependable rains each year

the earth is unable to produce its joy-bringing crops,

nor is the nature of living creatures, if deprived of food,

195 able to reproduce its race and safeguard its life.

You should thus believe all the more that many bodies are common to many things, as we see letters are common to words,

rather than that anything is able to exist without first beginnings. Next, why was nature unable to produce men

200 so large that they could cross the ocean by walking through the shallows,

rip apart huge mountains with their bare hands,

and succeed in living through many ages of living creatures,

unless it is because fixed matter has been assigned to things

for their growth, from which it is determined what is able to come to be?

205 So it must be confessed that nothing is able to come from nothing, since things have a need for seed by which they all can,

when created, be brought forth into the soft breezes of the air. Finally, since we see that cultivated lands are better than uncultivated, and produce better crops when they are cared for by our hands,

210 it is clear that there exist in the earth the first beginnings of things which we stir into being when we turn over the fertile clods

with a plough and work the soil of the earth from deep down.

But if there were not first beginnings, you would see everything come to be much better on its own without our efforts.

215 Next is this: nature dissolves each thing back
into its particles and does not destroy things into nothing.[14]
For if anything were mortal in all its parts, each thing
would perish by being snatched suddenly from before our eyes.
For no need would exist for a force that was able to arrange

220 the destruction of the parts of each thing and dissolve its structure. But as it is, since each
thing is composed out of eternal seed,
until a force is present that hammers apart the thing with a blow
or penetrates within through empty spaces and dissolves it,
nature does not allow the destruction of anything to be seen.

225 And if time annihilates whatever it removes through the aging process, consuming all the
matter, from where would Venus restore
the living race each according to kind, or from where
does earth the sweet artificer nourish and increase them
once restored, providing them with food each according to kind?

230 From where would internal springs and external, far-off rivers supply the sea? From where
would the sky feed the stars?
For infinite time gone by and the passing days
ought to have consumed everything that has a mortal structure.
But if in this duration and time gone by there have been

235 things from which this sum of things is restored and exists,
they are without any doubt endowed with an immortal nature. Therefore everything cannot
be changed back into nothing.
Next, the same force and cause would destroy everything indiscriminately, unless they were
held together by an eternal stuff

240 entangled to a lesser or greater degree in its interconnections with itself.
Indeed a mere touch would undoubtedly be a sufficient cause
of death, especially seeing that there would be nothing with eternal body
whose texture a special force would be required to dissolve.
But as things are, since there are various interconnections

245 of the first beginnings with themselves and matter is everlasting, things persist with their
bodies sound, until a force found sufficiently strong to overcome their textures meets them.
Thus not one thing returns to nothing, but all things
when they split apart return to the first bodies of matter.

---

14   This is the second major law of Epicurean physics: Nothing can be destroyed into nothing, or everything would cease to be. Cf. Epicurus' *Letter to Herodotus* 39 ("And if what disappears had perished into what is not, all things would have perished, since what they were dissolved into does not exist.").

250 Lastly, the rains pass away, when father sky
    sends them down into the lap of mother earth.
    But glistening crops erupt and branches turn green on trees,
    while the trees themselves grow and are weighed down by fruit. Hence further our race and
    the race of beasts are fed,
255 hence we see glad cities flower with children
    and lush forests everywhere sing with young birds.
    Hence cows exhausted by their fat lay their bodies
    down on the joyful pasture and the glistening moisture of milk
    drips from their distended udders. Hence new calves
260 play and frolic on shaky limbs in the soft grass,
    their tender young minds drunk on pure milk.
    Thus all things that are visible do not perish completely,
    since nature remakes one thing from another, nor does she allow anything to be born unless
    it is aided by another's death.
265 Come now, since I have shown that things cannot be created from nothing,
    and likewise that once created they cannot be reduced to nothing, lest by any chance you still
    begin to doubt my words,
    since you cannot see the first beginnings of things with your eyes,
    let me remind you besides that there are bodies which you must admit
270 exist in things and yet are not able to be seen.
    First, when the force of the wind is whipped up it lashes
    at the sea, overwhelming huge ships and scattering the clouds. Rushing along at times with a
    quick whirlwind it strews
    the plains with great trees and attacks the mountain tops
275 with forest-cracking blasts. So the wind with its shrill howling rages wildly, shrieking savagely
    and moaning with menace.
    It is therefore beyond doubt that there are invisible bodies of wind which sweep over the
    sea, the lands, and the clouds of the sky, buffeting them and snatching them up in a sudden
    whirlwind.
280 They flow along and breed destruction in the same way
    as when the soothing nature of water is carried off suddenly
    in an overflowing river, when it has been swollen after heavy rains by a tremendous rush of
    water coming off the high mountains.
    It tosses shattered branches from the forests and whole trees,
285 and not even sturdy bridges can withstand the sudden force
    of the approaching water. Stirred up by the heavy rains,
    the river rushes against the pilings with effective force.

It wreaks a deafening havoc and beneath its waves it rolls
huge rocks, rushing against whatever opposes its flow.
290 Therefore so too should the blasts of wind be carried along,
which, whenever they have spread out in any direction
like a powerful river, drive things before them and rush at them
with constant force, and now and then in a twisting gust
they seize them and quickly carry them off in a spinning whirlwind.
295 Therefore again and again there are invisible bodies of wind,
since they have been found to rival mighty rivers in what
they do and in how they act, and rivers have bodies we can see. Second, we experience the
different kinds of smells things have,
but nonetheless we never see the smells coming to our noses.
300 We do not see warm heat, nor can we apprehend
cold with our eyes, nor are we in the habit of seeing voices.
But it must be that all these things are bodily
by nature, since they are able to set the sense organs in motion.
For nothing is able to touch or be touched except body.
Third, clothes hung along the wave-beaten shore
grow damp, but they dry when spread out in the sun.
But we neither see how the dampness of the water settled on them, nor again how it was
forced out owing to the heat.
This shows that the moisture is split up into small
310 particles that the eye is in no way able to see.
Fourth, as the sun completes its journey year after year
a ring on the finger grows thinner beneath with wear,
the fall of water-drops hollows out a stone, the curved
iron plow of a farmer shrinks imperceptibly in the fields,
315 and we see that people's feet today are wearing down
the stone surfaces of the street. Then too near the gates of the city bronze statues extend right hands thinned
by the frequent touch of those who pass by and greet them.
These then we see diminish, since they have been worn away.
320 But the jealous nature of vision blocks our seeing which
bodies move away at any given time.
Finally, whatever time and nature gradually add
to things, compelling them to grow in due measure,
no sharpness of vision, no matter how it strains, is able to see.

325 Moreover, neither when things age by the wasting of time,
    nor when rocks overhanging the sea are eaten away by the devouring salt are you able to see
    at the time what they are losing.
    This is proof that nature conducts her business with invisible bodies.
    But all things are not held packed tightly
330 together everywhere by the nature of body, for there is void in things. Understanding this will
    be useful to you in many matters.
    It will prevent you from wandering around, always doubting and seeking
    after the nature of reality, and from lacking faith in my words. Therefore there exists intangible
    space, void, and emptiness.
335 If void did not exist, there is no way things
    would be able to move. For that which is the natural role[15] of body, to roll in the way and
    obstruct, would be present at all times
    for all things. Therefore nothing would be able
    to move forward, because nothing would provide a beginning of yielding.
340 Yet now through the oceans and lands and the heights of heaven
    we see before our eyes many things move by many
    means and in various ways. If void did not exist,
    these things would not only be deprived of and lack
    restless motion, but would never have been brought to birth at all,
345 since everywhere matter would be still, packed tightly together. Besides, however solid things
    might be thought to be,
    nevertheless you may tell their bodies are loose-knit from this:
    in rocks in caves the liquid moisture of water seeps
    and trickles through, and everything weeps with plentiful drops.
350 Food is distributed into every part of an animal's body.
    Trees grow and bear fruit at the proper time,
    because food is distributed throughout all the parts of trees,
    from the deepest roots, through the trunks, and throughout all the branches.
    Voices travel through walls and fly across closed-off
355 rooms in houses, stiffening cold penetrates to the bone.
    These things you would never see happen in any way
    unless there were empty spaces through which individual bodies pass. And next, why do we
    see that some things exceed
    others in weight, although they are no different in size?

---

15 "Role…roll" is an attempt to get at Lucretius' play on words with *officium* ("duty, function, job, role") and *officere* ("to block, get in the way").

360 For if there is the same amount of body in a ball of wool
as there is in a ball of lead, it is fair to suppose they weigh
the same, since it is the role of body to press everything downward. But in contrast it is the
nature of the void to persist without weight.
Therefore whatever is equal in size but is observed to be lighter
365 without doubt shows that it possesses more void.
But in contrast the heavier thing declares that there is more body in it and that it has within
much less empty space.
Therefore it is certain that what we have been searching for with keen reasoning, what we call
void, exists, mixed in things.
370 In order that what some assert in these matters not be able
to lead you from the truth, I feel compelled to outstrip their argument. They say that water
yields to scaly creatures as they strive
and opens fluid paths, because fish leave spaces
behind them where the waters as they yield are able to flow together.
375 So too they say that other things are able to move
among themselves and change place, although all is full.
This all has of course been accepted on false reasoning.
For where can the scaly creatures go forward after all,
if water does not give space? Furthermore where will the waves
380 be able to give place, when the fish will not be able to go?
Therefore either all bodies must be deprived of motion,
or it must be admitted that void is mixed in things, from which source each thing takes its
first beginning of motion.
Finally, if two broad bodies suddenly leap
385 apart from their union, it is of course necessary that air fill
up all the void which is created between the bodies.
Yet however fast the breezes circulate with which the air
flows together, still the entire space would never be able
to be filled up at one time. For the air must
390 occupy each space in succession, before all are occupied.
But if someone by chance should happen to think that this occurs when the bodies leap apart
because the air compresses itself,
he errs. For then a vacuum is created which did not exist
before and likewise a vacuum is filled which existed before,
395 nor is air able to be condensed in any such way
nor, if it could, could it, I think, without void
contract into itself and gather its parts into one.

Wherefore although you delay by raising many objections,
it is nevertheless necessary to admit that void is present in things.

400 And moreover by relating many arguments to you I am able
to scrape together trust in these words of mine.
But these little traces are enough for a keen intellect,
and by their means you are able to discover the rest on your own.
For just as dogs often find with their noses the resting places,

405 covered by foliage, of a wild beast that roams the mountains,
as soon as they set to work on the sure traces of its path,
so you yourself on your own will be able in such cases
to see one thing from another and to work your way into every
dark hiding place and drag back the truth from them.

410 But if you show hesitation or turn aside a little from your task,
I am able to promise this clearly to you, Memmius:
such large draughts from deep fountains will my sweet
tongue pour out from my well-stocked mind
that I am afraid that slow-moving old age will creep

415 through our limbs and dissolve the bonds of life in both of us
before the whole abundant supply of arguments in my poem
on any particular point has been sent flying through your ears.
But now to return to weave in words what I have begun:
the nature of the universe, then, as it is in itself, is made

420 up of two things; for there are bodies and void.
Bodies are located in the void and move in it this way and that.
For ordinary perception declares by itself that body exists.
Unless trust in perception is firmly founded and flourishes,
in the case of hidden things there will be nothing to which we can refer

425 to prove anything at all with the reasoning power of the mind.
Then again if there were no place and space, which we call void, bodies would never be able
to have location nor to travel
at all in this way and that in any direction.
This is what I have already showed you a little while ago.[16]

430 In addition to this, there is nothing you are able to name which is distinct
and separated off apart from all body and the void,
which can be discovered to be some third type of nature.

---

16   1.335–345, 370–383.

For whatever will exist, this will have to be something itself.

Now if it will be subject to touch, no matter how light and tiny, (435)

435 it will, by an increase either great or at least small, if it does exist, (434) increase the number
of body and be part of the sum of the whole.

But if it will not be subject to touch, and is able from no side
to stop anything which is traveling from passing through it,
it will of course be what we call empty void.

440 In addition, whatever will exist by itself either will act on something or will have to suffer
other things acting upon it,
or will be such that things are able to exist and move in it.
But nothing is able to act or be acted upon without body,
nor again to provide place unless what is void and empty.

445 Therefore besides void and bodies there can remain by itself
among the number of things no third nature
that could come and make contact with our senses at any time
or that anyone might be able to grasp with the reasoning power of the mind.
For all things that have a name, either you will find that they are properties

450 of these two things or you will see that they are accidents of them.
A property is that which is never able to be disjoined
and separated off without a fatally harmful disintegration,
as weight is to rocks, heat to fire, fluidity is to water,
tangibility to all bodies, and intangibility to void.

455 Slavery, on the other hand, and poverty and wealth,
freedom, war, peace, and other things at whose
arrival and departure the nature of things remains unharmed,
we are accustomed to call, as is right, accidents.
Time likewise does not exist independently, but from things themselves

460 comes a sense of what has happened in ages past, then what
thing looms before us, and then further what will follow.
No one, it must be confessed, senses time through itself,
separated off from the motion and the quiet immobility of things.
Indeed when they say the daughter of Tyndareus[17] was raped and the Trojan

465 peoples were subdued in war, we must beware that they do not accidentally
force us to admit that these things exist on their own
just because an age which is past and can't be called back
took away these races of men, whose accidents these were.

---

17 Helen of Troy.

For whatever will have happened will be able to be called an accident,
470 on the one hand of the lands, on the other of the regions of space themselves.
Indeed if there had been no material for things, nor place
and space, in which all things are carried out,
never would the fire, fanned by love for the beautiful shape
of Tyndareus' daughter, glistening in the Phrygian heart of Alexander,
475 have ignited the glowing contests of savage war,
nor unbeknownst to the Trojans would the wooden horse have set fire to Pergama by giving
birth to Greeks at night.
You can see, then, that absolutely all things that occur
never are nor exist through themselves as body does,
480 nor are they spoken of in the same sense as void is,
but rather so that you can rightly call them events
of body and place, in which all things are carried on.
Bodies, moreover, are partly the first beginnings of things,
partly the things that are formed by the assemblage of first beginnings.
485 But those that are the first beginnings of things, no force is strong enough
to destroy. For with solid body they are victorious in the end.[18]
And yet it seems difficult to believe that anything
can be found with solid body among things that exist.
For lightning from heaven makes its way through the walls of houses,
490 as do shouts and voices. Iron glows with heat in the fire,
and rocks burst apart because of fierce blazing heat.
The unyielding hardness of gold is loosened and dissolved by heat, and the ice of bronze is
overcome by flame and melts.
Heat and penetrating cold seep through silver,
495 seeing that we have felt both as we solemnly hold our cups
in hand and the dew of water is poured in from above.
To such an extent does there seem to be no solidity in things.
But nevertheless because true reason and the nature of things compels us, stand by me, until
I explain in a few verses
500 that there are things which exist with solid and eternal body,
which we are demonstrating to be the seeds and first beginnings of things,
from where now exists the entire created sum of things.
First, since the twofold nature of the two
things has been found to exist far different,

---

18 i.e., the first beginnings are so strong and solid that nothing can destroy them.

505 that is of body and of place, in which all things occur,

     each must be in and for itself, and unmixed.

     For wherever there is empty space, which we call void,

     there is no body. And wherever body is located,

     there empty space will never exist.

510 Therefore the first bodies are solid and without void.

     Moreover, since void is present in created things,

     it must be that solid matter exists around it.

     And there is nothing that can be shown by true reasoning

     to conceal void with its body and to have it within,

515 unless you admit that what holds it in is solid.

     Now that thing can be nothing except an assemblage

     of matter, which is able to contain the void in things.

     Matter, therefore, which exists with a solid body,

     is able to be eternal, when all other bodies are dissolved.

520 Then further, if there were nothing which was empty void,

     all would be solid. In contrast, unless there were definite bodies which fill up whatever places they hold,

     all that is would exist as vacant and empty space.

     Therefore without doubt body has been alternately marked off

525 from void, since the universe is neither completely full

     nor yet empty. There are, therefore, definite bodies

     which are able to mark off empty from occupied space.

     These bodies cannot be struck and dissolved by external

     blows, nor can they be penetrated and undone from deep within.

530 Nor can they be attacked and grow weak in another way,

     as I demonstrated to you above a little while ago.[19]

     For it seems clear that unless a thing has void in it

     it cannot be crushed, broken, or split by being cut in two,

     nor can it take in water, seeping cold,

535 and penetrating fire, by which all things are destroyed.

     And the more void each thing contains within,

     the more it is attacked by these things deep within and is weakened. Therefore if the primary

     bodies are solid and are without void,

     just as I have demonstrated, they must necessarily be eternal.

540 Moreover, unless matter had been eternal, before now

     all things would have been completely reduced to nothing

---

19 1.215–264, 485–502

and whatever we see would have been born again from nothing.
But since I have shown above that nothing is able to be created
from nothing and that what has been made cannot be recalled to nothing,

545   the first beginnings must be endowed with immortal bodies,
into which all things can be dissolved in their final moments,
so that matter can be supplied for the re-creation of things. Therefore primary bodies exist in
their solid singleness,
for in no other way can they be kept safe forever

550   from an infinite time past and recreate things again.
In addition, if nature had established no end
to the breaking apart of things, the bodies of matter now
would have been reduced to such a state by the breakage of earlier ages that nothing could be
conceived from them within a fixed amount

555   of time and reach the full limit of its age.
For we see that anything can be dissolved more quickly
than it can be rebuilt. Therefore whatever the infinitely long
span of days of all time that has gone before
had broken apart up until now by demolishing and dissolving,

560   never could it have been created again in the time that remains.
But of course a limit of breaking apart has been established
and remains fixed, since we see that each thing is recreated
and that a finite amount of time for each generation of things
exists, in which they are able to attain the flower of their life.

565   In addition, although the bodies of matter are totally solid,
it is still possible to explain how all those things
which are made soft (air, water, earth, and fires)[20]
are made and by what force they are all borne along,
when once void has been mixed up in things.

570   But on the contrary, if the first bodies of things were soft,
from what source strong flints and iron were created,
no explanation could be given. For all nature
will completely lack the starting point for a foundation.
Therefore the primary bodies are solid, powerful in their singleness.

575   Through a more tightly condensed union of them, all things
can be riveted together and display impressive strength.
Further, if no end has been appointed to the breaking apart

---

20   These are the four elements of the Presocratic philosopher Empedocles. Lucretius argues against Empedocles below in
lines 716–829.

of bodies, yet it is necessary that from time eternal bodies
of each kind of thing survive even now,
580   which have not yet been attacked by any danger.
But since they exist endowed with a fragile nature,
it is inconsistent to think that they have been able to survive for all time when they have been
buffeted by innumerable blows throughout the ages.
Next, since there has been appointed for things, each according
585   to their kind, a limit of growth and of remaining alive,
and seeing that what they each are capable of by the laws of nature, and further what they are
incapable of, stand ordained,
and since nothing is changed, but all things remain constant
to such an extent that all the different kinds of birds
590   in their order show the markings of their kind on their bodies,
they ought doubtless also to have a body of unchanging
matter. For if the first beginnings of things
are able to be mastered and changed in any way,
it would also be uncertain what can come to be,
595   what cannot, in short, by what process each thing
has its power limited and its deep-set boundary stone,
nor could the generations according to their kinds so often recall
the nature, behavior, way of life, and movements of their parents. Then further, since there is
an extreme point in each case
600   on that body our senses are no longer able to discern,
each point is undoubtedly without parts
and is endowed with the smallest nature possible, nor did it ever exist separately by itself, nor
will it ever have the power to do
so afterwards, since it is itself a primary and single part of another.
605   Thence more and more similar parts in their order
fill out the nature of the atom in a tight mass.
Since these points are unable to exist by themselves, they must
be fixed fast so that they can in no way be pulled away.
Therefore primary bodies exist in their solid singleness,
610   closely packed and tightly bound in their minimal parts.[21]
They were not assembled from a collection of minimal parts,

---

21   Unlike many other ancient philosophers, Epicurus held that both space and time were not infinitely divisible and that there were minimal units of space and time beyond which space and time could not be further divided. He taught that atoms were made up of "minimal parts" that could neither be physically nor conceptually divided. He also argued that atoms could never be split up into their component minimal parts. For more on minimal parts, see Epicurus' *Letter to Herodotus* 55–59.

but rather they are powerfully strong in their eternal singleness,
and from them nature, keeping safe the seeds of things,
has never allowed anything to be pulled away or diminished.

615 Moreover, unless a minimum exists, all the tiniest
bodies will be made up of an infinite number of parts,
since in that case the half of a half will always have
a half, nor will there be anything to set a limit.
Therefore what difference will there be between the sum of things

620 and the least of things? There will be none. For although the whole sum
of things be completely infinite, nevertheless, those things
that are tiniest will equally be made up out of infinite parts.
But since true reasoning shouts back and denies
that the mind can believe this, you should give in and admit

625 that these things now exist possessing no parts
and endowed with a minimal nature. And since they exist,
you must also admit that the atoms are solid and eternal.
Finally, if nature, the creator of things, had been accustomed to compel all things to be
dissolved into their minimal parts,

630 it would not now be able to create anything from them,
because things that are not augmented by any parts
are unable to have those things which generating matter
ought to have: different connections, weight, blows,
meetings, motions, through which all things take place.

635 Therefore those who think that the primary substance of things
is fire, and that the sum of things consists of fire alone,
are seen to have fallen far from true reasoning.
Heraclitus[22] was the first to enter the fray as their leader.
He was famous on account of his obscure language more among the foolish

640 than those thoughtful Greeks who seek the truth.
For stupid people find more impressive and attractive
all things that they see hidden beneath twisted words,
and they judge those things true which can caress
their ears prettily and which are colored with delightful sound.

645 For how are things able to be so varied, I ask,
if they are created from pure fire alone?

---

22   Heraclitus of Ephesus lived in the 6th to 5th century BC, and was one of the most famous Presocratic philosophers. He
taught that all things that existed were made up of different forms of fire.

For it would be no help for hot fire to become dense
or to be rarified, if the parts of fire had the same nature
that fire taken as a whole has as well.

650 For the heat would be more intense when its parts were condensed, and weaker when they
were pulled apart and dispersed.
Beyond this there is nothing you can imagine happening
under such conditions, still less that such a great variety
of things could exist because of condensed and rarified fire.

655 This too: If they were to assume that void is mixed
in things, fire will become dense or be left rarified.
But since they see many things that go against them,
and flee from allowing there to be pure void in things,
while they fear the steep path, they lose the true one,

660 nor again do they see that if void is removed from things, everything is condensed and one
body is created from all.
This body could not speed anything from itself,
like warming fire sends out light and heat,
so that you see that it is not composed of closely packed parts.

665 But if by chance they believe that fire can in some other way
be extinguished in its union and change its substance,
of course if they do not refrain from doing this in any part, doubtless all heat will perish
completely into nothing,
and all things that are created would come to be from nothing.

670 For whatever is changed and departs from its own limits,
this is immediately the death of that which it was before.[23] Accordingly it is necessary that
something be preserved safe for things, or else you would see all things return completely
to nothing
and from nothing the supply of things would be reborn and grow.

675 Now therefore since there are certain most definite bodies,
which always preserve the same nature,
by whose departure or arrival, and changed ordering,
things change their nature and bodies transform themselves,
you can be sure that these bodies of things are not made out of fire.

680 For it would make no difference that certain things separate and leave, and others are added,
and certain others change their ordering,
if all of them still retained the nature of fire.

---

23   1.670–671 = 1.792–793, 2.753–754, 3.519–520.

For whatever they would create would in all ways be fire.

The truth, as I think, is this: there are certain bodies,

685   whose coming-togethers, movements, order, positions, and configurations

create fire. When their order is changed, they change a thing's nature, and they are not like fire nor any other

thing which is able to send off bodies

to our sense organs and touch our touch by its contact.

690   Further, to say that all things are fire

and that nothing real exists in the number of things except fire,

as this same man[24] does, seems to be completely crazy.

For he himself fought back against his senses with his senses,

and thereby undermined the source on which all his beliefs depend,

695   and the source of his knowing that fire which he names.

For he believes that the senses truly perceive fire,

but not other things, which are no less clear.

This seems to me to be both silly and crazy.

What other criterion can we use? What can be more certain to us

700   than our senses themselves, by which we distinguish true and false? Besides, why would anyone exclude everything else

and desire to leave only the nature of fire,

anymore than to deny the existence of fire, while admitting the existence of something else?

It seems to be equal madness to say either.

705   Therefore those who think that the primary substance of things

is fire, and that the sum of things can consist of fire,

and those who have made air the first principle for the creation

of things,[25] and whoever has thought that water

alone by itself fabricates things[26] or that earth creates

710   all things and is changed into all the natures of things,[27]

seem to have wandered very far from the truth.

Add, too, those who double the first beginnings of things,

joining air to fire[28] and earth to water,[29]

and those who think that all things are able to develop

---

24   Heraclitus.

25   Anaximenes of Miletus (c. 585–525 BC) and Diogenes of Apollonia (5th century BC).

26   Thales of Miletus (c. 6th century BC)

27   The reference is uncertain.

28   The reference is uncertain.

29   Xenophanes of Colophon (c. 570–478 BC).

715 from four things: fire, earth, air, and water.[30]

Foremost among such men is Empedocles of Acragas,

whom an island[31] bore within the three-cornered shores of its lands. The Ionian sea flows around this island with its great

inlets and sprays salty brine from its green waves.

720 In its narrow strait the rushing sea divides with its waves

the shores of the lands of Aeolia[32] from the boundaries of Sicily. Here is destructive Charybdis[33] and here the rumblings of Etna[34] threaten to gather the anger of its flames together again,

so that its violence might once again spew forth flames

725 from its jaws and again launch shafts of fire to the sky.

Although this region seems great and marvelous in many

ways to the races of men, and is said to be worth seeing,

rich in good things, and protected by the great force of its men, nevertheless it seems to have had in it nothing more outstanding than

730 this man, nor holier, more wondrous, and precious.

Nay indeed the poems from his divine mind

shout aloud and set out his outstanding discoveries,

so that he seems scarcely to have been created from human stock. Nevertheless he and those I mentioned above, ranked

735 far below him in many ways and lesser by far,

although they made many fine and divine discoveries,

and issued responses from, so to speak, the shrine of their hearts with more holiness and with much more certain reasoning than

the Pythia[35] who speaks from the tripod and laurel of Apollo,

740 nevertheless about the first beginnings of things, they have come crashing down,

and though great, with a great fall they fell there mightily.[36]

First because although they take away void from things,

they posit motion and leave things soft and porous:

air, sun, rain, earth, animals, fruits,

---

30 Empedocles of Acragas (Sicily) (c.492–432 BC)

31 Sicily

32 Southern Italy.

33 A famous narrow whirlpool located in the straits of Messina between Sicily and the Italian mainland.

34 Etna = Mt. Etna, located in Eastern Sicily and the highest active volcano in Europe.

35 The Pythia was the priestess at the oracle of Delphi in Greece.

36 This line imitates Homer *Iliad* 16.776.

745 and yet they do not mix void into the bodies of these things.
Next because they establish no limit at all for dividing
bodies nor any cessation for the breaking up of things,
nor further does any minimum in things exist for them,
although we see that there is for each thing
750 that extreme point which to our senses appears to be a minimum,
so that from this you can infer that the extreme point in those things which you cannot see exists
as a minimum in them.
In addition, since they have made the primary elements
of things soft, things which we see are born
755 and endowed with mortal body, the whole sum of things
ought now to return completely to nothing,
and the supply of things ought to be reborn from nothing and thrive.
And how far each of these is from the truth you will understand by now.
Next, these elements are in many ways hostile and like poison
760 themselves to themselves among themselves. Therefore if they meet either they will perish, or
scatter just as, when a storm has gathered, we see thunderbolts, rain, and the winds scatter apart.
Again, if all things are created from four elements
and all are dissolved into these things again, how
765 can these elements be called the first beginnings of things any more than
on the contrary things be called the first beginnings of the elements, our thought reversed?
For they are begotten in alternation and change color
and their whole nature among themselves for all time.
[we see thunderbolts, rain, and the winds scatter apart.][37]
770 But if by chance you think that fire and the body of earth
and airy breezes and the dew of water come together
in a way that none of them changes its nature in the compound,
you will find that nothing will be able to be created from them,
not a living thing, nor one with a lifeless body, like a tree.
775 For each thing combined in a discordant heap will display
its own nature, and air will be seen to be mixed
together with earth, and fire to stand with water.
But the first beginnings in creating things must
of necessity possess a nature that is secret and invisible,
780 so that nothing can show forth which would fight against and hinder
whatever is created from being able to exist with its own character.

---

37 This line was repeated here from 763 by a copyist's error.

And furthermore, they[38] begin from the heaven and its fires
and maintain that fire first turns itself into the breezes
of the air, and then rain is produced, and then that earth is created
785 from rain, and that all things are changed back again from earth: first water, afterwards air, and finally heat,
and that these things never cease changing among themselves,
and travel from heaven to earth, from earth to the stars of the firmament. First beginnings ought never to do this in any way.
790 For something unchangeable must necessarily remain,
so that all things not be completely reduced to nothing.
For whatever is changed and departs from its own limits,
this is immediately the death of that which it was before.
Therefore since those things which I have just mentioned above
795 undergo change, they must be made up
of other things, which can never change, or else
you would see all things return completely to nothing.
Why not rather posit certain bodies endowed with such a nature that if they created, say, fire, these same bodies
800 would be able, with a few of them taken away and a few of them added, and with their ordering
and movement changed, to create the breezes of the air,
and in this way all other things could be changed into others? "But," you say, "it is a plain and obvious fact that all
things are nourished and grow from the earth into the breezes of the air;
805 and unless the weather gives free play at the right time
to the rains, so that by the melting of the clouds the trees may sway, and unless the sun for its part cradles and warms them,
crops, trees, and living creatures cannot grow."
Yes, and unless we have the benefit of dry food and soft
810 liquid, our flesh would soon be lost and all life
too would be released from all our sinews and bones.
Beyond a shadow of a doubt we are helped along and nourished
by specific things, as are other things by other specific things. Doubtless because many first beginnings, common
815 in many ways to many things, are mixed in things,
so different things are nourished by different things.

---

38 Who "they" are is unclear. Some scholars think Lucretius is attacking the Stoics, but others disagree and have suggested different possibilities.

And it often makes a great difference with these same
first beginnings with what and in what position they are held,
and what motions they impart and receive among themselves.

820 For sky, sea, earth, rivers, and sun are composed
of the same things, and so too crops, trees, and animals,
but they are mixed with different things and are moved in different ways.
And furthermore, here and there in our verses themselves
you see many letters shared by many words,

825 although it is still necessary to admit that the verses and words[39] differ among themselves in
meaning and in the sounding of their sounds.
So much can letters accomplish with only a change in ordering.
But the first beginnings of things can bring more differences into play,
from which the various things in their several kinds can be created.

830 Now let us also examine Anaxagoras' "homoeomeria,"[40]
as the Greeks call it, which the poverty of our native speech
does not allow us to name in our own language,
but nevertheless it is easy to explain the thing itself in words.
First, as to what he calls the homoeomeria of things,

835 he clearly thinks that bones are made of small and tiny
bones, and that flesh is made from small and tiny
pieces of flesh, and that blood is created when many
drops of blood intermingle with one another,
and that from flecks of gold there can be built up

840 gold, and that from small pieces of earth earth can grow,
and that fires can be from fires, and water from waters,
and he imagines and thinks of other things in the same way.
And nevertheless he does not allow that void is present in things
in any part, nor that there is an end to dividing bodies.

845 Therefore in both of these reasonings he seems to have made
the same errors as those people whom I discussed above.[41]
Add that he makes the first beginnings too weak,
if they are first beginnings at all which are endowed with a nature similar to the things themselves and suffer in the same way

---

39   1.823–825 = 2.688–690.
40   Anaxagoras was a Presocratic philosopher from Clazomenae (c.500–428 BC). Lucretius uses the Greek term "homoeo-meria" (ho-moi-o-MER-i-a, literally "having like parts") as the name for Anaxagoras' doctrine that there is a bit of everything in everything.
41   Heraclitus and Empedocles.

850 and perish, nor does anything hold them back from destruction.
    For which of them will endure when they are heavily crushed,
    so that they can escape death, when they are in the very teeth of destruction?
    Will it be fire? Water? Air? Which of these? Blood? Bones?
    None of these, I think, when everything will be as equally and completely
855 mortal as the clearly perceptible things we see
    with our own eyes perish when they are overcome by some force.
    But I appeal to the things we have proved before, that nothing
    can sink into nothingness nor again grow from nothing.
    Moreover, since food increases and nourishes the body,
860 we are able to know that veins and blood and bones
    <and sinews are composed of parts different in kind;>[42]
    or if they say that all foods are mixed in body
    and have in themselves small bodies of sinews,
    and bones and veins besides, and parts of blood,
    it will happen that all food itself, both dry and liquid,
865 will be supposed to be made out of things unlike itself,
    with bones and sinews and gore and blood mixed in.
    Moreover if whatever bodies grow from the earth,
    are in the earth, the earth must necessarily consist of
    things unlike itself which arise from the earth.
870 Take another case, and you may use the same words.
    If flame lies hidden in logs, and smoke and ashes,
    logs must consist of things unlike themselves,
873 of things unlike themselves which arise from the logs. (874)
874 Moreover whatever bodies earth nourishes and increases[43] (873)

      * * * * * * * * * * * *

875 There remains here some slight means of escaping detection,
    which Anaxagoras took for himself, that he thinks that all things
    are mixed with all things and escape detection, but that one
    thing is visible, whose particles have been mixed in the greatest numbers
    and are more visible and located right up front.

---

42   The text is corrupt here. I have translated Lambinus' suggested addition.
43   There is a lacuna in the text after line 874.

880 But this is far removed from true reasoning.
For it would be natural also for grains of wheat, when they are broken under the oppressive
strength of stone, to release a trace
of blood or something of those things which are nourished in our body. When we rub with
stone on stone, the blood should ooze out.

885 In a similar way it would be right for grass, too, and water
often to release sweet drops which are similar in taste
to the richness of the milk of wool-bearing sheep.
Yes, and it would be right, when clods of earth are crumbled up,
for types of grasses and wheat and foliage often to be seen

890 to lie hidden dispersed in tiny portions within the earth,
and finally it would be right, when logs would be broken open,
for ashes and smoke, and tiny fires, to be seen to be hidden.
Since the plain facts show that none of this happens,
we may know that things are not mixed in things in this way,

895 but rather that seeds, mixed up in many ways, and common
to many things, must lie hidden in things.
"But," you will object, "it often happens on great mountains
that the neighboring tops of high trees are rubbed together
among themselves when a strong south wind forces them

900 to do this until they burst and flash into a flower of flames."
And nevertheless fire is not implanted in firs, of course,
but there are many seeds of fire which when they flow together
by rubbing create fiery destruction in the woods.
But if there were fully formed flames hidden in the woods,

905 fires would not be able to be contained for a moment;
they would destroy woods everywhere, they would incinerate orchards. Now then, do you see,
as we said a little earlier,[44]
that it often is very important with these same first beginnings
with what and in what position they are held,

910 and what motions they impart and receive among themselves,
and that the same things, a little changed among themselves, create both fires and fir? This
is the way even with words themselves when the letters are changed around a little among
themselves,
since we designate firs and fires by a change in sound.[45]

---

44 Lines 817–819.
45 Lucretius uses the Latin terms ligna ("wood, firs") and ignis ("fires").

915 Finally, if you think that whatever you see in things
      that are visible cannot be created unless you posit
      bodies of matter endowed with a nature like the whole,
      by this reasoning the first beginnings perish on you.
      The first beginnings will rock with rolling laughter, howl

920 aloud, and with salty tears drench their faces and cheeks.[46]
      Now come, understand what remains and hear more clearly.
      I am very aware how obscure these things are. But great
      hope for praise strikes my heart with a sharp thyrsus[47]
      and at the same time strikes into my breast sweet love

925 for the Muses. Now roused by this in my lively mind
      I am traversing the remote places of the Pierides,[48] untrodden by the sole
      of anyone before. It is a joy to approach pure springs
      and to drink from them, and it is a joy to pick new flowers
      and to seek a preeminent crown for my head from that place

930 whence the Muses had wreathed the temples of no one before;[49]
      first because I am teaching about great things and proceeding
      to free the mind from the narrow bonds of religion,
      next because I am writing so clear a poem about so obscure
      a subject, touching everything with the charm of the Muses.

935 For this too seems to be not without reason.
      But just as when physicians try to give loathsome wormwood
      to children, they first touch the rim of the cup all
      around with the sweet, golden liquid of honey,
      so that the unsuspecting age of children may be tricked as far

940 as their lips, and so that meanwhile the child might drink down
      the bitter wormwood juice and though deceived, be not deceased,
      but rather by such means be restored and become well,
      so I now, since this system seems for the most part to be
      too bitter to those who have not tried it and

945 the common people shrink back from it, I wanted to explain
      our system to you in sweet-spoken Pierian[50] song

---

46 1.919-920 are nearly identical to 2.976–977.

47 A thyrsus was a wand whose tip was wrapped with ivy or vine leaves. It was a symbol of the worship of Dionysus and poetic inspiration.

48 Pierides = the daughters of Pierus, i.e. , the Muses.

49 Lucretius claims to be the first Roman to write a philosophic poem.

50 i.e. , sacred to the Muses.

and touch it, so to speak, with the sweet honey of the Muses.
I have done so in the hope I might in this way be able to hold
your attention in our verses, until you look into the whole

950 nature of things, with what shape it is endowed and exists.[51]
But since I have shown that the most solid bodies of matter
are indestructible and fly around forever without stopping,
now come, let us unfold whether there is a limit to their sum

955 or not; and likewise that which has been discovered to be void
or place or space, in which all things take place,
let us consider whether it is all at bottom bounded, or whether
it stretches out, limitless in extent and immensely deep.
Therefore all that exists is bounded in no direction
of its ways; for in that case it would have to have an end point.

960 And, moreover, it seems that there cannot be an endpoint for anything, unless there is something
beyond it which limits it, so that there is seen to be
a place beyond which this nature of our senses cannot follow.
Now since it must be confessed that there is nothing outside the universe, it does not have an
endpoint, and therefore lacks boundary and limit.

965 It does not matter in what region of the universe you place yourself; so true is it that whatever
place anyone occupies, he leaves
the universe infinite in all directions to the same extent.
Besides, suppose now that the totality of space
were to be limited: if someone were to run all the way

970 to its final boundaries and hurl a flying spear,
do you prefer to think that, spun with great strength,
it would go where it was sent, and fly far,
or do you think that something would be able to stop and block it? For you must admit and
accept one of the two alternatives.

975 Either choice will prevent your escape and force you
to concede that the universe stretches forth without limit.
For whether there is something that stops it and makes it so
that it cannot go where it was sent and reach its goal, or whether
it travels beyond, it did not set out from the end of the universe.

980 In this way I will proceed and, wherever you place the ultimate boundaries, I will ask, "What
finally happens to the spear?"
It will turn out that an end of the universe cannot be fixed,

---

51   1.926–950 = 4.1–25, with a few minor differences.

and that an opportunity for flight always extends the flight. Besides, if the whole space of the entire sum of things

985 had been shut in and were fixed with certain boundaries,

and had been enclosed, by now the supply of matter would everywhere have flowed to the bottom because of its solidity and weight. Nothing could move beneath the cover of the sky, nor would there be a sky at all nor light of the sun,

990 since all matter would lie gathered in a heap,

having by now sunk down in infinite time.

But as things are, of course, no rest has been given to the bodies

of the first beginnings, since there is absolutely no bottom

where they could flow together, so to speak, and take their places.

995 All things are always being carried along

in constant motion on all sides, and bodies of matter

are supplied from below, speeding out of infinite space.

Finally, before our eyes one thing is seen to limit

another: the air hedges in hills, and mountains the air.

1000 Land bounds the sea, and sea, in return, bounds all lands,

whereas truly there is nothing which could limit the universe from the outside.

Therefore the nature of place and the space of the abyss

is such that neither could shining thunderbolts traverse it on their endless

journey, gliding on through an eternal tract of time,

1005 nor, further, by their travelling make it so that there remained any less to go,

such an immense supply of space extends everywhere for things, with no limits anywhere in any direction.

Moreover, nature insures that the sum of things cannot

on its own set a limit to itself, and forces body

1010 to be bounded by void, and what is void to be bounded by body,

so that it thus renders the universe infinite by their alternation,

or else one of the two, if the other of them does not bound it,

in its single nature extends nevertheless without limit.[52]

<But if the void were limited, the infinite atoms would not

have a place to exist; and if matter were limited>

neither the sea nor the land nor the bright regions of the sky

1015 nor the human race nor the holy bodies of the gods

would be able to exist for even a small fraction of an hour.

For the supply of matter, wrenched apart from its union,

---

52   There is a lacuna after 1013. Following Diels' suggestion, I have supplied a possible rendering of what might be missing.

would have been dissolved and carried along through the great void, or, more accurately, it never would have come together and created

1020 anything, since in its scattered state it could not have been brought together.

For certainly not by design did the first beginnings of things arrange themselves in their order with keen intent, nor surely

did they reach an agreement about what motions each would take.

1025 But since many of them are moved in many ways throughout the universe

and from endless time are stirred up and excited by collisions,

by trying motions and unions of every kind

they finally arrive at arrangements like those

which produce and maintain this sum of things.[53]

1030 And it too, preserved for many great years

when once it had been cast into suitable motions,

insures that rivers replenish the greedy sea with the abundant waves of their streams, and that the earth, nurtured by the sun's heat, renews its offspring, and that the race of living things is bred and flourishes, and that the gliding fires of heaven live on.

1035 In no way would they do this, unless a supply

of matter could rise up from the infinite, from which they are accustomed to make up all that is lost in due time.

For just as the nature of living things, when deprived of food,

loses bulk and fades, so all things ought

1040 to be dissolved as soon as matter fails to be supplied

when it is for whatever reason diverted from its course.

Nor are blows from the outside in all directions able

to maintain every world that has been gathered together.

Indeed they can repeatedly pound and preserve a part,

1045 until others arrive and the sum is able to be supplied.

But sometimes they are forced to spring back, and in so doing provide for the first beginnings of things the space and opportunity for escape, so that they can be free and move away from their unions. Wherefore again and again it is necessary that many things

1050 be provided, and yet in order that even blows too be present,

it is necessary that the supply of matter be everywhere infinite.

In these matters flee far from believing, Memmius,

what some say:[54] that everything tends to the center of the universe,

and that thus the nature of the world stands firm without any

---

53 "This sum of things" = "our world"

54 Lucretius probably has the Aristotelian and perhaps Stoic conceptions of the world in mind.

1055external blows, and that top and bottom cannot be undone

in any direction, because all things tend toward the center

(if you can believe that anything is able to stand on itself!).

And they say that all heavy things that are under the earth

press upwards and rest on the earth upside down,

1060just like the images of things we now see in water.

And in a similar way they maintain that animals wander around upside down, and cannot fall from the earth

to the regions of space below, anymore than our bodies

of their own accord can fly off into regions of the sky.

1065And that when they see the sun, we gaze upon the stars

of the night, and that they share with us in alternation

the seasons of the sky, and have nights equal to our days.

But empty <error has commended> these false things to fools,[55] because they have tackled

<the problem with twisted reasoning.>

1070For there can be no center, <since the universe is>

infinite. Nor indeed, if there now <were a center,>

would anything be able to rest for all that, rather

than <be driven> far away for any other reason.

For all place and space, which <we call> void,

1075whether at the center or not at the center, <must> yield

equally to heavy bodies, wherever their movements tend.

Nor is there any place where when bodies reach it

the power of weight is lost and they stand still in the void.

Nor ought that which is void hold up anything,

1080but must, as its own nature requires, hasten to yield.

Therefore not at all in this manner can things be held

together in union, overcome by a longing for the center.

Moreover, since they posit that not all bodies

tend to the center, but those of earth and water,

1085the moisture of the sea and the great waters from the mountains,[56] (**1086**)

and the things which are contained in an earthly body, so to speak; (**1085**)

but on the contrary they explain that the light breezes of the air

and hot fires are carried away together from the center,

and so the entire aether[57] twinkles all around with stars

---

55   The text of lines 1068–1075 is damaged. I have translated the lines with Munro's suggested additions.

56   The text is uncertain. I have followed editors who transpose lines 1085 and 1086.

57   "Aether" = the upper air.

1090and the flames of the sun are fed in the sky-blue sky, because all heat, fleeing from the center, collects there, nor further could the highest branches of trees leaf out, unless each is fed little by little from the earth...[58]

* * * * * * * * * * * *

1102lest, in the winged way of flames the walls of the world
suddenly fly away and dissolve in the great void,
and lest other things follow in a similar way,
1105lest the thundering regions of the sky rush upwards,
the earth suddenly snatch itself from under our feet,
and all of it, among the scattered ruins of things and sky
that have let their bodies go, depart through the vast void,
so that in an instant of time nothing remains behind
1110except empty space and invisible first beginnings.
For from whatever part you will first decide bodies are missing, this part will be the door of death for things,
and by it the whole throng of matter will make its exit.
Thus you will learn these things, led with little effort.
1115For one thing will be clarified by another, nor will dark night deprive you of your way, until you see deeply into the ultimate principles of nature: so things will illuminate other things.

---

58   Lines 1094–1101 are lost.